SIGNIFICANT SUPREME COURT OPINIONS
OF
THE HONORABLE WARREN E. BURGER
CHIEF JUSTICE OF THE UNITED STATES

THE PHILIPPINE BAR ASSOCIATION
MANILA, PHILIPPINES
December 1984

CHIEF JUSTICE WARREN E. BURGER

PREFACE

The Philippine Bar Association is highly honored and privileged to publish significant decisions of the Honorable Warren E. Burger, the Chief Justice of the United States.

The Chief Justice has been a member of the Supreme Court of the United States since 1969. He has graciously selected thirty-nine (39) memorable opinions, including one dissenting opinion, that make up this volume; and they are grouped into five distinct sections, each dealing with an essential aspect of individual and democratic life.

For convenience and utility, the 39 opinions were reproduced from the original, 33 from *United States Reports*, and the 6 most recent from slip opinions; and all include the syllabus, footnotes, running heads and page numbers, so that those interested may directly cite them.

These learned decisions of the Chief Justice, which are clear, concise, solid and scholarly, are most useful not only to the members of the bench and the bar, but also to the layman interested in basic rights and the rule of law.

Moreover, their value and service extends beyond the United States, for these momentous decisions of its Supreme Court, the leading judicial court in the world, are relevant to all democracies and freedom-loving countries.

We are truly grateful to the eminent Chief Justice for kindly consenting to select significant decisions since his elevation in 1969, which are virtual landmarks in and of the law. I am personally thankful for all the courtesies extended during the several visits in connection with this project.

We are likewise obliged to the Honorable Howard T. Markey, Chief Judge of the U.S. Court of Appeals for the Federal Circuit, for his fine Foreword; and to the distinguished Burnett Anderson for his excellent Introduction.

In closing, we would like to express our sincere appreciation to Mark W. Cannon, Administrative Assistant to the Chief Justice, and to Edith S. Coliver, Representative of The Asia Foundation in the Philippines, for all their aid and assistance in making this worthy project possible.

ENRIQUE P. SYQUIA
President
Philippine Bar Association (1981-1984)
Vice-President
International Bar Association (1982-1984)

TABLE OF CONTENTS

Part I
The Powers of Governance:
Separation of Powers and Limited Government

Part II
Freedom of Communication

Part III
Religious Freedom

Part IV
Rights of the Accused

Part V
Equal Justice Under Law:
Racial and Non-Racial Discrimination

FOREWORD

Warren E. Burger has been the Chief Justice of the United States for 16 of this Nation's most tumultuous years. Amid wars, constitutional crises, and great social changes, Chief Justice Burger has stood firmly at the helm of the institution designed to ensure the stability of a free society and the primacy of its unique founding document, the Constitution.

The Chief Justice's heritage was forged in America's heartland, Minnesota, with a family tradition of work, loyalty and service to country. His grandfather, an emigrant from Austria, was awarded the nation's highest award for valor under fire while still a teenage Civil War soldier. He built on a childhood of warmth and accepted hard work to become a respected and able lawyer in private law practice while serving as an adjunct law professor, and a leader in his city and state. Even in those early years, he made time for extra service to the cause of justice in representing the poor and the unpopular. His abilities were recognized by his appointment as Assistant Attorney General and his elevation to a judgeship on the United States Court of Appeals, both appointments by President Eisenhower. He was a strong judge and an innovator in judicial administration. When he was appointed Chief Justice, his background was widely recognized and he was confirmed by the Democratic Senate in less than three weeks.

His broad experience and background enabled him to undertake the awesome responsibilities as Chief Justice with an equanimity and steadiness essential in a period of rapid, monumental, and continuing societal and technological change. His dedication to the constitutional balance of powers, freedom of speech and press, freedom of religion, the rights of the criminally accused, personal accountability, and to equal justice under law, has been clear and constant. When competing demands of modern society have threatened the balance between the rights of some and the rights of all, Warren Burger's sensitivity and thoughtfulness have helped to maintain the needed equilibrium and to avoid rents in the fabric of society that could have resulted from injudicious pronouncements. His leadership for better correctional institutions, and for changes in court administration and legal education programs, is characteristic.

That the Chief Justice has ably answered the call to service on the Nation's highest Court can be seen in the representative selections in this volume. Through them runs a theme of common sense and common language. He writes that all may understand. Yet the writing reflects a level of true scholarship remarkable in its clarity as well as its breadth and depth. It would do honor to one without other responsibilities, but as Chief Justice of the United States, the author of these selected opinions has served as Chairman of the Judicial Conference of the United States, Chairman of the Federal Judicial Center, as Chancellor of the Smithsonian, as Chairman and Trustee of the National Gallery of Art, Trustee of the National Geographic Society, and as Honorary Chairman of the Institute of Judicial Administration and the National Judicial College.

During the period of his innovative leadership as head of the Third Branch of Government, the federal judiciary has expanded by more than half in judgeships and one and a half times in cases decided. While dealing with the problems of increased caseload, he has continued to fulfill the more than 50 statutory administrative responsibilities of the Office of the Chief Justice. Only the stamina born of his heritage and dedication has enabled him to meet these increasing demands.

The selections in this volume have been divided into those dealing with five aspects of jurisprudence critical to American life. There are others, but these particularly illustrate Chief Justice Burger's dedication to fundamental principles. They reflect a consistency and order essential to continued reverence for the Constitution by the people of the United States. They are selections from the jurisprudential works of a great leader and a great judge.

Howard T. Markey
Chief Judge
U.S. Court of Appeals for the
Federal Circuit

INTRODUCTION

It has been observed by a number of authorities in the American government that few persons arrive at high office so ideally qualified by education, experience, and character as Warren Burger to be Chief Justice of the United States. His route to the pinnacle of the U.S. judicial system encompassed virtually every aspect of its workings, from practicing attorney for 21 years, followed by three years at the top levels of the executive branch as U.S. Assistant Attorney General for the Civil Division, to thirteen years as a judge of the U.S. Court of Appeals for the District of Columbia Circuit.

Warren Burger was born on September 17, 1907, in St. Paul, Minnesota, one of seven children. The Austrian-Swiss-German heritage of his immigrant grandparents and his parents undoubtedly impressed on him the value of work and self-discipline which has characterized his entire career. He was offered a scholarship to Princeton University on the basis of his distinguished high school record, but he could not accept it because of shared obligations for support of his family.

Warren Burger pursued his education in night classes at the University of Minnesota and gained his legal degree in night courses at the St. Paul (now William Mitchell) College of Law. He was awarded the LL.B *magna cum laude* in 1931, which led to employment by a highly respected law firm where he became a full partner within a few years.

His experience as a lawyer covered a wide range of practice, including all levels of state and federal courts and at the Supreme Bench over which he was later to preside. He participated fully in the civic and political life of his native city and state. Among other things, he organized the first Council on Human Relations to fight racial discrimination in St. Paul. When Japanese-Americans were forced to leave the West Coast in World War II, this Council created a special committee to facilitate finding them homes and employment.

As an honors graduate, he was appointed to the faculty of his law school immediately following his own graduation and became an adjunct professor of contracts. He served for many years as a trustee of the Mayo Foundation, which operates the famed medical center in Rochester, Minnesota, and as a trustee of Macalester College in St. Paul.

While it was not apparent even to him at the time, Warren Burger's career took a definitive turn in 1953, when President Eisenhower appointed him Assistant U.S. Attorney General for the Civil Division. Here he represented the U.S. not only in courts throughout the country but internationally as well. After three years of distinguished service, he was preparing to return to private practice in his home city when President Eisenhower persuaded him to accept appointment to the U.S. Court of Appeals for the District of Columbia Circuit.

At this juncture Judge Burger had acquired a remarkably broad and deep overview of the entire judicial system, state and federal, which was further enhanced by his service on the Court of Appeals. Here he carried his full share of decision-making, delving deeply into constitutional questions. The District of Columbia Appeals Circuit has sometimes been called "the Little Supreme Court" for the volume of significant litigation brought before it, and some of Judge Burger's opinions became precedents. He also sat by assignment in other circuits and in the District Courts as a trial judge.

Warren Burger's years on the Court of Appeals were highly productive off the bench as well as on it. He continued his own education both formally and informally; among other things he enrolled in a 1960 summer course in private international law at the Hague Academy of International Law in the Netherlands. During summer recess, year after year, he observed the courts and penal institutions of Europe, seeking better solutions to America's stubborn problems of crime and corrections. He participated in establishing the Appellate Judges' Seminar at New York University in 1957, and he has served on its faculty ever since. He began speaking out boldly on the great problems of the American judicial system: court management, case overload and delays, inefficiencies, inadequacies of judicial education, crime and punishment, and controversial constitutional questions.

On May 22, 1969, he was nominated Chief Justice of the United States. The Senate confirmed him 18 days later, on the unanimous recommendation of its Judiciary Committee.

Responding to a question in his hearing before the Committee, Judge Burger said he would conceive his duties to be, first of all, "basically the same as they have been as a member of the U.S. Court of Appeals — deciding cases." But, he went on, " . . . the Chief Justice of the United States is assigned many other duties, administrative in nature. I would think it was the duty of the Chief Justice . . . to make our system work better. And I would expect to devote every energy and every moment of the rest of my life to that end should I be confirmed."

The opinions in this volume are sufficient testimony to Warren Burger's fulfillment of the first part of that self-imposed mandate. That he is *primus inter pares* does not relieve him of his full share of writing opinions (and dissents), and the annual statistical summaries of the work of the nine Justices shows that he has carried at least his full share of the burden year in and year out.

This brief sketch of Warren Burger's career would be inadequate and one-dimensional without some mention of his unprecedented accomplishments under the second part, the "many other duties" of the Chief Justice of the United States. Immediately after taking office in 1969, he was invited to address the annual American Bar Association meeting in Dallas, Texas, and present any problems he wished. Since that time, he has made well over one hundred speeches, all of which have generally produced prompt and positive action.

Bernard G. Segal, former president of the American Bar Association, has said that more judicial improvements were made in the first three years of Chief Justice Burger's tenure than during the preceding quarter century. They included creation of the Institute for Court Management, in Colorado, to train professional court administrators; establishment of the National Center for State Courts; creation of State-Federal Judicial Councils in more than two-thirds of the states; and establishment of a program to provide trained and certified Circuit Executives for each of the eleven federal circuits.

Successively and repeatedly he has pressed for improvements in American correctional methods and institutions, for improved legal education, for higher ethical standards and civility in the profession both in and outside the courtroom, for expanded alternative dispute resolution, and for improved delivery of justice to all Americans. History will judge the results, but the preliminary returns suggest that Chief Justice Warren Burger has made a unique and unprecedented contribution. One evaluation came in 1983 from Chief Justice Vincent McCusick of Maine, who said, "It is impossible to exaggerate Chief Justice Burger's contributions to improving the courts, state quite as much as federal. [He] has done more than any other single person in history to improve the operation of all our nation's courts."

An amateur sculptor and painter, a voracious reader of history, a student of antiques, Warren Burger is also fully at home in some of the other statutory duties of the Chief Justice. He is Chancellor of the Smithsonian Institution, a member of the governing board (and for many years chairman) of the National Gallery of Art, and a trustee of the National Geographic Society. He takes an active and informed role in all of these assignments.

Although his opinions must be confined to interpretation of the law and Constitution, where personal preferences and convictions are rigidly excluded, the man cannot be separated from the Justice. Readers will find here repeated evidence of his high concept of public service, his insistence on responsibility as a *sine qua non* of the free society, and an unshakeable commitment to equal justice under law.

Burnett Anderson

PART I

THE POWERS OF GOVERNANCE:
SEPARATION OF POWERS AND LIMITED GOVERNMENT

1. SCHLESINGER, SECRETARY OF DEFENSE, et al. v. RESERVISTS COMMITTEE TO STOP THE WAR et al. (1974).

2. UNITED STATES v. BREWSTER (1972).

3. TENNESSEE VALLEY AUTHORITY v. HILL et al. (1978).

4. DIAMOND, COMMISSIONER OF PATENTS AND TRADEMARKS v. CHAKRABARTY (1980).

5. IMMIGRATION AND NATURALIZATION SERVICE v. CHADHA et al. (1983).

6. UNITED STATES v. NIXON, PRESIDENT OF THE UNITED STATES (1974).

7. UNITES STATES v. WILL et al. (1980).

---oOo---

SCHLESINGER, SECRETARY OF DEFENSE, ET AL. *v.* RESERVISTS COMMITTEE TO STOP THE WAR ET AL.

CERTIORARI TO THE UNITED STATES COURT OF APPEALS FOR THE DISTRICT OF COLUMBIA CIRCUIT

No. 72–1188. Argued January 14, 1974—Decided June 25, 1974

Respondents—an association of present and former members of the Armed Forces Reserve opposing United States involvement in Vietnam, and five association members who were United States citizens and taxpayers—brought a class action on behalf, *inter alia,* of all United States citizens and taxpayers against petitioners, the Secretary of Defense and the three Service Secretaries, challenging the Reserve membership of Members of Congress as violating the Incompatibility Clause of Art. I, § 6, cl. 2, of the Constitution, which provides that "no Person holding any Office under the United States, shall be a Member of either House during his Continuance in Office." The District Court held that respondents had standing to sue as citizens but not as taxpayers, and on the merits granted partial relief. The Court of Appeals affirmed. *Held:*

1. Respondents had no standing to sue as citizens, since the claimed nonobservance of the Incompatibility Clause which they assert deprives citizens of the faithful discharge of the legislative duties of reservist Members of Congress implicates only the generalized interest of all citizens in constitutional governance and is thus merely an abstract injury rather than the concrete injury that is essential to satisfy Art. III's "case or controversy" requirement. Pp. 216–227.

2. Respondents also lacked standing to sue as taxpayers, since they failed to establish the required "logical nexus between the [taxpayer] status asserted and the claim sought to be adjudicated." *Flast* v. *Cohen,* 392 U. S. 83, 102. Pp. 227–228.

162 U. S. App. D. C. 19, 495 F. 2d 1075, reversed and remanded.

BURGER, C. J., delivered the opinion of the Court, in which STEWART, WHITE, BLACKMUN, POWELL, and REHNQUIST, JJ., joined. STEWART, J., filed a concurring opinion, *post,* p. 228. DOUGLAS, J., filed a dissenting opinion, in which MARSHALL, J., joined, *post*, p. 229. BRENNAN, J., *post*, p. 235, and MARSHALL, J., *post*, p. 238, filed dissenting opinions.

Solicitor General Bork argued the cause for petitioners. With him on the brief were *Acting Assistant Attorney General Jaffe, Deputy Solicitor General Friedman, Leonard Schaitman,* and *William D. Appler.*

William A. Dobrovir argued the cause and filed a brief for respondents.*

MR. CHIEF JUSTICE BURGER delivered the opinion of the Court.

We granted certiorari, *sub nom. Richardson* v. *Reservists Committee to Stop the War,* 411 U. S. 947 (1973), to review the judgment of the Court of Appeals affirming, without opinion, the District Court's partial summary judgment for respondents declaring that "Article I, Section 6, Clause 2 of the Constitution renders a member of Congress ineligible to hold a commission in the Armed Forces Reserve during his continuance in office." *Reservists Committee to Stop the War* v. *Laird,* 323 F. Supp. 833, 843 (DC 1971). We hold that respondents do not have standing to sue as citizens or taxpayers. The judgment of the Court of Appeals is therefore reversed.

I

Article I, § 6, cl. 2, of the Federal Constitution provides:

"No Senator or Representative shall, during the Time for which he was elected, be appointed to any civil Office under the Authority of the United States, which shall have been created, or the Emoluments

---

Thomas H. King, Maurice F. Biddle, and *Harold Shapiro* filed a brief for the Reserve Officers Association of the United States as *amicus curiae.*

3

whereof shall have been encreased during such time; and no Person holding any Office under the United States, shall be a Member of either House during his Continuance in Office."

The Constitution thereby makes Members of Congress ineligible for appointment to certain offices through the limitation of the Ineligibility Clause, and prohibits Members of Congress from holding other offices through the latter limitation, the Incompatibility Clause.

Respondents, the Reservists Committee to Stop the War and certain named members thereof,[1] challenged the Reserve membership of Members of Congress[2] as being

---

[1] The Committee, located in California, is a national unincorporated association of present and former officers and enlisted members of the Reserves, organized for the purpose of opposing the military involvement of the United States in Vietnam and of using all lawful means to end that involvement, including efforts by its members individually to take all steps necessary and appropriate to end that involvement. The five individual respondents were all members of the Committee, residents of California, and United States citizens and taxpayers. At the time suit was filed, four of the individuals were in active Ready Reserve status; the status of the fifth, then the Committee cochairman, was unspecified.

[2] At the time suit was filed, 130 Members of the 91st Congress were also members of the Reserves, which are divided into Ready, Standby, and Retired components. By the end of the 92d Congress, 119 Members were reservists. As of November 2, 1973, the 93d Congress has seen the number of its reservists reduced to 107, all but one of whom are commissioned officers, App. 5, and none of whom can occupy the Ready Reserve status of the individual respondents, supra, n. 1. Dept. of Defense Directive 1200.7 § v, c. 2 (July 2, 1970); 32 CFR § 125.4 (c) (2). Of the 107, 20 (including the one enlisted man) are in the active, and 12 in the inactive, Standby Reserve; and 73 are in the Retired Reserve, 16 of whom receive retirement pay. Two other Members are in the Army National Guard, and thus in the Ready Reserve, 10 U. S. C. § 269 (b), but since the governors of the various States control appointments to offices in the Guard, petitioners could not provide

4

in violation of the Incompatibility Clause. They commenced a class action in the District Court against petitioners, the Secretary of Defense and the three Service
Secretaries, seeking (1) an order in the nature of mandamus directed to petitioners requiring them to strike from
the rolls of the Reserves all Members of Congress presently
thereon, to discharge any member of the Reserves who
subsequently became a Member of Congress, and to
seek to reclaim from Members and former Members of
Congress any Reserve pay said Members received while
serving as Members of Congress, (2) a permanent injunction preventing petitioners from placing on the rolls of
the Reserves any Member of Congress while serving in
Congress, and (3) a declaration that membership in the
Reserves is an office under the United States prohibited to
Members of Congress by Art. I, § 6, cl. 2, and incompatible
with membership in the Congress.

Respondents sought the above relief on behalf of
four classes of persons. The Committee and the individual respondents sought to represent the interests of
(1) all persons opposed to United States military involvement in Vietnam and purporting to use lawful means,
including communication with and persuasion of Members of Congress, to end that involvement. The individual respondents alone sought to represent the interests
of (2) all officers and enlisted members of the Reserves
who were not Members of Congress, (3) all taxpayers of
the United States, and (4) all citizens of the United
States. The interests of these four classes were alleged
to be adversely affected by the Reserve membership of
Members of Congress in various ways.

---

relief regarding such reservists. The judgment of the District
Court did not therefore extend to this category of reservist. 323
F. Supp. 833, 838 n. 3 (DC 1971).

As relevant here, citizens and taxpayers were alleged in respondents' complaint to have suffered injury because Members of Congress holding a Reserve position in the Executive Branch were said to be subject to the possibility of undue influence by the Executive Branch,[3] in violation of the concept of the independence of Congress implicit in Art. I of the Constitution. Reserve membership was also said to place upon Members of Congress possible inconsistent obligations which might cause them to violate their duty faithfully to perform as reservists or as Members of Congress. Reserve membership by Members of Congress thus, according to respondents' complaint,

> "deprives or may deprive the individual named plaintiffs and all other citizens and taxpayers of the United States of the faithful discharge by members of Congress who are members of the Reserves of their duties as members of Congress, to which all citizens and taxpayers are entitled." Pet. for Cert. 46.

Petitioners filed a motion to dismiss respondents' complaint on the ground that respondents lacked standing to bring the action, and because the complaint failed to state a cause of action upon which relief could be granted. The latter ground was based upon the contention that the Incompatibility Clause sets forth a qualification for Membership in the Congress, U. S. Const., Art. I, § 5, cl. 1, not a qualification for a position in the Executive Branch. The power to judge that qualification was as-

---

[3] Respondents appear to have had reference in part to pressure that conceivably could be applied to reservist Members of Congress through such offices as the President's power to call reservists to active duty without their consent, 10 U. S. C. §§ 672–675, or his power to discharge commissioned reservists, who serve only at his pleasure. 10 U. S. C. § 593.

serted to rest exclusively with Congress, not the courts, under *Powell* v. *McCormack,* 395 U. S. 486, 550 (1969).

The District Court concluded that it first had to determine whether respondents had standing to bring the action and, without citation to authority, stated:

> "In recent years the Supreme Court has greatly expanded the concept of standing and in this Circuit the concept has now been almost completely abandoned."   323 F. Supp., at 839.

The court then held that of the four classes respondents sought to represent, "[o]nly their status as citizens" gave them standing to sue in this case. *Id.,* at 840. The District Court denied standing to respondents as reservists, as opponents of our Vietnam involvement, and as taxpayers. The court acknowledged that there were very few instances in which the assertion of "merely the undifferentiated interest of citizens," *ibid.,* would be sufficient, but was persuaded to find that interest sufficient here by several considerations it found present in the nature of the dispute before it and by the asserted abandonment of standing limitations by the Court of Appeals, whose decisions were binding on the District Court.

In response to petitioners' contention that the Incompatibility Clause sets forth a qualification only for Membership in the Congress, which Congress alone might judge, the District Court characterized the issue as whether respondents presented a nonjusticiable "political question," resolution of which by the text of the Constitution was committed to the Congress under *Baker* v. *Carr,* 369 U. S. 186, 217 (1962). The court held that the failure of the Executive Branch to remove reservist Members of Congress from their Reserve positions was justiciable.

7

Having resolved the issues of standing and political question in favor of respondents, the District Court held on the merits that a commission in the Reserves is an "Office under the United States" within the meaning of the Incompatibility Clause. On the basis of the foregoing, the court in its final order granted partial summary judgment for respondents by declaring that the Incompatibility Clause renders a Member of Congress ineligible, during his continuance in office, to hold a Reserve "commission"; the court denied such parts of respondents' motion for summary judgment which sought a permanent injunction and relief in the nature of mandamus.[4] 323 F. Supp., at 843.

The Court of Appeals affirmed the judgment of the District Court in an unpublished opinion "on the basis of the memorandum opinion of the District Court." The Court of Appeals added that it was "also of the view that [respondents] have the requisite standing and that their claim is judicially enforceable under the rationale of" *Flast* v. *Cohen*, 392 U. S. 83 (1968), and *Baker* v. *Carr, supra.* Petitioners present three questions for review: (1) whether respondents have standing, "either as citizens or as federal taxpayers," to bring this claim, (2) whether respondents' claim presents a "political question" not subject to judicial review, and (3) whether "membership" in the Reserves constitutes an "Office under the United States" within the meaning of the Incompatibility Clause. Pet. for Cert. 2.

---

[4] Respondents did not, in the Court of Appeals, or by cross-petition here challenge the District Court's denial of injunctive and mandamus relief. In light of the ground for our disposition of the case, we need not and do not address ourselves to the validity or scope of the District Court's ruling on the merits of respondents' claim, or the relief it granted.

II

A

In *Flast* v. *Cohen, supra,* at 95, the Court noted that the concept of justiciability, which expresses the jurisdictional limitations imposed upon federal courts by the "case or controversy" requirement of Art. III, embodies both the standing and political question doctrines upon which petitioners in part rely. Each of these doctrines poses a distinct and separate limitation, *Powell* v. *McCormack,* 395 U. S., at 512; *Baker* v. *Carr, supra,* at 198, so that either the absence of standing or the presence of a political question suffices to prevent the power of the federal judiciary from being invoked by the complaining party. The more sensitive and complex task of determining whether a particular issue presents a political question causes courts, as did the District Court here, to turn initially, although not invariably,[5] to the question of standing to sue. In light of the District Court's action we turn to petitioners' contention that respondents lacked standing to bring the suit. Our conclusion that the District Court erred in holding that respondents had standing to sue as United States citizens,

---

[5] The lack of a fixed rule as to the proper sequence of judicial analysis of contentions involving more than one facet of the concept of justiciability was recently exhibited by the Court of Appeals for the Second Circuit, which bypassed a determination on standing to rule that a claim was not justiciable because it presented a political question:

"[T]he standing of a party need not come into question if a court determines that for other reasons the issue raised before the bench is non-justiciable."

That court thus held in effect that if no justiciable question is presented no one has standing. *DaCosta* v. *Laird,* 471 F. 2d 1146, 1152 (1973). See also *Sierra Club* v. *Morton,* 405 U. S. 727, 731 (1972); *Flast* v. *Cohen,* 392 U. S. 83, 100 (1968).

but was correct in denying respondents' standing as taxpayers, eliminates the need to consider the other questions presented by petitioners.

The District Court considered standing as to each of the four capacities in which respondents brought suit; it rejected standing as to three of the four, holding that respondents could sue only as citizens. The Court of Appeals' judgment of affirmance, based solely upon the opinion of the District Court, did not alter the District Court's ruling on standing. The standing question presented in the petition for certiorari is addressed to the District Court's holding on citizen standing and seeks to add the question whether respondents also had standing as taxpayers.[6] Respondents do not contend that the District Court erred in denying standing to them in the other two capacities in which they sought to proceed, i. e., as opponents of American military involvement in Vietnam, and as reservists. We therefore proceed to consideration of respondents' standing only as citizens and taxpayers.

B

Citizen Standing

To have standing to sue as a class representative it is essential that a plaintiff must be a part of that class, that is, he must possess the same interest and suffer the same injury shared by all members of the class he represents. *Indiana Employment Division* v. *Burney,* 409 U. S. 540 (1973); *Bailey* v. *Patterson,* 369 U. S. 31 (1962). In granting respondents standing to sue as representatives

---

[6] The Court of Appeals did no more than affirm the judgment of the District Court, including the latter's denial of respondents' standing as taxpayers. Petitioners may, however, have sought to raise the issue of taxpayer standing in this Court because of the ambiguous reference in the Court of Appeals' judgment of affirmance to *Flast* v. *Cohen, supra,* a taxpayer-standing case.

of the class of all United States citizens, the District Court therefore necessarily—and correctly—characterized respondents' interest as "undifferentiated" from that of all other citizens.

The only interest all citizens share in the claim advanced by respondents is one which presents injury in the abstract. Respondents seek to have the Judicial Branch compel the Executive Branch to act in conformity with the Incompatibility Clause, an interest shared by all citizens. The very language of respondents' complaint, *supra,* at 212, reveals that it is nothing more than a matter of speculation whether the claimed nonobservance of that Clause deprives citizens of the faithful discharge of the legislative duties of reservist Members of Congress. And that claimed nonobservance, standing alone, would adversely affect only the generalized interest of all citizens in constitutional governance, and that is an abstract injury.[7] The Court has previously declined to treat "generalized grievances" about the conduct of Government as a basis for taxpayer standing. *Flast* v. *Cohen,* 392 U. S., at 106. We consider now whether a citizen has standing to sue under such a generalized complaint.

Our analysis begins with *Baker* v. *Carr,* 369 U. S. 186 (1962), where the Court stated that the gist of the inquiry must be whether the complaining party has

> "alleged such a personal stake in the outcome of the controversy as to assure that concrete adverseness which sharpens the presentation of issues upon which

---

[7] The generalized nature of respondents' claim is revealed by the scope of relief sought, *i. e.,* removal of all reservist Members of Congress from Reserve status rather than the removal of only those reservist Members who manifested by their actions that they were influenced by their Reserve status to act adversely to respondents' interest.

11

the court so largely depends for illumination of difficult constitutional questions." *Id.*, at 204.

Although dealing with a case of claimed taxpayer standing, *Flast* v. *Cohen, supra,* gave further meaning to the need for a "personal stake" in noting that it was meant to assure that the complainant seeking to adjudicate his claim was the "proper party" to present the claim "in an adversary context and in a form historically viewed as capable of judicial resolution." 392 U. S., at 100, 101. In the circumstances of *Flast,* the Court held that the taxpayer-complainant before it had established a relationship between his status as a taxpayer and his claim under the Taxing and Spending Clause sufficient to give assurance

> "that the questions will be framed with the necessary specificity, that the issues will be contested with the necessary adverseness and that the litigation will be pursued with the necessary vigor to assure that the constitutional challenge will be made in a form traditionally thought to be capable of judicial resolution." *Id.*, at 106.

While *Flast* noted that the "case or controversy" limitation on the federal judicial power found in Art. III is a "blend of constitutional requirements and policy considerations," *id.*, at 97, the Court, subsequently, in the context of judicial review of regulatory agency action held that whatever else the "case or controversy" requirement embodied, its essence is a requirement of "injury in fact." *Association of Data Processing Service Organizations, Inc.* v. *Camp,* 397 U. S. 150, 152 (1970). Although we there noted that the categories of judicially cognizable injury were being broadened, *id.*, at 154, we have more recently stressed that the broadening of *categories* "is a different matter from abandoning the requirement that the party seeking review must himself have suffered an injury."

Sierra Club v. *Morton,* 405 U. S. 727, 738 (1972). And, in defining the nature of that injury, we have only recently stated flatly: "Abstract injury is not enough." *O'Shea* v. *Littleton,* 414 U. S. 488, 494 (1974).

Ex parte Lévitt, 302 U. S. 633 (1937), was the only other occasion in which the Court faced a question under Art. I, § 6, cl. 2, although that challenge was made under the Ineligibility Clause, not the Incompatibility Clause involved here. There a petition was filed in this Court seeking an order to show cause why one of the Justices should not be disqualified to serve as an Associate Justice. The petition asserted that the appointment and confirmation of the Justice in August 1937 was unlawful because the Act of March 1, 1937, permitting Justices to retire at full salary after a period of specified service, thereby increased the emoluments of the office and that the statute was enacted while the challenged Justice was a Senator. The appointment of the Justice by the President and his confirmation by the Senate were thus said to violate the Ineligibility Clause which provides:

> "No Senator or Representative shall, during the Time for which he was elected, be appointed to any civil Office under the Authority of the United States . . . the Emoluments whereof shall have been encreased during such time . . . ."

The Court held:

> "The motion papers disclose no interest upon the part of the petitioner other than that of a citizen and a member of the bar of this Court. That is insufficient. It is an established principle that to entitle a private individual to invoke the judicial power to determine the validity of executive or legislative action he must show that he has sustained or is immediately in danger of sustaining a direct injury as the result of that action and it is not

13

sufficient that he has merely a general interest common to all members of the public." 302 U. S., at 634.[8]

The Court has today recognized the continued vitality of *Lévitt*,[9] *United States* v. *Richardson, ante,* at 176–179; see also *Laird* v. *Tatum,* 408 U. S. 1, 13 (1972). We reaffirm *Lévitt* in holding that standing to sue may not be predicated upon an interest of the kind alleged here which is held in common by all members of the public, because of the necessarily abstract nature of the injury all citizens share. Concrete injury, whether actual or threatened, is that indispensable element of a dispute which serves in part to cast it in a form traditionally

---

[8] The Court cited a number of cases in support of its holding, nearly all of which contained language similar to that quoted in the text. See *Frothingham* v. *Mellon,* 262 U. S. 447, 488 (1923) (insufficient for a party to show "merely that he suffers in some indefinite way in common with people generally"); *Fairchild* v. *Hughes,* 258 U. S. 126, 129–130 (1922) ("Plaintiff has only the right, possessed by every citizen, to require that the Government be administered according to law and that the public moneys be not wasted. Obviously this general right does not entitle a private citizen to institute in the federal courts a suit"); *Tyler* v. *Judges of Court of Registration,* 179 U. S. 405, 406 (1900) ("even in a proceeding which he prosecutes for the benefit of the public . . . [the plaintiff] must generally aver an injury peculiar to himself, as distinguished from the great body of his fellow citizens"). See also *Giles* v. *Harris,* 189 U. S. 475, 486 (1903) (Holmes, J.) ("The plaintiff alleges that the whole registration scheme of the Alabama constitution is a fraud upon the Constitution of the United States, and asks us to declare it void. But of course he could not maintain a bill for a mere declaration in the air"). Cf. *Newman* v. *Frizzell,* 238 U. S. 537, 550 (1915).

[9] The Court has also recently cited with approval two of the principal cases relied upon in *Ex parte Lévitt,* 302 U. S. 633 (1937). *Frothingham* v. *Mellon, supra,* was used for support in *O'Shea* v. *Littleton,* 414 U. S. 488, 494 (1974), as was *Fairchild* v. *Hughes, supra,* used in *Baker* v. *Carr,* 369 U. S. 186, 208 (1962).

capable of judicial resolution. It adds the essential
dimension of specificity to the dispute by requiring that
the complaining party have suffered a particular injury
caused by the action challenged as unlawful. This
personal stake is what the Court has consistently held
enables a complainant authoritatively to present to a
court a complete perspective upon the adverse consequences flowing from the specific set of facts undergirding
his grievance. Such authoritative presentations are an
integral part of the judicial process, for a court must rely
on the parties' treatment of the facts and claims before
it to develop its rules of law.[10] Only concrete injury
presents the factual context within which a court, aided
by parties who argue within the context, is capable of
making decisions.

Moreover, when a court is asked to undertake constitutional adjudication, the most important and delicate of
its responsibilities, the requirement of concrete injury
further serves the function of insuring that such adjudication does not take place unnecessarily. This principle
is particularly applicable here, where respondents seek an
interpretation of a constitutional provision which has
never before been construed by the federal courts. First,
concrete injury removes from the realm of speculation
whether there is a real need to exercise the power of
judicial review in order to protect the interests of the
complaining party.

"The desire to obtain [sweeping relief] cannot be

---

[10] This is in sharp contrast to the political processes in which
the Congress can initiate inquiry and action, define issues and objectives, and exercise virtually unlimited power by way of hearings and
reports, thus making a record for plenary consideration and solutions. The legislative function is inherently general rather than
particular and is not intended to be responsive to adversaries asserting specific claims or interests peculiar to themselves.

accepted as a substitute for compliance with the general rule that the complainant must present facts sufficient to show that his individual need requires the remedy for which he asks." *McCabe* v. *Atchison, T. & S. F. R. Co.*, 235 U. S. 151, 164 (1914).

Second, the discrete factual context within which the concrete injury occurred or is threatened insures the framing of relief no broader than required by the precise facts to which the court's ruling would be applied. This is especially important when the relief sought produces a confrontation with one of the coordinate branches of the Government; here the relief sought would, in practical effect, bring about conflict with two coordinate branches.

To permit a complainant who has no concrete injury to require a court to rule on important constitutional issues in the abstract would create the potential for abuse of the judicial process, distort the role of the Judiciary in its relationship to the Executive and the Legislature and open the Judiciary to an arguable charge of providing "government by injunction."

"The powers of the federal judiciary will be adequate for the great burdens placed upon them only if they are employed prudently, with recognition of the strengths as well as the hazards that go with our kind of representative government." *Flast* v. *Cohen*, 392 U. S., at 131 (Harlan, J., dissenting).[11]

Our conclusion that there is no citizen standing here, apart from being in accord with all other federal courts of appeals that have considered the question, until the

---

[11] We have expressed apprehension about claims of standing based on "mere 'interest in a problem.'" See, *e. g., Sierra Club*, 405 U. S., at 739. Earlier cases of the Court evidenced comparable concern. See, *e. g., Newman* v. *Frizzell*, 238 U. S., at 552 n. 8.

Court of Appeals' holding now under review,[12] is also consistent with the recent holdings of this Court. It is one thing for a court to hear an individual's complaint that certain specific government action will cause that person private competitive injury, *Association of Data Processing Service Organizations, Inc.* v. *Camp*, 397 U. S. 150 (1970), or a complaint that individual enjoyment of certain natural resources has been impaired by such action, *United States* v. *SCRAP*, 412 U. S. 669, 687 (1973), but it is another matter to allow a citizen to call on the courts to resolve abstract questions.[13] The former provides the setting for a focused consideration of a concrete injury. In the latter, although allegations assert an arguable conflict with some limitation of the Constitution, it can be only a matter of speculation whether the claimed violation has caused concrete injury to the particular complainant.

----

[12] *Lamm* v. *Volpe*, 449 F. 2d 1202, 1204 (CA10 1971); *Pietsch* v. *President of United States*, 434 F. 2d 861, 863 (CA2 1970) (Clark, J.); *Troutman* v. *Shriver*, 417 F. 2d 171, 174 (CA5 1969) (citing *Lévitt, supra*); *Velvel* v. *Nixon*, 415 F. 2d 236, 239 (CA10 1969); *Pauling* v. *McElroy*, 107 U. S. App. D. C. 372, 374, 278 F. 2d 252, 254 (1960); cf. *Sharrow* v. *Brown*, 447 F. 2d 94, 97 (CA2 1971). And aside from the decision under review, the only other opinion that appears to have ruled otherwise is *Atlee* v. *Laird*, 339 F. Supp. 1347 (ED Pa. 1972), which relied upon the decision of the District Court here. *Id.*, at 1357 n. 8.

[13] The Court of Appeals' reliance on *Baker* v. *Carr*, 369 U. S. 186 (1962), is inapposite. *United States* v. *SCRAP*, 412 U. S. 669 (1973), pointed out that a personal stake in a fraction of a vote in *Baker* v. *Carr* was sufficient to support standing. *Id.*, at 689 n. 14. The injury asserted in *Baker* was thus a concrete injury to fundamental voting rights, as distinguished from the abstract injury in nonobservance of the Constitution asserted by respondents as citizens.

In *Baker* v. *Carr*, the Court cited with approval the early case of *Liverpool, N. Y. & Phila. S. S. Co.* v. *Comm'rs of Emigration*, 113 U. S. 33 (1885), where it was held that a federal court can adjudge rights only "in actual controversies." *Id.*, at 39.

Finally, the several considerations advanced by the District Court in support of respondents' standing as citizens do not militate against our conclusion that it was error to grant standing to respondents as citizens. First, the District Court acknowledged that any injury resulting from the reservist status of Members of Congress was hypothetical, but stressed that the Incompatibility Clause was designed to prohibit such potential for injury.[14] 323 F. Supp., at 840. This rationale fails, however, to compensate for the respondents' failure to present a claim under that Clause which alleges concrete injury. The claims of respondents here, like the claim under the Ineligibility Clause in *Levitt, supra,* would require courts to deal with a difficult and sensitive issue of constitutional adjudication on the complaint of one who does not allege "a personal stake in the outcome of the controversy." *Baker* v. *Carr,* 369 U. S., at 204. To support standing there must be concrete injury in a form which assures "the necessary specificity" called for by *Flast,* 392 U. S., at 106, and "that concrete adverseness . . . upon which the court so largely depends for illumination of difficult constitutional questions." *Baker* v. *Carr, supra,* at 204.

---

[14] The District Court made analogy to conflict-of-interest statutes which, it said, are directed at avoiding circumstances of potential, not actual, impropriety. We have no doubt that if the Congress enacted a statute creating such a legal right, the requisite injury for standing would be found in an invasion of that right. *O'Shea* v. *Littleton,* 414 U. S., at 493 n. 2; *Linda R. S.* v. *Richard D.,* 410 U. S. 614, 617 n. 3 (1973); *Association of Data Processing Service Organizations, Inc.* v. *Camp,* 397 U. S. 150, 154 (1970). But to satisfy the Art. III prerequisite the complaining party would still be required to allege a specific invasion of the right suffered by him. Standing could not be found—as it is not here—in a citizen who alleged no more than the right of all other citizens to have government conducted without what he perceived, without himself having suffered concrete harm, to be proscribed conflicts of interest.

Standing was thus found by premature evaluation of the merits of respondents' complaint.[15]

The District Court next acknowledged this Court's longstanding reluctance to entertain "generalized grievances about the conduct of government," *Flast* v. *Cohen*, 392 U. S., at 106, but distinguished respondents' complaint from such grievances by characterizing the Incompatibility Clause as "precise [and] self-operative." 323 F. Supp., at 840. Even accepting that characterization of the Clause it is not an adequate substitute for the judicially cognizable injury not present here. Moreover, that characterization rested, as did the preceding characterization, on an interpretation of the Clause by way of the Court's preliminary appraisal of the merits of respondents' claim before standing was found. In any event, the Ineligibility Clause involved in *Lévitt, supra,* is no less specific or less "precise [and] self-operative" than the Incompatibility Clause.

The District Court further relied on the fact that the adverse parties sharply conflicted in their interests and views and were supported by able briefs and arguments. *Id.,* at 841. We have no doubt about the sincerity of respondents' stated objectives and the depth of their commitment to them. But the essence of standing

> "is not a question of motivation but of possession of the requisite . . . interest that is, or is threatened

---

[15] Looking "to the substantive issues" which *Flast* stated to be both "appropriate and necessary" in relation to taxpayer standing was for the express purpose of determining "whether there is a logical nexus between the [taxpayer] status asserted and the claim sought to be adjudicated." 392 U. S., at 102. This step is not appropriate on a claim of citizen standing since the *Flast* nexus test is not applicable where the taxing and spending power is not challenged. Hence there was no occasion for the District Court or the Court of Appeals to reach or evaluate what it saw as the merits of respondents' complaint.

to be, injured by the unconstitutional conduct."
Doremus v. *Board of Education*, 342 U. S. 429, 435
(1952).

This same theme as to the inadequacy of motivation to
support standing is suggested in the Court's opinion in
Sierra Club, supra:

"But a mere 'interest in a problem,' no matter how
longstanding the interest and no matter how qualified the organization is in evaluating the problem,
is not sufficient by itself to render the organization
'adversely affected' or 'aggrieved' within the meaning of the APA." 405 U. S., at 739.

Respondents' motivation has indeed brought them
sharply into conflict with petitioners, but as the Court
has noted, motivation is not a substitute for the actual
injury needed by the courts and adversaries to focus
litigation efforts and judicial decisionmaking. Moreover,
the evaluation of the quality of the presentation on the
merits was a retrospective judgment that could have
properly been arrived at only after standing had been
found so as to permit the court to consider the merits.
A logical corollary to this approach would be the manifestly untenable view that the inadequacy of the presentation on the merits would be an appropriate basis for
denying standing.

Furthermore, to have reached the conclusion that respondents' interests as citizens were meant to be protected by the Incompatibility Clause because the primary
purpose of the Clause was to insure independence of each
of the branches of the Federal Government, similarly involved an appraisal of the merits before the issue of standing was resolved. All citizens, of course, share equally
an interest in the independence of each branch of Government. In some fashion, every provision of the Consti-

tution was meant to serve the interests of all. Such a generalized interest, however, is too abstract to constitute a "case or controversy" appropriate for judicial resolution.[16] The proposition that all constitutional provisions are enforceable by any citizen simply because citizens are the ultimate beneficiaries of those provisions has no boundaries.

Closely linked to the idea that generalized citizen interest is a sufficient basis for standing was the District Court's observation that it was not irrelevant that if respondents could not obtain judicial review of petitioners' action, "then as a practical matter no one can." Our system of government leaves many crucial decisions to the political processes. The assumption that if respondents have no standing to sue, no one would have standing, is not a reason to find standing. See *United States* v. *Richardson, ante,* at 179.

C

Taxpayer Standing

Consideration of whether respondents have standing to sue as taxpayers raises a different question from whether they may sue as citizens. *Flast* v. *Cohen, supra,* established that status as a taxpayer can, under certain limited circumstances, supply the personal stake essential to standing. There, the Court held that, in order to ensure the necessary personal stake, there must be "a logical

---

[16] Satisfaction of the *Data Processing* "zone of interest" requirement seemingly relied upon to find citizen standing does not support such standing for two reasons: first, that case involved judicial review under the Administrative Procedure Act of regulatory agency action alleged to have caused private competitive injury; second, *Data Processing* required a showing of injury in fact, in addition to the "zone of interest" requirement. Until a judicially cognizable injury is shown no other inquiry is relevant to consideration of citizen standing.

nexus between the [taxpayer] status asserted and the claim sought to be adjudicated," 392 U. S., at 102. In *Flast,* the Court determined that the taxpayer demonstrated such a "logical nexus" because, (1) he challenged the exercise of "congressional power under the taxing and spending clause of Art. I, § 8 . . ." and (2) "the challenged enactment exceed[ed] specific constitutional limitations imposed upon the exercise of the congressional taxing and spending power" under Art. I, § 8. *Id.,* at 102–103.

Here, the District Court, applying the *Flast* holding, denied respondents' standing as taxpayers for failure to satisfy the nexus test. We agree with that conclusion since respondents did not challenge an enactment under Art. I, § 8, but rather the action of the Executive Branch in permitting Members of Congress to maintain their Reserve status.[17]

Accordingly, the judgment of the Court of Appeals is reversed, and the case is remanded to the District Court for further proceedings consistent with this opinion.

It is so ordered.

---

[17] As noted earlier, *supra,* at 211, respondents requested the District Court to compel petitioners to seek to reclaim Reserve pay received by reservist Members of Congress. Such relief would follow from the invalidity of Executive action in paying persons who could not lawfully have been reservists, not from the invalidity of the statutes authorizing pay to those who lawfully were Reservists.

UNITED STATES *v.* BREWSTER

APPEAL FROM THE UNITED STATES DISTRICT COURT FOR THE
DISTRICT OF COLUMBIA

No. 70–45. Argued October 18, 1971—Reargued March 20, 1972—
Decided June 29, 1972

Appellee, a former United States Senator, was charged with the
solicitation and acceptance of bribes in violation of 18 U. S. C.
§§ 201 (c)(1) and 201 (g). The District Court, on appellee's pretrial motion, dismissed the indictment on the ground that the
Speech or Debate Clause of the Constitution shielded him "from
any prosecution for alleged bribery to perform a legislative act."
The United States filed a direct appeal to this Court under 18
U. S. C. § 3731 (1964 ed., Supp. V), which appellee contends this
Court does not have jurisdiction to entertain because the District
Court's action was not "a decision or judgment setting aside, or
dismissing" the indictment but was instead a summary judgment
on the merits based on the facts of the case. *Held:*

1. This Court has jurisdiction under 18 U. S. C. § 3731 (1964
ed., Supp. V) to hear the appeal, since the District Court's order
was based upon its determination of the constitutional invalidity
of 18 U. S. C. §§ 201 (c)(1) and 201 (g) on the facts as alleged in
the indictment. Pp. 504–507.

2. The prosecution of appellee is not prohibited by the Speech
or Debate Clause. Although that provision protects Members of
Congress from inquiry into legislative acts or the motivation for
performance of such acts, *United States* v. *Johnson,* 383 U. S. 169,
185, it does not protect all conduct *relating* to the legislative process. Since in this case prosecution of the bribery charges does not
necessitate inquiry into legislative acts or motivation, the District
Court erred in holding that the Speech or Debate Clause required
dismissal of the indictment. Pp. 507–529.

Reversed and remanded.

BURGER, C. J., delivered the opinion of the Court, in which STEW-
ART, MARSHALL, BLACKMUN, POWELL, and REHNQUIST, JJ., joined.
BRENNAN, J., filed a dissenting opinion in which DOUGLAS, J., joined,
post, p. 529. WHITE, J., filed a dissenting opinion, in which DOUGLAS
and BRENNAN, JJ., joined, *post,* p. 551.

Solicitor General Griswold reargued the cause for the United States. With him on the briefs on the original argument were *Assistant Attorney General Wilson, Jerome M. Feit,* and *Beatrice Rosenberg.* With him on the brief on the reargument were *Assistant Attorney General Petersen* and *Mr. Feit.*

Norman P. Ramsey reargued the cause for appellee. With him on the briefs were *Thomas Waxter, Jr.,* and *H. Thomas Howell.*

MR. CHIEF JUSTICE BURGER delivered the opinion of the Court.

This direct appeal from the District Court presents the question whether a Member of Congress may be prosecuted under 18 U. S. C. §§ 201 (c)(1), 201 (g), for accepting a bribe in exchange for a promise relating to an official act. Appellee, a former United States Senator, was charged in five counts of a 10-count indictment.[1] Counts one, three, five, and seven alleged that on four separate occasions, appellee, while he was a Senator and a member of the Senate Committee on Post Office and Civil Service,

> "directly and indirectly, corruptly asked, solicited, sought, accepted, received and agreed to receive [sums] . . . in return for being influenced in his performance of official acts in respect to his action, vote, and decision on postage rate legislation which might at any time be pending before him in his official capacity . . . in violation of Sections 201 (c)(1) and 2, Title 18, United States Code."[2]

[1] The remaining five counts charged the alleged bribers with offering and giving bribes in violation of 18 U. S. C. § 201 (b).

[2] Title 18 U. S. C. § 201 (c) provides: "Whoever, being a public official or person selected to be a public official, directly or indirectly, corruptly asks, demands, exacts, solicits, seeks, accepts, receives,

Count nine charged that appellee

"directly and indirectly, asked, demanded, exacted, solicited, sought, accepted, received and agreed to receive [a sum] . . . for and because of official acts performed by him in respect to his action, vote and decision on postage rate legislation which had been pending before him in his official capacity . . . in violation of Sections 201 (g) and 2, Title 18, United States Code." [3]

Before a trial date was set, the appellee moved to dismiss the indictment on the ground of immunity under the Speech or Debate Clause, Art. I, § 6, of the Constitution, which provides:

"[F]or any Speech or Debate in either House, they [Senators or Representatives] shall not be questioned in any other Place."

After hearing argument, the District Court ruled from the bench:

"Gentlemen, based on the facts of this case,

___

or agrees to receive anything of value for himself or for any other person or entity, in return for:

"(1) being influenced in his performance of any official act . . . [shall be guilty of an offense]."

Title 18 U. S. C. § 201 (a) defines "public official" to include "Member of Congress." The same subsection provides: " 'official act' means any decision or action on any question, matter, cause, suit, proceeding or controversy, which may at any time be pending, or which may by law be brought before any public official, in his official capacity, or in his place of trust or profit." Title 18 U. S. C. § 2 is the aiding or abetting statute.

[3] Title 18 U. S. C. § 201 (g) provides: "Whoever, being a public official, former public official, or person selected to be a public official, otherwise than as provided by law for the proper discharge of official duty, directly or indirectly asks, demands, exacts, solicits, seeks, accepts, receives, or agrees to receive anything of value for himself for or because of any official act performed or to be performed by him . . . [shall be guilty of an offense]."

25

it is admitted by the Government that the five counts of the indictment which charge Senator Brewster relate to the acceptance of bribes in connection with the performance of a legislative function by a Senator of the United States.

"It is the opinion of this Court that the immunity under the Speech and [sic] Debate Clause of the Constitution, particularly in view of the interpretation given that Clause by the Supreme Court in Johnson, shields Senator Brewster, constitutionally shields him from any prosecution for alleged bribery to perform a legislative act.

"I will, therefore, dismiss the odd counts of the indictment, 1, 3, 5, 7 and 9, as they apply to Senator Brewster."

The United States filed a direct appeal to this Court, pursuant to 18 U. S. C. § 3731 (1964 ed., Supp. V).[4] We postponed consideration of jurisdiction until hearing the case on the merits.   401 U. S. 935 (1971).

I

The United States asserts that this Court has jurisdiction under 18 U. S. C. § 3731 (1964 ed., Supp. V) to

---

[4] Title 18 U. S. C. § 3731 provided in relevant part:

"An appeal may be taken by and on behalf of the United States from the district courts direct to the Supreme Court of the United States in all criminal cases in the following instances:

"From a decision or judgment setting aside, or dismissing any indictment or information, or any count thereof, where such decision or judgment is based upon the invalidity or construction of the statute upon which the indictment or information is founded.

.   .   .   .   .

"From the decision or judgment sustaining a motion in bar, when the defendant has not been put in jeopardy."

The statute has since been amended to eliminate the direct appeal provision on which the United States relies.   18 U. S. C. § 3731. This appeal, however, was perfected under the old statute.

review the District Court's dismissal of the indictment against appellee. Specifically, the United States urges that the District Court decision was either "a decision or judgment setting aside, or dismissing [an] indictment . . . or any count thereof, where such decision or judgment is based upon the invalidity or construction of the statute upon which the indictment . . . is founded" or a "decision or judgment sustaining a motion in bar, when the defendant has not been put in jeopardy." If the District Court decision is correctly characterized by either of those descriptions, this Court has jurisdiction under the statute to hear the United States' appeal.

In *United States* v. *Knox,* 396 U. S. 77 (1969), we considered a direct appeal by the United States from the dismissal of an indictment that charged the appellee in that case with violating 18 U. S. C. § 1001, a general criminal provision punishing fraudulent statements made to any federal agency. The appellee, Knox, had been accused of willfully understating the number of employees accepting wagers on his behalf when he filed a form that persons engaged in the business of accepting wagers were required by law to file. The District Court dismissed the counts charging violations of § 1001 on the ground that the appellee could not be prosecuted for failure to answer the wagering form correctly since his Fifth Amendment privilege against self-incrimination prevented prosecution for failure to file the form in any respect. We found jurisdiction under § 3731 to hear the appeal in *Knox* on the theory that the District Court had passed on the validity of the statute on which the indictment rested. 396 U. S., at 79 n. 2. The District Court in that case held that "§ 1001, as applied to this class of cases, is constitutionally invalid." *Ibid.*

The counts of the indictment involved in the instant case were based on 18 U. S. C. § 201, a bribery statute.

27

Section 201 applies to "public officials," and that term
is defined explicitly to include Members of Congress
as well as other employees and officers of the United
States.   Subsections (c)(1) and (g) prohibit the accepting of a bribe in return for being influenced in or
performing an official act.   The ruling of the District
Court here was that "the Speech [or] Debate Clause of
the Constitution, particularly in view of the interpretation given . . . in Johnson, shields Senator Brewster . . .
from any prosecution for alleged bribery to perform a
legislative act."   Since § 201 applies only to bribery for
the performance of official acts, the District Court's
ruling is that, as applied to Members of Congress, § 201
is constitutionally invalid.

Appellee argues that the action of the District Court
was not "a decision or judgment setting aside, or dismissing" the indictment, but was instead a summary
judgment on the merits.   Appellee also argues that the
District Court did not rule that § 201 could never be
constitutionally applied to a Member of Congress, but
that "based on the facts of this case" the statute could not
be constitutionally applied.   Under *United States* v.
Sisson, 399 U. S. 267 (1970), an appeal does not lie
from a decision that rests, not upon the sufficiency of
the indictment alone, but upon extraneous facts.   If
an indictment is dismissed as a result of a stipulated
fact or the showing of evidentiary facts outside the
indictment, which facts would constitute a defense on
the merits at trial, no appeal is available.   See *United
States* v. *Findley,* 439 F. 2d 970 (CA1 1971).   Appellee
claims that the District Court relied on factual matter
other than facts alleged in the indictment.

An examination of the record, however, discloses that,
with the exception of a letter in which the United States
briefly outlined the theory of its case against appellee,
there were no "facts" on which the District Court could

28

act other than those recited in the indictment. Appellee contends that the statement "based on the facts of this case," used by the District Judge in announcing his decision, shows reliance on the Government's outline of its case. We read the District Judge's reference to "facts," in context, as a reference to the facts alleged in the indictment, and his ruling as holding that Members of Congress are totally immune from prosecution for accepting bribes for the performance of official, *i. e.,* legislative, acts by virtue of the Speech or Debate Clause. Under that interpretation of § 201, it cannot be applied to a Member of Congress who accepts bribes that relate in any way to his office. We conclude, therefore, that the District Court was relying only on facts alleged in the indictment and that the dismissal of the indictment was based on a determination that the statute on which the indictment was drawn was invalid under the Speech or Debate Clause. As a consequence, this Court has jurisdiction to hear the appeal.

II

The immunities of the Speech or Debate Clause were not written into the Constitution simply for the personal or private benefit of Members of Congress, but to protect the integrity of the legislative process by insuring the independence of individual legislators. The genesis of the Clause at common law is well known. In his opinion for the Court in *United States* v. *Johnson,* 383 U. S. 169 (1966), Mr. Justice Harlan canvassed the history of the Clause and concluded that it

> "was the culmination of a long struggle for parliamentary supremacy. Behind these simple phrases lies a history of conflict between the Commons and the Tudor and Stuart monarchs during which successive monarchs utilized the criminal and civil law to suppress and intimidate critical legisla-

tors. Since the Glorious Revolution in Britain, and throughout United States history, the privilege has been recognized as an important protection of the independence and integrity of the legislature." *Id.,* at 178 (footnote omitted).

Although the Speech or Debate Clause's historic roots are in English history, it must be interpreted in light of the American experience, and in the context of the American constitutional scheme of government rather than the English parliamentary system. We should bear in mind that the English system differs from ours in that their Parliament is the supreme authority, not a co-ordinate branch. Our speech or debate privilege was designed to preserve legislative independence, not supremacy.[5] Our task, therefore, is to apply the Clause in such a way as to insure the independence of the legislature without altering the historic balance of the three co-equal branches of Government.

It does not undermine the validity of the Framers' concern for the independence of the Legislative Branch to acknowledge that our history does not reflect a catalogue of abuses at the hands of the Executive that gave rise to the privilege in England. There is nothing in our history, for example, comparable to the imprisonment of a Member of Parliament in the Tower without a hearing and, owing to the subservience of some royal judges to the 17th and 18th century English kings, without meaningful recourse to a writ of habeas corpus.[6] In fact, on only one previous occasion has this Court ever

---

[5] Cella, The Doctrine of Legislative Privilege of Freedom of Speech and Debate: Its Past, Present and Future as a Bar to Criminal Prosecutions in the Courts, 2 Suffolk L. Rev. 1, 15 (1968); Note, The Bribed Congressman's Immunity from Prosecution, 75 Yale L. J. 335, 337–338 (1965).

[6] See C. Wittke, The History of English Parliamentary Privilege 23–32 (1921).

interpreted the Speech or Debate Clause in the context of a criminal charge against a Member of Congress.

(a) In *United States* v. *Johnson, supra,* the Court reviewed the conviction of a former Representative on seven counts of violating the federal conflict-of-interest statute, 18 U. S. C. § 281 (1964 ed.), and on one count of conspiracy to defraud the United States, 18 U. S. C. § 371. The Court of Appeals had set aside the conviction on the count for conspiracy to defraud as violating the Speech or Debate Clause. Mr. Justice Harlan, speaking for the Court, 383 U. S., at 183, cited the oft-quoted passage of Mr. Justice Lush in *Ex parte Wason,* L. R. 4 Q. B. 573 (1869):

> "I am clearly of opinion that we ought not to allow it to be doubted for a moment that the motives or intentions of members of either House cannot be inquired into by criminal proceedings *with respect to anything they may do or say in the House.*" *Id.,* at 577 (emphasis added).

In *Kilbourn* v. *Thompson,* 103 U. S. 168 (1881), the first case in which this Court interpreted the Speech or Debate Clause, the Court expressed a similar view of the ambit of the American privilege. There the Court said the Clause is to be read broadly to include anything "generally done in a session of the House by one of its members in relation to the business before it." *Id.,* at 204. This statement, too, was cited with approval in *Johnson,* 383 U. S., at 179. Our conclusion in *Johnson* was that the privilege protected Members from inquiry into legislative acts or the motivation for actual performance of legislative acts. *Id.,* at 185.

In applying the Speech or Debate Clause, the Court focused on the specific facts of the *Johnson* prosecution. The conspiracy-to-defraud count alleged an agreement among Representative Johnson and three co-

31

defendants to obtain the dismissal of pending indictments against officials of savings and loan institutions. For these services, which included a speech made by Johnson on the House floor, the Government claimed Johnson was paid a bribe. At trial, the Government questioned Johnson extensively, relative to the conspiracy-to-defraud count, concerning the authorship of the speech, the factual basis for certain statements made in the speech, and his motives for giving the speech. The Court held that the use of evidence of a speech to support a count under a broad conspiracy statute was prohibited by the Speech or Debate Clause. The Government was, therefore, precluded from prosecuting the conspiracy count on retrial, insofar as it depended on inquiries into speeches made in the House.

It is important to note the very narrow scope of the Court's holding in *Johnson:*

> "We hold that a prosecution under a general criminal statute dependent on such inquiries [into the speech or its preparation] necessarily contravenes the Speech or Debate Clause. We emphasize that our holding is limited to prosecutions involving circumstances such as those presented in the case before us." 383 U. S., at 184–185.

The opinion specifically left open the question of a prosecution which, though possibly entailing some reference to legislative acts, is founded upon a "narrowly drawn" statute passed by Congress in the exercise of its power to regulate its Members' conduct. Of more relevance to this case, the Court in *Johnson* emphasized that its decision did not affect a prosecution that, though founded on a criminal statute of general application, "does not draw in question the legislative acts of the defendant member of Congress or his motives for performing them." *Id.*, at 185. The Court did not

32

question the power of the United States to try Johnson on the conflict-of-interest counts, and it authorized a new trial on the conspiracy count, provided that all references to the making of the speech were eliminated.[7]

Three members of the Court would have affirmed Johnson's conviction. Mr. Chief Justice Warren, joined by MR. JUSTICE DOUGLAS and MR. JUSTICE BRENNAN, concurring in part and dissenting in part, stated:

"After reading the record, it is my conclusion that the Court of Appeals erred in determining that the evidence concerning the speech infected the jury's judgment on the [conflict-of-interest] counts. The evidence amply supports the prosecution's theory and the jury's verdict on these counts—that the respondent received over $20,000 for attempting to have the Justice Department dismiss an indictment against his [present] co-conspirators, without disclosing his role in the enterprise. This is the classic example of a violation of § 281 by a Member of the Congress. . . . The arguments of government counsel and the court's instructions separating the conspiracy from the substantive counts seem unimpeachable. The speech was a minor part of the prosecution. There was nothing in it to inflame the jury and the respondent pointed with pride to it as evidence of his vigilance in protecting the financial institutions of his State. The record further reveals that the trial participants were well aware that a finding of criminality on one count did not authorize sim-

---

[7] On remand, the District Court dismissed the conspiracy count without objection from the Government. Johnson was then found guilty on the remaining counts, and his conviction was affirmed. *United States* v. *Johnson,* 419 F. 2d 56 (CA4 1969), cert. denied, 397 U. S. 1010 (1970).

ilar conclusions as to other counts, and I believe that this salutary principle was conscientiously followed. Therefore, I would affirm the convictions on the substantive counts." *Id.,* at 188–189. (Footnote omitted.)

Johnson thus stands as a unanimous holding that a Member of Congress may be prosecuted under a criminal statute provided that the Government's case does not rely on legislative acts or the motivation for legislative acts. A legislative act has consistently been defined as an act generally done in Congress in relation to the business before it. In sum, the Speech or Debate Clause prohibits inquiry only into those things generally said or done in the House or the Senate in the performance of official duties and into the motivation for those acts.

It is well known, of course, that Members of the Congress engage in many activities other than the purely legislative activities protected by the Speech or Debate Clause. These include a wide range of legitimate "errands" performed for constituents, the making of appointments with Government agencies, assistance in securing Government contracts, preparing so-called "news letters" to constituents, news releases, and speeches delivered outside the Congress. The range of these related activities has grown over the years. They are performed in part because they have come to be expected by constituents, and because they are a means of developing continuing support for future elections. Although these are entirely legitimate activities, they are political in nature rather than legislative, in the sense that term has been used by the Court in prior cases. But it has never been seriously contended that these political matters, however appropriate, have the protection afforded by the Speech or Debate Clause. Careful examination of the decided cases reveals that the Court has regarded the protection as reaching only those things "generally done in a

session of the House by one of its members in relation
to the business before it," *Kilbourn* v. *Thompson, supra,*
at 204, or things "said or done by him, as a representative,
in the exercise of the functions of that office," *Coffin*
v. *Coffin,* 4 Mass. 1, 27 (1808).

(b) Appellee argues, however, that in *Johnson* we expressed a broader test for the coverage of the Speech or
Debate Clause. It is urged that we held that the Clause
protected from executive or judicial inquiry all conduct
"related to the due functioning of the legislative process." It is true that the quoted words appear in the
Johnson opinion, but appellee takes them out of context; in context they reflect a quite different meaning
from that now urged. Although the indictment against
Johnson contained eight counts, only one count was
challenged before this Court as in violation of the Speech
or Debate Clause. The other seven counts concerned
Johnson's attempts to influence staff members of the Justice Department to dismiss pending prosecutions. In explaining why those counts were not before the Court,
Mr. Justice Harlan wrote:

> "No argument is made, nor do we think that it
> could be successfully contended, that the Speech or
> Debate Clause reaches conduct, such as was in-
> volved in the attempt to influence the Department
> of Justice, that is in no wise *related to the due
> functioning of the legislative process.* It is the
> application of this broad conspiracy statute to an
> improperly motivated speech that raises the con-
> stitutional problem with which we deal." 383 U. S.,
> at 172. (Emphasis added; footnote omitted.)

In stating that those things "in no wise related to
the due functioning of the legislative process" were *not*
covered by the privilege, the Court did not in any sense
imply as a corollary that everything that "related" to the

office of a Member was shielded by the Clause. Quite the contrary, in *Johnson* we held, citing *Kilbourn* v. *Thompson, supra,* that only acts generally done in the course of the process of enacting legislation were protected.

Nor can we give *Kilbourn* a more expansive interpretation. In citing with approval, 103 U. S., at 203, the language of Chief Justice Parsons of the Supreme Judicial Court of Massachusetts in *Coffin* v. *Coffin*, 4 Mass. 1 (1808), the *Kilbourn* Court gave no thought to enlarging "legislative acts" to include illicit conduct outside the House. The *Coffin* language is:

> "[The Massachusetts legislative privilege] ought not to be construed strictly, but liberally, that the full design of it may be answered. I will not confine it to delivering an opinion, uttering a speech, or haranguing in debate; but will extend it to the giving of a vote, to the making of a written report, and to every other act resulting from the nature, and in the execution, of the office: and I would define the article, as securing to every member exemption from prosecution, *for every thing said or done by him, as a representative, in the exercise of the functions of that office* without enquiring whether the exercise was regular according to the rules of the house, or irregular and against their rules. I do not confine the member to his place in the house; and I am satisfied that there are cases, in which he is entitled to this privilege, when not within the walls of the representatives' chamber." *Id.,* at 27 (emphasis added).

It is suggested that in citing these words, which were also quoted with approval in *Tenney* v. *Brandhove,* 341 U. S. 367, 373–374 (1951), the Court was interpreting the sweep of the Speech or Debate Clause to be broader than *Johnson* seemed to indicate or than we today hold. Emphasis is placed on the statement that "there are cases in which [a Member] is entitled to this privilege, when not within the walls of the representatives' chamber." But the context of *Coffin* v. *Coffin* indicates that in this passage Chief Justice Parsons was referring only to legislative acts, such as committee meetings, which take place outside the physical confines of the legislative chamber. In another passage, the meaning is clarified:

"If a member . . . be out of the chamber, sitting in committee, executing the commission of the house, it appears to me that such member is within the reason of the article, and ought to be considered within the privilege. The body of which he is a member, is in session, and he, as a member of that body, is in fact discharging the duties of his office. He ought therefore to be protected from civil or criminal prosecutions for every thing said or done by him in the exercise of his functions, as a representative in committee, either in debating, in assenting to, or in draughting a report." [8] 4 Mass., at 28.

In no case has this Court ever treated the Clause as protecting all conduct *relating* to the legislative process.[9] In every case thus far before this Court, the Speech or Debate Clause has been limited to an act which was

---

[8] It is especially important to note that in *Coffin* v. *Coffin*, the court concluded that the defendant was not executing the duties of his office when he allegedly defamed the plaintiff and was hence not entitled to the claim of privilege.

[9] The "concession" MR. JUSTICE BRENNAN seeks to attribute to the Government lawyer who argued the case in the District Court reveals no more than the failure of the arguments in that court to focus on the distinction between true legislative acts and the myriad related political functions of a Member of Congress. The "concession" came in response to a question clearly revealing that the District Court treated as protected all acts "related" to the office rather than limiting the protection to what is "said or done by him, as a representative, in the exercise of the functions of that office."

clearly a part of the legislative process—the *due* functioning of the process.[10] Appellee's contention for a broader interpretation of the privilege draws essentially on the flavor of the rhetoric and the sweep of the language used by courts, not on the precise words used in any prior case, and surely not on the sense of those cases, fairly read.

(c) We would not think it sound or wise, simply out of an abundance of caution to doubly insure legislative independence, to extend the privilege beyond its intended scope, its literal language, and its history, to include all things in any way related to the legislative process. Given such a sweeping reading, we have no doubt that there are few activities in which a legislator engages that he would be unable somehow to "relate" to the legislative process. Admittedly, the Speech or Debate Clause must be read broadly to effectuate its purpose of protecting the independence of the Legislative Branch, but no more than the statutes we apply, was its purpose to make Members of Congress super-citizens, immune from criminal responsibility. In its narrowest scope, the Clause is a very large, albeit essential, grant of privilege. It has enabled reckless men to slander and even destroy others with impunity, but that was the conscious choice of the Framers.[11]

---

[10] See *Kilbourn* v. *Thompson*, 103 U. S. 168 (1881) (voting for a resolution); *Tenney* v. *Brandhove*, 341 U. S. 367 (1951) (harassment of witness by state legislator during a legislative hearing; not a Speech or Debate Clause case); *United States* v. *Johnson*, 383 U. S. 169 (1966) (making a speech on House floor); *Dombrowski* v. *Eastland*, 387 U. S. 82 (1967) (subpoenaing records for committee hearing); *Powell* v. *McCormack*, 395 U. S. 486 (1969) (voting for a resolution).

In *Coffin* v. *Coffin*, 4 Mass. 1 (1808), the state equivalent of the Speech or Debate Clause was held to be inapplicable to a legislator who was acting outside of his official duties.

[11] "To this construction of the article it is objected, that a private citizen may have his character basely defamed, without any pecuniary

The history of the privilege is by no means free from grave abuses by legislators. In one instance, abuses reached such a level in England that Parliament was compelled to enact curative legislation.

"The practice of granting the privilege of freedom from arrest and molestation to members' servants in time became a serious menace to individual liberty and to public order, and a form of protection by which offenders often tried—and they were often successful—to escape the penalties which their offences deserved and which the ordinary courts would not have hesitated to inflict. Indeed, the sale of 'protections' at one time proved a source of income to unscrupulous members, and these parliamentary 'indulgences' were on several occasions obtainable at a fixed market price." C. Wittke, The History of English Parliamentary Privilege 39 (1921).

The authors of our Constitution were well aware of the history of both the need for the privilege and the abuses that could flow from too sweeping safeguards. In order to preserve other values, they wrote the privilege so that it tolerates and protects behavior on the part of Members not tolerated and protected when done by other citizens, but the shield does not extend beyond what is necessary to preserve the integrity of the legislative process. Moreover, unlike England with no formal, written constitutional limitations on the monarch, we defined limits on the co-ordinate branches, pro-

---

recompense or satisfaction. The truth of the objection is admitted. . . . The injury to the reputation of a private citizen is of less importance to the commonwealth, than the free and unreserved exercise of the duties of a representative, unawed by the fear of legal prosecutions." *Coffin* v. *Coffin,* 4 Mass., at 28.

See *Cochran* v. *Couzens,* 59 App. D. C. 374, 42 F. 2d 783, cert. denied, 282 U. S. 874 (1930) (defamatory words uttered on Senate floor could not be basis of slander action).

viding other checks to protect against abuses of the kind
experienced in that country.

It is also suggested that, even if we interpreted the
Clause broadly so as to exempt from inquiry all matters
having any relationship to the legislative process, misconduct of Members would not necessarily go unpunished
because each House is empowered to discipline its Members. Article I, § 5, does indeed empower each House to
"determine the Rules of its Proceedings, punish its Members for disorderly Behavior, and, with the Concurrence of
two thirds, expel a Member," but Congress is ill-equipped
to investigate, try, and punish its Members for a wide
range of behavior that is loosely and incidentally related
to the legislative process. In this sense, the English
analogy on which the dissents place much emphasis, and
the reliance on *Ex parte Wason*, L. R. 4 Q. B. 573
(1869), are inapt. Parliament is itself "The High Court
of Parliament"—the highest court in the land—and its
judicial tradition better equips it for judicial tasks.

> "It is by no means an exaggeration to say that [the
> judicial characteristics of Parliament] colored and
> influenced some of the great struggles over [legisla-
> tive] privilege in and out of Parliament to the very
> close of the nineteenth century. It is not altogether
> certain whether they have been entirely forgotten
> even now. Nowhere has the theory that Parliament
> is a court—the highest court of the realm, often
> acting in a judicial capacity and in a judicial man-
> ner—persisted longer than in the history of privilege
> of Parliament." Wittke, *supra,* at 14.

The very fact of the supremacy of Parliament as England's highest tribunal explains the long tradition precluding trial for official misconduct of a member in any
other and lesser tribunal.

In Australia and Canada, "where provision for legisla-

40

tive free speech or debate exists but where the legislature
may not claim a tradition as the highest court of the
realm, courts have held that the privilege does not bar
the criminal prosecution of legislators for bribery." Note,
The Bribed Congressman's Immunity from Prosecution,
75 Yale L. J. 335, 338 (1965) (footnote omitted). Congress has shown little inclination to exert itself in this
area.[12] Moreover, if Congress did lay aside its normal
activities and take on itself the responsibility to police
and prosecute the myriad activities of its Members related to but not directly a part of the legislative function,
the independence of individual Members might actually
be impaired.

The process of disciplining a Member in the Congress is not without countervailing risks of abuse since
it is not surrounded with the panoply of protective
shields that are present in a criminal case. An
accused Member is judged by no specifically articulated
standards[13] and is at the mercy of an almost unbridled discretion of the charging body that functions
at once as accuser, prosecutor, judge, and jury from
whose decision there is no established right of review.
In short, a Member would be compelled to defend in what
would be comparable to a criminal prosecution without
the safeguards provided by the Constitution. Moreover, it would be somewhat naive to assume that the triers
would be wholly objective and free from considerations

---

[12] See Thomas, Freedom of Debate: Protector of the People or
Haven for the Criminal?, 3 The Harvard Rev. 74, 80–81 (No. 3,
1965); Note, The Bribed Congressman's Immunity from Prosecution,
75 Yale L. J. 335, 349 n. 84 (1965); Oppenheim, Congressional Free
Speech, 8 Loyola L. Rev. 1, 27–28 (1955–1956).

[13] See, *e. g.*, *In re Chapman*, 166 U. S. 661, 669–670 (1897):
"The right to expel extends to all cases where the offence is such
as in the judgment of the Senate is inconsistent with the trust and
duty of a member."

41

of party and politics and the passions of the moment.[14] Strong arguments can be made that trials conducted in a Congress with an entrenched majority from one political party could result in far greater harassment than a conventional criminal trial with the wide range of procedural protections for the accused, including indictment by grand jury, trial by jury under strict standards of proof with fixed rules of evidence, and extensive appellate review.

Finally, the jurisdiction of Congress to punish its Members is not all-embracing. For instance, it is unclear to what extent Congress would have jurisdiction over a case such as this in which the alleged illegal activity occurred outside the chamber, while the appellee was a Member, but was undiscovered or not brought before a grand jury until after he left office.[15]

The sweeping claims of appellee would render Members of Congress virtually immune from a wide range of crimes simply because the acts in question were peripherally related to their holding office. Such claims are inconsistent with the reading this Court has given, not only to the Speech or Debate Clause, but also to the other legislative privileges embodied in Art. I, § 6. The very sentence in which the Speech or Debate Clause appears provides that Members "shall in all Cases, ex-

---

[14] See the account of the impeachment of President Andrew Johnson in J. Kennedy, Profiles in Courage 126–151 (1955). See also the account of the impeachment of Mr. Justice Samuel Chase in 3 A. Beveridge, The Life of John Marshall 169–220 (1919).

[15] ". . . English Parliaments have historically reserved to themselves and still retain the sole and exclusive right to punish their members for the acceptance of a bribe in the discharge of their office. No member of Parliament may be tried for such an offense in any court of the land." Cella, supra, n. 5, at 15–16. That this is obviously not the case in this country is implicit in the remand of Representative Johnson to be retried on bribery charges.

cept Treason, Felony and Breach of the Peace, be privileged from Arrest during their Attendance at the Session of their Respective Houses. . . ." In *Williamson* v. *United States,* 207 U. S. 425 (1908), this Court rejected a claim, made by a Member convicted of subornation of perjury in proceedings for the purchase of public lands, that he could not be arrested, convicted, or imprisoned for any crime that was not treason, felony, or breach of the peace in the modern sense, *i. e.,* disturbing the peace. Mr. Justice Edward Douglass White noted that when the Constitution was written the term "breach of the peace" did not mean, as it came to mean later, a misdemeanor such as disorderly conduct but had a different 18th century usage, since it derived from breaching the King's peace and thus embraced the whole range of crimes at common law. Quoting Lord Mansfield, he noted, with respect to the claim of parliamentary privilege, "[t]he laws of this country allow no place or employment as a sanctuary for crime . . . ." *Id.,* at 439.

The subsequent case of *Long* v. *Ansell,* 293 U. S. 76 (1934), held that a Member's immunity from arrest in civil cases did not extend to civil process. Mr. Justice Brandeis wrote for the Court:

> "Clause 1 [of Art. I, § 6] defines the extent of the immunity. Its language is exact and leaves no room for a construction which would extend the privilege beyond the terms of the grant." *Id.,* at 82.

We recognize that the privilege against arrest is not identical with the Speech or Debate privilege, but it is closely related in purpose and origin. It can hardly be thought that the Speech or Debate Clause totally protects what the sentence preceding it has plainly left open to prosecution, *i. e.,* all criminal acts.

(d) MR. JUSTICE WHITE suggests that permitting the Executive to initiate the prosecution of a Member of Con-

43

gress for the specific crime of bribery is subject to serious potential abuse that might endanger the independence of the legislature—for example, a campaign contribution might be twisted by a ruthless prosecutor into a bribery indictment. But, as we have just noted, the Executive is not alone in possessing power potentially subject to abuse; such possibilities are inherent in a system of government that delegates to each of the three branches separate and independent powers.[16] In The Federalist

---

[16] The potential for harassment by an unscrupulous member of the Executive Branch may exist, but this country has no tradition of absolute congressional immunity from criminal prosecution. See *United States* v. *Quinn,* 141 F. Supp. 622 (SDNY 1956) (motion for acquittal granted because the defendant Member of Congress was unaware of receipt of fees by his law firm); *Burton* v. *United States,* 202 U. S. 344 (1906) (Senator convicted for accepting compensation to intervene before Post Office Department); *United States* v. *Dietrich,* 126 F. 671 (CC Neb. 1904) (Senator-elect's accepting payment to procure office for another not covered by statute); *May* v. *United States,* 84 U. S. App. D. C. 233, 175 F. 2d 994, cert. denied, 338 U. S. 830 (1949) (Congressman convicted of receiving compensation for services before an agency); *United States* v. *Bramblett,* 348 U. S. 503 (1955) (Congressman convicted of defrauding government agency). *Bramblett* concerned a Congressman's misuse of office funds via a "kick-back" scheme, which is surely "related" to the legislative office.

A strategically timed indictment could indeed cause serious harm to a Congressman. Representative Johnson, for example, was indicted while campaigning for re-election, and arguably his indictment contributed to his defeat. On the other hand, there is the classic case of Mayor Curley who was re-elected while under indictment. See N. Y. Times, Nov. 8, 1945, p. 12, col. 5; 4 New Catholic Encyclopedia 541 (1967). Moreover, we should not overlook the barriers a prosecutor, attempting to bring such a case, must face. First, he must persuade a grand jury to indict, and we are not prepared to assume that grand juries will act against a Member without solid evidence. Thereafter, he must convince a petit jury beyond a reasonable doubt, with the presumption of innocence favoring the accused. A prosecutor who fails to clear one of these hurdles faces serious practical consequences when the defendant is a Congressman. The Legislative Branch is not

44

No. 73, Hamilton expressed concern over the possible hazards that confronted an Executive dependent on Congress for financial support.

> "The Legislature, with a discretionary power over the salary and emoluments of the Chief Magistrate, could render him as obsequious to their will as they might think proper to make him. They might, in most cases, either reduce him by famine, or tempt him by largesses, to surrender at discretion his judgment to their inclinations."

Yet Hamilton's "parade of horribles" finds little real support in history. The check-and-balance mechanism, buttressed by unfettered debate in an open society with a free press, has not encouraged abuses of power or tolerated them long when they arose. This may be explained in part because the third branch has intervened with neutral authority. See, *e. g., United States* v. *Lovett,* 328 U. S. 303 (1946). The system of divided powers was expressly designed to check the abuses England experienced in the 16th to the 18th centuries.

Probably of more importance is the public reaction engendered by any attempt of one branch to dominate or harass another. Even traditional political attempts to establish dominance have met with little success owing to contrary popular sentiment. Attempts to "purge" uncooperative legislators, for example, have not been notably successful. We are not cited to any cases in which the bribery statutes, which have been applicable to Members of Congress for over 100 years,[17]

without weapons of its own and would no doubt use them if it thought the Executive were unjustly harassing one of its members. Perhaps more important is the omnipresence of the news media whose traditional function and competitive inclination afford no immunities to reckless or irresponsible official misconduct.

[17] The first bribery statute applicable to Congressmen was enacted in 1853. Act of Feb. 26, 1853, c. 81, § 6, 10 Stat. 171.

have been abused by the Executive Branch. When a powerful Executive sought to make the Judicial Branch more responsive to the combined will of the Executive and Legislative Branches, it was the Congress itself that checked the effort to enlarge the Court. 2 M. Pusey, Charles Evans Hughes 749–765 (1951).

We would be closing our eyes to the realities of the American political system if we failed to acknowledge that many non-legislative activities are an established and accepted part of the role of a Member, and are indeed "related" to the legislative process. But if the Executive may prosecute a Member's attempt, as in *Johnson,* to influence another branch of the Government in return for a bribe, its power to harass is not greatly enhanced if it can prosecute for a promise relating to a legislative act in return for a bribe. We therefore see no substantial increase in the power of the Executive and Judicial Branches over the Legislative Branch resulting from our holding today. If we underestimate the potential for harassment, the Congress, of course, is free to exempt its Members from the ambit of federal bribery laws, but it has deliberately allowed the instant statute to remain on the books for over a century.

We do not discount entirely the possibility that an abuse might occur, but this possibility, which we consider remote, must be balanced against the potential danger flowing from either the absence of a bribery statute applicable to Members of Congress or a holding that the statute violates the Constitution. As we noted at the outset, the purpose of the Speech or Debate Clause is to protect the individual legislator, not simply for his own sake, but to preserve the independence and thereby the integrity of the legislative process. But financial abuses by way of bribes, perhaps even more than Executive power, would gravely undermine legislative integrity and defeat the right of the public to honest representation. Depriving the Executive of the power to investigate and prosecute and the Judiciary of the power to punish bribery of Members of Congress is unlikely to enhance legislative independence. Given the disinclination and limitations of each House to police these matters, it is understandable that both Houses deliberately delegated this function to the courts, as they did with the power to punish persons committing contempts of Congress. 2 U. S. C. § 194.

It is beyond doubt that the Speech or Debate Clause protects against inquiry into acts that occur in the regular course of the legislative process and into the motivation for those acts. So expressed, the privilege is broad enough to insure the historic independence of the Legislative Branch, essential to our separation of powers, but narrow enough to guard against the excesses of those who would corrupt the process by corrupting its Members. We turn next to determine whether the subject of this criminal inquiry is within the scope of the privilege.

III

An examination of the indictment brought against appellee and the statutes on which it is founded reveals that no inquiry into legislative acts or motivation for legislative acts is necessary for the Government to make out a prima facie case. Four of the five counts charge that appellee "corruptly asked, solicited, sought, accepted, received and agreed to receive" money "in return for being influenced . . . in respect to his action, vote, and decision on postage rate legislation which might at any time be pending before him in his official capacity." This is said to be a violation of 18 U. S. C. § 201 (c), which provides that a Member who "corruptly asks, demands, exacts, solicits, seeks, accepts, receives, or agrees to receive anything of value . . . in return for . . . (1) being influenced in his performance of any official act" is guilty of an offense.

The question is whether it is necessary to inquire into how appellee spoke, how he debated, how he voted, or anything he did in the chamber or in committee in order to make out a violation of this statute. The illegal conduct is taking or agreeing to take money for a promise to act in a certain way. There is no need for the Government to show that appellee fulfilled the alleged illegal bargain; acceptance of the bribe is the violation of the statute, not performance of the illegal promise.

Taking a bribe is, obviously, no part of the legislative process or function; it is not a legislative act. It is not, by any conceivable interpretation, an act performed as a part of or even incidental to the role of a legislator. It is not an "act resulting from the nature, and in the execution, of the office." Nor is it a "thing said or done by him, as a representative, in the exercise of the functions of that office," 4 Mass., at 27. Nor is inquiry into a legislative act or the motivation for a legislative act necessary to a prosecution under this statute or this indictment. When a bribe is taken, it does not matter whether the promise for which the bribe was given was for the performance of a legislative act as here or, as in *Johnson,* for use of a Congressman's influence with the Executive Branch. And an inquiry into the purpose of a bribe "does not draw in question the legislative acts of the defendant member of Congress or his motives for performing them." 383 U. S., at 185.

Nor does it matter if the Member defaults on his illegal bargain. To make a prima facie case under this indictment, the Government need not show any act of appellee subsequent to the corrupt promise for payment, for it is *taking* the bribe, not performance of the illicit compact, that is a criminal act. If, for example, there were undisputed evidence that a Member took a bribe in exchange

48

for an agreement to vote for a given bill and if there were also undisputed evidence that he, in fact, voted against the bill, can it be thought that this alters the nature of the bribery or removes it from the area of wrongdoing the Congress sought to make a crime?

Another count of the indictment against appellee alleges that he "asked, demanded, exacted, solicited, sought, accepted, received and agreed to receive" money "for and because of official acts performed by him in respect to his action, vote and decision on postage rate legislation which had been pending before him in his official capacity . . . ." This count is founded on 18 U. S. C. § 201 (g), which provides that a Member of Congress who "asks, demands, exacts, solicits, seeks, accepts, receives, or agrees to receive anything of value for himself for or because of any official act performed or to be performed by him" is guilty of an offense. Although the indictment alleges that the bribe was given for an act that was actually performed, it is, once again, unnecessary to inquire into the act or its motivation. To sustain a conviction it is necessary to show that appellee solicited, received, or agreed to receive, money with knowledge that the donor was paying him compensation for an official act. Inquiry into the legislative performance itself is not necessary; evidence of the Member's knowledge of the alleged briber's illicit reasons for paying the money is sufficient to carry the case to the jury.

Mr. Justice White rests heavily on the fact that the indictment charges the offense as being in part linked to Brewster's "action, vote and decision on postage rate legislation." This is true, of course, but our holding in *Johnson* precludes any showing of how he acted, voted, or decided. The dissenting position stands on the fragile proposition that it "would take the Government at its word" with respect to wanting to prove what we all agree are protected acts that cannot be shown in evidence. Perhaps the Government would make a more appealing case if it could do so, but here, as in that case, evidence of acts protected by the Clause is inadmissible. The Government, as we have noted, need not prove any specific act, speech, debate, or decision to establish a violation of the statute under which appellee was indicted. To accept the arguments of the dissent would be to retreat from the Court's position in *Johnson* that a Member may be convicted if no showing of legislative act is required.

MR. JUSTICE BRENNAN suggests that inquiry into the alleged bribe is inquiry into the motivation for a legislative act, and it is urged that this very inquiry was condemned as impermissible in *Johnson.* That argument misconstrues the concept of motivation for legislative acts. The Speech or Debate Clause does not prohibit inquiry into illegal conduct simply because it has some nexus to legislative functions. In *Johnson,* the Court held that, on remand, Johnson could be retried on the conspiracy-to-defraud count, so long as evidence concerning his speech on the House floor was not admitted. The Court's opinion plainly implies that had the Government chosen to retry Johnson on that count, he could not have obtained immunity from prosecution by asserting that the matter being inquired into was related to the motivation for his House speech. See n. 7, *supra.*

The only reasonable reading of the Clause, consistent with its history and purpose, is that it does not prohibit inquiry into activities that are casually or incidentally related to legislative affairs but not a part of the legislative process itself. Under this indictment and these statutes no such proof is needed.

We hold that under these statutes and this indictment, prosecution of appellee is not prohibited by the Speech or Debate Clause.[18]   Accordingly, the judgment of the District Court is reversed and the case is remanded for further proceedings consistent with this opinion.

Reversed and remanded.

---

[18] In reversing the District Court's ruling that a Member of Congress may not be constitutionally tried for a violation of the federal bribery statutes, we express no views on the question left open in *Johnson* as to the constitutionality of an inquiry that probes into legislative acts or the motivation for legislative acts if Congress specifically authorizes such in a narrowly drawn statute. Should such an inquiry be made and should a conviction be sustained, then we would face the question whether inquiry into legislative acts and motivation is permissible under such a narrowly drawn statute.

TENNESSEE VALLEY AUTHORITY v. HILL ET AL.

CERTIORARI TO THE UNITED STATES COURT OF APPEALS FOR THE SIXTH CIRCUIT

No. 76–1701.   Argued April 18, 1978—Decided June 15, 1978

The Endangered Species Act of 1973 (Act) authorizes the Secretary of the Interior (Secretary) in § 4 to declare a species of life "endangered." Section 7 specifies that all "Federal departments and agencies shall, . . . with the assistance of the Secretary, utilize their authorities in further-ance of the purposes of [the] Act by carrying out programs for the conservation of endangered species . . . and by taking such action necessary to insure that actions authorized, funded, or carried out by them do not jeopardize the continued existence of such endangered species and threatened species or result in the destruction or modifica-tion of habitat of such species which is determined by the Secretary . . . to be critical."   Shortly after the Act's passage the Secretary was peti-tioned to list a small fish popularly known as the snail darter as an endangered species under the Act.   Thereafter the Secretary made the designation.   Having determined that the snail darter apparently lives only in that portion of the Little Tennessee River that would be com-pletely inundated by the impoundment of the reservoir created as a consequence of the completion of the Tellico Dam, he declared that area as the snail darter's "critical habitat."   Notwithstanding the near completion of the multimillion-dollar dam, the Secretary issued a regula-tion in which it was declared that, pursuant to § 7, "all Federal agencies must take such action as is necessary to ensure that actions author-ized, funded, or carried out by them do not result in the destruction or modification of this critical habitat area."   Respondents brought this suit to enjoin completion of the dam and impoundment of the reservoir, claiming that those actions would violate the Act by causing the snail darter's extinction.   The District Court after trial denied relief and dis-missed the complaint.   Though finding that the impoundment of the reservoir would probably jeopardize the snail darter's continued exist-ence, the court noted that Congress, though fully aware of the snail darter problem, had continued Tellico's appropriations, and concluded that "[a]t some point in time a federal project becomes so near com-pletion and so incapable of modification that a court of equity should not apply a statute enacted long after inception of the project to pro-duce an unreasonable result. . . ."   The Court of Appeals reversed and ordered the District Court permanently to enjoin completion of the project "until Congress, by appropriate legislation, exempts Tellico from compliance with the Act or the snail darter has been deleted from the list of endangered species or its critical habitat materially redefined." The court held that the record revealed a prima facie violation of § 7 in that the Tennessee Valley Authority had failed to take necessary action to avoid jeopardizing the snail darter's critical habitat by its "actions." The court thus rejected the contention that the word "actions" as used in § 7 was not intended by Congress to encompass the terminal phases of ongoing projects. At various times before, during, and after the foregoing judicial proceedings, TVA represented to congressional Appropriations Committees that the Act did not prohibit completion of the Tellico Project and described its efforts to transplant the snail darter. The Committees consistently recommended appropriations for the dam, sometimes stating their views that the Act did not prohibit completion of the dam at its advanced stage, and Congress each time approved TVA's general budget, which contained funds for the dam's continued construction. *Held:*

1. The Endangered Species Act prohibits impoundment of the Little Tennessee River by the Tellico Dam. Pp. 172–193.

(a) The language of § 7 is plain and makes no exception such as that urged by petitioner whereby the Act would not apply to a project like Tellico that was well under way when Congress passed the Act. Pp. 172–174.

(b) It is clear from the Act's legislative history that Congress intended to halt and reverse the trend toward species extinction— whatever the cost. The pointed omission of the type of qualified language previously included in endangered species legislation reveals a conscious congressional design to give endangered species priority over the "primary missions" of federal agencies. Congress, moreover, foresaw that § 7 would on occasion require agencies to alter ongoing projects in order to fulfill the Act's goals. Pp. 174–187.

(c) None of the limited "hardship exemptions" provided in the Act would even remotely apply to the Tellico Project. P. 188.

(d) Though statements in Appropriations Committee Reports reflected the view of the Committees either that the Act did not apply to Tellico or that the dam should be completed regardless of the Act's provisions, nothing in the TVA appropriations measures passed by Congress stated that the Tellico Project was to be completed regardless of the Act's requirements. To find a repeal under these circumstances, as petitioner has urged, would violate the " 'cardinal rule . . . that repeals by implication are not favored.' " *Morton* v. *Mancari,* 417 U. S. 535, 549. The doctrine disfavoring repeals by implication applies with full vigor when the subsequent legislation is an appropriations measure. When voting on appropriations measures, legislators are entitled to assume that the funds will be devoted to purposes that are lawful and not for any purpose forbidden. A contrary policy would violate the express rules of both Houses of Congress, which provide that appropriations measures may not change existing substantive law. An appropriations committee's expression does not operate to repeal or modify substantive legislation. Pp. 189–193.

2. The Court of Appeals did not err in ordering that completion of the Tellico Dam, which would have violated the Act, be enjoined. Congress has spoken in the plainest words, making it clear that endangered species are to be accorded the highest priorities. Since that legislative power has been exercised, it is up to the Executive Branch to administer the law and for the Judiciary to enforce it when, as here, enforcement has been sought. Pp. 193–194.

549 F. 2d 1064, affirmed.

BURGER, C. J., delivered the opinion of the Court, in which BRENNAN, STEWART, WHITE, MARSHALL, and STEVENS, JJ., joined. POWELL, J., filed a dissenting opinion, in which BLACKMUN, J., joined, *post*, p. 195. REHNQUIST, J., filed a dissenting opinion, *post*, p. 211.

Attorney General Bell argued the cause for petitioner. On the briefs were *Acting Solicitor General Friedman, Deputy Solicitor General Barnett, Herbert S. Sanger, Jr., Richard A. Allen, Charles A. Wagner III, Thomas A. Pedersen,* and *Nicholas A. Della Volpe.*

Zygmunt J. B. Plater argued the cause for respondents. With him on the brief was *W. P. Boone Dougherty.**

---

*Briefs of *amici curiae* urging reversal were filed by *Robert J. Pennington* for Monroe County et al.; and by *Ronald A. Zumbrun, Raymond M. Momboisse, Robert K. Best, Albert Ferri, Jr., Donald C. Simpson,* and *W. Hugh O'Riordan* for the Pacific Legal Foundation.

Briefs of *amici curiae* urging affirmance were filed by *Ben Oshel Bridgers* for the Eastern Band of Cherokee Indians; by *William A. Butler* for the Environmental Defense Fund et al.; and by *Howell H. Sherrod, Jr.,* for the East Tennessee Valley Landowners' Assn.

Ben B. Blackburn and *Wayne T. Elliott* filed a brief for the Southeastern Legal Foundation as *amicus curiae.*

MR. CHIEF JUSTICE BURGER delivered the opinion of the Court.

The questions presented in this case are (a) whether the Endangered Species Act of 1973 requires a court to enjoin the operation of a virtually completed federal dam—which had been authorized prior to 1973—when, pursuant to authority vested in him by Congress, the Secretary of the Interior has determined that operation of the dam would eradicate an endangered species; and (b) whether continued congressional appropriations for the dam after 1973 constituted an implied repeal of the Endangered Species Act, at least as to the particular dam.

I

The Little Tennessee River originates in the mountains of northern Georgia and flows through the national forest lands of North Carolina into Tennessee, where it converges with the Big Tennessee River near Knoxville. The lower 33 miles of the Little Tennessee takes the river's clear, free-flowing waters through an area of great natural beauty. Among other environmental amenities, this stretch of river is said to contain abundant trout. Considerable historical importance attaches to the areas immediately adjacent to this portion of the Little Tennessee's banks. To the south of the river's edge lies Fort Loudon, established in 1756 as England's southwestern outpost in the French and Indian War. Nearby are also the ancient sites of several native American villages, the archeological stores of which are to a large extent unexplored.[1] These include the Cherokee towns of Echota and Tennase, the former

---

[1] This description is taken from the opinion of the District Judge in the first litigation involving the Tellico Dam and Reservoir Project. *Environmental Defense Fund* v. *TVA*, 339 F. Supp. 806, 808 (ED Tenn. 1972). In his opinion, "all of these benefits of the present Little Tennessee River Valley will be destroyed by impoundment of the river . . . ." *Ibid.* The District Judge noted that "[t]he free-flowing river is the likely habitat of one or more of seven rare or endangered fish species." *Ibid.*

being the sacred capital of the Cherokee Nation as early as the 16th century and the latter providing the linguistic basis from which the State of Tennessee derives its name.[2]

In this area of the Little Tennessee River the Tennessee Valley Authority, a wholly owned public corporation of the United States, began constructing the Tellico Dam and Reservoir Project in 1967, shortly after Congress appropriated initial funds for its development.[3] Tellico is a multipurpose regional development project designed principally to stimulate shoreline development, generate sufficient electric current to heat 20,000 homes,[4] and provide flatwater recreation and flood control, as well as improve economic conditions in "an area characterized by underutilization of human resources and outmigration of young people." Hearings on Public Works for Power and Energy Research Appropriation Bill, 1977, before a Subcommittee of the House Committee on Appropriations, 94th Cong., 2d Sess., pt. 5, p. 261 (1976). Of particular relevance to this case is one aspect of the project, a dam which TVA determined to place on the Little Tennessee, a short distance from where the river's waters meet with the Big Tennessee. When fully operational, the dam would impound water covering some 16,500 acres—much of which represents valuable and productive farmland—thereby converting the river's shallow, fast-flowing waters into a deep reservoir over 30 miles in length.

The Tellico Dam has never opened, however, despite the fact that construction has been virtually completed and the

---

[2] See Brief for the Eastern Band of Cherokee Indians as *Amicus Curiae* 2. See also Mooney, Myths of the Cherokee, 19 Bureau of American Ethnology Ann. Rep. 11 (1900); H. Timberlake, Memoirs, 1756–1765 (Watauga Press 1927); A. Brewer & C. Brewer, Valley So Wild: A Folk History (East Tenn. Historical Soc. 1975).

[3] Public Works Appropriation Act, 1967, 80 Stat. 1002, 1014.

[4] Tellico Dam itself will contain no electric generators; however, an interreservoir canal connecting Tellico Reservoir with a nearby hydroelectric plant will augment the latter's capacity.

dam is essentially ready for operation. Although Congress has appropriated monies for Tellico every year since 1967, progress was delayed, and ultimately stopped, by a tangle of lawsuits and administrative proceedings. After unsuccessfully urging TVA to consider alternatives to damming the Little Tennessee, local citizens and national conservation groups brought suit in the District Court, claiming that the project did not conform to the requirements of the National Environmental Policy Act of 1969 (NEPA), 83 Stat. 852, 42 U. S. C. § 4321 *et seq.* After finding TVA to be in violation of NEPA, the District Court enjoined the dam's completion pending the filing of an appropriate environmental impact statement. *Environmental Defense Fund* v. *TVA*, 339 F. Supp. 806 (ED Tenn.), aff'd, 468 F. 2d 1164 (CA6 1972). The injunction remained in effect until late 1973, when the District Court concluded that TVA's final environmental impact statement for Tellico was in compliance with the law. *Environmental Defense Fund* v. *TVA*, 371 F. Supp. 1004 (ED Tenn. 1973), aff'd, 492 F. 2d 466 (CA6 1974).[5]

A few months prior to the District Court's decision dissolving the NEPA injunction, a discovery was made in the waters of the Little Tennessee which would profoundly affect the Tellico Project. Exploring the area around Coytee Springs, which is about seven miles from the mouth of the river, a University of Tennessee ichthyologist, Dr. David A. Etnier, found a previously unknown species of perch, the snail darter, or *Percina (Imostoma) tanasi.*[6] This three-inch, tannish-colored fish,

---

[5] The NEPA injunction was in effect some 21 months; when it was entered TVA had spent some $29 million on the project. Most of these funds have gone to purchase land, construct the concrete portions of the dam, and build a four-lane steel-span bridge to carry a state highway over the proposed reservoir. 339 F. Supp., at 808.

[6] The snail darter was scientifically described by Dr. Etnier in the Proceedings of the Biological Society of Washington, Vol. 88, No. 44, pp. 469–488 (Jan. 22, 1976). The scientific merit and content of Dr. Etnier's

whose numbers are estimated to be in the range of 10,000 to 15,000, would soon engage the attention of environmentalists, the TVA, the Department of the Interior, the Congress of the United States, and ultimately the federal courts, as a new and additional basis to halt construction of the dam.

Until recently the finding of a new species of animal life would hardly generate a cause célèbre. This is particularly so in the case of darters, of which there are approximately 130 known species, 8 to 10 of these having been identified only in the last five years.[7] The moving force behind the snail darter's sudden fame came some four months after its discovery, when the Congress passed the Endangered Species Act of 1973 (Act), 87 Stat. 884, 16 U. S. C. § 1531 *et seq.* (1976 ed.). This legislation, among other things, authorizes the Secretary of the Interior to declare species of animal life "endangered"[8] and to

_____

paper on the snail darter were checked by a panel from the Smithsonian Institution prior to publication. See App. 111.

[7] In Tennessee alone there are 85 to 90 species of darters, *id.*, at 131, of which upward to 45 live in the Tennessee River system. *Id.*, at 130. New species of darters are being constantly discovered and classified—at the rate of about one per year. *Id.*, at 131. This is a difficult task for even trained ichthyologists since species of darters are often hard to differentiate from one another. *Ibid.*

[8] An "endangered species" is defined by the Act to mean "any species which is in danger of extinction throughout all or a significant portion of its range other than a species of the Class Insecta determined by the Secretary to constitute a pest whose protection under the provisions of this chapter would present an overwhelming and overriding risk to man." 16 U. S. C. § 1532 (4) (1976 ed.).

" 'The act covers every animal and plant species, subspecies, and population in the world needing protection. There are approximately 1.4 million full species of animals and 600,000 full species of plants in the world. Various authorities calculate as many as 10% of them—some 200,000—may need to be listed as Endangered or Threatened. When one counts in subspecies, not to mention individual populations, the total could increase to three to five times that number.' " Keith Shreiner, Associate Director and Endangered Species Program Manager of the U. S. Fish and Wildlife Service, quoted in a letter from A. J. Wagner, Chairman, TVA, to identify the "critical habitat" [9] of these creatures. When a species or its habitat is so listed, the following portion of the Act—relevant here—becomes effective:

> "The Secretary [of the Interior] shall review other programs administered by him and utilize such programs in furtherance of the purposes of this chapter. All other Federal departments and agencies shall, in consultation with and with the assistance of the Secretary, utilize their authorities in furtherance of the purposes of this chapter by carrying out programs for the conservation of endangered species and threatened species listed pursuant to section 1533 of this title and *by taking such action necessary to insure that actions authorized, funded, or carried out by them do not jeopardize the continued existence of such endangered species and threatened species or result in the destruction or modification of habitat of such species* which is determined by the Secretary, after consultation as appropriate with the affected States, to be critical." 16 U. S. C. § 1536 (1976 ed.) (emphasis added).

Chairman, House Committee on Merchant Marine and Fisheries, dated Apr. 25, 1977, quoted in Wood, On Protecting an Endangered Statute: The Endangered Species Act of 1973, 37 Federal B. J. 25, 27 (1978).

[9] The Act does not define "critical habitat," but the Secretary of the Interior has administratively construed the term:

"'Critical habitat' means any air, land, or water area (exclusive of those existing man-made structures or settlements which are not necessary to the survival and recovery of a listed species) and constituent elements thereof, the loss of which would appreciably decrease the likelihood of the survival and recovery of a listed species or a distinct segment of its population. The constituent elements of critical habitat include, but are not limited to: physical structures and topography, biota, climate, human activity, and the quality and chemical content of land, water, and air. Critical habitat may represent any portion of the present habitat of a listed species and may include additional areas for reasonable population expansion." 43 Fed. Reg. 874 (1978) (to be codified as 50 CFR § 402.02).

In January 1975, the respondents in this case [10] and others petitioned the Secretary of the Interior [11] to list the snail darter as an endangered species. After receiving comments from various interested parties, including TVA and the State of Tennessee, the Secretary formally listed the snail darter as an endangered species on October 8, 1975. 40 Fed. Reg. 47505–47506; see 50 CFR § 17.11 (i) (1976). In so acting, it was noted that "the snail darter is a living entity which is genetically distinct and reproductively isolated from other fishes." 40 Fed. Reg. 47505. More important for the purposes of this case, the Secretary determined that the snail darter apparently lives only in that portion of the Little Tennessee River which would be completely inundated by the reservoir created as a consequence of the Tellico Dam's completion. *Id.,* at 47506.[12]

---

[10] Respondents are a regional association of biological scientists, a Tennessee conservation group, and individuals who are citizens or users of the Little Tennessee Valley area which would be affected by the Tellico Project.

[11] The Act authorizes "interested person[s]" to petition the Secretary of the Interior to list a species as endangered. 16 U. S. C. § 1533 (c) (2) (1976 ed.); see 5 U. S. C. § 553 (e) (1976 ed.).

[12] Searches by TVA in more than 60 watercourses have failed to find other populations of snail darters. App. 36, 410–412. The Secretary has noted that "more than 1,000 collections in recent years and additional earlier collections from central and east Tennessee have not revealed the presence of the snail darter outside the Little Tennessee River." 40 Fed. Reg. 47505 (1975). It is estimated, however, that the snail darter's range once extended throughout the upper main Tennessee River and the lower portions of its major tributaries above Chattanooga—all of which are now the sites of dam impoundments. See Hearings on Public Works for Water and Power Development and Energy Research Appropriation Bill, 1978, before a Subcommittee of the House Committee on Appropriations, 95th Cong., 1st Sess., pt. 4, pp. 240–241 (1977) (statement of witness for TVA); Hearings on Endangered Species Act Oversight, before the Subcommittee on Resource Protection of the Senate Committee on Environment and Public Works, 95th Cong., 1st Sess., 291 (1977); App. 139.

The Secretary went on to explain the significance of the dam
to the habitat of the snail darter:

"[T]he snail darter occurs only in the swifter portions of
shoals over clean gravel substrate in cool, low-turbidity
water. Food of the snail darter is almost exclusively
snails which require a clean gravel substrate for their
survival. *The proposed impoundment of water behind
the proposed Tellico Dam would result in total destruction of the snail darter's habitat.*" *Ibid.* (emphasis
added).

Subsequent to this determination, the Secretary declared the
area of the Little Tennessee which would be affected by the
Tellico Dam to be the "critical habitat" of the snail darter.
41 Fed. Reg. 13926–13928 (1976) (to be codified as 50 CFR
§ 17.81). Using these determinations as a predicate, and notwithstanding the near completion of the dam, the Secretary
declared that pursuant to § 7 of the Act, "all Federal agencies
must take such action as is necessary to insure that actions
authorized, funded, or carried out by them do not result in the
destruction or modification of this critical habitat area." 41
Fed. Reg. 13928 (1976) (to be codified as 50 CFR § 17.81 (b)).
This notice, of course, was pointedly directed at TVA and
clearly aimed at halting completion or operation of the dam.

During the pendency of these administrative actions, other
developments of relevance to the snail darter issue were tran-
spiring. Communication was occurring between the Department of the Interior's Fish and Wildlife Service and TVA with
a view toward settling the issue informally. These negotiations were to no avail, however, since TVA consistently took
the position that the only available alternative was to attempt
relocating the snail darter population to another suitable location. To this end, TVA conducted a search of alternative sites
which might sustain the fish, culminating in the experimental
transplantation of a number of snail darters to the nearby
Hiwassee River. However, the Secretary of the Interior was

not satisfied with the results of these efforts, finding that TVA had presented "little evidence that they have carefully studied the Hiwassee to determine whether or not" there were "biological and other factors in this river that [would] negate a successful transplant." [13] 40 Fed. Reg. 47506 (1975).

Meanwhile, Congress had also become involved in the fate of the snail darter. Appearing before a Subcommittee of the House Committee on Appropriations in April 1975—some seven months before the snail darter was listed as endangered—TVA representatives described the discovery of the fish and the relevance of the Endangered Species Act to the Tellico Project. Hearings on Public Works for Water and Power Development and Energy Research Appropriation Bill, 1976, before a Subcommittee of the House Committee on Appropriations, 94th Cong., 1st Sess., pt. 7, pp. 466–467 (1975); Hearings on H. R. 8122, Public Works for Water and Power Development and Energy Research Appropriations for Fiscal Year 1976, before a Subcommittee of the Senate Committee on Appropriations, 94th Cong., 1st Sess., pt. 4, pp. 3775–3777 (1975). At that time TVA presented a position which it would advance in successive forums thereafter, namely, that the Act did not prohibit the completion of a project authorized, funded, and substantially constructed before the Act was passed. TVA also described its efforts to transplant the snail darter, but contended that the dam should be finished regardless of the

---

[13] The Fish and Wildlife Service and Dr. Etnier have stated that it may take from 5 to 15 years for scientists to determine whether the snail darter can successfully survive and reproduce in this new environment. See General Accounting Office, The Tennessee Valley Authority's Tellico Dam Project—Costs, Alternatives, and Benefits 4 (Oct. 14, 1977). In expressing doubt over the long-term future of the Hiwassee transplant, the Secretary noted: "That the snail darter does not already inhabit the Hiwassee River, despite the fact that the fish has had access to it in the past, is a strong indication that there may be biological and other factors in this river that negate a successful transplant." 40 Fed. Reg. 47506 (1975).

experiment's success. Thereafter, the House Committee on
Appropriations, in its June 20, 1975, Report, stated the following in the course of recommending that an additional $29
million be appropriated for Tellico:

> "The *Committee* directs that the project, for which an
> environmental impact statement has been completed and
> provided the Committee, should be completed as promptly
> as possible . . . ." H. R. Rep. No. 94–319, p. 76 (1975).
> (Emphasis added.)

Congress then approved the TVA general budget, which contained funds for continued construction of the Tellico Project.[14]
In December 1975, one month after the snail darter was declared an endangered species, the President signed the bill into
law. Public Works for Water and Power Development and
Energy Research Appropriation Act, 1976, 89 Stat. 1035, 1047.

In February 1976, pursuant to § 11 (g) of the Endangered
Species Act, 87 Stat. 900, 16 U. S. C. § 1540 (g) (1976 ed.),[15]
respondents filed the case now under review, seeking to enjoin
completion of the dam and impoundment of the reservoir on
the ground that those actions would violate the Act by directly
causing the extinction of the species *Percina* (*Imostoma*)
tanasi. The District Court denied respondents' request for a
preliminary injunction and set the matter for trial. Shortly
thereafter the House and Senate held appropriations hearings
which would include discussions of the Tellico budget.

---

[14] TVA projects generally are authorized by the Authority itself and are
funded—without the need for specific congressional authorization—from
lump-sum appropriations provided in yearly budget grants. See 16
U. S. C. §§ 831c (j) and 831z (1976 ed.).

[15] Section 11 (g) allows "any person" to commence a civil action in a
United States District Court to, *inter alia,* "enjoin any person, including
the United States and any other governmental instrumentality or agency
(to the extent permitted by the eleventh amendment to the Constitution),
who is alleged to be in violation of any provision" of the Act "or regulation
issued under the authority thereof . . . ."

At these hearings, TVA Chairman Wagner reiterated the agency's position that the Act did not apply to a project which was over 50% finished by the time the Act became effective and some 70% to 80% complete when the snail darter was officially listed as endangered. It also notified the Committees of the recently filed lawsuit's status and reported that TVA's efforts to transplant the snail darter had "been very encouraging." Hearings on Public Works for Water and Power Development and Energy Research Appropriation Bill, 1977, before a Subcommittee of the House Committee on Appropriations, 94th Cong., 2d Sess., pt. 5, pp. 261–262 (1976); Hearings on Public Works for Water and Power Development and Energy Research Appropriations for Fiscal Year 1977, before a Subcommittee of the Senate Committee on Appropriations, 94th Cong., 2d Sess., pt. 4, pp. 3096–3099 (1976).

Trial was held in the District Court on April 29 and 30, 1976, and on May 25, 1976, the court entered its memorandum opinion and order denying respondents their requested relief and dismissing the complaint. The District Court found that closure of the dam and the consequent impoundment of the reservoir would "result in the adverse modification, if not complete destruction, of the snail darter's critical habitat," [16]

---

[16] The District Court made the following findings with respect to the dam's effect on the ecology of the snail darter:

"The evidence introduced at trial showed that the snail darter requires for its survival a clear, gravel substrate, in a large-to-medium, flowing river. The snail darter has a fairly high requirement for oxygen and since it tends to exist in the bottom of the river, the flowing water provides the necessary oxygen at greater depths. Reservoirs, unlike flowing rivers, tend to have a low oxygen content at greater depths.

"Reservoirs also tend to have more silt on the bottom than flowing rivers, and this factor, combined with the lower oxygen content, would make it highly probable that snail darter eggs would smother in such an environment. Furthermore, the adult snail darters would probably find this type of reservoir environment unsuitable for spawning.

"Another factor that would tend to make a reservoir habitat unsuitable for snail darters is that their primary source of food, snails, probably making it "highly probable" that "the continued existence of the snail darter" would be "jeopardize[d]." 419 F. Supp. 753, 757 (ED Tenn.). Despite these findings, the District Court declined to embrace the plaintiffs' position on the merits: that once a federal project was shown to jeopardize an endangered species, a court of equity is compelled to issue an injunction restraining violation of the Endangered Species Act.

In reaching this result, the District Court stressed that the entire project was then about 80% complete and, based on available evidence, "there [were] no alternatives to impoundment of the reservoir, short of scrapping the entire project." *Id.*, at 758. The District Court also found that if the Tellico Project was permanently enjoined, "some $53 million would be lost in nonrecoverable obligations," *id.*, at 759, meaning that a large portion of the $78 million already expended would be wasted. The court also noted that the Endangered Species Act of 1973 was passed some seven years after construction on the dam commenced and that Congress had continued appropriations for Tellico, with full awareness of the snail darter problem. Assessing these various factors, the District Court concluded:

> "At some point in time a federal project becomes so near completion and so incapable of modification that a court of equity should not apply a statute enacted long after inception of the project to produce an unreasonable result. . . . Where there has been an irreversible and irretrievable commitment of resources by Congress to a project over a span of almost a decade, the Court should proceed with a great deal of circumspection." *Id.*, at 760.

To accept the plaintiffs' position, the District Court argued, would inexorably lead to what it characterized as the absurd result of requiring "a court to halt impoundment of water

----

would not survive in such an environment." 419 F. Supp. 753, 756 (ED Tenn. 1976).

behind a fully completed dam if an endangered species were discovered in the river on the day before such impoundment was scheduled to take place. We cannot conceive that Congress intended such a result." *Id.,* at 763.

Less than a month after the District Court decision, the Senate and House Appropriations Committees recommended the full budget request of $9 million for continued work on Tellico. See S. Rep. No. 94–960, p. 96 (1976); H. R. Rep. No. 94–1223, p. 83 (1976). In its Report accompanying the appropriations bill, the Senate Committee stated:

> "During subcommittee hearings, TVA was questioned about the relationship between the Tellico project's completion and the November 1975 listing of the snail darter (a small 3-inch fish which was discovered in 1973) as an endangered species under the Endangered Species Act. TVA informed the Committee that it was continuing its efforts to preserve the darter, while working towards the scheduled 1977 completion date. TVA repeated its view that the Endangered Species Act did not prevent the completion of the Tellico project, which has been under construction for nearly a decade. The subcommittee brought this matter, as well as the recent U. S. District Court's decision upholding TVA's decision to complete the project, to the attention of the full Committee. *The Committee does not view* the Endangered Species Act as prohibiting the completion of the Tellico project at its advanced stage and directs that this project be completed as promptly as possible in the public interest." S. Rep. No. 94–960, *supra,* at 96. (Emphasis added.)

On June 29, 1976, both Houses of Congress passed TVA's general budget, which included funds for Tellico; the President signed the bill on July 12, 1976. Public Works for Water and Power Development and Energy Research Appropriation Act, 1977, 90 Stat. 889, 899.

Thereafter, in the Court of Appeals, respondents argued that the District Court had abused its discretion by not issuing an injunction in the face of "a blatant statutory violation." 549 F. 2d 1064, 1069 (CA6 1977). The Court of Appeals agreed, and on January 31, 1977, it reversed, remanding "with instructions that a permanent injunction issue halting all activities incident to the Tellico Project which may destroy or modify the critical habitat of the snail darter." *Id.*, at 1075. The Court of Appeals directed that the injunction "remain in effect until Congress, by appropriate legislation, exempts Tellico from compliance with the Act or the snail darter has been deleted from the list of endangered species or its critical habitat materially redefined." *Ibid.*

The Court of Appeals accepted the District Court's finding that closure of the dam would result in the known population of snail darters being "significantly reduced if not completely extirpated." *Id.*, at 1069. TVA, in fact, had conceded as much in the Court of Appeals, but argued that "closure of the Tellico Dam, as the last stage of a ten-year project, falls outside the legitimate purview of the Act if it is rationally construed." *Id.*, at 1070. Disagreeing, the Court of Appeals held that the record revealed a prima facie violation of § 7 of the Act, namely that TVA had failed to take "such action . . . necessary to insure" that its "actions" did not jeopardize the snail darter or its critical habitat.

The reviewing court thus rejected TVA's contention that the word "actions" in § 7 of the Act was not intended by Congress to encompass the terminal phases of ongoing projects. Not only could the court find no "positive reinforcement" for TVA's argument in the Act's legislative history, but also such an interpretation was seen as being "inimical to . . . its objectives." 549 F. 2d, at 1070. By way of illustration, that court pointed out that "the detrimental impact of a project upon an endangered species may not always be clearly perceived before construction is well underway." *Id.*, at 1071. Given such a likelihood, the Court of Appeals was of the opinion that TVA's position would require the District Court, sitting as a chancellor, to balance the worth of an endangered species against the value of an ongoing public works measure, a result which the appellate court was not willing to accept. Emphasizing the limits on judicial power in this setting, the court stated:

"Current project status cannot be translated into a workable standard of judicial review. Whether a dam is 50% or 90% completed is irrelevant in calculating the social and scientific costs attributable to the disappearance of a unique form of life. Courts are ill-equipped to calculate how many dollars must be invested before the value of a dam exceeds that of the endangered species. Our responsibility under § 1540 (g)(1)(A) is merely to preserve the status quo where endangered species are threatened, thereby guaranteeing the legislative or executive branches sufficient opportunity to grapple with the alternatives." *Ibid.*

As far as the Court of Appeals was concerned, it made no difference that Congress had repeatedly approved appropriations for Tellico, referring to such legislative approval as an "advisory opinio[n]" concerning the proper application of an existing statute. In that court's view, the only relevant legislation was the Act itself, "[t]he meaning and spirit" of which was "clear on its face." *Id.,* at 1072.

Turning to the question of an appropriate remedy, the Court of Appeals ruled that the District Court had erred by not issuing an injunction. While recognizing the irretrievable loss of millions of dollars of public funds which would accompany injunctive relief, the court nonetheless decided that the Act explicitly commanded precisely that result:

"It is conceivable that the welfare of an endangered species may weigh more heavily upon the public conscience, as expressed by the final will of Congress, than the writeoff of those millions of dollars already expended

for Tellico in excess of its present salvageable value."
Id., at 1074.

Following the issuance of the permanent injunction, members of TVA's Board of Directors appeared before Subcommittees of the House and Senate Appropriations Committees to testify in support of continued appropriations for Tellico. The Subcommittees were apprised of all aspects of Tellico's status, including the Court of Appeals' decision. TVA reported that the dam stood "ready for the gates to be closed and the reservoir filled," Hearings on Public Works for Water and Power Development and Energy Research Appropriation Bill, 1978, before a Subcommittee of the House Committee on Appropriations, 95th Cong., 1st Sess., pt. 4, p. 234 (1977), and requested funds for completion of certain ancillary parts of the project, such as public use areas, roads, and bridges. As to the snail darter itself, TVA commented optimistically on its transplantation efforts, expressing the opinion that the relocated fish were "doing well and ha[d] reproduced." *Id.,* at 235, 261–262.

Both Appropriations Committees subsequently recommended the full amount requested for completion of the Tellico Project. In its June 2, 1977, Report, the House Appropriations Committee stated:

> "It is *the Committee's view* that the Endangered Species Act was not intended to halt projects such as these in their advanced stage of completion, and [the Committee] strongly recommends that these projects not be stopped because of misuse of the Act." H. R. Rep. No. 95–379, p. 104.   (Emphasis added.)

As a solution to the problem, the House Committee advised that TVA should cooperate with the Department of the Interior "to relocate the endangered species to another suitable habitat so as to permit the project to proceed as rapidly as possible." *Id.,* at 11. Toward this end, the Committee recommended a special appropriation of $2 million to facilitate relocation of the snail darter and other endangered species which threatened to delay or stop TVA projects. Much the same occurred on the Senate side, with its Appropriations Committee recommending both the amount requested to complete Tellico and the special appropriation for transplantation of endangered species. Reporting to the Senate on these measures, the Appropriations Committee took a particularly strong stand on the snail darter issue:

> "This *committee has not viewed* the Endangered Species Act as preventing the completion and use of these projects which were well under way at the time the affected species were listed as endangered. If the act has such an effect, which is contrary to *the Committee's understanding* of the intent of Congress in enacting the Endangered Species Act, funds should be appropriated to allow these projects to be completed and their benefits realized in the public interest, the Endangered Species Act notwithstanding." S. Rep. No. 95–301, p. 99 (1977). (Emphasis added.)

TVA's budget, including funds for completion of Tellico and relocation of the snail darter, passed both Houses of Congress and was signed into law on August 7, 1977. Public Works for Water and Power Development and Energy Research Appropriation Act, 1978, 91 Stat. 797.

We granted certiorari, 434 U. S. 954 (1977), to review the judgment of the Court of Appeals.

II

We begin with the premise that operation of the Tellico Dam will either eradicate the known population of snail darters or destroy their critical habitat. Petitioner does not now seriously dispute this fact.[17] In any event, under § 4 (a)(1)

---

[17] The District Court findings are to the same effect and are unchallenged here.

of the Act, 87 Stat. 886, 16 U. S. C. § 1533 (a)(1) (1976 ed.), the Secretary of the Interior is vested with exclusive authority to determine whether a species such as the snail darter is "endangered" or "threatened" and to ascertain the factors which have led to such a precarious existence. By § 4 (d) Congress has authorized—indeed commanded—the Secretary to "issue such regulations as he deems necessary and advisable to provide for the conservation of such species." 16 U. S. C. § 1533 (d) (1976 ed.). As we have seen, the Secretary promulgated regulations which declared the snail darter an endangered species whose critical habitat would be destroyed by creation of the Tellico Reservoir. Doubtless petitioner would prefer not to have these regulations on the books, but there is no suggestion that the Secretary exceeded his authority or abused his discretion in issuing the regulations. Indeed, no judicial review of the Secretary's determinations has ever been sought and hence the validity of his actions are not open to review in this Court.

Starting from the above premise, two questions are presented: (a) would TVA be in violation of the Act if it completed and operated the Tellico Dam as planned? (b) if TVA's actions would offend the Act, is an injunction the appropriate remedy for the violation? For the reasons stated hereinafter, we hold that both questions must be answered in the affirmative.

(A)

It may seem curious to some that the survival of a relatively small number of three-inch fish among all the countless millions of species extant would require the permanent halting of a virtually completed dam for which Congress has expended more than $100 million. The paradox is not minimized by the fact that Congress continued to appropriate large sums of public money for the project, even after congressional Appropriations Committees were apprised of its apparent impact upon the survival of the snail darter. We conclude, however, that the explicit provisions of the Endangered Species Act require precisely that result.

One would be hard pressed to find a statutory provision whose terms were any plainer than those in § 7 of the Endangered Species Act.   Its very words affirmatively command all federal agencies "to *insure* that actions *authorized, funded,* or *carried out* by them do not *jeopardize* the continued existence" of an endangered species or *"result* in the destruction or modification of habitat of such species . . . ."   16 U. S. C. § 1536 (1976 ed.).   (Emphasis added.)   This language admits of no exception.   Nonetheless, petitioner urges, as do the dissenters, that the Act cannot reasonably be interpreted as applying to a federal project which was well under way when Congress passed the Endangered Species Act of 1973.   To sustain that position, however, we would be forced to ignore the ordinary meaning of plain language.   It has not been shown, for example, how TVA can close the gates of the Tellico Dam without "carrying out" an action that has been "authorized" and "funded" by a federal agency.   Nor can we understand how such action will *"insure"* that the snail darter's habitat is not disrupted.[18]   Accepting the Secretary's determinations, as

---

[18] In dissent, MR. JUSTICE POWELL argues that the meaning of "actions" in § 7 is "far from 'plain,'" and that "it seems evident that the 'actions' referred to are not all actions that an agency can ever take, but rather actions that the agency is *deciding whether* to authorize, to fund, or to carry out." *Post,* at 205. Aside from this bare assertion, however, no explanation is given to support the proffered interpretation. This recalls Lewis Carroll's classic advice on the construction of language:

" 'When *I* use a word,' Humpty Dumpty said, in rather a scornful tone, 'it means just what *I* choose it to mean—neither more nor less.' " Through the Looking Glass, in The Complete Works of Lewis Carroll 196 (1939).

Aside from being unexplicated, the dissent's reading of § 7 is flawed on several counts. First, under its view, the words "or carry out" in § 7 would be superfluous since all prospective actions of an agency remain to be "authorized" or "funded." Second, the dissent's position logically means that an agency would be obligated to comply with § 7 only when a project is in the planning stage. But if Congress had meant to so limit the Act, it we must, it is clear that TVA's proposed operation of the dam will have precisely the opposite effect, namely the *eradication* of an endangered species.

Concededly, this view of the Act will produce results requiring the sacrifice of the anticipated benefits of the project and of many millions of dollars in public funds.[19]   But examination of the language, history, and structure of the legislation under review here indicates beyond doubt that Congress intended endangered species to be afforded the highest of priorities.

When Congress passed the Act in 1973, it was not legislating on a clean slate.   The first major congressional concern for the preservation of the endangered species had come with passage of the Endangered Species Act of 1966, 80 Stat. 926, repealed, 87 Stat. 903.[20]   In that legislation Congress gave the

───────────

surely would have used words to that effect, as it did in the National Environmental Policy Act, 42 U. S. C. §§ 4332 (2) (A), (C).

[19] The District Court determined that failure to complete the Tellico Dam would result in the loss of some $53 million in nonrecoverable obligations; see *supra,* at 166.   Respondents dispute this figure, and point to a recent study by the General Accounting Office, which suggests that the figure could be considerably less.   See GAO Study, n. 13, *supra,* at 5–14; see also Cook, Cook, & Gove, The Snail Darter & the Dam, 51 National Parks & Conservation Magazine 10 (1977); Conservation Foundation Letter 1–2 (Apr. 1978).   The GAO study also concludes that TVA and Congress should explore alternatives to impoundment of the reservoir, such as the creation of a regional development program based on a free-flowing river.   None of these considerations are relevant to our decision, however; they are properly addressed to the Executive and Congress.

[20] Prior federal involvement with endangered species had been quite limited.   For example, the Lacey Act of 1900, 31 Stat. 187, partially codified in 16 U. S. C. §§ 667e and 701 (1976 ed.), and the Black Bass Act of 1926, 44 Stat. 576, as amended, 16 U. S. C. § 851 *et seq.* (1976 ed.), prohibited the transportation in interstate commerce of fish or wildlife taken in violation of national, state, or foreign law.   The effect of both of these statutes was constrained, however, by the fact that prior to passage of the Endangered Species Act of 1973, there were few laws regulating these

73

Secretary power to identify "the names of the species of native
fish and wildlife found to be threatened with extinction,"
§ 1 (c), 80 Stat. 926, as well as authorization to purchase land
for the conservation, protection, restoration, and propagation
of "selected species" of "native fish and wildlife" threatened
with extinction. §§ 2 (a)–(c), 80 Stat. 926–927. Declaring
the preservation of endangered species a national policy, the
1966 Act directed all federal agencies both to protect these
species and *"insofar as is practicable and consistent with
the*[ir] *primary purposes,"* § 1 (b), 80 Stat. 926, "preserve the
habitats of such threatened species on lands under their
jurisdiction." *Ibid.* (Emphasis added.) The 1966 statute
was not a sweeping prohibition on the taking of endangered
species, however, except on federal lands, § 4 (c), 80 Stat. 928,
and even in those federal areas the Secretary was authorized
to allow the hunting and fishing of endangered species. § 4
(d)(1), 80 Stat. 928.

In 1969 Congress enacted the Endangered Species Conservation Act, 83 Stat. 275, repealed, 87 Stat. 903, which continued
the provisions of the 1966 Act while at the same time broadening federal involvement in the preservation of endangered
species. Under the 1969 legislation, the Secretary was empowered to list species "threatened with worldwide extinction,"
§ 3 (a), 83 Stat. 275; in addition, the importation of any
species so recognized into the United States was prohibited.
§ 2, 83 Stat. 275. An indirect approach to the taking of

---

creatures. See Coggins, Conserving Wildlife Resources: An Overview of
the Endangered Species Act of 1973, 51 N. D. L. Rev. 315, 317–318 (1975).
The Migratory Bird Treaty Act, passed in 1918, 40 Stat. 755, as amended,
16 U. S. C. § 703 *et seq.* (1976 ed.), was more extensive, giving the Secretary of the Interior power to adopt regulations for the protection of migratory birds. Other measures concentrated on establishing refuges for wildlife. See, *e. g.*, Land and Water Conservation Fund Act of 1965, 78 Stat.
897, 16 U. S. C. § 460*l*–4 *et seq.* (1976 ed.). See generally Environmental
Law Institute, The Evolution of National Wildlife Law (1977).

endangered species was also adopted in the Conservation Act by way of a ban on the transportation and sale of wildlife taken in violation of any federal, state, or foreign law. §§ 7 (a)–(b), 83 Stat. 279.[21]

Despite the fact that the 1966 and 1969 legislation represented "the most comprehensive of its type to be enacted by any nation" [22] up to that time, Congress was soon persuaded that a more expansive approach was needed if the newly declared national policy of preserving endangered species was to be realized.   By 1973, when Congress held hearings on what would later become the Endangered Species Act of 1973, it was informed that species were still being lost at the rate of about one per year, 1973 House Hearings 306 (statement of Stephen R. Seater, for Defenders of Wildlife), and "the pace of disappearance of species" appeared to be "accelerating." H. R. Rep. No. 93–412, p. 4 (1973).   Moreover, Congress was also told that the primary cause of this trend was something other than the normal process of natural selection:

> "[M]an and his technology has [sic] continued at an ever-increasing rate to disrupt the natural ecosystem. This has resulted in a dramatic rise in the number and severity of the threats faced by the world's wildlife.   The truth in this is apparent when one realizes that half of the recorded extinctions of mammals over the past 2,000 years have occurred in the most recent 50-year period." 1973 House Hearings 202 (statement of Assistant Secretary of the Interior).

_____

[21] This approach to the problem of taking, of course, contained the same inherent limitations as the Lacey and Black Bass Acts, discussed, n. 20, *supra*.

[22] Hearings on Endangered Species before the Subcommittee of the House Committee on Merchant Marine and Fisheries, 93d Cong., 1st Sess., 202 (1973) (statement of Assistant Secretary of the Interior) (hereinafter cited as 1973 House Hearings).

That Congress did not view these developments lightly was stressed by one commentator:

"The dominant theme pervading all Congressional discussion of the proposed [Endangered Species Act of 1973] was the overriding need *to devote whatever effort and resources were necessary* to avoid further diminution of national and worldwide wildlife resources. Much of the testimony at the hearings and much debate was devoted to the biological problem of extinction. Senators and Congressmen uniformly deplored the irreplaceable loss to aesthetics, science, ecology, and the national heritage should more species disappear." Coggins, Conserving Wildlife Resources: An Overview of the Endangered Species Act of 1973, 51 N. D. L. Rev. 315, 321 (1975). (Emphasis added.)

The legislative proceedings in 1973 are, in fact, replete with expressions of concern over the risk that might lie in the loss of *any* endangered species.[23] Typifying these sentiments is the Report of the House Committee on Merchant Marine and

---

[23] See, *e. g.*, 1973 House Hearings 280 (statement of Rep. Roe); *id.*, at 281 (statement of Rep. Whitehurst); *id.*, at 301 (statement of Friends of the Earth); *id.*, at 306–307 (statement of Defenders of Wildlife). One statement, made by the Assistant Secretary of the Interior, particularly deserves notice:

"I have watched in my lifetime a vast array of mollusks in southern streams totally disappear as a result of damming, channelization, and pollution. It is often asked of me, 'what is the importance of the mollusks for example in Alabama.' I do not know, and I do not know whether any of us will ever have the insight to know exactly why these mollusks evolved over millions of years or what their importance is in the total ecosystem. However, I have great trouble being party to their destruction without ever having gained such knowledge." *Id.*, at 207.

One member of the mollusk family existing in these southern rivers is the snail, see 12 Encyclopedia Britannica 326 (15th ed. 1974), which ironically enough provides the principal food for snail darters. See *supra*, at 162, 165–166, n. 16.

Fisheries on H. R. 37, a bill which contained the essential features of the subsequently enacted Act of 1973; in explaining the need for the legislation, the Report stated:

"As we homogenize the habitats in which these plants and animals evolved, and as we increase the pressure for products that they are in a position to supply (usually unwillingly) we threaten their—and our own—genetic heritage.

The value of this genetic heritage is, quite literally, incalculable.

.   .   .   .   .

"From the most narrow possible point of view, *it is in the best interests of mankind to minimize the losses of genetic variations.*   The reason is simple: they are potential resources.   They are keys to puzzles which we cannot solve, and may provide answers to questions which we have not yet learned to ask.

"To take a homely, but apt, example: one of the critical chemicals in the regulation of ovulations in humans was found in a common plant.   Once discovered, and analyzed, humans could duplicate it synthetically, but had it never existed—or had it been driven out of existence before we knew its potentialities—we would never have tried to synthesize it in the first place.

"Who knows, or can say, what potential cures for cancer or other scourges, present or future, may lie locked up in the structures of plants which may yet be undiscovered, much less analyzed?   . . .   Sheer self-interest impels us to be cautious.

"The institutionalization of that caution lies at the heart of H. R. 37 . . . ."   H. R. Rep. No. 93–412, pp. 4–5 (1973).   (Emphasis added.)

As the examples cited here demonstrate, Congress was concerned about the *unknown* uses that endangered species might have and about the *unforeseeable* place such creatures may have in the chain of life on this planet.

In shaping legislation to deal with the problem thus presented, Congress started from the finding that "[t]he two major causes of extinction are hunting and destruction of natural habitat." S. Rep. No. 93–307, p. 2 (1973). Of these twin threats, Congress was informed that the greatest was destruction of natural habitats; see 1973 House Hearings 236 (statement of Associate Deputy Chief for National Forest System, Dept. of Agriculture); *id.*, at 241 (statement of Director of Mich. Dept. of Natural Resources); *id.*, at 306 (statement of Stephen R. Seater, Defenders of Wildlife); Lachenmeier, The Endangered Species Act of 1973: Preservation or Pandemonium?, 5 Environ. Law 29, 31 (1974). Witnesses recommended, among other things, that Congress require all land-managing agencies "to avoid damaging critical habitat for endangered species and to take positive steps to improve such habitat." 1973 House Hearings 241 (statement of Director of Mich. Dept. of Natural Resources). Virtually every bill introduced in Congress during the 1973 session responded to this concern by incorporating language similar, if not identical, to that found in the present § 7 of the Act.[24] These provisions were designed, in the words of an administration witness, "for the first time [to] *prohibit* [a] federal agency from taking action which does jeopardize the status of endangered species," Hearings on S. 1592 and S. 1983 before the Subcommittee on Environment of the Senate Committee on Commerce, 93d Cong., 1st Sess., 68 (1973) (statement of

---

[24] For provisions in the House bills, see § 5 (d) of H. R. 37, 470, 471, 1511, 2669, 3696, and 3795; § 3 (d) of H. R. 1461 and 4755; § 5 (d) of H. R. 2735; § 3 (d) of H. R. 4758. For provisions in the Senate bills, see § 3 (d) of S. 1592; § 5 (d) of S. 1983. The House bills are collected in 1973 House Hearings 87–185; the Senate bills are found in the Hearings on S. 1592 and S. 1983 before the Subcommittee on Environment of the Senate Committee on Commerce, 93d Cong., 1st Sess., 3–49 (1973).

Deputy Assistant Secretary of the Interior) (emphasis added);
furthermore, the proposed bills would *"direc[t]* all . . . Federal
agencies to utilize their authorities for carrying out programs
for the protection of endangered animals." 1973 House Hearings 205 (statement of Assistant Secretary of the Interior).
(Emphasis added.)

As it was finally passed, the Endangered Species Act of 1973
represented the most comprehensive legislation for the preservation of endangered species ever enacted by any nation. Its
stated purposes were "to provide a means whereby the ecosystems upon which endangered species and threatened species
depend may be conserved," and "to provide a program for the
conservation of such . . . species . . . ." 16 U. S. C. § 1531 (b)
(1976 ed.). In furtherance of these goals, Congress expressly
stated in § 2 (c) that "all Federal departments and agencies
shall seek *to conserve endangered species* and threatened
species . . . ." 16 U. S. C. § 1531 (c) (1976 ed.). (Emphasis
added.) Lest there be any ambiguity as to the meaning of
this statutory directive, the Act specifically defined "conserve"
as meaning "to use and the use of *all methods and procedures
which are necessary* to bring *any endangered species* or threatened species to the point at which the measures provided
pursuant to this chapter are no longer necessary." § 1532 (2).
(Emphasis added.) Aside from § 7, other provisions indicated
the seriousness with which Congress viewed this issue: Virtually all dealings with endangered species, including taking,
possession, transportation, and sale, were prohibited, 16 U. S. C.
§ 1538 (1976 ed.), except in extremely narrow circumstances,
see § 1539 (b). The Secretary was also given extensive power
to develop regulations and programs for the preservation of
endangered and threatened species.[25] § 1533 (d). Citizen

---

[25] A further indication of the comprehensive scope of the 1973 Act lies
in Congress' inclusion of "threatened species" as a class deserving federal
protection. Threatened species are defined as those which are "likely to
become an endangered species within the foreseeable future throughout all

involvement was encouraged by the Act, with provisions allowing interested persons to petition the Secretary to list a species as endangered or threatened, § 1533 (c)(2), see n. 11, *supra,* and bring civil suits in United States district courts to force compliance with any provision of the Act, §§ 1540 (c) and (g).

Section 7 of the Act, which of course is relied upon by respondents in this case, provides a particularly good gauge of congressional intent. As we have seen, this provision had its genesis in the Endangered Species Act of 1966, but that legislation qualified the obligation of federal agencies by stating that they should seek to preserve endangered species only *"insofar as is practicable and consistent with the*[*ir*] *primary purposes . . . ."* Likewise, every bill introduced in 1973 contained a qualification similar to that found in the earlier statutes.[26] Exemplary of these was the administration bill, H. R. 4758, which in § 2 (b) would direct federal agencies to use their authorities to further the ends of the Act *"insofar as is practicable and consistent with the*[*ir*] *primary purposes . . . ."* (Emphasis added.) Explaining the idea behind this language, an administration spokesman told Congress that it "would further signal to all . . . agencies of the Government that this is the *first priority, consistent with their primary objectives."* 1973 House Hearings 213 (statement of Deputy Assistant Secretary of the Interior). (Emphasis added.) This type of language did not go unnoticed by those advocating strong endangered species legislation. A representative of the

---

or a significant portion of [their] range." 16 U. S. C. § 1532 (15) (1976 ed.).

[26] For provisions in the House bills, see §§ 2 (c) and 5 (d) of H. R. 37, 470, 471, 1511, 2669, 3310, 3696, and 3795; § 3 (d) of H. R. 1461 and 4755; § 5 (d) of H. R. 2735; § 2 (b) of H. R. 4758; one other House bill, H. R. 2169, imposed no requirements on federal agencies. For provisions in the Senate bills, see § 2 (b) of S. 1592; §§ 2 (b), and 5 (d) of S. 1983.

Sierra Club, for example, attacked the use of the phrase
"consistent with the primary purpose" in proposed H. R. 4758,
cautioning that the qualification "could be construed to be a
declaration of congressional policy that other agency purposes
are necessarily more important than protection of endangered
species and would always prevail if conflict were to occur."
1973 House Hearings 335 (statement of the chairman of the
Sierra Club's National Wildlife Committee); see *id.*, at 251
(statement for the National Audubon Society).

What is very significant in this sequence is that the final
version of the 1973 Act carefully omitted all of the reservations
described above.   In the bill which the Senate initially approved (S. 1983), however, the version of the current § 7
merely required federal agencies to "carry out such programs
as are practicable for the protection of species listed . . . ." [27]
S. 1983, § 7 (a).   (Emphasis added.)   By way of contrast,
the bill that originally passed the House, H. R. 37, contained a
provision which was essentially a mirror image of the subsequently passed § 7—indeed all phrases which might have
qualified an agency's responsibilities had been omitted from
the bill.[28]   In explaining the expected impact of this provision
in H. R. 37 on federal agencies, the House Committee's Report
states:

> "This subsection *requires* the Secretary and the heads of
> all other Federal departments and agencies to use their
> authorities in order to carry out programs for the pro-

---

[27] We note, however, that in the version of S. 1983 which was sent to
the floor of the Senate by the Senate Committee on Commerce, the qualifying language "wherever practicable" had been omitted from one part of
the bill, that being § 2 (b).   See 119 Cong. Rec. 25663 (1973).   Section
2 (b) was the portion of S. 1983 that stated the "purposes and policy" of
Congress.   But the Committee's version of S. 1983—which was reported
to the full Senate—retained the limitation on § 7 that we note here.   119
Cong. Rec. 25664 (1973).

[28] See *id.*, at 30157–30162.

tection of endangered species, and it further *requires* that those agencies take *the necessary action* that will *not jeopardize* the continuing existence of endangered species or result in the destruction of critical habitat of those species." H. R. Rep. No. 93–412, p. 14 (1973). (Emphasis added.)

Resolution of this difference in statutory language, as well as other variations between the House and Senate bills, was the task of a Conference Committee. See 119 Cong. Rec. 30174–30175, 31183 (1973). The Conference Report, H. R. Conf. Rep. No. 93–740 (1973), basically adopted the Senate bill, S. 1983; but the conferees rejected the Senate version of § 7 and adopted the stringent, mandatory language in H. R. 37. While the Conference Report made no specific reference to this choice of provisions, the House manager of the bill, Representative Dingell, provided an interpretation of what the Conference bill would require, making it clear that the mandatory provisions of § 7 were not casually or inadvertently included:

"[Section 7] substantially amplifie[s] the obligation of [federal agencies] to take steps within their power to carry out the purposes of this act. A recent article . . . illustrates the problem which might occur absent this new language in the bill. It appears that the whooping cranes of this country, perhaps the best known of our endangered species, are being threatened by Air Force bombing activities along the gulf coast of Texas. Under existing law, the Secretary of Defense has some discretion as to whether or not he will take the necessary action to see that this threat disappears . . . . [O]nce the bill is enacted, [the Secretary of Defense] *would be required to take the proper steps.* . . .

"Another example . . . [has] to do with the continental population of grizzly bears which may or may not be endangered, but which is surely threatened. . . . Once this bill is enacted, the appropriate Secretary, whether of Interior, Agriculture or whatever, *will have to take action* to see that this situation is not permitted to worsen, and that these bears are not driven to extinction. The purposes of the bill included the conservation of the species and of the ecosystems upon which they depend, and *every agency of government is committed* to see that those purposes are carried out. . . . [T]he agencies of Government can no longer plead that they can do nothing about it. *They can, and they must. The law is clear.*" 119 Cong. Rec. 42913 (1973). (Emphasis added.)

It is against this legislative background [29] that we must measure TVA's claim that the Act was not intended to stop operation of a project which, like Tellico Dam, was near completion when an endangered species was discovered in its path. While there is no discussion in the legislative history of precisely this problem, the totality of congressional action makes it abundantly clear that the result we reach today is wholly in accord with both the words of the statute and the intent of Congress. The plain intent of Congress in enacting this statute was to halt and reverse the trend toward species extinction, whatever the cost. This is reflected not only in the stated policies of the Act, but in literally every section of the statute. All persons, including federal agencies, are specifically instructed not to "take" endangered species, meaning that no one is "to harass, harm,[30] pursue, hunt, shoot,

---

[29] When confronted with a statute which is plain and unambiguous on its face, we ordinarily do not look to legislative history as a guide to its meaning. *Ex parte Collett,* 337 U. S. 55, 61 (1949), and cases cited therein. Here it is not *necessary* to look beyond the words of the statute. We have undertaken such an analysis only to meet MR. JUSTICE POWELL's suggestion that the "absurd" result reached in this case, *post,* at 196, is not in accord with congressional intent.

[30] We do not understand how TVA intends to operate Tellico Dam without "harming" the snail darter. The Secretary of the Interior has defined the term "harm" to mean "an act or omission which actually

wound, kill, trap, capture, or collect" such life forms. 16
U. S. C. §§ 1532 (14), 1538 (a)(1)(B) (1976 ed.). Agencies in
particular are directed by §§ 2 (c) and 3 (2) of the Act to
"use . . . *all methods* and procedures which are necessary" to
preserve endangered species. 16 U. S. C. §§ 1531 (c), 1532 (2)
(1976 ed.) (emphasis added). In addition, the legislative
history undergirding § 7 reveals an explicit congressional decision to require agencies to afford first priority to the declared
national policy of saving endangered species. The pointed
omission of the type of qualifying language previously included
in endangered species legislation reveals a conscious decision
by Congress to give endangered species priority over the
"primary missions" of federal agencies.

It is not for us to speculate, much less act, on whether
Congress would have altered its stance had the specific events
of this case been anticipated. In any event, we discern no
hint in the deliberations of Congress relating to the 1973 Act
that would compel a different result than we reach here.[31]

---

injures or kills wildlife, including acts which annoy it to such an extent as
to significantly disrupt essential behavioral patterns, which include, but
are not limited to, breeding, feeding or sheltering; *significant environmental modification or degradation which has such effects is included
within the meaning of 'harm.'* "   50 CFR § 17.3 (1976) (emphasis added);
see S. Rep. No. 93–307, p. 7 (1973).

[31] The *only* portion of the legislative history which petitioner cites as
being favorable to its position consists of certain statements made by
Senator Tunney on the floor of the Senate during debates on S. 1983; see 119
Cong. Rec. 25691–25692 (1973). Senator Tunney was asked whether the
proposed bill would affect the Army Corps of Engineers' decision to build
a road through a particular area of Kentucky. Responding to this question, Senator Tunney opined that § 7 of S. 1983 would require consultation among the agencies involved, but that the Corps of Engineers "would
not be prohibited from building such a road if they deemed it necessary
to do so." 119 Cong. Rec. 25689 (1973). Petitioner interprets these
remarks to mean that an agency, after balancing the respective interests
involved, could decide to take action which would extirpate an endangered
species. If that is what Senator Tunney meant, his views are in distinct

Indeed, the repeated expressions of congressional concern over
what it saw as the potentially enormous danger presented by
the eradication of *any* endangered species suggest how the
balance would have been struck had the issue been presented
to Congress in 1973.

Furthermore, it is clear Congress foresaw that § 7 would,
on occasion, require agencies to alter ongoing projects in
order to fulfill the goals of the Act.[32] Congressman Dingell's
discussion of Air Force practice bombing, for instance, obviously pinpoints a particular activity—intimately related to

contrast to every other expression in the legislative history as to the meaning of § 7. For example, when the Kentucky example was brought up in
the Senate hearings, an administration spokesman interpreted an analogous provision in S. 1592 as "prohibit[ing] [a] federal agency from taking
action which does jeopardize the status of endangered species." *Supra*, at
179. Moreover, we note that the version of S. 1983 being discussed by
Senator Tunney contained the "as practicable" limitation in § 7 (a) which
we have previously mentioned. See *supra*, at 182. Senator Tunney's
remarks perhaps explain why the Conference Committee subsequently
deleted all such qualifying expressions. We construe the Senator's remarks
as simply meaning that under the 1973 Act the agency responsible for the
project would have the "final decision," 119 Cong. Rec. 25690 (1973), as
to whether the action should proceed, notwithstanding contrary advice
from the Secretary of the Interior. The Secretary's recourse would be to
either appeal to higher authority in the administration, or proceed to
federal court under the relevant provisions of the Act; citizens may likewise seek enforcement under 16 U. S. C. § 1540 (g) (1976 ed.), as has been
done in this case.

[32] MR. JUSTICE POWELL characterizes the result reached here as giving
"retroactive" effect to the Endangered Species Act of 1973. We cannot
accept that contention. Our holding merely gives effect to the plain words
of the statute, namely, that § 7 affects all projects which remain to be authorized, funded, or carried out. Indeed, under the Act there could be no
"retroactive" application since, by definition, any *prior* action of a federal
agency which *would* have come under the scope of the Act must have
already *resulted* in the destruction of an endangered species or its critical
habitat. In that circumstance the species would have already been extirpated or its habitat destroyed; the Act would then have no subject matter
to which it might apply.

the national defense—which a major federal department would be obliged to alter in deference to the strictures of § 7. A similar example is provided by the House Committee Report:

> "Under the authority of [§ 7], the Director of the Park Service would be required *to conform the practices of his agency* to the need for protecting the rapidly dwindling stock of grizzly bears within Yellowstone Park. These bears, which may be endangered, and are undeniably threatened, should at least be protected by supplying them with carcasses from excess elk within the park, *by curtailing the destruction of habitat by clearcutting National Forests surrounding the Park,* and by preventing hunting until their numbers have recovered sufficiently to withstand these pressures." H. R. Rep. No. 93–412, p. 14 (1973). (Emphasis added.)

One might dispute the applicability of these examples to the Tellico Dam by saying that in this case the burden on the public through the loss of millions of unrecoverable dollars would greatly outweigh the loss of the snail darter.[33] But neither the Endangered Species Act nor Art. III of the Constitution provides federal courts with authority to make such fine utilitarian calculations. On the contrary, the plain language of the Act, buttressed by its legislative history, shows clearly that Congress viewed the value of endangered species as "incalculable." Quite obviously, it would be difficult for

---

[33] MR. JUSTICE POWELL's dissent places great reliance on *Church of the Holy Trinity* v. *United States,* 143 U. S. 457, 459 (1892), *post,* at 204, to support his view of the 1973 Act's legislative history. This Court, however, later explained *Holy Trinity* as applying only in "rare and exceptional circumstances. . . . And there must be something to make plain the intent of Congress that the letter of the statute is not to prevail." *Crooks* v. *Harrelson,* 282 U. S. 55, 60 (1930). As we have seen from our explication of the structure and history of the 1973 Act, there is nothing to support the assertion that the literal meaning of § 7 should not apply in this case.

a court to balance the loss of a sum certain—even $100 million—against a congressionally declared "incalculable" value, even assuming we had the power to engage in such a weighing process, which we emphatically do not.

In passing the Endangered Species Act of 1973, Congress was also aware of certain instances in which exceptions to the statute's broad sweep would be necessary. Thus, § 10, 16 U. S. C. § 1539 (1976 ed.), creates a number of limited "hardship exemptions," none of which would even remotely apply to the Tellico Project. In fact, there are no exemptions in the Endangered Species Act for federal agencies, meaning that under the maxim *expressio unius est exclusio alterius*, we must presume that these were the only "hardship cases" Congress intended to exempt. Cf. *National Railroad Passenger Corp.* v. *National Assn. of Railroad Passengers*, 414 U. S. 453, 458 (1974).[34]

---

[34] MR. JUSTICE POWELL's dissent relies on cases decided under the National Environmental Policy Act to support its position that the 1973 Act should only apply to prospective actions of an agency. *Post*, at 205–206. The NEPA decisions, however, are completely inapposite. First, the two statutes serve different purposes. NEPA essentially imposes a procedural requirement on agencies, requiring them to engage in an extensive *inquiry* as to the effect of federal actions on the environment; by way of contrast, the 1973 Act is substantive in effect, designed to *prevent* the loss of any endangered species, regardless of the cost. Thus, it would make sense to hold NEPA inapplicable at some point in the life of a project, because the agency would no longer have a meaningful opportunity to *weigh* the benefits of the project versus the detrimental effects on the environment. Section 7, on the other hand, compels agencies not only to *consider* the effect of their projects on endangered species, but to take such actions as are necessary to *insure* that species are not extirpated as a result of federal activities. Second, even the NEPA cases have generally required agencies to file environmental impact statements when the remaining governmental action would be environmentally "significant." See, *c. g.*, *Environmental Defense Fund* v. *TVA*, 468 F. 2d 1164, 1177 (CA6 1972). Under § 7, the loss of *any* endangered species has been determined by Congress to be environmentally "significant." See *supra*, at 177–179.

Notwithstanding Congress' expression of intent in 1973, we are urged to find that the continuing appropriations for Tellico Dam constitute an implied repeal of the 1973 Act, at least insofar as it applies to the Tellico Project. In support of this view, TVA points to the statements found in various House and Senate Appropriations Committees' Reports; as described in Part I, *supra,* those Reports generally reflected the attitude of the *Committees* either that the Act did not apply to Tellico or that the dam should be completed regardless of the provisions of the Act. Since we are unwilling to assume that these latter Committee statements constituted advice to ignore the provisions of a duly enacted law, we assume that these Committees believed that the Act simply was not applicable in this situation. But even under this interpretation of the Committees' actions, we are unable to conclude that the Act has been in any respect amended or repealed.

There is nothing in the appropriations measures, as passed, which states that the Tellico Project was to be completed irrespective of the requirements of the Endangered Species Act. These appropriations, in fact, represented relatively minor components of the lump-sum amounts for the *entire* TVA budget.[35] To find a repeal of the Endangered Species Act under these circumstances would surely do violence to the " 'cardinal rule . . . that repeals by implication are not favored.' " *Morton* v. *Mancari,* 417 U. S. 535, 549 (1974), quoting *Posadas* v. *National City Bank,* 296 U. S. 497, 503 (1936). In *Posadas* this Court held, in no uncertain terms, that "the intention of the legislature to repeal must be clear and manifest." *Ibid.* See *Georgia* v. *Pennsylvania R. Co.,*

---

[35] The Appropriations Acts did not themselves identify the projects for which the sums had been appropriated; identification of these projects requires reference to the legislative history. See n. 14, *supra.* Thus, unless a Member scrutinized in detail the Committee proceedings concerning the appropriations, he would have no knowledge of the possible conflict between the continued funding and the Endangered Species Act.

324 U. S. 439, 456–457 (1945) ("Only a clear repugnancy between the old . . . and the new [law] results in the former giving way . . ."); *United States* v. *Borden Co.,* 308 U. S. 188, 198–199 (1939) ("[I]ntention of the legislature to repeal 'must be clear and manifest'. . . . '[A] positive repugnancy [between the old and the new laws]' "); *Wood* v. *United States,* 16 Pet. 342, 363 (1842) ("[T]here must be a positive repugnancy . . ."). In practical terms, this "cardinal rule" means that "[i]n the absence of some affirmative showing of an intention to repeal, the only permissible justification for a repeal by implication is when the earlier and later statutes are irreconcilable." *Mancari, supra,* at 550.

The doctrine disfavoring repeals by implication "applies with full vigor when . . . the subsequent legislation is an *appropriations* measure." *Committee for Nuclear Responsibility* v. *Seaborg,* 149 U. S. App. D. C. 380, 382, 463 F. 2d 783, 785 (1971) (emphasis added); *Environmental Defense Fund* v. *Froehlke,* 473 F. 2d 346, 355 (CA8 1972). This is perhaps an understatement since it would be more accurate to say that the policy applies with even *greater* force when the claimed repeal rests solely on an Appropriations Act. We recognize that both substantive enactments and appropriations measures are "Acts of Congress," but the latter have the limited and specific purpose of providing funds for authorized programs. When voting on appropriations measures, legislators are entitled to operate under the assumption that the funds will be devoted to purposes which are lawful and not for any purpose forbidden. Without such an assurance, every appropriations measure would be pregnant with prospects of altering substantive legislation, repealing by implication any prior statute which might prohibit the expenditure. Not only would this lead to the absurd result of requiring Members to review exhaustively the background of every authorization before voting on an appropriation, but it would flout the very rules the Congress carefully adopted to avoid this need. House Rule XXI (2), for instance, specifically provides:

> "No appropriation shall be reported in any general appropriation bill, or be in order as an amendment thereto, for any expenditure not previously authorized by law, unless in continuation of appropriations for such public works as are already in progress. *Nor shall any provision in any such bill or amendment thereto changing existing law be in order.*" (Emphasis added.)

See also Standing Rules of the Senate, Rule 16.4. Thus, to sustain petitioner's position, we would be obliged to assume that Congress meant to repeal *pro tanto* § 7 of the Act by means of a procedure expressly prohibited under the rules of Congress.

Perhaps mindful of the fact that it is "swimming upstream" against a strong current of well-established precedent, TVA argues for an exception to the rule against implied repealers in a circumstance where, as here, Appropriations Committees have expressly stated their "understanding" that the earlier legislation would not prohibit the proposed expenditure. We cannot accept such a proposition. Expressions of committees dealing with requests for appropriations cannot be equated with statutes enacted by Congress, particularly not in the circumstances presented by this case. First, the Appropriations Committees had no jurisdiction over the subject of endangered species, much less did they conduct the type of extensive hearings which preceded passage of the earlier Endangered Species Acts, especially the 1973 Act. We venture to suggest that the House Committee on Merchant Marine and Fisheries and the Senate Committee on Commerce would be somewhat surprised to learn that their careful work on the substantive legislation had been undone by the simple—and brief— insertion of some inconsistent language in Appropriations Committees' Reports.

Second, there is no indication that Congress as a whole was aware of TVA's position, although the Appropriations Committees apparently agreed with petitioner's views. Only recently, in *SEC* v. *Sloan,* 436 U. S. 103 (1978), we declined to presume general congressional acquiescence in a 34-year-old practice of the Securities and Exchange Commission, despite the fact that the Senate Committee *having jurisdiction over the Commission's activities* had long expressed approval of the practice. MR. JUSTICE REHNQUIST, speaking for the Court, observed that we should be "extremely hesitant to presume general congressional awareness of the Commission's construction based only upon a few isolated statements in the thousands of pages of legislative documents." *Id.,* at 121. *A fortiori,* we should not assume that petitioner's views—and the Appropriations Committees' acceptance of them—were any better known, especially when the TVA is not the agency with primary responsibility for administering the Endangered Species Act.

Quite apart from the foregoing factors, we would still be unable to find that in this case "the earlier and later statutes are irreconcilable," *Mancari,* 417 U. S., at 550; here it is entirely possible "to regard each as effective." *Id.,* at 551. The starting point in this analysis must be the legislative proceedings leading to the 1977 appropriations since the earlier funding of the dam occurred prior to the listing of the snail darter as an endangered species. In all successive years, TVA confidently reported to the Appropriations Committees that efforts to transplant the snail darter appeared to be successful; this surely gave those Committees some basis for the impression that there was no direct conflict between the Tellico Project and the Endangered Species Act. Indeed, the special appropriation for 1978 of $2 million for transplantation of endangered species supports the view that the Committees saw such relocation as the means whereby collision between Tellico and the Endangered Species Act could be avoided. It should also

be noted that the Reports issued by the Senate and House
Appropriations Committees in 1976 came within a month of
the District Court's decision in this case, which hardly could
have given the Members cause for concern over the possible
applicability of the Act. This leaves only the 1978 appropriations, the Reports for which issued after the Court of Appeals'
decision now before us. At that point very little remained to
be accomplished on the project; the Committees understandably advised TVA to cooperate with the Department of the
Interior "to relocate the endangered species to another suitable
habitat so as to permit the project to proceed as rapidly as
possible." H. R. Rep. No. 95–379, p. 11 (1977). It is true
that the *Committees* repeated their earlier expressed "view"
that the Act did not prevent completion of the Tellico Project.
Considering these statements in context, however, it is evident
that they " 'represent only the personal views of these legislators,' " and "however explicit, [they] cannot serve to change
the legislative intent of Congress expressed before the Act's
passage." *Regional Rail Reorganization Act Cases*, 419 U. S.
102, 132 (1974).

(B)

Having determined that there is an irreconcilable conflict
between operation of the Tellico Dam and the explicit provisions of § 7 of the Endangered Species Act, we must now
consider what remedy, if any, is appropriate. It is correct, of
course, that a federal judge sitting as a chancellor is not
mechanically obligated to grant an injunction for every violation of law. This Court made plain in *Hecht Co.* v. *Bowles,*
321 U. S. 321, 329 (1944), that "[a] grant of *jurisdiction* to
issue compliance orders hardly suggests an absolute duty to do
so under any and all circumstances." As a general matter it
may be said that "[s]ince all or almost all equitable remedies
are discretionary, the balancing of equities and hardships is
appropriate in almost any case as a guide to the chancellor's
discretion." D. Dobbs, Remedies 52 (1973). Thus, in *Hecht*

Co. the Court refused to grant an injunction when it appeared from the District Court findings that "the issuance of an injunction would have 'no effect by way of insuring better compliance in the future' and would [have been] 'unjust' to [the] petitioner and not 'in the public interest.'" 321 U. S., at 326.

But these principles take a court only so far. Our system of government is, after all, a tripartite one, with each branch having certain defined functions delegated to it by the Constitution. While "[i]t is emphatically the province and duty of the judicial department to say what the law is," *Marbury* v. *Madison,* 1 Cranch 137, 177 (1803), it is equally—and emphatically—the exclusive province of the Congress not only to formulate legislative policies and mandate programs and projects, but also to establish their relative priority for the Nation. Once Congress, exercising its delegated powers, has decided the order of priorities in a given area, it is for the Executive to administer the laws and for the courts to enforce them when enforcement is sought.

Here we are urged to view the Endangered Species Act "reasonably," and hence shape a remedy "that accords with some modicum of common sense and the public weal." *Post,* at 196. But is that our function? We have no expert knowledge on the subject of endangered species, much less do we have a mandate from the people to strike a balance of equities on the side of the Tellico Dam. Congress has spoken in the plainest of words, making it abundantly clear that the balance has been struck in favor of affording endangered species the highest of priorities, thereby adopting a policy which it described as "institutionalized caution."

Our individual appraisal of the wisdom or unwisdom of a particular course consciously selected by the Congress is to be put aside in the process of interpreting a statute. Once the meaning of an enactment is discerned and its constitutionality determined, the judicial process comes to an end. We do not sit as a committee of review, nor are we vested with the power of veto. The lines ascribed to Sir Thomas More by Robert Bolt are not without relevance here:

"The law, Roper, the law. I know what's legal, not what's right. And I'll stick to what's legal. . . . I'm *not* God. The currents and eddies of right and wrong, which you find such plain-sailing, I can't navigate, I'm no voyager. But in the thickets of the law, oh there I'm a forester. . . . What would you do? Cut a great road through the law to get after the Devil? . . . And when the last law was down, and the Devil turned round on you—where would you hide, Roper, the laws all being flat? . . . This country's planted thick with laws from coast to coast—Man's laws, not God's—and if you cut them down . . . d'you really think you could stand upright in the winds that would blow them? . . . Yes, I'd give the Devil benefit of law, for my own safety's sake." R. Bolt, A Man for All Seasons, Act I, p. 147 (Three Plays, Heinemann ed. 1967).

We agree with the Court of Appeals that in our constitutional system the commitment to the separation of powers is too fundamental for us to pre-empt congressional action by judicially decreeing what accords with "common sense and the public weal." Our Constitution vests such responsibilities in the political branches.

Affirmed.

DIAMOND, COMMISSIONER OF PATENTS AND TRADEMARKS *v.* CHAKRABARTY

CERTIORARI TO THE UNITED STATES COURT OF CUSTOMS AND PATENT APPEALS

No. 79–136. Argued March 17, 1980—Decided June 16, 1980

Title 35 U. S. C. § 101 provides for the issuance of a patent to a person who invents or discovers "any" new and useful "manufacture" or "composition of matter." Respondent filed a patent application relating to his invention of a human-made, genetically engineered bacterium capable of breaking down crude oil, a property which is possessed by no naturally occurring bacteria. A patent examiner's rejection of the patent application's claims for the new bacteria was affirmed by the Patent Office Board of Appeals on the ground that living things are not patentable subject matter under § 101. The Court of Customs and Patent Appeals reversed, concluding that the fact that micro-organisms are alive is without legal significance for purposes of the patent law.

Held: A live, human-made micro-organism is patentable subject matter under § 101. Respondent's micro-organism constitutes a "manufacture" or "composition of matter" within that statute. Pp. 308–318.

  (a) In choosing such expansive terms as "manufacture" and "composition of matter," modified by the comprehensive "any," Congress contemplated that the patent laws should be given wide scope, and the relevant legislative history also supports a broad construction. While laws of nature, physical phenomena, and abstract ideas are not patentable, respondent's claim is not to a hitherto unknown natural phenomenon, but to a nonnaturally occurring manufacture or composition of matter—a product of human ingenuity "having a distinctive name, character [and] use." *Hartranft* v. *Wiegmann*, 121 U. S. 609, 615. *Funk Brothers Seed Co.* v. *Kalo Inoculant Co.*, 333 U. S. 127, distinguished. Pp. 308–310.

  (b) The passage of the 1930 Plant Patent Act, which afforded patent protection to certain asexually reproduced plants, and the 1970 Plant Variety Protection Act, which authorized protection for certain sexually reproduced plants but excluded bacteria from its protection, does not evidence congressional understanding that the terms "manufacture" or "composition of matter" in § 101 do not include living things. Pp. 310–314.

(c) Nor does the fact that genetic technology was unforeseen when Congress enacted § 101 require the conclusion that micro-organisms cannot qualify as patentable subject matter until Congress expressly authorizes such protection. The unambiguous language of § 101 fairly embraces respondent's invention. Arguments against patentability under § 101, based on potential hazards that may be generated by genetic research, should be addressed to the Congress and the Executive, not to the Judiciary. Pp. 314–318.

596 F. 2d 952, affirmed.

BURGER, C. J., delivered the opinion of the Court, in which STEWART, BLACKMUN, REHNQUIST, and STEVENS, JJ., joined. BRENNAN, J., filed a dissenting opinion, in which WHITE, MARSHALL, and POWELL, JJ., joined, *post*, p. 318.

Deputy Solicitor General Wallace argued the cause for petitioner. With him on the briefs were *Solicitor General McCree, Assistant Attorney General Shenefield, Harriet S. Shapiro, Robert B. Nicholson, Frederic Freilicher,* and *Joseph F. Nakamura.*

Edward F. McKie, Jr., argued the cause for respondent. With him on the brief were *Leo I. MaLossi, William E. Schuyler, Jr.,* and *Dale H. Hoscheit.**

Leonard S. Rubenstein filed a brief for the Peoples Business Commission as *amicus curiae* urging reversal.

Briefs of *amici curiae* urging affirmance were filed by *George W. Whitney, Bruce M. Collins,* and *Karl F. Jorda* for the American Patent Law Association, Inc.; by *Thomas D. Kiley* for Genentech, Inc.; by *Jerome G. Lee, William F. Dudine, Jr.,* and *Paul H. Heller* for the New York Patent Law Association, Inc.; by *Peter R. Taft, Joseph A. Keyes, Jr.,* and *Sheldon Elloit Steinbach* for Dr. Leroy E. Hood et al.; and by *Lorance L. Greenlee* for Dr. George Pieczenik.

Briefs of *amici curiae* were filed by *William I. Althen* for the American Society for Microbiology; by *Donald R. Dunner* for the Pharmaceutical Manufacturers Association; by *Edward S. Irons, Mary Helen Sears,* and *Donald Reidhaar* for the Regents of the University of California; and by *Cornell D. Cornish, pro se.*

MR. CHIEF JUSTICE BURGER delivered the opinion of the Court.

We granted certiorari to determine whether a live, human-made micro-organism is patentable subject matter under 35 U. S. C. § 101.

I

In 1972, respondent Chakrabarty, a microbiologist, filed a patent application, assigned to the General Electric Co. The application asserted 36 claims related to Chakrabarty's invention of "a bacterium from the genus *Pseudomonas* containing therein at least two stable energy-generating plasmids, each of said plasmids providing a separate hydrocarbon degradative pathway." [1] This human-made, genetically engineered bacterium is capable of breaking down multiple components of crude oil. Because of this property, which is possessed by no naturally occurring bacteria, Chakrabarty's invention is believed to have significant value for the treatment of oil spills. [2]

Chakrabarty's patent claims were of three types: first, process claims for the method of producing the bacteria;

---

[1] Plasmids are hereditary units physically separate from the chromosomes of the cell. In prior research, Chakrabarty and an associate discovered that plasmids control the oil degradation abilities of certain bacteria. In particular, the two researchers discovered plasmids capable of degrading camphor and octane, two components of crude oil. In the work represented by the patent application at issue here, Chakrabarty discovered a process by which four different plasmids, capable of degrading four different oil components, could be transferred to and maintained stably in a single *Pseudomonas* bacterum, which itself has no capacity for degrading oil.

[2] At present, biological control of oil spills requires the use of a mixture of naturally occurring bacteria, each capable of degrading one component of the oil complex. In this way, oil is decomposed into simpler substances which can serve as food for aquatic life. However, for various reasons, only a portion of any such mixed culture survives to attack the oil spill. By breaking down multiple components of oil, Chakrabarty's micro-organism promises more efficient and rapid oil-spill control.

second, claims for an inoculum comprised of a carrier material floating on water, such as straw, and the new bacteria; and third, claims to the bacteria themselves. The patent examiner allowed the claims falling into the first two categories, but rejected claims for the bacteria. His decision rested on two grounds: (1) that micro-organisms are "products of nature," and (2) that as living things they are not patentable subject matter under 35 U. S. C. § 101.

Chakrabarty appealed the rejection of these claims to the Patent Office Board of Appeals, and the Board affirmed the examiner on the second ground.[3] Relying on the legislative history of the 1930 Plant Patent Act, in which Congress extended patent protection to certain asexually reproduced plants, the Board concluded that § 101 was not intended to cover living things such as these laboratory created micro-organisms.

The Court of Customs and Patent Appeals, by a divided vote, reversed on the authority of its prior decision in *In re Bergy,* 563 F. 2d 1031, 1038 (1977), which held that "the fact that microorganisms . . . are alive . . . [is] without legal significance" for purposes of the patent law.[4] Subsequently, we granted the Acting Commissioner of Patents and Trademarks' petition for certiorari in *Bergy,* vacated the judgment, and remanded the case "for further consideration in light of *Parker* v. *Flook,* 437 U. S. 584 (1978)." 438 U. S. 902 (1978). The Court of Customs and Patent Appeals then vacated its judgment in *Chakrabarty* and consolidated the case with *Bergy* for reconsideration. After re-examining both cases in the light of our holding in *Flook,* that court, with one dissent, reaffirmed its earlier judgments. 596 F. 2d 952 (1979).

---

[3] The Board concluded that the new bacteria were not "products of nature," because *Pseudomonas* bacteria containing two or more different energy-generating plasmids are not naturally occurring.

[4] *Bergy* involved a patent application for a pure culture of the micro-organism *Streptomyces vellosus* found to be useful in the production of lincomycin, an antibiotic.

The Commissioner of Patents and Trademarks again sought certiorari, and we granted the writ as to both *Bergy* and *Chakrabarty*. 444 U. S. 924 (1979). Since then, *Bergy* has been dismissed as moot, 444 U. S. 1028 (1980), leaving only *Chakrabarty* for decision.

II

The Constitution grants Congress broad power to legislate to "promote the Progress of Science and useful Arts, by securing for limited Times to Authors and Inventors the exclusive Right to their respective Writings and Discoveries." Art. I, § 8, cl. 8. The patent laws promote this progress by offering inventors exclusive rights for a limited period as an incentive for their inventiveness and research efforts. *Kewanee Oil Co.* v. *Bicron Corp.*, 416 U. S. 470, 480–481 (1974); *Universal Oil Co.* v. *Globe Co.*, 322 U. S. 471, 484 (1944). The authority of Congress is exercised in the hope that "[t]he productive effort thereby fostered will have a positive effect on society through the introduction of new products and processes of manufacture into the economy, and the emanations by way of increased employment and better lives for our citizens." *Kewanee, supra,* at 480.

The question before us in this case is a narrow one of statutory interpretation requiring us to construe 35 U. S. C. § 101, which provides:

> "Whoever invents or discovers any new and useful process, machine, manufacture, or composition of matter, or any new and useful improvement thereof, may obtain a patent therefor, subject to the conditions and requirements of this title."

Specifically, we must determine whether respondent's microorganism constitutes a "manufacture" or "composition of matter" within the meaning of the statute.[5]

---

[5] This case does not involve the other "conditions and requirements" of the patent laws, such as novelty and nonobviousness. 35 U. S. C. §§ 102, 103.

III

In cases of statutory construction we begin, of course, with the language of the statute. *Southeastern Community College* v. *Davis*, 442 U. S. 397, 405 (1979). And "unless otherwise defined, words will be interpreted as taking their ordinary, contemporary, common meaning." *Perrin* v. *United States*, 444 U. S. 37, 42 (1979). We have also cautioned that courts "should not read into the patent laws limitations and conditions which the legislature has not expressed." *United States* v. *Dubilier Condenser Corp.*, 289 U. S. 178, 199 (1933).

Guided by these canons of construction, this Court has read the term "manufacture" in § 101 in accordance with its dictionary definition to mean "the production of articles for use from raw or prepared materials by giving to these materials new forms, qualities, properties, or combinations, whether by hand-labor or by machinery." *American Fruit Growers, Inc.* v. *Brogdex Co.*, 283 U. S. 1, 11 (1931). Similarly, "composition of matter" has been construed consistent with its common usage to include "all compositions of two or more substances and . . . all composite articles, whether they be the results of chemical union, or of mechanical mixture, or whether they be gases, fluids, powders or solids." *Shell Development Co.* v. *Watson*, 149 F. Supp. 279, 280 (DC 1957) (citing 1 A. Deller, Walker on Patents § 14, p. 55 (1st ed. 1937)). In choosing such expansive terms as "manufacture" and "composition of matter," modified by the comprehensive "any," Congress plainly contemplated that the patent laws would be given wide scope.

The relevant legislative history also supports a broad construction. The Patent Act of 1793, authored by Thomas Jefferson, defined statutory subject matter as "any new and useful art, machine, manufacture, or composition of matter, or any new or useful improvement [thereof]." Act of Feb. 21, 1793, § 1, 1 Stat. 319. The Act embodied Jefferson's philosophy that "ingenuity should receive a liberal encouragement."

5 Writings of Thomas Jefferson 75–76 (Washington ed. 1871). See *Graham* v. *John Deere Co.*, 383 U. S. 1, 7–10 (1966). Subsequent patent statutes in 1836, 1870, and 1874 employed this same broad language. In 1952, when the patent laws were recodified, Congress replaced the word "art" with "process," but otherwise left Jefferson's language intact. The Committee Reports accompanying the 1952 Act inform us that Congress intended statutory subject matter to "include anything under the sun that is made by man." S. Rep. No. 1979, 82d Cong., 2d Sess., 5 (1952); H. R. Rep. No. 1923, 82d Cong., 2d Sess., 6 (1952).[6]

This is not to suggest that § 101 has no limits or that it embraces every discovery. The laws of nature, physical phenomena, and abstract ideas have been held not patentable. See *Parker* v. *Flook*, 437 U. S. 584 (1978); *Gottschalk* v. *Benson*, 409 U. S. 63, 67 (1972); *Funk Brothers Seed Co.* v. *Kalo Inoculant Co.*, 333 U. S. 127, 130 (1948); *O'Reilly* v. *Morse*, 15 How. 62, 112–121 (1854); *Le Roy* v. *Tatham*, 14 How. 156, 175 (1853). Thus, a new mineral discovered in the earth or a new plant found in the wild is not patentable subject matter. Likewise, Einstein could not patent his celebrated law that $E=mc^2$; nor could Newton have patented the law of gravity. Such discoveries are "manifestations of . . . nature, free to all men and reserved exclusively to none." *Funk, supra,* at 130.

Judged in this light, respondent's micro-organism plainly qualifies as patentable subject matter. His claim is not to a hitherto unknown natural phenomenon, but to a nonnaturally occurring manufacture or composition of matter—a product of human ingenuity "having a distinctive name, character [and]

---

[6] This same language was employed by P. J. Federico, a principal draftsman of the 1952 recodification, in his testimony regarding that legislation: "[U]nder section 101 a person may have invented a machine or a manufacture, which may include anything under the sun that is made by man. . . ." Hearings on H. R. 3760 before Subcommittee No. 3 of the House Committee on the Judiciary, 82d Cong., 1st Sess., 37 (1951).

use." *Hartranft* v. *Wiegmann,* 121 U. S. 609, 615 (1887). The point is underscored dramatically by comparison of the invention here with that in *Funk.* There, the patentee had discovered that there existed in nature certain species of root-nodule bacteria which did not exert a mutually inhibitive effect on each other. He used that discovery to produce a mixed culture capable of inoculating the seeds of leguminous plants. Concluding that the patentee had discovered "only some of the handiwork of nature," the Court ruled the product nonpatentable:

> "Each of the species of root-nodule bacteria contained in the package infects the same group of leguminous plants which it always infected. No species acquires a different use. The combination of species produces no new bacteria, no change in the six species of bacteria, and no enlargement of the range of their utility. Each species has the same effect it always had. The bacteria perform in their natural way. Their use in combination does not improve in any way their natural functioning. They serve the ends nature originally provided and act quite independently of any effort of the patentee." 333 U. S., at 131.

Here, by contrast, the patentee has produced a new bacterium with markedly different characteristics from any found in nature and one having the potential for significant utility. His discovery is not nature's handiwork, but his own; accordingly it is patentable subject matter under § 101.

IV

Two contrary arguments are advanced, neither of which we find persuasive.

(A)

The petitioner's first argument rests on the enactment of the 1930 Plant Patent Act, which afforded patent protection to certain asexually reproduced plants, and the 1970 Plant

Variety Protection Act, which authorized protection for certain sexually reproduced plants but excluded bacteria from its protection.[7] In the petitioner's view, the passage of these Acts evidences congressional understanding that the terms "manufacture" or "composition of matter" do not include living things; if they did, the petitioner argues, neither Act would have been necessary.

We reject this argument. Prior to 1930, two factors were thought to remove plants from patent protection. The first was the belief that plants, even those artificially bred, were products of nature for purposes of the patent law. This position appears to have derived from the decision of the Patent Office in *Ex parte Latimer,* 1889 Dec. Com. Pat. 123, in which a patent claim for fiber found in the needle of the *Pinus australis* was rejected. The Commissioner reasoned that a contrary result would permit "patents [to] be obtained upon the trees of the forest and the plants of the earth, which of course would be unreasonable and impossible." *Id.,* at 126. The *Latimer* case, it seems, came to "se[t] forth the general stand taken in these matters" that plants were natural products not subject to patent protection. Thorne, Relation of Patent Law to Natural Products, 6 J. Pat. Off. Soc. 23, 24

---

[7] The Plant Patent Act of 1930, 35 U. S. C. § 161, provides in relevant part:

"Whoever invents or discovers and asexually reproduces any distinct and new variety of plant, including cultivated sports, mutants, hybrids, and newly found seedlings, other than a tuber propogated plant or a plant found in an uncultivated state, may obtain a patent therefor. . . ."

The Plant Variety Protection Act of 1970, provides in relevant part:

"The breeder of any novel variety of sexually reproduced plant (other than fungi, bacteria, or first generation hybrids) who has so reproduced the variety, or his successor in interest, shall be entitled to plant variety protection therefor. . . ." 84 Stat. 1547, 7 U. S. C. § 2402 (a).

See generally, 3 A. Deller, Walker on Patents, ch. IX (2d ed. 1964); R. Allyn, The First Plant Patents (1934).

(1923).[8] The second obstacle to patent protection for plants was the fact that plants were thought not amenable to the "written description" requirement of the patent law. See 35 U. S. C. § 112. Because new plants may differ from old only in color or perfume, differentiation by written description was often impossible. See Hearings on H. R. 11372 before the House Committee on Patents, 71st Cong., 2d Sess., 7 (1930) (memorandum of Patent Commissioner Robertson).

In enacting the Plant Patent Act, Congress addressed both of these concerns. It explained at length its belief that the work of the plant breeder "in aid of nature" was patentable invention. S. Rep. No. 315, 71st Cong., 2d Sess., 6–8 (1930); H. R. Rep. No. 1129, 71st Cong., 2d Sess., 7–9 (1930). And it relaxed the written description requirement in favor of "a description . . . as complete as is reasonably possible." 35 U. S. C. § 162. No Committee or Member of Congress, however, expressed the broader view, now urged by the petitioner, that the terms "manufacture" or "composition of matter" exclude living things. The sole support for that position in the legislative history of the 1930 Act is found in the conclusory statement of Secretary of Agriculture Hyde, in a letter to the Chairmen of the House and Senate Committees considering the 1930 Act, that "the patent laws . . . at the present time are understood to cover only inventions or discoveries in the field of inanimate nature." See S. Rep. No. 315, *supra,* at Appendix A; H. R. Rep. No. 1129, *supra,* at Appendix A. Secretary Hyde's opinion, however, is not entitled to controlling weight. His views were solicited on the administration of the new law and not on the scope of patent-

---

[8] Writing three years after the passage of the 1930 Act, R. Cook, Editor of the Journal of Heredity, commented: "It is a little hard for plant men to understand why [Art. I, § 8] of the Constitution should not have been earlier construed to include the promotion of the art of plant breeding. The reason for this is probably to be found in the principle that natural products are not patentable." Florists Exchange and Horticultural Trade World, July 15, 1933, p. 9.

able subject matter—an area beyond his competence. Moreover, there is language in the House and Senate Committee Reports suggesting that to the extent Congress considered the matter it found the Secretary's dichotomy unpersuasive. The Reports observe:

> "There is a clear and logical distinction *between the discovery of a new variety of plant and of certain inanimate things,* such, for example, as a new and useful natural mineral. The mineral is created wholly by nature unassisted by man. . . . On the other hand, a plant discovery resulting from cultivation is unique, isolated, and is not repeated by nature, nor can it be reproduced by nature unaided by man. . . ." S. Rep. No. 315, *supra,* at 6; H. R. Rep. No. 1129, *supra,* at 7 (emphasis added).

Congress thus recognized that the relevant distinction was not between living and inanimate things, but between products of nature, whether living or not, and human-made inventions. Here, respondent's micro-organism is the result of human ingenuity and research. Hence, the passage of the Plant Patent Act affords the Government no support.

Nor does the passage of the 1970 Plant Variety Protection Act support the Government's position. As the Government acknowledges, sexually reproduced plants were not included under the 1930 Act because new varieties could not be reproduced true-to-type through seedlings. Brief for Petitioner 27, n. 31. By 1970, however, it was generally recognized that true-to-type reproduction was possible and that plant patent protection was therefore appropriate. The 1970 Act extended that protection. There is nothing in its language or history to suggest that it was enacted because § 101 did not include living things.

In particular, we find nothing in the exclusion of bacteria from plant variety protection to support the petitioner's position. See n. 7, *supra.* The legislative history gives no reason for this exclusion. As the Court of Customs and

Patent Appeals suggested, it may simply reflect congressional agreement with the result reached by that court in deciding *In re Arzberger,* 27 C. C. P. A. (Pat.) 1315, 112 F. 2d 834 (1940), which held that bacteria were not plants for the purposes of the 1930 Act. Or it may reflect the fact that prior to 1970 the Patent Office had issued patents for bacteria under § 101.[9] In any event, absent some clear indication that Congress "focused on [the] issues . . . directly related to the one presently before the Court," *SEC* v. *Sloan,* 436 U. S. 103, 120–121 (1978), there is no basis for reading into its actions an intent to modify the plain meaning of the words found in § 101. See *TVA* v. *Hill,* 437 U. S. 153, 189–193 (1978); *United States* v. *Price,* 361 U. S. 304, 313 (1960).

(B)

The petitioner's second argument is that micro-organisms cannot qualify as patentable subject matter until Congress expressly authorizes such protection. His position rests on the fact that genetic technology was unforeseen when Congress enacted § 101. From this it is argued that resolution of the patentability of inventions such as respondent's should be left to Congress. The legislative process, the petitioner argues, is best equipped to weigh the competing economic, social, and scientific considerations involved, and to determine whether living organisms produced by genetic engineering should receive patent protection. In support of this position, the petitioner relies on our recent holding in *Parker* v. *Flook,* 437 U. S. 584 (1978), and the statement that the judiciary "must proceed cautiously when . . . asked to extend

---

[9] In 1873, the Patent Office granted Louis Pasteur a patent on "yeast, free from organic germs of disease, as an article of manufacture." And in 1967 and 1968, immediately prior to the passage of the Plant Variety Protection Act, that Office granted two patents which, as the petitioner concedes, state claims for living micro-organisms. See Reply Brief for Petitioner 3, and n. 2.

patent rights into areas wholly unforeseen by Congress." *Id.*, at 596.

It is, of course, correct that Congress, not the courts, must define the limits of patentability; but it is equally true that once Congress has spoken it is "the province and duty of the judicial department to say what the law is." *Marbury* v. *Madison*, 1 Cranch 137, 177 (1803). Congress has performed its constitutional role in defining patentable subject matter in § 101; we perform ours in construing the language Congress has employed. In so doing, our obligation is to take statutes as we find them, guided, if ambiguity appears, by the legislative history and statutory purpose. Here, we perceive no ambiguity. The subject-matter provisions of the patent law have been cast in broad terms to fulfill the constitutional and statutory goal of promoting "the Progress of Science and the useful Arts" with all that means for the social and economic benefits envisioned by Jefferson. Broad general language is not necessarily ambiguous when congressional objectives require broad terms.

Nothing in *Flook* is to the contrary. That case applied our prior precedents to determine that a "claim for an improved method of calculation, even when tied to a specific end use, is unpatentable subject matter under § 101." 437 U. S., at 595, n. 18. The Court carefully scrutinized the claim at issue to determine whether it was precluded from patent protection under "the principles underlying the prohibition against patents for 'ideas' or phenomena of nature." *Id.*, at 593. We have done that here. *Flook* did not announce a new principle that inventions in areas not contemplated by Congress when the patent laws were enacted are unpatentable *per se*.

To read that concept into *Flook* would frustrate the purposes of the patent law. This Court frequently has observed that a statute is not to be confined to the "particular application[s] . . . contemplated by the legislators." *Barr* v. *United States*, 324 U. S. 83, 90 (1945). Accord, *Browder* v. *United States*, 312 U. S. 335, 339 (1941); *Puerto Rico* v. *Shell Co.*,

302 U. S. 253, 257 (1937). This is especially true in the field of patent law. A rule that unanticipated inventions are without protection would conflict with the core concept of the patent law that anticipation undermines patentability. See *Graham* v. *John Deere Co.*, 383 U. S., at 12–17. Mr. Justice Douglas reminded that the inventions most benefiting mankind are those that "push back the frontiers of chemistry, physics, and the like." *Great A. & P. Tea Co.* v. *Supermarket Corp.*, 340 U. S. 147, 154 (1950) (concurring opinion). Congress employed broad general language in drafting § 101 precisely because such inventions are often unforeseeable.[10]

To buttress his argument, the petitioner, with the support of *amicus,* points to grave risks that may be generated by research endeavors such as respondent's. The briefs present a gruesome parade of horribles. Scientists, among them Nobel laureates, are quoted suggesting that genetic research may pose a serious threat to the human race, or, at the very least, that the dangers are far too substantial to permit such research to proceed apace at this time. We are told that genetic research and related technological developments may spread pollution and disease, that it may result in a loss of genetic diversity, and that its practice may tend to depreciate the value of human life. These arguments are forcefully, even passionately, presented; they remind us that, at times, human ingenuity seems unable to control fully the forces it creates—that, with Hamlet, it is sometimes better "to bear those ills we have than fly to others that we know not of."

It is argued that this Court should weigh these potential hazards in considering whether respondent's invention is

---

[10] Even an abbreviated list of patented inventions underscores the point: telegraph (Morse, No. 1,647); telephone (Bell, No. 174,465); electric lamp (Edison, No. 223,898); airplane (the Wrights, No. 821,393); transistor (Bardeen & Brattain, No. 2,524,035); neutronic reactor (Fermi & Szilard, No. 2,708,656); laser (Schawlow & Townes, No. 2,929,922). See generally Revolutionary Ideas, Patents & Progress in America, United States Patent and Trademark Office (1976).

patentable subject matter under § 101. We disagree. The grant or denial of patents on micro-organisms is not likely to put an end to genetic research or to its attendant risks. The large amount of research that has already occurred when no researcher had sure knowledge that patent protection would be available suggests that legislative or judicial fiat as to patentability will not deter the scientific mind from probing into the unknown any more than Canute could command the tides. Whether respondent's claims are patentable may determine whether research efforts are accelerated by the hope of reward or slowed by want of incentives, but that is all.

What is more important is that we are without competence to entertain these arguments—either to brush them aside as fantasies generated by fear of the unknown, or to act on them. The choice we are urged to make is a matter of high policy for resolution within the legislative process after the kind of investigation, examination, and study that legislative bodies can provide and courts cannot. That process involves the balancing of competing values and interests, which in our democratic system is the business of elected representatives. Whatever their validity, the contentions now pressed on us should be addressed to the political branches of the Government, the Congress and the Executive, and not to the courts.[11]

---

[11] We are not to be understood as suggesting that the political branches have been laggard in the consideration of the problems related to genetic research and technology. They have already taken action. In 1976, for example, the National Institutes of Health released guidelines for NIH-sponsored genetic research which established conditions under which such research could be performed. 41 Fed. Reg. 27902. In 1978 those guidelines were revised and relaxed. 43 Fed. Reg. 60080, 60108, 60134. And Committees of the Congress have held extensive hearings on these matters. See, e. g., Hearings on Genetic Engineering before the Subcommittee on Health of the Senate Committee on Labor and Public Welfare, 94th Cong., 1st Sess. (1975); Hearings before the Subcommittee on Science, Technology, and Space of the Senate Committee on Commerce, Science, and Transportation, 95th Cong., 1st Sess. (1977); Hearings on H. R. 4759 et al. before the Subcommittee on Health and the Environment of the

We have emphasized in the recent past that "[o]ur individual appraisal of the wisdom or unwisdom of a particular [legislative] course . . . is to be put aside in the process of interpreting a statute." *TVA* v. *Hill*, 437 U. S., at 194. Our task, rather, is the narrow one of determining what Congress meant by the words it used in the statute; once that is done our powers are exhausted. Congress is free to amend § 101 so as to exclude from patent protection organisms produced by genetic engineering. Cf. 42 U. S. C. § 2181 (a), exempting from patent protection inventions "useful solely in the utilization of special nuclear material or atomic energy in an atomic weapon." Or it may choose to craft a statute specifically designed for such living things. But, until Congress takes such action, this Court must construe the language of § 101 as it is. The language of that section fairly embraces respondent's invention.

Accordingly, the judgment of the Court of Customs and Patent Appeals is

Affirmed.

SUPREME COURT OF THE UNITED STATES

Nos. 80–1832, 80–2170 AND 80–2171

IMMIGRATION AND NATURALIZATION SERVICE, APPELLANT

80–1832   *v.*

JAGDISH RAI CHADHA ET AL.

ON APPEAL FROM THE UNITED STATES COURT OF APPEALS FOR THE NINTH CIRCUIT

UNITED STATES HOUSE OF REPRESENTATIVES, PETITIONER

80–2170   *v.*

IMMIGRATION AND NATURALIZATION SERVICE ET AL.

UNITED STATES SENATE, PETITIONER

80–2171   *v.*

IMMIGRATION AND NATURALIZATION SERVICE ET AL.

ON WRITS OF CERTIORARI TO THE UNITED STATES COURT OF APPEALS FOR THE NINTH CIRCUIT

[June 23, 1983]

CHIEF JUSTICE BURGER delivered the opinion of the Court.

We granted certiorari in Nos. 80–2170 and 80–2171, and postponed consideration of the question of jurisdiction in No. 80–1832. Each presents a challenge to the constitutionality of the provision in § 244(c)(2) of the Immigration and Nationality Act, 8 U. S. C. § 1254(c)(2), authorizing one House of

tion for review of the deportation order in the Court of Appeals, and the
INS joined him in arguing that § 244(c)(2) is unconstitutional. The
Court of Appeals held that § 244(c)(2) violates the constitutional doctrine
of separation of powers, and accordingly directed the Attorney General
to cease taking any steps to deport Chadha based upon the House
Resolution.

Held:

1. This Court has jurisdiction to entertain the INS's appeal in No.
80–1832 under 28 U. S. C. § 1252, which provides that "[a]ny party" may
appeal to the Supreme Court from a judgment of "any court of the
United States" holding an Act of Congress unconstitutional in "any civil
action, suit or proceeding" to which the United States or any of its agencies is a party. A court of appeals is "a court of the United States" for
purposes of § 1252, the proceeding below was a "civil action, suit or proceeding," the INS is an agency of the United States and was a party to
the proceeding below, and the judgment below held an Act of Congress
unconstitutional. Moreover, for purposes of deciding whether the INS
was "any party" within the grant of appellate jurisdiction in § 1252, the
INS was sufficiently aggrieved by the Court of Appeals' decision prohibiting it from taking action it would otherwise take. An agency's status
as an aggrieved party under § 1252 is not altered by the fact that the Executive may agree with the holding that the statute in question is unconstitutional. Pp. 8–10.

2. Section 244(c)(2) is severable from the remainder of § 244. Section
406 of the Act provides that if any particular provision of the Act is held
invalid, the remainder of the Act shall not be affected. This gives rise
to a presumption that Congress did not intend the validity of the Act as a
whole, or any part thereof, to depend upon whether the veto clause of
§ 244(c)(2) was invalid. This presumption is supported by § 244's legislative history. Moreover, a provision is further presumed severable if
what remains after severance is fully operative as a law. Here, § 244
can survive as a "fully operative" and workable administrative mechanism without the one-house veto. Pp. 10–14.

3. Chadha has standing to challenge the constitutionality of § 244(c)(2)
since he has demonstrated "injury in fact and a substantial likelihood
that the judicial relief requested will prevent or redress the claimed injury." *Duke Power Co.* v. *Carolina Environmental Study Group,* 438
U. S. 59, 79. Pp. 14–15.

4. The fact that Chadha may have other statutory relief available to
him does not preclude him from challenging the constitutionality of
§ 244(c)(2), especially where the other avenues of relief are at most speculative. Pp. 15–16.

Syllabus

5. The Court of Appeals had jurisdiction under § 106(a) of the Act, which provides that a petition for review in a court of appeals "shall be the sole and exclusive procedure for the judicial review of all final orders of deportation . . . made against aliens within the United States pursuant to administrative proceedings" under § 242(b) of the Act. Section 106(a) includes all matters on which the final deportation order is contingent, rather than only those determinations made at the deportation hearing. Here, Chadha's deportation stands or falls on the validity of the challenged veto, the final deportation order having been entered only to implement that veto. Pp. 16–18.

6. A case or controversy is presented by these cases. From the time of the House's formal intervention, there was concrete adverseness, and prior to such intervention, there was adequate Art. III adverseness even though the only parties were the INS and Chadha. The INS's agreement with Chadha's position does not alter the fact that the INS would have deported him absent the Court of Appeals' judgment. Moreover, Congress is the proper party to defend the validity of a statute when a Government agency, as a defendant charged with enforcing the statute, agrees with plaintiffs that the statute is unconstitutional. Pp. 18–19.

7. These cases do not present a nonjusticiable political question on the asserted ground that Chadha is merely challenging Congress' authority under the Naturalization and Necessary and Proper Clauses of the Constitution. The presence of constitutional issues with significant political overtones does not automatically invoke the political question doctrine. Resolution of litigation challenging the constitutional authority of one of the three branches cannot be evaded by the courts simply because the issues have political implications. Pp. 19–23.

8. The congressional veto provision in § 244(c)(2) is unconstitutional. Pp. 23–37.

(a) The prescription for legislative action in Art. I, § 1—requiring all legislative powers to be vested in a Congress consisting of a Senate and a House of Representatives—and § 7—requiring every bill passed by the House and Senate, before becoming law, to be presented to the President, and, if he disapproves, to be repassed by two-thirds of the Senate and House—represents the Framers' decision that the legislative power of the Federal Government be exercised in accord with a single, finely wrought and exhaustively considered procedure. This procedure is an integral part of the constitutional design for the separation of powers. Pp. 23–30.

(b) Here, the action taken by the House pursuant to § 244(c)(2) was essentially legislative in purpose and effect and thus was subject to the

procedural requirements of Art. I, § 7, for *legislative* action: passage by
a majority of both Houses and presentation to the President. The one-
House veto operated to overrule the Attorney General and mandate
Chadha's deportation. The veto's legislative character is confirmed by
the character of the congressional action it supplants; *i.e.*, absent the
veto provision of § 244(c)(2), neither the House nor the Senate, or both
acting together, could effectively require the Attorney General to deport
an alien once the Attorney General, in the exercise of legislatively delegated authority, had determined that the alien should remain in the
United States. Without the veto provision, this could have been
achieved only by legislation requiring deportation. A veto by one
House under § 244(c)(2) cannot be justified as an attempt at amending
the standards set out in § 244(a)(1), or as a repeal of § 244 as applied to
Chadha. The nature of the decision implemented by the one-House veto
further manifests its legislative character. Congress must abide by its
delegation of authority to the Attorney General until that delegation is
legislatively altered or revoked. Finally, the veto's legislative character is confirmed by the fact that when the Framers intended to authorize
either House of Congress to act alone and outside of its prescribed bicameral legislative role, they narrowly and precisely defined the procedure for such action in the Constitution. Pp. 30–37.

634 F. 2d 408, affirmed.

BURGER, C. J., delivered the opinion of the Court, in which BRENNAN,
MARSHALL, BLACKMUN, STEVENS, and O'CONNOR, JJ., joined. POWELL,
J., filed an opinion concurring in the judgment. WHITE, J., filed a dissent-
ing opinion. REHNQUIST, J., filed a dissenting opinion, in which WHITE,
J., joined.

(Slip Opinion)

SUPREME COURT OF THE UNITED STATES

Syllabus

IMMIGRATION AND NATURALIZATION SERVICE *v.* CHADHA ET AL.

APPEAL FROM THE UNITED STATES COURT OF APPEALS FOR THE NINTH CIRCUIT

No. 80–1832. Argued February 22, 1982—Reargued December 7, 1982— Decided June 23, 1983*

Section 244(c)(2) of the Immigration and Nationality Act (Act) authorizes either House of Congress, by resolution, to invalidate the decision of the Executive Branch, pursuant to authority delegated by Congress to the Attorney General, to allow a particular deportable alien to remain in the United States. Appellee-respondent Chadha, an alien who had been lawfully admitted to the United States on a nonimmigrant student visa, remained in the United States after his visa had expired and was ordered by the Immigration and Naturalization Service (INS) to show cause why he should not be deported. He then applied for suspension of the deportation, and, after a hearing, an Immigration Judge, acting pursuant to § 244(a)(1) of the Act, which authorizes the Attorney General, in his discretion, to suspend deportation, ordered the suspension, and reported the suspension to Congress as required by § 244(c)(1). Thereafter, the House of Representatives passed a Resolution pursuant to § 244(c)(2) vetoing the suspension, and the Immigration Judge reopened the deportation proceedings. Chadha moved to terminate the proceedings on the ground that § 244(c)(2) is unconstitutional, but the judge held that he had no authority to rule on its constitutionality and ordered Chadha deported pursuant to the House Resolution. Chadha's appeal to the Board of Immigration Appeals was dismissed, the Board also holding that it had no power to declare § 244(c)(2) unconstitutional. Chadha then filed a peti-

---

*Together with No. 80–2170, *United States House of Representatives* v. *Immigration and Naturalization Service et al.*, and No. 80–2171, *United States Senate* v. *Immigration and Naturalization Service et al.*, on certiorari to the same court.

I

115

Congress, by resolution, to invalidate the decision of the Executive Branch, pursuant to authority delegated by Congress to the Attorney General of the United States, to allow a particular deportable alien to remain in the United States.

I

Chadha is an East Indian who was born in Kenya and holds a British passport. He was lawfully admitted to the United States in 1966 on a nonimmigrant student visa. His visa expired on June 30, 1972. On October 11, 1973, the District Director of the Immigration and Naturalization Service ordered Chadha to show cause why he should not be deported for having "remained in the United States for a longer time than permitted." App. 6. Pursuant to § 242(b) of the Immigration and Nationality Act (Act), 8 U. S. C. § 1254(b), a deportation hearing was held before an immigration judge on January 11, 1974. Chadha conceded that he was deportable for overstaying his visa and the hearing was adjourned to enable him to file an application for suspension of deportation under § 244(a)(1) of the Act, 8 U. S. C. § 1254(a)(1). Section 244(a)(1) provides:

> "(a) As hereinafter prescribed in this section, the Attorney General may, in his discretion, suspend deportation and adjust the status to that of an alien lawfully admitted for permanent residence, in the case of an alien who applies to the Attorney General for suspension of deportation and—

> (1) is deportable under any law of the United States except the provisions specified in paragraph (2) of this subsection; has been physically present in the United States for a continuous period of not less than seven years immediately preceding the date of such application, and proves that during all of such period he was and is a person of good moral character; and is a person whose deportation would, in the opinion of the Attorney

General, result in extreme hardship to the alien or to his spouse, parent, or child, who is a citizen of the United States or an alien lawfully admitted for permanent residence." [1]

After Chadha submitted his application for suspension of deportation, the deportation hearing was resumed on February 7, 1974. On the basis of evidence adduced at the hearing, affidavits submitted with the application, and the results of a character investigation conducted by the INS, the immigration judge, on June 25, 1974, ordered that Chadha's deportation be suspended. The immigration judge found that Chadha met the requirements of § 244(a)(1): he had resided continuously in the United States for over seven years, was of good moral character, and would suffer "extreme hardship" if deported.

Pursuant to § 244(c)(1) of the Act, 8 U. S. C. § 1254(c)(1), the immigration judge suspended Chadha's deportation and a report of the suspension was transmitted to Congress. Section 244(c)(1) provides:

> "Upon application by any alien who is found by the Attorney General to meet the requirements of subsection (a) of this section the Attorney General may in his discretion suspend deportation of such alien. If the deportation of any alien is suspended under the provisions of this subsection, a complete and detailed statement of the facts and pertinent provisions of law in the case shall be reported to the Congress with the reasons for such suspension. Such reports shall be submitted on the first day of each calendar month in which Congress is in session."

---

[1] Congress delegated the major responsibilities for enforcement of the Immigration and Nationality Act to the Attorney General. 8 U. S. C. § 1103(a). The Attorney General discharges his responsibilities through the Immigration and Naturalization Service, a division of the Department of Justice. *Ibid.*

Once the Attorney General's recommendation for suspension of Chadha's deportation was conveyed to Congress, Congress had the power under § 244(c)(2) of the Act, 8 U. S. C. § 1254(c)(2), to veto[2] the Attorney General's determination that Chadha should not be deported. Section 244(c)(2) provides:

> "(2) In the case of an alien specified in paragraph (1) of subsection (a) of this subsection—
> if during the session of the Congress at which a case is reported, or prior to the close of the session of the Congress next following the session at which a case is reported, either the Senate or the House of Representatives passes a resolution stating in substance that it does not favor the suspension of such deportation, the Attorney General shall thereupon deport such alien or authorize the alien's voluntary departure at his own expense under the order of deportation in the manner provided by law. If, within the time above specified, neither the Senate nor the House of Representatives shall pass such a resolution, the Attorney General shall cancel deportation proceedings."

The June 25, 1974 order of the immigration judge suspending Chadha's deportation remained outstanding as a valid order for a year and a half. For reasons not disclosed by the record, Congress did not exercise the veto authority re-

---

[2] In constitutional terms, "veto" is used to describe the President's power under Art. I, § 7 of the Constitution. See Black's Law Dictionary 1403 (5th ed. 1979). It appears, however, that Congressional devices of the type authorized by § 244(c)(2) have come to be commonly referred to as a "veto." See, *e. g.*, Martin, The Legislative Veto and the Responsible Exercise of Congressional Power, 68 Va. L. Rev. 253 (1982); Miller and Knapp, The Congressional Veto: Preserving the Constitutional Framework, 52 Ind. L.J. 367 (1977). We refer to the Congressional "resolution" authorized by § 244(c)(2) as a "one-House veto" of the Attorney General's decision to allow a particular deportable alien to remain in the United States.

served to it under § 244(c)(2) until the first session of the 94th Congress. This was the final session in which Congress, pursuant to § 244(c)(2), could act to veto the Attorney General's determination that Chadha should not be deported. The session ended on December 19, 1975. 121 Cong. Rec. 42014, 42277 (1975). Absent Congressional action, Chadha's deportation proceedings would have been cancelled after this date and his status adjusted to that of a permanent resident alien. See 8 U. S. C. § 1254(d).

On December 12, 1975, Representative Eilberg, Chairman of the Judiciary Subcommittee on Immigration, Citizenship, and International Law, introduced a resolution opposing "the granting of permanent residence in the United States to [six] aliens", including Chadha. H. R. Res. 926, 94th Cong., 1st Sess.; 121 Cong Rec. 40247 (1975). The resolution was referred to the House Committee on the Judiciary. On December 16, 1975, the resolution was discharged from further consideration by the House Committee on the Judiciary and submitted to the House of Representatives for a vote. 121 Cong. Rec. 40800. The resolution had not been printed and was not made available to other Members of the House prior to or at the time it was voted on. *Ibid.* So far as the record before us shows, the House consideration of the resolution was based on Representative Eilberg's statement from the floor that

> "[i]t was the feeling of the committee, after reviewing 340 cases, that the aliens contained in the resolution [Chadha and five others] did not meet these statutory requirements, particularly as it relates to hardship; and it is the opinion of the committee that their deportation should not be suspended." *Ibid.*

The resolution was passed without debate or recorded vote.[3]

---

[3] It is not at all clear whether the House generally, or Subcommittee Chairman Eilberg in particular, correctly understood the relationship be-

Since the House action was pursuant to § 244(c)(2), the resolution was not treated as an Article I legislative act; it was not submitted to the Senate or presented to the President for his action.

After the House veto of the Attorney General's decision to allow Chadha to remain in the United States, the immigra-

---

tween H. R. Res. 926 and the Attorney General's decision to suspend Chadha's deportation. Exactly one year previous to the House veto of the Attorney General's decision in this case, Representative Eilberg introduced a similar resolution disapproving the Attorney General's suspension of deportation in the case of six other aliens. H. R. Res. 1518, 93d Cong., 2d Sess. The following colloquy occurred on the floor of the House:

"Mr. WYLIE. Mr. Speaker, further reserving the right to object, is this procedure to expedite the ongoing operations of the Department of Justice, as far as these people are concerned. Is it in any way contrary to whatever action the Attorney General has taken on the question of deportation; does the gentleman know?

Mr. EILBERG. Mr. Speaker, the answer is no to the gentleman's final question. These aliens have been found to be deportable and the Special Inquiry Officer's decision denying suspension of deportation has been reversed by the Board of Immigration Appeals. We are complying with the law since all of these decisions have been referred to us for approval or disapproval, and there are hundreds of cases in this category. In these six cases however, we believe it would be grossly improper to allow these people to acquire the status of permanent resident aliens.

Mr. WYLIE. In other words, the gentleman has been working with the Attorney General's office?

Mr. EILBERG. Yes.

Mr. WYLIE. This bill then is in fact a confirmation of what the Attorney General intends to do?

Mr. EILBERG. The gentleman is correct insofar as it relates to the determination of deportability which has been made by the Department of Justice in these cases.

Mr. WYLIE. Mr. Speaker, I withdraw my reservation of objection." 120 Cong. Rec. 41412 (1974).

Clearly, this was an obfuscation of the effect of a veto under § 244(c)(2). Such a veto in no way constitutes "a confirmation of what the Attorney General intends to do." To the contrary, such a resolution was meant to overrule and set aside, or "veto," the Attorney General's determination that, in a particular case, cancellation of deportation would be appropriate under the standards set forth in § 244(a)(1).

tion judge reopened the deportation proceedings to implement the House order deporting Chadha. Chadha moved to terminate the proceedings on the ground that § 244(c)(2) is unconstitutional. The immigration judge held that he had no authority to rule on the constitutional validity of § 244(c)(2). On November 8, 1976, Chadha was ordered deported pursuant to the House action.

Chadha appealed the deportation order to the Board of Immigration Appeals again contending that § 244(c)(2) is unconstitutional. The Board held that it had "no power to declare unconstitutional an act of Congress" and Chadha's appeal was dismissed. App. 55–56.

Pursuant to § 106(a) of the Act, 8 U. S. C. § 1105a(a), Chadha filed a petition for review of the deportation order in the United States Court of Appeals for the Ninth Circuit. The Immigration and Naturalization Service agreed with Chadha's position before the Court of Appeals and joined him in arguing that § 244(c)(2) is unconstitutional. In light of the importance of the question, the Court of Appeals invited both the Senate and the House of Representatives to file briefs *amici curiae.*

After full briefing and oral argument, the Court of Appeals held that the House was without constitutional authority to order Chadha's deportation; accordingly it directed the Attorney General "to cease and desist from taking any steps to deport this alien based upon the resolution enacted by the House of Representatives." *Chadha* v. *INS*, 634 F. 2d 408, 436 (CA9 1980). The essence of its holding was that § 244(c)(2) violates the constitutional doctrine of separation of powers.

We granted certiorari in Nos. 80–2170 and 80–2171, and postponed consideration of our jurisdiction over the appeal in No. 80–1832, 454 U. S. 812 (1981), and we now affirm.

II

Before we address the important question of the constitutionality of the one-House veto provision of § 244(c)(2), we

first consider several challenges to the authority of this Court
to resolve the issue raised.

A

Appellate Jurisdiction

Both Houses of Congress[4] contend that we are without jurisdiction under 28 U. S. C. § 1252 to entertain the INS appeal in No. 80–1832.   Section 1252 provides:

> "Any party may appeal to the Supreme Court from an
> interlocutory or final judgment, decree or order of any
> court of the United States, the United States District
> Court for the District of the Canal Zone, the District
> Court of Guam and the District Court of the Virgin Is-
> lands and any court of record of Puerto Rico, holding an
> Act of Congress unconstitutional in any civil action, suit,
> or proceeding to which the United States or any of its
> agencies, or any officer or employee thereof, as such offi-
> cer or employee, is a party."

Parker v. *Levy*, 417 U. S. 733, 742 n. 10 (1974), makes
clear that a court of appeals is a "court of the United States"
for purposes of § 1252.   It is likewise clear that the proceeding below was a "civil action, suit or proceeding," that the
INS is an agency of the United States and was a party to the
proceeding below, and that that proceeding held an Act of
Congress—namely,   the   one-House   veto   provision   in
§ 244(c)(2)—unconstitutional.   The express requisites for an
appeal under § 1252, therefore, have been met.

In motions to dismiss the INS appeal, the Congressional
parties[5] direct attention, however, to our statement that "[a]

---

[4] Nine Members of the House of Representatives disagree with the position taken in the briefs filed by the Senate and the House of Representatives and have filed a brief *amicus curiae* urging that the decision of the
Court of Appeals be affirmed in this case.

[5] The Senate and House authorized intervention in this case, S. Res. 40
and H. R. Res. 49, 97th Cong., 1st Sess. (1981), and, on February 3, 1981,

party who receives all that he has sought generally is not aggrieved by the judgment affording relief and cannot appeal from it." *Deposit Guaranty National Bank* v. *Roper*, 445 U. S. 326, 333 (1980). Here, the INS sought the invalidation of § 244(c)(2) and the Court of Appeals granted that relief. Both Houses contend that the INS has already received what it sought from the Court of Appeals, is not an aggrieved party, and therefore cannot appeal from the decision of the Court of Appeals. We cannot agree.

The INS was ordered by one House of Congress to deport Chadha. As we have set out more fully, *ante* at 7, the INS concluded that it had no power to rule on the constitutionality of that order and accordingly proceeded to implement it. Chadha's appeal challenged that decision and the INS presented the Executive's views on the constitutionality of the House action to the Court of Appeals. But the INS brief to the Court of Appeals did not alter the agency's decision to comply with the House action ordering deportation of Chadha. The Court of Appeals set aside the deportation proceedings and ordered the Attorney General to cease and desist from taking any steps to deport Chadha; steps that the Attorney General would have taken were it not for that decision.

At least for purposes of deciding whether the INS is "any party" within the grant of appellate jurisdiction in § 1252, we hold that the INS was sufficiently aggrieved by the Court of Appeals decision prohibiting it from taking action it would otherwise take. It is apparent that Congress intended that this Court take notice of cases that meet the technical prerequisites of § 1252; in other cases where an Act of Congress is held unconstitutional by a federal court, review in this Court

---

filed motions to intervene and petitioned for rehearing. The Court of Appeals granted the motions to intervene. Both Houses are therefore proper "parties" within the meaning of that term in 28 U. S. C. § 1254(1). See *Batterton* v. *Francis*, 432 U. S. 416, 424, n. 7 (1977).

is available only by writ of certiorari.   When an agency of the United States is a party to a case in which the Act of Congress it administers is held unconstitutional, it is an aggrieved party for purposes of taking an appeal under § 1252. The agency's status as an aggrieved party under § 1252 is not altered by the fact that the Executive may agree with the holding that the statute in question is unconstitutional.   The appeal in No. 80–1832 is therefore properly before us.[6]

B

Severability

Congress also contends that the provision for the one-House veto in § 244(c)(2) cannot be severed from § 244.   Congress argues that if the provision for the one-House veto is held unconstitutional, all of § 244 must fall.   If § 244 in its entirety is violative of the Constitution, it follows that the Attorney General has no authority to suspend Chadha's deportation under § 244(a)(1) and Chadha would be deported. From this, Congress argues that Chadha lacks standing to challenge the constitutionality of the one-House veto provision because he could receive no relief even if his constitutional challenge proves successful.[7]

Only recently this Court reaffirmed that the invalid portions of a statute are to be severed " '[u]nless it is evident that the Legislature would not have enacted those provisions which are within its power, independently of that which is not.' "   *Buckley* v. *Valeo,* 424 U. S. 1, 108 (1976), quoting

---

[6] In addition to meeting the statutory requisites of § 1252, of course, an appeal must present a justiciable case or controversy under Art. III. Such a controversy clearly exists in No. 80–1832, as in the other two cases, because of the presence of the two Houses of Congress as adverse parties. See *infra,* at 18; see also *Director, OWCP* v. *Perini North River Associates,* —— U. S. ——, —— (1982).

[7] In this case we deem it appropriate to address questions of severability first.   But see *Buckley* v. *Valeo,* 424 U. S. 1, 108–109 (1976); *United States* v. *Jackson,* 390 U. S. 570, 585 (1968).

Champlin Refining Co. v. *Corporation Comm'n,* 286 U. S.
210, 234 (1932). Here, however, we need not embark on
that elusive inquiry since Congress itself has provided the answer to the question of severability in § 406 of the Immigration and Nationality Act, 8 U. S. C. § 1101, which provides:

> "If *any* particular provision of this Act, or the applica-
> tion thereof to *any* person or circumstance, is held
> invalid, *the remainder of the Act and the application of
> such provision to other persons or circumstances shall
> not be affected thereby.*" (Emphasis added.)

This language is unambiguous and gives rise to a presumption that Congress did not intend the validity of the Act as a
whole, or of any part of the Act, to depend upon whether the
veto clause of § 244(c)(2) was invalid. The one-House veto
provision in § 244(c)(2) is clearly a "particular provision" of
the Act as that language is used in the severability clause.
Congress clearly intended "the remainder of the Act" to
stand if "any particular provision" were held invalid. Congress could not have more plainly authorized the presumption
that the provision for a one-House veto in § 244(c)(2) is severable from the remainder of § 244 and the Act of which it is a
part. See *Electric Bond & Share Co.* v. *SEC,* 303 U. S. 419,
434 (1938).

The presumption as to the severability of the one-House
veto provision in § 244(c)(2) is supported by the legislative
history of § 244. That section and its precursors supplanted
the long established pattern of dealing with deportations like
Chadha's on a case-by-case basis through private bills. Although it may be that Congress was reluctant to delegate final authority over cancellation of deportations, such reluctance is not sufficient to overcome the presumption of
severability raised by § 406.

The Immigration Act of 1924, Pub. L. No. 139, § 14, 43
Stat. 153, 162, required the Secretary of Labor to deport any
alien who entered or remained in the United States unlaw-

fully.   The only means by which a deportable alien could lawfully remain in the United States was to have his status altered by a private bill enacted by both Houses and presented to the President pursuant to the procedures set out in Art. I, § 7 of the Constitution.   These private bills were found intolerable by Congress.   In the debate on a 1937 bill introduced by Representative Dies to authorize the Secretary to grant permanent residence in "meritorious" cases, Dies stated:

> "It was my original thought that the way to handle all these meritorious cases was through special bills.   I am absolutely convinced as a result of what has occurred in this House that it is impossible to deal with the situation through special bills.   We had a demonstration of that fact not long ago when 15 special bills were before the House.   The House consumed 5½ hours considering four bills and made no disposition of any of these bills."   81 Cong. Rec. 5542 (1937).

Representative Dies' bill passed the House, *id.*, at 5574, but did not come to a vote in the Senate.   83 Cong. Rec. 8992–8996 (1938).

Congress first authorized the Attorney General to suspend the deportation of certain aliens in the Alien Registration Act of 1940, ch. 439, § 20, 54 Stat. 671.   That Act provided that an alien was to be deported, despite the Attorney General's decision to the contrary, if both Houses, by concurrent resolution, disapproved the suspension.

In 1948, Congress amended the Act to broaden the category of aliens eligible for suspension of deportation.   In addition, however, Congress limited the authority of the Attorney General to suspend deportations by providing that the Attorney General could not cancel a deportation unless both Houses affirmatively voted by concurrent resolution to *approve* the Attorney General's action.   Act of July 1, 1948, ch. 783, 62 Stat. 1206.   The provision for approval by concurrent resolution in the 1948 Act proved almost as burdensome as

private bills. Just four years later, the House Judiciary
Committee, in support of the predecessor to §244(c)(2),
stated in a report:

"In the light of experience of the last several months, the
committee came to the conclusion that the requirements
of affirmative action by both Houses of the Congress in
many thousands of individual cases which are submitted
by the Attorney General every year, is not workable and
places upon the Congress and particularly on the Committee on the Judiciary responsibilities which it cannot
assume. The new responsibilities placed upon the Committee on the Judiciary [by the concurrent resolution
mechanism] are of purely administrative nature and they
seriously interfere with the legislative work of the Committee on the Judiciary and would, in time, interfere
with the legislative work of the House." H. R. Rep.
No. 362, 81st Cong., 1st Sess. 2 (1949).

The proposal to permit one House of Congress to veto the
Attorney General's suspension of an alien's deportation was
incorporated in the Immigration and Nationality Act of 1952,
Pub. L. No. 414, 66 Stat. 163, 214. Plainly, Congress' desire
to retain a veto in this area cannot be considered in isolation
but must be viewed in the context of Congress' irritation with
the burden of private immigration bills. This legislative history is not sufficient to rebut the presumption of severability
raised by §406 because there is insufficient evidence that
Congress would have continued to subject itself to the oner-
ous burdens of private bills had it known that §244(c)(2)
would be held unconstitutional.

A provision is further presumed severable if what remains
after severance "is fully operative as a law." *Champlin Refining Co.* v. *Corporation Comm'n, supra,* 286 U. S., at 234.
There can be no doubt that §244 is "fully operative" and
workable administrative machinery without the veto provision in §244(c)(2). Entirely independent of the one-House

veto, the administrative process enacted by Congress authorizes the Attorney General to suspend an alien's deportation under § 244(a). Congress' oversight of the exercise of this delegated authority is preserved since all such suspensions will continue to be reported to it under § 244(c)(1). Absent the passage of a bill to the contrary,[8] deportation proceedings will be cancelled when the period specified in § 244(c)(2) has expired.[9] Clearly, § 244 survives as a workable administrative mechanism without the one-House veto.

C

Standing

We must also reject the contention that Chadha lacks

---

[8] Without the provision for one-House veto, Congress would presumably retain the power, during the time allotted in § 244(c)(2), to enact a law, in accordance with the requirements of Article I of the Constitution, mandating a particular alien's deportation, unless, of course, other constitutional principles place substantive limitations on such action. Cf. Attorney General Jackson's attack on H. R. 9766, 76th Cong., 3d Sess. (1940), a bill to require the Attorney General to deport an individual alien. The Attorney General called the bill "an historical departure from an unbroken American practice and tradition. It would be the first time that an act of Congress singled out a named individual for deportation." S. Rep. No. 2031, 76th Cong., 3d Sess. 9 (1940) (reprinting Jackson's letter of June 18, 1940). See n. 17, *infra.*

[9] Without the one-House veto, § 244 resembles the "report and wait" provision approved by the Court in *Sibbach* v. *Wilson,* 312 U. S. 1 (1941). The statute examined in *Sibbach* provided that the newly promulgated Federal Rules of Civil Procedure "shall not take effect until they shall have been reported to Congress by the Attorney General at the beginning of a regular session thereof and until after the close of such session." Act of June 19, 1934, ch. 651, § 2, 48 Stat. 1064. This statute did *not* provide that Congress could unilaterally veto the Federal Rules. Rather, it gave Congress the opportunity to review the Rules before they became effective and to pass legislation barring their effectiveness if the Rules were found objectionable. This technique was used by Congress when it acted in 1973 to stay, and ultimately to revise, the proposed Rules of Evidence. *Compare* Act of March 30, 1973, Pub. L. No. 93–12, 87 Stat. 9, *with* Act of Jan. 2, 1975, Pub. L. 93–595, 88 Stat. 1926.

standing because a consequence of his prevailing will advance the interests of the Executive Branch in a separation of powers dispute with Congress, rather than simply Chadha's private interests. Chadha has demonstrated "injury in fact and a substantial likelihood that the judicial relief requested will prevent or redress the claimed injury. . . ." *Duke Power Co.* v. *Carolina Environmental Study Group,* 438 U. S. 59, 79 (1978). If the veto provision violates the Constitution, and is severable, the deportation order against Chadha will be cancelled. Chadha therefore has standing to challenge the order of the Executive mandated by the House veto.

D

Alternative Relief

It is contended that the Court should decline to decide the constitutional question presented by this case because Chadha may have other statutory relief available to him. It is argued that since Chadha married a United States citizen on August 10, 1980, it is possible that other avenues of relief may be open under §§ 201(b), 204, and 245 of the Act, 8 U. S. C. §§ 1151(b), 1154, 1255. It is true that Chadha may be eligible for classification as an "immediate relative" and, as such, could lawfully be accorded permanent residence. Moreover, in March 1980, just prior to the decision of the Court of Appeals in this case, Congress enacted the Refugee Act of 1980, Pub. L. No. 96–212, 94 Stat. 102, under which the Attorney General is authorized to grant asylum, and then permanent residence, to any alien who is unable to return to his country of nationality because of "a well-founded fear of persecution on account of race."

It is urged that these two intervening factors constitute a prudential bar to our consideration of the constitutional question presented in this case. See *Ashwander* v. *Tennessee Valley Authority,* 297 U. S. 288, 346 (1936) (Brandeis, J., concurring). If we could perceive merit in this contention we might well seek to avoid deciding the constitutional claim advanced. But at most these other avenues of relief are speculative. It is by no means certain, for example, that Chadha's classification as an immediate relative would result in the adjustment of Chadha's status from nonimmigrant to permanent resident. See *Menezes* v. *INS*, 601 F. 2d 1028 (CA9 1979). If Chadha is successful in his present challenge he will not be deported and will automatically become eligible to apply for citizenship.[10] A person threatened with deportation cannot be denied the right to challenge the constitutional validity of the process which led to his status merely on the basis of speculation over the availability of other forms of relief.

E

Jurisdiction

It is contended that the Court of Appeals lacked jurisdiction under § 106(a) of the Act, 8 U. S. C. § 1105a(a). That section provides that a petition for review in the Court of Appeals "shall be the sole and exclusive procedure for the judicial review of all final orders of deportation . . . made against aliens within the United States pursuant to administrative proceedings under section 242(b) of this Act." Congress argues that the one-House veto authorized by § 244(c)(2) takes place outside the administrative proceedings conducted under § 242(b), and that the jurisdictional grant contained in § 106(a) does not encompass Chadha's constitutional

---

[10] Depending on how the INS interprets its statutory duty under § 244 apart from the challenged portion of § 244(c)(2), Chadha's status may be retroactively adjusted to that of a permanent resident as of December 19, 1975—the last session in which Congress could have attempted to stop the suspension of Chadha's deportation from ripening into cancellation of deportation. See 8 U. S. C. § 1254(d). In that event, Chadha's five-year waiting period to become a citizen under § 316(a) of the Act, 8 U. S. C. § 1427(a), would have elapsed.

challenge.

In *Cheng Fan Kwok* v. *INS*, 392 U. S. 206, 216 (1968), this Court held that "§ 106(a) embrace[s] only those determinations made during a proceeding conducted under § 242(b), including those determinations made incident to a motion to reopen such proceedings." It is true that one court has read *Cheng Fan Kwok* to preclude appeals similar to Chadha's. See *Dastmalchi* v. *INS*, 660 F. 2d 880 (CA3 1981).[11] However, we agree with the Court of Appeals in this case that the term "final orders" in § 106(a) "includes all matters on which the validity of the final order is contingent, rather than only those determinations actually made at the hearing." 634 F. 2d, at 412. Here, Chadha's deportation stands or falls on the validity of the challenged veto; the final order of deportation was entered against Chadha only to implement the action of the House of Representatives. Although the Attorney General was satisfied that the House action was invalid and that it should not have any effect on his decision to suspend deportation, he appropriately let the controversy take its course through the courts.

This Court's decision in *Cheng Fan Kwok*, *supra*, does not bar Chadha's appeal. There, after an order of deportation had been entered, the affected alien requested the INS to stay the execution of that order. When that request was de-

---

[11] Under the Third Circuit's reasoning, judicial review under § 106(a) would not extend to the constitutionality of § 244(c)(2) because that issue could not have been tested during the administrative deportation proceedings conducted under § 242(b). *Dastmalchi* v. *INS*, 660 F. 2d 880 (CA3 1981). The facts in *Dastmalchi* are distinguishable, however. In *Dastmalchi*, Iranian aliens who had entered the United States on nonimmigrant student visas challenged a regulation that required them to report to the District Director of the INS during the Iranian hostage crisis. The aliens reported and were ordered deported after a § 242(b) proceeding. The aliens in *Dastmalchi* could have been deported irrespective of the challenged regulation. Here, in contrast, Chadha's deportation would have been *cancelled* but for § 242(c)(2).

nied, the alien sought review in the Court of Appeals under
§ 106(a). This Court's holding that the Court of Appeals
lacked jurisdiction was based on the fact that the alien "did
not 'attack the deportation order itself but instead [sought]
relief not inconsistent with it.'" 392 U. S., at 213, quoting
Mui v. *Esperdy*, 371 F. 2d 772, 777 (CA2 1966). Here, in
contrast, Chadha directly attacks the deportation order itself
and the relief he seeks—cancellation of deportation—is
plainly inconsistent with the deportation order. Accordingly, the Court of Appeals had jurisdiction under § 106(a) to
decide this case.

F

Case or Controversy

It is also contended that this is not a genuine controversy
but "a friendly, non-adversary, proceeding," *Ashwander* v.
Tennessee Valley Authority, supra, 297 U. S., at 346 (Brandeis, J., concurring), upon which the Court should not pass.
This argument rests on the fact that Chadha and the INS
take the same position on the constitutionality of the one-
House veto. But it would be a curious result if, in the administration of justice, a person could be denied access to the
courts because the Attorney General of the United States
agreed with the legal arguments asserted by the individual.

A case or controversy is presented by this case. First,
from the time of Congress' formal intervention, see note 5,
supra, the concrete adverseness is beyond doubt. Congress
is both a proper party to defend the constitutionality of
§ 244(c)(2) and a proper petitioner under § 1254(1). Second,
prior to Congress' intervention, there was adequate Art. III
adverseness even though the only parties were the INS and
Chadha. We have already held that the INS's agreement
with the Court of Appeals' decision that § 244(c)(2) is unconstitutional does not affect that agency's "aggrieved" status
for purposes of appealing that decision under 28 U. S. C.
§ 1252, see *ante*, at 8–10. For similar reasons, the INS's

agreement with Chadha's position does not alter the fact that the INS would have deported Chadha absent the Court of Appeals' judgment. We agree with the Court of Appeals that "Chadha has asserted a concrete controversy, and our decision will have real meaning: if we rule for Chadha, he will not be deported; if we uphold § 244(c)(2), the INS will execute its order and deport him." 634 F. 2d, at 419.[12]

Of course, there may be prudential, as opposed to Art. III, concerns about sanctioning the adjudication of this case in the absence of any participant supporting the validity of § 244(c)(2). The Court of Appeals properly dispelled any such concerns by inviting and accepting briefs from both Houses of Congress. We have long held that Congress is the proper party to defend the validity of a statute when an agency of government, as a defendant charged with enforcing the statute, agrees with plaintiffs that the statue is inapplicable or unconstitutional. See *Cheng Fan Kwok* v. *INS, supra,* 392 U. S., at 210 n. 9; *United States* v. *Lovett,* 328 U. S. 303 (1946).

G

Political Question

It is also argued that this case presents a nonjusticiable political question because Chadha is merely challenging Congress' authority under the Naturalization Clause, U. S. Const. art. I, § 8, cl. 4, and the Necessary and Proper Clause,

---

[12] A relevant parallel can be found in our recent decision in *Bob Jones University* v. *United States,* —— U. S. —— (1983). There, the United States agreed with Bob Jones University and Goldsboro Christian Schools that certain Revenue Rulings denying tax exempt status to schools that discriminated on the basis of race were invalid. Despite its agreement with the schools, however, the United States was complying with a court order enjoining it from granting tax-exempt status to any school that discriminated on the basis of race. Even though the government largely agreed with the opposing party on the merits of the controversy, we found an adequate basis for jurisdiction in the fact that the government intended to enforce the challenged law against that party. See *id.,* at —— n. 9.

U. S. Const. art. I, § 8, cl. 18.   It is argued that Congress' Article I power "To establish a uniform Rule of Naturalization", combined with the Necessary and Proper Clause, grants it unreviewable authority over the regulation of aliens.   The plenary authority of Congress over aliens under Art. I, § 8, cl. 4 is not open to question, but what is challenged here is whether Congress has chosen a constitutionally permissible means of implementing that power.   As we made clear in *Buckley* v. *Valeo*, 424 U. S. 1 (1976); "Congress has plenary authority in all cases in which it has substantive legislative jurisdiction, *M'Culloch* v. *Maryland*, 4 Wheat. 316 (1819), so long as the exercise of that authority does not offend some other constitutional restriction." *Id.*, at 132.

A brief review of those factors which may indicate the presence of a nonjusticiable political question satisfies us that our assertion of jurisdiction over this case does no violence to the political question doctrine.   As identified in *Baker* v. *Carr*, 369 U. S. 186, 217 (1962), a political question may arise when any one of the following circumstances is present:

> "a textually demonstrable constitutional commitment of the issue to a coordinate political department; or a lack of judicially discoverable and manageable standards for resolving it; or the impossibility of deciding without an initial policy determination of a kind clearly for nonjudicial discretion; or the impossibility of a court's undertaking independent resolution without expressing lack of the respect due coordinate branches of government; or an unusual need for unquestioning adherence to a political decision already made; or the potentiality of embarrassment from multifarious pronouncements by various departments on one question."

Congress apparently directs its assertion of nonjusticiability to the first of the *Baker* factors by asserting that Chadha's claim is "an assault on the legislative authority to enact Section 244(c)(2)."   Brief for the United States House of Representatives 48.   But if this turns the question into a political question virtually every challenge to the constitutionality of a statute would be a political question.   Chadha indeed argues that one House of Congress cannot constitutionally veto the Attorney General's decision to allow him to remain in this country.   No policy underlying the political question doctrine suggests that Congress or the Executive, or both acting in concert and in compliance with Art. I, can decide the constitutionality of a statute; that is a decision for the courts.[13]

Other *Baker* factors are likewise inapplicable to this case. As we discuss more fully below, Art. I provides the "judicially discoverable and manageable standards" of *Baker* for resolving the question presented by this case.   Those standards forestall reliance by this Court on nonjudicial "policy

---

[13] The suggestion is made that § 244(c)(2) is somehow immunized from constitutional scrutiny because the Act containing § 244(c)(2) was passed by Congress and approved by the President.   *Marbury* v. *Madison*, 1 Cranch 137 (1803), resolved that question.   The assent of the Executive to a bill which contains a provision contrary to the Constitution does not shield it from judicial review.   See *Smith* v. *Maryland*, 442 U. S. 735, 740 n. 5 (1979); *National League of Cities* v. *Usery*, 426 U. S. 833, 841 n. 12 (1976); *Buckley* v. *Valeo*, 424 U. S. 1 (1976); *Myers* v. *United States*, 272 U. S. 52 (1926).   See also n. 22, *infra*.   In any event, eleven Presidents, from Mr. Wilson through Mr. Reagan, who have been presented with this issue have gone on record at some point to challenge Congressional vetoes as unconstitutional.   See Henry, The Legislative Veto: In Search of Constitutional Limits, 16 Harv. J. Legis. 735, 737–738 n. 7 (1979) (collecting citations to presidential statements).   Perhaps the earliest Executive expression on the constitutionality of the Congressional veto is found in Attorney General William D. Mitchell's opinion of January 24, 1933 to President Hoover.   37 Op. Atty. Gen. 56. (1933).   Furthermore, it is not uncommon for Presidents to approve legislation containing parts which are objectionable on constitutional grounds.   For example, after President Roosevelt signed the Lend-Lease Act of 1941, Attorney General Jackson released a memorandum explaining the President's view that the provision allowing the Act's authorization to be terminated by concurrent resolution was unconstitutional.   Jackson, A Presidential Legal Opinion, 66 Harv. L. Rev. 1353 (1953).

determinations" or any showing of disrespect for a coordinate branch. Similarly, if Chadha's arguments are accepted, § 244(c)(2) cannot stand, and, since the constitutionality of that statute is for this Court to resolve, there is no possibility of "multifarious pronouncements" on this question.

It is correct that this controversy may, in a sense, be termed "political." But the presence of constitutional issues with significant political overtones does not automatically invoke the political question doctrine. Resolution of litigation challenging the constitutional authority of one of the three branches cannot be evaded by courts because the issues have political implications in the sense urged by Congress. *Marbury* v. *Madison*, 1 Cranch 137 (1803), was also a "political" case, involving as it did claims under a judicial commission alleged to have been duly signed by the President but not delivered. But "courts cannot reject as 'no law suit' a bona fide controversy as to whether some action denominated 'political' exceeds constitutional authority." *Baker* v. *Carr, supra,* 369 U. S. at 217.

In *Field* v. *Clark,* 143 U. S. 649 (1892), this Court addressed and resolved the question whether

> "a bill signed by the Speaker of the House of Representatives and by the President of the Senate, presented to and approved by the President of the United States, and delivered by the latter to the Secretary of State, as an act passed by Congress, does not become a law of the United States if it had not in fact been passed by Congress.
>
> . . . . .
>
> We recognize, on one hand, the duty of this court, from the performance of which it may not shrink, to give full effect to the provisions of the Constitution relating to the enactment of laws that are to operate wherever the authority and jurisdiction of the United States extend. On the other hand, we cannot be unmindful of the conse-

quences that must result if this court should feel obliged, in fidelity to the Constitution, to declare that an enrolled bill, on which depend public and private interests of vast magnitude, and which has been . . . deposited in the public archives, *as an act of Congress,* . . . did not become law." *Id.,* at 669, 670 (emphasis in original).

H

The contentions on standing and justiciability have been fully examined and we are satisfied the parties are properly before us. The important issues have been fully briefed and twice argued, —— U. S. —— (1982). The Court's duty in this case, as Chief Justice Marshall declared in *Cohens* v. *Virginia,* 6 Wheat. 264, 404 (1821), is clear:

"Questions may occur which we would gladly avoid; but we cannot avoid them. All we can do is, to exercise our best judgment, and conscientiously to perform our duty."

III

A

We turn now to the question whether action of one House of Congress under § 244(c)(2) violates strictures of the Constitution. We begin, of course, with the presumption that the challenged statute is valid. Its wisdom is not the concern of the courts; if a challenged action does not violate the Constitution, it must be sustained:

"Once the meaning of an enactment is discerned and its constitutionality determined, the judicial process comes to an end. We do not sit as a committee of review, nor are we vested with the power of veto." *Tennessee Valley Authority* v. *Hill,* 437 U. S. 153, 194–195 (1978).

By the same token, the fact that a given law or procedure is efficient, convenient, and useful in facilitating functions of government, standing alone, will not save it if it is contrary to the Constitution. Convenience and efficiency are not the primary objectives—or the hallmarks—of democratic government and our inquiry is sharpened rather than blunted by the fact that Congressional veto provisions are appearing with increasing frequency in statutes which delegate authority to executive and independent agencies:

> "Since 1932, when the first veto provision was enacted into law, 295 congressional veto-type procedures have been inserted in 196 different statutes as follows: from 1932 to 1939, five statutes were affected; from 1940–49, nineteen statutes; between 1950–59, thirty-four statutes; and from 1960–69, forty-nine. From the year 1970 through 1975, at least one hundred sixty-three such provisions were included in eighty-nine laws." Abourezk, The Congressional Veto: A Contemporary Response to Executive Encroachment on Legislative Prerogatives, 52 Ind. L. Rev. 323, 324 (1977). See also Appendix 1 to JUSTICE WHITE's dissent, *post*, at ——.

JUSTICE WHITE undertakes to make a case for the proposition that the one-House veto is a useful "political invention," *post*, at ——, and we need not challenge that assertion. We can even concede this utilitarian argument although the long range political wisdom of this "invention" is arguable. It has been vigorously debated and it is instructive to compare the views of the protagonists. See, e. g., Javits & Klein, Congressional Oversight and the Legislative Veto: A Constitutional Analysis, 52 N.Y.U. L. Rev. 455 (1977), and Martin, The Legislative Veto and the Responsible Exercise of Congressional Power, 68 Va. L. Rev. 253 (1982). But policy arguments supporting even useful "political inventions" are subject to the demands of the Constitution which defines powers and, with respect to this subject, sets out just how those powers are to be exercised.

Explicit and unambiguous provisions of the Constitution

prescribe and define the respective functions of the Congress and of the Executive in the legislative process. Since the precise terms of those familiar provisions are critical to the resolution of this case, we set them out verbatim. Art. I provides:

> "All legislative Powers herein granted shall be vested in a Congress of the United States, which shall consist of a Senate *and* a House of Representatives." Art. I, §1. (Emphasis added).

> "Every Bill which shall have passed the House of Representatives *and* the Senate, *shall*, before it become a Law, be presented to the President of the United States; . . ." Art. I, §7, cl. 2. (Emphasis added).

> "*Every* Order, Resolution, or Vote to which the Concurrence of the Senate and House of Representatives may be necessary (except on a question of Adjournment) *shall be* presented to the President of the United States; and before the Same shall take Effect, *shall be* approved by him, or being disapproved by him, *shall be* repassed by two thirds of the Senate and House of Representatives, according to the Rules and Limitations prescribed in the Case of a Bill." Art. I, §7, cl. 3. (Emphasis added).

These provisions of Art. I are integral parts of the constitutional design for the separation of powers. We have recently noted that "[t]he principle of separation of powers was not simply an abstract generalization in the minds of the Framers: it was woven into the documents that they drafted in Philadelphia in the summer of 1787." *Buckley* v. *Valeo,* *supra,* 424 U. S., at 124. Just as we relied on the textual provision of Art. II, §2, cl. 2, to vindicate the principle of separation of powers in *Buckley,* we find that the purposes underlying the Presentment Clauses, Art. I, §7, cls. 2, 3, and the bicameral requirement of Art. I, § 1 and § 7, cl. 2, guide our resolution of the important question presented in this case. The very structure of the articles delegating and separating powers under Arts. I, II, and III exemplify the concept of separation of powers and we now turn to Art. I.

B

The Presentment Clauses

The records of the Constitutional Convention reveal that the requirement that all legislation be presented to the President before becoming law was uniformly accepted by the Framers.[14] Presentment to the President and the Presidential veto were considered so imperative that the draftsmen took special pains to assure that these requirements could not be circumvented. During the final debate on Art. I, § 7, cl. 2, James Madison expressed concern that it might easily be evaded by the simple expedient of calling a proposed law a "resolution" or "vote" rather than a "bill." 2 M. Farrand, The Records of the Federal Convention of 1787 301–302. As a consequence, Art. I, § 7, cl. 3, *ante*, at 25, was added. *Id.*, at 304–305.

The decision to provide the President with a limited and

---

[14] The widespread approval of the delegates was commented on by Joseph Story:

"In the convention there does not seem to have been much diversity of opinion on the subject of the propriety of giving to the president a negative on the laws. The principal points of discussion seem to have been, whether the negative should be absolute, or qualified; and if the latter, by what number of each house the bill should subsequently be passed, in order to become a law; and whether the negative should in either case be exclusively vested in the president alone, or in him jointly with some other department of government." 1 J. Story, Commentaries on the Constitution of the United States 611 (1858). See 1 M. Farrand, The Records of the Federal Convention of 1787 21, 97–104, 138–140; *id.*, at 73–80, 181, 298, 301–305.

qualified power to nullify proposed legislation by veto was based on the profound conviction of the Framers that the powers conferred on Congress were the powers to be most carefully circumscribed. It is beyond doubt that lawmaking was a power to be shared by both Houses and the President. In The Federalist No. 73 (H. Lodge ed. 1888), Hamilton focused on the President's role in making laws:

> "If even no propensity had ever discovered itself in the legislative body to invade the rights of the Executive, the rules of just reasoning and theoretic propriety would of themselves teach us that the one ought not to be left to the mercy of the other, but ought to possess a constitutional and effectual power of self-defense." *Id.*, at 457–458.

See also The Federalist No. 51. In his Commentaries on the Constitution, Joseph Story makes the same point. 1 J. Story, Commentaries on the Constitution of the United States 614–615 (1858).

The President's role in the lawmaking process also reflects the Framers' careful efforts to check whatever propensity a particular Congress might have to enact oppressive, improvident, or ill-considered measures. The President's veto role in the legislative process was described later during public debate on ratification:

> "It establishes a salutary check upon the legislative body, calculated to guard the community against the effects of faction, precipitancy, or of any impulse unfriendly to the public good which may happen to influence a majority of that body. . . . The primary inducement to conferring the power in question upon the Executive is to enable him to defend himself; the secondary one is to increase the chances in favor of the community against the passing of bad laws through haste, inad-

vertence, or design." The Federalist No. 73, *supra*, at 458 (A. Hamilton).

See also *The Pocket Veto Case*, 279 U. S. 655, 678 (1929); *Myers* v. *United States*, 272 U. S. 52, 123 (1926). The Court also has observed that the Presentment Clauses serve the important purpose of assuring that a "national" perspective is grafted on the legislative process:

> "The President is a representative of the people just as the members of the Senate and of the House are, and it may be, at some times, on some subjects, that the President elected by all the people is rather more representative of them all than are the members of either body of the Legislature whose constituencies are local and not countrywide. . . .". *Myers* v. *United States*, *supra*, 272 U. S., at 123.

C

Bicameralism

The bicameral requirement of Art. I, §§ 1, 7 was of scarcely less concern to the Framers than was the Presidential veto and indeed the two concepts are interdependent. By providing that no law could take effect without the concurrence of the prescribed majority of the Members of both Houses, the Framers reemphasized their belief, already remarked upon in connection with the Presentment Clauses, that legislation should not be enacted unless it has been carefully and fully considered by the Nation's elected officials. In the Constitutional Convention debates on the need for a bicameral legislature, James Wilson, later to become a Justice of this Court, commented:

> "Despotism comes on mankind in different shapes. Sometimes in an Executive, sometimes in a military, one. Is there danger of a Legislative despotism? Theory & practice both proclaim it. If the Legislative authority be not restrained, there can be neither liberty nor stabil-

ity; and it can only be restrained by dividing it within itself, into distinct and independent branches. In a single house there is no check, but the inadequate one, of the virtue & good sense of those who compose it." 1 M. Farrand, *supra,* at 254.

Hamilton argued that a Congress comprised of a single House was antithetical to the very purposes of the Constitution. Were the Nation to adopt a Constitution providing for only one legislative organ, he warned:

"we shall finally accumulate, in a single body, all the most important prerogatives of sovereignty, and thus entail upon our posterity one of the most execrable forms of government that human infatuation ever contrived. Thus we should create in reality that very tyranny which the adversaries of the new Constitution either are, or affect to be, solicitous to avert." The Federalist No. 22, *supra,* at 135.

This view was rooted in a general skepticism regarding the fallibility of human nature later commented on by Joseph Story:

"Public bodies, like private persons, are occasionally under the dominion of strong passions and excitements; impatient, irritable, and impetuous. . . . If [a legislature] feels no check but its own will, it rarely has the firmness to insist upon holding a question long enough under its own view, to see and mark it in all its bearings and relations to society." 1 J. Story, *supra,* at 383–384.

These observations are consistent with what many of the Framers expressed, none more cogently than Hamilton in pointing up the need to divide and disperse power in order to protect liberty:

"In republican government, the legislative authority

necessarily predominates. The remedy for this inconveniency is to divide the legislature into different branches; and to render them, by different modes of election and different principles of action, as little connected with each other as the nature of their common functions and their common dependence on the society will admit." The Federalist No. 51, *supra,* at 324.

See also The Federalist No. 62.

However familiar, it is useful to recall that apart from their fear that special interests could be favored at the expense of public needs, the Framers were also concerned, although not of one mind, over the apprehensions of the smaller states. Those states feared a commonality of interest among the larger states would work to their disadvantage; representatives of the larger states, on the other hand, were skeptical of a legislature that could pass laws favoring a minority of the people. See 1 M. Farrand, *supra,* 176–177, 484–491. It need hardly be repeated here that the Great Compromise, under which one House was viewed as representing the people and the other the states, allayed the fears of both the large and small states.[15]

We see therefore that the Framers were acutely conscious that the bicameral requirement and the Presentment Clauses would serve essential constitutional functions. The President's participation in the legislative process was to protect the Executive Branch from Congress and to protect the whole people from improvident laws. The division of the Congress into two distinctive bodies assures that the legislative power would be exercised only after opportunity for full study and debate in separate settings. The President's unilateral veto power, in turn, was limited by the power of two thirds of both Houses of Congress to overrule a veto thereby

---

[15] The Great Compromise was considered so important by the Framers that they inserted a special provision to ensure that it could not be altered, even by constitutional amendment, except with the consent of the states affected. See U. S. Const. **Art V.**

precluding final arbitrary action of one person. See 1 M. Farrand, *supra*, at 99–104. It emerges clearly that the prescription for legislative action in Art. I, §§ 1, 7 represents the Framers' decision that the legislative power of the Federal government be exercised in accord with a single, finely wrought and exhaustively considered, procedure.

IV

The Constitution sought to divide the delegated powers of the new federal government into three defined categories, legislative, executive and judicial, to assure, as nearly as possible, that each Branch of government would confine itself to its assigned responsibility. The hydraulic pressure inherent within each of the separate Branches to exceed the outer limits of its power, even to accomplish desirable objectives, must be resisted.

Although not "hermetically" sealed from one another, *Buckley* v. *Valeo, supra,* 424 U. S., at 121, the powers delegated to the three Branches are functionally identifiable. When any Branch acts, it is presumptively exercising the power the Constitution has delegated to it. See *Hampton & Co.* v. *United States,* 276 U. S. 394, 406 (1928). When the Executive acts, it presumptively acts in an executive or administrative capacity as defined in Art. II. And when, as here, one House of Congress purports to act, it is presumptively acting within its assigned sphere.

Beginning with this presumption, we must nevertheless establish that the challenged action under § 244(c)(2) is of the kind to which the procedural requirements of Art. I, § 7 apply. Not every action taken by either House is subject to the bicameralism and presentment requirements of Art. I. See *post,* at 35. Whether actions taken by either House are, in law and fact, an exercise of legislative power depends not on their form but upon "whether they contain matter which is properly to be regarded as legislative in its character and effect." S. Rep. No. 1335, 54th Cong., 2d Sess., 8 (1897).

145

Examination of the action taken here by one House pursuant to § 244(c)(2) reveals that it was essentially legislative in purpose and effect. In purporting to exercise power defined in Art. I, § 8, cl. 4 to "establish an uniform Rule of Naturalization," the House took action that had the purpose and effect of altering the legal rights, duties and relations of persons, including the Attorney General, Executive Branch officials and Chadha, all outside the legislative branch. Section 244(c)(2) purports to authorize one House of Congress to require the Attorney General to deport an individual alien whose deportation otherwise would be cancelled under § 244. The one-House veto operated in this case to overrule the Attorney General and mandate Chadha's deportation; absent the House action, Chadha would remain in the United States. Congress has *acted* and its action has altered Chadha's status.

The legislative character of the one-House veto in this case is confirmed by the character of the Congressional action it supplants. Neither the House of Representatives nor the Senate contends that, absent the veto provision in § 244(c)(2), either of them, or both of them acting together, could effectively require the Attorney General to deport an alien once the Attorney General, in the exercise of legislatively delegated authority,[16] had determined the alien should remain in

---

[16] Congress protests that affirming the Court of Appeals in this case will sanction "lawmaking by the Attorney General. . . . Why is the Attorney General exempt from submitting his proposed changes in the law to the full bicameral process?" Brief of the United States House of Representatives 40. To be sure, some administrative agency action—rule making, for example—may resemble "lawmaking." See 5 U. S. C. § 551(4), which defines an agency's "rule" as "the whole or part of an agency statement of general or particular applicability and future effect designed to implement, interpret, or prescribe *law* or policy. . . ." This Court has referred to agency activity as being "quasi-legislative" in character. *Humphrey's Executor* v. *United States*, 295 U. S. 602, 628 (1935). Clearly, however, "[i]n the framework of our Constitution, the President's power to see that the laws are faithfully executed refutes the idea that he is to be a lawmaker." *Youngstown Sheet & Tube Co.* v. *Sawyer*, 343 U. S. 579, 587 (1952). See

the United States. Without the challenged provision in
§ 244(c)(2), this could have been achieved, if at all, only by
legislation requiring deportation.[17] Similarly, a veto by one
House of Congress under § 244(c)(2) cannot be justified as an
attempt at amending the standards set out in § 244(a)(1), or
as a repeal of § 244 as applied to Chadha. Amendment and
repeal of statutes, no less than enactment, must conform
with Art. I.[18]

Buckley v. *Valeo,* 424 U. S. 1, 123 (1976). When the Attorney General
performs his duties pursuant to § 244, he does not exercise "legislative"
power. See *Ernst & Ernst* v. *Hochfelder,* 425 U. S. 185, 213–214 (1976).
The bicameral process is not necessary as a check on the Executive's administration of the laws because his administrative activity cannot reach
beyond the limits of the statute that created it—a statute duly enacted pursuant to Art. I, §§ 1, 7. The constitutionality of the Attorney General's
execution of the authority delegated to him by § 244 involves only a question of delegation doctrine. The courts, when a case or controversy arises,
can always "ascertain whether the will of Congress has been obeyed,"
Yakus v. *United States,* 321 U. S. 414, 425 (1944), and can enforce adherence to statutory standards. See *Youngstown Sheet & Tube Co.* v. *Sawyer,* 343 U. S. 579, 585 (1952); *Ethyl Corp.* v. *EPA,* 541 F. 2d 1, 68
(CADC) (en banc) (separate statement of Leventhal, J.), *cert. denied,* 426
U. S. 941 (1976); L. Jaffe, Judicial Control of Administrative Action 320
(1965). It is clear, therefore, that the Attorney General acts in his presumptively Art. II capacity when he administers the Immigration and Nationality Act. Executive action under legislatively delegated authority
that might resemble "legislative" action in some respects is not subject to
the approval of both Houses of Congress and the President for the reason
that the Constitution does not so require. That kind of Executive action is
always subject to check by the terms of the legislation that authorized it;
and if that authority is exceeded it is open to judicial review as well as the
power of Congress to modify or revoke the authority entirely. A one-
House veto is clearly legislative in both character and effect and is not so
checked; the need for the check provided by Art. I, §§ 1, 7 is therefore
clear. Congress' authority to delegate portions of its power to administrative agencies provides no support for the argument that Congress can
constitutionally control administration of the laws by way of a Congressional veto.

[17] We express no opinion as to whether such legislation would violate any
constitutional provision. See note 8, *supra.*

[18] During the Convention of 1787, the application of the President's veto

The nature of the decision implemented by the one-House veto in this case further manifests its legislative character. After long experience with the clumsy, time consuming private bill procedure, Congress made a deliberate choice to delegate to the Executive Branch, and specifically to the Attorney General, the authority to allow deportable aliens to remain in this country in certain specified circumstances. It is not disputed that this choice to delegate authority is precisely the kind of decision that can be implemented only in accordance with the procedures set out in Art. I. Disagreement with the Attorney General's decision on Chadha's deportation—that is, Congress' decision to deport Chadha—no less than Congress' original choice to delegate to the Attorney General the authority to make that decision, involves determinations of policy that Congress can implement in only one way; bicameral passage followed by presentment to the President. Congress must abide by its delegation of authority until that delegation is legislatively altered or revoked.[19]

---

to repeals of statutes was addressed and the Framers were apparently content with Madison's comment that "[a]s to the difficulty of repeals, it was probable that in doubtful cases the policy would soon take place of limiting the duration of laws as to require renewal instead of repeal." 2 M. Farrand, *supra*, at 587. See Ginnane, The Control of Federal Administration by Congressional Resolutions and Committees, 66 Harv. L. Rev. 569, 587–599 (1953). There is no provision allowing Congress to repeal or amend laws by other than legislative means pursuant to Art. I.

[19] This does not mean that Congress is required to capitulate to "the accretion of policy control by forces outside its chambers." Javits and Klein, Congresional Oversight and the Legislative Veto: A Constitutional Analysis, 52 N.Y.U. L. Rev. 455, 462 (1977). The Constitution provides Congress with abundant means to oversee and control its administrative creatures. Beyond the obvious fact that Congress ultimately controls administrative agencies in the legislation that creates them, other means of control, such as durational limits on authorizations and formal reporting requirements, lie well within Congress' constitutional power. See *id.*, at 460–461; Kaiser, Congressional Action to Overturn Agency Rules: Alternatives to the "Legislative Veto", 32 Ad. L. Rev. 667 (1980). See also note 9, *supra*.

Finally, we see that when the Framers intended to authorize either House of Congress to act alone and outside of its prescribed bicameral legislative role, they narrowly and precisely defined the procedure for such action. There are but four provisions in the Constitution, explicit and unambiguous, by which one House may act alone with the unreviewable force of law, not subject to the President's veto:

(a) The House of Representatives alone was given the power to initiate impeachments. Art. I, §2, cl. 6;

(b) The Senate alone was given the power to conduct trials following impeachment on charges inititated by the House and to convict following trial. Art. I, §3, cl. 5;

(c) The Senate alone was given final unreviewable power to approve or to disapprove presidential appointments. Art. II, §2, cl. 2;

(d) The Senate alone was given unreviewable power to ratify treaties negotiated by the President. Art. II, §2, cl. 2.

Clearly, when the Draftsmen sought to confer special powers on one House, independent of the other House, or of the President, they did so in explicit, unambiguous terms.[20]

---

[20] An exception from the Presentment Clauses was ratified in *Hollingsworth* v. *Virginia*, 3 Dall. 378 (1798). There the Court held presidential approval was unnecessary for a proposed constitutional amendment which had passed both Houses of Congress by the requisite two-thirds majority. See U. S. Const. Art. V.

One might also include another "exception" to the rule that Congressional action having the force of law be subject to the bicameral requirement and the Presentment Clauses. Each House has the power to act alone in determining specified internal matters. Art. I, §7, cl. 2, 3, and §5, cl. 2. However, this "exception" only empowers Congress to bind itself and is noteworthy only insofar as it further indicates the Framers' intent that Congress not act in any legally binding manner outside a closely circumscribed legislative arena, except in specific and enumerated instances.

Although the bicameral check was not provided for in any of these provisions for independent Congressional action, precautionary alternative

These carefully defined exceptions from presentment and bicameralism underscore the difference between the legislative
functions of Congress and other unilateral but important and
binding one-House acts provided for in the Constitution.
These exceptions are narrow, explicit, and separately justified; none of them authorize the action challenged here.   On
the contrary, they provide further support for the conclusion
that Congressional authority is not to be implied and for the
conclusion that the veto provided for in § 244(c)(2) is not authorized by the constitutional design of the powers of the
Legislative Branch.

Since it is clear that the action by the House under
§ 244(c)(2) was not within any of the express constitutional
exceptions authorizing one House to act alone, and equally
clear that it was an exercise of legislative power, that action
was subject to the standards prescribed in Article I.[21]   The

---

checks are evident.   For example, Art. II., § 2 requires that two-thirds of
the Senators present concur in the Senate's consent to a treaty, rather than
the simple majority required for passage of legislation.   See The Federalist No. 64 (J. Jay); The Federalist No. 66 (A. Hamilton); The Federalist
No. 75 (A. Hamilton).   Similarly, the Framers adopted an alternative protection, in the stead of Presidential veto and bicameralism, by requiring
the concurrence of two-thirds of the Senators present for a conviction of
impeachment.   Art. I, § 3.   We also note that the Court's holding in
Hollingsworth, supra, that a resolution proposing an amendment to the
Constitution need not be presented to the President, is subject to two alternative protections.   First, a constitutional amendment must command
the votes of two-thirds of each House.   Second, three-fourths of the states
must ratify any amendment.

[21] JUSTICE POWELL's position is that the one-House veto in this case is a
judicial act and therefore unconstitutional as beyond the authority vested
in Congress by the Constitution.   We agree that there is a sense in which
one-House action pursuant to § 244(c)(2) has a judicial cast, since it purports to "review" Executive action.   In this case, for example, the sponsor
of the resolution vetoing the suspension of Chadha's deportation argued
that Chadha "did not meet [the] statutory requirements" for suspension of
deportation.   *Ante,* at 5.   To be sure, it is normally up to the courts to
decide whether an agency has complied with its statutory mandate.   See

bicameral requirement, the Presentment Clauses, the President's veto, and Congress' power to override a veto were intended to erect enduring checks on each Branch and to protect the people from the improvident exercise of power by mandating certain prescribed steps. To preserve those checks, and maintain the separation of powers, the carefully defined limits on the power of each Branch must not be eroded. To accomplish what has been attempted by one House of Congress in this case requires action in conformity with the express procedures of the Constitution's prescription for legislative action: passage by a majority of both Houses and presentment to the President.[22]

----

note 16, *supra*. But the attempted analogy between judicial action and the one-House veto is less than perfect. Federal courts do not enjoy a roving mandate to correct alleged excesses of administrative agencies; we are limited by Art. III to hearing cases and controversies and no justiciable case or controversy was presented by the Attorney General's decision to allow Chadha to remain in this country. We are aware of no decision, and JUSTICE POWELL has cited none, where a federal court has reviewed a decision of the Attorney General suspending deportation of an alien pursuant to the standards set out in § 244(a)(1). This is not surprising, given that no party to such action has either the motivation or the right to appeal from it. As JUSTICE WHITE correctly notes, *post*, at ——, "the courts have not been given the authority to review whether an alien should be given permanent status; review is limited to whether the Attorney General has properly applied the statutory standards for" *denying* a request for suspension of deportation. *Foti* v. *INS*, 375 U. S. 217 (1963), relied on by JUSTICE POWELL, addressed only "whether a refusal by the Attorney General to grant a suspension of deportation is one of these 'final orders of deportation' of which direct review by Courts of Appeals is authorized under § 106(a) of the Act." *Id.*, at 221. Thus, JUSTICE POWELL's statement that the one-House veto in this case is "clearly adjudicatory," *post*, at ——, simply is not supported by his accompanying assertion that the House has "assumed a function ordinarily entrusted to the federal courts." *Ibid.* We are satisfied that the one-House veto is legislative in purpose and effect and subject to the procedures set out in Art. I.

[22] Neither can we accept the suggestion that the one-House veto provision in § 244(c)(2) either removes or modifies the bicameralism and presentation requirements for the enactment of future legislation affecting aliens.

The veto authorized by § 244(c)(2) doubtless has been in many respects a convenient shortcut; the "sharing" with the Executive by Congress of its authority over aliens in this manner is, on its face, an appealing compromise. In purely practical terms, it is obviously easier for action to be taken by one House without submission to the President; but it is crystal clear from the records of the Convention, contemporaneous writings and debates, that the Framers ranked other values higher than efficiency. The records of the Convention and debates in the States preceding ratification underscore the common desire to define and limit the exercise of the newly created federal powers affecting the states and the people. There is unmistakable expression of a determination that legislation by the national Congress be a step-by-

---

See *Atkins* v. *United States,* 556 F. 2d 1028, 1063–1064 (Ct. Cl. 1977), cert denied, 431 U. S. 1009 (1978); Brief for the United States House of Representatives 40. The explicit prescription for legislative action contained in Art. I cannot be amended by legislation. See n. 13, *supra.*

JUSTICE WHITE suggests that the Attorney General's action under § 244(c)(1) suspending deportation is equivalent to a *proposal* for legislation and that because Congressional approval is indicated "by failure to veto, the one-House veto satisfies the requirement of bicameral approval." *Post,* at ——. However, as the Court of Appeals noted, that approach "would analogize the effect of the one house disapproval to the failure of one house to vote affirmatively on a private bill." 634 F. 2d, at 435. Even if it were clear that Congress entertained such an arcane theory when it enacted § 244(c)(2), which JUSTICE WHITE does not suggest, this would amount to nothing less than an amending of Art. I. The legislative steps outlined in Art. I are not empty formalities; they were designed to assure that both Houses of Congress and the President participate in the exercise of lawmaking authority. This does not mean that legislation must always be preceded by debate; on the contrary, we have said that it is not necessary for a legislative body to "articulate its reasons for enacting a statute." *United States Railroad Retirement Board* v. *Fritz,* 449 U. S. 166, 179 (1980). But the steps required by Art. I, §§ 1, 7 make certain that there is an opportunity for deliberation and debate. To allow Congress to evade the strictures of the Constitution and in effect enact Executive proposals into law by mere silence cannot be squared with Art. I.

step, deliberate and deliberative process.

The choices we discern as having been made in the Constitutional Convention impose burdens on governmental processes that often seem clumsy, inefficient, even unworkable, but those hard choices were consciously made by men who had lived under a form of government that permitted arbitrary govermental acts to go unchecked. There is no support in the Constitution or decisions of this Court for the proposition that the cumbersomeness and delays often encountered in complying with explicit Constitutional standards may be avoided, either by the Congress or by the President. See *Youngstown Sheet & Tube Co.* v. *Sawyer*, 343 U. S. 579 (1952). With all the obvious flaws of delay, untidiness, and potential for abuse, we have not yet found a better way to preserve freedom than by making the exercise of power subject to the carefully crafted restraints spelled out in the Constitution.

V

We hold that the Congressional veto provision in § 244(c)(2) is severable from the Act and that it is unconstitutional. Accordingly, the judgment of the Court of Appeals is

Affirmed.

UNITED STATES *v.* NIXON, PRESIDENT OF THE UNITED STATES, ET AL.

CERTIORARI BEFORE JUDGMENT TO THE UNITED STATES COURT OF APPEALS FOR THE DISTRICT OF COLUMBIA CIRCUIT

No. 73–1766. Argued July 8, 1974—Decided July 24, 1974*

Following indictment alleging violation of federal statutes by certain staff members of the White House and political supporters of the President, the Special Prosecutor filed a motion under Fed. Rule Crim. Proc. 17 (c) for a subpoena *duces tecum* for the production before trial of certain tapes and documents relating to precisely identified conversations and meetings between the President and others. The President, claiming executive privilege, filed a motion to quash the subpoena. The District Court, after treating the subpoenaed material as presumptively privileged, concluded that the Special Prosecutor had made a sufficient showing to rebut the presumption and that the requirements of Rule 17 (c) had been satisfied. The court thereafter issued an order for an *in camera* examination of the subpoenaed material, having rejected the President's contentions (a) that the dispute between him and the Special Prosecutor was nonjusticiable as an "intra-executive" conflict and (b) that the judiciary lacked authority to review the President's assertion of executive privilege. The court stayed its order pending appellate review, which the President then sought in the Court of Appeals. The Special Prosecutor then filed in this Court a petition for a writ of certiorari before judgment (No. 73–1766) and the President filed a cross-petition for such a writ challenging the grand-jury action (No. 73–1834). The Court granted both petitions. *Held:*

1. The District Court's order was appealable as a "final" order under 28 U. S. C. § 1291, was therefore properly "in" the Court of Appeals, 28 U. S. C. § 1254, when the petition for certiorari before judgment was filed in this Court, and is now properly before this Court for review. Although such an order is normally not final and subject to appeal, an exception is made in a "limited class of

---

*Together with No. 73–1834, *Nixon, President of the United States v. United States,* also on certiorari before judgment to the same court.

cases where denial of immediate review would render impossible any review whatsoever of an individual's claims," *United States* v. *Ryan*, 402 U. S. 530, 533. Such an exception is proper in the unique circumstances of this case where it would be inappropriate to subject the President to the procedure of securing review by resisting the order and inappropriate to require that the District Court proceed by a traditional contempt citation in order to provide appellate review. Pp. 690–692.

2. The dispute between the Special Prosecutor and the President presents a justiciable controversy. Pp. 692–697.

(a) The mere assertion of an "intra-branch dispute," without more, does not defeat federal jurisdiction. *United States* v. *ICC*, 337 U. S. 426. P. 693.

(b) The Attorney General by regulation has conferred upon the Special Prosecutor unique tenure and authority to represent the United States and has given the Special Prosecutor explicit power to contest the invocation of executive privilege in seeking evidence deemed relevant to the performance of his specially delegated duties. While the regulation remains in effect, the Executive Branch is bound by it. *United States ex rel. Accardi* v. *Shaughnessy*, 347 U. S. 260. Pp. 694–696.

(c) The action of the Special Prosecutor within the scope of his express authority seeking specified evidence preliminarily determined to be relevant and admissible in the pending criminal case, and the President's assertion of privilege in opposition thereto, present issues "of a type which are traditionally justiciable," *United States* v. *ICC, supra*, at 430, and the fact that both litigants are officers of the Executive Branch is not a bar to justiciability. Pp. 696–697.

3. From this Court's examination of the material submitted by the Special Prosecutor in support of his motion for the subpoena, much of which is under seal, it is clear that the District Court's denial of the motion to quash comported with Rule 17 (c) and that the Special Prosecutor has made a sufficient showing to justify a subpoena for production *before* trial. Pp. 697–702.

4. Neither the doctrine of separation of powers nor the generalized need for confidentiality of high-level communications, without more, can sustain an absolute, unqualified Presidential privilege of immunity from judicial process under all circumstances. See, *e. g., Marbury* v. *Madison*, 1 Cranch 137, 177; *Baker* v. *Carr*, 369 U. S. 186, 211. Absent a claim of need to protect military, diplomatic, or sensitive national security secrets, the confidentiality of

Presidential communications is not significantly diminished by producing material for a criminal trial under the protected conditions of *in camera* inspection, and any absolute executive privilege under Art. II of the Constitution would plainly conflict with the function of the courts under the Constitution. Pp. 703–707.

5. Although the courts will afford the utmost deference to Presidential acts in the performance of an Art. II function, *United States* v. *Burr*, 25 F. Cas. 187, 190, 191–192 (No. 14,694), when a claim of Presidential privilege as to materials subpoenaed for use in a criminal trial is based, as it is here, not on the ground that military or diplomatic secrets are implicated, but merely on the ground of a generalized interest in confidentiality, the President's generalized assertion of privilege must yield to the demonstrated, specific need for evidence in a pending criminal trial and the fundamental demands of due process of law in the fair administration of criminal justice. Pp. 707–713.

6. On the basis of this Court's examination of the record, it cannot be concluded that the District Court erred in ordering *in camera* examination of the subpoenaed material, which shall now forthwith be transmitted to the District Court. Pp. 713–714.

7. Since a President's communications encompass a vastly wider range of sensitive material than would be true of an ordinary individual, the public interest requires that Presidential confidentiality be afforded the greatest protection consistent with the fair administration of justice, and the District Court has a heavy responsibility to ensure that material involving Presidential conversations irrelevant to or inadmissible in the criminal prosecution be accorded the high degree of respect due a President and that such material be returned under seal to its lawful custodian. Until released to the Special Prosecutor no *in camera* material is to be released to anyone. Pp. 714–716.

No. 73–1766, 377 F. Supp. 1326, affirmed; No. 73–1834, certiorari dismissed as improvidently granted.

BURGER, C. J., delivered the opinion of the Court, in which all Members joined except REHNQUIST, J., who took no part in the consideration or decision of the cases.

Leon Jaworski and *Philip A. Lacovara* argued the cause and filed briefs for the United States in both cases.

James D. St. Clair argued the cause for the President

in both cases. With him on the briefs were *Charles Alan Wright, Leonard Garment, Michael A. Sterlacci, Jerome J. Murphy, Loren A. Smith, James R. Prochnow, Theodore J. Garrish, James J. Tansey,* and *Larry G. Gutterridge. William Snow Frates, Andrew C. Hall, Spencer H. Boyer,* and *Henry H. Jones* filed a brief for respondent Ehrlichman in No. 73–1766. *John M. Bray* filed a brief for respondent Strachan in No. 73–1766.†

MR. CHIEF JUSTICE BURGER delivered the opinion of the Court.

This litigation presents for review the denial of a motion, filed in the District Court on behalf of the President of the United States, in the case of *United States* v. *Mitchell* (D. C. Crim. No. 74–110), to quash a third-party subpoena *duces tecum* issued by the United States District Court for the District of Columbia, pursuant to Fed. Rule Crim. Proc. 17 (c). The subpoena directed the President to produce certain tape recordings and documents relating to his conversations with aides and advisers. The court rejected the President's claims of absolute executive privilege, of lack of jurisdiction, and of failure to satisfy the requirements of Rule 17 (c). The President appealed to the Court of Appeals. We granted both the United States' petition for certiorari before judgment (No. 73–1766),[1] and also the President's cross-petition for certio-

----

†*Norman Dorsen* and *Melvin L Wulf* filed a brief for the American Civil Liberties Union as *amicus curiae* urging affirmance of the District Court judgment.

[1] See 28 U. S. C. §§ 1254 (1) and 2101 (e) and our Rule 20. See, *e. g., Youngstown Sheet & Tube Co.* v. *Sawyer,* 343 U. S. 579 (1952); *United States* v. *United Mine Workers,* 330 U. S. 258 (1947); *Carter* v. *Carter Coal Co,* 298 U. S. 238 (1936); *Rickert Rice Mills* v. *Fontenot,* 297 U. S. 110 (1936); *Railroad Retirement Board* v. *Alton R. Co.,* 295 U. S. 330 (1935); *Norman* v. *Baltimore & Ohio R. Co,* 294 U. S. 240 (1935).

rari before judgment (No. 73–1834),[2] because of the public importance of the issues presented and the need for their prompt resolution. 417 U. S. 927 and 960 (1974).

On March 1, 1974, a grand jury of the United States District Court for the District of Columbia returned an indictment charging seven named individuals[3] with various offenses, including conspiracy to defraud the United States and to obstruct justice. Although he was not designated as such in the indictment, the grand jury named the President, among others, as an unindicted coconspirator.[4] On April 18, 1974, upon motion of the Spe-

---

[2] The cross-petition in No. 73–1834 raised the issue whether the grand jury acted within its authority in naming the President as an unindicted coconspirator. Since we find resolution of this issue unnecessary to resolution of the question whether the claim of privilege is to prevail, the cross-petition for certiorari is dismissed as improvidently granted and the remainder of this opinion is concerned with the issues raised in No. 73–1766. On June 19, 1974, the President's counsel moved for disclosure and transmittal to this Court of all evidence presented to the grand jury relating to its action in naming the President as an unindicted coconspirator. Action on this motion was deferred pending oral argument of the case and is now denied.

[3] The seven defendants were John N. Mitchell, H. R. Haldeman, John D. Ehrlichman, Charles W. Colson, Robert C. Mardian, Kenneth W. Parkinson, and Gordon Strachan. Each had occupied either a position of responsibility on the White House staff or a position with the Committee for the Re-election of the President. Colson entered a guilty plea on another charge and is no longer a defendant.

[4] The President entered a special appearance in the District Court on June 6 and requested that court to lift its protective order regarding the naming of certain individuals as coconspirators and to any additional extent deemed appropriate by the Court. This motion of the President was based on the ground that the disclosures to the news media made the reasons for continuance of the protective order no longer meaningful. On June 7, the District Court removed its protective order and, on June 10, counsel for both parties jointly moved this Court to unseal those parts of the record which related to the action of the grand jury regarding the President. After receiv-

cial Prosecutor, see n. 8, *infra*, a subpoena *duces tecum* was issued pursuant to Rule 17 (c) to the President by the United States District Court and made returnable on May 2, 1974. This subpoena required the production, in advance of the September 9 trial date, of certain tapes, memoranda, papers, transcripts, or other writings relating to certain precisely identified meetings between the President and others.[5] The Special Prosecutor was able to fix the time, place, and persons present at these discussions because the White House daily logs and appointment records had been delivered to him. On April 30, the President publicly released edited transcripts of 43 conversations; portions of 20 conversations subject to subpoena in the present case were included. On May 1, 1974, the President's counsel filed a "special appearance" and a motion to quash the subpoena under Rule 17 (c). This motion was accompanied by a formal claim of privilege. At a subsequent hearing,[6] further motions to expunge the grand jury's action naming the President as an unindicted coconspirator and for protective orders against the disclosure of that information were filed or raised orally by counsel for the President.

On May 20, 1974, the District Court denied the motion to quash and the motions to expunge and for protective orders. 377 F. Supp. 1326. It further ordered "the President or any subordinate officer, official, or employee with custody or control of the documents or

---

ing a statement in opposition from the defendants, this Court denied that motion on June 15, 1974, except for the grand jury's immediate finding relating to the status of the President as an unindicted coconspirator. 417 U. S. 960.

[5] The specific meetings and conversations are enumerated in a schedule attached to the subpoena. App. 42a–46a.

[6] At the joint suggestion of the Special Prosecutor and counsel for the President, and with the approval of counsel for the defendants, further proceedings in the District Court were held *in camera*.

objects subpoenaed," *id.*, at 1331, to deliver to the District Court, on or before May 31, 1974, the originals of all subpoenaed items, as well as an index and analysis of those items, together with tape copies of those portions of the subpoenaed recordings for which transcripts had been released to the public by the President on April 30. The District Court rejected jurisdictional challenges based on a contention that the dispute was nonjusticiable because it was between the Special Prosecutor and the Chief Executive and hence "intra-executive" in character; it also rejected the contention that the Judiciary was without authority to review an assertion of executive privilege by the President. The court's rejection of the first challenge was based on the authority and powers vested in the Special Prosecutor by the regulation promulgated by the Attorney General; the court concluded that a justiciable controversy was presented. The second challenge was held to be foreclosed by the decision in *Nixon* v. *Sirica,* 159 U. S. App. D. C. 58, 487 F. 2d 700 (1973).

The District Court held that the judiciary, not the President, was the final arbiter of a claim of executive privilege. The court concluded that, under the circumstances of this case, the presumptive privilege was overcome by the Special Prosecutor's prima facie "demonstration of need sufficiently compelling to warrant judicial examination in chambers . . . ." 377 F. Supp., at 1330. The court held, finally, that the Special Prosecutor had satisfied the requirements of Rule 17 (c). The District Court stayed its order pending appellate review on condition that review was sought before 4 p. m., May 24. The court further provided that matters filed under seal remain under seal when transmitted as part of the record.

On May 24, 1974, the President filed a timely notice of appeal from the District Court order, and the certified record from the District Court was docketed in the United

States Court of Appeals for the District of Columbia Circuit. On the same day, the President also filed a petition for writ of mandamus in the Court of Appeals seeking review of the District Court order.

Later on May 24, the Special Prosecutor also filed, in this Court, a petition for a writ of certiorari before judgment. On May 31, the petition was granted with an expedited briefing schedule. 417 U. S. 927. On June 6, the President filed, under seal, a cross-petition for writ of certiorari before judgment. This cross-petition was granted June 15, 1974, 417 U. S. 960, and the case was set for argument on July 8, 1974.

I

JURISDICTION

The threshold question presented is whether the May 20, 1974, order of the District Court was an appealable order and whether this case was properly "in" the Court of Appeals when the petition for certiorari was filed in this Court. 28 U. S. C. § 1254. The Court of Appeals' jurisdiction under 28 U. S. C. § 1291 encompasses only "final decisions of the district courts." Since the appeal was timely filed and all other procedural requirements were met, the petition is properly before this Court for consideration if the District Court order was final. 28 U. S. C. §§ 1254 (1), 2101 (e).

The finality requirement of 28 U. S. C. § 1291 embodies a strong congressional policy against piecemeal reviews, and against obstructing or impeding an ongoing judicial proceeding by interlocutory appeals. See, e. g., Cobbledick v. United States, 309 U. S. 323, 324–326 (1940). This requirement ordinarily promotes judicial efficiency and hastens the ultimate termination of litigation. In applying this principle to an order denying a motion to quash and requiring the production of evidence pursuant to a subpoena *duces tecum,* it has been repeatedly held that the order is not final and hence not appealable. *United States* v. *Ryan,* 402 U. S. 530, 532 (1971); *Cobbledick* v. *United States, supra; Alexander* v. *United States,* 201 U. S. 117 (1906). This Court has

> "consistently held that the necessity for expedition in the administration of the criminal law justifies putting one who seeks to resist the production of desired information to a choice between compliance with a trial court's order to produce prior to any review of that order, and resistance to that order with the concomitant possibility of an adjudication of contempt if his claims are rejected on appeal." *United States* v. *Ryan, supra,* at 533.

The requirement of submitting to contempt, however, is not without exception and in some instances the purposes underlying the finality rule require a different result. For example, in *Perlman* v. *United States,* 247 U. S. 7 (1918), a subpoena had been directed to a third party requesting certain exhibits; the appellant, who owned the exhibits, sought to raise a claim of privilege. The Court held an order compelling production was appealable because it was unlikely that the third party would risk a contempt citation in order to allow immediate review of the appellant's claim of privilege. *Id.,* at 12–13. That case fell within the "limited class of cases where denial of immediate review would render impossible any review whatsoever of an individual's claims." *United States* v. *Ryan, supra,* at 533.

Here too, the traditional contempt avenue to immediate appeal is peculiarly inappropriate due to the unique setting in which the question arises. To require a President of the United States to place himself in the posture of disobeying an order of a court merely to trigger the procedural mechanism for review of the ruling would be unseemly, and would present an unnecessary occasion for constitutional confrontation between two branches of the Government. Similarly, a federal judge should not be placed in the posture of issuing a citation to a President simply in order to invoke review. The issue whether a President can be cited for contempt could itself engender protracted litigation, and would further delay both review on the merits of his claim of privilege and the ultimate termination of the underlying criminal action for which his evidence is sought. These considerations lead us to conclude that the order of the District Court was an appealable order. The appeal from that order was therefore properly "in" the Court of Appeals, and the case is now properly before this Court on the writ of certiorari before judgment. 28 U. S. C. § 1254; 28 U. S. C. § 2101 (e). *Gay* v. *Ruff,* 292 U. S. 25, 30 (1934).[7]

II

JUSTICIABILITY

In the District Court, the President's counsel argued that the court lacked jurisdiction to issue the subpoena because the matter was an intra-branch dispute between a subordinate and superior officer of the Executive Branch and hence not subject to judicial resolution. That argument has been renewed in this Court with emphasis on the contention that the dispute does not present a "case" or "controversy" which can be adjudicated in the federal courts. The President's counsel argues that the federal courts should not intrude into areas committed to the other branches of Government.

---

[7] The parties have suggested that this Court has jurisdiction on other grounds. In view of our conclusion that there is jurisdiction under 28 U. S. C. § 1254 (1) because the District Court's order was appealable, we need not decide whether other jurisdictional vehicles are available.

He views the present dispute as essentially a "jurisdictional" dispute within the Executive Branch which he analogizes to a dispute between two congressional committees. Since the Executive Branch has exclusive authority and absolute discretion to decide whether to prosecute a case, *Confiscation Cases,* 7 Wall. 454 (1869); *United States* v. *Cox,* 342 F. 2d 167, 171 (CA5), cert. denied *sub nom. Cox* v. *Hauberg,* 381 U. S. 935 (1965), it is contended that a President's decision is final in determining what evidence is to be used in a given criminal case. Although his counsel concedes that the President has delegated certain specific powers to the Special Prosecutor, he has not "waived nor delegated to the Special Prosecutor the President's duty to claim privilege as to all materials . . . which fall within the President's inherent authority to refuse to disclose to any executive officer." Brief for the President 42. The Special Prosecutor's demand for the items therefore presents, in the view of the President's counsel, a political question under *Baker* v. *Carr,* 369 U. S. 186 (1962), since it involves a "textually demonstrable" grant of power under Art. II.

The mere assertion of a claim of an "intra-branch dispute," without more, has never operated to defeat federal jurisdiction; justiciability does not depend on such a surface inquiry. In *United States* v. *ICC,* 337 U. S. 426 (1949), the Court observed, "courts must look behind names that symbolize the parties to determine whether a justiciable case or controversy is presented." *Id.,* at 430. See also *Powell* v. *McCormack,* 395 U. S. 486 (1969); *ICC* v. *Jersey City,* 322 U. S. 503 (1944); *United States ex rel. Chapman* v. *FPC,* 345 U. S. 153 (1953); *Secretary of Agriculture* v. *United States,* 347 U. S. 645 (1954); *FMB* v. *Isbrandtsen Co.,* 356 U. S. 481, 483 n. 2 (1958); *United States* v. *Marine Bancorporation, ante,* p. 602; and *United States* v. *Connecticut National Bank, ante,* p. 656.

Our starting point is the nature of the proceeding for which the evidence is sought—here a pending criminal prosecution. It is a judicial proceeding in a federal court alleging violation of federal laws and is brought in the name of the United States as sovereign. *Berger* v. *United States,* 295 U. S. 78, 88 (1935). Under the authority of Art. II, § 2, Congress has vested in the Attorney General the power to conduct the criminal litigation of the United States Government. 28 U. S. C. § 516. It has also vested in him the power to appoint subordinate officers to assist him in the discharge of his duties. 28 U. S. C. §§ 509, 510, 515, 533. Acting pursuant to those statutes, the Attorney General has delegated the authority to represent the United States in these particular matters to a Special Prosecutor with unique authority and tenure.[8] The regulation gives the

---

[8] The regulation issued by the Attorney General pursuant to his statutory authority, vests in the Special Prosecutor plenary authority to control the course of investigations and litigation related to "all offenses arising out of the 1972 Presidential Election for which the Special Prosecutor deems it necessary and appropriate to assume responsibility, allegations involving the President, members of the White House staff, or Presidential appointees, and any other matters which he consents to have assigned to him by the Attorney General." 38 Fed. Reg. 30739, as amended by 38 Fed. Reg. 32805. In particular, the Special Prosecutor was given full authority, *inter alia,* "to contest the assertion of 'Executive Privilege' . . . and handl[e] all aspects of any cases within his jurisdiction." *Id.,* at 30739. The regulation then goes on to provide:

"In exercising this authority, the Special Prosecutor will have the greatest degree of independence that is consistent with the Attorney General's statutory accountability for all matters falling within the jurisdiction of the Department of Justice. The Attorney General will not countermand or interfere with the Special Prosecutor's decisions or actions. The Special Prosecutor will determine whether and to what extent he will inform or consult with the Attorney General about the conduct of his duties and responsibilities. In accordance with assurances given by the President to the Attorney

Special Prosecutor explicit power to contest the invocation of executive privilege in the process of seeking evidence deemed relevant to the performance of these specially delegated duties.[9] 38 Fed. Reg. 30739, as amended by 38 Fed. Reg. 32805.

So long as this regulation is extant it has the force of law. In *United States ex rel. Accardi* v. *Shaughnessy,* 347 U. S. 260 (1954), regulations of the Attorney General delegated certain of his discretionary powers to the Board

General that the President will not exercise his Constitutional powers to effect the discharge of the Special Prosecutor or to limit the independence that he is hereby given, the Special Prosecutor will not be removed from his duties except for extraordinary improprieties on his part and without the President's first consulting the Majority and the Minority Leaders and Chairmen and ranking Minority Members of the Judiciary Committees of the Senate and House of Representatives and ascertaining that their consensus is in accord with his proposed action."

[9] That this was the understanding of Acting Attorney General Robert Bork, the author of the regulation establishing the independence of the Special Prosecutor, is shown by his testimony before the Senate Judiciary Committee:

"Although it is anticipated that Mr. Jaworski will receive cooperation from the White House in getting any evidence he feels he needs to conduct investigations and prosecutions, it is clear and understood on all sides that he has the power to use judicial processes to pursue evidence if disagreement should develop."

Hearings on the Special Prosecutor before the Senate Committee on the Judiciary, 93d Cong., 1st Sess., pt. 2, p. 450 (1973). Acting Attorney General Bork gave similar assurances to the House Subcommittee on Criminal Justice. Hearings on H. J. Res. 784 and H. R. 10937 before the Subcommittee on Criminal Justice of the House Committee on the Judiciary, 93d Cong., 1st Sess., 266 (1973). At his confirmation hearings, Attorney General William Saxbe testified that he shared Acting Attorney General Bork's views concerning the Special Prosecutor's authority to test any claim of executive privilege in the courts. Hearings on the Nomination of William B. Saxbe to be Attorney General before the Senate Committee on the Judiciary, 93d Cong., 1st Sess., 9 (1973).

of Immigration Appeals and required that Board to exercise its own discretion on appeals in deportation cases. The Court held that so long as the Attorney General's regulations remained operative, he denied himself the authority to exercise the discretion delegated to the Board even though the original authority was his and he could reassert it by amending the regulations. *Service* v. *Dulles,* 354 U. S. 363, 388 (1957), and *Vitarelli* v. *Seaton,* 359 U. S. 535 (1959), reaffirmed the basic holding of *Accardi.*

Here, as in *Accardi,* it is theoretically possible for the Attorney General to amend or revoke the regulation defining the Special Prosecutor's authority. But he has not done so.[10] So long as this regulation remains in force the Executive Branch is bound by it, and indeed the United States as the sovereign composed of the three branches is bound to respect and to enforce it. Moreover, the delegation of authority to the Special Prosecutor in this case is not an ordinary delegation by the Attorney General to a subordinate officer: with the authorization of the President, the Acting Attorney General provided in the regulation that the Special Prosecutor was not to be removed without the "consensus" of eight designated leaders of Congress. N. 8, *supra.*

The demands of and the resistance to the subpoena present an obvious controversy in the ordinary sense, but that alone is not sufficient to meet constitutional standards. In the constitutional sense, controversy means more than disagreement and conflict; rather it means the kind of controversy courts traditionally resolve. Here

---

[10] At his confirmation hearings, Attorney General William Saxbe testified that he agreed with the regulation adopted by Acting Attorney General Bork and would not remove the Special Prosecutor except for "gross impropriety." *Id.,* at 5–6, 8–10. There is no contention here that the Special Prosecutor is guilty of any such impropriety.

at issue is the production or nonproduction of specified evidence deemed by the Special Prosecutor to be relevant and admissible in a pending criminal case. It is sought by one official of the Executive Branch within the scope of his express authority; it is resisted by the Chief Executive on the ground of his duty to preserve the confidentiality of the communications of the President. Whatever the correct answer on the merits, these issues are "of a type which are traditionally justiciable." *United States* v. *ICC,* 337 U. S., at 430. The independent Special Prosecutor with his asserted need for the subpoenaed material in the underlying criminal prosecution is opposed by the President with his steadfast assertion of privilege against disclosure of the material. This setting assures there is "that concrete adverseness which sharpens the presentation of issues upon which the court so largely depends for illumination of difficult constitutional questions." *Baker* v. *Carr,* 369 U. S., at 204. Moreover, since the matter is one arising in the regular course of a federal criminal prosecution, it is within the traditional scope of Art. III power. *Id.,* at 198.

In light of the uniqueness of the setting in which the conflict arises, the fact that both parties are officers of the Executive Branch cannot be viewed as a barrier to justiciability. It would be inconsistent with the applicable law and regulation, and the unique facts of this case to conclude other than that the Special Prosecutor has standing to bring this action and that a justiciable controversy is presented for decision.

III

RULE 17 (c)

The subpoena *duces tecum* is challenged on the ground that the Special Prosecutor failed to satisfy the requirements of Fed. Rule Crim. Proc. 17 (c), which governs the issuance of subpoenas *duces tecum* in federal criminal proceedings. If we sustained this challenge, there would be no occasion to reach the claim of privilege asserted with respect to the subpoenaed material. Thus we turn to the question whether the requirements of Rule 17 (c) have been satisfied. See *Arkansas Louisiana Gas Co.* v. *Dept. of Public Utilities,* 304 U. S. 61, 64 (1938); *Ashwander* v. *TVA,* 297 U. S. 288, 346–347 (1936) (Brandeis, J., concurring).

Rule 17 (c) provides:

> "A subpoena may also command the person to whom it is directed to produce the books, papers, documents or other objects designated therein. The court on motion made promptly may quash or modify the subpoena if compliance would be unreasonable or oppressive. The court may direct that books, papers, documents or objects designated in the subpoena be produced before the court at a time prior to the trial or prior to the time when they are to be offered in evidence and may upon their production permit the books, papers, documents or objects or portions thereof to be inspected by the parties and their attorneys."

A subpoena for documents may be quashed if their production would be "unreasonable or oppressive," but not otherwise. The leading case in this Court interpreting this standard is *Bowman Dairy Co.* v. *United States,* 341 U. S. 214 (1951). This case recognized certain fundamental characteristics of the subpoena *duces tecum* in criminal cases: (1) it was not intended to provide a means of discovery for criminal cases, *id.,* at 220; (2) its chief innovation was to expedite the trial by providing a time and place *before* trial for the inspection of

subpoenaed materials,[11] *ibid.* As both parties agree,
cases decided in the wake of *Bowman* have generally
followed Judge Weinfeld's formulation in *United States*
v. *Iozia*, 13 F. R. D. 335, 338 (SDNY 1952), as to
the required showing. Under this test, in order to
require production prior to trial, the moving party must
show: (1) that the documents are evidentiary [12] and
relevant; (2) that they are not otherwise procurable
reasonably in advance of trial by exercise of due diligence; (3) that the party cannot properly prepare for
trial without such production and inspection in advance
of trial and that the failure to obtain such inspection
may tend unreasonably to delay the trial; and (4) that

---

[11] The Court quoted a statement of a member of the advisory
committee that the purpose of the Rule was to bring documents into
court "in advance of the time that they are offered in evidence, so
that they may then be inspected in advance, for the purpose . . . of
enabling the party to see whether he can use [them] or whether he
wants to use [them]." 341 U. S., at 220 n. 5. The Manual for Complex and Multidistrict Litigation published by the Federal Judicial
Center recommends that use of Rule 17 (c) be encouraged in complex criminal cases in order that each party may be compelled to
produce its documentary evidence well in advance of trial and in advance of the time it is to be offered. P. 150.

[12] The District Court found here that it was faced with "the more
unusual situation . . . where the subpoena, rather than being directed to the government by defendants, issues to what, as a
practical matter, is a third party." *United States* v. *Mitchell*, 377
F. Supp. 1326, 1330 (DC 1974). The Special Prosecutor suggests that
the evidentiary requirement of *Bowman Dairy Co.* and *Iozia* does not
apply in its full vigor when the subpoena *duces tecum* is issued to
third parties rather than to government prosecutors. Brief for
United States 128–129. We need not decide whether a lower
standard exists because we are satisfied that the relevance and
evidentiary nature of the subpoenaed tapes were sufficiently shown
as a preliminary matter to warrant the District Court's refusal to
quash the subpoena.

the application is made in good faith and is not intended as a general "fishing expedition."

Against this background, the Special Prosecutor, in order to carry his burden, must clear three hurdles: (1) relevancy; (2) admissibility; (3) specificity. Our own review of the record necessarily affords a less comprehensive view of the total situation than was available to the trial judge and we are unwilling to conclude that the District Court erred in the evaluation of the Special Prosecutor's showing under Rule 17 (c). Our conclusion is based on the record before us, much of which is under seal. Of course, the contents of the subpoenaed tapes could not at that stage be described fully by the Special Prosecutor, but there was a sufficient likelihood that each of the tapes contains conversations relevant to the offenses charged in the indictment. *United States* v. *Gross,* 24 F. R. D. 138 (SDNY 1959). With respect to many of the tapes, the Special Prosecutor offered the sworn testimony or statements of one or more of the participants in the conversations as to what was said at the time. As for the remainder of the tapes, the identity of the participants and the time and place of the conversations, taken in their total context, permit a rational inference that at least part of the conversations relate to the offenses charged in the indictment.

We also conclude there was a sufficient preliminary showing that each of the subpoenaed tapes contains evidence admissible with respect to the offenses charged in the indictment. The most cogent objection to the admissibility of the taped conversations here at issue is that they are a collection of out-of-court statements by declarants who will not be subject to cross-examination and that the statements are therefore inadmissible hearsay. Here, however, most of the tapes apparently contain conversations to which one or more of the defendants named in the indictment were party. The hearsay rule does not automatically bar all out-of-court statements by a defendant in a criminal case.[13] Declarations by one defendant may also be admissible against other defendants upon a sufficient showing, by independent evidence,[14] of a conspiracy among one or more other defendants and the declarant and if the declarations at issue were in furtherance of that conspiracy. The same is true of declarations of coconspirators who are not defendants in the case on trial. *Dutton* v. *Evans,* 400 U. S. 74, 81 (1970). Recorded conversations may also be admissible for the limited purpose of impeaching the credibility of any defendant who testifies or any other coconspirator who testifies. Generally, the need for evidence to impeach witnesses is insufficient to require its production in advance of trial. See, *e. g., United States* v. *Carter,* 15 F. R. D. 367,

---

[13] Such statements are declarations by a party defendant that "would surmount all objections based on the hearsay rule . . ." and, at least as to the declarant himself, "would be admissible for whatever inferences" might be reasonably drawn. *United States* v. *Matlock,* 415 U. S. 164, 172 (1974). *On Lee* v. *United States,* 343 U. S. 747, 757 (1952). See also C. McCormick, Evidence § 270, pp. 651–652 (2d ed. 1972).

[14] As a preliminary matter, there must be substantial, independent evidence of the conspiracy, at least enough to take the question to the jury. *United States* v. *Vaught,* 485 F. 2d 320, 323 (CA4 1973); *United States* v. *Hoffa,* 349 F. 2d 20, 41–42 (CA6 1965), aff'd on other grounds, 385 U. S. 293 (1966); *United States* v. *Santos,* 385 F. 2d 43, 45 (CA7 1967), cert. denied, 390 U. S. 954 (1968); *United States* v. *Morton,* 483 F. 2d 573, 576 (CA8 1973); *United States* v. *Spanos,* 462 F. 2d 1012, 1014 (CA9 1972); *Carbo* v. *United States,* 314 F. 2d 718, 737 (CA9 1963), cert. denied, 377 U. S. 953 (1964). Whether the standard has been satisfied is a question of admissibility of evidence to be decided by the trial judge.

371 (DC 1954). Here, however, there are other valid potential evidentiary uses for the same material, and the analysis and possible transcription of the tapes may take a significant period of time. Accordingly, we cannot conclude that the District Court erred in authorizing the issuance of the subpoena *duces tecum*.

Enforcement of a pretrial subpoena *duces tecum* must necessarily be committed to the sound discretion of the trial court since the necessity for the subpoena most often turns upon a determination of factual issues. Without a determination of arbitrariness or that the trial court finding was without record support, an appellate court will not ordinarily disturb a finding that the applicant for a subpoena complied with Rule 17 (c). See, *e. g., Sue* v. *Chicago Transit Authority,* 279 F. 2d 416, 419 (CA7 1960); *Shotkin* v. *Nelson,* 146 F. 2d 402 (CA10 1944).

In a case such as this, however, where a subpoena is directed to a President of the United States, appellate review, in deference to a coordinate branch of Government, should be particularly meticulous to ensure that the standards of Rule 17 (c) have been correctly applied. *United States* v. *Burr,* 25 F. Cas. 30, 34 (No. 14,692d) (CC Va. 1807). From our examination of the materials submitted by the Special Prosecutor to the District Court in support of his motion for the subpoena, we are persuaded that the District Court's denial of the President's motion to quash the subpoena was consistent with Rule 17 (c). We also conclude that the Special Prosecutor has made a sufficient showing to justify a subpoena for production *before* trial. The subpoenaed materials are not available from any other source, and their examination and processing should not await trial in the circumstances shown. *Bowman Dairy Co.* v. *United States,* 341 U. S. 214 (1951); *United States* v. *Iozia,* 13 F. R. D. 335 (SDNY 1952).

IV

THE CLAIM OF PRIVILEGE

A

Having determined that the requirements of Rule 17 (c) were satisfied, we turn to the claim that the subpoena should be quashed because it demands "confidential conversations between a President and his close advisors that it would be inconsistent with the public interest to produce." App. 48a. The first contention is a broad claim that the separation of powers doctrine precludes judicial review of a President's claim of privilege. The second contention is that if he does not prevail on the claim of absolute privilege, the court should hold as a matter of constitutional law that the privilege prevails over the subpoena *duces tecum.*

In the performance of assigned constitutional duties each branch of the Government must initially interpret the Constitution, and the interpretation of its powers by any branch is due great respect from the others. The President's counsel, as we have noted, reads the Constitution as providing an absolute privilege of confidentiality for all Presidential communications. Many decisions of this Court, however, have unequivocally reaffirmed the holding of *Marbury* v. *Madison,* 1 Cranch 137 (1803), that "[i]t is emphatically the province and duty of the judicial department to say what the law is." *Id.,* at 177.

No holding of the Court has defined the scope of judicial power specifically relating to the enforcement of a subpoena for confidential Presidential communications for use in a criminal prosecution, but other exercises of power by the Executive Branch and the Legislative Branch have been found invalid as in conflict with the Constitution. *Powell* v. *McCormack,* 395 U. S. 486 (1969); *Youngstown Sheet & Tube Co.* v. *Sawyer,* 343 U. S. 579 (1952). In a series of cases, the Court interpreted the explicit immunity conferred by express provisions of the Constitution on Members of the House and Senate by the Speech or Debate Clause, U. S. Const. Art. I, § 6. *Doe* v. *McMillan,* 412 U. S. 306 (1973); *Gravel* v. *United States,* 408 U. S. 606 (1972); *United States* v. *Brewster,* 408 U. S. 501 (1972); *United States* v. *Johnson,* 383 U. S. 169 (1966). Since this Court has consistently exercised the power to construe and delineate claims arising under express powers, it must follow that the Court has authority to interpret claims with respect to powers alleged to derive from enumerated powers.

Our system of government "requires that federal courts on occasion interpret the Constitution in a manner at variance with the construction given the document by another branch." *Powell* v. *McCormack, supra,* at 549. And in *Baker* v. *Carr,* 369 U. S., at 211, the Court stated:

> "Deciding whether a matter has in any measure been committed by the Constitution to another branch of government, or whether the action of that branch exceeds whatever authority has been committed, is itself a delicate exercise in constitutional interpretation, and is a responsibility of this Court as ultimate interpreter of the Constitution."

Notwithstanding the deference each branch must accord the others, the "judicial Power of the United States" vested in the federal courts by Art. III, § 1, of the Constitution can no more be shared with the Executive Branch than the Chief Executive, for example, can share with the Judiciary the veto power, or the Congress share with the Judiciary the power to override a Presidential veto. Any other conclusion would be contrary to the basic concept of separation of powers and the checks and balances that flow from the scheme of a tripartite government. The Federalist, No. 47, p. 313 (S. Mittell ed.

1938).   We therefore reaffirm that it is the province and duty of this Court "to say what the law is" with respect to the claim of privilege presented in this case.   *Marbury* v. *Madison, supra,* at 177.

B

In support of his claim of absolute privilege, the President's counsel urges two grounds, one of which is common to all governments and one of which is peculiar to our system of separation of powers.   The first ground is the valid need for protection of communications between high Government officials and those who advise and assist them in the performance of their manifold duties; the importance of this confidentiality is too plain to require further discussion.   Human experience teaches that those who expect public dissemination of their remarks may well temper candor with a concern for appearances and for their own interests to the detriment of the decisionmaking process.[15]   Whatever the nature of the privilege of confidentiality of Presidential communications in the exercise of Art. II powers, the privilege can be said to derive from the supremacy of each branch within its own assigned area of constitutional duties.   Certain powers and privileges flow from the nature of enumerated powers;[16] the protection of the confidentiality of

---

[15] There is nothing novel about governmental confidentiality.   The meetings of the Constitutional Convention in 1787 were conducted in complete privacy.   1 M. Farrand, The Records of the Federal Convention of 1787, pp. xi-xxv (1911).   Moreover, all records of those meetings were sealed for more than 30 years after the Convention.   See 3 Stat. 475, 15th Cong., 1st Sess., Res. 8 (1818).   Most of the Framers acknowledged that without secrecy no constitution of the kind that was developed could have been written.   C. Warren, The Making of the Constitution 134–139 (1937).

[16] The Special Prosecutor argues that there is no provision in the Constitution for a Presidential privilege as to the President's com-

Presidential communications has similar constitutional underpinnings.

The second ground asserted by the President's counsel in support of the claim of absolute privilege rests on the doctrine of separation of powers. Here it is argued that the independence of the Executive Branch within its own sphere, *Humphrey's Executor* v. *United States,* 295 U. S. 602, 629–630 (1935); *Kilbourn* v. *Thompson,* 103 U. S. 168, 190–191 (1881), insulates a President from a judicial subpoena in an ongoing criminal prosecution, and thereby protects confidential Presidential communications.

However, neither the doctrine of separation of powers, nor the need for confidentiality of high-level communications, without more, can sustain an absolute, unqualified Presidential privilege of immunity from judicial process under all circumstances. The President's need for complete candor and objectivity from advisers calls for great deference from the courts. However, when the privilege depends solely on the broad, undifferentiated claim of public interest in the confidentiality of such conversations, a confrontation with other values arises. Absent a claim of need to protect military, diplomatic, or sensitive national security secrets, we find it difficult to accept the argument that even the very important interest in confidentiality of Presidential communications is significantly diminished by production of such material for *in camera* inspection with all the protection that a district court will be obliged to provide.

---

munications corresponding to the privilege of Members of Congress under the Speech or Debate Clause. But the silence of the Constitution on this score is not dispositive. "The rule of constitutional interpretation announced in *McCulloch* v. *Maryland,* 4 Wheat. 316, that that which was reasonably appropriate and relevant to the exercise of a granted power was to be considered as accompanying the grant, has been so universally applied that it suffices merely to state it." *Marshall* v. *Gordon,* 243 U. S. 521, 537 (1917).

The impediment that an absolute, unqualified privilege would place in the way of the primary constitutional duty of the Judicial Branch to do justice in criminal prosecutions would plainly conflict with the function of the courts under Art. III.   In designing the structure of our Government and dividing and allocating the sovereign power among three co-equal branches, the Framers of the Constitution sought to provide a comprehensive system, but the separate powers were not intended to operate with absolute independence.

"While the Constitution diffuses power the better to secure liberty, it also contemplates that practice will integrate the dispersed powers into a workable government.   It enjoins upon its branches separateness but interdependence, autonomy but reciprocity." *Youngstown Sheet & Tube Co.* v. *Sawyer,* 343 U. S., at 635 (Jackson, J., concurring).

To read the Art. II powers of the President as providing an absolute privilege as against a subpoena essential to enforcement of criminal statutes on no more than a generalized claim of the public interest in confidentiality of nonmilitary and nondiplomatic discussions would upset the constitutional balance of "a workable government" and gravely impair the role of the courts under Art. III.

C

Since we conclude that the legitimate needs of the judicial process may outweigh Presidential privilege, it is necessary to resolve those competing interests in a manner that preserves the essential functions of each branch. The right and indeed the duty to resolve that question does not free the Judiciary from according high respect to the representations made on behalf of the President. *United States* v. *Burr,* 25 F. Cas. 187, 190, 191–192 (No. 14,694) (CC Va. 1807).

The expectation of a President to the confidentiality of his conversations and correspondence, like the claim of confidentiality of judicial deliberations, for example, has all the values to which we accord deference for the privacy of all citizens and, added to those values, is the necessity for protection of the public interest in candid, objective, and even blunt or harsh opinions in Presidential decision-making. A President and those who assist him must be free to explore alternatives in the process of shaping policies and making decisions and to do so in a way many would be unwilling to express except privately. These are the considerations justifying a presumptive privilege for Presidential communications. The privilege is fundamental to the operation of Government and inextricably rooted in the separation of powers under the Constitution.[17] In *Nixon* v. *Sirica,* 159 U. S. App. D. C. 58, 487 F. 2d 700 (1973), the Court of Appeals held that such Presidential communications are "presumptively privileged," *id.,* at 75, 487 F. 2d, at 717, and this position is accepted by both parties in the present litigation. We agree with Mr. Chief Justice Marshall's observation, therefore, that "[i]n no case of this kind would a court be required to proceed against the president as against an ordinary individual." *United States* v. *Burr,* 25 F. Cas., at 192.

But this presumptive privilege must be considered in light of our historic commitment to the rule of law. This

---

[17] "Freedom of communication vital to fulfillment of the aims of wholesome relationships is obtained only by removing the specter of compelled disclosure. . . . [G]overnment . . . needs open but protected channels for the kind of plain talk that is essential to the quality of its functioning." *Carl Zeiss Stiftung* v. *V. E. B. Carl Zeiss, Jena,* 40 F. R. D. 318, 325 (DC 1966). See *Nixon* v. *Sirica,* 159 U. S. App. D. C. 58, 71, 487 F. 2d 700, 713 (1973); *Kaiser Aluminum & Chem. Corp.* v. *United States,* 141 Ct. Cl. 38, 157 F. Supp. 939 (1958) (Reed, J.); The Federalist, No. 64 (S. Mittell ed. 1938).

is nowhere more profoundly manifest than in our view that "the twofold aim [of criminal justice] is that guilt shall not escape or innocence suffer." *Berger* v. *United States,* 295 U. S., at 88. We have elected to employ an adversary system of criminal justice in which the parties contest all issues before a court of law. The need to develop all relevant facts in the adversary system is both fundamental and comprehensive. The ends of criminal justice would be defeated if judgments were to be founded on a partial or speculative presentation of the facts. The very integrity of the judicial system and public confidence in the system depend on full disclosure of all the facts, within the framework of the rules of evidence. To ensure that justice is done, it is imperative to the function of courts that compulsory process be available for the production of evidence needed either by the prosecution or by the defense.

Only recently the Court restated the ancient proposition of law, albeit in the context of a grand jury inquiry rather than a trial,

> "that 'the public . . . has a right to every man's evidence,' except for those persons protected by a constitutional, common-law, or statutory privilege, *United States* v. *Bryan,* 339 U. S. [323, 331 (1950)]; *Blackmer* v. *United States,* 284 U. S. 421, 438 (1932) . . . ." *Branzburg* v. *Hayes,* 408 U. S. 665, 688 (1972).

The privileges referred to by the Court are designed to protect weighty and legitimate competing interests. Thus, the Fifth Amendment to the Constitution provides that no man "shall be compelled in any criminal case to be a witness against himself." And, generally, an attorney or a priest may not be required to disclose what has been revealed in professional confidence. These and other interests are recognized in law by privileges against forced disclosure, established in the Constitution, by statute, or at common law.   Whatever their origins, these exceptions to the demand for every man's evidence are not lightly created nor expansively construed, for they are in derogation of the search for truth.[18]

In this case the President challenges a subpoena served on him as a third party requiring the production of materials for use in a criminal prosecution; he does so on the claim that he has a privilege against disclosure of confidential communications.   He does not place his claim of privilege on the ground they are military or diplomatic secrets.   As to these areas of Art. II duties the courts have traditionally shown the utmost deference to Presidential responsibilities.   In *C. & S. Air Lines* v. *Waterman S. S. Corp.*, 333 U. S. 103, 111 (1948), dealing with Presidential authority involving foreign policy considerations, the Court said:

> "The President, both as Commander-in-Chief and as the Nation's organ for foreign affairs, has available intelligence services whose reports are not and ought not to be published to the world.   It would be intolerable that courts, without the relevant information, should review and perhaps nullify actions of the Executive taken on information properly held secret."

In *United States* v. *Reynolds,* 345 U. S. 1 (1953), deal-

---

[18] Because of the key role of the testimony of witnesses in the judicial process, courts have historically been cautious about privileges. Mr. Justice Frankfurter, dissenting in *Elkins* v. *United States*, 364 U. S. 206, 234 (1960), said of this: "Limitations are properly placed upon the operation of this general principle only to the very limited extent that permitting a refusal to testify or excluding relevant evidence has a public good transcending the normally predominant principle of utilizing all rational means for ascertaining truth."

ing with a claimant's demand for evidence in a Tort Claims Act case against the Government, the Court said:

> "It may be possible to satisfy the court, from all the circumstances of the case, that there is a reasonable danger that compulsion of the evidence will expose military matters which, in the interest of national security, should not be divulged. When this is the case, the occasion for the privilege is appropriate, and the court should not jeopardize the security which the privilege is meant to protect by insisting upon an examination of the evidence, even by the judge alone, in chambers." *Id.*, at 10.

No case of the Court, however, has extended this high degree of deference to a President's generalized interest in confidentiality. Nowhere in the Constitution, as we have noted earlier, is there any explicit reference to a privilege of confidentiality, yet to the extent this interest relates to the effective discharge of a President's powers, it is constitutionally based.

The right to the production of all evidence at a criminal trial similarly has constitutional dimensions. The Sixth Amendment explicitly confers upon every defendant in a criminal trial the right "to be confronted with the witnesses against him" and "to have compulsory process for obtaining witnesses in his favor." Moreover, the Fifth Amendment also guarantees that no person shall be deprived of liberty without due process of law. It is the manifest duty of the courts to vindicate those guarantees, and to accomplish that it is essential that all relevant and admissible evidence be produced.

In this case we must weigh the importance of the general privilege of confidentiality of Presidential communications in performance of the President's responsibilities against the inroads of such a privilege on the fair administration of criminal justice.[19] The interest in preserving confidentiality is weighty indeed and entitled to great respect. However, we cannot conclude that advisers will be moved to temper the candor of their remarks by the infrequent occasions of disclosure because of the possibility that such conversations will be called for in the context of a criminal prosecution.[20]

On the other hand, the allowance of the privilege to withhold evidence that is demonstrably relevant in a criminal trial would cut deeply into the guarantee of due process of law and gravely impair the basic function of the courts. A President's acknowledged need for con-

---

[19] We are not here concerned with the balance between the President's generalized interest in confidentiality and the need for relevant evidence in civil litigation, nor with that between the confidentiality interest and congressional demands for information, nor with the President's interest in preserving state secrets. We address only the conflict between the President's assertion of a generalized privilege of confidentiality and the constitutional need for relevant evidence in criminal trials.

[20] Mr. Justice Cardozo made this point in an analogous context. Speaking for a unanimous Court in *Clark* v. *United States,* 289 U. S. 1 (1933), he emphasized the importance of maintaining the secrecy of the deliberations of a petit jury in a criminal case. "Freedom of debate might be stifled and independence of thought checked if jurors were made to feel that their arguments and ballots were to be freely published to the world." *Id.,* at 13. Nonetheless, the Court also recognized that isolated inroads on confidentiality designed to serve the paramount need of the criminal law would not vitiate the interests served by secrecy:

"A juror of integrity and reasonable firmness will not fear to speak his mind if the confidences of debate are barred to the ears of mere impertinence or malice. He will not expect to be shielded against the disclosure of his conduct in the event that there is evidence reflecting upon his honor. The chance that now and then there may be found some timid soul who will take counsel of his fears and give way to their repressive power is too remote and shadowy to shape the course of justice." *Id.,* at 16.

183

fidentiality in the communications of his office is general in nature, whereas the constitutional need for production of relevant evidence in a criminal proceeding is specific and central to the fair adjudication of a particular criminal case in the administration of justice. Without access to specific facts a criminal prosecution may be totally frustrated. The President's broad interest in confidentiality of communications will not be vitiated by disclosure of a limited number of conversations preliminarily shown to have some bearing on the pending criminal cases.

We conclude that when the ground for asserting privilege as to subpoenaed materials sought for use in a criminal trial is based only on the generalized interest in confidentiality, it cannot prevail over the fundamental demands of due process of law in the fair administration of criminal justice. The generalized assertion of privilege must yield to the demonstrated, specific need for evidence in a pending criminal trial.

D

We have earlier determined that the District Court did not err in authorizing the issuance of the subpoena. If a President concludes that compliance with a subpoena would be injurious to the public interest he may properly, as was done here, invoke a claim of privilege on the return of the subpoena. Upon receiving a claim of privilege from the Chief Executive, it became the further duty of the District Court to treat the subpoenaed material as presumptively privileged and to require the Special Prosecutor to demonstrate that the Presidential material was "essential to the justice of the [pending criminal] case." *United States* v. *Burr,* 25 F. Cas., at 192. Here the District Court treated the material as presumptively privileged, proceeded to find that the Special

Prosecutor had made a sufficient showing to rebut the presumption, and ordered an *in camera* examination of the subpoenaed material. On the basis of our examination of the record we are unable to conclude that the District Court erred in ordering the inspection. Accordingly we affirm the order of the District Court that subpoenaed materials be transmitted to that court. We now turn to the important question of the District Court's responsibilities in conducting the *in camera* examination of Presidential materials or communications delivered under the compulsion of the subpoena *duces tecum.*

E

Enforcement of the subpoena *duces tecum* was stayed pending this Court's resolution of the issues raised by the petitions for certiorari. Those issues now having been disposed of, the matter of implementation will rest with the District Court. "[T]he guard, furnished to [the President] to protect him from being harassed by vexatious and unnecessary subpoenas, is to be looked for in the conduct of a [district] court after those subpoenas have issued; not in any circumstance which is to precede their being issued." *United States* v. *Burr,* 25 F. Cas., at 34. Statements that meet the test of admissibility and relevance must be isolated; all other material must be excised. At this stage the District Court is not limited to representations of the Special Prosecutor as to the evidence sought by the subpoena; the material will be available to the District Court. It is elementary that *in camera* inspection of evidence is always a procedure calling for scrupulous protection against any release or publication of material not found by the court, at that stage, probably admissible in evidence and relevant to the issues of the trial for which it is sought. That being true of an ordinary situation, it is obvious that the District Court has a very heavy responsibility to see to it that Presidential conversations, which are either not relevant or not admissible, are accorded that high degree of respect due the President of the United States. Mr. Chief Justice Marshall, sitting as a trial judge in the *Burr* case, *supra*, was extraordinarily careful to point out that

> "[i]n no case of this kind would a court be required to proceed against the president as against an ordinary individual." 25 F. Cas., at 192.

Marshall's statement cannot be read to mean in any sense that a President is above the law, but relates to the singularly unique role under Art. II of a President's communications and activities, related to the performance of duties under that Article. Moreover, a President's communications and activities encompass a vastly wider range of sensitive material than would be true of any "ordinary individual." It is therefore necessary [21] in the public interest to afford Presidential confidentiality the greatest protection consistent with the fair administration of justice. The need for confidentiality even as to idle conversations with associates in which casual reference might be made concerning political leaders within the country or foreign statesmen is too obvious to call for further treatment. We have no doubt that the District Judge will at all times accord to Presidential records that high degree of deference suggested in *United States* v. *Burr, supra,* and will discharge his responsibility to see to

---

[21] When the subpoenaed material is delivered to the District Judge *in camera,* questions may arise as to the excising of parts, and it lies within the discretion of that court to seek the aid of the Special Prosecutor and the President's counsel for *in camera* consideration of the validity of particular excisions, whether the basis of excision is relevancy or admissibility or under such cases as *United States* v. *Reynolds,* 345 U. S. 1 (1953), or *C. & S. Air Lines* v. *Waterman S. S. Corp.,* 333 U. S. 103 (1948).

it that until released to the Special Prosecutor no *in camera* material is revealed to anyone. This burden applies with even greater force to excised material; once the decision is made to excise, the material is restored to its privileged status and should be returned under seal to its lawful custodian.

Since this matter came before the Court during the pendency of a criminal prosecution, and on representations that time is of the essence, the mandate shall issue forthwith.

Affirmed.

UNITED STATES v. WILL ET AL.

APPEAL FROM THE UNITED STATES DISTRICT COURT FOR THE NORTHERN DISTRICT OF ILLINOIS

No. 79–983. Argued October 13, 1980—Decided December 15, 1980*

An interlocking network of federal statutes fixes the compensation of high-level federal officials, including federal judges, and provides for annual cost-of-living adjustments in salary determined in the same way as those for federal employees generally. In four consecutive fiscal years (hereafter Years 1, 2, 3, and 4), Congress, with respect to these high-level officials, enacted statutes to stop or reduce previously authorized cost-of-living increases initially intended to be automatically operative under that statutory scheme. In Years 2 and 3, the statutes became law before the start of the fiscal year, and in Years 1 and 4 became law on or after the first day of the fiscal year. A number of United States District Court Judges (appellees) filed class actions against the United States in District Court, challenging the validity of the statutes under the Compensation Clause of the Constitution, which provides that federal judges shall receive compensation which "shall not be diminished during their Continuance in Office." The District Court granted summary judgments for appellees.

Held:

  1. This Court has jurisdiction of the appeals under 28 U. S. C. § 1252, providing for appeals to this Court from judgments holding an Act of Congress unconstitutional in any civil action to which the United States is a party. And the District Court had jurisdiction over the actions under 28 U. S. C. § 1346 (a) (2), which confers on district courts and the Court of Claims concurrent jurisdiction over actions against the United States based on the Constitution when the amount in controversy does not exceed $10,000, none of the individual claims here having been alleged to have exceeded that amount. Pp. 210–211.

  2. Title 28 U. S. C. § 455—which requires a federal judge to disqualify himself in any proceeding in which his impartiality might reasonably be questioned or where he has a financial interest in the subject matter in controversy or is a party to the proceeding—by reason of the Rule of

---

*Together with No. 79–1689, *United States* v. *Will et al.*, also on appeal from the same court.

Necessity does not operate to disqualify all federal judges, including the Justices of this Court, from deciding the issues presented by these cases. Where, under the circumstances of these cases, all Article III judges have an interest in the outcome so that it was not possible to assign a substitute district judge or for the Chief Justice to remit the appeal, as he is authorized to do by statute, to a division of the Court of Appeals with judges who are not subject to the disqualification provisions of § 455, the common-law Rule of Necessity, under which a judge, even though he has an interest in the case, has a duty to hear and decide the case if it cannot otherwise be heard, prevails over the disqualification standards of § 455. Far from promoting § 455's purpose of reaching disqualification of an individual judge when there is another to whom the case may be assigned, failure to apply the Rule of Necessity in these cases would have a contrary effect by denying some litigants their right to a forum. And the public might be denied resolution of the crucial matter involved if first the District Judge and now all the Justices of this Court were to ignore the mandate of the Rule of Necessity and decline to answer the questions presented. Pp. 211–217.

3. The statutes in question in Years 1 and 4, but not in Years 2 and 3, violated the Compensation Clause. Pp. 217–230.

(a) In each of the four years in question, Congress intended in effect to repeal or postpone previously authorized salary increases for federal judges, not simply to consign such increases to the fiscal limbo of an account due but not payable. Pp. 221–224.

(b) Since the statute applying to Year 1 became law on the first day of the fiscal year, by which time the salary increases already had taken effect, it purported to repeal a salary increase already in force and thus "diminished" the compensation of federal judges. That the statute included in the salary "freeze" other federal officials who are not protected by the Compensation Clause did not insulate a direct diminution in judges' salaries from the clear mandate of that Clause. Pp. 224–226.

(c) But the statutes applying to Years 2 and 3 became law before the scheduled salary increases for federal judges had taken effect, *i. e.,* before they had become a part of the compensation due Article III judges, and hence in no sense diminished the compensation such judges were receiving. Pp. 226–229.

(d) Even though the statute applying to Year 4 referred only to "executive employees, which includes Members of Congress," and did not expressly mention judges, it appears that Congress intended to include Article III judges. Accordingly, where such statute, similarly to the statute applying to Year 1, purported to revoke an increase in judges' compensation after the statutes granting the increase had taken effect, it violated the Compensation Clause. Pp. 229–230.

No. 79–983, 478 F. Supp. 621, and No. 79–1689, affirmed in part, reversed in part, and remanded.

BURGER, C. J., delivered the opinion of the Court, in which all other Members joined, except BLACKMUN, J., who took no part in the decision of the cases.

Acting Solicitor General Geller argued the cause for the United States. With him on the briefs were *Assistant Attorney General Daniel, Mark I. Levy, Anthony J. Steinmeyer, Neil H. Koslowe,* and *Mark N. Mutterperl.*

Kevin M. Forde argued the cause for appellees. With him on the brief was *Richard J. Prendergast.*†

CHIEF JUSTICE BURGER delivered the opinion of the Court.

These appeals present the questions whether under the Compensation Clause, Art. III, § 1, Congress may repeal or modify a statutorily defined formula for annual cost-of-living increases in the compensation of federal judges, and, if so, whether it must act before the particular increases take effect.

I

Congress has enacted an interlocking network of statutes to fix the compensation of high-level officials in the Executive, Legislative, and Judicial Branches, including federal judges. It provides for quadrennial review of overall salary levels and annual cost-of-living adjustments determined in the same fashion as those for federal employees generally. In four consecutive fiscal years, Congress, with respect to these high-level

---

†Briefs of *amici curiae* urging affirmance in both cases were filed by *Leonard F. Janofsky, John A. Sutro, Francis R. Kirkham,* and *C. Douglas Floyd* for the American Bar Association; by *Richard William Austin* and *John F. McCarthy* for the Chicago Bar Association; and by *Nancy Y. Bekavac* and *Richard Coleman* for the Los Angeles County Bar Association.

Executive Branch, Legislative, and Judicial salaries, enacted
statutes to stop or to reduce previously authorized cost-of-
living increases initially intended to be automatically operative under that statutory scheme, once the Executive had
determined the amount.   In two of these years, the legislation
was signed by the President and became law before the start
of the fiscal year; in the other two years, on or after the first
day of the fiscal year.

A

The salaries of high-level Executive, Legislative, and Judicial officials are set under the Postal Revenue and Federal
Salary Act of 1967, 81 Stat. 642, as amended, 2 U. S. C.
§§ 351–361 (1976 ed. and Supp. III).   The Salary Act provides for a quadrennial review, starting in 1969, of these officials' compensation.   A Commission on Executive, Legislative, and Judicial Salaries periodically examines the salary
levels for these positions in relation to one another and to the
General Schedule (GS), the matrix of grades and steps that
determines the salaries of most federal employees.   Its recommendations are submitted to the President, who in turn
submits that report with his recommendations to Congress
in the next budget.   Each House of Congress must vote on
the President's proposal within 60 days.   If both Houses
approve, the adjustment takes effect at the start of the first
pay period beginning 30 days thereafter.[1]

In 1975, Congress adopted the Executive Salary Cost-of-
Living Adjustment Act, Pub. L. 94–82, 89 Stat. 419.   The
Adjustment Act subjects the salaries covered by the Salary
Act to the same annual adjustment made in the General
Schedule under the Federal Pay Comparability Act of 1970,
5 U. S. C. §§ 5305–5306.   The Comparability Act requires
that each year the President designate an agent to compare
federal salaries to data on private-sector salaries compiled by

---

[1] The Salary Act, as amended, does not expressly prescribe what occurs
if either House of Congress disapproves.   See 2 U. S. C. § 359 (1976 ed.,
Supp. III).

the Bureau of Labor Statistics. The agent must undertake certain steps in his investigation and, ultimately, submit a report to the President recommending adjustments as deemed appropriate to bring federal employees' salaries in line with prevailing rates in the private sector. A separate Advisory Committee on Federal Pay then reviews that report and makes its own independent recommendation. Thereafter, the President issues an order adjusting the salaries of federal employees and submits a report to Congress listing the overall percentage of the adjustment and including the reports and recommendations submitted to him on the subject. If the President believes that economic conditions or conditions of national emergency make the planned adjustment inappropriate, he may submit to Congress before September 1 an alternative plan for adjusting federal employees' salaries. This alternative plan controls unless within 30 days of continuous legislative session either House of Congress adopts a resolution disapproving of the President's proposed plan. If one House disapproves, the agent's recommendation governs. The increases take effect with the start of the first pay period starting on or after the beginning of the federal fiscal year on October 1.

This complex web of base salaries adjusted annually for civil service employees and again quadrennially for higher-rank positions has led to the following statutory definition of a United States district judge's compensation:

> "Each judge of a district court of the United States shall receive a salary at an annual rate determined under section 225 of the Federal Salary Act of 1967 (2 U. S. C. 351–361), as adjusted by section 461 of this title." 28 U. S. C. § 135.

Similarly phrased statutes apply to all other Article III judges.[2] Title 28 U. S. C. § 461 in turn provides that the an-

---

[2] See 28 U. S. C. § 5 (the Chief Justice and each Associate Justice of the Supreme Court); 28 U. S. C. § 44 (d) (circuit judges); 28 U. S. C.

nual GS adjustment, rounded to the nearest multiple of $100, shall apply to salaries subject to that section, effective at the start of the next pay period. Compensation of judges is set at an annual figure and paid monthly, with each pay period coinciding with the calendar month. See 5 U. S. C. § 5505. Accordingly, any annual change in salary under the Adjustment Act takes effect at the beginning of October, the start of the fiscal year.

B

In October 1975, GS salaries were increased by an average of 5% under the terms of the Comparability Act. Federal judges and the other officials covered by the Adjustment Act received similar increases. In each of the following four years, however, Congress adopted a statute that altered the application of the Adjustment Act for the officials of the three branches subject to it. To avoid the confusion generated by a fiscal year's having a number different from the calendar year in which it begins, we refer to these as Years 1, 2, 3, and 4. We turn now to the specific actions taken for each of the four years in question.

Year 1

In October 1976, GS salaries were increased by an average of 4.8% under the procedures of the Comparability Act outlined earlier. On October 1, the first day of the new fiscal year and the first day of the relevant pay period, the President signed the Legislative Branch Appropriation Act, 1977, Pub. L. 94–440, 90 Stat. 1439. Title II of that statute provided:

> "[N]one of the funds contained in this Act shall be used to increase salaries of Members of the House of Representatives . . . . No part of the funds appropriated in

---

§ 173 (Court of Claims); 28 U. S. C. § 213 (Court of Customs and Patent Appeals); 28 U. S. C. § 252 (Court of International Trade (formerly Customs Court)).

this Act or any other Act shall be used to pay the salary of an individual in a position or office referred to in section 225 (f) of the Federal Salary Act of 1967, as amended (2 U. S. C. 356), including a Delegate to the House of Representatives, at a rate which exceeds the salary rate in effect on September 30, 1976, for such position or office . . . ."

By virtue of the reference to the Salary Act, this statute applied to federal judges; its import, therefore, was to prohibit paying the 4.8% raise on October 1, 1976, under the Adjustment Act to federal judges, as well as Members of Congress and high-level officials in the Executive Branch.

In March 1977, Members of Congress, federal judges, and high-ranking employees in the Executive Branch received raises pursuant to the quadrennial review under the Salary Act. The salary of a United States district judge, for example, increased to $54,500; circuit judges and special appellate judges, to $57,500; Associate Justices of the Supreme Court, to $72,000. 42 Fed. Reg. 10297 (1977).[3]

Year 2

In October 1977, GS salaries, which generally are not subject to the quadrennial review under the Salary Act, were increased an average of 7.1% under the Comparability Act. On July 11, 1977, the President signed Pub. L. 95–66, 91 Stat. 270, which provided:

"[T]he first adjustment which, but for this Act, would be made after the date of enactment of this Act under the following provisions of law in the salary or rate of pay

---

[3] These amounts exceeded the levels these salaries would have achieved had Congress left in effect the 4.8% increase from October 1, 1976. Therefore, appellees' complaint in No. 79–983 challenged the statute in Year 1 only insofar as it affected judicial compensation from October 1, 1976, to March 1, 1977. See n. 6, infra.

of positions or individuals to which such provisions apply [the 7.1% in October 1977], shall not take effect:

. . . . .

"(3) section 461 of title 28, United States Code, relating to comparability adjustments in the salary and rate of pay of justices, judges, commissioners, and referees . . . ."

Parallel subdivisions applied to the other officials under the Salary Act. According to the House Report on this measure, an Adjustment Act increase would be inappropriate following the Comparability Act increase earlier in the same calendar year. H. R. Rep. No. 95–458, p. 2 (1977).[4] The effect of this statute was to nullify the contemplated 7.1% increase for these high-level executive employees, Members of Congress, and federal judges.

Year 3

For the fiscal year beginning October 1, 1978, the President approved the recommendation to increase GS salaries an average of 5.5%. On September 30, 1978, the final day of the preceding fiscal year, however, the President signed the Legislative Branch Appropriation Act, 1979, Pub. L. 95–391, 92 Stat. 763. Section 304 (a) of that Act stated:

"No part of the funds appropriated for the fiscal year ending September 30, 1979, by this Act or any other Act may be used to pay the salary or pay of any individual in any office or position in the legislative, executive, or judicial branch, or in the government of the District of Columbia, at a rate which exceeds the rate (or maximum rate, if higher) of salary or basic pay payable for such office or position for September 30, 1978 . . . ."

---

[4] See also 123 Cong. Rec. 7126 (1977) (remarks of Sen. Scott) ("prevents people . . . from receiving two pay raises in 1 year"); *id.*, at 21121 (remarks of Rep. Solarz) ("individuals who have already received one increase during the course of the current year should not be entitled to receive a second increase as well"); *infra*, at 222, and n. 24.

The effect of this provision was to prohibit paying the 5.5%
increase authorized by the Adjustment Act for the fiscal year
beginning October 1, 1978.

Year 4

For the fiscal year beginning October 1, 1979, the President's
statutory agent transmitted a recommendation for an average
increase of 10.41%. However, on August 31, the President
invoked his power under the Comparability Act to alter this
rate; he reduced the proposed increase to 7% from the 10.41%
recommended. These increases, the Government concedes,
took effect on October 1, 1979. Moreover, because the September 30, 1978, statute (Year 3) prohibited paying the 5.5%
increase only during fiscal year 1979, that increase took effect
as well; along with the 7% adjustment, this brought the total
to 12.9%.[5] Nevertheless, the Government now contends that
this increase was in effect for only 11 days, since on October
12, the President signed Pub. L. 96–86, 93 Stat. 656. Section
101 (c) of this statute stated, in relevant part:

> "For fiscal year 1980, funds available for payment to
> executive employees, which includes Members of Con-
> gress, who under existing law are entitled to approximately
> 12.9 percent increase in pay, shall not be used to pay any
> such employee or elected or appointed official any sum
> in excess of 5.5 percent increase in existing pay and such
> sum if accepted shall be in lieu of the 12.9 percent due
> for such fiscal year."

None of the appellees have exercised the statutory option to
accept the 5.5% increase pursuant to the final clause of this
statute; in terms that statute provides such acceptance of the
5.5% operates as a waiver of all claims to rates higher than

---

[5] The 7% increase was computed on the salary levels as they stood
after the addition of the 5.5% increase deferred from Year 3. The com-
pounding of the two increases means that the employees affected felt a
combined increase of 12.9%. This explains the additional 0.4%.

the 5.5%. The Government concedes the 5.5% increase has continued in effect.

C

On February 7, 1978, 13 United States District Judges filed an action (No. 79–983 in this Court) in the District Court for the Northern District of Illinois. The complaint, which named the United States as defendant, challenged the validity of the statutes in Years 1 and 2 under the Compensation Clause, U. S. Const., Art. III, § 1.[6] The plaintiff judges were certified as representatives of two classes of Article III judges, the classes defined with reference to Years 1 and 2.[7] The Government, while not opposing certification of the classes, defended the validity of both statutes.

In an opinion filed August 29, 1979, the District Court granted summary judgment for the plaintiffs, appellees here. 478 F. Supp. 621. A corresponding judgment order was entered September 24. On appeal by the Government, we postponed decision on jurisdiction to the hearing on the merits and directed the parties to address the effect of 28 U. S. C. § 455, if any, on the jurisdiction of the District Court and this Court. 444 U. S. 1068 (1980).

No. 79–1689 comes to us from a similar complaint filed in the United States District Court for the Northern District of

---

[6] The plaintiffs challenged the statute in Year 1 only insofar as it applied to compensation earned from October 1, 1976, until March 1, 1977, the date the quadrennial increase under the Comparability Act took effect. See n. 3, *supra.*

[7] For Year 1, the class was defined as all Article III judges serving during part or all of the period October 1, 1976, to March 1, 1977, the date the quadrennial increase under the Comparability Act took effect. See n. 6, *supra.* For Year 2, the class was defined as all Article III judges taking office prior to July 11, 1977, the date the statute was passed, and continuing in office after October 1, 1977, the date the Adjustment Act increase was due to take effect.

The case was referred to a newly appointed member of the District Court who had taken office after October 1, 1977, and thus was not a member of either class.

Illinois on October 19, 1979, after the District Court had entered judgment in No. 79–983. At issue this time were the statutes in Years 3 and 4. The same 13 judges, joined by one other, again sought to represent two classes of Article III judges defined by the years.[8] The United States is defendant. The case was referred to the same member of the District Court who had presided over the proceedings in No. 79–983.

On January 31, 1980, the District Court entered an order certifying the classes and granting summary judgment for the plaintiffs, appellees in No. 79–1689. Based on its decision in No. 79–983, the court held that the statute in Year 3 violated the Compensation Clause. The court noted with respect to Year 4 that the relevant statute referred only to "executive employees." It then held that while it was doubtful Congress intended the statute to apply to judges, the statute would be unconstitutional if Congress did so intend. In either case, the Adjustment Act increase for Year 4 took effect. Judgment for appellees was formally entered February 12. On the Government's appeal to this Court, we postponed consideration of jurisdiction to the merits and consolidated this case with No. 79–983 for briefing and oral argument. 447 U. S. 919 (1980).

II

A

Jurisdiction

Although it is clear that the District Judge and all Justices of this Court have an interest in the outcome of these cases, there is no doubt whatever as to this Court's jurisdiction

---

[8] For Year 3, the class was defined as all Article III judges in office on October 1, 1978, the date of the scheduled Adjustment Act increase, and continuing in office thereafter. For Year 4, the class was defined as all Article III judges in office on October 1, 1979, the date the Adjustment Act increase took effect, and continuing in office through October 12, 1979, the date the Year 4 statute was signed.

under 28 U. S. C. § 1252 [9] or that of the District Court under 28 U. S. C. § 1346 (a)(2) (1976 ed., Supp. III).[10] Section 455 of Title 28 [11] neither expressly nor by implication purports to deal with jurisdiction. On its face § 455 provides for disqualification of individual judges under specified circumstances; it does not affect the jurisdiction of a court. Nothing in the text or the history of § 455 suggests that Congress intended, by that section, to amend the vast array of statutes conferring jurisdiction over certain matters on various federal courts.

B

Disqualification

Jurisdiction being clear, our next inquiry is whether 28 U. S. C. § 455 or traditional judicial canons [12] operate to dis-

---

[9] This section provides in part:

"Any party may appeal to the Supreme Court from an interlocutory or final judgment, decree or order of any court of the United States . . . holding an Act of Congress unconstitutional in any civil action, suit, or proceeding to which the United States or any of its agencies, or any officer or employee thereof, as such officer or employee, is a party."

[10] This provision confers on the district courts and the Court of Claims concurrent jurisdiction over actions against the United States based on the Constitution when the amount in controversy does not exceed $10,000. The complaints in both No. 79–983 and No. 79–1689 state that the claims of individual members of the classes do not exceed $10,000, an allegation the Government has not disputed. See App. 9a, 62a.

[11] This section provides in relevant part:

"(a) Any justice, judge, or magistrate of the United States shall disqualify himself in any proceeding in which his impartiality might reasonably be questioned.

"(b) He shall also disqualify himself in the following circumstances:

.   .   .   .   .

"(4) He knows that he . . . has a financial interest in the subject matter in controversy . . . ;

"(5) He . . .

"(i) Is a party to the proceeding . . . ."

[12] See, *e. g.*, ABA, Code of Judicial Conduct, Canon 3 (C).

qualify all United States judges, including the Justices of this Court, from deciding these issues. This threshold question reaches us with both the Government and the appellees in full agreement that § 455 did not require the District Judge, and does not now require each Justice of this Court, to disqualify himself. Rather, they agree the ancient Rule of Necessity prevails over the disqualification standards of § 455. Notwithstanding this concurrence of views resulting from the Government's concession, the sensitivity of the issues leads us to address the applicability of § 455 with the same degree of care and attention we would employ if the Government asserted that the District Court lacked jurisdiction or that § 455 mandates disqualification of all judges and Justices without exception.

In federal courts generally, when an individual judge is disqualified from a particular case by reason of § 455, the disqualified judge simply steps aside and allows the normal administrative processes of the court to assign the case to another judge not disqualified. In the cases now before us, however, all Article III judges have an interest in the outcome; assignment of a substitute District Judge was not possible. And in this Court, when one or more Justices are recused but a statutory quorum of six Justices eligible to act remains available, see 28 U. S. C. § 1, the Court may continue to hear the case. Even if all Justices are disqualified in a particular case under § 455, 28 U. S. C. § 2109 authorizes the Chief Justice to remit a direct appeal to the Court of Appeals for final decision by judges not so disqualified.[13]

---

[13] Section 2109 provides, in relevant part:

"If a case brought to the Supreme Court by direct appeal from a district court cannot be heard and determined because of the absence of a quorum of qualified justices, the Chief Justice of the United States may order it remitted to the court of appeals for the circuit including the district in which the case arose, to be heard and determined by that court either sitting in banc or specially constituted and composed of the three

However, in the highly unusual setting of these cases, even with the authority to assign other federal judges to sit temporarily under 28 U. S. C. §§ 291–296 (1976 ed. and Supp. III), it is not possible to convene a division of the Court of Appeals with judges who are not subject to the disqualification provisions of § 455. It was precisely considerations of this kind that gave rise to the Rule of Necessity, a well-settled principle at common law that, as Pollack put it, "although a judge had better not, if it can be avoided, take part in the decision of a case in which he has any personal interest, yet he not only may but must do so if the case cannot be heard otherwise."   F. Pollack, A First Book of Jurisprudence 270 (6th ed. 1929).

C

Rule of Necessity

The Rule of Necessity had its genesis at least five and a half centuries ago.   Its earliest recorded invocation was in 1430, when it was held that the Chancellor of Oxford could act as judge of a case in which he was a party when there was no provision for appointment of another judge.   Y. B. Hil.

---

circuit judges senior in commission who are able to sit, as such order may direct.   The decision of such court shall be final and conclusive.   In the event of the disqualification or disability of one or more of such circuit judges, such court shall be filled as provided in chapter 15 of this title."

The second paragraph of the section provides that, in all other cases when a quorum of qualified Justices is unable to sit, the Court shall enter an order affirming the judgment extant, which shall have the precedential effect of an affirmance by an equally divided Court.

The original version of this section was designed to ensure that the parties in antitrust and Interstate Commerce Commission cases, which at that time could be appealed directly to this Court, would always have some form of appellate review.   See H. R. Rep. No. 1317, 78th Cong., 2d Sess., 2 (1944).   Congress broadened this right in the 1948 revision of Title 28 to include all cases of direct review.   H. R. Rep. No. 308, 80th Cong., 1st Sess., A175–A176 (1947).

8 Hen. VI, f. 19, pl. 6.[14]   Early cases in this country confirmed the vitality of the Rule.[15]

The Rule of Necessity has been consistently applied in this country in both state and federal courts.   In *State ex rel. Mitchell* v. *Sage Stores Co.*, 157 Kan. 622, 143 P. 2d 652 (1943), the Supreme Court of Kansas observed:

> "[I]t is well established that actual disqualification of a member of a court of last resort will not excuse such member from performing his official duty if failure to do so would result in a denial of a litigant's constitutional right to have a question, properly presented to such court, adjudicated."   *Id.*, at 629, 143 P. 2d, at 656.

Similarly, the Supreme Court of Pennsylvania held:

> "The true rule unquestionably is that wherever it becomes necessary for a judge to sit even where he has an interest—where no provision is made for calling another in, or where no one else can take his place—it is his duty to hear and decide, however disagreeable it may be." *Philadelphia* v. *Fox*, 64 Pa. 169, 185 (1870).

Other state [16] and federal [17] courts also have recognized the Rule.

---

[14] Rolle's Abridgment summarized this holding as follows: "If an action is sued in the bench against all the Judges there, then by necessity they shall be their own Judges." 2 H. Rolle, An Abridgment of Many Cases and Resolutions at Common Law 93 (1668) (translation).

[15] For example, in *Mooers* v. *White*, 6 Johns. Ch. 360 (N. Y. 1822), Chancellor Kent continued to sit despite his brother-in-law's being a party; New York law made no provision for a substitute chancellor. See *In re Leefe*, 2 Barb. Ch. 39 (N. Y. 1846).   See also cases cited in Annot., 39 A. L. R. 1476 (1925).

[16] *E. g., Moulton* v. *Byrd*, 224 Ala. 403, 140 So. 384 (1932); *Olson* v. *Cory*, 26 Cal. 3d 672, 609 P. 2d 991 (1980); *Nellius* v. *Stiftel*, 402 A. 2d 359 (Del. 1978); *Dacey* v. *Connecticut Bar Assn.*, 170 Conn. 520, 368 A. 2d 125 (1976); *Wheeler* v. *Board of Trustees of Fargo Consol. School*

[*Footnote 17 is on p. 215*]

The concept of the absolute duty of judges to hear and decide cases within their jurisdiction revealed in *Pollack, supra,* and *Philadelphia* v. *Fox, supra,* is reflected in decisions of this Court. Our earlier cases dealing with the Compensation Clause did not directly involve the compensation of Justices or name them as parties, and no express reference to the Rule is found. See, *e. g., O'Malley* v. *Woodrough,* 307 U. S. 277 (1939); *O'Donoghue* v. *United States,* 289 U. S. 516 (1933); *Evans* v. *Gore,* 253 U. S. 245 (1920). In *Evans,* however, an action brought by an individual judge in his own behalf, the Court by clear implication dealt with the Rule:

> "Because of the individual relation of the members of this court to the question . . . , we cannot but regret that its solution falls to us . . . . But jurisdiction of the present case cannot be declined or renounced. The plaintiff was entitled by law to invoke our decision on the question as respects his own compensation, in which no other judge can have any direct personal interest; and there was no other appellate tribunal to which under the law he could go." *Id.,* at 247–248.[18]

Dist., 200 Ga. 323, 37 S. E. 2d 322 (1946); *Schward* v. *Ariyoshi,* 57 Haw. 348, 555 P. 2d 1329 (1976); *Higer* v. *Hansen,* 67 Idaho 45, 170 P. 2d 411 (1946); *Gordy* v. *Dennis,* 176 Md. 106, 5 A. 2d 69 (1936); *State ex rel. Gardner* v. *Holm,* 241 Minn. 125, 62 N. W. 2d 52 (1954); *State ex rel. West Jersey Traction Co.* v. *Board of Public Works,* 56 N. J. L. 431, 29 A. 163 (1894); *Long* v. *Watts,* 183 N. C. 99, 110 S. E. 765 (1922); *First American Bank & Trust Co.* v. *Ellwein,* 221 N. W. 2d 509 (N. D.), cert. denied, 419 U. S. 1026 (1974); *McCoy* v. *Handlin,* 35 S. D. 487, 153 N. W. 361 (1915); *Alamo Title Co.* v. *San Antonio Bar Assn.,* 360 S. W. 2d 814 (Tex. Civ. App.), writ ref'd, no rev. error (Tex. 1962).

[17] *E. g., Atkins* v. *United States,* 214 Ct. Cl. 186, 556 F. 2d 1028 (1977), cert. denied, 434 U. S. 1009 (1978); *Pilla* v. *American Bar Assn.,* 542 F. 2d 56 (CA8 1976); *Brinkley* v. *Hassig,* 83 F. 2d 351 (CA10 1936); *United States* v. *Corrigan,* 401 F. Supp. 795 (Wyo. 1975).

[18] *O'Malley* cast doubt on the substantive holding of *Evans,* see n. 31, *infra,* but the fact that the Court reached the issue indicates that it did not question this aspect of the *Evans* opinion.

It would appear, therefore, that this Court so took for granted the continuing validity of the Rule of Necessity that no express reference to it or extended discussion of it was needed.[19]

D

Limited Purpose of Section 455

The objective of § 455 was to deal with the reality of a positive disqualification by reason of an interest or the appearance of possible bias. The House and Senate Reports on § 455 reflect a constant assumption that upon disqualification of a particular judge, another would be assigned to the case. For example:

> "[I]f there is [any] reasonable factual basis for doubting the judge's impartiality, he should disqualify himself *and let another judge preside over the case.*" S. Rep. No. 93–419, p. 5 (1973) (emphasis added); H. R. Rep. No. 93–1453, p. 5 (1973) (emphasis added).

The Reports of the two Houses continued:

> "The statutes contain ample authority for chief judges *to assign other judges* to replace either a circuit or district court judge who become disqualified [under § 455]." S. Rep. No. 93–419, *supra,* at 7 (emphasis added); H. R. Rep. No. 93–1453, *supra,* at 7 (emphasis added).

---

[19] In another, not unrelated context, Chief Justice Marshall's exposition in *Cohens* v. *Virginia,* 6 Wheat. 264 (1821), could well have been the explanation of the Rule of Necessity; he wrote that a court "must take jurisdiction if it should. The judiciary cannot, as the legislature may, avoid a measure because it approaches the confines of the constitution. We cannot pass it by, because it is doubtful. With whatever doubts, with whatever difficulties, a case may be attended, we must decide it, if it be brought before us. *We have no more right to decline the exercise of jurisdiction which is given, than to usurp that which is not given.* The one or the other would be treason to the constitution. Questions may occur which we would gladly avoid; but we cannot avoid them." *Id.,* at 404 (emphasis added).

The congressional purpose so clearly expressed in the Reports gives no hint of altering the ancient Rule of Necessity, a doctrine that had not been questioned under prior judicial disqualification statutes.[20]   The declared purpose of § 455 is to guarantee litigants a fair forum in which they can pursue their claims.   Far from promoting this purpose, failure to apply the Rule of Necessity would have a contrary effect, for without the Rule, some litigants would be denied their right to a forum.   The availability of a forum becomes especially important in these cases.   As this Court has observed elsewhere, the Compensation Clause is designed to benefit, not the judges as individuals, but the public interest in a competent and independent judiciary. *Evans* v. *Gore, supra,* at 253.   The public might be denied resolution of this crucial matter if first the District Judge, and now all the Justices of this Court, were to ignore the mandate of the Rule of Necessity and decline to answer the questions presented.   On balance, the public interest would not be served by requiring disqualification under § 455.

We therefore hold that § 455 was not intended by Congress to alter the time-honored Rule of Necessity.   And we would not casually infer that the Legislative and Executive Branches sought by the enactment of § 455 to foreclose federal courts from exercising "the province and duty of the judicial department to say what the law is." *Marbury* v. *Madison,* 1 Cranch 137, 177 (1803).

III

The Compensation Clause

The Compensation Clause has its roots in the longstanding Anglo-American tradition of an independent Judiciary.   A

---

[20] See Act of Mar. 3, 1911, ch. 231, §§ 20, 21, 36 Stat. 1090 (current version at 28 U. S. C. §§ 144, 455 (1976 ed. and Supp. III)). This statute applied only to district judges, but its existence demonstrates that the Rule of Necessity has continued in force side by side with statutory disqualification standards.

Judiciary free from control by the Executive and the Legislature is essential if there is a right to have claims decided by judges who are free from potential domination by other branches of government. Our Constitution promotes that independence specifically by providing:

> "The Judges, both of the supreme and inferior Courts, shall hold their Offices during good Behaviour, and shall, at stated Times, receive for their Services, a Compensation, which shall not be diminished during their Continuance in Office." Art. III, § 1.

Hamilton, in The Federalist No. 79, p. 491 (1818) (emphasis deleted), emphasized the importance of protecting judicial compensation:

> "In the general course of human nature, a power over a man's subsistence amounts to a power over his will."

The relationship of judges' compensation to their independence was by no means a new idea initiated by the authors of the Constitution. The Act of Settlement in 1701, designed to correct abuses prevalent under the reign of the Stuart Kings, includes a provision that, upon the accession of the successor to then Princess Anne,

> "Judges Commissions be made *Quamdiu se bene gesserint* [during good behavior], and their Salaries ascertained and established . . . ." 12 & 13 Will. III, ch. 2, § III, cl. 7 (1701).

This English statute is the earliest legislative acknowledgment that control over the tenure and compensation of judges is incompatible with a truly independent judiciary, free of improper influence from other forces within government. Later, Parliament passed, and the King assented to, a statute implementing the Act of Settlement providing that a judge's salary would not be decreased "so long as the Patents and Commissions of them, or any of them respectively, shall continue and remain in force." 1 Geo. III, ch. 23, § III (1760). These two statutes were designed "to maintain both the dignity and independence of the judges." 1 W. Blackstone, Commentaries *267.

Originally, these same protections applied to colonial judges as well. In 1761, however, the King converted the tenure of colonial judges to service at his pleasure.[21] The interference this change brought to the administration of justice in the Colonies soon became one of the major objections voiced against the Crown. Indeed, the Declaration of Independence, in listing the grievances against the King, complained:

> "He has made Judges dependent on his Will alone, for the tenure of their offices, and the amount and payment of their salaries."

Independence won, the colonists did not forget the reasons that caused them to separate from the Mother Country. Thus, when the Framers met in Philadelphia in 1787 to draft our organic law, they made certain that in the judicial articles both the tenure and the compensation of judges would be protected from one of the evils that had brought on the Revolution and separation.

Madison's notes of the Constitutional Convention reveal that the draftsmen first reached a tentative arrangement whereby the Congress could neither increase nor decrease the compensation of judges. Later, Gouverneur Morris succeeded in striking the prohibition on increases; with others, he believed the Congress should be at liberty to raise salaries to meet such contingencies as inflation, a phenomenon known in that day as it is in ours. Madison opposed the change on the ground judges might tend to defer unduly to the Congress when that body was considering pay increases.

---

[21] See, *e. g.,* W. Carpenter, Judicial Tenure in the United States 2–3 (1918).

The concern for the ravages of inflation is revealed in Madison's comment:

> "The variations in the value of money, may be guarded agst. by taking for a standard wheat or some other thing of permanent value. 2 M. Farrand, The Records of the Federal Convention of 1787, p. 45 (1911).

Morris criticized the proposal for overlooking changes in the state of the economy; the value of wheat may change, he said, and leave the judges undercompensated. The Convention finally adopted Morris' motion to allow increases by the Congress, thereby accepting a limited risk of external influence in order to accommodate the need to raise judges' salaries when times changed.[22] As Hamilton later explained:

> "It will readily be understood, that the fluctuations in the value of money, and in the state of society, rendered a fixed rate of compensation [of judges] in the Constitution inadmissible. What might be extravagant to-day might in half a century become penurious and inadequate. It was therefore necessary to leave it to the discretion of the legislature to vary its provisions in conformity to the variations in circumstances; yet under such restrictions as to put it out of the power of that body to change the condition of the individual for the worse." The Federalist No. 79, pp. 491–492 (1818).

This Court has recognized that the Compensation Clause

---

[22] The rejection of Madison's suggestion of tying judicial salaries to the price of some commodity may have arisen from colonial Virginia's unsatisfactory experience with a similar scheme for paying the clergy with a set amount of tobacco. See generally L. Gipson, The Coming of the Revolution, 1763–1775, pp. 46–54 (1954); Scott, The Constitutional Aspects of the "Parson's Cause," 31 Pol. Sci. Q. 558 (1916). Although ultimately the tobacco statutes and the subsequent cases are more important as indications of early dissatisfaction with the Crown, the widespread publicity surrounding them surely made the Framers wary of indexing salaries by reference to some commodity.

also serves another, related purpose. As well as promoting judicial independence, it ensures a prospective judge that, in abandoning private practice—more often than not more lucrative than the bench—the compensation of the new post will not diminish. Beyond doubt, such assurance has served to attract able lawyers to the bench and thereby enhances the quality of justice. *Evans* v. *Gore,* 253 U. S., at 253; 1 J. Kent, Commentaries on American Law 276 (1826).

IV

The four statutes now before us present an issue never before addressed by this Court: when, if ever, does the Compensation Clause prohibit the Congress from repealing salary increases that otherwise take effect automatically pursuant to a formula previously enacted? We must decide when a salary increase authorized by Congress under such a formula "vests"—*i. e.,* becomes irreversible under the Compensation Clause. Is the protection of the Clause first invoked when the formula is *enacted* or when increases *take effect?*

A

Appellees argue that we need not reach this constitutional question. They contend that Congress intended these four statutes do no more than halt *funding* for the salary increases under the Adjustment Act. If, as appellees contend, the statutes are appropriations measures that do not alter substantive law, the increases in all four years nevertheless are now in effect and the Government is obliged to pay them; it has simply to authorize that payment. Accordingly, appellees submit, these congressional actions violate the Compensation Clause regardless of whether Congress could have rescinded increases previously passed.

As a general rule, "repeals by implication are not favored." *Posadas* v. *National City Bank,* 296 U. S. 497, 503 (1936). See also *TVA* v. *Hill,* 437 U. S. 153, 189 (1978), and *Morton* v. *Mancari,* 417 U. S. 535, 549 (1974). This rule applies with especial force when the provision advanced as the repealing measure was enacted in an appropriations bill. *TVA v. Hill, supra,* at 190. Indeed, the rules of both Houses limit the ability to change substantive law through appropriations measures. See Senate Standing Rule XVI (4); House of Representatives Rule XXI (2). Nevertheless, when Congress desires to suspend or repeal a statute in force, "[t]here can be no doubt that . . . it could accomplish its purpose by an amendment to an appropriation bill, or otherwise." *United States v. Dickerson,* 310 U. S. 554, 555 (1940). "The whole question depends on the intention of Congress as expressed in the statutes." *United States v. Mitchell,* 109 U. S. 146, 150 (1883). See also *Belknap v. United States,* 150 U. S. 588, 594 (1893).[23]

In the cases now before us, we conclude that in each of the four years in question Congress intended to repeal or postpone previously authorized increases. In the statute for Year 2, Congress expressly stated that the Adjustment Act increase due the following October "shall not take effect." Pub. L. 95–66, 91 Stat. 270. Thus, the plain words of the statute reveal an intention to repeal the Adjustment Act insofar as it would increase salaries in October 1977. This reading finds support in the House Report on the bill, which repeatedly uses language such as "eliminate the expected October 1977 comparability adjustment." See H. R. Rep. No. 95–458, pp. 1, 3 (1977). The floor remarks of Senators and Representatives confirm that this construction was generally understood.[24]

---

[23] Indeed, in both *Mitchell* and *Belknap,* the Court held that provisions in appropriations statutes funding certain officials' salaries at amounts below those established under previous statutes operated to repeal the relevant provisions of those statutes and set new salary levels.

[24] See, *e. g.* 123 Cong. Rec. 7095 (1977) (remarks of Sen. Byrd) ("salaries . . . shall not be increased . . . thus obviat[ing] the effect of the comparability pay provisions"); *ibid.* (remarks of Sen. Baker) ("forgo and rescind that adjustment"); *id.,* at 21121 (remarks of Rep. Solarz)

The statutes in Years 1, 3, and 4, although phrased in terms of limiting funds, see *supra,* at 205–206, 207, 208, nevertheless were intended by Congress to block the increases the Adjustment Act otherwise would generate. Representative Shipley introduced the rider in relation to Year 1 to "preven[t] the automatic cost-of-living pay increase . . . ." 122 Cong. Rec. 28872 (1976).[25] Floor remarks in both Houses reflected this view.[26] In Year 3, the House Report characterized the statute as a "change [in] the application of existing law," H. R. Rep. No. 95–1254, p. 31 (1978), and described its effect as creating a one-year "pay freeze," *id.,* at 35. The Senate Re-

_____

("knock[s] out the comparability increase for this year"); *id.,* at 21125 (remarks of Rep. Ammerman) ("deny the October 1 cost-of-living pay increase").

[25] Representative Shipley's original amendment applied only to Members of the House of Representatives. The provision was expanded to cover all officials subject to the Salary Act. See 122 Cong. Rec. 28877 (1976). The Senate Committee studying the bill recommended the provision be deleted altogether, see S. Rep. No. 94–1201, p. 2 (1976), but the Senate ultimately passed a version applying the freeze to all Members of Congress, see 122 Cong. Rec. 29132–29133 (1976). The Conference Committee recommended that the freeze apply to all Salary Act positions, see H. R. Conf. Rep. No. 94–1559, p. 3 (1976). This recommendation prevailed.

[26] See, *e. g.,* 122 Cong. Rec. 28865 (1976) (remarks of Rep. Armstrong) (a "freeze of the salaries"); *ibid.* (remarks of Rep. Yates) ("freeze the salaries"); *ibid.* (remarks of Rep. McClory) ("effectively eliminate the . . . cost-of-living increases"); *id.,* at 28870 (remarks of Rep. Derwinski) ("freezing . . . pay at its current level"); *id.,* at 28871 (remarks of Rep. Miller) ("stopping the pay raise"); *id.,* at 28879 (remarks of Rep. Anderson) ("block a cost-of-living pay increase"); *id.,* at 29132 (remarks of Sen. Taft) ("effectively freeze those salaries—the employees would not be given a cost-of-living raise on October 1, or a salary increase"); *id.,* at 29164 (remarks of Sen. Allen) ("freezing the compensation"); *id.,* at 29172 (remarks of Sen. Allen) ("denied the upcoming increase"; "salaries frozen at the September 30, 1976, level"); *id.,* at 29372 (remarks of Sen. Bartlett) ("automatic pay raises . . . eliminated"); *id.,* at 31892 (remarks of Rep. Shipley) ("no October cost-of-living increases would be made"; bill "proscribe[s] . . . the October cost-of-living pay increase[s]"); *id.,* at 31896 (remarks of Rep. Riegle) ("elimination of the cost-of-living raise").

port stated that the statute would "continu[e] . . . the so called 'cap' " on salaries for the next fiscal year. S. Rep. No. 95–1024, p. 50 (1978). Floor debate once again expressed agreement with this construction.[27] The House Report on the statute for Year 4 characterized it as "reduc[ing] Federal executive pay increases from the mandatory entitlement of 12.9 per centum to 5.5 per centum." H. R. Rep. No. 96–500, p. 7 (1979). The Report referred to the bill as a change in existing law. See id., at 3. Later the Conference Report stated that the statute "restricts Cost-of-Living increases to 5.5 percent" for the fiscal year just begun. H. R. Conf. Rep. No. 96–513, p. 3 (1979). The floor debates also confirm this understanding.[28]

These passages indicate clearly that Congress intended to rescind these raises entirely, not simply to consign them to the fiscal limbo of an account due but not payable. The clear intent of Congress in each year was to stop for that year the application of the Adjustment Act. The issue thus resolves itself into whether Congress could do so without violating the Compensation Clause.

B

Year 1

The statute applying to Year 1 was signed by the President during the business day of October 1, 1976. By that time, the 4.8% increase under the Adjustment Act already had

---

[27] See, e. g., 124 Cong. Rec. 17603 (1978) (remarks of Rep. Shipley) ("pay freeze"); id., at 17604 (remarks of Rep. Armstrong) ("automatic cost-of-living increases will not be permitted"); id., at 24375 (remarks of Sen. Sasser) ("freeze, during fiscal year 1979, the pay").

[28] See, e. g., 125 Cong. Rec. 27532 (1979) (remarks of Rep. Whitten) ("sharply decreas[es] such automatic increases"); id., at 27533 (remarks of Rep. Jacobs) ("rollback of the automatic 12.9-percent salary increase"); id., at 28019 (remarks of Sen. Byrd) ("put a cap on that pay increase"); id., at 28020 (remarks of Sen. Magnuson) ("this is in the nature of a cap, a limitation"); id., at 28108 (remarks of Rep. Conte) ("reduces from 12.9 to 5.5 percent the increase in pay").

taken effect, since it was operative with the start of the month—and the new fiscal year—at the beginning of the day. The statute became law only upon the President's signing it on October 1; it therefore purported to repeal a salary increase already in force. Thus it "diminished" the compensation of federal judges.[29]

---

[29] The Government asks us to invoke the rule that the law does not recognize fractions of a day, see, *e. g., Lapeyre* v. *United States,* 17 Wall. 191 (1873); it is argued that we should treat the President's assent as having been given at the start of October 1, the same time the Year 1 increase was to take effect. It is correct that "the law generally reject[s] all fractions of a day, in order to avoid disputes." 2 W. Blackstone, Commentaries *141. Here, however, the Government acknowledges that the statute was signed by the President *after* the Year 1 increase had taken effect. This Court, almost a century ago, stated:

" '[W]henever it becomes important to the ends of justice, or in order to decide upon conflicting interests, the law will look into fractions of a day, as readily as into the fractions of any other unit of time. The rule is purely one of convenience, which must give way whenever the rights of parties require it. . . . The law is not made of such unreasonable and arbitrary rules.' " *Louisville* v. *Savings Bank,* 104 U. S. 469, 474–475 (1881) (quoting *Grosvenor* v. *Magill,* 37 Ill. 239, 240–241 (1865); citations omitted).

Accord, *Combe* v. *Pitt,* 3 Burr. 1423, 97 Eng. Rep. 907 (K. B. 1763); 2 C. Sands, Sutherland on Statutory Construction § 33.10 (4th ed. 1973).

In *Burgess* v. *Salmon,* 97 U. S. 381 (1878), this Court was required to look to the time of day when a statute was enacted as compared to another and related event. This Court held that, notwithstanding the general rule, a person could not be subjected to a civil fine for violating a statute passed on the same day he engaged in the conduct but after that conduct had occurred. To impose a penalty on an act innocent when performed would render the statute an *ex post facto* law. *Id.,* at 384–385. Thus *Burgess* dealt not so much with benefits and penalties as it did with constitutional limitations on the legislative authority of Congress and the Executive. In the context of periodic increases, the Compensation Clause, like the *Ex Post Facto* Clause of Art. I, § 9, places limits on Congress and the President. Because of the constitutional implications, the logic of *Burgess* applies to the statute for Year 1 and requires us to look to the precise time the statute became law by the President's action.

The Government contends that Congress could reduce compensation as long as it did not "discriminate" against judges, as such, during the process. That the "freeze" applied to various officials in the Legislative and the Executive Branches, as well as judges, does not save the statute, however. This is quite different from the situation in *O'Malley* v. *Woodrough*, 307 U. S. 277 (1939). There the Court held that the Compensation Clause was not offended by an income tax levied on Article III judges as well as on all other taxpayers; there was no discrimination against the plaintiff judge. Federal judges, like all citizens, must share "the material burden of the government . . . ." *Id.*, at 282. The inclusion in the freeze of other officials who are not protected by the Compensation Clause does not insulate a direct diminution in judges' salaries from the clear mandate of that Clause; the Constitution makes no exceptions for "nondiscriminatory" reductions.[30] Accordingly, we hold that the statute with respect to Year 1, as applied to compensation of members of the certified class, violates the Compensation Clause of Art. III.

Year 2

Unlike the statute for Year 1, the statute for Year 2 was signed by the President before October 1, when the 7.1% raise under the Comparability Act was due to take effect. Year 2 thus confronts us squarely with the question of whether Congress may, before the effective date of a salary increase, rescind such an increase scheduled to take effect at a later date. The District Court held that by including an annual cost-of-living adjustment in the statutory definitions of the salaries of Article III judges, see *supra*, at 204, and n. 2, Congress made the annual adjustment, from that moment on,

---

[30] We need not address the question of whether evidence of an intent to influence the Judiciary would invalidate a statute that on its face does not directly reduce judicial compensation. See *Evans* v. *Gore*, 253 U. S. 245, 252 (1920).

a part of judges' compensation for constitutional purposes. Subsequent action reducing those adjustments "diminishes" compensation within the meaning of the Compensation Clause. Relying on *Evans* v. *Gore,* 253 U. S., at 254, the District Court held that such action reduces the amount "a judge . . . has been promised," and all amounts thus promised fall within the protection of the Clause.

We are unable to agree with the District Court's analysis and result. Our discussion of the Framers' debates over the Compensation Clause, *supra,* at 219–220, led to a conclusion that the Compensation Clause does not erect an absolute ban on all legislation that conceivably could have an adverse effect on compensation of judges.[31] Rather, that provision embodies a clear rule prohibiting decreases but allowing increases, a practical balancing by the Framers of the need to increase compensation to meet economic changes, such as substantial inflation, against the need for judges to be free from undue congressional influence. The Constitution delegated to Congress the discretion to fix salaries and of necessity placed faith in the integrity and sound judgment of the elected representatives to enact increases when changing conditions demand.

Congress enacted the Adjustment Act based on this delegated power to fix and, periodically, increase judicial compensation. It did not thereby alter the *compensation* of judges; it modified only the *formula* for determining that compensation. Later, Congress decided to abandon the for-

---

[31] In *O'Malley* v. *Woodrough,* 307 U. S. 277 (1939), this Court held that the immunity in the Compensation Clause would not extend to exempting judges from paying taxes, a duty shared by all citizens. The Court thus recognized that the Compensation Clause does not forbid everything that might adversely affect judges. The opinion concluded by saying that to the extent *Miles* v. *Graham,* 268 U. S. 501 (1925), was inconsistent, it "cannot survive." 307 U. S., at 282–283. Because *Miles* relied on *Evans* v. *Gore, O'Malley* must also be read to undermine the reasoning of *Evans,* on which the District Court relied in reaching its decision.

mula as to the particular years in question. For Year 2, as opposed to Year 1, the statute was passed before the Adjustment Act increases had taken effect—before they had become a part of the compensation due Article III judges. Thus, the departure from the Adjustment Act policy in no sense diminished the compensation Article III judges were receiving; it refused only to apply a previously enacted formula.[32]

A paramount—indeed, an indispensable—ingredient of the concept of powers delegated to coequal branches is that each branch must recognize and respect the limits on its own authority and the boundaries of the authority delegated to the other branches. To say that the Congress could not alter a method of calculating salaries before it was executed would mean the Judicial Branch could command Congress to carry out an announced future intent as to a decision the Constitution vests exclusively in the Congress.[33] We therefore conclude

---

[32] *United States* v. *More* (CC DC 1803), writ of error dism'd for want of jurisdiction, 3 Cranch 159 (1805), is not to the contrary. Congress had enacted a system of fees for compensating justices of the peace in the District of Columbia but subsequently abolished the fees. The Government brought an indictment against a justice of the peace who had continued to charge the fees, and the defendant demurred. The Circuit Court for the District of Columbia held that the compensation of justices of the peace in the District of Columbia was subject to the Compensation Clause and that a statute diminishing (here, abolishing) the fees violated the Constitution. *Id.,* at 161, n. In *More,* the fee system was already in place as part of the justices' compensation when Congress repealed it. Here, by contrast, the increase in Year 2 had not yet become part of the compensation of Article III judges when the statute repealing it was passed and signed by the President.

[33] Indeed, it would be particularly ironic if we were to bind Congress to an indexing scheme for salaries when the Framers themselves rejected an indexing proposal. See *supra,* at 220. Of course, indexing techniques have improved since 1787. Nevertheless, Congress' repeated rejections of specific adjustments indicates some dissatisfaction with automatic adjustments according to a predetermined formula, even if not with the formula itself.

that a salary increase "vests" for purposes of the Compensation Clause only when it takes effect as part of the compensation due and payable to Article III judges. With regard to Year 2, we hold that the Compensation Clause did not prohibit Congress from repealing the planned but not yet effective cost-of-living adjustment of October 1, 1977, when it did so before October 1, the time it first was scheduled to become part of judges' compensation. The statute in Year 2 thus represents a constitutionally valid exercise of legislative authority.

Year 3

For our purposes, the legal issues presented by the statute in Year 3 are indistinguishable from those in Year 2. Each statute eliminated—before October 1—the Adjustment Act salary increases contemplated but not yet implemented. Each statute was passed and signed by the President *before* the Adjustment Act increases took effect, in the case of Year 3, on September 30. For the reasons set forth in our discussion of the issues for Year 2, we hold that the statute in Year 3 did not violate the Compensation Clause.

Year 4

Before reaching the constitutional issues implicated in Year 4, we must resolve a problem of statutory construction. On its face, the statute in Year 4 applies in terms to "executive employees, which includes Members of Congress." See *supra*, at 208. It does not expressly mention judges. Appellees contend that even if Congress constitutionally could freeze the salaries of Article III judges, it did not do so in this statute.

We are satisfied that Congress' use of the phrase "executive employees," in context, was intended to include Article III judges. The full title of the Adjustment Act is the *Executive Salary Cost-of-Living Adjustment Act*, but it is clear that it was intended to apply to officials in the Legislative and the

Judicial Branches as well.[34] The title does not control over
the terms of the statute. The statutes in the three preceding years undeniably applied to judges, and we can discern
no indication that the Congress chose to single them out for
an exemption when it was including Executive and Legislative officials. Most important, both the Conference Report
and the Chairman of the House Appropriations Committee,
speaking on the floor, made explicit what already was implicit: the limiting statute would apply to judges as well.
See H. R. Conf. Rep. No. 96–513, p. 3 (1979); 125 Cong.
Rec. 27530, 27532 (1979) (remarks of Rep. Whitten).[35]

Having concluded that the statute in Year 4 was intended
to apply to judges as well as other high-level federal officials,
we are confronted with a situation similar to that in Year 1.
Here again, the statute purported to revoke an increase in
judges' compensation *after* those statutes had taken effect.
For the reasons governing the statute as to Year 1, we hold
that the statute revoking the increase for Year 4 violated the
Compensation Clause insofar as it applied to members of the
certified class.

V

The District Court has not yet calculated the precise dollar amounts involved in Years 1 and 4, the years in which
we hold the statutes violated the Compensation Clause. Further proceedings are required to resolve these questions.
Accordingly, the judgment of the District Court in No. 79–983

---

[34] Most positions covered, of course, are in the Executive Branch, which
may explain the limited title.

[35] Several Members of Congress acknowledged the potential constitutional problem with rolling back the salary increase already in effect for
judges. See 125 Cong. Rec. 27529–27530 (1979) (remarks of Rep. Latta);
id., at 27531–27533 (remarks of Rep. Whitten); *id.,* at 27533 (remarks
of Rep. Jacobs); *id.,* at 28022 (remarks of Sen. Stevens). Representative
Whitten, the Chairman of the House Appropriations Committee, stated
that "the courts will have to make a final determination regarding this
issue." *Id.,* at 27532.

is affirmed in part and reversed in part, the judgment in No. 79-1689 is affirmed in part and reversed in part, and the cases are remanded for further proceedings consistent with this opinion.

It is so ordered.

PART II

FREEDOM OF COMMUNICATION

1. ORGANIZATION FOR A BETTER AUSTIN et al. v. KEEFE (1971).

2. PARIS ADULT THEATRE I et al. v. SLATON, DISTRICT ATTORNEY, et al. (1973).

3. MILLER v. CALIFORNIA (1973).

4. COLUMBIA BROADCASTING SYSTEM, INC. v. DEMOCRATIC NATIONAL COMMITTEE (1973).

5. GOLDFARB et ux. v. VIRGINIA STATE BAR et al. (1975).

6. RICHMOND NEWSPAPERS, INC. et al. v. VIRGINIA et al. (1980).

7. CBS, INC. v. FEDERAL COMMUNICATIONS COMMISSION et al. (1981).

—oOo—

ORGANIZATION FOR A BETTER AUSTIN
ET AL. *v.* KEEFE

CERTIORARI TO THE APPELLATE COURT OF ILLINOIS, FIRST DISTRICT

No. 135.   Argued January 20, 1971—Decided May 17, 1971

Respondent real estate broker applied for and obtained from the Illinois courts an injunction enjoining petitioners from distributing any literature in the City of Westchester, on the ground that their leaflets, critical of respondent's alleged "blockbusting" and "panic peddling" activities in the Austin area of Chicago, invaded respondent's right of privacy, and were coercive and intimidating rather than informative, thus not being entitled to First Amendment protection. *Held:* Respondent has not met the heavy burden of justifying the imposition of the prior restraint of petitioners' peaceful distribution of informational literature of the nature disclosed by this record.   Pp. 418–420.

115 Ill. App. 2d 236, 253 N. E. 2d 76, reversed.

BURGER, C. J., delivered the opinion of the Court in which BLACK, DOUGLAS, BRENNAN, STEWART, WHITE, MARSHALL, and BLACKMUN, JJ., joined.   HARLAN, J., filed a dissenting opinion, *post,* p. 420.

David C. Long argued the cause for petitioners.   With him on the briefs was *Willard J. Lassers.*

Thomas W. McNamara argued the cause for respondent.   With him on the brief was *John C. Tucker.*

MR. CHIEF JUSTICE BURGER delivered the opinion of the Court.

We granted the writ in this case to consider the claim that an order of the Circuit Court of Cook County, Illinois, enjoining petitioners from distributing leaflets anywhere in the town of Westchester, Illinois, violates petitioners' rights under the Federal Constitution.

Petitioner Organization for a Better Austin (OBA) is a racially integrated community organization in the

Austin neighborhood of Chicago. Respondent is a real estate broker whose office and business activities are in the Austin neighborhood. He resides in Westchester, Illinois, a suburb of Chicago some seven miles from the Austin area.

OBA is an organization whose stated purpose is to "stabilize" the racial ratio in the Austin area. For a number of years the boundary of the Negro segregated area of Chicago has moved progressively west to Austin. OBA, in its efforts to "stabilize" the area—so it describes its program—has opposed and protested various real estate tactics and activities generally known as "blockbusting" or "panic peddling."

It was the contention of OBA that respondent had been one of those who engaged in such tactics, specifically that he aroused the fears of the local white residents that Negroes were coming into the area and then, exploiting the reactions and emotions so aroused, was able to secure listings and sell homes to Negroes. OBA alleged that since 1961 respondent had from time to time actively promoted sales in this manner by means of flyers, phone calls, and personal visits to residents of the area in which his office is located, without regard to whether the persons solicited had expressed any desire to sell their homes. As the "boundary" marking the furthest westward advance of Negroes moved into the Austin area, respondent is alleged to have moved his office along with it.

Community meetings were arranged with respondent to try to persuade him to change his real estate practices. Several other real estate agents were prevailed on to sign an agreement whereby they would not solicit property, by phone, flyer, or visit, in the Austin community. Respondent who has consistently denied that he is engaging in "panic peddling" or "blockbusting" refused to sign, contending that it was his right under Illinois law to solicit real estate business as he saw fit.

Thereafter, during September and October of 1967, members of petitioner organization distributed leaflets in Westchester describing respondent's activities. There was no evidence of picketing in Westchester. The challenged publications, now enjoined, were critical of respondent's real estate practices in the Austin neighborhood; one of the leaflets set out the business card respondent used to solicit listings, quoted him as saying "I only sell to Negroes," cited a Chicago Daily News article describing his real estate activities and accused him of being a "panic peddler." Another leaflet, of the same general order, stated that: "When he signs the agreement, we stop coming to Westchester." Two of the leaflets requested recipients to call respondent at his home phone number and urge him to sign the "no solicitation" agreement. On several days leaflets were given to persons in a Westchester shopping center. On two other occasions leaflets were passed out to some parishioners on their way to or from respondent's church in Westchester. Leaflets were also left at the doors of his neighbors. The trial court found that petitioners' "distribution of leaflets was on all occasions conducted in a peaceful and orderly manner, did not cause any disruption of pedestrian or vehicular traffic, and did not precipitate any fights, disturbances or other breaches of the peace." One of the officers of OBA testified at trial that he hoped that respondent would be induced to sign the no-solicitation agreement by letting "his neighbors know what he was doing to us."

Respondent sought an injunction in the Circuit Court of Cook County, Illinois, on December 20, 1967. After an adversary hearing the trial court entered a temporary injunction enjoining petitioners "from passing out pamphlets, leaflets or literature of any kind, and from picketing, anywhere in the City of Westchester, Illinois."

223

On appeal to the Appellate Court of Illinois, First District, that court affirmed. It sustained the finding of fact that petitioners' activities in Westchester had invaded respondent's right of privacy, had caused irreparable harm, and were without adequate remedy at law. The Appellate Court appears to have viewed the alleged activities as coercive and intimidating, rather than informative and therefore as not entitled to First Amendment protection. The Appellate Court rested its holding on its belief that the public policy of the State of Illinois strongly favored protection of the privacy of home and family from encroachment of the nature of petitioners' activities.*

It is elementary, of course, that in a case of this kind the courts do not concern themselves with the truth or validity of the publication. Under *Near* v. *Minnesota,* 283 U. S. 697 (1931), the injunction, so far as it imposes prior restraint on speech and publication, constitutes an impermissible restraint on First Amendment rights. Here, as in that case, the injunction operates, not to redress alleged private wrongs, but to suppress, on the

---

*The injunction is termed a "temporary" injunction by the Illinois courts. We have therefore considered whether we may properly decide this case. 28 U. S. C. § 1257. We see nothing in the record that would indicate that the Illinois courts applied a less rigorous standard in issuing and sustaining this injunction than they would with any permanent injunction in the case. Nor is there any indication that the injunction rests on a disputed question of fact that might be resolved differently upon further hearing. Indeed, our reading of the record leads to the conclusion that the issuance of a permanent injunction upon termination of these proceedings will be little more than a formality. Moreover, the temporary injunction here, which has been in effect for over three years, has already had marked impact on petitioners' First Amendment rights. Although the record in this case is not such as to leave the matter entirely free from doubt we conclude we are not without power to decide this case. *Mills* v. *Alabama,* 384 U. S. 214 (1966); *Construction Laborers' Local 438* v. *Curry,* 371 U. S. 542 (1963).

basis of previous publications, distribution of literature "of any kind" in a city of 18,000.

This Court has often recognized that the activity of peaceful pamphleteering is a form of communication protected by the First Amendment. *E. g., Martin* v. *City of Struthers,* 319 U. S. 141 (1943); *Schneider* v. *State,* 308 U. S. 147 (1939); *Lovell* v. *Griffin,* 303 U. S. 444 (1938). In sustaining the injunction, however, the Appellate Court was apparently of the view that petitioners' purpose in distributing their literature was not to inform the public, but to "force" respondent to sign a no-solicitation agreement. The claim that the expressions were intended to exercise a coercive impact on respondent does not remove them from the reach of the First Amendment. Petitioners plainly intended to influence respondent's conduct by their activities; this is not fundamentally different from the function of a newspaper. See *Schneider* v. *State, supra; Thornhill* v. *Alabama,* 310 U. S. 88 (1940). Petitioners were engaged openly and vigorously in making the public aware of respondent's real estate practices. Those practices were offensive to them, as the views and practices of petitioners are no doubt offensive to others. But so long as the means are peaceful, the communication need not meet standards of acceptability.

Any prior restraint on expression comes to this Court with a "heavy presumption" against its constitutional validity. *Carroll* v. *Princess Anne,* 393 U. S. 175, 181 (1968); *Bantam Books, Inc.* v. *Sullivan,* 372 U. S. 58, 70 (1963). Respondent thus carries a heavy burden of showing justification for the imposition of such a restraint. He has not met that burden. No prior decisions support the claim that the interest of an individual in being free from public criticism of his business practices in pamphlets or leaflets warrants use of the injunctive power of a court. Designating the conduct as an invasion of privacy, the apparent basis for the injunction here, is not sufficient to support an injunction against peaceful distribution of informational literature of the nature revealed by this record. *Rowan* v. *United States Post Office Dept.*, 397 U. S. 728 (1970), relied on by respondent, is not in point; the right of privacy involved in that case is not shown here. Among other important distinctions, respondent is not attempting to stop the flow of information into his own household, but to the public. Accordingly, the injunction issued by the Illinois court must be vacated.

Reversed.

PARIS ADULT THEATRE I et al. *v.* SLATON, DISTRICT ATTORNEY, et al.

CERTIORARI TO THE SUPREME COURT OF GEORGIA

No. 71–1051. Argued October 19, 1972—Decided June 21, 1973

Respondents sued under Georgia civil law to enjoin the exhibiting by petitioners of two allegedly obscene films. There was no prior restraint. In a jury-waived trial, the trial court (which did not require "expert" affirmative evidence of obscenity) viewed the films and thereafter dismissed the complaints on the ground that the display of the films in commercial theaters to consenting adult audiences (reasonable precautions having been taken to exclude minors) was "constitutionally permissible." The Georgia Supreme Court reversed, holding that the films constituted "hard core" pornography not within the protection of the First Amendment. *Held:*

   1. Obscene material is not speech entitled to First Amendment protection. *Miller* v. *California, ante,* p. 15; *Roth* v. *United States,* 354 U. S. 476. P. 54.

   2. The Georgia civil procedure followed here (assuming use of a constitutionally acceptable standard for determining what is unprotected by the First Amendment) comported with the standards of *Teitel Film Corp.* v. *Cusack,* 390 U. S. 139; *Freedman* v. *Maryland,* 380 U. S. 51; and *Kingsley Books, Inc.* v. *Brown,* 354 U. S. 436. Pp. 54–55.

   3. It was not error to fail to require expert affirmative evidence of the films' obscenity, since the films (which were the best evidence of what they depicted) were themselves placed in evidence. P. 56.

   4. States have a legitimate interest in regulating commerce in obscene material and its exhibition in places of public accommodation, including "adult" theaters. Pp. 57–69.

   (a) There is a proper state concern with safeguarding against crime and the other arguably ill effects of obscenity by prohibiting the public or commercial exhibition of obscene material. Though conclusive proof is lacking, the States may reasonably determine that a nexus does or might exist between antisocial behavior and obscene material, just as States have acted on unprovable assumptions in other areas of public control. Pp. 57–63.

   (b) Though States are free to adopt a laissez-faire policy toward commercialized obscenity, they are not constitutionally obliged to do so. P. 64.

(c) Exhibition of obscene material in places of public accommodation is not protected by any constitutional doctrine of privacy. A commercial theater cannot be equated with a private home; nor is there here a privacy right arising from a special relationship, such as marriage. *Stanley* v. *Georgia*, 394 U. S. 557; *Griswold* v. *Connecticut*, 381 U. S. 479, distinguished. Nor can the privacy of the home be equated with a "zone" of "privacy" that follows a consumer of obscene materials wherever he goes. *United States* v. *Orito, post,* p. 139; *United States* v. *12 200-ft. Reels of Film, post,* p. 123. Pp. 65–67.

(d) Preventing the unlimited display of obscene material is not thought control. Pp. 67–68.

(e) Not all conduct directly involving "consenting adults" only has a claim to constitutional protection. Pp. 68–69.

5. The Georgia obscenity laws involved herein should now be re-evaluated in the light of the First Amendment standards newly enunciated by the Court in *Miller* v. *California, ante,* p. 15. Pp. 69–70.

228 Ga. 343, 185 S. E. 2d 768, vacated and remanded.

BURGER, C. J., delivered the opinion of the Court, in which WHITE, BLACKMUN, POWELL, and REHNQUIST, JJ., joined. DOUGLAS, J., filed a dissenting opinion, *post,* p. 70. BRENNAN, J., filed a dissenting opinion, in which STEWART and MARSHALL, JJ., joined, *post,* p. 73.

Robert Eugene Smith argued the cause for petitioners. With him on the brief were *Mel S. Friedman* and *D. Freeman Hutton.*

Thomas E. Moran argued the cause for respondents. With him on the brief was *Joel M. Feldman.**

MR. CHIEF JUSTICE BURGER delivered the opinion of the Court.

Petitioners are two Atlanta, Georgia, movie theaters and their owners and managers, operating in the

---

**Charles H. Keating, Jr.,* pro se, *Richard M. Bertsch, James J. Clancy,* and *Albert S. Johnston III* filed a brief for Charles H. Keating, Jr., as *amicus curiae* urging affirmance.

style of "adult" theaters. On December 28, 1970, respondents, the local state district attorney and the solicitor for the local state trial court, filed civil complaints in that court alleging that petitioners were exhibiting to the public for paid admission two allegedly obscene films, contrary to Georgia Code Ann. § 26–2101.[1] The two films in question, "Magic Mirror" and "It All Comes Out in the End," depict sexual conduct char-

---

[1] This is a civil proceeding. Georgia Code Ann. § 26–2101 defines a criminal offense, but the exhibition of materials found to be "obscene" as defined by that statute may be enjoined in a civil proceeding under Georgia case law. *1024 Peachtree Corp.* v. *Slaton,* 228 Ga. 102, 184 S. E. 2d 144 (1971); *Walter* v. *Slaton,* 227 Ga. 676, 182 S. E. 2d 464 (1971); *Evans Theatre Corp.* v. *Slaton,* 227 Ga. 377, 180 S. E. 2d 712 (1971). See *infra,* at 54. Georgia Code Ann. § 26–2101 reads in relevant part:

"Distributing obscene materials.

"(a) A person commits the offense of distributing obscene materials when he sells, lends, rents, leases, gives, advertises, publishes, exhibits or otherwise disseminates to any person any obscene material of any description, knowing the obscene nature thereof, or who offers to do so, or who possesses such material with the intent so to do . . . .

"(b) Material is obscene if considered as a whole, applying community standards, its predominant appeal is to prurient interest, that is, a shameful or morbid interest in nudity, sex or excretion, and utterly without redeeming social value and if, in addition, it goes substantially beyond customary limits of candor in describing or representing such matters. . . .

.   .   .   .   .

"(d) A person convicted of distributing obscene material shall for the first offense be punished as for a misdemeanor, and for any subsequent offense shall be punished by imprisonment for not less than one nor more than five years, or by a fine not to exceed $5,000, or both."

The constitutionality of Georgia Code Ann. § 26–2101 was upheld against First Amendment and due process challenges in *Gable* v. *Jenkins,* 309 F. Supp. 998 (ND Ga. 1969), aff'd *per curiam,* 397 U. S. 592 (1970).

acterized by the Georgia Supreme Court as "hard core pornography" leaving "little to the imagination."

Respondents' complaints, made on behalf of the State of Georgia, demanded that the two films be declared obscene and that petitioners be enjoined from exhibiting the films. The exhibition of the films was not enjoined, but a temporary injunction was granted *ex parte* by the local trial court, restraining petitioners from destroying the films or removing them from the jurisdiction. Petitioners were further ordered to have one print each of the films in court on January 13, 1971, together with the proper viewing equipment.

On January 13, 1971, 15 days after the proceedings began, the films were produced by petitioners at a jury-waived trial. Certain photographs, also produced at trial, were stipulated to portray the single entrance to both Paris Adult Theatre I and Paris Adult Theatre II as it appeared at the time of the complaints. These photographs show a conventional, inoffensive theater entrance, without any pictures, but with signs indicating that the theaters exhibit "Atlanta's Finest Mature Feature Films." On the door itself is a sign saying: "Adult Theatre—You must be 21 and able to prove it. If viewing the nude body offends you, Please Do Not Enter."

The two films were exhibited to the trial court. The only other state evidence was testimony by criminal investigators that they had paid admission to see the films and that nothing on the outside of the theater indicated the full nature of what was shown. In particular, nothing indicated that the films depicted—as they did—scenes of simulated fellatio, cunnilingus, and group sex intercourse. There was no evidence presented that minors had ever entered the theaters. Nor was there evidence presented that petitioners had a systematic policy of barring minors, apart from posting signs at the entrance. On April 12, 1971, the trial judge dismissed respondents' complaints. He assumed "that obscenity is established," but stated:

> "It appears to the Court that the display of these films in a commercial theatre, when surrounded by requisite notice to the public of their nature and by reasonable protection against the exposure of these films to minors, is constitutionally permissible."

On appeal, the Georgia Supreme Court unanimously reversed. It assumed that the adult theaters in question barred minors and gave a full warning to the general public of the nature of the films shown, but held that the films were without protection under the First Amendment. Citing the opinion of this Court in *United States* v. *Reidel,* 402 U. S. 351 (1971), the Georgia court stated that "the sale and delivery of obscene material to willing adults is not protected under the first amendment." The Georgia court also held *Stanley* v. *Georgia,* 394 U. S. 557 (1969), to be inapposite since it did not deal with "the commercial distribution of pornography, but with the right of Stanley to possess, in the privacy of his home, pornographic films." 228 Ga. 343, 345, 185 S. E. 2d 768, 769 (1971). After viewing the films, the Georgia Supreme Court held that their exhibition should have been enjoined, stating:

> "The films in this case leave little to the imagination. It is plain what they purport to depict, that is, conduct of the most salacious character. We hold that these films are also hard core pornography, and the showing of such films should have been enjoined since their exhibition is not protected by the first amendment." *Id.,* at 347, 185 S. E. 2d, at 770.

I

It should be clear from the outset that we do not undertake to tell the States what they must do, but rather to define the area in which they may chart their own course in dealing with obscene material. This Court has consistently held that obscene material is not protected by the First Amendment as a limitation on the state police power by virtue of the Fourteenth Amendment. *Miller* v. *California, ante,* at 23–25; *Kois* v. *Wisconsin,* 408 U. S. 229, 230 (1972); *United States* v. *Reidel, supra,* at 354; *Roth* v. *United States,* 354 U. S. 476, 485 (1957).

Georgia case law permits a civil injunction of the exhibition of obscene materials. See *1024 Peachtree Corp.* v. *Slaton,* 228 Ga. 102, 184 S. E. 2d 144 (1971); *Walter* v. *Slaton,* 227 Ga. 676, 182 S. E. 2d 464 (1971); *Evans Theatre Corp.* v. *Slaton,* 227 Ga. 377, 180 S. E. 2d 712 (1971). While this procedure is civil in nature, and does not directly involve the state criminal statute proscribing exhibition of obscene material,[2] the Georgia case law permitting civil injunction does adopt the definition of "obscene materials" used by the criminal statute.[3] Today, in *Miller* v. *California, supra,* we have

_____

[2] See Georgia Code Ann. § 26–2101, set out *supra,* at 51 n. 1.

[3] In *Walter* v. *Slaton,* 227 Ga. 676, 182 S. E. 2d 464 (1971), the Georgia Supreme Court described the cases before it as follows: "Each case was commenced as a civil action by the District Attorney of the Superior Court of Fulton County jointly with the Solicitor of the Criminal Court of Fulton County. In each case the plaintiffs alleged that the defendants named therein were conducting a business of exhibiting motion picture films to members of the public; that they were in control and possession of the described motion picture film which they were exhibiting to the public on a fee basis; that said film 'constitutes a flagrant violation of Ga. Code § 26–2101 in that the sole and dominant theme of the motion picture film . . . considered as a whole, and applying contemporary standards, appeals to the prurient interest in sex and nudity, and that said motion picture film is utterly and absolutely without any redeeming social value whatsoever and transgresses beyond the customary limits of candor in describing and discussing sexual matters.' " *Id.,* at 676–677, 182 S. E. 2d, at 465.

sought to clarify the constitutional definition of obscene material subject to regulation by the States, and we vacate and remand this case for reconsideration in light of *Miller.*

This is not to be read as disapproval of the Georgia civil procedure employed in this case, assuming the use of a constitutionally acceptable standard for determining what is unprotected by the First Amendment. On the contrary, such a procedure provides an exhibitor or purveyor of materials the best possible notice, prior to any criminal indictments, as to whether the materials are unprotected by the First Amendment and subject to state regulation.[4] See *Kingsley Books, Inc.* v. *Brown,* 354 U. S. 436, 441–444 (1957). Here, Georgia imposed no restraint on the exhibition of the films involved in this case until after a full adversary proceeding and a final judicial determination by the Georgia Supreme Court that the materials were constitutionally unprotected.[5] Thus the standards of *Blount* v. *Rizzi,* 400 U. S. 410, 417 (1971); *Teitel Film Corp.* v. *Cusack,* 390 U. S. 139, 141–142 (1968); *Freedman* v. *Maryland,* 380 U. S. 51, 58–59 (1965), and *Kingsley Books, Inc.* v. *Brown, supra,* at 443–445, were met. Cf. *United States* v. *Thirty-seven Photographs,* 402 U. S. 363, 367–369 (1971) (opinion of WHITE, J.).

---

[4] This procedure would have even more merit if the exhibitor or purveyor could also test the issue of obscenity in a similar civil action, prior to any exposure to criminal penalty. We are not here presented with the problem of whether a holding that materials were not obscene could be circumvented in a later proceeding by evidence of pandering. See *Memoirs* v. *Massachusetts,* 383 U. S. 413, 458 n. 3 (1966) (Harlan, J., dissenting); *Ginzburg* v. *United States,* 383 U. S. 463, 496 (1966) (Harlan, J., dissenting).

[5] At the specific request of petitioners' counsel, the copies of the films produced for the trial court were placed in the "administrative custody" of that court pending the outcome of this litigation.

Nor was it error to fail to require "expert" affirmative evidence that the materials were obscene when the materials themselves were actually placed in evidence. *United States* v. *Groner,* 479 F. 2d 577, 579–586 (CA5 1973); *id.,* at 586–588 (Ainsworth, J., concurring); *id.,* at 588–589 (Clark, J., concurring); *United States* v. *Wild,* 422 F. 2d 34, 35–36 (CA2 1969), cert. denied, 402 U. S. 986 (1971); *Kahm* v. *United States,* 300 F. 2d 78, 84 (CA5), cert. denied, 369 U. S. 859 (1962); *State* v. *Amato,* 49 Wis. 2d 638, 645, 183 N. W. 2d 29, 32 (1971), cert. denied *sub nom. Amato* v. *Wisconsin,* 404 U. S. 1063 (1972). See *Smith* v. *California,* 361 U. S. 147, 172 (1959) (Harlan, J., concurring and dissenting); *United States* v. *Brown,* 328 F. Supp. 196, 199 (ED Va. 1971). The films, obviously, are the best evidence of what they represent.[6] "In the cases in which this Court has decided obscenity questions since *Roth,* it has regarded the materials as sufficient in themselves for the determination of the question." *Ginzburg* v. *United States,* 383 U. S. 463, 465 (1966).

---

[6] This is not a subject that lends itself to the traditional use of expert testimony. Such testimony is usually admitted for the purpose of explaining to lay jurors what they otherwise could not understand. Cf. 2 J. Wigmore, Evidence §§ 556, 559 (3d ed. 1940). No such assistance is needed by jurors in obscenity cases; indeed the "expert witness" practices employed in these cases have often made a mockery out of the otherwise sound concept of expert testimony. See *United States* v. *Groner,* 479 F. 2d 577, 585–586 (CA5 1973); *id.,* at 587–588 (Ainsworth, J., concurring). "Simply stated, hard core pornography . . . can and does speak for itself." *United States* v. *Wild,* 422 F. 2d 34, 36 (CA2 1970), cert. denied, 402 U. S. 986 (1971). We reserve judgment, however, on the extreme case, not presented here, where contested materials are directed at such a bizarre deviant group that the experience of the trier of fact would be plainly inadequate to judge whether the material appeals to the prurient interest. See *Mishkin* v. *New York,* 383 U. S. 502, 508–510 (1966); *United States* v. *Klaw,* 350 F. 2d 155, 167–168 (CA2 1965).

II

We categorically disapprove the theory, apparently adopted by the trial judge, that obscene, pornographic films acquire constitutional immunity from state regulation simply because they are exhibited for consenting adults only. This holding was properly rejected by the Georgia Supreme Court. Although we have often pointedly recognized the high importance of the state interest in regulating the exposure of obscene materials to juveniles and unconsenting adults, see *Miller* v. *California, ante,* at 18–20; *Stanley* v. *Georgia,* 394 U. S., at 567; *Redrup* v. *New York,* 386 U. S. 767, 769 (1967), this Court has never declared these to be the only legitimate state interests permitting regulation of obscene material. The States have a long-recognized legitimate interest in regulating the use of obscene material in local commerce and in all places of public accommodation, as long as these regulations do not run afoul of specific constitutional prohibitions. See *United States* v. *Thirty-seven Photographs, supra,* at 376–377 (opinion of White, J.); *United States* v. *Reidel,* 402 U. S., at 354–356. Cf. *United States* v. *Thirty-seven Photographs, supra,* at 378 (Stewart, J., concurring). "In an unbroken series of cases extending over a long stretch of this Court's history, it has been accepted as a postulate that 'the primary requirements of decency may be enforced against obscene publications.' [*Near* v. *Minnesota,* 283 U. S. 697, 716 (1931)]." *Kingsley Books, Inc.* v. *Brown, supra,* at 440.

In particular, we hold that there are legitimate state interests at stake in stemming the tide of commercialized obscenity, even assuming it is feasible to enforce effective safeguards against exposure to juveniles and to passersby.[7] Rights and interests "other than those of the advocates are involved." *Breard* v. *Alexandria*, 341 U. S. 622, 642 (1951). These include the interest of the public in the quality of life and the total community environment, the tone of commerce in the great city centers, and, possibly, the public safety itself. The Hill-Link Minority Report of the Commission on Obscenity and Pornography indicates that there is at least an arguable correlation between obscene material and crime.[8] Quite

---

[7] It is conceivable that an "adult" theater can—if it really insists—prevent the exposure of its obscene wares to juveniles. An "adult" bookstore, dealing in obscene books, magazines, and pictures, cannot realistically make this claim. The Hill-Link Minority Report of the Commission on Obscenity and Pornography emphasizes evidence (the Abelson National Survey of Youth and Adults) that, although most pornography may be bought by elders, "the heavy users and most highly exposed people to pornography are adolescent females (among women) and adolescent and young adult males (among men)." The Report of the Commission on Obscenity and Pornography 401 (1970). The legitimate interest in preventing exposure of juveniles to obscene material cannot be fully served by simply barring juveniles from the immediate physical premises of "adult" bookstores, when there is a flourishing "outside business" in these materials.

[8] The Report of the Commission on Obscenity and Pornography 390–412 (1970). For a discussion of earlier studies indicating "a division of thought [among behavioral scientists] on the correlation between obscenity and socially deleterious behavior," *Memoirs* v. *Massachusetts, supra,* at 451, and references to expert opinions that obscene material may induce crime and antisocial conduct, see *id.*, at 451–453 (Clark, J., dissenting). Mr. Justice Clark emphasized:

"While erotic stimulation caused by pornography may be legally insignificant in itself, there are medical experts who believe that such stimulation frequently manifests itself in criminal sexual behavior or other antisocial conduct. For example, Dr. George W. Henry of Cornell University has expressed the opinion that obscenity, with its exaggerated and morbid emphasis on sex, particularly abnormal and perverted practices, and its unrealistic pres-

apart from sex crimes, however, there remains one problem of large proportions aptly described by Professor Bickel:

> "It concerns the tone of the society, the mode, or to use terms that have perhaps greater currency, the style and quality of life, now and in the future. A man may be entitled to read an obscene book in his room, or expose himself indecently there . . . . We should protect his privacy. But if he demands a right to obtain the books and pictures he wants in the market, and to foregather in public places—discreet, if you will, but accessible to all—with others who share his tastes, *then to grant him his right is to affect the world about the rest of us, and to impinge on other privacies.* Even supposing that each of us can, if he wishes, effectively avert the eye and stop the ear (which, in truth, we cannot), what is commonly read and seen and heard and done intrudes upon us all, want it or not." 22 The Public Interest 25–26 (Winter 1971).[9] (Emphasis added.)

As Mr. Chief Justice Warren stated, there is a "right of the Nation and of the States to maintain a decent soci-

---

entation of sexual behavior and attitudes, may induce antisocial conduct by the average person. A number of sociologists think that this material may have adverse effects upon individual mental health, with potentially disruptive consequences for the community.

.   .   .   .   .

"Congress and the legislatures of every State have enacted measures to restrict the distribution of erotic and pornographic material, justifying these controls by reference to evidence that antisocial behavior may result in part from reading obscenity." *Id.,* at 452–453 (footnotes omitted).

[9] See also Berns, Pornography vs. Democracy: The Case for Censorship, in 22 The Public Interest 3 (Winter 1971); van den Haag, in Censorship: For & Against 156–157 (H. Hart ed. 1971).

ety . . . ," *Jacobellis* v. *Ohio,* 378 U. S. 184, 199 (1964)
(dissenting opinion).[10] See *Memoirs* v. *Massachusetts,*
383 U. S. 413, 457 (1966) (Harlan, J., dissenting);
Beauharnais v. *Illinois,* 343 U. S. 250, 256–257 (1952);
Kovacs v. *Cooper,* 336 U. S. 77, 86–88 (1949).

But, it is argued, there are no scientific data which conclusively demonstrate that exposure to obscene material adversely affects men and women or their society.
It is urged on behalf of the petitioners that, absent such
a demonstration, any kind of state regulation is "impermissible." We reject this argument. It is not for us
to resolve empirical uncertainties underlying state legislation, save in the exceptional case where that legislation
plainly impinges upon rights protected by the Constitution itself.[11] MR. JUSTICE BRENNAN, speaking for the
Court in *Ginsberg* v. *New York,* 390 U. S. 629, 642–643
(1968), said: "We do not demand of legislatures 'scientifically certain criteria of legislation.' *Noble State Bank*
v. *Haskell,* 219 U. S. 104, 110." Although there is no conclusive proof of a connection between antisocial behavior

---

[10] "In this and other cases in this area of the law, which are coming
to us in ever-increasing numbers, we are faced with the resolution
of rights basic both to individuals and to society as a whole. Specifically, we are called upon to reconcile the right of the Nation and of
the States to maintain a decent society and, on the other hand, the
right of individuals to express themselves freely in accordance with
the guarantees of the First and Fourteenth Amendments." *Jacobellis*
v. *Ohio, supra,* at 199 (Warren, C. J., dissenting).

[11] Mr. Justice Holmes stated in another context, that:

"[T]he proper course is to recognize that a state legislature can do
whatever it sees fit to do unless it is restrained by some express
prohibition in the Constitution of the United States or of the State,
and that Courts should be careful not to extend such prohibitions
beyond their obvious meaning by reading into them conceptions of
public policy that the particular Court may happen to entertain."
Tyson & Brother v. *Banton,* 273 U. S. 418, 446 (1927) (dissenting
opinion joined by Brandeis, J.).

and obscene material, the legislature of Georgia could quite reasonably determine that such a connection does or might exist. In deciding *Roth,* this Court implicitly accepted that a legislature could legitimately act on such a conclusion to protect *"the social interest in order and morality." Roth* v. *United States,* 354 U. S., at 485, quoting *Chaplinsky* v. *New Hampshire,* 315 U. S. 568, 572 (1942) (emphasis added in *Roth*).[12]

From the beginning of civilized societies, legislators and judges have acted on various unprovable assumptions. Such assumptions underlie much lawful state regulation of commercial and business affairs. See *Ferguson* v. *Skrupa,* 372 U. S. 726, 730 (1963); *Breard* v. *Alexandria,* 341 U. S., at 632–633, 641–645; *Lincoln Federal Labor Union* v. *Northwestern Iron & Metal Co.,* 335 U. S. 525, 536–537 (1949). The same is true of the federal securities and antitrust laws and a host of federal regulations. See *SEC* v. *Capital Gains Research Bureau, Inc.,* 375 U. S. 180, 186–195 (1963); *American Power & Light Co.* v. *SEC,* 329 U. S. 90, 99–103 (1946); *North American Co.* v. *SEC,* 327 U. S. 686, 705–707 (1946), and cases cited. See also *Brooks* v. *United States,* 267 U. S. 432, 436–437 (1925), and *Hoke* v. *United States,* 227 U. S. 308, 322 (1913). On the basis of these assumptions both Congress and state legislatures have, for example, drastically restricted associational rights by adopting antitrust laws, and have strictly regulated public expression by issuers of and dealers in securities, profit sharing "coupons," and "trading stamps,"

---

[12] *"It has been well observed that such* [lewd and obscene] *utterances are no essential part of any exposition of ideas, and are of such slight social value as a step to truth that any benefit that may be derived from them is clearly outweighed by the social interest in order and morality." Roth* v. *United States,* 354 U. S. 476, 485 (1957), quoting *Chaplinsky* v. *New Hampshire,* 315 U. S. 568, 572 (1942) (emphasis added in *Roth*).

commanding what they must and must not publish
and announce. See *Sugar Institute, Inc.* v. *United
States,* 297 U. S. 553, 597–602 (1936); *Merrick*
v. *N. W. Halsey & Co.,* 242 U. S. 568, 584–589 (1917);
Caldwell v. *Sioux Falls Stock Yards Co.,* 242 U. S. 559,
567–568 (1917); *Hall* v. *Geiger-Jones Co.,* 242 U. S.
539, 548–552 (1917); *Tanner* v. *Little,* 240 U. S. 369, 383–
386 (1916); *Rast* v. *Van Deman & Lewis Co.,* 240 U. S.
342, 363–368 (1916). Understandably those who entertain an absolutist view of the First Amendment find it
uncomfortable to explain why rights of association,
speech, and press should be severely restrained in the
marketplace of goods and money, but not in the marketplace of pornography.

Likewise, when legislatures and administrators act to
protect the physical environment from pollution and to
preserve our resources of forests, streams, and parks, they
must act on such imponderables as the impact of a new
highway near or through an existing park or wilderness
area. See *Citizens to Preserve Overton Park* v. *Volpe,*
401 U. S. 402, 417–420 (1971). Thus, § 18 (a) of the
Federal-Aid Highway Act of 1968, 23 U. S. C. § 138, and
the Department of Transportation Act of 1966, as
amended, 82 Stat. 824, 49 U. S. C. § 1653 (f), have been
described by Mr. Justice Black as "a solemn determination of the highest law-making body of this Nation that
the beauty and health-giving facilities of our parks are
not to be taken away for public roads without hearings,
factfindings, and policy determinations under the supervision of a Cabinet officer . . . ." *Citizens to Preserve
Overton Park, supra,* at 421 (separate opinion joined by
BRENNAN, J.). The fact that a congressional directive
reflects unprovable assumptions about what is good for
the people, including imponderable aesthetic assumptions, is not a sufficient reason to find that statute
unconstitutional.

If we accept the unprovable assumption that a complete education requires the reading of certain books, see *Board of Education* v. *Allen,* 392 U. S. 236, 245 (1968), and *Johnson* v. *New York State Education Dept.,* 449 F. 2d 871, 882–883 (CA2 1971) (dissenting opinion), vacated and remanded to consider mootness, 409 U. S. 75 (1972), *id.,* at 76–77 (MARSHALL, J., concurring), and the well nigh universal belief that good books, plays, and art lift the spirit, improve the mind, enrich the human personality, and develop character, can we then say that a state legislature may not act on the corollary assumption that commerce in obscene books, or public exhibitions focused on obscene conduct, have a tendency to exert a corrupting and debasing impact leading to antisocial behavior? "Many of these effects may be intangible and indistinct, but they are nonetheless real." *American Power & Light Co.* v. *SEC, supra,* at 103. Mr. Justice Cardozo said that all laws in Western civilization are "guided by a robust common sense . . . ." *Steward Machine Co.* v. *Davis,* 301 U. S. 548, 590 (1937). The sum of experience, including that of the past two decades, affords an ample basis for legislatures to conclude that a sensitive, key relationship of human existence, central to family life, community welfare, and the development of human personality, can be debased and distorted by crass commercial exploitation of sex. Nothing in the Constitution prohibits a State from reaching such a conclusion and acting on it legislatively simply because there is no conclusive evidence or empirical data.

It is argued that individual "free will" must govern, even in activities beyond the protection of the First Amendment and other constitutional guarantees of privacy, and that government cannot legitimately impede an individual's desire to see or acquire obscene plays, movies, and books. We do indeed base our society on certain assumptions that people have the capacity for free choice. Most exercises of individual free choice— those in politics, religion, and expression of ideas— are explicitly protected by the Constitution. Totally unlimited play for free will, however, is not allowed in our or any other society. We have just noted, for example, that neither the First Amendment nor "free will" precludes States from having "blue sky" laws to regulate what sellers of securities may write or publish about their wares. See *supra,* at 61–62. Such laws are to protect the weak, the uninformed, the unsuspecting, and the gullible from the exercise of their own volition. Nor do modern societies leave disposal of garbage and sewage up to the individual "free will," but impose regulation to protect both public health and the appearance of public places. States are told by some that they must await a "laissez-faire" market solution to the obscenity-pornography problem, paradoxically "by people who have never otherwise had a kind word to say for laissez-faire," particularly in solving urban, commercial, and environmental pollution problems. See I. Kristol, On the Democratic Idea in America 37 (1972).

The States, of course, may follow such a "laissez-faire" policy and drop all controls on commercialized obscenity, if that is what they prefer, just as they can ignore consumer protection in the marketplace, but nothing in the Constitution *compels* the States to do so with regard to matters falling within state jurisdiction. See *United States* v. *Reidel,* 402 U. S., at 357; *Memoirs* v. *Massachusetts,* 383 U. S., at 462 (WHITE, J., dissenting). "We do not sit as a super-legislature to determine the wisdom, need, and propriety of laws that touch economic problems, business affairs, or social conditions." *Griswold* v. *Connecticut,* 381 U. S. 479, 482 (1965). See *Ferguson* v. *Skrupa,* 372 U. S., at 731; *Day-Brite Lighting, Inc.* v. *Missouri,* 342 U. S. 421, 423 (1952).

It is asserted, however, that standards for evaluating state commercial regulations are inapposite in the present context, as state regulation of access by consenting adults to obscene material violates the constitutionally protected right to privacy enjoyed by petitioners' customers. Even assuming that petitioners have vicarious standing to assert potential customers' rights, it is unavailing to compare a theater open to the public for a fee, with the private home of *Stanley* v. *Georgia,* 394 U. S., at 568, and the marital bedroom of *Griswold* v. *Connecticut, supra,* at 485–486. This Court, has, on numerous occasions, refused to hold that commercial ventures such as a motion-picture house are "private" for the purpose of civil rights litigation and civil rights statutes. See *Sullivan* v. *Little Hunting Park, Inc.,* 396 U. S. 229, 236 (1969); *Daniel* v. *Paul,* 395 U. S. 298, 305–308 (1969); *Blow* v. *North Carolina,* 379 U. S. 684, 685–686 (1965); *Hamm* v. *Rock Hill,* 379 U. S. 306, 307–308 (1964); *Heart of Atlanta Motel, Inc.* v. *United States,* 379 U. S. 241, 247, 260–261 (1964). The Civil Rights Act of 1964 specifically defines motion-picture houses and theaters as places of "public accommodation" covered by the Act as operations affecting commerce. 78 Stat. 243, 42 U. S. C. §§ 2000a (b)(3), (c).

Our prior decisions recognizing a right to privacy guaranteed by the Fourteenth Amendment included "only personal rights that can be deemed 'fundamental' or 'implicit in the concept of ordered liberty.' *Palko* v. *Connecticut,* 302 U. S. 319, 325 (1937)." *Roe* v. *Wade,* 410 U. S. 113, 152 (1973). This privacy right encompasses and protects the personal intimacies of the home, the family, marriage, motherhood, procreation, and child rearing. Cf. *Eisenstadt* v. *Baird,* 405 U. S. 438, 453–454 (1972); *id.,* at 460, 463–465 (WHITE, J., concurring); *Stanley* v. *Georgia, supra,* at 568; *Loving* v. *Virginia,* 388

U. S. 1, 12 (1967); *Griswold* v. *Connecticut, supra,* at 486; *Prince* v. *Massachusetts,* 321 U. S. 158, 166 (1944); *Skinner* v. *Oklahoma,* 316 U. S. 535, 541 (1942); *Pierce* v. *Society of Sisters,* 268 U. S. 510, 535 (1925); *Meyer* v. *Nebraska,* 262 U. S. 390, 399 (1923). Nothing, however, in this Court's decisions intimates that there is any "fundamental" privacy right "implicit in the concept of ordered liberty" to watch obscene movies in places of public accommodation.

If obscene material unprotected by the First Amendment in itself carried with it a "penumbra" of constitutionally protected privacy, this Court would not have found it necessary to decide *Stanley* on the narrow basis of the "privacy of the home," which was hardly more than a reaffirmation that "a man's home is his castle." Cf. *Stanley* v. *Georgia, supra,* at 564.[13] Moreover, we have declined to equate the privacy of the home relied on in *Stanley* with a "zone" of "privacy" that follows a distributor or a consumer of obscene materials wherever he goes. See *United States* v. *Orito, post,* at 141–143; *United States* v. *12 200-ft. Reels of Film, post,* at 126–129; *United States* v. *Thirty-seven Photographs,* 402 U. S., at 376–377 (opinion of WHITE, J.); *United States* v. *Reidel, supra,* at 355. The idea of a "privacy" right and a place of public accommodation are, in this context,

---

[13] The protection afforded by *Stanley* v. *Georgia,* 394 U. S. 557 (1969), is restricted to a place, the home. In contrast, the constitutionally protected privacy of family, marriage, motherhood, procreation, and child rearing is not just concerned with a particular place, but with a protected intimate relationship. Such protected privacy extends to the doctor's office, the hospital, the hotel room, or as otherwise required to safeguard the right to intimacy involved. Cf. *Roe* v. *Wade,* 410 U. S. 113, 152–154 (1973); *Griswold* v. *Connecticut,* 381 U. S. 479, 485–486 (1965). Obviously, there is no necessary or legitimate expectation of privacy which would extend to marital intercourse on a street corner or a theater stage.

mutually exclusive. Conduct or depictions of conduct that the state police power can prohibit on a public street do not become automatically protected by the Constitution merely because the conduct is moved to a bar or a "live" theater stage, any more than a "live" performance of a man and woman locked in a sexual embrace at high noon in Times Square is protected by the Constitution because they simultaneously engage in a valid political dialogue.

It is also argued that the State has no legitimate interest in "control [of] the moral content of a person's thoughts," *Stanley* v. *Georgia, supra,* at 565, and we need not quarrel with this. But we reject the claim that the State of Georgia is here attempting to control the minds or thoughts of those who patronize theaters. Preventing unlimited display or distribution of obscene material, which by definition lacks any serious literary, artistic, political, or scientific value as communication, *Miller* v. *California, ante,* at 24, 34, is distinct from a control of reason and the intellect. Cf. *Kois* v. *Wisconsin,* 408 U. S. 229 (1972); *Roth* v. *United States, supra,* at 485–487; *Thornhill* v. *Alabama,* 310 U. S. 88, 101–102 (1940); Finnis, "Reason and Passion": The Constitutional Dialectic of Free Speech and Obscenity, 116 U. Pa. L. Rev. 222, 229–230, 241–243 (1967). Where communication of ideas, protected by the First Amendment, is not involved, or the particular privacy of the home protected by *Stanley,* or any of the other "areas or zones" of constitutionally protected privacy, the mere fact that, as a consequence, some human "utterances" or "thoughts" may be incidentally affected does not bar the State from acting to protect legitimate state interests. Cf. *Roth* v. *United States, supra,* at 483, 485–487; *Beauharnais* v. *Illinois,* 343 U. S., at 256–257. The fantasies of a drug addict are his own and beyond the reach of government, but government regulation of drug sales is not prohibited by the Constitution. Cf. *United States* v. *Reidel, supra,* at 359–360 (Harlan, J., concurring).

Finally, petitioners argue that conduct which directly involves "consenting adults" only has, for that sole reason, a special claim to constitutional protection. Our Constitution establishes a broad range of conditions on the exercise of power by the States, but for us to say that our Constitution incorporates the proposition that conduct involving consenting adults only is always beyond state regulation,[14] is a step we are unable to take.[15] Commercial exploitation of depictions, descriptions, or exhibitions of obscene conduct on commercial premises open to the adult public falls within a State's broad power to regulate commerce and protect the public

---

[14] Cf. J. Mill, On Liberty 13 (1955 ed.).

[15] The state statute books are replete with constitutionally unchallenged laws against prostitution, suicide, voluntary self-mutilation, brutalizing "bare fist" prize fights, and duels, although these crimes may only directly involve "consenting adults." Statutes making bigamy a crime surely cut into an individual's freedom to associate, but few today seriously claim such statutes violate the First Amendment or any other constitutional provision. See *Davis* v. *Beason,* 133 U. S. 333, 344–345 (1890). Consider also the language of this Court in *McLaughlin* v. *Florida,* 379 U. S. 184, 196 (1964), as to adultery; *Southern Surety Co.* v. *Oklahoma,* 241 U. S. 582, 586 (1916), as to fornication; *Hoke* v. *United States,* 227 U. S. 308, 320–322 (1913), and *Caminetti* v. *United States,* 242 U. S. 470, 484–487, 491–492 (1917), as to "white slavery"; *Murphy* v. *California,* 225 U. S. 623, 629 (1912), as to billiard halls; and the *Lottery Case,* 188 U. S. 321, 355–356 (1903), as to gambling. See also the summary of state statutes prohibiting bearbaiting, cockfighting, and other brutalizing animal "sports," in Stevens, Fighting and Baiting, in Animals and Their Legal Rights 112–127 (Leavitt ed. 1970). As Professor Irving Kristol has observed: "Bearbaiting and cockfighting are prohibited only in part out of compassion for the suffering animals; the main reason they were abolished was because it was felt that they debased and brutalized the citizenry who flocked to witness such spectacles." On the Democratic Idea in America 33 (1972).

environment. The issue in this context goes beyond whether someone, or even the majority, considers the conduct depicted as "wrong" or "sinful." The States have the power to make a morally neutral judgment that public exhibition of obscene material, or commerce in such material, has a tendency to injure the community as a whole, to endanger the public safety, or to jeopardize, in Mr. Chief Justice Warren's words, the States' "right . . . to maintain a decent society." *Jacobellis* v. *Ohio,* 378 U. S., at 199 (dissenting opinion).

To summarize, we have today reaffirmed the basic holding of *Roth* v. *United States, supra,* that obscene material has no protection under the First Amendment. See *Miller* v. *California, supra,* and *Kaplan* v. *California, post,* p. 115. We have directed our holdings, not at thoughts or speech, but at depiction and description of specifically defined sexual conduct that States may regulate within limits designed to prevent infringement of First Amendment rights. We have also reaffirmed the holdings of *United States* v. *Reidel, supra,* and *United States* v. *Thirty-seven Photographs, supra,* that commerce in obscene material is unprotected by any constitutional doctrine of privacy. *United States* v. *Orito, post,* at 141–143; *United States* v. *12 200-ft. Reels of Film, post,* at 126–129. In this case we hold that the States have a legitimate interest in regulating commerce in obscene material and in regulating exhibition of obscene material in places of public accommodation, including so-called "adult" theaters from which minors are excluded. In light of these holdings, nothing precludes the State of Georgia from the regulation of the allegedly obscene material exhibited in Paris Adult Theatre I or II, provided that the applicable Georgia law, as written or authoritatively interpreted by the Georgia courts, meets the First Amendment standards set forth in *Miller* v. *California, ante,* at 23–25. The judgment is vacated and the case remanded to the Georgia Supreme Court for further proceedings not inconsistent with this opinion and *Miller* v. *California, supra.* See *United States* v. *12 200-ft. Reels of Film, post,* at 130 n. 7.

Vacated and remanded.

MILLER *v.* CALIFORNIA

APPEAL FROM THE APPELLATE DEPARTMENT, SUPERIOR
COURT OF CALIFORNIA, COUNTY OF ORANGE

No. 70–73.   Argued January 18–19, 1972—Reargued November 7,
1972—Decided June 21, 1973

Appellant was convicted of mailing unsolicited sexually explicit material in violation of a California statute that approximately incorporated the obscenity test formulated in *Memoirs* v. *Massachusetts,* 383 U. S. 413, 418 (plurality opinion). The trial court instructed the jury to evaluate the materials by the contemporary community standards of California. Appellant's conviction was affirmed on appeal. In lieu of the obscenity criteria enunciated by the *Memoirs* plurality, it is *held:*

1. Obscene material is not protected by the First Amendment. *Roth* v. *United States,* 354 U. S. 476, reaffirmed. A work may be subject to state regulation where that work, taken as a whole, appeals to the prurient interest in sex; portrays, in a patently offensive way, sexual conduct specifically defined by the applicable state law; and, taken as a whole, does not have serious literary, artistic, political, or scientific value. Pp. 23–24.

2. The basic guidelines for the trier of fact must be: (a) whether "the average person, applying contemporary community standards" would find that the work, taken as a whole, appeals to the prurient interest, *Roth, supra,* at 489, (b) whether the work depicts or describes, in a patently offensive way, sexual conduct specifically defined by the applicable state law, and (c) whether the work, taken as a whole, lacks serious literary, artistic, political, or scientific value. If a state obscenity law is thus limited, First Amendment values are adequately protected by ultimate independent appellate review of constitutional claims when necessary. Pp. 24–25.

3. The test of *"utterly* without redeeming social value" articulated in *Memoirs, supra,* is rejected as a constitutional standard. Pp. 24–25.

4. The jury may measure the essentially factual issues of prurient appeal and patent offensiveness by the standard that prevails in the forum community, and need not employ a "national standard." Pp. 30–34.

Vacated and remanded.

BURGER, C. J., delivered the opinion of the Court, in which WHITE,
BLACKMUN, POWELL, and REHNQUIST, JJ., joined. DOUGLAS, J.,
filed a dissenting opinion, *post*, p. 37. BRENNAN, J., filed a dissenting opinion, in which STEWART and MARSHALL, JJ., joined,
post, p. 47.

Burton Marks reargued the cause and filed a brief for
appellant.

Michael R. Capizzi reargued the cause for appellee.
With him on the brief was *Cecil Hicks.**

MR. CHIEF JUSTICE BURGER delivered the opinion of
the Court.

This is one of a group of "obscenity-pornography"
cases being reviewed by the Court in a re-examination
of standards enunciated in earlier cases involving what
Mr. Justice Harlan called "the intractable obscenity problem." *Interstate Circuit, Inc.* v. *Dallas*, 390 U. S. 676,
704 (1968) (concurring and dissenting).

Appellant conducted a mass mailing campaign to advertise the sale of illustrated books, euphemistically called
"adult" material. After a jury trial, he was convicted
of violating California Penal Code § 311.2 (a), a misdemeanor, by knowingly distributing obscene matter,[1]

---

*Samuel Rosenwein, A. L. Wirin, Fred Okrand, Laurence R.
Sperber, Melvin L. Wulf,* and *Joel M. Gora* filed a brief for the
American Civil Liberties Union of Southern California et al. as
amici curiae urging reversal.

[1] At the time of the commission of the alleged offense, which was
prior to June 25, 1969, §§ 311.2 (a) and 311 of the California Penal
Code read in relevant part:

"§ 311.2 Sending or bringing into state for sale or distribution;
printing, exhibiting, distributing or possessing within state

"(a) Every person who knowingly: sends or causes to be sent,
or brings or causes to be brought, into this state for sale or distribution, or in this state prepares, publishes, prints, exhibits, distributes,
or offers to distribute, or has in his possession with intent to dis-

and the Appellate Department, Superior Court of California, County of Orange, summarily affirmed the judgment without opinion. Appellant's conviction was spe-

tribute or to exhibit or offer to distribute, any obscene matter is guilty of a misdemeanor. . . ."

"§ 311. Definitions

"As used in this chapter:

"(a) 'Obscene' means that to the average person, applying contemporary standards, the predominant appeal of the matter, taken as a whole, is to prurient interest, i. e., a shameful or morbid interest in nudity, sex, or excretion, which goes substantially beyond customary limits of candor in description or representation of such matters and is matter which is utterly without redeeming social importance.

"(b) 'Matter' means any book, magazine, newspaper, or other printed or written material or any picture, drawing, photograph, motion picture, or other pictorial representation or any statue or other figure, or any recording, transcription or mechanical, chemical or electrical reproduction or any other articles, equipment, machines or materials.

"(c) 'Person' means any individual, partnership, firm, association, corporation, or other legal entity.

"(d) 'Distribute' means to transfer possession of, whether with or without consideration.

"(e) 'Knowingly' means having knowledge that the matter is obscene."

Section 311 (e) of the California Penal Code, supra, was amended on June 25, 1969, to read as follows:

"(e) 'Knowingly' means being aware of the character of the matter."

Cal. Amended Stats. 1969, c. 249, § 1, p. 598. Despite appellant's contentions to the contrary, the record indicates that the new § 311 (e) was not applied ex post facto to his case, but only the old § 311 (e) as construed by state decisions prior to the commission of the alleged offense. See People v. Pinkus, 256 Cal. App. 2d 941, 948–950, 63 Cal. Rptr. 680, 685–686 (App. Dept., Superior Ct., Los Angeles, 1967); People v. Campise, 242 Cal. App. 2d 905, 914, 51 Cal. Rptr. 815, 821 (App. Dept., Superior Ct., San Diego, 1966). Cf. Bouie v. City of Columbia, 378 U. S. 347 (1964). Nor did § 311.2, supra, as applied, create any "direct, immediate burden on the percifically based on his conduct in causing five unsolicited advertising brochures to be sent through the mail in an envelope addressed to a restaurant in Newport Beach, California. The envelope was opened by the manager of the restaurant and his mother. They had not requested the brochures; they complained to the police.

The brochures advertise four books entitled "Intercourse," "Man-Woman," "Sex Orgies Illustrated," and "An Illustrated History of Pornography," and a film entitled "Marital Intercourse." While the brochures contain some descriptive printed material, primarily they consist of pictures and drawings very explicitly depicting men and women in groups of two or more engaging in a variety of sexual activities, with genitals often prominently displayed.

I

This case involves the application of a State's criminal obscenity statute to a situation in which sexually explicit materials have been thrust by aggressive sales action upon unwilling recipients who had in no way indicated any desire to receive such materials. This Court has recognized that the States have a legitimate interest in prohibiting dissemination or exhibition of obscene material [2]

---

formance of the postal functions," or infringe on congressional commerce powers under Art. I, § 8, cl. 3. *Roth* v. *United States,* 354 U. S. 476, 494 (1957), quoting *Railway Mail Assn.* v. *Corsi,* 326 U. S. 88, 96 (1945). See also *Mishkin* v. *New York,* 383 U. S. 502, 506 (1966); *Smith* v. *California,* 361 U. S. 147, 150–152 (1959).

[2] This Court has defined "obscene material" as "material which deals with sex in a manner appealing to prurient interest," *Roth* v. *United States, supra,* at 487, but the *Roth* definition does not reflect the precise meaning of "obscene" as traditionally used in the English language. Derived from the Latin *obscaenus, ob,* to, plus *caenum,* filth, "obscene" is defined in the Webster's Third New International Dictionary (Unabridged 1969) as "1a: dis-

when the mode of dissemination carries with it a significant danger of offending the sensibilities of unwilling recipients or of exposure to juveniles. *Stanley* v. *Georgia,* 394 U. S. 557, 567 (1969); *Ginsberg* v. *New York,* 390 U. S. 629, 637–643 (1968); *Interstate Circuit, Inc.* v. *Dallas, supra,* at 690; *Redrup* v. *New York,* 386 U. S. 767, 769 (1967); *Jacobellis* v. *Ohio,* 378 U. S. 184, 195 (1964). See *Rabe* v. *Washington,* 405 U. S. 313, 317 (1972) (BURGER, C. J., concurring); *United States* v. *Reidel,* 402 U. S. 351, 360–362 (1971) (opinion of MARSHALL, J.); *Joseph Burstyn, Inc.* v. *Wilson,* 343 U. S. 495, 502 (1952); *Breard* v. *Alexandria,* 341 U. S. 622, 644–645 (1951); *Kovacs* v. *Cooper,* 336 U. S. 77, 88–89 (1949); *Prince* v. *Massachusetts,* 321 U. S. 158, 169–170 (1944). Cf. *Butler* v. *Michigan,* 352 U. S. 380, 382–383 (1957); *Public Utilities Comm'n* v. *Pollak,* 343 U. S. 451, 464–465 (1952). It is in this context that we are called

---

gusting to the senses . . . b: grossly repugnant to the generally accepted notions of what is appropriate . . . 2: offensive or revolting as countering or violating some ideal or principle." The Oxford English Dictionary (1933 ed.) gives a similar definition, "[o]ffensive to the senses, or to taste or refinement; disgusting, repulsive, filthy, foul, abominable, loathsome."

The material we are discussing in this case is more accurately defined as "pornography" or "pornographic material." "Pornography" derives from the Greek (*pornè,* harlot, and *graphos,* writing). The word now means "1: a description of prostitutes or prostitution 2: a depiction (as in writing or painting) of licentiousness or lewdness: a portrayal of erotic behavior designed to cause sexual excitement." Webster's Third New International Dictionary, *supra.* Pornographic material which is obscene forms a sub-group of all "obscene" expression, but not the whole, at least as the word "obscene" is now used in our language. We note, therefore, that the words "obscene material," as used in this case, have a specific judicial meaning which derives from the *Roth* case, *i. e.,* obscene material "which deals with sex." *Roth, supra,* at 487. See also ALI Model Penal Code § 251.4 (1) "Obscene Defined." (Official Draft 1962.)

on to define the standards which must be used to identify
obscene material that a State may regulate without in-
fringing on the First Amendment as applicable to the
States through the Fourteenth Amendment.

The dissent of MR. JUSTICE BRENNAN reviews the
background of the obscenity problem, but since the
Court now undertakes to formulate standards more concrete than those in the past, it is useful for us to focus
on two of the landmark cases in the somewhat tortured
history of the Court's obscenity decisions. In *Roth* v.
United States, 354 U. S. 476 (1957), the Court sustained
a conviction under a federal statute punishing the mailing
of "obscene, lewd, lascivious or filthy . . ." materials. The
key to that holding was the Court's rejection of the claim
that obscene materials were protected by the First
Amendment. Five Justices joined in the opinion stating:

"All ideas having even the slightest redeeming
social importance—unorthodox ideas, controversial
ideas, even ideas hateful to the prevailing climate
of opinion—have the full protection of the [First
Amendment] guaranties, unless excludable because
they encroach upon the limited area of more important interests. But implicit in the history of
the First Amendment is the rejection of obscenity
as utterly without redeeming social importance. . . .
This is the same judgment expressed by this Court
in *Chaplinsky* v. *New Hampshire,* 315 U. S. 568,
571–572:

"'. . . There are certain well-defined and narrowly limited classes of speech, the prevention and
punishment of which have never been thought to
raise any Constitutional problem. *These include
the lewd and obscene . . . . It has been well observed that such utterances are no essential part of
any exposition of ideas, and are of such slight social*

*value as a step to truth that any benefit that may
be derived from them is clearly outweighed by the
social interest in order and morality. . . .'* [Empha-
sis by Court in *Roth* opinion.]

"We hold that obscenity is not within the area of
constitutionally protected speech or press." 354
U. S., at 484–485 (footnotes omitted).

Nine years later, in *Memoirs* v. *Massachusetts,* 383 U. S.
413 (1966), the Court veered sharply away from the
Roth concept and, with only three Justices in the plurality opinion, articulated a new test of obscenity. The plurality held that under the *Roth* definition

"as elaborated in subsequent cases, three elements must coalesce: it must be established that
(a) the dominant theme of the material taken as a
whole appeals to a prurient interest in sex; (b) the
material is patently offensive because it affronts contemporary community standards relating to the description or representation of sexual matters; and
(c) the material is utterly without redeeming social
value." *Id.,* at 418.

The sharpness of the break with *Roth,* represented by the
third element of the *Memoirs* test and emphasized by
MR. JUSTICE WHITE's dissent, *id.,* at 460–462, was
further underscored when the *Memoirs* plurality went on
to state:

"The Supreme Judicial Court erred in holding that
a book need not be 'unqualifiedly worthless before it
can be deemed obscene.' A book cannot be proscribed unless it is found to be *utterly* without redeeming social value." *Id.,* at 419 (emphasis in
original).

While *Roth* presumed "obscenity" to be "utterly
without redeeming social importance," *Memoirs* required

that to prove obscenity it must be affirmatively established that the material is "*utterly* without redeeming
social value." Thus, even as they repeated the words of
Roth, the *Memoirs* plurality produced a drastically altered
test that called on the prosecution to prove a negative,
i. e., that the material was "*utterly* without redeeming
social value"—a burden virtually impossible to discharge
under our criminal standards of proof. Such considerations caused Mr. Justice Harlan to wonder if the "*utterly*
without redeeming social value" test had any meaning
at all. See *Memoirs* v. *Massachusetts, id.,* at 459 (Harlan, J., dissenting). See also *id.,* at 461 (WHITE, J.,
dissenting); *United States* v. *Groner,* 479 F. 2d 577, 579–
581 (CA5 1973).

Apart from the initial formulation in the *Roth* case, no
majority of the Court has at any given time been able
to agree on a standard to determine what constitutes
obscene, pornographic material subject to regulation
under the States' police power. See, *e. g., Redrup* v.
New York, 386 U. S., at 770–771. We have seen "a
variety of views among the members of the Court un-
matched in any other course of constitutional adjudication." *Interstate Circuit, Inc.* v. *Dallas,* 390 U. S.,
at 704–705 (Harlan, J., concurring and dissenting) (footnote omitted).[3] This is not remarkable, for in the area

---

[3] In the absence of a majority view, this Court was compelled
to embark on the practice of summarily reversing convictions for
the dissemination of materials that at least five members of
the Court, applying their separate tests, found to be protected
by the First Amendment. *Redrup* v. *New York,* 386 U. S. 767
(1967). Thirty-one cases have been decided in this manner. Beyond the necessity of circumstances, however, no justification has
ever been offered in support of the *Redrup* "policy." See *Walker* v.
Ohio, 398 U. S. 434–435 (1970) (dissenting opinions of BURGER,
C. J., and Harlan, J.). The *Redrup* procedure has cast us in the role
of an unreviewable board of censorship for the 50 States, subjectively
judging each piece of material brought before us.

of freedom of speech and press the courts must always remain sensitive to any infringement on genuinely serious literary, artistic, political, or scientific expression. This is an area in which there are few eternal verities.

The case we now review was tried on the theory that the California Penal Code § 311 approximately incorporates the three-stage *Memoirs* test, *supra*. But now the *Memoirs* test has been abandoned as unworkable by its author,[4] and no Member of the Court today supports the *Memoirs* formulation.

II

This much has been categorically settled by the Court, that obscene material is unprotected by the First Amendment. *Kois* v. *Wisconsin,* 408 U. S. 229 (1972); *United States* v. *Reidel,* 402 U. S., at 354; *Roth* v. *United States, supra,* at 485.[5] "The First and Fourteenth Amendments have never been treated as absolutes [footnote omitted]." *Breard* v. *Alexandria,* 341 U. S., at 642, and cases cited. See *Times Film Corp.* v. *Chicago,* 365 U. S. 43, 47–50 (1961); *Joseph Burstyn, Inc.* v. *Wilson,* 343 U. S., at 502. We acknowledge, however, the inherent dangers of undertaking to regulate any form of expression. State statutes designed to regulate obscene materials must be

---

[4] See the dissenting opinion of MR. JUSTICE BRENNAN in *Paris Adult Theatre I* v. *Slaton, post,* p. 73.

[5] As Mr. Chief Justice Warren stated, dissenting, in *Jacobellis* v. *Ohio,* 378 U. S. 184, 200 (1964):

"For all the sound and fury that the *Roth* test has generated, it has not been proved unsound, and I believe that we should try to live with it—at least until a more satisfactory definition is evolved. No government—be it federal, state, or local—should be forced to choose between repressing all material, including that within the realm of decency, and allowing unrestrained license to publish any material, no matter how vile. There must be a rule of reason in this as in other areas of the law, and we have attempted in the *Roth* case to provide such a rule."

carefully limited. See *Interstate Circuit, Inc.* v. *Dallas,
supra,* at 682–685. As a result, we now confine the
permissible scope of such regulation to works which
depict or describe sexual conduct. That conduct must
be specifically defined by the applicable state law, as
written or authoritatively construed.[6] A state offense
must also be limited to works which, taken as a whole,
appeal to the prurient interest in sex, which portray
sexual conduct in a patently offensive way, and which,
taken as a whole, do not have serious literary, artistic,
political, or scientific value.

The basic guidelines for the trier of fact must be:
(a) whether "the average person, applying contemporary
community standards" would find that the work, taken
as a whole, appeals to the prurient interest, *Kois* v. *Wisconsin, supra,* at 230, quoting *Roth* v. *United States,
supra,* at 489; (b) whether the work depicts or describes,
in a patently offensive way, sexual conduct specifically
defined by the applicable state law; and (c) whether
the work, taken as a whole, lacks serious literary,
artistic, political, or scientific value. We do not adopt
as a constitutional standard the "*utterly* without redeeming social value" test of *Memoirs* v. *Massachusetts,*

---

[6] See, *e. g.,* Oregon Laws 1971, c. 743, Art. 29, §§ 255–262, and
Hawaii Penal Code, Tit. 37, §§ 1210–1216, 1972 Hawaii Session Laws,
Act 9, c. 12, pt. II, pp. 126–129, as examples of state laws directed at
depiction of defined physical conduct, as opposed to expression. Other
state formulations could be equally valid in this respect. In giving
the Oregon and Hawaii statutes as examples, we do not wish to be
understood as approving of them in all other respects nor as establishing their limits as the extent of state power.

We do not hold, as MR. JUSTICE BRENNAN intimates, that all
States other than Oregon must now enact new obscenity statutes.
Other existing state statutes, as construed heretofore or hereafter,
may well be adequate. See *United States* v. *12 200-ft. Reels of
Film, post,* at 130 n. 7.

383 U. S., at 419; that concept has never commanded the adherence of more than three Justices at one time.[7] See *supra,* at 21. If a state law that regulates obscene material is thus limited, as written or construed, the First Amendment values applicable to the States through the Fourteenth Amendment are adequately protected by the ultimate power of appellate courts to conduct an independent review of constitutional claims when necessary. See *Kois* v. *Wisconsin, supra,* at 232; *Memoirs* v. *Massachusetts, supra,* at 459–460 (Harlan, J., dissenting); *Jacobellis* v. *Ohio,* 378 U. S., at 204 (Harlan, J., dissenting); *New York Times Co.* v. *Sullivan,* 376 U. S. 254, 284–285 (1964); *Roth* v. *United States, supra,* at 497–498 (Harlan, J., concurring and dissenting).

We emphasize that it is not our function to propose regulatory schemes for the States. That must await their concrete legislative efforts. It is possible, however, to give a few plain examples of what a state statute could define for regulation under part (b) of the standard announced in this opinion, *supra:*

(a) Patently offensive representations or descriptions of ultimate sexual acts, normal or perverted, actual or simulated.

(b) Patently offensive representations or descriptions of masturbation, excretory functions, and lewd exhibition of the genitals.

Sex and nudity may not be exploited without limit by films or pictures exhibited or sold in places of public accommodation any more than live sex and nudity can

---

[7] "A quotation from Voltaire in the flyleaf of a book will not constitutionally redeem an otherwise obscene publication . . . ." *Kois* v. *Wisconsin,* 408 U. S. 229, 231 (1972). See *Memoirs* v. *Massachusetts,* 383 U. S. 413, 461 (1966) (WHITE, J., dissenting). We also reject, as a constitutional standard, the ambiguous concept of "social importance." See *id.,* at 462 (WHITE, J., dissenting).

be exhibited or sold without limit in such public places.[8]
At a minimum, prurient, patently offensive depiction or
description of sexual conduct must have serious literary,
artistic, political, or scientific value to merit First
Amendment protection. See *Kois* v. *Wisconsin, supra,*
at 230–232; *Roth* v. *United States, supra,* at 487; *Thornhill* v. *Alabama,* 310 U. S. 88, 101–102 (1940). For example, medical books for the education of physicians and
related personnel necessarily use graphic illustrations and
descriptions of human anatomy. In resolving the inevitably sensitive questions of fact and law, we must continue to rely on the jury system, accompanied by the
safeguards that judges, rules of evidence, presumption of
innocence, and other protective features provide, as we
do with rape, murder, and a host of other offenses
against society and its individual members.[9]

   MR. JUSTICE BRENNAN, author of the opinions of the
Court, or the plurality opinions, in *Roth* v. *United States,
supra; Jacobellis* v. *Ohio, supra; Ginzburg* v. *United*

---

[8] Although we are not presented here with the problem of regulating lewd public conduct itself, the States have greater power to
regulate nonverbal, physical conduct than to suppress depictions or
descriptions of the same behavior. In *United States* v. *O'Brien,*
391 U. S. 367, 377 (1968), a case not dealing with obscenity, the
Court held a State regulation of conduct which itself embodied both
speech and nonspeech elements to be "sufficiently justified if . . .
it furthers an important or substantial governmental interest; if the
governmental interest is unrelated to the suppression of free expression; and if the incidental restriction on alleged First Amendment
freedoms is no greater than is essential to the furtherance of that
interest." See *California* v. *LaRue,* 409 U. S. 109, 117–118 (1972).

[9] The mere fact juries may reach different conclusions as to the
same material does not mean that constitutional rights are abridged.
As this Court observed in *Roth* v. *United States,* 354 U. S., at 492
n. 30, "it is common experience that different juries may reach
different results under any criminal statute. That is one of the
consequences we accept under our jury system. Cf. *Dunlop* v.
United States, 165 U. S. 486, 499–500."

States, 383 U. S. 463 (1966), *Mishkin* v. *New York,* 383 U. S. 502 (1966); and *Memoirs* v. *Massachusetts, supra,* has abandoned his former position and now maintains that no formulation of this Court, the Congress, or the States can adequately distinguish obscene material unprotected by the First Amendment from protected expression, *Paris Adult Theatre I* v. *Slaton, post,* p. 73 (BRENNAN, J., dissenting). Paradoxically, MR. JUSTICE BRENNAN indicates that suppression of unprotected obscene material is permissible to avoid exposure to unconsenting adults, as in this case, and to juveniles, although he gives no indication of how the division between protected and nonprotected materials may be drawn with greater precision for these purposes than for regulation of commercial exposure to consenting adults only. Nor does he indicate where in the Constitution he finds the authority to distinguish between a willing "adult" one month past the state law age of majority and a willing "juvenile" one month younger.

Under the holdings announced today, no one will be subject to prosecution for the sale or exposure of obscene materials unless these materials depict or describe patently offensive "hard core" sexual conduct specifically defined by the regulating state law, as written or construed. We are satisfied that these specific prerequisites will provide fair notice to a dealer in such materials that his public and commercial activities may bring prosecution. See *Roth* v. *United States, supra,* at 491–492. Cf. *Ginsberg* v. *New York,* 390 U. S., at 643.[10] If

---

[10] As MR. JUSTICE BRENNAN stated for the Court in *Roth* v. *United States, supra,* at 491–492:

"Many decisions have recognized that these terms of obscenity statutes are not precise. [Footnote omitted.] This Court, however, has consistently held that lack of precision is not itself offensive to the requirements of due process. '. . . [T]he Constitution does not require impossible standards'; all that is required is that the

the inability to define regulated materials with ultimate, god-like precision altogether removes the power of the States or the Congress to regulate, then "hard core" pornography may be exposed without limit to the juvenile, the passerby, and the consenting adult alike, as, indeed, MR. JUSTICE DOUGLAS contends. As to MR. JUSTICE DOUGLAS' position, see *United States* v. *Thirty-seven Photographs,* 402 U. S. 363, 379–380 (1971) (Black, J., joined by DOUGLAS, J., dissenting); *Ginzburg* v. *United States, supra,* at 476, 491–492 (Black, J., and DOUGLAS, J., dissenting); *Jacobellis* v. *Ohio, supra,* at 196 (Black, J., joined by DOUGLAS, J., concurring); *Roth, supra,* at 508–514 (DOUGLAS, J., dissenting). In this belief, however, MR. JUSTICE DOUGLAS now stands alone.

MR. JUSTICE BRENNAN also emphasizes "institutional stress" in justification of his change of view. Noting that "[t]he number of obscenity cases on our docket gives ample testimony to the burden that has been placed upon this Court," he quite rightly remarks that the examination of contested materials "is hardly a source of edification to the members of this Court." *Paris Adult*

---

language 'conveys sufficiently definite warning as to the proscribed conduct when measured by common understanding and practices. . . .' *United States* v. *Petrillo,* 332 U. S. 1, 7–8. These words, applied according to the proper standard for judging obscenity, already discussed, give adequate warning of the conduct proscribed and mark '. . . boundaries sufficiently distinct for judges and juries fairly to administer the law . . . . That there may be marginal cases in which it is difficult to determine the side of the line on which a particular fact situation falls is no sufficient reason to hold the language too ambiguous to define a criminal offense. . . .' *Id.,* at 7. See also *United States* v. *Harriss,* 347 U. S. 612, 624, n. 15; *Boyce Motor Lines, Inc.* v. *United States,* 342 U. S. 337, 340; *United States* v. *Ragen,* 314 U. S. 513, 523–524; *United States* v. *Wurzbach,* 280 U. S. 396; *Hygrade Provision Co.* v. *Sherman,* 266 U. S. 497; *Fox* v. *Washington,* 236 U. S. 273; *Nash* v. *United States,* 229 U. S. 373."

Theatre I v. *Slaton, post,* at 92, 93. He also notes, and we agree, that "uncertainty of the standards creates a continuing source of tension between state and federal courts . . . ." "The problem is . . . that one cannot say with certainty that material is obscene until at least five members of this Court, applying inevitably obscure standards, have pronounced it so." *Id.,* at 93, 92.

It is certainly true that the absence, since *Roth,* of a single majority view of this Court as to proper standards for testing obscenity has placed a strain on both state and federal courts. But today, for the first time since *Roth* was decided in 1957, a majority of this Court has agreed on concrete guidelines to isolate "hard core" pornography from expression protected by the First Amendment. Now we may abandon the casual practice of *Redrup* v. *New York,* 386 U. S. 767 (1967), and attempt to provide positive guidance to federal and state courts alike.

This may not be an easy road, free from difficulty. But no amount of "fatigue" should lead us to adopt a convenient "institutional" rationale—an absolutist, "anything goes" view of the First Amendment—because it will lighten our burdens.[11] "Such an abnegation of judicial supervision in this field would be inconsistent with our duty to uphold the constitutional guarantees." *Jacobellis* v. *Ohio, supra,* at 187–188 (opinion of Brennan, J.). Nor should we remedy "tension between state and federal courts" by arbitrarily depriving the States of a power reserved to them under the Constitution, a power which they have enjoyed and exercised continuously from before the adoption of the First Amendment to this day. See *Roth* v. *United States, supra,* at 482–485. "Our duty admits of no 'substitute for facing up

---

[11] We must note, in addition, that any assumption concerning the relative burdens of the past and the probable burden under the standards now adopted is pure speculation.

to the tough individual problems of constitutional judg-
ment involved in every obscenity case.' [*Roth* v. *United
States, supra,* at 498]; see *Manual Enterprises, Inc.* v.
Day, 370 U. S. 478, 488 (opinion of Harlan, J.) [footnote
omitted]." *Jacobellis* v. *Ohio, supra,* at 188 (opinion of
BRENNAN, J.).

III

Under a National Constitution, fundamental First
Amendment limitations on the powers of the States do
not vary from community to community, but this does
not mean that there are, or should or can be, fixed,
uniform national standards of precisely what appeals
to the "prurient interest" or is "patently offensive."
These are essentially questions of fact, and our Nation
is simply too big and too diverse for this Court to reasonably expect that such standards could be articulated for
all 50 States in a single formulation, even assuming the
prerequisite consensus exists. When triers of fact are
asked to decide whether "the average person, applying
contemporary community standards" would consider certain materials "prurient," it would be unrealistic to require that the answer be based on some abstract
formulation. The adversary system, with lay jurors as
the usual ultimate factfinders in criminal prosecutions,
has historically permitted triers of fact to draw on the
standards of their community, guided always by limiting
instructions on the law. To require a State to structure
obscenity proceedings around evidence of a *national*
"community standard" would be an exercise in futility.

As noted before, this case was tried on the theory that
the California obscenity statute sought to incorporate the
tripartite test of *Memoirs.* This, a "national" standard
of First Amendment protection enumerated by a plurality
of this Court, was correctly regarded at the time of trial
as limiting state prosecution under the controlling case

law. The jury, however, was explicitly instructed that, in determining whether the "dominant theme of the material as a whole . . . appeals to the prurient interest" and in determining whether the material "goes substantially beyond customary limits of candor and affronts contemporary community standards of decency," it was to apply "contemporary community standards of the State of California."

During the trial, both the prosecution and the defense assumed that the relevant "community standards" in making the factual determination of obscenity were those of the State of California, not some hypothetical standard of the entire United States of America. Defense counsel at trial never objected to the testimony of the State's expert on community standards [12] or to the instructions of the trial judge on "statewide" standards. On appeal to the Appellate Department, Superior Court of California, County of Orange, appellant for the first time contended that application of state, rather than national, standards violated the First and Fourteenth Amendments.

We conclude that neither the State's alleged failure to offer evidence of "national standards," nor the trial court's charge that the jury consider state community standards, were constitutional errors. Nothing in the First Amendment requires that a jury must consider hypothetical and unascertainable "national standards" when attempting to determine whether certain materials are obscene as a mat-

---

[12] The record simply does not support appellant's contention, belatedly raised on appeal, that the State's expert was unqualified to give evidence on California "community standards." The expert, a police officer with many years of specialization in obscenity offenses, had conducted an extensive statewide survey and had given expert evidence on 26 occasions in the year prior to this trial. Allowing such expert testimony was certainly not constitutional error. Cf. *United States* v. *Augenblick,* 393 U. S. 348, 356 (1969).

ter of fact. Mr. Chief Justice Warren pointedly commented in his dissent in *Jacobellis* v. *Ohio, supra,* at 200:

> "It is my belief that when the Court said in *Roth* that obscenity is to be defined by reference to 'community standards,' it meant community standards—not a national standard, as is sometimes argued. I believe that there is no provable 'national standard' .... At all events, this Court has not been able to enunciate one, and it would be unreasonable to expect local courts to divine one."

It is neither realistic nor constitutionally sound to read the First Amendment as requiring that the people of Maine or Mississippi accept public depiction of conduct found tolerable in Las Vegas, or New York City.[13]

---

[13] In *Jacobellis* v. *Ohio,* 378 U. S. 184 (1964), two Justices argued that application of "local" community standards would run the risk of preventing dissemination of materials in some places because sellers would be unwilling to risk criminal conviction by testing variations in standards from place to place. *Id.,* at 193–195 (opinion of BRENNAN, J., joined by Goldberg, J.). The use of "national" standards, however, necessarily implies that materials found tolerable in some places, but not under the "national" criteria, will nevertheless be unavailable where they are acceptable. Thus, in terms of danger to free expression, the potential for suppression seems at least as great in the application of a single nationwide standard as in allowing distribution in accordance with local tastes, a point which Mr. Justice Harlan often emphasized. See *Roth* v. *United States,* 354 U. S., at 506.

Appellant also argues that adherence to a "national standard" is necessary "in order to avoid unconscionable burdens on the free flow of interstate commerce." As noted *supra,* at 18 n. 1, the application of domestic state police powers in this case did not intrude on any congressional powers under Art. I, § 8, cl. 3, for there is no indication that appellant's materials were ever distributed interstate. Appellant's argument would appear without substance in any event. Obscene material may be validly regulated by a State in the exercise of its traditional local power to protect the

See *Hoyt* v. *Minnesota,* 399 U. S. 524–525 (1970) (BLACK-MUN, J., dissenting); *Walker* v. *Ohio,* 398 U. S. 434 (1970) (BURGER, C. J., dissenting); *id.,* at 434–435 (Harlan, J., dissenting); *Cain* v. *Kentucky,* 397 U. S. 319 (1970) (BURGER, C. J., dissenting); *id.,* at 319–320 (Harlan, J., dissenting); *United States* v. *Groner,* 479 F. 2d, at 581–583; O'Meara & Shaffer, Obscenity in The Supreme Court: A Note on *Jacobellis* v. *Ohio,* 40 Notre Dame Law. 1, 6–7 (1964). See also *Memoirs* v. *Massachusetts,* 383 U. S., at 458 (Harlan, J., dissenting); *Jacobellis* v. *Ohio, supra,* at 203–204 (Harlan, J., dissenting); *Roth* v. *United States, supra,* at 505–506 (Harlan, J., concurring and dissenting). People in different States vary in their tastes and attitudes, and this diversity is not to be strangled by the absolutism of imposed uniformity. As the Court made clear in *Mishkin* v. *New York,* 383 U. S., at 508–509, the primary concern with requiring a jury to apply the standard of "the average person, applying contemporary community standards" is to be certain that, so far as material is not aimed at a deviant group, it will be judged by its impact on an average person, rather than a particularly susceptible or sensitive person—or indeed a totally insensitive one. See *Roth* v. *United States, supra,* at 489. Cf. the now discredited test in *Regina* v. *Hicklin,* [1868] L. R. 3 Q. B. 360. We hold that the requirement that the jury evaluate the materials with reference to "contemporary

---

general welfare of its population despite some possible incidental effect on the flow of such materials across state lines. See, *e. g., Head* v. *New Mexico Board,* 374 U. S. 424 (1963); *Huron Portland Cement Co.* v. *Detroit,* 362 U. S. 440 (1960); *Breard* v. *Alexandria,* 341 U. S. 622 (1951); *H. P. Hood & Sons* v. *Du Mond,* 336 U. S. 525 (1949); *Southern Pacific Co.* v. *Arizona,* 325 U. S. 761 (1945); *Baldwin* v. *G. A. F. Seelig, Inc.,* 294 U. S. 511 (1935); *Sligh* v. *Kirkwood,* 237 U. S. 52 (1915).

standards of the State of California" serves this protective purpose and is constitutionally adequate.[14]

IV

The dissenting Justices sound the alarm of repression. But, in our view, to equate the free and robust exchange of ideas and political debate with commercial exploitation of obscene material demeans the grand conception of the First Amendment and its high purposes in the historic struggle for freedom. It is a "misuse of the great guarantees of free speech and free press . . . ." *Breard* v. *Alexandria*, 341 U. S., at 645. The First Amendment protects works which, taken as a whole, have serious literary, artistic, political, or scientific value, regardless of whether the government or a majority of the people approve of the ideas these works represent. "The protection given speech and press was fashioned to assure unfettered interchange of *ideas* for the bringing about of

---

[14] Appellant's jurisdictional statement contends that he was subjected to "double jeopardy" because a Los Angeles County trial judge dismissed, before trial, a prior prosecution based on the same brochures, but apparently alleging exposures at a different time in a different setting. Appellant argues that once material has been found not to be obscene in one proceeding, the State is "collaterally estopped" from ever alleging it to be obscene in a different proceeding. It is not clear from the record that appellant properly raised this issue, better regarded as a question of procedural due process than a "double jeopardy" claim, in the state courts below. Appellant failed to address any portion of his brief on the merits to this issue, and appellee contends that the question was waived under California law because it was improperly pleaded at trial. Nor is it totally clear from the record before us what collateral effect the pretrial dismissal might have under state law. The dismissal was based, at least in part, on a failure of the prosecution to present affirmative evidence required by state law, evidence which was apparently presented in this case. Appellant's contention, therefore, is best left to the California courts for further consideration on remand. The issue is not, in any event, a proper subject for appeal. See *Mishkin* v. *New York*, 383 U. S. 502, 512–514 (1966).

political and social changes desired by the people," *Roth*
v. *United States, supra,* at 484 (emphasis added). See
Kois v. *Wisconsin,* 408 U. S., at 230–232; *Thornhill* v.
Alabama, 310 U. S., at 101–102. But the public portrayal of hard-core sexual conduct for its own sake, and
for the ensuing commercial gain, is a different matter.[15]
There is no evidence, empirical or historical, that
the stern 19th century American censorship of public
distribution and display of material relating to sex,
see *Roth* v. *United States, supra,* at 482–485, in
any way limited or affected expression of serious literary,
artistic, political, or scientific ideas. On the contrary,
it is beyond any question that the era following Thomas
Jefferson to Theodore Roosevelt was an "extraordinarily
vigorous period," not just in economics and politics, but
in *belles lettres* and in "the outlying fields of social and
political philosophies." [16] We do not see the harsh hand

---

[15] In the apt words of Mr. Chief Justice Warren, appellant in
this case was "plainly engaged in the commercial exploitation of
the morbid and shameful craving for materials with prurient effect.
I believe that the State and Federal Governments can constitutionally
punish such conduct. That is all that these cases present to us,
and that is all we need to decide." *Roth* v. *United States, supra,* at
496 (concurring opinion).

[16] See 2 V. Parrington, Main Currents in American Thought
ix et seq. (1930). As to the latter part of the 19th century, Parrington observed "A new age had come and other dreams—the age and
the dreams of a middle-class sovereignty . . . . From the crude and
vast romanticisms of that vigorous sovereignty emerged eventually a
spirit of realistic criticism, seeking to evaluate the worth of this new
America, and discover if possible other philosophies to take the
place of those which had gone down in the fierce battles of the
Civil War." *Id.,* at 474. Cf. 2 S. Morison, H. Commager & W.
Leuchtenburg, The Growth of the American Republic 197–233 (6th
ed. 1969); Paths of American Thought 123–166, 203–290 (A.
Schlesinger & M. White ed. 1963) (articles of Fleming, Lerner, Morton
& Lucia White, E. Rostow, Samuelson, Kazin, Hofstadter); and
H. Wish, Society and Thought in Modern America 337–386 (1952).

of censorship of ideas—good or bad, sound or unsound—
and "repression" of political liberty lurking in every state
regulation of commercial exploitation of human interest
in sex.

MR. JUSTICE BRENNAN finds "it is hard to see how
state-ordered regimentation of our minds can ever be
forestalled." *Paris Adult Theatre I* v. *Slaton, post,* at
110 (BRENNAN, J., dissenting). These doleful anticipa-
tions assume that courts cannot distinguish commerce in
ideas, protected by the First Amendment, from commercial exploitation of obscene material. Moreover, state
regulation of hard-core pornography so as to make it
unavailable to nonadults, a regulation which MR. JUS-
TICE BRENNAN finds constitutionally permissible, has
all the elements of "censorship" for adults; indeed
even more rigid enforcement techniques may be called
for with such dichotomy of regulation. See *Interstate
Circuit, Inc.* v. *Dallas,* 390 U. S., at 690.[17] One can
concede that the "sexual revolution" of recent years may
have had useful byproducts in striking layers of prudery
from a subject long irrationally kept from needed ventilation. But it does not follow that no regulation of
patently offensive "hard core" materials is needed or
permissible; civilized people do not allow unregulated
access to heroin because it is a derivative of medicinal
morphine.

In sum, we (a) reaffirm the *Roth* holding that obscene
material is not protected by the First Amendment;
(b) hold that such material can be regulated by the
States, subject to the specific safeguards enunciated

---

[17] "[W]e have indicated . . . that because of its strong and
abiding interest in youth, a State may regulate the dissemination to
juveniles of, and their access to, material objectionable as to them,
but which a State clearly could not regulate as to adults. *Ginsberg*
v. *New York,* . . . [390 U. S. 629 (1968)]." *Interstate Circuit, Inc.*
v. *Dallas,* 390 U. S. 676, 690 (1968) (footnote omitted).

15

above, without a showing that the material is *"utterly without redeeming social value"*; and (c) hold that obscenity is to be determined by applying "contemporary community standards," see *Kois* v. *Wisconsin, supra,* at 230, and *Roth* v. *United States, supra,* at 489, not "national standards." The judgment of the Appellate Department of the Superior Court, Orange County, California, is vacated and the case remanded to that court for further proceedings not inconsistent with the First Amendment standards established by this opinion. See *United States* v. *12 200-ft. Reels of Film, post,* at 130 n. 7.

Vacated and remanded.

COLUMBIA BROADCASTING SYSTEM, INC. v. DEMOCRATIC NATIONAL COMMITTEE

CERTIORARI TO THE UNITED STATES COURT OF APPEALS FOR THE DISTRICT OF COLUMBIA CIRCUIT

No. 71–863. Argued October 16, 1972—Decided May 29, 1973*

The Democratic National Committee requested a declaratory ruling from the Federal Communications Commission (FCC) that the Communications Act or the First Amendment precluded a licensee from having a general policy of refusing to sell time to "responsible entities" to present their views on public issues. The Business Executives' Move for Vietnam Peace filed a complaint with the FCC, alleging that a broadcaster had violated the First Amendment by refusing to sell it time to broadcast spot announcements expressing the group's views on the Vietnam conflict and that the station's coverage of antiwar views did not meet the requirements of the Fairness Doctrine. The FCC rejected the Fairness Doctrine challenge and ruled that a broadcaster was not prohibited from having a policy of refusing to accept paid editorial advertisements by individuals and organizations like respondents. The Court of Appeals reversed, holding that "a flat ban on paid public issue announcements is in violation of the First Amendment, at least when other sorts of paid announcements are accepted," and remanded the causes to the FCC to develop regulations governing which, and how many, editorial announcements would be aired. *Held:* Neither the Communications Act nor the First Amendment requires broadcasters to accept paid editorial advertisements. Pp. 101–114; 121–170.

146 U. S. App. D. C. 181, 450 F. 2d 642, reversed.

Mr. Chief Justice Burger delivered the opinion of the Court with respect to Parts I, II, and IV, finding that:

1. The basic criterion governing use of broadcast frequencies is the right of the public to be informed; the manner by which this

---

*Together with Nos. 71–864, *Federal Communications Commission et al.* v. *Business Executives' Move for Vietnam Peace et al.;* 71–865, *Post-Newsweek Stations, Capital Area, Inc.* v. *Business Executives' Move for Vietnam Peace;* and 71–866, *American Broadcasting Cos., Inc.* v. *Democratic National Committee,* also on certiorari to the same court.

interest is best served is dispositive of the respondents' statutory and First Amendment contentions. Pp. 101–114.

(a) In evaluating respondents' claims, great weight must be afforded the decisions of Congress and the experience of the FCC. Pp. 101–103.

(b) Congress has consistently rejected efforts to impose on broadcasters a "common carrier" right of access for all persons wishing to speak out on public issues. Instead, it reposed in the FCC regulatory authority by which the Fairness Doctrine was evolved to require that the broadcaster's coverage of important public issues must be adequate and must fairly reflect differing viewpoints; thus, no private individual or group has a right to command the use of broadcast facilities. Pp. 103–114.

2. The "public interest" standard of the Communications Act, which incorporates First Amendment principles, does not require broadcasters to accept editorial advertisements. Pp. 121–131.

(a) The FCC was justified in concluding that the public interest in having access to the marketplace of "ideas and experiences" would not be served by ordering a right of access to advertising time. There is substantial risk that such a system would be monopolized by those who could and would pay the costs, that the effective operation of the Fairness Doctrine itself would be undermined, and that the public accountability which now rests with the broadcaster would be diluted. Pp. 121–125.

(b) The difficult problems involved in implementing an absolute right of access would inevitably implicate the FCC in a case-by-case determination of who should be heard and when, thus enlarging the involvement of the Government in broadcasting operations. The FCC could properly take into account the fact that listeners and viewers constitute a kind of "captive audience" and that the public interest requires that a substantial degree of journalistic discretion must remain with broadcasters. Pp. 126–130.

THE CHIEF JUSTICE, joined by MR. JUSTICE STEWART and MR. JUSTICE REHNQUIST, concluded, in Part III, that a broadcast licensee's refusal to accept a paid editorial advertisement does not constitute "governmental action" for First Amendment purposes. The Government is neither a "partner" to the action complained of nor engaged in a "symbiotic relationship" with the licensee. Pp. 114–121.

(a) Under the Communications Act a broadcast licensee is vested with substantial journalistic discretion in deciding how to meet its statutory obligations as a "public trustee." Pp. 114–117.

(b) The licensee's policy against accepting editorial advertising is compatible with the Communications Act and with the
broadcaster's obligation to provide a balanced treatment of controversial questions. Pp. 118–121.

(c) The FCC has not fostered the licensee policy against accepting editorial advertisements; it has merely declined to command acceptance because the subject was a matter within the area
of journalistic discretion. P. 118.

BURGER, C. J., announced the Court's judgment and delivered an
opinion of the Court with respect to Parts I, II, and IV, in which
WHITE, BLACKMUN, POWELL, and REHNQUIST, JJ., joined, and
in which as to Parts I, II, and III STEWART and REHNQUIST, JJ.,
joined. STEWART, J., filed an opinion concurring in Parts I, II,
and III, *post*, p. 132. WHITE, J., filed an opinion concurring in
Parts I, II, and IV, *post*, p. 146. BLACKMUN, J., filed an opinion
concurring in Parts I, II, and IV, in which POWELL, J., joined, *post*,
p. 147. DOUGLAS, J., filed an opinion concurring in the judgment,
post, p. 148. BRENNAN, J., filed a dissenting opinion, in which
MARSHALL, J., joined, *post*, p. 170.

J. Roger Wollenberg argued the cause for petitioner
in No. 71–863. With him on the briefs were *Lloyd N.
Cutler, Timothy B. Dyk, Daniel Marcus, Robert V.
Evans, John D. Appel,* and *Joseph DeFranco. Solicitor
General Griswold* argued the cause for petitioners in No.
71–864. With him on the brief were *Acting Assistant
Attorney General Comegys, Howard E. Shapiro,* and
John W. Pettit. Ernest W. Jennes argued the cause for
petitioner in No. 71–865. With him on the briefs were
Charles A. Miller and *Michael Boudin. Vernon L.
Wilkinson* argued the cause for petitioner in No. 71–866.
With him on the brief were *James A. McKenna, Jr.,* and
Carl R. Ramey.

Joseph A. Califano, Jr., argued the cause for respondent
Democratic National Committee in Nos. 71–863, 71–864,
and 71–866. With him on the brief was *John G. Kester.
Thomas R. Asher* argued the cause for respondent Busi-

ness Executives' Move for Vietnam Peace in Nos. 71–864 and 71–865. With him on the brief was *Albert H. Kramer.*†

MR. CHIEF JUSTICE BURGER delivered the opinion of the Court (Parts I, II, and IV) together with an opinion (Part III), in which MR. JUSTICE STEWART and MR. JUSTICE REHNQUIST joined.

We granted the writs of certiorari in these cases to consider whether a broadcast licensee's general policy of not selling advertising time to individuals or groups wishing to speak out on issues they consider important violates the Federal Communications Act of 1934, 48 Stat. 1064, as amended, 47 U. S. C. § 151 *et seq.,* or the First Amendment.

In two orders announced the same day, the Federal Communications Commission ruled that a broadcaster who meets his public obligation to provide full and fair coverage of public issues is not required to accept editorial advertisements. *Democratic National Committee,* 25 F. C. C. 2d 216; *Business Executives' Move for Vietnam Peace,* 25 F. C. C. 2d 242. A divided Court of Appeals reversed the Commission, holding that a broadcaster's fixed policy of refusing editorial advertisements violates the First Amendment; the court remanded the cases to the Commission to develop procedures and guidelines for administering a First Amendment right of access. *Business Executives' Move For Vietnam Peace v. FCC,* 146 U. S. App. D. C. 181, 450 F. 2d 642 (1971).

The complainants in these actions are the Democratic

---

†*Floyd Abrams* and *Corydon B. Dunham* filed a brief for National Broadcasting Co., Inc., as *amicus curiae* urging reversal.

J. Albert Woll, Laurence Gold, and *Thomas E. Harris* filed a brief for the American Federation of Labor and Congress of Industrial Organizations as *amicus curiae* urging affirmance.

National Committee (DNC) and the Business Executives' Move for Vietnam Peace (BEM), a national organization of businessmen opposed to United States involvement in the Vietnam conflict. In January 1970, BEM filed a complaint with the Commission charging that radio station WTOP in Washington, D. C., had refused to sell it time to broadcast a series of one-minute spot announcements expressing BEM views on Vietnam. WTOP, in common with many, but not all, broadcasters, followed a policy of refusing to sell time for spot announcements to individuals and groups who wished to expound their views on controversial issues. WTOP took the position that since it presented full and fair coverage of important public questions, including the Vietnam conflict, it was justified in refusing to accept editorial advertisements. WTOP also submitted evidence showing that the station had aired the views of critics of our Vietnam policy on numerous occasions. BEM challenged the fairness of WTOP's coverage of criticism of that policy, but it presented no evidence in support of that claim.

Four months later, in May 1970, DNC filed with the Commission a request for a declaratory ruling:

> "That under the First Amendment to the Constitution and the Communications Act, a broadcaster may not, as a general policy, refuse to sell time to responsible entities, such as the DNC, for the solicitation of funds and for comment on public issues."

DNC claimed that it intended to purchase time from radio and television stations and from the national networks in order to present the views of the Democratic Party and to solicit funds. Unlike BEM, DNC did not object to the policies of any particular broadcaster but claimed that its prior "experiences in this area make it clear that it will encounter considerable difficulty—if not total frustration of its efforts—in carrying out its plans in the event the Commission should decline to issue a ruling as requested."   DNC cited *Red Lion Broadcasting Co.* v. *FCC*, 395 U. S. 367 (1969), as establishing a limited constitutional right of access to the airwaves.

In two separate opinions, the Commission rejected respondents' claims that "responsible" individuals and groups have a right to purchase advertising time to comment on public issues without regard to whether the broadcaster has complied with the Fairness Doctrine. The Commission viewed the issue as one of major significance in administering the regulatory scheme relating to the electronic media, one going "to the heart of the system of broadcasting which has developed in this country . . . ."   25 F. C. C. 2d, at 221.   After reviewing the legislative history of the Communications Act, the provisions of the Act itself, the Commission's decisions under the Act, and the difficult problems inherent in administering a right of access, the Commission rejected the demands of BEM and DNC.

The Commission also rejected BEM's claim that WTOP had violated the Fairness Doctrine by failing to air views such as those held by members of BEM; the Commission pointed out that BEM had made only a "general allegation" of unfairness in WTOP's coverage of the Vietnam conflict and that the station had adequately rebutted the charge by affidavit.   The Commission did, however, uphold DNC's position that the statute recognized a right of political parties to purchase broadcast time for the purpose of soliciting funds.   The Commission noted that Congress has accorded special consideration for access by political parties, see 47 U. S. C. § 315 (a), and that solicitation of funds by political parties is both feasible and appropriate in the short space of time generally allotted to spot advertisements.[1]

A majority of the Court of Appeals reversed the Commission, holding that "a flat ban on paid public issue announcements is in violation of the First Amendment, at least when other sorts of paid announcements are accepted." 146 U. S. App. D. C., at 185, 450 F. 2d, at 646. Recognizing that the broadcast frequencies are a scarce resource inherently unavailable to all, the court nevertheless concluded that the First Amendment mandated an "abridgeable" right to present editorial advertisements. The court reasoned that a broadcaster's policy of airing commercial advertisements but not editorial advertisements constitutes unconstitutional discrimination. The court did not, however, order that either BEM's or DNC's proposed announcements must be accepted by the broadcasters; rather, it remanded the cases to the Commission to develop "reasonable procedures and regulations determining which and how many 'editorial advertisements' will be put on the air." *Ibid.*

Judge McGowan dissented; in his view, the First Amendment did not compel the Commission to undertake the task assigned to it by the majority:

> "It is presently the obligation of a licensee to advance the public's right to know by devoting a substantial amount of time to the presentation of controversial views on issues of public importance, striking a balance which is always subject to redress by reference to the fairness doctrine. Failure to do so puts continuation of the license at risk—a sanction of tremendous potency, and one which the Commission is under increasing pressure to employ.

---

[1] The Commission's rulings against BEM's Fairness Doctrine complaint and in favor of DNC's claim that political parties should be permitted to purchase air time for solicitation of funds were not appealed to the Court of Appeals and are not before us here.

"This is the system which Congress has, wisely or not, provided as the alternative to public ownership and operation of radio and television communications facilities. This approach has never been thought to be other than within the permissible limits of constitutional choice." 146 U. S. App. D. C., at 205, 450 F. 2d, at 666.

Judge McGowan concluded that the court's decision to overrule the Commission and to remand for development and implementation of a constitutional right of access put the Commission in a "constitutional straitjacket" on a highly complex and far-reaching issue.

I

MR. JUSTICE WHITE's opinion for the Court in *Red Lion Broadcasting Co.* v. *FCC*, 395 U. S. 367 (1969), makes clear that the broadcast media pose unique and special problems not present in the traditional free speech case. Unlike other media, broadcasting is subject to an inherent physical limitation. Broadcast frequencies are a scarce resource; they must be portioned out among applicants. All who possess the financial resources and the desire to communicate by television or radio cannot be satisfactorily accommodated. The Court spoke to this reality when, in *Red Lion*, we said "it is idle to posit an unabridgeable First Amendment right to broadcast comparable to the right of every individual to speak, write, or publish." *Id.*, at 388.

Because the broadcast media utilize a valuable and limited public resource, there is also present an unusual order of First Amendment values. *Red Lion* discussed at length the application of the First Amendment to the broadcast media. In analyzing the broadcasters' claim that the Fairness Doctrine and two of its component rules violated their freedom of expression, we

279

held that "[n]o one has a First Amendment right to a license or to monopolize a radio frequency; to deny a station license because 'the public interest' requires it 'is not a denial of free speech.'" *Id.,* at 389. Although the broadcaster is not without protection under the First Amendment, *United States* v. *Paramount Pictures, Inc.,* 334 U. S. 131, 166 (1948), "[i]t is the right of the viewers and listeners, not the right of the broadcasters, which is paramount. . . . It is the right of the public to receive suitable access to social, political, esthetic, moral, and other ideas and experiences which is crucial here. That right may not constitutionally be abridged either by Congress or by the FCC." *Red Lion, supra,* at 390.

Balancing the various First Amendment interests involved in the broadcast media and determining what best serves the public's right to be informed is a task of a great delicacy and difficulty. The process must necessarily be undertaken within the framework of the regulatory scheme that has evolved over the course of the past half century. For, during that time, Congress and its chosen regulatory agency have established a delicately balanced system of regulation intended to serve the interests of all concerned. The problems of regulation are rendered more difficult because the broadcast industry is dynamic in terms of technological change; solutions adequate a decade ago are not necessarily so now, and those acceptable today may well be outmoded 10 years hence.

Thus, in evaluating the First Amendment claims of respondents, we must afford great weight to the decisions of Congress and the experience of the Commission. Professor Chafee aptly observed:

"Once we get away from the bare words of the [First] Amendment, we must construe it as part of a Constitution which creates a government for the purpose of performing several very important tasks.

The [First] Amendment should be interpreted so as not to cripple the regular work of the government. A part of this work is the regulation of interstate and foreign commerce, and this has come in our modern age to include the job of parceling out the air among broadcasters, which Congress has entrusted to the FCC. Therefore, every free-speech problem in the radio has to be considered with reference to the satisfactory performance of this job as well as to the value of open discussion. Although free speech should weigh heavily in the scale in the event of conflict, still the Commission should be given ample scope to do its job." 2 Z. Chafee, Government and Mass Communications 640–641 (1947).

The judgment of the Legislative Branch cannot be ignored or undervalued simply because one segment of the broadcast constituency casts its claims under the umbrella of the First Amendment. That is not to say we "defer" to the judgment of the Congress and the Commission on a constitutional question, or that we would hesitate to invoke the Constitution should we determine that the Commission has not fulfilled its task with appropriate sensitivity to the interests in free expression. The point is, rather, that when we face a complex problem with many hard questions and few easy answers we do well to pay careful attention to how the other branches of Government have addressed the same problem. Thus, before confronting the specific legal issues in these cases, we turn to an examination of the legislative and administrative development of our broadcast system over the last half century.

II

This Court has on numerous occasions recounted the origins of our modern system of broadcast regulation. See, *e. g., Red Lion, supra,* at 375–386; *National Broad-*

casting Co. v. *United States,* 319 U. S. 190, 210–217
(1943); *FCC* v. *Sanders Brothers Radio Station,* 309
U. S. 470, 474 (1940); *FCC* v. *Pottsville Broadcasting Co.,* 309 U. S. 134, 137–138 (1940). We have
noted that prior to the passage of the Radio Act of 1927,
44 Stat. 1162, broadcasting was marked by chaos. The
unregulated and burgeoning private use of the new
media in the 1920's had resulted in an intolerable situation demanding congressional action:

> "It quickly became apparent that broadcast fre-
> quencies constituted a scarce resource whose use
> could be regulated and rationalized only by the Gov-
> ernment. Without government control, the medium
> would be of little use because of the cacaphony of
> competing voices, none of which could be clearly
> and predictably heard." *Red Lion, supra,* at 376.

But, once it was accepted that broadcasting was subject
to regulation, Congress was confronted with a major
dilemma: how to strike a proper balance between private and public control. Cf. *Farmers Union* v. *WDAY,*
360 U. S. 525, 528 (1959).

One of the earliest and most frequently quoted statements of this dilemma is that of Herbert Hoover, when
he was Secretary of Commerce. While his Department
was making exploratory attempts to deal with the infant
broadcasting industry in the early 1920's, he testified before a House Committee:

> "We can not allow any single person or group to
> place themselves in [a] position where they can
> censor the material which shall be broadcasted to the
> public, nor do I believe that the Government should
> ever be placed in the position of censoring this
> material." Hearings on H. R. 7357 before the House
> Committee on the Merchant Marine and Fisheries,
> 68th Cong., 1st Sess., 8 (1924).

That statement foreshadowed the "tightrope" aspects of Government regulation of the broadcast media, a problem the Congress, the Commission, and the courts have struggled with ever since. Congress appears to have concluded, however, that of these two choices—private or official censorship—Government censorship would be the most pervasive, the most self-serving, the most difficult to restrain and hence the one most to be avoided.

The legislative history of the Radio Act of 1927, the model for our present statutory scheme, see *FCC v. Pottsville Broadcasting Co., supra,* at 137, reveals that in the area of discussion of public issues Congress chose to leave broad journalistic discretion with the licensee. Congress specifically dealt with—and firmly rejected—the argument that the broadcast facilities should be open on a nonselective basis to all persons wishing to talk about public issues. Some members of Congress—those whose views were ultimately rejected—strenuously objected to the unregulated power of broadcasters to reject applications for service. See, *e. g.,* H. R. Rep. No. 404, 69th Cong., 1st Sess., 18 (minority report). They regarded the exercise of such power to be "private censorship," which should be controlled by treating broadcasters as public utilities.[2] The provision that came closest to imposing an unlimited right of access to broadcast time was part of the bill reported to the Senate by the Committee on Interstate Commerce. The

---

[2] Congressman Davis, for example, stated on the floor of the House the view that Congress found unacceptable:

"I do not think any member of the committee will deny that it is absolutely inevitable that we are going to have to regulate the radio public utilities just as we regulate other public utilities. We are going to have to regulate the rates and the service, and to force them to give equal service and equal treatment to all." 67 Cong. Rec. 5483 (1926). See also *id.,* at 5484.

bill that emerged from the Committee contained the following provision:

"[I]f any licensee shall permit a broadcasting station to be used . . . by a candidate or candidates for any public office, *or for the discussion of any question affecting the public,* he shall make no discrimination as to the use of such broadcasting station, *and with respect to said matters the licensee shall be deemed a common carrier in interstate commerce:* Provided, that such licensee shall have no power to censor the material broadcast." 67 Cong. Rec. 12503 (1926) (emphasis added).

When the bill came to the Senate floor, the principal architect of the Radio Act of 1927, Senator Dill, offered an amendment to the provision to eliminate the common carrier obligation and to restrict the right of access to candidates for public office. Senator Dill explained the need for the amendment:

"When we recall that broadcasting today is purely voluntary, and the listener-in pays nothing for it, that the broadcaster gives it for the purpose of building up his reputation, it seemed unwise to put the broadcaster under the hampering control of being a common carrier and compelled to accept anything and everything that was offered him so long as the price was paid." 67 Cong. Rec. 12502.

The Senators were also sensitive to the problems involved in legislating "equal opportunities" with respect to the discussion of public issues. Senator Dill stated:

"['Public questions'] is such a general term that there is probably no question of any interest whatsoever that could be discussed but that the other side of it could demand time; and thus a radio station

would be placed in the position that the Senator
from Iowa mentions about candidates, namely, that
they would have to give all their time to that kind
of discussion, or no public question could be discussed." *Id.,* at 12504.

The Senate adopted Senator Dill's amendment. The
provision finally enacted, § 18 of the Radio Act of 1927,
44 Stat. 1170, was later re-enacted as § 315 (a) of the
Communications Act of 1934,[3] but only after Congress
rejected another proposal that would have imposed a
limited obligation on broadcasters to turn over their
microphones to persons wishing to speak out on certain

---

[3] Section 315 (a) now reads:

"If any licensee shall permit any person who is a legally qualified
candidate for any public office to use a broadcasting station, he
shall afford equal opportunities to all other such candidates for that
office in the use of such broadcasting station: *Provided,* That such
licensee shall have no power of censorship over the material broadcast under the provisions of this section. No obligation is imposed
under this subsection upon any licensee to allow the use of its station
by any such candidate. Appearance by a legally qualified candidate
on any—

"(1) bona fide newscast,

"(2) bona fide news interview,

"(3) bona fide news documentary (if the appearance of the candidate is incidental to the presentation of the subject or subjects
covered by the news documentary), or

"(4) on-the-spot coverage of bona fide news events (including
but not limited to political conventions and activities incidental
thereto),

"shall not be deemed to be use of a broadcasting station within
the meaning of this subsection. Nothing in the foregoing sentence
shall be construed as relieving broadcasters, in connection with the
presentation of newscasts, news interviews, news documentaries, and
on-the-spot coverage of news events, from the obligation imposed
upon them under this chapter to operate in the public interest and
to afford reasonable opportunity for the discussion of conflicting
views on issues of public importance." 47 U. S. C. § 315 (a).

public issues.⁴ Instead, Congress after prolonged consideration adopted § 3 (h), which specifically provides that "a person engaged in radio broadcasting shall not,

---

⁴ The Senate passed a provision stating that:

"[I]f any licensee shall permit any person to use a broadcasting station in support of or in opposition to any candidate for public office, *or in the presentation of views on a public question to be voted upon at an election, he shall afford equal opportunity to an equal number of other persons to use such station* in support of an opposing candidate for such public office, or to reply to a person who has used such broadcasting station in support of or in opposition to a candidate, *or for the presentation of opposite views on such public questions."*

See Hearings on S. 2910 before the Senate Committee on Interstate Commerce, 73d Cong., 2d Sess., 19 (1934) (emphasis added). The provision for discussion of public issues was deleted by the House-Senate Conference. See H. R. Conf. Rep. No. 1918 on S. 3285, 73d Cong., 2d Sess., 49.

Also noteworthy are two bills offered in 1934 that would have restricted the control of broadcasters over the discussion of certain issues. Congressman McFadden proposed a bill that would have forbidden broadcasters to discriminate against programs sponsored by religious, charitable, or educational associations. H. R. 7986, 73d Cong., 2d Sess. The bill was not reported out of committee. And, during the debates on the 1934 Act, Senators Wagner and Hatfield offered an amendment that would have ordered the Commission to "reserve and allocate only to educational, religious, agricultural, labor, cooperative, and similar non-profit-making associations one-fourth of all the radio broadcasting facilities within its jurisdiction." 78 Cong. Rec. 8828. Senator Dill explained why the Committee had rejected the proposed amendment, indicating that the practical difficulties and the dangers of censorship were crucial:

"MR. DILL. . . . If we should provide that 25 percent of time shall be allocated to nonprofit organizations, someone would have to determine—Congress or somebody else—how much of the 25 percent should go to education, how much of it to religion, and how much of it to agriculture, how much of it to labor, how much of it to fraternal organizations, and so forth. When we enter this insofar as such person is so engaged, be deemed a common carrier." [5]

Other provisions of the 1934 Act also evince a legislative desire to preserve values of private journalism under a regulatory scheme which would insure fulfillment of certain public obligations. Although the Commission was given the authority to issue renewable three-year licenses to broadcasters [6] and to promulgate rules and regulations governing the use of those licenses,[7] both con-

---

field we must determine how much to give to the Catholics probably and how much to the Protestants and how much to the Jews." 78 Cong. Rec. 8843.

Senator Dill went on to say that the problem of determining the proper allocation of time for discussion of these subjects should be worked out by the Commission. *Id.,* at 8844. The Senate rejected the amendment. *Id.,* at 8846.

[5] Section 3 (h) provides as follows:

" 'Common carrier' or 'carrier' means any person engaged as a common carrier for hire, in interstate or foreign communication by wire or radio or in interstate or foreign radio transmission of energy, except where reference is made to common carriers not subject to this chapter; but a person engaged in radio broadcasting shall not, insofar as such person is so engaged, be deemed a common carrier." 48 Stat. 1066, as amended, 47 U. S. C. § 153 (h).

[6] 48 Stat. 1083, as amended, 47 U. S. C. § 307.

[7] Section 303, 48 Stat. 1082, as amended, 47 U. S. C. § 303, provides in relevant part:

"Except as otherwise provided in this chapter, the Commission from time to time, as public convenience, interest, or necessity requires, shall—

.   .   .   .   .

"(b) Prescribe the nature of the service to be rendered by each class of licensed stations and each station within any class;

.   .   .   .   .

"(r) Make such rules and regulations and prescribe such restrictions and conditions, not inconsistent with law, as may be necessary to carry out the provisions of this chapter . . . ."

287

sistent with the "public convenience, interest, or necessity," § 326 of the Act specifically provides that:

> "Nothing in this chapter shall be understood or
> construed to give the Commission the power of
> censorship over the radio communications or signals
> transmitted by any radio station, and no regulation
> or condition shall be promulgated or fixed by the
> Commission which shall interfere with the right of
> free speech by means of radio communication." 47
> U. S. C. § 326.

From these provisions it seems clear that Congress
intended to permit private broadcasting to develop with
the widest journalistic freedom consistent with its public obligations. Only when the interests of the public
are found to outweigh the private journalistic interests
of the broadcasters will government power be asserted
within the framework of the Act. License renewal proceedings, in which the listening public can be heard, are
a principal means of such regulation. See *Office of Communication of United Church of Christ* v. *FCC,* 123 U. S.
App. D. C. 328, 359 F. 2d 994 (1966), and 138 U. S.
App. D. C. 112, 425 F. 2d 543 (1969).

Subsequent developments in broadcast regulation illustrate how this regulatory scheme has evolved. Of particular importance, in light of Congress' flat refusal to
impose a "common carrier" right of access for all persons
wishing to speak out on public issues, is the Commission's "Fairness Doctrine," which evolved gradually over
the years spanning federal regulation of the broadcast
media.[8] Formulated under the Commission's power to

---

[8] In 1959, Congress amended § 315 of the Act to give statutory
approval to the Fairness Doctrine. Act of Sept. 14, 1959, § 1, 73
Stat. 557, 47 U. S. C. § 315 (a).

For a summary of the development and nature of the Fairness
Doctrine, see *Red Lion Broadcasting Co.* v. *FCC,* 395 U. S. 367,
375–386 (1969).

issue regulations consistent with the "public interest," the doctrine imposes two affirmative responsibilities on the broadcaster: coverage of issues of public importance must be adequate and must fairly reflect differing viewpoints. See *Red Lion,* 395 U. S., at 377. In fulfilling the Fairness Doctrine obligations, the broadcaster must provide free time for the presentation of opposing views if a paid sponsor is unavailable, *Cullman Broadcasting Co.,* 25 P & F Radio Reg. 895 (1963), and must initiate programming on public issues if no one else seeks to do so. See *John J. Dempsey,* 6 P & F Radio Reg. 615 (1950); *Red Lion, supra,* at 378.

Since it is physically impossible to provide time for all viewpoints, however, the right to exercise editorial judgment was granted to the broadcaster. The broadcaster, therefore, is allowed significant journalistic discretion in deciding how best to fulfill the Fairness Doctrine obligations,[9] although that discretion is bounded by rules designed to assure that the public interest in fairness is furthered. In its decision in the instant cases, the Commission described the boundaries as follows:

> "The most basic consideration in this respect is that the licensee cannot rule off the air coverage of important issues or views because of his private ends or beliefs. As a public trustee, he must present

---

[9] See *Madalyn Murray,* 5 P & F Radio Reg. 2d 263 (1965). Factors that the broadcaster must take into account in exercising his discretion include the following:

"In determining whether to honor specific requests for time, the station will inevitably be confronted with such questions as whether the subject is worth considering, whether the viewpoint of the requesting party has already received a sufficient amount of broadcast time, or whether there may not be other available groups or individuals who might be more appropriate spokesmen for the particular point of view than the person [or group] making the request." Report on Editorializing by Broadcast Licensees, 13 F. C. C. 1246, 1251–1252 (1949).

representative community views and voices on controversial issues which are of importance to his
listeners. . . . This means also that some of the
voices must be partisan. A licensee policy of excluding partisan voices and always itself presenting
views in a bland, inoffensive manner would run
counter to the 'profound national commitment that
debate on public issues should be uninhibited, robust,
and wide-open.' *New York Times Co.* v. *Sullivan,*
376 U. S. 254, 270 (1964); see also *Red Lion Broadcasting Co., Inc.* v. *F. C. C.,* 395 U. S. 367, 392 (n. 18)
(1969) . . . ." 25 F. C. C. 2d, at 222–223.

Thus, under the Fairness Doctrine broadcasters are
responsible for providing the listening and viewing public
with access to a balanced presentation of information
on issues of public importance.[10] The basic principle
underlying that responsibility is "the right of the public
to be informed, rather than any right on the part of the

---

[10] The Commission has also adopted various component regulations under the Fairness Doctrine, the most notable of which are
the "personal attack" and "political editorializing" rules which we
upheld in *Red Lion.* The "personal attack" rule provides that
"[w]hen, during the presentation of views on a controversial issue
of public importance, an attack is made upon the honesty, character,
integrity or like personal qualities of an identified person," the
licensee must notify the person attacked and give him an opportunity to respond. *E. g.,* 47 CFR § 73.123. Similarly, the "political
editorializing" rule provides that, when a licensee endorses a political
candidate in an editorial, he must give other candidates or their
spokesmen an opportunity to respond. *E. g., id.,* § 73.123.

The Commission, of course, has taken other steps beyond the
Fairness Doctrine to expand the diversity of expression on radio and
television. The chain broadcasting and multiple ownership rules
are established examples. *E. g., id.,* §§ 73.131, 73.240. More recently, the Commission promulgated rules limiting television network
syndication practices and reserving 25% of prime time for non-
network programs. *Id.,* §§ 73.658 (j), (k).

Government, any broadcast licensee or any individual member of the public to broadcast his own particular views on any matter . . . ."   Report on Editorializing by Broadcast Licensees, 13 F. C. C. 1246, 1249 (1949). Consistent with that philosophy, the Commission on several occasions has ruled that no private individual or group has a right to command the use of broadcast facilities.[11]   See, *e. g., Dowie A. Crittenden,* 18 F. C. C. 2d 499 (1969); *Margaret Z. Scherbina,* 21 F. C. C. 2d 141 (1969); *Boalt Hall Student Assn.,* 20 F. C. C. 2d 612 (1969); *Madalyn Murray,* 40 F. C. C. 647 (1965); *Democratic State Central Committee of California,* 19 F. C. C. 2d 833 (1968); *U. S. Broadcasting Corp.,* 2 F. C. C. 208 (1935).   Congress has not yet seen fit to alter that policy, although since 1934 it has amended the Act on several occasions[12] and considered various

---

[11] The Court of Appeals, respondents, and the dissent in this case have relied on dictum in *United Broadcasting Co.,* 10 F. C. C. 515 (1945), as illustrating Commission approval of a private right to purchase air time for the discussion of controversial issues.   In that case the complaint alleged, not only that the station had a policy of refusing to sell time for the discussion of public issues, but also that the station had applied its policy in a discriminatory manner, a factor not shown in the cases presently before us.   Furthermore, the decision was handed down four years before the Commission had fully developed and articulated the Fairness Doctrine.   See Report on Editorializing by Broadcast Licensees, 13 F. C. C. 1246 (1949).   Thus, even if the decision is read without reference to the allegation of discrimination, it stands as merely an isolated statement, made during the period in which the Commission was still working out the problems associated with the discussion of public issues; the dictum has not been followed since and has been modified by the Fairness Doctrine.

[12] In 1959, as noted earlier, Congress amended § 315 (a) of the Act to give statutory approval to the Commission's Fairness Doctrine.   Act of Sept. 14, 1959, § 1, 73 Stat. 557, 47 U. S. C. § 315 (a).   Very recently, Congress amended § 312 (a) of the 1934 Act to authorize the Commission to revoke a station license "for willful

proposals that would have vested private individuals with a right of access.[13]

With this background in mind, we next proceed to consider whether a broadcaster's refusal to accept editorial advertisements is governmental action violative of the First Amendment.

III

That "Congress shall make no law . . . abridging the freedom of speech, or of the press" is a restraint on government action, not that of private persons. *Public Utilities Comm'n* v. *Pollak,* 343 U. S. 451, 461 (1952). The Court has not previously considered whether the action of a broadcast licensee such as that challenged here is "governmental action" for purposes of the First

---

or repeated failure to allow reasonable access to or to permit purchase of reasonable amounts of time for the use of a broadcasting station by a legally qualified candidate for Federal elective office on behalf of his candidacy." Campaign Communications Reform Act of 1972, Pub. L. 92–225, 86 Stat. 4. This amendment essentially codified the Commission's prior interpretation of § 315 (a) as requiring broadcasters to make time available to political candidates. *Farmers Union* v. *WDAY,* 360 U. S. 525, 534 (1959). See FCC Memorandum on Second Sentence of Section 315 (a), in Political Broadcasts—Equal Time, Hearings before Subcommittee of the House Committee on Interstate and Foreign Commerce, 88th Cong., 1st Sess., on H. J. Res. 247, pp. 84–90.

[13] See, *e. g.,* H. R. 3595, 80th Cong., 1st Sess. (1947). A more recent proposal was offered by Senator Fulbright. His bill would have amended § 315 of the Act to provide:

"(d) Licensees shall provide a reasonable amount of public service time to authorized representatives of the Senate of the United States, and the House of Representatives of the United States, to present the views of the Senate and the House of Representatives on issues of public importance. The public service time required to be provided under this subsection shall be made available to each such authorized representative at least, but not limited to, four times during each calendar year." S. J. Res. 209, 91st Cong., 2d Sess. (1970).

Amendment.   The holding under review thus presents a
novel question, and one with far-reaching implications.
See Jaffe, The Editorial Responsibility of the Broadcaster: Reflections on Fairness and Access, 85 Harv.
L. Rev. 768, 782–787 (1972).

The Court of Appeals held that broadcasters are instrumentalities of the Government for First Amendment
purposes, relying on the thesis, familiar in other contexts, that broadcast licensees are granted use of part of
the public domain and are regulated as "proxies" or
"'fiduciaries' of the people."   146 U. S. App. D. C., at
191, 450 F. 2d, at 652.   These characterizations are not
without validity for some purposes, but they do not
resolve the sensitive constitutional issues inherent in
deciding whether a particular licensee action is subject
to First Amendment restraints.[14]

In dealing with the broadcast media, as in other contexts, the line between private conduct and governmental
action cannot be defined by reference to any general formula unrelated to particular exercises of governmental
authority.   When governmental action is alleged there
must be cautious analysis of the quality and degree of
Government relationship to the particular acts in question.   "Only by sifting facts and weighing circumstances
can the nonobvious involvement of the State in private
conduct be attributed its true significance."   Burton v.
Wilmington Parking Authority, 365 U. S. 715, 722 (1961).

---

[14] The dissent offers the same analysis as the Court of Appeals.
As one distinguished commentator has recognized, this line of reasoning "stretch[es] the concept of state action very far."   Jaffe,
The Editorial Responsibility of the Broadcaster: Reflections on
Fairness and Access, 85 Harv. L. Rev. 768, 784 (1972).   The notion
that broadcasters are engaged in "governmental action" because
they are licensed to utilize the "public" frequencies and because they
are regulated is superficially appealing but, as Professor Jaffe ob-
serves, "not entirely satisfactory."   Id., at 783.

In deciding whether the First Amendment encompasses the conduct challenged here, it must be kept in
mind that we are dealing with a vital part of our system
of communication. The electronic media have swiftly become a major factor in the dissemination of ideas and
information. More than 7,000 licensed broadcast stations undertake to perform this important function. To
a large extent they share with the printed media the role
of keeping people informed.

As we have seen, with the advent of radio a half century ago, Congress was faced with a fundamental choice
between total Government ownership and control of the
new medium—the choice of most other countries—or
some other alternative. Long before the impact and potential of the medium was realized, Congress opted for
a system of private broadcasters licensed and regulated
by Government. The legislative history suggests that
this choice was influenced not only by traditional attitudes toward private enterprise, but by a desire to maintain for licensees, so far as consistent with necessary
regulation, a traditional journalistic role. The historic
aversion to censorship led Congress to enact § 326 of
the Act, which explicitly prohibits the Commission from
interfering with the exercise of free speech over the
broadcast frequencies. Congress pointedly refrained from
divesting broadcasters of their control over the selection
of voices; § 3 (h) of the Act stands as a firm congressional
statement that broadcast licensees are not to be treated
as common carriers, obliged to accept whatever is tendered by members of the public. Both these provisions
clearly manifest the intention of Congress to maintain
a substantial measure of journalistic independence for
the broadcast licensee.[15]

---

[15] The dissenting view would appear to "want to have it both
ways" on the question of Government control of the broadcast media.
In finding governmental action, the dissent stresses what is per-

The regulatory scheme evolved slowly, but very early the licensee's role developed in terms of a "public trustee" charged with the duty of fairly and impartially informing the public audience. In this structure the Commission acts in essence as an "overseer," but the initial and primary responsibility for fairness, balance, and objectivity rests with the licensee. This role of the Government as an "overseer" and ultimate arbiter and guardian of the public interest and the role of the licensee as a journalistic "free agent" call for a delicate balancing of competing interests. The maintenance of this balance for more than 40 years has called on both the regulators and the licensees to walk a "tightrope" to preserve the First Amendment values written into the Radio Act and its successor, the Communications Act.

The tensions inherent in such a regulatory structure emerge more clearly when we compare a private newspaper with a broadcast licensee. The power of a privately owned newspaper to advance its own political, social, and economic views is bounded by only two factors: first, the acceptance of a sufficient number of readers—and hence advertisers—to assure financial success; and, second, the journalistic integrity of its editors and publishers. A broadcast licensee has a large measure of journalistic freedom but not as large as that exercised by

---

ceived as an "elaborate statutory scheme governing virtually all aspects of the broadcast industry." "Indeed," the dissent suggests, "federal agency review and guidance of broadcaster conduct is automatic, continuing, and pervasive." *Post,* at 176–177. Yet later in the dissent, when discussing the constitutional need for a right of access, the dissent objects to the substantial independence afforded broadcasters in covering issues of public importance. Thus, it is said that "broadcasters retain almost exclusive control over the selection of issues and viewpoints to be covered, the manner of presentation and, perhaps most important, who shall speak." *Post,* at 187.

a newspaper. A licensee must balance what it might prefer to do as a private entrepreneur with what it is required to do as a "public trustee." To perform its statutory duties, the Commission must oversee without censoring. This suggests something of the difficulty and delicacy of administering the Communications Act—a function calling for flexibility and the capacity to adjust and readjust the regulatory mechanism to meet changing problems and needs.

The licensee policy challenged in this case is intimately related to the journalistic role of a licensee for which it has been given initial and primary responsibility by Congress. The licensee's policy against accepting editorial advertising cannot be examined as an abstract proposition, but must be viewed in the context of its journalistic role. It does not help to press on us the idea that editorial ads are "like" commercial ads, for the licensee's policy against editorial spot ads is expressly based on a journalistic judgment that 10- to 60-second spot announcements are ill-suited to intelligible and intelligent treatment of public issues; the broadcaster has chosen to provide a balanced treatment of controversial questions in a more comprehensive form. Obviously the licensee's evaluation is based on its own journalistic judgment of priorities and newsworthiness.

Moreover, the Commission has not fostered the licensee policy challenged here; it has simply declined to command particular action because it fell within the area of journalistic discretion. The Commission explicitly emphasized that "there is of course no Commission policy thwarting the sale of time to comment on public issues." 25 F. C. C. 2d, at 226. The Commission's reasoning, consistent with nearly 40 years of precedent, is that so long as a licensee meets its "public trustee" obligation to provide balanced coverage of issues and events, it has broad discretion to decide how that obligation will be met. We do not reach the question whether the First Amendment or the Act can be read to preclude the Commission from determining that in some situations the public interest requires licensees to re-examine their policies with respect to editorial advertisements. The Commission has not yet made such a determination; it has, for the present at least, found the policy to be within the sphere of journalistic discretion which Congress has left with the licensee.

Thus, it cannot be said that the Government is a "partner" to the action of the broadcast licensee complained of here, nor is it engaged in a "symbiotic relationship" with the licensee, profiting from the invidious discrimination of its proxy. Compare *Moose Lodge No. 107* v. *Irvis,* 407 U. S. 163, 174–177 (1972), with *Burton* v. *Wilmington Parking Authority,* 365 U. S., at 723–724. The First Amendment does not reach acts of private parties in every instance where the Congress or the Commission has merely permitted or failed to prohibit such acts.

Our conclusion is not altered merely because the Commission rejected the claims of BEM and DNC and concluded that the challenged licensee policy is not inconsistent with the public interest. It is true that in *Public Utilities Comm'n* v. *Pollak,* 343 U. S. 451 (1952), we found governmental action sufficient to trigger First Amendment protections on a record involving agency approval of the conduct of a public utility. Though we held that the decision of a District of Columbia bus company to install radio receivers in its public buses was within the reach of the First Amendment, there Congress had expressly authorized the agency to undertake plenary intervention into the affairs of the carrier and it was pursuant to that authorization that the agency investigated the challenged policy and approved it on public interest standards. *Id.,* at 462.

Here, Congress has not established a regulatory scheme for broadcast licensees as pervasive as the regulation of public transportation in *Pollak*. More important, as we have noted, Congress has affirmatively indicated in the Communications Act that certain journalistic decisions are for the licensee, subject only to the restrictions imposed by evaluation of its overall performance under the public interest standard. In *Pollak* there was no suggestion that Congress had considered worthy of protection the carrier's interest in exercising discretion over the content of communications forced on passengers. A more basic distinction, perhaps, between *Pollak* and this case is that *Pollak* was concerned with a transportation utility that itself derives no protection from the First Amendment. See *United States* v. *Paramount Pictures, Inc.*, 334 U. S. 131, 166 (1948).

Were we to read the First Amendment to spell out governmental action in the circumstances presented here, few licensee decisions on the content of broadcasts or the processes of editorial evaluation would escape constitutional scrutiny. In this sensitive area so sweeping a concept of governmental action would go far in practical effect to undermine nearly a half century of unmistakable congressional purpose to maintain—no matter how difficult the task—essentially private broadcast journalism held only broadly accountable to public interest standards. To do this Congress, and the Commission as its agent, must remain in a posture of flexibility to chart a workable "middle course" in its quest to preserve a balance between the essential public accountability and the desired private control of the media.

More profoundly, it would be anomalous for us to hold, in the name of promoting the constitutional guarantees of free expression, that the day-to-day editorial decisions of broadcast licensees are subject to the kind of restraints urged by respondents. To do so in the name of the First Amendment would be a contradiction. Journalistic discretion would in many ways be lost to the rigid limitations that the First Amendment imposes on Government. Application of such standards to broadcast licensees would be antithetical to the very ideal of vigorous, challenging debate on issues of public interest. Every licensee is already held accountable for the totality of its performance of public interest obligations.

The concept of private, independent broadcast journalism, regulated by Government to assure protection of the public interest, has evolved slowly and cautiously over more than 40 years and has been nurtured by processes of adjudication. That concept of journalistic independence could not co-exist with a reading of the challenged conduct of the licensee as governmental action. Nor could it exist without administrative flexibility to meet changing needs and swift technological developments. We therefore conclude that the policies complained of do not constitute governmental action violative of the First Amendment. See *McIntire* v. *William Penn Broadcasting Co.,* 151 F. 2d 597, 601 (CA3 1945), cert. denied, 327 U. S. 779 (1946); *Massachusetts Universalist Convention* v. *Hildreth & Rogers Co.,* 183 F. 2d 497 (CA1 1950); *Post* v. *Payton,* 323 F. Supp. 799, 803 (EDNY 1971).

IV

There remains for consideration the question whether the "public interest" standard of the Communications Act requires broadcasters to accept editorial advertisements or, whether, assuming governmental action, broadcasters are required to do so by reason of the First Amendment. In resolving those issues, we are guided by the "venerable principle that the construction of a statute by those charged with its execution should be followed unless there are compelling indications that it is wrong . . . ." *Red Lion,* 395 U. S., at 381. Whether there are "compelling indications" of error in these cases must be answered by a careful evaluation of the Commission's reasoning in light of the policies embodied by Congress in the "public interest" standard of the Act. Many of those policies, as the legislative history makes clear, were drawn from the First Amendment itself; the "public interest" standard necessarily invites reference to First Amendment principles. Thus, the question before us is whether the various interests in free expression of the public, the broadcaster, and the individuals require broadcasters to sell commercial time to persons wishing to discuss controversial issues. In resolving that issue it must constantly be kept in mind that the interest of the public is our foremost concern. With broadcasting, where the available means of communication are limited in both space and time, the admonition of Professor Alexander Meiklejohn that "[w]hat is essential is not that everyone shall speak, but that everything worth saying shall be said" is peculiarly appropriate. Political Freedom 26 (1948).

At the outset we reiterate what was made clear earlier that nothing in the language of the Communications Act or its legislative history compels a conclusion different from that reached by the Commission. As we have seen, Congress has time and again rejected various legislative attempts that would have mandated a variety of forms of individual access. That is not to say that Congress' rejection of such proposals must be taken to mean that Congress is opposed to private rights of access under all circumstances. Rather, the point is that Congress has chosen to leave such questions with the Commission, to which it has given the flexibility to experiment with new ideas as changing conditions require. In this case, the Commission has decided that on balance the undesirable effects of the right of access urged by respondents would outweigh the asserted benefits. The Court of

Appeals failed to give due weight to the Commission's judgment on these matters.

The Commission was justified in concluding that the public interest in providing access to the marketplace of "ideas and experiences" would scarcely be served by a system so heavily weighted in favor of the financially affluent, or those with access to wealth. Cf. *Red Lion, supra,* at 392. Even under a first-come-first-served system, proposed by the dissenting Commissioner in these cases,[16] the views of the affluent could well prevail over those of others, since they would have it within their power to purchase time more frequently. Moreover, there is the substantial danger, as the Court of Appeals acknowledged, 146 U. S. App. D. C., at 203, 450 F. 2d, at 664, that the time allotted for editorial advertising could be monopolized by those of one political persuasion.

These problems would not necessarily be solved by applying the Fairness Doctrine, including the *Cullman* doctrine, to editorial advertising. If broadcasters were required to provide time, free when necessary, for the discussion of the various shades of opinion on the issue discussed in the advertisement, the affluent could still determine in large part the issues to be discussed. Thus, the very premise of the Court of Appeals' holding—that a right of access is necessary to allow individuals and groups the opportunity for self-initiated speech—would have little meaning to those who could not afford to purchase time in the first instance.[17]

---

[16] See 25 F. C. C. 2d 216, 230, 234–235 (Johnson, dissenting).

[17] To overcome this inconsistency it has been suggested that a "submarket rate system" be established for those unable to afford the normal cost for air time. See Note, 85 Harv. L. Rev. 689, 695–696 (1972). That proposal has been criticized, we think justifiably, as raising "incredible administrative problems." Jaffe, The Editorial Responsibility of the Broadcaster: Reflections on Fairness and Access, 85 Harv. L. Rev. 768, 789 (1972).

If the Fairness Doctrine were applied to editorial advertising, there is also the substantial danger that the effective operation of that doctrine would be jeopardized. To minimize financial hardship and to comply fully with its public responsibilities a broadcaster might well be forced to make regular programming time available to those holding a view different from that expressed in an editorial advertisement; indeed, BEM has suggested as much in its brief. The result would be a further erosion of the journalistic discretion of broadcasters in the coverage of public issues, and a transfer of control over the treatment of public issues from the licensees who are accountable for broadcast performance to private individuals who are not. The public interest would no longer be "paramount" but, rather, subordinate to private whim especially since, under the Court of Appeals' decision, a broadcaster would be largely precluded from rejecting editorial advertisements that dealt with matters trivial or insignificant or already fairly covered by the broadcaster. 146 U. S. App. D. C., at 196 n. 36, 197, 450 F. 2d, at 657 n. 36, 658. If the Fairness Doctrine and the *Cullman* doctrine were suspended to alleviate these problems, as respondents suggest might be appropriate, the question arises whether we would have abandoned more than we have gained. Under such a regime the congressional objective of balanced coverage of public issues would be seriously threatened.

Nor can we accept the Court of Appeals' view that every potential speaker is "the best judge" of what the listening public ought to hear or indeed the best judge of the merits of his or her views. All journalistic tradition and experience is to the contrary. For better or worse, editing is what editors are for; and editing is selection and choice of material. That editors—newspaper or broadcast—can and do abuse this power is beyond doubt, but that is no reason to deny the discretion Congress provided. Calculated risks of abuse are taken in order to preserve higher values. The presence of these risks is nothing new; the authors of the Bill of Rights accepted the reality that these risks were evils for which there was no acceptable remedy other than a spirit of moderation and a sense of responsibility—and civility—on the part of those who exercise the guaranteed freedoms of expression.

It was reasonable for Congress to conclude that the public interest in being informed requires periodic accountability on the part of those who are entrusted with the use of broadcast frequencies, scarce as they are. In the delicate balancing historically followed in the regulation of broadcasting Congress and the Commission could appropriately conclude that the allocation of journalistic priorities should be concentrated in the licensee rather than diffused among many. This policy gives the public some assurance that the broadcaster will be answerable if he fails to meet its legitimate needs. No such accountability attaches to the private individual, whose only qualifications for using the broadcast facility may be abundant funds and a point of view. To agree that debate on public issues should be "robust, and wide-open" does not mean that we should exchange "public trustee" broadcasting, with all its limitations, for a system of self-appointed editorial commentators.

The Court of Appeals discounted those difficulties by stressing that it was merely mandating a "modest reform," requiring only that broadcasters be required to accept some editorial advertising. 146 U. S. App. D. C., at 202, 450 F. 2d, at 663. The court suggested that broadcasters could place an "outside limit on the total amount of editorial advertising they will sell" and that the Commission and the broadcasters could develop " 'reasonable regulations' designed to prevent domination by a few groups or a few viewpoints." *Id.,* at 202,

203, 450 F. 2d, at 663, 664. If the Commission decided to apply the Fairness Doctrine to editorial advertisements and as a result broadcasters suffered financial
harm, the court thought the "Commission could make
necessary adjustments." *Id.*, at 203, 450 F. 2d, at 664.
Thus, without providing any specific answers to the substantial objections raised by the Commission and the
broadcasters, other than to express repeatedly its "confidence" in the Commission's ability to overcome any
difficulties, the court remanded the cases to the Commission for the development of regulations to implement a
constitutional right of access.

By minimizing the difficult problems involved in implementing such a right of access, the Court of Appeals
failed to come to grips with another problem of critical
importance to broadcast regulation and the First Amendment—the risk of an enlargement of Government control
over the content of broadcast discussion of public issues.
See, *e. g., Fowler* v. *Rhode Island,* 345 U. S. 67 (1953);
Niemotko v. *Maryland,* 340 U. S. 268 (1951). This risk
is inherent in the Court of Appeals' remand requiring
regulations and procedures to sort out requests to be
heard—a process involving the very editing that licensees now perform as to regular programming. Although the use of a public resource by the broadcast
media permits a limited degree of Government surveillance, as is not true with respect to private media, see
National Broadcasting Co. v. *United States,* 319 U. S.,
at 216–219, the Government's power over licensees, as
we have noted, is by no means absolute and is carefully
circumscribed by the Act itself.[18]

Under a constitutionally commanded and Government
supervised right-of-access system urged by respondents
and mandated by the Court of Appeals, the Commission

[18] See n. 8, *supra.*

would be required to oversee far more of the day-to-day operations of broadcasters' conduct, deciding such questions as whether a particular individual or group has had sufficient opportunity to present its viewpoint and whether a particular viewpoint has already been sufficiently aired. Regimenting broadcasters is too radical a therapy for the ailment respondents complain of.

Under the Fairness Doctrine the Commission's responsibility is to judge whether a licensee's overall performance indicates a sustained good-faith effort to meet the public interest in being fully and fairly informed.[19] The Commission's responsibilities under a right-of-access system would tend to draw it into a continuing case-by-case determination of who should be heard and when. Indeed, the likelihood of Government involvement is so great that it has been suggested that the accepted constitutional principles against control of speech content would need to be relaxed with respect to editorial advertisements.[20] To sacrifice First Amendment protections for so speculative a gain is not warranted, and it was well within the Commission's discretion to construe the Act so as to avoid such a result.[21]

The Commission is also entitled to take into account the reality that in a very real sense listeners and viewers constitute a "captive audience." Cf. *Public Utilities Comm'n* v. *Pollak,* 343 U. S., at 463; *Kovacs* v. *Cooper,* 336 U. S. 77 (1949). The "captive" nature of the broadcast audience was recognized as early as 1924,

---

[19] See Report on Editorializing by Broadcast Licensees, 13 F. C. C., at 1251–1252.

[20] See Note, 85 Harv. L. Rev. 689, 697 (1973).

[21] DNC has urged in this Court that we at least recognize a right of our national parties to purchase air time for the purpose of discussing public issues. We see no principled means under the First Amendment of favoring access by organized political parties over other groups and individuals

when Commerce Secretary Hoover remarked at the Fourth National Radio Conference that "the radio listener does not have the same option that the reader of publications has—to ignore advertising in which he is not interested—and he may resent its invasion of his set." [22] As the broadcast media became more pervasive in our society, the problem has become more acute. In a recent decision upholding the Commission's power to promulgate rules regarding cigarette advertising, Judge Bazelon, writing for a unanimous Court of Appeals, noted some of the effects of the ubiquitous commercial:

> "Written messages are not communicated unless they are read, and reading requires an affirmative act. Broadcast messages, in contrast, are 'in the air.' In an age of omnipresent radio, there scarcely breathes a citizen who does not know some part of a leading cigarette jingle by heart. Similarly, an ordinary habitual television watcher can *avoid* these commercials only by frequently leaving the room, changing the channel, or doing some other such affirmative act. It is difficult to calculate the subliminal impact of this pervasive propaganda, which may be heard even if not listened to, but it may reasonably be thought greater than the impact of the written word." *Banzhaf* v. *FCC*, 132 U. S. App. D. C. 14, 32–33, 405 F. 2d 1082, 1100–1101 (1968), cert. denied, 396 U. S. 842 (1969).

It is no answer to say that because we tolerate pervasive commercial advertisements we can also live with its political counterparts.

The rationale for the Court of Appeals' decision imposing a constitutional right of access on the broadcast media was that the licensee impermissibly discriminates

---

[22] Reprinted in Hearings before the Senate Committee on Interstate Commerce on Radio Control, 69th Cong., 1st Sess., 54 (1926).

by accepting commercial advertisements while refusing editorial advertisements. The court relied on decisions holding that state-supported school newspapers and public transit companies were prohibited by the First Amendment from excluding controversial editorial advertisements in favor of commercial advertisements.[23] The court also attempted to analogize this case to some of our decisions holding that States may not constitutionally ban certain protected speech while at the same time permitting other speech in public areas. *Cox* v. *Louisiana*, 379 U. S. 536 (1965); *Fowler* v. *Rhode Island*, 345 U. S. 67 (1953); *Niemotko* v. *Maryland*, 340 U. S. 268 (1951). This theme of "invidious discrimination" against protected speech is echoed in the briefs of BEM and DNC to this Court. Respondents also rely on our recent decisions in *Grayned* v. *City of Rockford*, 408 U. S. 104 (1972), and *Police Dept. of Chicago* v. *Mosley*, 408 U. S. 92 (1972), where we held unconstitutional city ordinances that permitted "peaceful picketing of any school involved in a labor dispute," *id.*, at 93, but prohibited demonstrations for any other purposes on the streets and sidewalks within 150 feet of the school.

Those decisions provide little guidance, however, in resolving the question whether the First Amendment requires the Commission to mandate a private right of access to the broadcast media. In none of those cases did the forum sought for expression have an affirmative and independent statutory obligation to provide full and fair coverage of public issues, such as Congress has imposed on

---

[23] *Lee* v. *Board of Regents of State Colleges*, 306 F. Supp. 1097 (WD Wis. 1969), aff'd, 441 F. 2d 1257 (CA7 1971); *Zucker* v. *Panitz*, 299 F. Supp. 102 (SDNY 1969); *Kissinger* v. *New York City Transit Authority*, 274 F. Supp. 438 (SDNY 1967); *Hillside Community Church, Inc.* v. *City of Tacoma*, 76 Wash. 2d 63, 455 P. 2d 350 (1969); *Wirta* v. *Alameda-Contra Costa Transit District*, 68 Cal. 2d 51, 434 P. 2d 982 (1967).

all broadcast licensees. In short, there is no "discrimination" against controversial speech present in this case. The question here is not whether there is to be discussion of controversial issues of public importance on the broadcast media, but rather who shall determine what issues are to be discussed by whom, and when.

The opinion of the Court of Appeals asserted that the Fairness Doctrine, insofar as it allows broadcasters to exercise certain journalistic judgments over the discussion of public issues, is inadequate to meet the public's interest in being informed. The present system, the court held, "conforms . . . to a paternalistic structure in which licensees and bureaucrats decide what issues are 'important,' and how 'fully' to cover them, and the format, time and style of the coverage." 146 U. S. App. D. C., at 195, 450 F. 2d, at 656. The forced sale of advertising time for editorial spot announcements would, according to the Court of Appeals majority, remedy this deficiency. That conclusion was premised on the notion that advertising time, as opposed to programming time, involves a "special and separate mode of expression" because advertising content, unlike programming content, is generally prepared and edited by the advertiser. Thus, that court concluded, a broadcaster's policy against using advertising time for editorial messages "may well ignore opportunities to enliven and enrich the public's overall information." Id., at 197, 450 F. 2d, at 658. The Court of Appeals' holding would serve to transfer a large share of responsibility for balanced broadcasting from an identifiable, regulated entity—the licensee—to unregulated speakers who could afford the cost.

We reject the suggestion that the Fairness Doctrine permits broadcasters to preside over a "paternalistic" regime. See Red Lion, 395 U. S., at 390. That doctrine admittedly has not always brought to the public perfect or, indeed, even consistently high-quality treatment of all public events and issues; but the remedy does not lie in diluting licensee responsibility. The Commission stressed that, while the licensee has discretion in fulfilling its obligations under the Fairness Doctrine, it is required to "present representative community views and voices on controversial issues which are of importance to [its] listeners," and it is prohibited from "excluding partisan voices and always itself presenting views in a bland, inoffensive manner . . . ." 25 F. C. C. 2d, at 222. A broadcaster neglects that obligation only at the risk of losing his license.

Conceivably at some future date Congress or the Commission—or the broadcasters—may devise some kind of limited right of access that is both practicable and desirable. Indeed, the Commission noted in these proceedings that the advent of cable television will afford increased opportunities for the discussion of public issues. In its proposed rules on cable television the Commission has provided that cable systems in major television markets

> "shall maintain at least one specially designated, noncommercial public access channel available on a first-come, nondiscriminatory basis. The system shall maintain and have available for public use at least the minimal equipment and facilities necessary for the production of programming for such a channel." 37 Fed Reg. 3289, § 76.251 (a)(4).

For the present, the Commission is conducting a wide-ranging study into the effectiveness of the Fairness Doctrine to see what needs to be done to improve the coverage and presentation of public issues on the broadcast media. Notice of Inquiry in Docket 19260, 30 F. C. C. 2d 26, 36 Fed. Reg. 11825. Among other things, the study will attempt to determine whether "there is any feasible method of providing access for discussion of public issues

outside the requirements of the fairness doctrine." 30
F. C. C. 2d, at 33. The Commission made it clear, however, that it does not intend to discard the Fairness
Doctrine or to require broadcasters to accept all private
demands for air time.[24] The Commission's inquiry on
this score was announced prior to the decision of the
Court of Appeals in this case and hearings are under way.

The problems perceived by the Court of Appeals majority are by no means new; as we have seen, the history
of the Communications Act and the activities of the
Commission over a period of 40 years reflect a continuing
search for means to achieve reasonable regulation compatible with the First Amendment rights of the public
and the licensees. The Commission's pending hearings
are but one step in this continuing process. At the very
least, courts should not freeze this necessarily dynamic
process into a constitutional holding. See *American
Commercial Lines, Inc.* v. *Louisville & N. R. Co.,* 392
U. S. 571, 590–593 (1968).

The judgment of the Court of Appeals is

Reversed.

---

[24] Subsequent to the announcement of the Court of Appeals' decision, the Commission expanded the scope of the inquiry to comply
with the Court of Appeals' mandate. Further Notice of Inquiry
in Docket 19260, 33 F. C. C. 2d 554, 37 Fed. Reg. 3383. After
we granted certiorari and stayed the mandate of the Court of Appeals, the Commission withdrew that notice of an expanded inquiry
and continued its study as originally planned. Order and Further
Notice of Inquiry in Docket 19260, 33 F. C. C. 2d 798, 37 Fed.
Reg. 4980.

GOLDFARB ET UX. *v.* VIRGINIA STATE BAR ET AL.

CERTIORARI TO THE UNITED STATES COURT OF APPEALS FOR THE FOURTH CIRCUIT

No. 74–70. Argued March 25, 1975—Decided June 16, 1975

Petitioners, husband and wife, contracted to buy a home in Fairfax County, Va., and the lender who financed the purchase required them to obtain title insurance, which necessitated a title examination that could be performed legally only by a member of respondent Virginia State Bar. Petitioners unsuccessfully tried to find a lawyer who would examine the title for less than the fee prescribed in a minimum-fee schedule published by respondent Fairfax County Bar Association and enforced by respondent Virginia State Bar. Petitioners then brought this class action against respondents, seeking injunctive relief and damages, and alleging that the minimum-fee schedule and its enforcement mechanism, as applied to fees for legal services relating to residential real estate transactions, constitute price fixing in violation of § 1 of the Sherman Act. Although holding that the State Bar was exempt from the Sherman Act, the District Court granted judgment against the County Bar Association and enjoined the publication of the fee schedule. The Court of Appeals reversed, holding not only that the State Bar's actions were immune from liability as "state action," *Parker* v. *Brown,* 317 U. S. 341, but also that the County Bar Association was immune because the practice of law, as a "learned profession," is not "trade or commerce" under the Sherman Act; and that, in any event, respondents' activities did not have sufficient effect on interstate commerce to support Sherman Act jurisdiction. *Held:* The minimum-fee schedule, as published by the County Bar Association and enforced by the State Bar, violates § 1 of the Sherman Act. Pp. 780–793.

(a) The schedule and its enforcement mechanism constitute price fixing since the record shows that the schedule, rather than being purely advisory, operated as a fixed, rigid price floor. The fee schedule was enforced through the prospect of professional discipline by the State Bar, by reason of attorneys' desire to comply with announced professional norms, and by the assurance that other lawyers would not compete by underbidding. Pp. 781–783.

(b) Since a significant amount of funds furnished for financing the purchase of homes in Fairfax County comes from outside the State, and since a title examination is an integral part of such interstate transactions, interstate commerce is sufficiently affected for Sherman Act purposes notwithstanding that there is no showing that prospective purchasers were discouraged from buying homes in Fairfax County by the challenged activities, and no showing that the fee schedule resulted in raising fees. Pp. 783–785.

(c) Congress did not intend any sweeping "learned profession" exclusion from the Sherman Act; a title examination is a service, and the exchange of such a service for money is "commerce" in the common usage of that term. Pp. 785–788.

(d) Respondents' activities are not exempt from the Sherman Act as "state action" within the meaning of *Parker* v. *Brown, supra.* Neither the Virginia Supreme Court nor any Virginia statute required such activities, and, although the State Bar has the power to issue ethical opinions, it does not appear that the Supreme Court approves them. It is not enough that the anticompetitive conduct is "prompted" by state action; to be exempt, such conduct must be compelled by direction of the State acting as a sovereign. Here the State Bar, by providing that deviation from the minimum fees may lead to disciplinary action, has voluntarily joined in what is essentially a private anticompetitive activity and hence cannot claim it is beyond the Sherman Act's reach. Pp. 788–792.

497 F. 2d 1, reversed and remanded.

BURGER, C. J., delivered the opinion of the Court, in which all other Members joined except POWELL, J., who took no part in the consideration or decision of the case.

Alan B. Morrison argued the cause and filed briefs for petitioners.

Andrew P. Miller, Attorney General of Virginia, argued the cause for respondent Virginia State Bar. With him on the brief were *Anthony F. Troy,* Deputy Attorney General, and *Stuart H. Dunn,* Assistant Attorney General. *Lewis T. Booker* argued the cause for respondent Fairfax County Bar Assn. With him on the brief was *John H. Shenefield.*

Solicitor General Bork argued the cause for the United States as *amicus curiae* urging reversal. With him on the brief were *Assistant Attorney General Kauper, Gerald P. Norton,* and *Howard E. Shapiro.* *

MR. CHIEF JUSTICE BURGER delivered the opinion of the Court.

We granted certiorari to decide whether a minimum-fee schedule for lawyers published by the Fairfax County Bar Association and enforced by the Virginia State Bar violates § 1 of the Sherman Act, 26 Stat. 209, as amended, 15 U. S. C. § 1. The Court of Appeals held that, although the fee schedule and enforcement mechanism substantially restrained competition among lawyers, publication of the schedule by the County Bar was outside the scope of the Act because the practice of law is not "trade or commerce," and enforcement of the schedule by the State Bar was exempt from the Sherman Act as state action as defined in *Parker* v. *Brown,* 317 U. S. 341 (1943).

I

In 1971 petitioners, husband and wife, contracted to buy a home in Fairfax County, Va. The financing agency required them to secure title insurance; this required a title examination, and only a member of the Virginia State Bar could legally perform that service.[1]

---

*Eleanor M. Fox filed a brief for the Association of the Bar of the City of New York as *amicus curiae* urging reversal.

Briefs of *amici curiae* urging affirmance were filed by *James D. Fellers* and *H. Blair White* for the American Bar Assn.; by *Richard C. McFarlain* for the National Organization of Bar Counsel; by *Leroy Jeffers* for the State Bar of Texas; by *Warren H. Resh* for the State Bar of Wisconsin; by *E. Robert Wallach* and *Walter J. Robinson* for the Bar Association of San Francisco; and by *Owen Rall* and *Peter M. Sfikas* for the American Dental Assn.

[1] Unauthorized Practice of Law, Opinion No. 17, Aug. 5, 1942, Virginia State Bar—Opinions 239 (1965).

Petitioners therefore contacted a lawyer who quoted them the precise fee suggested in a minimum-fee schedule published by respondent Fairfax County Bar Association; the lawyer told them that it was his policy to keep his charges in line with the minimum-fee schedule which provided for a fee of 1% of the value of the property involved. Petitioners then tried to find a lawyer who would examine the title for less than the fee fixed by the schedule. They sent letters to 36 other Fairfax County lawyers requesting their fees. Nineteen replied, and none indicated that he would charge less than the rate fixed by the schedule; several stated that they knew of no attorney who would do so.

The fee schedule the lawyers referred to is a list of recommended minimum prices for common legal services. Respondent Fairfax County Bar Association published the fee schedule although, as a purely voluntary association of attorneys, the County Bar has no formal power to enforce it. Enforcement has been provided by respondent Virginia State Bar which is the administrative agency [2] through which the Virginia Supreme Court regulates the practice of law in that State; membership in the State Bar is required in order to practice in Virginia.[3] Although the State Bar has never taken formal disciplinary action to compel adherence to any fee sched-

_____

[2] Virginia Code Ann. § 54-49 (1972) provides:

"The Supreme Court of Appeals may, from time to time, prescribe, adopt, promulgate and amend rules and regulations organizing and governing the association known as the Virginia State Bar, composed of the attorneys at law of this State, to act as an administrative agency of the Court for the purpose of investigating and reporting the violation of such rules and regulations as are adopted by the Court under this article to a court of competent jurisdiction for such proceedings as may be necessary, and requiring all persons practicing law in this State to be members thereof in good standing."

[3] Ibid.

ule, it has published reports[4] condoning fee schedules, and has issued two ethical opinions[5] indicating that fee schedules cannot be ignored. The most recent opinion states that "evidence that an attorney *habitually* charges

---

[4] In 1962 the State Bar published a minimum-fee-schedule report that listed a series of fees and stated that they "represent the considered judgment of the Committee [on Economics of Law Practice] as to [a] fair minimum fee in each instance." The report stated, however, that the fees were not mandatory, and it recommended only that the State Bar *consider* adopting such a schedule. Nevertheless, shortly thereafter the County Bar adopted its own minimum-fee schedule that purported to be "a conscientious effort to show lawyers in their true perspective of dignity, training and integrity." The suggested fees for title examination were virtually identical to those in the State Bar report. In accord with Opinion 98 of the State Bar Committee on Legal Ethics the schedule stated that, although there is an ethical duty to charge a lower fee in a deserving case, if a lawyer

" 'purely for his own advancement, intentionally and regularly bills less than the customary charges of the bar for similar services . . . [in order to] increase his business with resulting personal gain, it becomes a form of solicitation contrary to Canon 27 and also a violation of Canon 7, which forbids the efforts of one lawyer to encroach upon the employment of another.' " App. 30.

In 1969 the State Bar published a second fee-schedule report that, as it candidly stated, "reflect[ed] a general scaling up of fees for legal services." The report again stated that no local bar association was bound by its recommendations; however, respondent County Bar again quickly moved to publish an updated minimum-fee schedule, and generally to raise fees. The new schedule stated that the fees were not mandatory, but tempered that by referring again to Opinion 98. This time the schedule also stated that lawyers should feel free to charge *more* than the recommended fees; and to avoid condemnation of higher fees charged by some lawyers, it cautioned County Bar members that "to . . . publicly criticize lawyers who charge more than the suggested fees herein might in itself be evidence of solicitation . . . ."

[5] Virginia State Bar Committee on Legal Ethics, Opinion No. 98, June 1, 1960; Virginia State Bar Committee on Legal Ethics, Opinion No. 170, May 28, 1971.

less than the suggested minimum fee schedule adopted by his local bar Association, raises a presumption that such lawyer is guilty of misconduct . . . ."[6]

Because petitioners could not find a lawyer willing to charge a fee lower than the schedule dictated, they had their title examined by the lawyer they had first contacted. They then brought this class action against the State Bar and the County Bar[7] alleging that the operation of the minimum-fee schedule, as applied to fees for legal services relating to residential real estate transactions, constitutes price fixing in violation of § 1 of the Sherman Act. Petitioners sought both injunctive relief and damages.

After a trial solely on the issue of liability the District Court held that the minimum-fee schedule violated the Sherman Act.[8] 355 F. Supp. 491 (ED Va. 1973). The

[6] *Ibid.* The parties stipulated that these opinions are a substantial influencing factor in lawyers' adherence to the fee schedules. One reason for this may be because the State Bar is required by statute to "investigat[e] and report . . . the violation of . . . rules and regulations as are adopted by the [Virginia Supreme Court] to a court of competent jurisdiction for such proceedings as may be necessary . . . ." Va. Code Ann. § 54–49 (1972). Therefore any lawyer who contemplated ignoring the fee schedule must have been aware that professional sanctions were possible, and that an enforcement mechanism existed to administer them.

[7] Two additional county bar associations were originally named as defendants but they agreed to a consent judgment under which they were directed to cancel their existing fee schedules, and were enjoined from adopting, publishing, or distributing any future schedules of minimum or suggested fees. Damage claims against these associations were then dismissed with prejudice.

[8] The court was satisfied that interstate commerce was sufficiently affected to sustain jurisdiction under the Sherman Act because a significant portion of the funds and insurance involved in the purchase of homes in Fairfax County comes from outside the State of Virginia. 355 F. Supp 491, 497 (ED Va. 1973).

court viewed the fee-schedule system as a significant reason for petitioners' failure to obtain legal services for less than the minimum fee, and it rejected the County Bar's contention that as a "learned profession" the practice of law is exempt from the Sherman Act.

Both respondents argued that their actions were also exempt from the Sherman Act as state action. *Parker* v. *Brown, supra.* The District Court agreed that the Virginia State Bar was exempt under that doctrine because it is an administrative agency of the Virginia Supreme Court, and more important, because its "minor role in this matter . . . derived from the judicial and 'legislative command of the State and was not intended to operate or become effective without that command.'" The County Bar, on the other hand, is a private organization and was under no compulsion to adopt the fee schedule recommended by the State Bar. Since the County Bar chose its own course of conduct the District Court held that the antitrust laws "remain in full force and effect as to it." The court enjoined the fee schedule, 15 U. S. C. § 26, and set the case down for trial to ascertain damages. 15 U. S. C. § 15.

The Court of Appeals reversed as to liability. 497 F. 2d 1 (CA4 1974). Despite its conclusion that it "is abundantly clear from the record before us that the fee schedule and the enforcement mechanism supporting it act as a substantial restraint upon competition among attorneys practicing in Fairfax County," *id.,* at 13, the Court of Appeals held the State Bar immune under *Parker* v. *Brown, supra,* and held the County Bar immune because the practice of law is not "trade or commerce" under the Sherman Act. There has long been judicial recognition of a limited exclusion of "learned professions" from the scope of the antitrust laws, the court said; that exclusion is based upon the special form

317

of regulation imposed upon the professions by the States, and the incompatibility of certain competitive practices with such professional regulation. It concluded that the promulgation of a minimum-fee schedule is one of "those matters with respect to which an accord must be reached between the necessities of professional regulation and the dictates of the antitrust laws." The accord reached by that court was to hold the practice of law exempt from the antitrust laws.

Alternatively, the Court of Appeals held that respondents' activities did not have sufficient effect on interstate commerce to support Sherman Act jurisdiction. Petitioners had argued that the fee schedule restrained the business of financing and insuring home mortgages by inflating a component part of the total cost of housing, but the court concluded that a title examination is generally a local service, and even where it is part of a transaction which crosses state lines its effect on commerce is only "incidental," and does not justify federal regulation.

We granted certiorari, 419 U. S. 963 (1974), and are thus confronted for the first time with the question of whether the Sherman Act applies to services performed by attorneys in examining titles in connection with financing the purchase of real estate.

II

Our inquiry can be divided into four steps: did respondents engage in price fixing? If so, are their activities in interstate commerce or do they affect interstate commerce? If so, are the activities exempt from the Sherman Act because they involve a "learned profession?" If not, are the activities "state action" within the meaning of Parker v. Brown, 317 U. S. 341 (1943), and therefore exempt from the Sherman Act?

A

The County Bar argues that because the fee schedule is merely advisory, the schedule and its enforcement mechanism do not constitute price fixing. Its purpose, the argument continues, is only to provide legitimate information to aid member lawyers in complying with Virginia professional regulations. Moreover, the County Bar contends that in practice the schedule has not had the effect of producing fixed fees. The facts found by the trier belie these contentions, and nothing in the record suggests these findings lack support.

A purely advisory fee schedule issued to provide guidelines, or an exchange of price information without a showing of an actual restraint on trade, would present us with a different question, *e. g., American Column Co.* v. *United States,* 257 U. S. 377 (1921); *Maple Flooring Assn.* v. *United States,* 268 U. S. 563, 580 (1925). But see *United States* v. *National Assn. of Real Estate Boards,* 339 U. S. 485, 488–489, 495 (1950). The record here, however, reveals a situation quite different from what would occur under a purely advisory fee schedule. Here a fixed, rigid price floor arose from respondents' activities: every lawyer who responded to petitioners' inquiries adhered to the fee schedule, and no lawyer asked for additional information in order to set an individualized fee. The price information disseminated did not concern past standards, cf. *Cement Mfrs. Protective Assn.* v. *United States,* 268 U. S. 588 (1925), but rather minimum fees to be charged in future transactions, and those minimum rates were increased over time. The fee schedule was enforced through the prospect of professional discipline from the State Bar, and the desire of attorneys to comply with announced professional norms, see generally *American Column Co., supra,* at 411;

319

the motivation to conform was reinforced by the assurance that other lawyers would not compete by underbidding. This is not merely a case of an agreement that may be inferred from an exchange of price information, *United States* v. *Container Corp.,* 393 U. S. 333, 337 (1969), for here a naked agreement was clearly shown, and the effect on prices is plain.[9] *Id.,* at 339 (Fortas, J., concurring).

Moreover, in terms of restraining competition and harming consumers like petitioners the price-fixing activities found here are unusually damaging. A title examination is indispensable in the process of financing a real estate purchase, and since only an attorney licensed to practice in Virginia may legally examine a title, see n. 1, *supra,* consumers could not turn to alternative sources for the necessary service. All attorneys, of course, were practicing under the constraint of the fee schedule. See generally *United States* v. *Container Corp., supra,* at 337. The County Bar makes much of the fact that it is a voluntary organization; however, the ethical opinions issued by the State Bar provide that any lawyer, whether or not a member of his county bar associ-

---

[9] The Court of Appeals accurately depicted the situation:

"[I]t is clear from the record that all or nearly all of the [County Bar] members charged fees equal to or exceeding the fees set forth in the schedule for title examinations and other services involving real estate." 497 F. 2d 1, 12 (CA4 1974).

"'A significant reason for the inability of [petitioners] to obtain legal services . . . for less than the fee set forth in the Minimum Fee Schedule . . . was the operation of the minimum fee schedule system.'" *Id.,* at 4.

"It is abundantly clear from the record before us that the fee schedule and the enforcement mechanism supporting it act as a substantial restraint upon competition among attorneys practicing in Fairfax County." *Id.,* at 13.

ation, may be disciplined for "*habitually* charg[ing] less than the suggested minimum fee schedule adopted by his local bar Association . . . ." See *supra*, at 777–778, and n. 4. These factors coalesced to create a pricing system that consumers could not realistically escape. On this record respondents' activities constitute a classic illustration of price fixing.

B

The County Bar argues, as the Court of Appeals held, that any effect on interstate commerce caused by the fee schedule's restraint on legal services was incidental and remote. In its view the legal services, which are performed wholly intrastate, are essentially local in nature and therefore a restraint with respect to them can never substantially affect interstate commerce. Further, the County Bar maintains, there was no showing here that the fee schedule and its enforcement mechanism increased fees, and that even if they did there was no showing that such an increase deterred any prospective homeowner from buying in Fairfax County.

These arguments misconceive the nature of the transactions at issue and the place legal services play in those transactions. As the District Court found,[10] "a significant portion of funds furnished for the purchasing of homes in Fairfax County comes from without the State of Virginia," and "significant amounts of loans on Fairfax County real estate are guaranteed by the United States Veterans Administration and Department of Housing and Urban Development, both headquartered in the District of Columbia." Thus in this class action the transactions which create the need for the particular legal

---

[10] The Court of Appeals did not disturb the District Court's findings of fact. It simply disagreed on the conclusions of law drawn therefrom.

services in question frequently are interstate transactions. The necessary connection between the interstate transactions and the restraint of trade provided by the minimum-fee schedule is present because, in a practical sense,[11] title examinations are necessary in real estate transactions to assure a lien on a valid title of the borrower. In financing realty purchases lenders require, "as a condition of making the loan, that the title to the property involved be examined . . . ."[12] Thus a title examination is an integral part of an interstate transaction[13] and this Court has long held that

> "there is an obvious distinction to be drawn between a course of conduct wholly within a state and conduct which is an inseparable element of a larger program dependent for its success upon activity which affects commerce between the states."

---

[11] It is in a practical sense that we must view an effect on interstate commerce, *Swift & Co.* v. *United States,* 196 U. S. 375, 398 (1905); *Mandeville Island Farms, Inc.* v. *American Crystal Sugar Co.,* 334 U. S. 219, 233 (1948).

[12] 355 F. Supp., at 494.

[13] The County Bar relies on *United States* v. *Yellow Cab Co.,* 332 U. S. 218 (1947), to support its argument that the "essentially local" legal services at issue here are beyond the Sherman Act. There we held, *inter alia,* that intrastate taxi trips that occurred at the start and finish of interstate rail travel were "too unrelated to interstate commerce to constitute a part thereof within the meaning of the Sherman Act." *Id.,* at 230. The ride to the railway station, we said, "[f]rom the standpoints of time and continuity . . . may be quite distinct and separate from the interstate journey." *Id.,* at 232. Here, on the contrary, the legal services are coincidental with interstate real estate transactions in terms of time, and, more important, in terms of continuity they are essential. Indeed, it would be more apt to compare the legal services here with a taxi trip between stations to change trains in the midst of an interstate journey. In *Yellow Cab* we held that such a trip was a part of the stream of commerce. *Id.,* at 228–229.

United States v. *Frankfort Distilleries,* 324 U. S. 293, 297 (1945).

See *United States* v. *Yellow Cab Co.,* 332 U. S. 218, 228–229 (1947).

Given the substantial volume of commerce involved,[14] and the inseparability of this particular legal service from the interstate aspects of real estate transactions, we conclude that interstate commerce has been sufficiently affected. See *Montague & Co.* v. *Lowry,* 193 U. S. 38, 45–46 (1904); *United States* v. *Women's Sportswear Assn.,* 336 U. S. 460, 464–465 (1949).

The fact that there was no showing that home buyers were discouraged by the challenged activities does not mean that interstate commerce was not affected. Otherwise, the magnitude of the effect would control, and our cases have shown that, once an effect is shown, no specific magnitude need be proved. *E. g., United States* v. *McKesson & Robbins, Inc.,* 351 U. S. 305, 310 (1956). Nor was it necessary for petitioners to prove that the fee schedule raised fees. Petitioners clearly proved that the fee schedule fixed fees and thus "deprive[d] purchasers or consumers of the advantages which they derive from free competition." *Apex Hosiery Co.* v. *Leader,* 310 U. S. 469, 501 (1940). See *United States* v. *Socony-Vacuum Oil Co.,* 310 U. S. 150 (1940).

Where, as a matter of law or practical necessity, legal services are an integral part of an interstate transaction, a restraint on those services may substantially affect commerce for Sherman Act purposes. Of course, there may be legal services that involve interstate commerce in other fashions, just as there may be legal services that

---

[14] 355 F. Supp., at 497.

have no nexus with interstate commerce and thus are beyond the reach of the Sherman Act.

C

The County Bar argues that Congress never intended to include the learned professions within the terms "trade or commerce" in § 1 of the Sherman Act,[15] and therefore the sale of professional services is exempt from the Act. No explicit exemption or legislative history is provided to support this contention; rather, the existence of state regulation seems to be its primary basis. Also, the County Bar maintains that competition is inconsistent with the practice of a profession because enhancing profit is not the goal of professional activities; the goal is to provide services necessary to the community.[16] That, indeed, is the classic basis traditionally

---

[15] The County Bar cites phrases in several cases that implied the practice of a learned profession is not "trade or commerce" under the antitrust laws. E. g., Federal Club v. National League, 259 U. S. 200, 209 (1922) ("a firm of lawyers sending out a member to argue a case . . . does not engage in . . . commerce because the lawyer . . . goes to another State"); FTC v. Raladam Co., 283 U. S. 643, 653 (1931) ("medical practitioners . . . follow a profession and not a trade . . ."); Atlantic Cleaners & Dyers v. United States, 286 U. S. 427, 436 (1932); United States v. National Assn. of Real Estate Boards, 339 U. S. 485, 490 (1950). These citations are to passing references in cases concerned with other issues; and, more important, until the present case it is clear that we have not attempted to decide whether the practice of a learned profession falls within § 1 of the Sherman Act. In National Assn. of Real Estate Boards, we specifically stated that the question was still open, 339 U. S., at 492, as we had done earlier in American Medical Assn. v. United States, 317 U. S. 519, 528 (1943).

[16] The reason for adopting the fee schedule does not appear to have been wholly altruistic. The first sentence in respondent State Bar's 1962 Minimum Fee Schedule Report states:

"'The lawyers have slowly, but surely, been committing economic suicide as a profession.'" Virginia State Bar, Minimum Fee Schedule Report 1962, p. 3, App. 20.

advanced to distinguish professions from trades, businesses, and other occupations, but it loses some of its
force when used to support the fee control activities involved here.

In arguing that learned professions are not "trade or
commerce" the County Bar seeks a total exclusion from
antitrust regulation. Whether state regulation is active
or dormant, real or theoretical, lawyers would be able
to adopt anticompetitive practices with impunity. We
cannot find support for the proposition that Congress intended any such sweeping exclusion. The nature of an
occupation, standing alone, does not provide sanctuary
from the Sherman Act, *Associated Press* v. *United States*,
326 U. S. 1, 7 (1945), nor is the public-service aspect of
professional practice controlling in determining whether
§ 1 includes professions. *United States* v. *National Assn.
of Real Estate Boards*, 339 U. S., at 489. Congress intended to strike as broadly as it could in § 1
of the Sherman Act, and to read into it so wide an
exemption as that urged on us would be at odds with that
purpose.

The language of § 1 of the Sherman Act, of course,
contains no exception. "Language more comprehensive
is difficult to conceive." *United States* v. *South-Eastern
Underwriters Assn.*, 322 U. S. 533, 553 (1944). And
our cases have repeatedly established that there is a
heavy presumption against implicit exemptions, *United
States* v. *Philadelphia National Bank*, 374 U. S. 321, 350–
351 (1963); *California* v. *FPC*, 369 U. S. 482, 485 (1962).
Indeed, our cases have specifically included the sale of
services within § 1. *E. g., American Medical Assn.* v.
United States, 317 U. S. 519 (1943); *Radovich* v. *National Football League*, 352 U. S. 445 (1957). Whatever
else it may be, the examination of a land title is a service;
the exchange of such a service for money is "commerce"

325

in the most common usage of that word. It is no disparagement of the practice of law as a profession to acknowledge that it has this business aspect,[17] and § 1 of the Sherman Act

"[o]n its face . . . shows a carefully studied attempt to bring within the Act every person engaged in business whose activities might restrain or monopolize commercial intercourse among the states." *United States* v. *South-Eastern Underwriters Assn., supra,* at 553.

In the modern world it cannot be denied that the activities of lawyers play an important part in commercial intercourse, and that anticompetitive activities by lawyers may exert a restraint on commerce.

D

In *Parker* v. *Brown,* 317 U. S. 341 (1943), the Court held that an anticompetitive marketing program which "derived its authority and its efficacy from the legislative command of the state" was not a violation of the Sherman Act because the Act was intended to regulate private practices and not to prohibit a State from imposing a restraint as an act of government. *Id.,* at 350–352; *Olsen* v. *Smith,* 195 U. S. 332, 344–345 (1904). Respondent State Bar and respondent County Bar both seek to avail themselves of this so-called state-action exemption.

---

[17] The fact that a restraint operates upon a profession as distinguished from a business is, of course, relevant in determining whether that particular restraint violates the Sherman Act. It would be unrealistic to view the practice of professions as interchangeable with other business activities, and automatically to apply to the professions antitrust concepts which originated in other areas. The public service aspect, and other features of the professions, may

Through its legislature Virginia has authorized its highest court to regulate the practice of law.[18] That court has adopted ethical codes which deal in part with fees, and far from exercising state power to authorize binding price fixing, explicitly directed lawyers not "to be controlled" by fee schedules.[19] The State Bar,

---

require that a particular practice, which could properly be viewed as a violation of the Sherman Act in another context, be treated differently. We intimate no view on any other situation than the one with which we are confronted today.

[18] Virginia Code Ann. § 54–48 (1972) provides:

"Rules and regulations defining practice of law and prescribing codes of ethics and disciplinary procedure.—The Supreme Court of Appeals may, from time to time, prescribe, adopt, promulgate and amend rules and regulations:

"(a) Defining the practice of law.

"(b) Prescribing a code of ethics governing the professional conduct of attorneys at law and a code of judicial ethics.

"(c) Prescribing procedure for disciplining, suspending, and disbarring attorneys at law."

In addition, the Supreme Court of Virginia, has inherent power to regulate the practice of law in that State. *Button* v. *Day,* 204 Va. 547, 132 S. E. 2d 292 (1963). See *Lathrop* v. *Donohue,* 367 U. S. 820 (1961).

[19] In 1938 the Supreme Court of Virginia adopted Rules for the Integration of the Virginia State Bar, and Rule II, § 12, dealt with the procedure for setting fees. Among six factors that court directed to be considered in setting a fee were "the customary charges of the Bar for similar services." The court also directed that

"[i]n determining the customary charges of the Bar for similar services, it is proper for a lawyer to consider a schedule of minimum fees adopted by a Bar Association, but *no lawyer should permit himself to be controlled* thereby or to follow it as his sole guide in determining the amount of his fee." Rules for Integration of the Virginia State Bar, 171 Va. xvii, xxiii. (Emphasis supplied.)

In 1970 the Virginia Supreme Court amended the 1938 rules in part, and adopted the Code of Professional Responsibility, effective Jan-a state agency by law,[20] argues that in issuing fee schedule reports and ethical opinions dealing with fee schedules it was merely implementing the fee provisions of the ethical codes. The County Bar, although it is a voluntary association and not a state agency, claims that the ethical codes and the activities of the State Bar "prompted" it to issue fee schedules and thus its actions, too, are state action for Sherman Act purposes.

The threshold inquiry in determining if an anticompetitive activity is state action of the type the Sherman Act was not meant to proscribe is whether the activity is required by the State acting as sovereign. *Parker v. Brown*, 317 U. S., at 350–352; *Continental Co. v. Union Carbide*, 370 U. S. 690, 706–707 (1962). Here we need not inquire further into the state-action question because it cannot fairly be said that the State of Virginia through its Supreme Court Rules required the anticompetitive activities of either respondent. Respondents have pointed to no Virginia statute requiring their activities; state law simply does not refer to fees, leaving regulation of the profession to the Virginia Supreme Court; although the Supreme Court's ethical codes mention advisory fee schedules they do not direct either respondent to supply them, or require the type of price floor which arose from respondents' activities.

---

uary 1, 1971. 211 Va. 295 (1970). Certain of its provisions also dealt with the fee-setting procedure. In EC 2–18 lawyers were told again that fees vary according to many factors, but that "[s]uggested fee schedules and economic reports of state and local bar associations provide some guidance on the subject of reasonable fees." 211 Va., at 302. In DR 2–106 (B), which detailed eight factors that should be considered in avoiding an excessive fee, one of the factors was "[t]he fee customarily charged in the locality for similar legal services." DR 2–106 (B)(3). 211 Va., at 313.

[20] See *supra*, at 776 n. 2.

Although the State Bar apparently has been granted the power to issue ethical opinions, there is no indication in this record that the Virginia Supreme Court approves the opinions. Respondents' arguments, at most, constitute the contention that their activities complemented the objective of the ethical codes. In our view that is not state action for Sherman Act purposes. It is not enough that, as the County Bar puts it, anticompetitive conduct is "prompted" by state action; rather, anticompetitive activities must be compelled by direction of the State acting as a sovereign.

The fact that the State Bar is a state agency for some limited purposes does not create an antitrust shield that allows it to foster anticompetitive practices for the benefit of its members.[21] Cf. *Gibson* v. *Berryhill*, 411 U. S. 564, 578–579 (1973). The State Bar, by providing that

---

[21] The District Court stated that the State Bar acted in only a "minor role" as far as the price fixing was concerned, 355 F. Supp., at 496, and one member of the Court of Appeals panel was prepared to exonerate the State Bar because its participation was so minimal as to be insufficient to impose Sherman Act liability. 497 F. 2d, at 21 (Craven, J., concurring and dissenting). Of course, an alleged participant in a restraint of trade may have so insubstantial a connection with the restraint that liability under the Sherman Act would not be found, see *United States* v. *National Assn. of Real Estate Boards*, 339 U. S., at 495; however, that is not the case here. The State Bar's fee schedule reports provided the impetus for the County Bar, on two occasions, to adopt minimum-fee schedules. More important, the State Bar's ethical opinions provided substantial reason for lawyers to comply with the minimum-fee schedules. Those opinions threatened professional discipline for habitual disregard of fee schedules, and thus attorneys knew their livelihood was in jeopardy if they did so. Even without that threat the opinions would have constituted substantial reason to adhere to the schedules because attorneys could be expected to comply in order to assure that they did not discredit themselves by departing from professional norms, and perhaps betraying their professional oaths.

deviation from County Bar minimum fees may lead to disciplinary action, has voluntarily joined in what is essentially a private anticompetitive activity, and in that posture cannot claim it is beyond the reach of the Sherman Act.[22] *Parker* v. *Brown, supra,* at 351–352. Its activities resulted in a rigid price floor from which petitioners, as consumers, could not escape if they wished to borrow money to buy a home.

III

We recognize that the States have a compelling interest in the practice of professions within their boundaries, and that as part of their power to protect the public health, safety, and other valid interests they have broad power to establish standards for licensing practitioners and regulating the practice of professions. We also recognize that in some instances the State may decide that "forms of competition usual in the business world may be demoralizing to the ethical standards of a profession." *United States* v. *Oregon State Medical Society,* 343 U. S. 326, 336 (1952). See also *Semler* v. *Oregon State Board of Dental Examiners,* 294 U. S. 608, 611–613 (1935). The interest of the States in regulating lawyers is especially great since lawyers are essential to the primary governmental function of administering justice, and have historically been "officers of the courts." See *Sperry* v. *Florida ex rel. Florida Bar,* 373 U. S. 379, 383 (1963); *Cohen* v. *Hurley,* 366 U. S. 117, 123–124 (1961); *Law Students Research Council* v. *Wadmond,* 401 U. S. 154,

---

[22] The State Bar also contends that it is protected by the Eleventh Amendment. See *Edelman* v. *Jordan,* 415 U. S. 651 (1974). Petitioners dispute this contention, and the District Court had no occasion to reach it in view of its holding. Given the record before us we intimate no view on the issue, leaving it for the District Court on remand.

157 (1971). In holding that certain anticompetitive conduct by lawyers is within the reach of the Sherman Act we intend no diminution of the authority of the State to regulate its professions.

The judgment of the Court of Appeals is reversed and the case is remanded to that court with orders to remand to the District Court for further proceedings consistent with this opinion.

Reversed and remanded.

RICHMOND NEWSPAPERS, INC., ET AL. *v.* VIRGINIA ET AL.

APPEAL FROM THE SUPREME COURT OF VIRGINIA

No. 79–243.   Argued February 19, 1980—Decided July 2, 1980

At the commencement of a fourth trial on a murder charge (the defendant's conviction after the first trial having been reversed on appeal, and two subsequent retrials having ended in mistrials), the Virginia trial court granted defense counsel's motion that the trial be closed to the public without any objections having been made by the prosecutor or by appellants, a newspaper and two of its reporters who were present in the courtroom, defense counsel having stated that he did not "want any information being shuffled back and forth when we have a recess as to . . . who testified to what." Later that same day, however, the trial judge granted appellants' request for a hearing on a motion to vacate the closure order, and appellants' counsel contended that constitutional considerations mandated that before ordering closure the court should first decide that the defendant's rights could be protected in no other way. But the trial judge denied the motion, saying that if he felt that the defendant's rights were infringed in any way and others' rights were not overridden he was inclined to order closure, and ordered the trial to continue "with the press and public excluded." The next day, the court granted defendant's motion to strike the prosecution's evidence, excused the jury, and found the defendant not guilty. Thereafter, the court granted appellants' motion to intervene *nunc pro tunc* in the case, and the Virginia Supreme Court dismissed their mandamus and prohibition petitions and, finding no reversible error, denied their petition for appeal from the closure order.

Held: The judgment is reversed. Pp. 563–581; 584–598; 598–601; 601–604.

Reversed.

MR. CHIEF JUSTICE BURGER, joined by MR. JUSTICE WHITE and MR. JUSTICE STEVENS, concluded that the right of the public and press to attend criminal trials is guaranteed under the First and Fourteenth Amendments. Absent an overriding interest articulated in findings, the trial of a criminal case must be open to the public. *Gannett Co.* v. *DePasquale,* 443 U. S. 368, distinguished. Pp. 563–581.

(a) The historical evidence of the evolution of the criminal trial in Anglo-American justice demonstrates conclusively that at the time this Nation's organic laws were adopted, criminal trials both here and in England had long been presumptively open, thus giving assurance that the proceedings were conducted fairly to all concerned and discouraging perjury, the misconduct of participants, or decisions based on secret bias or partiality. In addition, the significant community therapeutic value of public trials was recognized: when a shocking crime occurs, a community reaction of outrage and public protest often follows, and thereafter the open processes of justice serve an important prophylactic purpose, providing an outlet for community concern, hostility, and emotion. To work effectively, it is important that society's criminal process "satisfy the appearance of justice," *Offutt* v. *United States*, 348 U. S. 11, 14, which can best be provided by allowing people to observe such process. From this unbroken, uncontradicted history, supported by reasons as valid today as in centuries past, it must be concluded that a presumption of openness inheres in the very nature of a criminal trial under this Nation's system of justice. Cf., *e. g.*, *Levine* v. *United States*, 362 U. S. 610. Pp. 563–575.

(b) The freedoms of speech, press, and assembly, expressly guaranteed by the First Amendment, share a common core purpose of assuring freedom of communication on matters relating to the functioning of government. In guaranteeing freedoms such as those of speech and press, the First Amendment can be read as protecting the right of everyone to attend trials so as to give meaning to those explicit guarantees; the First Amendment right to receive information and ideas means, in the context of trials, that the guarantees of speech and press, standing alone, prohibit government from summarily closing courtroom doors which had long been open to the public at the time the First Amendment was adopted. Moreover, the right of assembly is also relevant, having been regarded not only as an independent right but also as a catalyst to augment the free exercise of the other First Amendment rights with which it was deliberately linked by the draftsmen. A trial courtroom is a public place where the people generally— and representatives of the media—have a right to be present, and where their presence historically has been thought to enhance the integrity and quality of what takes place. Pp. 575–578.

(c) Even though the Constitution contains no provision which by its terms guarantees to the public the right to attend criminal trials, various fundamental rights, not expressly guaranteed, have been recognized as indispensable to the enjoyment of enumerated rights. The right to attend criminal trials is implicit in the guarantees of the First Amendment; without the freedom to attend such trials, which people have exercised for centuries, important aspects of freedom of speech and of the press could be eviscerated. Pp. 579–580.

(d) With respect to the closure order in this case, despite the fact that this was the accused's fourth trial, the trial judge made no findings to support closure; no inquiry was made as to whether alternative solutions would have met the need to ensure fairness; there was no recognition of any right under the Constitution for the public or press to attend the trial; and there was no suggestion that any problems with witnesses could not have been dealt with by exclusion from the courtroom or sequestration during the trial, or that sequestration of the jurors would not have guarded against their being subjected to any improper information. Pp. 580–581.

MR. JUSTICE BRENNAN, joined by MR. JUSTICE MARSHALL, concluded that the First Amendment—of itself and as applied to the States through the Fourteenth Amendment—secures the public a right of access to trial proceedings, and that, without more, agreement of the trial judge and the parties cannot constitutionally close a trial to the public. Historically and functionally, open trials have been closely associated with the development of the fundamental procedure of trial by jury, and trial access assumes structural importance in this Nation's government of laws by assuring the public that procedural rights are respected and that justice is afforded equally, by serving as an effective restraint on possible abuse of judicial power, and by aiding the accuracy of the trial factfinding process. It was further concluded that it was not necessary to consider in this case what countervailing interests might be sufficiently compelling to reverse the presumption of openness of trials, since the Virginia statute involved—authorizing trial closures at the unfettered discretion of the judge and parties—violated the First and Fourteenth Amendments. Pp. 584–598.

MR. JUSTICE STEWART concluded that the First and Fourteenth Amendments clearly give the press and the public a right of access to trials, civil as well as criminal; that such right is not absolute, since various considerations may sometimes justify limitations upon the unrestricted presence of spectators in the courtroom; but that in the present case the trial judge apparently gave no recognition to the right of representatives of the press and members of the public to be present at the trial. Pp. 598–601.

MR. JUSTICE BLACKMUN, while being of the view that *Gannett Co.* v. *DePasquale, supra,* was in error, both in its interpretation of the Sixth Amendment generally, and in its application to the suppression hearing involved there, and that the right to a public trial is to be found in the Sixth Amendment, concluded, as a secondary position, that the First Amendment must provide some measure of protection for public access to the trial, and that here, by closing the trial, the trial judge abridged these First Amendment interests of the public. Pp. 601–604.

Burger, C. J., announced the Court's judgment and delivered an opinion, in which White and Stevens, JJ., joined. White, J., *post*, p. 581, and Stevens, J., *post*, p. 582, filed concurring opinions. Brennan, J., filed an opinion concurring in the judgment, in which Marshall, J., joined, *post*, p. 584. Stewart, J., *post*, p. 598, and Blackmun, J., *post*, p. 601, filed opinions concurring in the judgment. Rehnquist, J., filed a dissenting opinion, *post*, p. 604. Powell, J., took no part in the consideration or decision of the case.

Laurence H. Tribe argued the cause for appellants. With him on the briefs were *Andrew J. Brent, Alexander Wellford, Leslie W. Mullins,* and *David Rosenberg.*

Marshall Coleman, Attorney General of Virginia, argued the cause for appellees. With him on the brief were *James E. Moore, Leonard L. Hopkins, Jr., Martin A. Donlan, Jr.,* and *Jerry P. Slonaker,* Assistant Attorneys General.*

Mr. Chief Justice Burger announced the judgment of the Court and delivered an opinion, in which Mr. Justice White and Mr. Justice Stevens joined.

The narrow question presented in this case is whether the right of the public and press to attend criminal trials is guaranteed under the United States Constitution.

---

*Briefs of *amici curiae* urging reversal were filed by *John J. Degnan,* Attorney General, and *John De Cicco, Anthony J. Parrillo,* and *Debra L. Stone,* Deputy Attorneys General, for the State of New Jersey; by *Stephen Bricker* and *Bruce J. Ennis* for the American Civil Liberties Union et al.; by *Arthur B. Hanson, Frank M. Northam, Mitchell W. Dale,* and *Richard M. Schmidt, Jr.,* for the American Newspaper Publishers Association et al.; by *E. Barrett Prettyman, Jr., Erwin G. Krasnow, Arthur B. Sackler,* and *J. Laurent Scharff* for The Reporters Committee for Freedom of the Press et al.; and by *Edward Bennett Williams, John B. Kuhns,* and *Kevin T. Baine* for The Washington Post et al.

I

In March 1976, one Stevenson was indicted for the murder of a hotel manager who had been found stabbed to death on December 2, 1975. Tried promptly in July 1976, Stevenson was convicted of second-degree murder in the Circuit Court of Hanover County, Va. The Virginia Supreme Court reversed the conviction in October 1977, holding that a bloodstained shirt purportedly belonging to Stevenson had been improperly admitted into evidence. *Stevenson* v. *Commonwealth,* 218 Va. 462, 237 S. E. 2d 779.

Stevenson was retried in the same court. This second trial ended in a mistrial on May 30, 1978, when a juror asked to be excused after trial had begun and no alternate was available.[1]

A third trial, which began in the same court on June 6, 1978, also ended in a mistrial. It appears that the mistrial may have been declared because a prospective juror had read about Stevenson's previous trials in a newspaper and had told other prospective jurors about the case before the retrial began. See App. 35a–36a.

Stevenson was tried in the same court for a fourth time beginning on September 11, 1978. Present in the courtroom when the case was called were appellants Wheeler and McCarthy, reporters for appellant Richmond Newspapers, Inc. Before the trial began, counsel for the defendant moved that it be closed to the public:

> "[T]here was this woman that was with the family of the deceased when we were here before. She had sat in the Courtroom. I would like to ask that everybody be excluded from the Courtroom because I don't want any information being shuffled back and forth when we have

---

[1] A newspaper account published the next day reported the mistrial and went on to note that "[a] key piece of evidence in Stevenson's original conviction was a bloodstained shirt obtained from Stevenson's wife soon after the killing. The Virginia Supreme Court, however, ruled that the shirt was entered into evidence improperly." App. 34a.

a recess as to what—who testified to what." Tr. of
Sept. 11, 1978 Hearing on Defendant's Motion to Close
Trial to the Public 2–3.

The trial judge, who had presided over two of the three
previous trials, asked if the prosecution had any objection
to clearing the courtroom. The prosecutor stated he had no
objection and would leave it to the discretion of the court.
Id., at 4. Presumably referring to Va. Code § 19.2–266
(Supp. 1980), the trial judge then announced: "[T]he statute
gives me that power specifically and the defendant has made
the motion." He then ordered "that the Courtroom be kept
clear of all parties except the witnesses when they testify."
Tr., *supra,* at 4–5.[2] The record does not show that any objections to the closure order were made by anyone present at
the time, including appellants Wheeler and McCarthy.

Later that same day, however, appellants sought a hearing
on a motion to vacate the closure order. The trial judge
granted the request and scheduled a hearing to follow the
close of the day's proceedings. When the hearing began, the
court ruled that the hearing was to be treated as part of the
trial; accordingly, he again ordered the reporters to leave
the courtroom, and they complied.

At the closed hearing, counsel for appellants observed that
no evidentiary findings had been made by the court prior to
the entry of its closure order and pointed out that the court
had failed to consider any other, less drastic measures within
its power to ensure a fair trial. Tr. of Sept. 11, 1978 Hearing on Motion to Vacate 11–12. Counsel for appellants
argued that constitutional considerations mandated that before
ordering closure, the court should first decide that the rights
of the defendant could be protected in no other way.

---

[2] Virginia Code § 19.2–266 (Supp. 1980) provides in part:
"In the trial of all criminal cases, whether the same be felony or misdemeanor cases, the court may, in its discretion, exclude from the trial any
persons whose presence would impair the conduct of a fair trial, provided
that the right of the accused to a public trial shall not be violated."

Counsel for defendant Stevenson pointed out that this was the fourth time he was standing trial. He also referred to "difficulty with information between the jurors," and stated that he "didn't want information to leak out," be published by the media, perhaps inaccurately, and then be seen by the jurors. Defense counsel argued that these things, plus the fact that "this is a small community," made this a proper case for closure. *Id.,* at 16–18.

The trial judge noted that counsel for the defendant had made similar statements at the morning hearing. The court also stated:

> "[O]ne of the other points that we take into consideration in this particular Courtroom is layout of the Courtroom. I think that having people in the Courtroom is distracting to the jury. Now, we have to have certain people in here and maybe that's not a very good reason. When we get into our new Court Building, people can sit in the audience so the jury can't see them. The rule of the Court may be different under those circumstances. . . ." *Id.,* at 19.

The prosecutor again declined comment, and the court summed up by saying:

> "I'm inclined to agree with [defense counsel] that, if I feel that the rights of the defendant are infringed in any way, [when] he makes the motion to do something and it doesn't completely override all rights of everyone else, then I'm inclined to go along with the defendant's motion." *Id.,* at 20.

The court denied the motion to vacate and ordered the trial to continue the following morning "with the press and public excluded." *Id.,* at 27; App. 21a.

What transpired when the closed trial resumed the next day was disclosed in the following manner by an order of the court entered September 12, 1978:

> "[I]n the absence of the jury, the defendant by counsel

made a Motion that a mis-trial be declared, which motion was taken under advisement.

"At the conclusion of the Commonwealth's evidence, the attorney for the defendant moved the Court to strike the Commonwealth's evidence on grounds stated to the record, which Motion was sustained by the Court.

"And the jury having been excused, the Court doth find the accused NOT GUILTY of Murder, as charged in the Indictment, and he was allowed to depart." *Id.,* at 22a.[3]

On September 27, 1978, the trial court granted appellants' motion to intervene *nunc pro tunc* in the Stevenson case. Appellants then petitioned the Virginia Supreme Court for writs of mandamus and prohibition and filed an appeal from the trial court's closure order. On July 9, 1979, the Virginia Supreme Court dismissed the mandamus and prohibition petitions and, finding no reversible error, denied the petition for appeal. *Id.,* at 23a–28a.

Appellants then sought review in this Court, invoking both our appellate, 28 U. S. C. § 1257 (2), and certiorari jurisdiction. § 1257 (3). We postponed further consideration of the question of our jurisdiction to the hearing of the case on the merits. 444 U. S. 896 (1979). We conclude that jurisdiction by appeal does not lie;[4] however, treating the filed

---

[3] At oral argument, it was represented to the Court that tapes of the trial were available to the public as soon as the trial terminated. Tr. of Oral Arg. 36.

[4] In our view, the validity of Va. Code § 19.2–266 (Supp. 1980) was not sufficiently drawn in question by appellants before the Virginia courts to invoke our appellate jurisdiction. "It is essential to our jurisdiction on appeal . . . that there be an explicit and timely insistence in the state courts that a state statute, as applied, is repugnant to the federal Constitution, treaties or laws." *Charleston Federal Savings & Loan Assn.* v. *Alderson,* 324 U. S. 182, 185 (1945). Appellants never explicitly challenged the statute's validity. In both the trial court and the State Supreme Court, appellants argued that constitutional rights of the public and the press prevented the court from closing a trial without first

papers as a petition for a writ of certiorari pursuant to 28 U. S. C. § 2103, we grant the petition.

The criminal trial which appellants sought to attend has long since ended, and there is thus some suggestion that the case is moot. This Court has frequently recognized, however, that its jurisdiction is not necessarily defeated by the practical termination of a contest which is short-lived by nature. See, *e. g., Gannett Co.* v. *DePasquale,* 443 U. S. 368, 377–378 (1979); *Nebraska Press Assn.* v. *Stuart,* 427 U. S. 539, 546–547 (1976). If the underlying dispute is "capable of repetition, yet evading review," *Southern Pacific Terminal Co.* v. *ICC,* 219 U. S. 498, 515 (1911), it is not moot.

Since the Virginia Supreme Court declined plenary review, it is reasonably foreseeable that other trials may be closed by other judges without any more showing of need than is presented on this record. More often than not, criminal trials will be of sufficiently short duration that a closure order "will evade review, or at least considered plenary review in this Court." *Nebraska Press, supra,* at 547. Accordingly, we turn to the merits.

II

We begin consideration of this case by noting that the precise issue presented here has not previously been before this

---

giving notice and an opportunity for a hearing to the public and the press and exhausting every alternative means of protecting the defendant's right to a fair trial. Given appellants' failure explicitly to challenge the statute, we view these arguments as constituting claims of rights under the Constitution, which rights are said to limit the exercise of the discretion conferred by the statute on the trial court. Cf. *Phillips* v. *United States,* 312 U. S. 246, 252 (1941) ("[A]n attack on lawless exercise of authority in a particular case is not an attack upon the constitutionality of a statute conferring the authority . . ."). Such claims are properly brought before this Court by way of our certiorari, rather than appellate, jurisdiction. See, *e. g., Kulko* v. *California Superior Court,* 436 U. S. 84, 90, n. 4 (1978); *Hanson* v. *Denckla,* 357 U. S. 235, 244, and n. 4 (1958). We shall, however, continue to refer to the parties as appellants and appellee. See *Kulko, supra.*

Court for decision. In *Gannett Co.* v. *DePasquale, supra,* the Court was not required to decide whether a right of access to *trials,* as distingushed from hearings on *pretrial* motions, was constitutionally guaranteed. The Court held that the Sixth Amendment's guarantee to the accused of a public trial gave neither the public nor the press an enforce- able right of access to a *pretrial* suppression hearing. One concurring opinion specifically emphasized that "a hearing on a motion before trial to suppress evidence is not a *trial.* . . ." 443 U. S., at 394 (BURGER, C. J., concurring). Moreover, the Court did not decide whether the First and Fourteenth Amendments guarantee a right of the public to attend trials, *id.,* at 392, and n. 24; nor did the dissenting opinion reach this issue. *Id.,* at 447 (opinion of BLACKMUN, J.).

In prior cases the Court has treated questions involving con- flicts between publicity and a defendant's right to a fair trial; as we observed in *Nebraska Press Assn.* v. *Stuart, supra,* at 547, "[t]he problems presented by this [conflict] are almost as old as the Republic." See also, *e. g., Gannett, supra; Murphy* v. *Florida,* 421 U. S. 794 (1975); *Sheppard* v. *Max- well,* 384 U. S. 333 (1966); *Estes* v. *Texas,* 381 U. S. 532 (1965). But here for the first time the Court is asked to decide whether a criminal trial itself may be closed to the public upon the unopposed request of a defendant, without any demonstration that closure is required to protect the defendant's superior right to a fair trial, or that some other overriding consideration requires closure.

A

The origins of the proceeding which has become the modern criminal trial in Anglo-American justice can be traced back beyond reliable historical records. We need not here review all details of its development, but a summary of that history is instructive. What is significant for present purposes is that throughout its evolution, the trial has been open to all who cared to observe.

In the days before the Norman Conquest, cases in England were generally brought before moots, such as the local court of the hundred or the county court, which were attended by the freemen of the community. Pollock, English Law Before the Norman Conquest, in 1 Select Essays in Anglo-American Legal History 88, 89 (1907). Somewhat like modern jury duty, attendance at these early meetings was compulsory on the part of the freemen, who were called upon to render judgment. *Id.,* at 89–90; see also 1 W. Holdsworth, A History of English Law 10, 12 (1927).[5]

With the gradual evolution of the jury system in the years after the Norman Conquest, see, *e. g., id.,* at 316, the duty of all freemen to attend trials to render judgment was relaxed, but there is no indication that criminal trials did not remain public. When certain groups were excused from compelled attendance, see the Statute of Marlborough, 52 Hen. 3, ch. 10 (1267); 1 Holdsworth, *supra,* at 79, and n. 4, the statutory exemption did not prevent them from attending; Lord Coke observed that those excused "are not compellable to come, but left to their own liberty." 2 E. Coke, Institutes of the Laws of England 121 (6th ed. 1681).[6]

Although there appear to be few contemporary statements

---

[5] That there is little in the way of a contemporary record from this period is not surprising. It has been noted by historians, see E. Jenks, A Short History of English Law 3–4 (2d ed. 1922), that the early Anglo-Saxon laws "deal rather with the novel and uncertain, than with the normal and undoubted rules of law. . . . Why trouble to record that which every village elder knows? Only when a disputed point has long caused bloodshed and disturbance, or when a successful invader . . . insists on a change, is it necessary to draw up a code." *Ibid.*

[6] Coke interpreted certain language of an earlier chapter of the same statute as specifically indicating that court proceedings were to be public in nature: "These words [*In curia Domini Regis*] are of great importance, for all Causes ought to be heard, ordered, and determined before the Judges of the King's Courts *openly* in the King's Courts, *whither all persons may resort. . . .*" 2 E. Coke, Institutes of the Laws of England 103 (6th ed. 1681) (emphasis added).

on the subject, reports of the Eyre of Kent, a general court held in 1313–1314, evince a recognition of the importance of public attendance apart from the "jury duty" aspect. It was explained that

> "the King's will was that all evil doers should be punished after their deserts, and that justice should be ministered indifferently to rich as to poor; *and for the better accomplishing of this,* he prayed the community of the county *by their attendance* there to lend him their aid in the establishing of a happy and certain peace that should be both for the honour of the realm and for their own welfare." 1 Holdsworth, *supra,* at 268, quoting from the S. S. edition of the Eyre of Kent, vol. i., p. 2 (emphasis added).

From these early times, although great changes in courts and procedure took place, one thing remained constant: the public character of the trial at which guilt or innocence was decided. Sir Thomas Smith, writing in 1565 about "the definitive proceedinges in causes criminall," explained that, while the indictment was put in writing as in civil law countries:

> "All the rest is doone openlie in the presence of the Judges, the Justices, the enquest, the prisoner, *and so manie as will or can come so neare as to heare it,* and all depositions and witnesses given aloude, *that all men may heare from the mouth of the depositors and witnesses what is saide."* T. Smith, De Republica Anglorum 101 (Alston ed. 1972) (emphasis added).

Three centuries later, Sir Frederick Pollock was able to state of the "rule of publicity" that, "[h]ere we have one tradition, at any rate, which has persisted through all changes." F. Pollock, The Expansion of the Common Law 31–32 (1904). See also E. Jenks, The Book of English Law 73–74 (6th ed. 1967): "[O]ne of the most conspicuous features of English justice, that all judicial trials are held in open court, to which the public have free access, . . . appears to have been the rule in England from time immemorial."

We have found nothing to suggest that the presumptive openness of the trial, which English courts were later to call "one of the essential qualities of a court of justice," *Daubney* v. *Cooper,* 10 B. & C. 237, 240, 109 Eng. Rep. 438, 440 (K. B. 1829), was not also an attribute of the judicial systems of colonial America. In Virginia, for example, such records as there are of early criminal trials indicate that they were open, and nothing to the contrary has been cited. See A. Scott, Criminal Law in Colonial Virginia 128–129 (1930); Reinsch, The English Common Law in the Early American Colonies, in 1 Select Essays in Anglo-American Legal History 367, 405 (1907). Indeed, when in the mid-1600's the Virginia Assembly felt that the respect due the courts was "by the clamorous unmannerlynes of the people lost, and order, gravity and decoram which should manifest the authority of a court in the court it selfe neglected," the response was not to restrict the openness of the trials to the public, but instead to prescribe rules for the conduct of those attending them. See Scott, *supra,* at 132.

In some instances, the openness of trials was explicitly recognized as part of the fundamental law of the Colony. The 1677 Concessions and Agreements of West New Jersey, for example, provided:

> "That in all publick courts of justice for tryals of causes, civil or criminal, any person or persons, inhabitants of the said Province may freely come into, and attend the said courts, and hear and be present, at all or any such tryals as shall be there had or passed, that justice may not be done in a corner nor in any covert manner." Reprinted in Sources of Our Liberties 188 (R. Perry ed. 1959).

See also 1 B. Schwartz, The Bill of Rights: A Documentary History 129 (1971).

The Pennsylvania Frame of Government of 1682 also provided "[t]hat all courts shall be open . . . ," Sources of Our Liberties, *supra*, at 217; 1 Schwartz, *supra*, at 140, and this declaration was reaffirmed in § 26 of the Constitution adopted by Pennsylvania in 1776. See 1 Schwartz, *supra*, at 271. See also §§ 12 and 76 of the Massachusetts Body of Liberties, 1641, reprinted in 1 Schwartz, *supra*, at 73, 80.

Other contemporary writings confirm the recognition that part of the very nature of a criminal trial was its openness to those who wished to attend. Perhaps the best indication of this is found in an address to the inhabitants of Quebec which was drafted by a committee consisting of Thomas Cushing, Richard Henry Lee, and John Dickinson and approved by the First Continental Congress on October 26, 1774. 1 Journals of the Continental Congress, 1774–1789, pp. 101, 105 (1904) (Journals). This address, written to explain the position of the Colonies and to gain the support of the people of Quebec, is an "exposition of the fundamental rights of the colonists, as they were understood by a representative assembly chosen from all the colonies." 1 Schwartz, *supra*, at 221. Because it was intended for the inhabitants of Quebec, who had been "educated under another form of government" and had only recently become English subjects, it was thought desirable for the Continental Congress to explain "the inestimable advantages of a free English constitution of government, which it is the privilege of all English subjects to enjoy." 1 Journals 106.

"[One] great right is that of trial by jury. This provides, that neither life, liberty nor property, can be taken from the possessor, until twelve of his unexceptionable countrymen and peers of his vicinage, who from that neighbourhood may reasonably be supposed to be acquainted with his character, and the characters of the witnesses, upon a fair trial, and full enquiry, face to face, *in open Court, before as many of the people as chuse to*

345

attend, shall pass their sentence upon oath against him. . . ." *Id.,* at 107 (emphasis added).

B

As we have shown, and as was shown in both the Court's opinion and the dissent in *Gannett,* 443 U. S., at 384, 386, n. 15, 418–425, the historical evidence demonstrates conclusively that at the time when our organic laws were adopted, criminal trials both here and in England had long been presumptively open. This is no quirk of history; rather, it has long been recognized as an indispensable attribute of an Anglo-American trial. Both Hale in the 17th century and Blackstone in the 18th saw the importance of openness to the proper functioning of a trial; it gave assurance that the proceedings were conducted fairly to all concerned, and it discouraged perjury, the misconduct of participants, and decisions based on secret bias or partiality. See, *e. g.,* M. Hale, The History of the Common Law of England 343–345 (6th ed. 1820); 3 W. Blackstone, Commentaries *372–*373. Jeremy Bentham not only recognized the therapeutic value of open justice but regarded it as the keystone:

> "Without publicity, all other checks are insufficient: in comparison of publicity, all other checks are of small account. Recordation, appeal, whatever other institutions might present themselves in the character of checks, would be found to operate rather as cloaks than checks; as cloaks in reality, as checks only in appearance." 1 J. Bentham, Rationale of Judicial Evidence 524 (1827).[7]

Panegyrics on the values of openness were by no means confined to self-praise by the English. Foreign observers of English criminal procedure in the 18th and early 19th cen-

---

[7] Bentham also emphasized that open proceedings enhanced the performance of all involved, protected the judge from imputations of dishonesty, and served to educate the public. Rationale of Judicial Evidence, at 522–525.

turies came away impressed by the very fact that they had
been freely admitted to the courts, as many were not in their
own homelands. See L. Radzinowicz, A History of English
Criminal Law 715, and n. 96 (1948). They marveled that
"the whole juridical procedure passes in public," 2 P. Grosley,
A Tour to London; or New Observations on England 142
(Nugent trans. 1772), quoted in Radzinowicz, *supra,* at 717,
and one commentator declared:

> "The main excellence of the English judicature consists
> in publicity, in the free trial by jury, and in the extraor-
> dinary despatch with which business is transacted. The
> publicity of their proceedings is indeed astonishing. *Free
> access to the courts is universally granted."* C. Goede,
> A Foreigner's Opinion of England 214 (Horne trans.
> 1822). (Emphasis added.)

The nexus between openness, fairness, and the perception of
fairness was not lost on them:

> "[T]he judge, the counsel, and the jury, are constantly
> exposed to public animadversion; and this greatly tends
> to augment the extraordinary confidence, which the
> English repose in the administration of justice." *Id.,*
> at 215.

This observation raises the important point that "[t]he
publicity of a judicial proceeding is a requirement of much
broader bearing than its mere effect upon the quality of testimony." 6 J. Wigmore, Evidence § 1834, p. 435 (J. Chadbourn
rev. 1976).[8] The early history of open trials in part reflects
the widespread acknowledgment, long before there were behavioral scientists, that public trials had significant community therapeutic value. Even without such experts to frame

---

[8] A collateral aspect seen by Wigmore was the possibility that someone
in attendance at the trial or who learns of the proceedings through publicity may be able to furnish evidence in chief or contradict "falsifiers."
6 Wigmore, at 436. Wigmore gives examples of such occurrences. *Id.,*
at 436, and n. 2.

the concept in words, people sensed from experience and observation that, especially in the administration of criminal justice, the means used to achieve justice must have the support derived from public acceptance of both the process and its results.

When a shocking crime occurs, a community reaction of outrage and public protest often follows. See H. Weihofen, The Urge to Punish 130–131 (1956). Thereafter the open processes of justice serve an important prophylactic purpose, providing an outlet for community concern, hostility, and emotion. Without an awareness that society's responses to criminal conduct are underway, natural human reactions of outrage and protest are frustrated and may manifest themselves in some form of vengeful "self-help," as indeed they did regularly in the activities of vigilante "committees" on our frontiers. "The accusation and conviction or acquittal, as much perhaps as the execution of punishment, operat[e] to restore the imbalance which was created by the offense or public charge, to reaffirm the temporarily lost feeling of security and, perhaps, to satisfy that latent 'urge to punish.'" Mueller, Problems Posed by Publicity to Crime and Criminal Proceedings, 110 U. Pa. L. Rev. 1, 6 (1961).

Civilized societies withdraw both from the victim and the vigilante the enforcement of criminal laws, but they cannot erase from people's consciousness the fundamental, natural yearning to see justice done—or even the urge for retribution. The crucial prophylactic aspects of the administration of justice cannot function in the dark; no community catharsis can occur if justice is "done in a corner [or] in any covert manner." *Supra,* at 567. It is not enough to say that results alone will satiate the natural community desire for "satisfaction." A result considered untoward may undermine public confidence, and where the trial has been concealed from public view an unexpected outcome can cause a reaction that the system at best has failed and at worst has been corrupted. To work effectively, it is important that society's criminal process "satisfy the appearance of justice," *Offutt* v. *United States*, 348 U. S. 11, 14 (1954), and the appearance of justice can best be provided by allowing people to observe it.

Looking back, we see that when the ancient "town meeting" form of trial became too cumbersome, 12 members of the community were delegated to act as its surrogates, but the community did not surrender its right to observe the conduct of trials. The people retained a "right of visitation" which enabled them to satisfy themselves that justice was in fact being done.

People in an open society do not demand infallibility from their institutions, but it is difficult for them to accept what they are prohibited from observing. When a criminal trial is conducted in the open, there is at least an opportunity both for understanding the system in general and its workings in a particular case:

> "The educative effect of public attendance is a material advantage. Not only is respect for the law increased and intelligent acquaintance acquired with the methods of government, but a strong confidence in judicial remedies is secured which could never be inspired by a system of secrecy." 6 Wigmore, *supra*, at 438. See also 1 J. Bentham, Rationale of Judicial Evidence, at 525.

In earlier times, both in England and America, attendance at court was a common mode of "passing the time." See, *e. g.*, 6 Wigmore, *supra*, at 436; Mueller, *supra*, at 6. With the press, cinema, and electronic media now supplying the representations or reality of the real life drama once available only in the courtroom, attendance at court is no longer a widespread pastime. Yet "[i]t is not unrealistic even in this day to believe that public inclusion affords citizens a form of legal education and hopefully promotes confidence in the fair administration of justice." *State* v. *Schmit*, 273 Minn. 78, 87–88, 139 N. W. 2d 800, 807 (1966). Instead of acquiring information about trials by firsthand observation or by word of mouth from those who attended, people now acquire it chiefly through the print and electronic media. In a sense, this validates the media claim of functioning as surrogates for the public. While media representatives enjoy the same right of access as the public, they often are provided special seating and priority of entry so that they may report what people in attendance have seen and heard. This "contribute[s] to public understanding of the rule of law and to comprehension of the functioning of the entire criminal justice system. . . ." *Nebraska Press Assn.* v. *Stuart,* 427 U. S., at 587 (BRENNAN, J., concurring in judgment).

C

From this unbroken, uncontradicted history, supported by reasons as valid today as in centuries past, we are bound to conclude that a presumption of openness inheres in the very nature of a criminal trial under our system of justice. This conclusion is hardly novel; without a direct holding on the issue, the Court has voiced its recognition of it in a variety of contexts over the years.[9] Even while holding, in *Levine* v.

---

[9] "Of course trials must be public and the public have a deep interest in trials." *Pennekamp* v. *Florida,* 328 U. S. 331, 361 (1946) (Frankfurter, J, concurring).

"A trial is a public event. What transpires in the court room is public property." *Craig* v. *Harney,* 331 U. S. 367, 374 (1947) (Douglas, J.).

"[W]e have been unable to find a single instance of a criminal trial conducted in camera in any federal, state, or municipal court during the history of this country. Nor have we found any record of even one such secret criminal trial in England since abolition of the Court of Star Chamber in 1641, and whether that court ever convicted people secretly is in dispute. . . .

"This nation's accepted practice of guaranteeing a public trial to an accused has its roots in our English common law heritage. The exact date of its origin is obscure, but it likely evolved long before the settlement of our land as an accompaniment of the ancient institution of jury trial." *In re Oliver,* 333 U. S. 257, 266 (1948) (Black, J.) (footnotes omitted).

"One of the demands of a democratic society is that the public should know what goes on in courts by being told by the press what happens

United States, 362 U. S. 610 (1960), that a criminal contempt
proceeding was not a "criminal prosecution" within the meaning of the Sixth Amendment, the Court was careful to note
that more than the Sixth Amendment was involved:

> "[W]hile the right to a 'public trial' is explicitly guaran-
> teed by the Sixth Amendment only for 'criminal prosecu-
> tions,' that provision is a reflection of the notion, deeply
> rooted in the common law, that 'justice must satisfy the
> appearance of justice.' . . .   [D]ue process demands ap-
> propriate regard for the requirements of a public pro-
> ceeding in cases of criminal contempt . . . as it does
> for all adjudications through the exercise of the judi-
> cial power, barring narrowly limited categories of excep-
> tions. . . ." *Id.*, at 616.[10]

And recently in *Gannett Co.* v. *DePasquale*, 443 U. S. 368
(1979), both the majority, *id.*, at 384, 386, n. 15, and dissenting opinion, *id.*, at 423, agreed that open trials were part of
the common-law tradition.

---

there, to the end that the public may judge whether our system of criminal justice is fair and right." *Maryland* v. *Baltimore Radio Show, Inc.*,
338 U. S. 912, 920 (1950) (Frankfurter, J., dissenting from denial of
certiorari).

"It is true that the public has the right to be informed as to what occurs
in its courts, . . . reporters of all media, including television, are always
present if they wish to be and are plainly free to report whatever occurs
in open court. . . ." *Estes* v. *Texas*, 381 U. S. 532, 541–542 (1965)
(Clark, J.); see also *id.*, at 583–584 (Warren, C. J., concurring). (The
Court ruled, however, that the televising of the criminal trial over the
defendant's objections violated his due process right to a fair trial.)

"The principle that justice cannot survive behind walls of silence has
long been reflected in the 'Anglo-American distrust for secret trials.'"
Sheppard v. *Maxwell*, 384 U. S. 333, 349 (1966) (Clark, J.).

[10] The Court went on to hold that, "on the particular circumstances
of the case," 362 U. S., at 616, the accused could not complain on appeal
of the "so-called 'secrecy' of the proceedings," *id.*, at 617, because, with
counsel present, he had failed to object or to request the judge to open
the courtroom at the time.

Despite the history of criminal trials being presumptively open since long before the Constitution, the State presses its contention that neither the Constitution nor the Bill of Rights contains any provision which by its terms guarantees to the public the right to attend criminal trials. Standing alone, this is correct, but there remains the question whether, absent an explicit provision, the Constitution affords protection against exclusion of the public from criminal trials.

III

A

The First Amendment, in conjunction with the Fourteenth, prohibits governments from "abridging the freedom of speech, or of the press; or the right of the people peaceably to assemble, and to petition the Government for a redress of grievances." These expressly guaranteed freedoms share a common core purpose of assuring freedom of communication on matters relating to the functioning of government. Plainly it would be difficult to single out any aspect of government of higher concern and importance to the people than the manner in which criminal trials are conducted; as we have shown, recognition of this pervades the centuries-old history of open trials and the opinions of this Court. *Supra,* at 564–575, and n. 9.

The Bill of Rights was enacted against the backdrop of the long history of trials being presumptively open. Public access to trials was then regarded as an important aspect of the process itself; the conduct of trials "before as many of the people as chuse to attend" was regarded as one of "the inestimable advantages of a free English constitution of government." 1 Journals 106, 107. In guaranteeing freedoms such as those of speech and press, the First Amendment can be read as protecting the right of everyone to attend trials so as to give meaning to those explicit guarantees. "[T]he First Amendment goes beyond protection of the press and the self-

352

expression of individuals to prohibit government from limiting the stock of information from which members of the public may draw." *First National Bank of Boston* v. *Bellotti,* 435 U. S. 765, 783 (1978). Free speech carries with it some freedom to listen. "In a variety of contexts this Court has referred to a First Amendment right to 'receive information and ideas.'" *Kleindienst* v. *Mandel,* 408 U. S. 753, 762 (1972). What this means in the context of trials is that the First Amendment guarantees of speech and press, standing alone, prohibit government from summarily closing courtroom doors which had long been open to the public at the time that Amendment was adopted. "For the First Amendment does not speak equivocally. . . . It must be taken as a command of the broadest scope that explicit language, read in the context of a liberty-loving society, will allow." *Bridges* v. *California,* 314 U. S. 252, 263 (1941) (footnote omitted).

It is not crucial whether we describe this right to attend criminal trials to hear, see, and communicate observations concerning them as a "right of access," cf. *Gannett, supra,* at 397 (POWELL, J., concurring); *Saxbe* v. *Washington Post Co.,* 417 U. S. 843 (1974); *Pell* v. *Procunier,* 417 U. S. 817 (1974),[11] or a "right to gather information," for we have recognized that "without some protection for seeking out the news, freedom of the press could be eviscerated." *Branzburg* v. *Hayes,* 408 U. S. 665, 681 (1972). The explicit, guaranteed rights to speak and to publish concerning what takes place at a

---

[11] *Procunier* and *Saxbe* are distinguishable in the sense that they were concerned with penal institutions which, by definition, are not "open" or public places. Penal institutions do not share the long tradition of openness, although traditionally there have been visiting committees of citizens, and there is no doubt that legislative committees could exercise plenary oversight and "visitation rights." *Saxbe,* 417 U. S., at 849, noted that "limitation on visitations is justified by what the Court of Appeals acknowledged as 'the truism that prisons are institutions where public access is generally limited.' 161 U. S. App. D. C., at 80, 494 F. 2d, at 999. See *Adderley* v. *Florida,* 385 U. S. 39, 41 (1966) [jails]." See also *Greer* v. *Spock,* 424 U. S. 828 (1976) (military bases).

trial would lose much meaning if access to observe the trial could, as it was here, be foreclosed arbitrarily.[12]

B

The right of access to places traditionally open to the public, as criminal trials have long been, may be seen as assured by the amalgam of the First Amendment guarantees of speech and press; and their affinity to the right of assembly is not without relevance. From the outset, the right of assembly was regarded not only as an independent right but also as a catalyst to augment the free exercise of the other First Amendment rights with which it was deliberately linked by the draftsmen.[13]

---

[12] That the right to attend may be exercised by people less frequently today when information as to trials generally reaches them by way of print and electronic media in no way alters the basic right. Instead of relying on personal observation or reports from neighbors as in the past, most people receive information concerning trials through the media whose representatives "are entitled to the same rights [to attend trials] as the general public." *Estes* v. *Texas*, 381 U. S., at 540.

[13] When the First Congress was debating the Bill of Rights, it was contended that there was no need separately to assert the right of assembly because it was subsumed in freedom of speech. Mr. Sedgwick of Massachusetts argued that inclusion of "assembly" among the enumerated rights would tend to make the Congress "appear trifling in the eyes of their constituents. . . . If people freely converse together, they must assemble for that purpose; it is a self-evident, unalienable right which the people possess; it is certainly a thing that never would be called in question. . . ." 1 Annals of Cong. 731 (1789).

Since the right existed independent of any written guarantee, Sedgwick went on to argue that if it were the drafting committee's purpose to protect all inherent rights of the people by listing them, "they might have gone into a very lengthy enumeration of rights," but this was unnecessary, he said, "in a Government where none of them were intended to be infringed." *Id.*, at 732.

Mr. Page of Virginia responded, however, that at times "such rights have been opposed," and that "people have . . . been prevented from assembling together on their lawful occasions":

"[T]herefore it is well to guard against such stretches of authority, by inserting the privilege in the declaration of rights. If the people could

"The right of peaceable assembly is a right cognate to those of free speech and free press and is equally fundamental." *De Jonge* v. *Oregon,* 299 U. S. 353, 364 (1937). People assemble in public places not only to speak or to take action, but also to listen, observe, and learn; indeed, they may "assembl[e] for any lawful purpose," *Hague* v. *CIO,* 307 U. S. 496, 519 (1939) (opinion of Stone, J.). Subject to the traditional time, place, and manner restrictions, see, *e. g., Cox* v. *New Hampshire,* 312 U. S. 569 (1941); see also *Cox* v. *Louisiana,* 379 U. S. 559, 560–564 (1965), streets, sidewalks, and parks are places traditionally open, where First Amendment rights may be exercised, see *Hague* v. *CIO, supra,* at 515 (opinion of Roberts, J.); a trial courtroom also is a public place where the people generally—and representatives of the media—have a right to be present, and where their presence historically has been thought to enhance the integrity and quality of what takes place.[14]

---

be deprived of the power of assembling under any pretext whatsoever, they might be deprived of every other privilege contained in the clause." *Ibid.* The motion to strike "assembly" was defeated. *Id.,* at 733.

[14] It is of course true that the right of assembly in our Bill of Rights was in large part drafted in reaction to restrictions on such rights in England. See, *e. g.,* 1 Geo. 1, stat. 2, ch. 5 (1714); cf. 36 Geo. 3, ch. 8 (1795). As we have shown, the right of Englishmen to attend trials was not similarly limited; but it would be ironic indeed if the very historic openness of the trial could militate against protection of the right to attend it. The Constitution guarantees more than simply freedom from those abuses which led the Framers to single out particular rights. The very purpose of the First Amendment is to guarantee all facets of each right described; its draftsmen sought both to protect the "rights of Englishmen" and to enlarge their scope. See *Bridges* v. *California,* 314 U. S. 252, 263–265 (1941).

"There are no contrary implications in any part of the history of the period in which the First Amendment was framed and adopted. No purpose in ratifying the Bill of Rights was clearer than that of securing for the people of the United States much greater freedom of religion, expression, assembly, and petition than the people of Great Britain had ever enjoyed." *Id.,* at 265.

C

The State argues that the Constitution nowhere spells out a guarantee for the right of the public to attend trials, and that accordingly no such right is protected. The possibility that such a contention could be made did not escape the notice of the Constitution's draftsmen; they were concerned that some important rights might be thought disparaged because not specifically guaranteed. It was even argued that because of this danger no Bill of Rights should be adopted. See, *e. g.,* The Federalist No. 84 (A. Hamilton). In a letter to Thomas Jefferson in October 1788, James Madison explained why he, although "in favor of a bill of rights," had "not viewed it in an important light" up to that time: "I conceive that in a certain degree . . . the rights in question are reserved by the manner in which the federal powers are granted." He went on to state that "there is great reason to fear that a positive declaration of some of the most essential rights could not be obtained in the requisite latitude." 5 Writings of James Madison 271 (G. Hunt ed. 1904).[15]

But arguments such as the State makes have not precluded recognition of important rights not enumerated. Notwithstanding the appropriate caution against reading into the Constitution rights not explicitly defined, the Court has acknowledged that certain unarticulated rights are implicit in enumerated guarantees. For example, the rights of association and of privacy, the right to be presumed innocent, and the right to be judged by a standard of proof beyond a rea-

---

[15] Madison's comments in Congress also reveal the perceived need for some sort of constitutional "saving clause," which, among other things, would serve to foreclose application to the Bill of Rights of the maxim that the affirmation of particular rights implies a negation of those not expressly defined. See 1 Annals of Cong. 438–440 (1789). See also, *e. g.,* 2 J. Story, Commentaries on the Constitution of the United States 651 (5th ed. 1891). Madison's efforts, culminating in the Ninth Amendment, served to allay the fears of those who were concerned that expressing certain guarantees could be read as excluding others.

sonable doubt in a criminal trial, as well as the right to travel, appear nowhere in the Constitution or Bill of Rights. Yet these important but unarticulated rights have nonetheless been found to share constitutional protection in common with explicit guarantees.[16] The concerns expressed by Madison and others have thus been resolved; fundamental rights, even though not expressly guaranteed, have been recognized by the Court as indispensable to the enjoyment of rights explicitly defined.

We hold that the right to attend criminal trials [17] is implicit in the guarantees of the First Amendment; without the freedom to attend such trials, which people have exercised for centuries, important aspects of freedom of speech and "of the press could be eviscerated." *Branzburg,* 408 U. S., at 681.

D

Having concluded there was a guaranteed right of the public under the First and Fourteenth Amendments to attend the trial of Stevenson's case, we return to the closure order challenged by appellants. The Court in *Gannett* made clear that although the Sixth Amendment guarantees the accused a right to a public trial, it does not give a right to a private trial. 443 U. S., at 382. Despite the fact that this was the fourth trial of the accused, the trial judge made no findings to support closure; no inquiry was made as to whether alterna-

---

[16] See, *e. g., NAACP* v. *Alabama,* 357 U. S. 449 (1958) (right of association); *Griswold* v. *Connecticut,* 381 U. S. 479 (1965), and *Stanley* v. *Georgia,* 394 U. S. 557 (1969) (right to privacy); *Estelle* v. *Williams,* 425 U. S. 501, 503 (1976), and *Taylor* v. *Kentucky,* 436 U. S. 478, 483–486 (1978) (presumption of innocence); *In re Winship,* 397 U. S. 358 (1970) (standard of proof beyond a reasonable doubt); *United States* v. *Guest,* 383 U. S. 745, 757–759 (1966), and *Shapiro* v. *Thompson,* 394 U. S. 618, 630 (1969) (right to interstate travel).

[17] Whether the public has a right to attend trials of civil cases is a question not raised by this case, but we note that historically both civil and criminal trials have been presumptively open.

tive solutions would have met the need to ensure fairness; there was no recognition of any right under the Constitution for the public or press to attend the trial. In contrast to the pretrial proceeding dealt with in *Gannett,* there exist in the context of the trial itself various tested alternatives to satisfy the constitutional demands of fairness. See, *e. g., Nebraska Press Assn.* v. *Stuart,* 427 U. S., at 563–565; *Sheppard* v. *Maxwell,* 384 U. S., at 357–362. There was no suggestion that any problems with witnesses could not have been dealt with by their exclusion from the courtroom or their sequestration during the trial. See *id.,* at 359. Nor is there anything to indicate that sequestration of the jurors would not have guarded against their being subjected to any improper information. All of the alternatives admittedly present difficulties for trial courts, but none of the factors relied on here was beyond the realm of the manageable. Absent an overriding interest articulated in findings, the trial of a criminal case must be open to the public.[18] Accordingly, the judgment under review is

Reversed.

---

[18] We have no occasion here to define the circumstances in which all or parts of a criminal trial may be closed to the public, cf., *e. g.,* 6 J. Wigmore, Evidence § 1835 (J. Chadbourn rev. 1976), but our holding today does not mean that the First Amendment rights of the public and representatives of the press are absolute. Just as a government may impose reasonable time, place, and manner restrictions upon the use of its streets in the interest of such objectives as the free flow of traffic, see, *e. g., Cox* v. *New Hampshire,* 312 U. S. 569 (1941), so may a trial judge, in the interest of the fair administration of justice, impose reasonable limitations on access to a trial.

CBS, INC. *v.* FEDERAL COMMUNICATIONS COMMISSION ET AL.

CERTIORARI TO THE UNITED STATES COURT OF APPEALS FOR THE DISTRICT OF COLUMBIA CIRCUIT

No. 80–207. Argued March 3, 1981—Decided July 1, 1981*

Section 312 (a)(7) of the Communications Act of 1934, as added by Title I of the Federal Election Campaign Act of 1971, authorizes the Federal Communications Commission (FCC) to revoke any broadcasting station license "for willful or repeated failure to allow reasonable access to or to permit purchase of reasonable amounts of time for the use of a broadcasting station by a legally qualified candidate for Federal elective office on behalf of his candidacy." On October 11, 1979, the Carter-Mondale Presidential Committee (Committee) requested each of the three major television networks (petitioners) to provide time for a 30-minute program between 8 p. m. and 10:30 p. m. on any day from the 4th through the 7th of December 1979. The Committee intended to present, in conjunction with President Carter's formal announcement of his candidacy, a documentary outlining the record of his administration. The petitioners refused to make the requested time available. CBS emphasized the large number of candidates for the Presidential nominations and the potential disruption of regular programming to accommodate requests for equal treatment, but offered to sell a 5-minute segment at 10:55 p. m. on December 8 and a 5-minute segment in the daytime; American Broadcasting Cos. replied that it had not yet decided when it would begin selling political time for the 1980 Presidential campaign, but later indicated that it would allow such sales in January 1980; and National Broadcasting Co., noting the number of potential requests for time from Presidential candidates, stated that it was not prepared to sell time for political programs as early as December 1979. The Committee then filed a complaint with the FCC, charging that the networks had violated their obligation to provide "reasonable access" under § 312 (a)(7). The FCC ruled that the networks had violated the statute, concluding that their reasons for refusing to sell the time requested were "deficient" under the FCC's standards

---

*Together with No. 80–213, *American Broadcasting Cos., Inc.* v. *Federal Communications Commission et al.*, and No. 80–214, *National Broadcasting Co., Inc.* v. *Federal Communications Commission et al.*, also on certiorari to the same court.

of reasonableness, and directing the networks to indicate by a specified date how they intended to fulfill their statutory obligations. On the networks' petition for review, the Court of Appeals affirmed the FCC's orders, holding that the statute created a new, affirmative right of access to the broadcast media for individual candidates for federal elective office and that the FCC has the authority to independently evaluate whether a campaign has begun for purposes of the statute. The court approved the FCC's insistence that in responding to a candidate's request for time broadcasters must weigh certain factors, including the individual needs of the candidate (as expressed by the candidate); the amount of time previously provided to the candidate; potential disruption of regular programming; the number of other candidates likely to invoke equal opportunity rights if the broadcaster granted the request before it; and the timing of the request. The court determined that the record supported the FCC's conclusion that the networks failed to apply the proper standards and had thus violated the statute's "reasonable access" requirement. The court also rejected petitioners' First Amendment challenge to § 312 (a)(7) as applied.

Held:

1. Section 312 (a)(7) created an affirmative, promptly enforceable right of reasonable access to the use of broadcast stations for individual candidates seeking federal elective office. It went beyond merely codifying prior FCC policies developed under the public interest standard. Pp. 376–386.

(a) It is clear on the face of the statute that Congress did not prescribe simply a general duty to afford some measure of political programming, which the public interest obligation of broadcasters already provided for. Rather, § 312 (a)(7) focuses on the individual "legally qualified candidate" seeking air time to advocate *"his* candidacy," and guarantees him "reasonable access" enforceable by specific governmental sanction. Further, the sanction may be imposed for either "willful or repeated" failure to afford reasonable access. Pp. 377–379.

(b) The legislative history confirms that § 312 (a)(7) created a right of access that enlarged the political broadcasting responsibilities of licensees. Pp. 379–382.

(c) Since the enactment of § 312 (a)(7), the FCC has consistently construed the statute as extending beyond the prior public interest policy and as imposing the additional requirement that reasonable access and purchase of reasonable amounts of time be afforded candidates for federal office. This repeated construction of the statute comports with its language and legislative history and has received congressional review, so that departure from that construction is unwarranted. Pp. 382–385.

(d) The qualified observation in *Columbia Broadcasting System, Inc.* v. *Democratic National Committee,* 412 U. S. 94, 113–114, n. 12, relied on by petitioners, that § 312 (a)(7) "essentially codified" existing FCC practice was not a conclusion that the statute was in all respects coextensive with that practice and imposed no additional duties on broadcasters. That case did not purport to rule on the precise contours of the responsibilities created by § 312 (a)(7) since that issue was not before the Court. Pp. 385–386.

2. Contrary to petitioners' contentions, certain of the FCC's standards to effectuate the guarantees of § 312 (a)(7)—which standards evolved principally on a case-by-case basis and are not embodied in formalized rules—do not contravene the statutory objectives or unduly intrude on petitioners' editorial discretion, and the statute was properly applied to petitioners in determining that they had failed to grant the "reasonable access" required by the statute. Pp. 386–394.

(a) The FCC's practice of independently determining—by examining objective evidence and considering the position of both the candidate and the networks as well as other factors—whether a campaign has begun and the obligations imposed by the statute have attached does not improperly involve the FCC in the electoral process or significantly impair broadcasters' editorial discretion. Nor is the FCC's standard requiring broadcasters to evaluate access requests on an individualized basis improper on the alleged ground that it attaches inordinate significance to candidates' needs, thereby precluding fair assessment of broadcasters' concerns. The FCC mandates careful consideration of, not blind assent to, candidates' desires for air time. Although the standard does proscribe blanket rules concerning access, such as a broadcaster's rule of granting only time spots of a fixed duration to all candidates, the standard is consistent with § 312 (a)(7)'s guarantee of reasonable access to *individual* candidates for federal elective office. The FCC's standards are not arbitrary and capricious, but represent a reasoned attempt to effectuate the statute's access requirement, giving broadcasters room to exercise their discretion but demanding that they act in good faith. Pp. 388–390.

(b) On the basis of prior FCC decisions and interpretations, petitioners had adequate notice that their conduct in responding to the Committee's request for access would contravene the statute. The FCC's conclusion about the status of the campaign accorded with its announced position on the vesting of § 312 (a)(7) rights and was adequately supported by the objective factors on which it relied. And under the circumstances here, it cannot be concluded that the FCC abused its discretion in finding that petitioners failed to grant the "reasonable access" required by § 312 (a)(7). Pp. 390–394.

3. The right of access to the media under § 312 (a)(7), as defined by the FCC and applied here, does not violate the First Amendment rights of broadcasters by unduly circumscribing their editorial discretion, but instead properly balances the First Amendment rights of federal candidates, the public, and broadcasters. Although the broadcasting industry is entitled under the First Amendment to exercise "the widest journalistic freedom consistent with its public [duties]," *Columbia Broadcasting System, Inc.* v. *Democratic National Committee, supra,* at 110, "[i]t is the right of the viewers and listeners, not the right of the broadcasters, which is paramount." *Red Lion Broadcasting Co.* v. *FCC,* 395 U. S. 367, 390. Section 312 (a)(7), which creates only a *limited* right of access to the media, makes a significant contribution to freedom of expression by enhancing the ability of candidates to present, and the public to receive, information necessary for the effective operation of the democratic process. Pp. 394–397.

202 U. S. App. D. C. 369, 629 F. 2d 1, affirmed.

BURGER, C. J., delivered the opinion of the Court, in which BRENNAN, STEWART, MARSHALL, BLACKMUN, and POWELL, JJ., joined. WHITE, J., filed a dissenting opinion, in which REHNQUIST and STEVENS, JJ., joined, *post,* p. 397. STEVENS, J., filed a dissenting opinion, *post,* p. 418.

Floyd Abrams argued the cause for petitioners in all cases. On the briefs in No. 80–207 were *J. Roger Wollenberg, Timothy B. Dyk, Ralph E. Goldberg,* and *Joseph DeFranco.* On the briefs in No. 80–213 were *James A. McKenna, Jr., Thomas N. Frohock, Carl R. Ramey,* and *Robert J. Kaufman.* With Mr. Abrams on the briefs in No. 80–214 were *Dean Ringel, Patricia A. Pickrel, Corydon B. Dunham,* and *Howard Monderer. Erwin G. Krasnow* filed a brief for the National Association of Broadcasters, respondent under this Court's Rule 19.6, urging reversal.

Stephen M. Shapiro argued the cause for the federal respondents in all cases. With him on the brief were *Solicitor General McCree, Deputy Solicitor General Claiborne, Robert R. Bruce,* and *C. Grey Pash, Jr.*†

---

†*Heidi P. Sanchez* and *Andrew Jay Schwartzman* filed a brief for the

CHIEF JUSTICE BURGER delivered the opinion of the Court.

We granted certiorari to consider whether the Federal Communications Commission properly construed 47 U. S. C. § 312 (a)(7) and determined that petitioners failed to provide "reasonable access to . . . the use of a broadcasting station" as required by the statute. 449 U. S. 950 (1980).

I

A

On October 11, 1979, Gerald M. Rafshoon, President of the Carter-Mondale Presidential Committee, requested each of the three major television networks to provide time for a 30-minute program between 8 p. m. and 10:30 p. m. on either the 4th, 5th, 6th, or 7th of December 1979.[1] The Committee

---

National Citizens Committee for Broadcasting et al. as *amici curiae* urging affirmance.

[1] The text of Mr. Rafshoon's letter to the three networks read as follows:

"On behalf of the Carter/Mondale Presidential Committee, Inc., I am requesting availabilities for a thirty (30) minute program on [ABC, CBS, or NBC] between 8:00 p. m. and 10:30 p. m. E. S. T. on December 4, December 5, December 6, or December 7, 1979. This program, to be run in conjunction with an announcement concerning his candidacy by President Carter for the Democratic nomination for President, consists of a documentary outlining the President's record and that of his administration. At the time this program is aired, it may be assumed that President Carter will be a legally qualified candidate under the Communications Act of 1934, as amended, and that the President would appear on the program.

"As you know, the first official contest to select delegates to the Democratic National Convention occurs January 21, 1980, in Iowa, which is 47 days after December 7, 1979, our last requested date for availabilities.

"Unlike all previous Presidential election years, the news media has chosen to focus enormous attention on the Florida Caucus (October 13, 1979) and Convention (November 16–18, 1979) as well as other aspects of the 1980 campaign. As illustration, I have noted that in the six-week period from September 1 through October 9, 1979, ABC devoted 51 minutes, 22 seconds to the 1980 campaign; CBS devoted 51 minutes, 17 seconds to this subject; and NBC devoted 70 minutes. Therefore, our request for the above intended to present, in conjunction with President Carter's formal announcement of his candidacy, a documentary outlining the record of his administration.

The networks declined to make the requested time available. Petitioner CBS emphasized the large number of candidates for the Republican and Democratic Presidential nominations and the potential disruption of regular programming to accommodate requests for equal treatment, but it offered to sell two 5-minute segments to the Committee, one at 10:55 p. m. on December 8 and one in the daytime.[2] Peti-

---

time seems eminently appropriate in view of the escalating political climate already generated by both print and broadcast media.

"I will expect to hear from one of your sales representatives within the next week regarding a selection of times in order that we may choose a mutually agreeable date." App. 35–40.

[2] The letter (dated October 17, 1979) to Mr. Rafshoon from Raymond E. Dillon, Director of Political Sales at CBS, read in pertinent part:

"Because of the large number of present and potential candidates for the Republican and Democratic presidential nominations, we are at this time unable to accede to your request to purchase a half-hour program. We note that three Democrats and eleven Republicans have already announced, or may reasonably be expected shortly to announce, their presidential candidacies; indeed two candidates for the Republican presidential nomination have already requested to purchase half-hour programs on the CBS Television Network, and their requests have been declined on the same basis as indicated below.

"In light of the above circumstances, were we to provide the half-hour program you seek, accommodating potential requests for equal treatment from other candidates for presidential nomination would involve massive disruptions of the regular entertainment and information schedule of the CBS Television Network. Accordingly, we must respectfully reject your request.

"We are, however, prepared to make one 5-minute segment in prime time and one 5-minute daytime segment available for purchase by your committee. We note that this is the same offer made to the Republican candidates referred to above in response to their requests to purchase half-hour time periods.

"While we are unable to make available time on the dates you have specified, we are able to offer for your purchase a 5-minute period on

tioner American Broadcasting Cos. replied that it had not yet
decided when it would begin selling political time for the 1980
Presidential campaign,[3] but subsequently indicated that it
would allow such sales in January 1980.   App. 58.   Petitioner
National Broadcasting Co., noting the number of potential
requests for time from Presidential candidates, stated that
it was not prepared to sell time for political programs as early
as December 1979.[4]

On October 29, 1979, the Carter-Mondale Presidential
Committee filed a complaint with the Federal Communications Commission, charging that the networks had violated

---

December 8 between approximately 10:55 and 11:00 PM.   We will also
provide a specific 5-minute daytime availability for your purchase on
request."   *Id.*, at 44–45.

[3] The letter (dated October 23, 1979) to Mr. Rafshoon from Charles
C. Allen, Vice President for Sales Administration at ABC, read in pertinent part:

"[T]he ABC Television Network has not reached a decision as to when it
will start selling political time for the 1980 Presidential campaign, and,
accordingly, we are not in a position to comply with your request.   As I
mentioned on the telephone, I believe that later this year a decision will
be made to make political time for the Presidential campaign available on
ABC–TV early next year."   *Id.*, at 41.

[4] The letter (dated October 23, 1979) to Mr. Rafshoon from Joseph J.
Iaricci, Vice President for Sales and Administration at NBC, read in
pertinent part:

"We have evaluated your request carefully.   Based upon our experience
with past campaigns, we believe it is too early in the political season for
nationwide broadcast time to be made available for paid political purposes.
In addition, we believe that honoring your request at this early stage of
the Presidential campaign would require NBC to honor similar requests
from a number of other Presidential aspirants.   The impact of such an
undertaking at this time is, of course, a significant factor in our decision.

"Insofar as the nomination process is now focused on political activities
in individual states like Iowa, you may wish to contact stations serving
those particular states.

"Please be assured that NBC News will continue to cover important and
newsworthy aspects of President Carter's political activities."   *Id.*, at
42–43.

their obligation to provide "reasonable access" under § 312
(a)(7) of the Communications Act of 1934, as amended.
Title 47 U. S. C. § 312 (a)(7), as added to the Act, 86 Stat. 4,
states:

> "The Commission may revoke any station license or
> construction permit—
>
> .   .   .   .   .
>
> "(7) for willful or repeated failure to allow reasonable
> access to or to permit purchase of reasonable amounts
> of time for the use of a broadcasting station by a legally
> qualified candidate for Federal elective office on behalf
> of his candidacy."

At an open meeting on November 20, 1979, the Commission,
by a 4-to-3 vote, ruled that the networks had violated
§ 312 (a)(7).   In its memorandum opinion and order, the
Commission concluded that the networks' reasons for refusing
to sell the time requested were "deficient" under its standards of reasonableness, and directed the networks to indicate
by November 26, 1979, how they intended to fulfill their statutory obligations.   74 F. C. C. 2d 631.

Petitioners sought reconsideration of the FCC's decision.
The reconsideration petitions were denied by the same 4-to-3
vote, and, on November 28, 1979, the Commission issued a
second memorandum opinion and order clarifying its previous
decision.   It rejected petitioners' arguments that § 312 (a)(7)
was not intended to create a new right of access to the broadcast media and that the Commission had improperly substituted its judgment for that of the networks in evaluating the
Carter-Mondale Presidential Committee's request for time.
November 29, 1979, was set as the date for the networks to
file their plans for compliance with the statute.   74 F. C. C.
2d 657.

The networks, pursuant to 47 U. S. C. § 402, then petitioned
for review of the Commission's orders in the United States
Court of Appeals for the District of Columbia Circuit.   The

court allowed the Committee and the National Association of Broadcasters to intervene, and granted a stay of the Commission's orders pending review.

Following the seizure of American Embassy personnel in Iran, the Carter-Mondale Presidential Committee decided to postpone to early January 1980 the 30-minute program it had planned to broadcast during the period of December 4–7, 1979. However, believing that some time was needed in conjunction with the President's announcement of his candidacy, the Committee sought and subsequently obtained from CBS the purchase of five minutes of time on December 4. In addition, the Committee sought and obtained from ABC and NBC offers of time for a 30-minute program in January, and the ABC offer eventually was accepted. Throughout these negotiations, the Committee and the networks reserved all rights relating to the appeal.

B

The Court of Appeals affirmed the Commission's orders, 202 U. S. App. D. C. 369, 629 F. 2d 1 (1980), holding that the statute created a new, affirmative right of access to the broadcast media for individual candidates for federal elective office. As to the implementation of § 312 (a)(7), the court concluded that the Commission has the authority to independently evaluate whether a campaign has begun for purposes of the statute, and approved the Commission's insistence that "broadcasters consider and address all non-frivolous matters in responding to a candidate's request for time." *Id.*, at 386, 629 F. 2d, at 18. For example, a broadcaster must weigh such factors as: "(a) the individual needs of the candidate (as expressed by the candidate); (b) the amount of time previously provided to the candidate; (c) potential disruption of regular programming; (d) the number of other candidates likely to invoke equal opportunity rights if the broadcaster grants the request before him; and, (e) the timing of the request." *Id.*, at 387, 629 F. 2d, at 19. And in reviewing a broadcaster's decision, the Commission will confine itself to two questions: "(1) has the broadcaster adverted to the proper standards in deciding whether to grant a request for access, and (2) is the broadcaster's explanation for his decision reasonable in terms of those standards?" *Id.*, at 386, 629 F. 2d, at 18.

Applying these principles, the Court of Appeals sustained the Commission's determination that the Presidential campaign had begun by November 1979, and, accordingly, the obligations imposed by § 312 (a)(7) had attached. Further, the court decided that "the record . . . adequately supports the Commission's conclusion that the networks failed to apply the proper standards." *Id.*, at 389, 629 F. 2d, at 21. In particular, the "across-the-board" policies of all three networks failed to address the specific needs asserted by the Carter-Mondale Presidential Committee. *Id.*, at 390, 629 F. 2d, at 22. From this the court concluded that the Commission was correct in holding that the networks had violated the statute's "reasonable access" requirement.

Finally, the Court of Appeals rejected petitioners' First Amendment challenge to § 312 (a)(7) as applied, reasoning that the statute as construed by the Commission "is a constitutionally acceptable accommodation between, on the one hand, the public's right to be informed about elections and the right of candidates to speak and, on the other hand, the editorial rights of broadcasters." *Id.*, at 389, 629 F. 2d, at 25. In a concurring opinion adopted by the majority, *id.*, at 389, n. 117, 629 F. 2d, at 25, n. 117, Judge Tamm expressed the view that § 312 (a)(7) is saved from constitutional infirmity "as long as the [Commission] . . . maintains a very limited 'overseer' role consistent with its obligation of careful neutrality . . . ." *Id.*, at 402, 629 F. 2d, at 34.

II

We consider first the scope of § 312 (a)(7). Petitioners CBS and NBC contend that the statute did not impose any additional obligations on broadcasters, but merely codified prior policies developed by the Federal Communications Commission under the public interest standard. The Commission, however, argues that § 312 (a)(7) created an affirmative, promptly enforceable right of reasonable access to the use of broadcast stations for individual candidates seeking federal elective office.

A

The Federal Election Campaign Act of 1971, which Congress enacted in 1972, included as one of its four Titles the Campaign Communications Reform Act (Title I). Title I contained the provision that was codified as 47 U. S. C. § 312 (a)(7).[5]

We have often observed that the starting point in every case involving statutory construction is "the language employed by Congress." *Reiter* v. *Sonotone Corp.*, 442 U. S. 330, 337 (1979). In unambiguous language, § 312 (a)(7) authorizes the Commission to revoke a broadcaster's license

> "for willful or repeated failure to allow reasonable access to or to permit purchase of reasonable amounts of time for the use of a broadcasting station by a legally qualified candidate for Federal elective office on behalf of his candidacy."

It is clear on the face of the statute that Congress did not prescribe merely a general duty to afford some measure of political programming, which the public interest obligation

---

[5] Title I also provided: (a) that during a specified period before a primary or general election, a broadcast station was not permitted to charge a legally qualified candidate for any public office a fee in excess of its "lowest unit charge . . . for the same class and amount of time for the same period," 47 U. S. C. § 315 (b)(1); and (b) that in using the communications media, candidates for federal elective office were not allowed to exceed established spending limits, 47 U. S. C. § 803 (1970 ed., Supp. II), repealed, Pub. L. 93–443, 88 Stat. 1278 (1974).

of broadcasters already provided for. Rather, § 312 (a)(7) focuses on the individual "legally qualified candidate" seeking air time to advocate *"his* candidacy," and guarantees him "reasonable access" enforceable by specific governmental sanction. Further, the sanction may be imposed for "willful *or* repeated" failure to afford reasonable access. This suggests that, if a legally qualified candidate for federal office is denied a reasonable amount of broadcast time, license revocation may follow even a single instance of such denial so long as it is willful; where the denial is recurring, the penalty may be imposed in the absence of a showing of willfulness.

The command of § 312 (a)(7) differs from the limited duty of broadcasters under the public interest standard. The practice preceding the adoption of § 312 (a)(7) has been described by the Commission as follows:

> "Prior to the enactment of the [statute], we recognized political broadcasting as one of the fourteen basic elements necessary to meet the public interest, needs and desires of the community. No legally qualified candidate had, at that time, a specific right of access to a broadcasting station. However, stations were required to make reasonable, good faith judgments about the importance and interest of particular races. Based upon those judgments, licensees were to 'determine how much time should be made available for candidates in each race on either a paid or unpaid basis.' There was no requirement that such time be made available for specific 'uses' of a broadcasting station to which Section 315 'equal opportunities' would be applicable." (Footnotes omitted.) *Report and Order: Commission Policy in Enforcing Section 312 (a)(7) of the Communications Act,* 68 F. C. C. 2d 1079, 1087–1088 (1978) (1978 Report and Order).

Under the pre-1971 public interest requirement, compliance with which was necessary to assure license renewal, some time

370

had to be given to political issues, but an individual candidate could claim no personal right of access unless his opponent used the station and no distinction was drawn between federal, state, and local elections.[6] See *Farmers Educational & Cooperative Union* v. *WDAY, Inc.*, 360 U. S. 525, 534 (1959). By its terms, however, § 312 (a)(7) singles out legally qualified candidates for *federal* elective office and grants them a special right of access on an individual basis, violation of which carries the serious consequence of license revocation. The conclusion is inescapable that the statute did more than simply codify the pre-existing public interest standard.

B

The legislative history confirms that § 312 (a)(7) created a right of access that enlarged the political broadcasting responsibilities of licensees. When the subject of campaign reform was taken up by Congress in 1971, three bills were introduced in the Senate—S. 1, S. 382, and S. 956. All three measures, while differing in approach, were "intended to increase a candidate's accessibility to the media and to reduce the level of spending for its use." Federal Election Campaign Act of 1971: Hearings on S. 1, S. 382, and S. 956 before the Subcommittee on Communications of the Senate Committee on Commerce, 92d Cong., 1st Sess., 2 (1971) (remarks of Sen. Pastore). The subsequent Report of the Senate Commerce Committee stated that one of the primary purposes of the Federal Election Campaign Act of 1971 was to "give candidates for public office *greater access to the media* so that they may better explain their stand on the issues, and thereby more fully and completely inform the voters." S. Rep. No. 92–96, p. 20 (1971) (emphasis added). The Report con-

---

[6] The public interest requirement still governs the obligations of broadcasters with respect to political races at the state and local levels. See *Public Notice: The Law of Political Broadcasting and Cablecasting*, 69 F. C. C. 2d 2209, 2290 (1978) (1978 Primer).

tained neither an explicit interpretation of the provision that
became § 312 (a)(7) nor a discussion of its intended impact,
but simply noted:

> "[The amendment] provide[s] that willful or repeated
> failure by a broadcast licensee to allow reasonable access
> to or to permit purchase of reasonable amounts of time
> for the use of his station's facilities by a lagally [sic]
> qualified candidate for Federal elective office on behalf
> of his candidacy shall be grounds for adverse action by
> the FCC.

> "The duty of broadcast licensees generally to permit
> the use of their facilities by legally qualified candidates
> for these public offices is inherent in the requirement
> that licensees serve the needs and interests of the [com-
> munities] of license. The Federal Communications Com-
> mission has recognized this obligation . . . ." Id., at 34.

While acknowledging the "general" public interest requirement, the Report treated it separately from the specific obligation prescribed by the proposed legislation. See also id.,
at 28.

As initially reported in the Senate, § 312 (a)(7) applied
broadly to "the use of a broadcasting station by any person
who is a legally qualified candidate on behalf of his candidacy."
Id., at 3. The Conference Committee confined the provision
to candidates seeking *federal* elective office. S. Conf. Rep. No.
92–580, p. 22 (1971); H. Conf. Rep. No. 92–752, p. 22 (1971).
During floor debate on the Conference Report in the House,
attention was called to the substantial impact § 312 (a)(7)
would have on the broadcasting industry:

> "[B]roadcasters [are required] to permit any legally
> qualified candidate [for federal office] to purchase a
> 'reasonable amount of time' for his campaign advertis-
> ing. Any broadcaster found in willful or repeated vio-
> lation of this requirement could lose his license and be

thrown out of business, his total record of public service notwithstanding.

.   .   .   .   .

"[U]nder this provision, a broadcaster, whose license is obtained and retained on basis of performance in the public interest, may be charged with being unreasonable and, therefore, fall subject to revocation of his license." 118 Cong. Rec. 326 (1972) (remarks of Rep. Keith).

Such emphasis on the thrust of the statute would seem unnecessary if it did nothing more than reiterate the public interest standard.

Perhaps the most telling evidence of congressional intent, however, is the contemporaneous amendment of § 315 (a) of the Communications Act.[7] That amendment was described by the Conference Committee as a "conforming amendment" necessitated by the enactment of § 312 (a)(7). S. Conf. Rep. No. 92–580, *supra,* at 22; H. Conf. Rep. No. 92–752, *supra,* at 22. Prior to the "conforming amendment," the second sentence of 47 U. S. C. § 315 (a) (1970 ed.) read: "No obligation is imposed upon any licensee to allow the use of its station by any such candidate." This language made clear that broadcasters were not common carriers as to affirmative, rather than responsive, requests for access. As a result of the amendment, the second sentence now contains an important qualification: "No obligation is imposed *under this subsection* upon any licensee to allow the use of its station by any such candidate." 47 U. S. C. § 315 (a) (emphasis added). Congress retreated from its statement that "no obligation" exists to afford individual access presumably because § 312 (a)(7) compels such access in the context of federal elections. If § 312 (a)(7) simply reaffirmed the pre-existing public inter-

---

[7] Title 47 U. S. C. § 315 (a) provides that, if a legally qualified candidate for public office is permitted to use a broadcasting station, the licensee must afford "equal opportunities to all other . . . candidates for that office in the use of [the] station."

est requirement with the added sanction of license revocation, no conforming amendment to § 315 (a) would have been needed.

Thus, the legislative history supports the plain meaning of the statute that individual candidates for federal elective office have a right of reasonable access to the use of stations for paid political broadcasts on behalf of their candidacies,[8] without reference to whether an opponent has secured time.

C

We have held that "the construction of a statute by those charged with its execution should be followed unless there are compelling indications that it is wrong, especially when Congress has refused to alter the administrative construction." *Red Lion Broadcasting Co.* v. *FCC,* 395 U. S. 367, 381 (1969) (footnotes omitted). Accord *Columbia Broadcasting System, Inc.* v. *Democratic National Committee,* 412 U. S. 94, 121 (1973). Such deference "is particularly appropriate where, as here, an agency's interpretation involves issues of considerable public controversy, and Congress has not acted to correct any misperception of its statutory objectives." *United States* v. *Rutherford,* 442 U. S. 544, 554 (1979).

Since the enactment of § 312 (a)(7), the Commission has consistently construed the statute as extending beyond the prior public interest policy. In 1972, the Commission made clear that § 312 (a)(7) "now imposes on the overall obligation to operate in the public interest *the additional specific requirement* that reasonable access and purchase of reasonable amounts of time be afforded candidates for Federal office." *Use of Broadcast and Cablecast Facilities by Candidates for Public Office,* 34 F. C. C. 2d 510, 537–538 (1972)

---

[8] No request for access must be honored under § 312 (a)(7) unless the candidate is willing to pay for the time sought. See *Kennedy for President Comm.* v. *FCC,* 204 U. S. App. D. C. 160, 174–178, 636 F. 2d 432, 446–450 (1980); 1978 Primer, at 2288.

(1972 Policy Statement) (emphasis added). Accord, *Public Notice Concerning Licensee Responsibility Under Amendments to the Communications Act Made by the Federal Election Campaign Act of 1971*, 47 F. C. C. 2d 516 (1974). In its 1978 Report and Order, the Commission stated:

"When Congress enacted Section 312 (a)(7), it imposed an additional obligation on the general mandate to operate in the public interest. Licensees were specifically required to afford reasonable access to or to permit the purchase of reasonable amounts of broadcast time for the 'use' of Federal candidates.

"We see no merit to the contention that Section 312 (a)(7) was meant merely as a codification of the Commission's already existing policy concerning political broadcasts. There was no reason to commit that policy to statute since it was already being enforced by the Commission. . . ." 68 F. C. C. 2d, at 1088.

See also 1978 Primer, 69 F. C. C. 2d, at 2286–2289. The Commission has adhered to this view of the statute in its rulings on individual inquiries and complaints. See, *e. g., The Labor Party*, 67 F. C. C. 2d 589, 590 (1978); *Ken Bauder*, 62 F. C. C. 2d 849 (Broadcast Bureau 1976); *Don C. Smith*, 49 F. C. C. 2d 678, 679 (Broadcast Bureau 1974); *Summa Corp.*, 43 F. C. C. 2d 602, 603–605 (1973); *Robert H. Hauslein*, 39 F. C. C. 2d 1064, 1065 (Broadcast Bureau 1973).

Congress has been made aware of the Commission's interpretation of § 312 (a)(7). In 1973, hearings were conducted to review the operation of the Federal Election Campaign Act of 1971. Federal Election Campaign Act of 1973: Hearings on S. 372 before the Subcommittee on Communications of the Senate Committee on Commerce, 93d Cong., 1st Sess. (1973). Commission Chairman Dean Burch testified regarding the agency's experience with § 312 (a)(7). *Id.*, at 136–137. He noted that the Commission's 1972 Policy Statement was "widely distributed and represented our best judgment as to the requirements of the law and the intent of Congress." *Id.*, at 135. Chairman Burch discussed some of the difficult questions implicit in determining whether a station has afforded "reasonable access" to a candidate for federal office, and in conclusion stated: "We have brought our approach to these problems in the form of the 1972 Public Notice to the attention of Congress. If we have erred in some important construction, we would, of course, welcome congressional guidance." *Id.*, at 137. Senator Pastore, Chairman of the Communications Subcommittee, replied:

> "We didn't draw the provision any differently than we did because when you begin to legislate on guidelines, and on standards, and on criteria, you know what you run up against. I think what we did was reasonable enough, and I think what you did was reasonable enough as well.
>
> .	.	.	.	.
>
> "I would suppose that in cases of that kind, you would get some complaints. But, frankly, I think it has worked out pretty well." *Id.*, at 137–138.

The issue was joined when CBS Vice Chairman Frank Stanton also testified at the hearings and objected to the fact that § 312 (a)(7) "grants rights to all legally qualified candidates for Federal office . . . ." *Id.*, at 190. He strongly urged "repeal" of the statute, but his plea was unsuccessful. *Ibid.*[9]

The Commission's repeated construction of § 312 (a)(7) as affording an affirmative right of reasonable access to in-

---

[9] Broadcasters have continued to register their complaints about § 312 (a)(7) with Congress. See First Amendment Clarification Act of 1977: Hearing on S. 22 before the Subcommittee on Communications of the Senate Committee on Commerce, Science, and Transportation, 95th Cong., 2d Sess., 67 (1978). And Congress has considered specific proposals to repeal the statute, but has declined to do so. See S. 22, 95th Cong., 1st Sess., § 3 (1977); S. 1178, 94th Cong., 1st Sess., § 2 (1975). Indeed when the Federal Election Campaign Act was amended in 1974, § 312 (a)(7) was left undisturbed. See Pub. L. 93–443, 88 Stat. 1272.

dividual candidates for federal elective office comports with
the statute's language and legislative history and has received
congressional review. Therefore, departure from that construction is unwarranted. "Congress' failure to repeal or
revise [the statute] in the face of such administrative interpretation [is] persuasive evidence that that interpretation is
the one intended by Congress." *Zemel* v. *Rusk,* 381 U. S. 1,
11 (1965).

D

In support of their narrow reading of § 312 (a)(7) as simply a restatement of the public interest obligation, petitioners cite our decision in *Columbia Broadcasting System,
Inc.* v. *Democratic National Committee,* 412 U. S. 94 (1973),
which held that neither the First Amendment nor the Communications Act requires broadcasters to accept paid editorial advertisements from citizens at large. The Court in
Democratic National Committee observed that "the Commission on several occasions has ruled that no private individual
or group has a right to command the use of broadcast facilities," and that Congress has not altered that policy even
though it has amended the Communications Act several times.
Id., at 113. In a footnote, on which petitioners here rely, we
referred to the then recently enacted § 312 (a)(7) as one such
amendment, stating that it had "essentially codified the Commission's prior interpretation of § 315 (a) as requiring broadcasters to make time available to political candidates." *Id.,*
at 113–114, n. 12.

However, "the language of an opinion is not always to be
parsed as though we were dealing with language of a statute."
Reiter v. *Sonotone Corp.,* 442 U. S., at 341. The qualified
observation that § 312 (a)(7) "essentially codified" existing
Commission practice was not a conclusion that the statute
was in all respects coextensive with that practice and imposed
no additional duties on broadcasters. In *Democratic National
Committee,* we did not purport to rule on the precise con-

tours of the responsibilities created by § 312 (a)(7) since that
issue was not before us. Like the general public interest
standard and the equal opportunities provision of § 315 (a),
§ 312 (a)(7) reflects the importance attached to the use of
the public airwaves by political candidates. Yet we now
hold that § 312 (a)(7) expanded on those predecessor requirements and granted a new right of access to persons seeking election to federal office.[10]

III

A

Although Congress provided in § 312 (a)(7) for greater
use of broadcasting stations by federal candidates, it did not
give guidance on how the Commission should implement the
statute's access requirement. Essentially, Congress adopted
a "rule of reason" and charged the Commission with its enforcement. Pursuant to 47 U. S. C. § 303 (r), which empowers the Commission to "[m]ake such rules and regulations
and prescribe such restrictions and conditions, not inconsistent with law, as may be necessary to carry out the provisions
of [the Communications Act]," the agency has developed
standards to effectuate the guarantees of § 312 (a)(7). See
also 47 U. S. C. § 154 (i). The Commission has issued some
general interpretative statements, but its standards implementing § 312 (a)(7) have evolved principally on a case-by-
case basis and are not embodied in formalized rules. The
relevant criteria broadcasters must employ in evaluating access requests under the statute can be summarized from the
Commission's 1978 Report and Order and the memorandum
opinions and orders in these cases.

Broadcasters are free to deny the sale of air time prior to

---

[10] See generally Note, The Right of "Reasonable Access" for Federal
Political Candidates Under Section 312 (a)(7) of the Communications Act,
78 Colum. L. Rev. 1287 (1978).

the commencement of a campaign, but once a campaign has begun, they must give reasonable and good-faith attention to access requests from "legally qualified" candidates [11] for federal elective office. Such requests must be considered on an individualized basis, and broadcasters are required to tailor their responses to accommodate, as much as reasonably possible, a candidate's stated purposes in seeking air time. In responding to access requests, however, broadcasters may also give weight to such factors as the amount of time previously sold to the candidate, the disruptive impact on regular programming, and the likelihood of requests for time by rival candidates under the equal opportunities provision of § 315 (a). These considerations may not be invoked as pretexts for denying access; to justify a negative response, broadcasters must cite a realistic danger of substantial program disruption—perhaps caused by insufficient notice to allow adjustments in the schedule—or of an excessive number of equal time requests. Further, in order to facilitate review by the Commission, broadcasters must explain their reasons for refusing time or making a more limited counteroffer. If broadcasters take the appropriate factors into account and act reasonably and in good faith, their decisions will be entitled to deference even if the Commission's analysis would have differed in the first instance. But if broadcasters adopt "across-the-board policies" and do not attempt to respond to

[11] In order to be "legally qualified" under the Commission's rules, a candidate must: (a) be eligible under law to hold the office he seeks; (b) announce his candidacy; and (c) qualify for a place on the ballot or be eligible under law for election as a write-in candidate. Persons seeking nomination for the Presidency or Vice Presidency are "legally qualified" in: (a) those states in which they or their proposed delegates have qualified for the primary or Presidential preference ballot; or (b) those states in which they have made a substantial showing of being serious candidates for nomination. Such persons will be considered "legally qualified" in all states if they have qualified in 10 or more states. See 1978 Primer, 69 F. C. C. 2d, at 2216–2218.

the individualized situation of a particular candidate, the Commission is not compelled to sustain their denial of access. See 74 F. C. C. 2d, at 665–674; 74 F. C. C. 2d, at 642–651; 1978 Report and Order, 68 F. C. C. 2d, at 1089–1092, 1094. Petitioners argue that certain of these standards are contrary to the statutory objectives of § 312 (a)(7).

(1)

The Commission has concluded that, as a threshold matter, it will independently determine whether a campaign has begun and the obligations imposed by § 312 (a)(7) have attached. 74 F. C. C. 2d, at 665–666. Petitioners assert that, in undertaking such a task, the Commission becomes improperly involved in the electoral process and seriously impairs broadcaster discretion.

However, petitioners fail to recognize that the Commission does not set the starting date for a campaign. Rather, on review of a complaint alleging denial of "reasonable access," it examines objective evidence to find whether the campaign has already commenced, "taking into account the position of the candidate *and the networks* as well as other factors." *Id.*, at 665 (emphasis added). As the Court of Appeals noted, the "determination of when the statutory obligations attach does not control the electoral process. . . . the determination is controlled by the process." 202 U. S. App. D. C., at 384, 629 F. 2d, at 16. Such a decision is not, and cannot be, purely one of editorial judgment.

Moreover, the Commission's approach serves to narrow § 312 (a)(7), which might be read as vesting access rights in an individual candidate as soon as he becomes "legally qualified" without regard to the status of the campaign. See n. 11, *supra*. By confining the applicability of the statute to the period after a campaign commences, the Commission has limited its impact on broadcasters and given substance to its command of *reasonable* access.

(2)

Petitioners also challenge the Commission's requirement that broadcasters evaluate and respond to access requests on an individualized basis. In petitioners' view, the agency has attached inordinate significance to candidates' needs, thereby precluding fair assessment of broadcasters' concerns and prohibiting the adoption of uniform policies regarding requests for access.

While admonishing broadcasters not to " 'second guess' the 'political' wisdom or . . . effectiveness" of the particular format sought by a candidate, the Commission has clearly acknowledged that "the candidate's . . . request is by no means conclusive of the question of how much time, if any, is appropriate. Other . . . factors, such as the disruption or displacement of regular programming (particularly as affected by a reasonable probability of requests by other candidates), must be considered in the balance." 74 F. C. C. 2d, at 667–668. Thus, the Commission mandates careful consideration of, not blind assent to, candidates' desires for air time.

Petitioners are correct that the Commission's standards proscribe blanket rules concerning access; each request must be examined on its own merits. While the adoption of uniform policies might well prove more convenient for broadcasters, such an approach would allow personal campaign strategies and the exigencies of the political process to be ignored. A broadcaster's "evenhanded" response of granting only time spots of a fixed duration to candidates may be "unreasonable" where a particular candidate desires less time for an advertisement or a longer format to discuss substantive issues. In essence, petitioners seek the unilateral right to determine in advance how much time to afford *all* candidates. Yet § 312 (a)(7) assures a right of reasonable access to *individual* candidates for federal elective office, and the Commission's requirement that their requests be considered on an *individualized* basis is consistent with that guarantee.

(3)

The Federal Communications Commission is the experienced administrative agency long entrusted by Congress with the regulation of broadcasting, and the Commission is responsible for implementing and enforcing § 312 (a)(7) of the Communications Act. Accordingly, its construction of the statute is entitled to judicial deference "unless there are compelling indications that it is wrong." *Red Lion Broadcasting Co.* v. *FCC,* 395 U. S., at 381. As we held in *Columbia Broadcasting System, Inc.* v. *Democratic National Committee,* 412 U. S., at 120, the Commission must be allowed to "remain in a posture of flexibility to chart a workable 'middle course' in its quest to preserve a balance between the essential public accountability and the desired private control of the media." Like the Court of Appeals, we cannot say that the Commission's standards are arbitrary and capricious or at odds with the language and purposes of § 312 (a)(7). See 5 U. S. C. § 706 (2)(A). Indeed, we are satisfied that the Commission's action represents a reasoned attempt to effectuate the statute's access requirement, giving broadcasters room to exercise their discretion but demanding that they act in good faith.[12]

B

There can be no doubt that the Commission's standards have achieved greater clarity as a result of the orders in these cases.[13] However laudable that may be, it raises the question

---

[12] The dissenters place great emphasis on the preservation of broadcaster discretion. However, endowing licensees with a "blank check" to determine what constitutes "reasonable access" would eviscerate § 312 (a)(7).

[13] In 1978, the Commission issued a Notice of Inquiry, which asked whether rulemaking proceedings should be commenced in order to clarify licensee obligations under § 312 (a)(7). 43 Fed. Reg. 12938. Petitioners and others in the broadcasting industry expressed strong opposition to the promulgation of specific rules, and none were formulated. 1978 Report and Order, 68 F. C. C. 2d, at 1079–1081. Petitioners, therefore, must share responsibility for any vagueness and confusion in the Commission's standards.

whether § 312 (a)(7) was properly applied to petitioners.[14] Based upon the Commission's prior decisions and 1978 Report and Order, however, we must conclude that petitioners had adequate notice that their conduct in responding to the Carter-Mondale Presidential Committee's request for access would contravene the statute.

In the 1978 Report and Order, the Commission stated that it could not establish a precise point at which § 312 (a)(7) obligations would attach for all campaigns because each is unique:

> "For instance, *a presidential campaign may be in full swing almost a year before an election;* other campaigns may be limited to a short concentrated period. . . . [W]e believe that, generally, a licensee would be unreasonable if it refused to afford access to Federal candidates at least during those time periods [when the 'lowest unit charge' provision of § 315 applied]. Moreover, it may be required to afford reasonable access before these periods; however, the determination of whether 'reasonable access' must be afforded before these periods for particular races must be made in each case under all the facts and circumstances present. . . . [W]e expect licensees to afford access at a reasonable time prior to a convention or caucus. We will review a licensee's decisions in

---

[14] Section 312 (a) empowers the Commission to "revoke any *station* license or construction permit." (Emphasis added.) In the Court of Appeals, petitioners argued that the statute applies only to licensees, not to networks. However, the court rejected that contention, reasoning that the Commission's jurisdiction to "mandate reasonable network access . . . is reasonably ancillary' to the effective enforcement of the individual licensee's Section 312 (a)(7) obligations . . . ." 202 U. S. App. D. C., at 393–395, 629 F. 2d, at 25–27. Petitioners do not contest that holding in this Court. See Tr. of Oral Arg. 16–17. In any event, as the Commission noted, each petitioner is "a multi-station licensee fully reachable [as to its licenses] by [the express] revocation authority" granted under § 312 (a)(7). 74 F. C. C. 2d, at 640, n. 10.

this area on a case-by-case basis." 68 F. C. C. 2d, at 1091–1092 (emphasis added).

In *Anthony R. Martin-Trigona,* 67 F. C. C. 2d 743 (1978), the Commission observed: "[T]he licensee, *and ultimately the Commission,* must look to the circumstances of each particular case to determine when it is reasonable for a candidate's access to begin . . . ." *Id.,* at 746, n. 4 (emphasis added). Further, the 1978 Report and Order made clear that "Federal candidates are the intended beneficiary of Section 312 (a)(7) and therefore a candidate's desires as to the method of conducting his or her media campaign should be considered by licensees in granting reasonable access." 68 F. C. C. 2d, at 1089, n. 14. The agency also stated:

> "[A]n arbitrary 'blanket' ban on the use by a candidate of a particular class or length of time in a particular period cannot be considered reasonable. A Federal candidate's decisions as to the best method of pursuing his or her media campaign should be honored as much as possible under the 'reasonable' limits imposed by the licensee." *Id.,* at 1090.

Here, the Carter-Mondale Presidential Committee sought broadcast time approximately 11 months before the 1980 Presidential election and 8 months before the Democratic National Convention. In determining that a national campaign was underway at that point, the Commission stressed: (a) that 10 candidates formally had announced their intention to seek the Republican nomination, and 2 candidates had done so for the Democratic nomination; (b) that various states had started the delegate selection process; (c) that candidates were traveling across the country making speeches and attempting to raise funds; (d) that national campaign organizations were established and operating; (e) that the Iowa caucus would be held the following month; (f) that public officials and private groups were making endorsements; and (g) that the national print media had given campaign activities prominent coverage for almost two months. 74 F. C. C. 2d, at 645–647. The Commission's conclusion about the status of the campaign accorded with its announced position on the vesting of § 312 (a)(7) rights and was adequately supported by the objective factors on which it relied.

Nevertheless, petitioners ABC and NBC refused to sell the Carter-Mondale Presidential Committee any time in December 1979 on the ground that it was "too early in the political season." App. 41–43, 52–74; nn. 3 and 4, *supra.* These petitioners made no counteroffers, but adopted "blanket" policies refusing access despite the admonition against such an approach in the 1978 Report and Order. Cf. *Donald W. Riegle,* 59 F. C. C. 2d 1314 (1976); *WALB–TV, Inc.,* 59 F. C. C. 2d 1246 (1976). Likewise, petitioner CBS, while not barring access completely, had an across-the-board policy of selling only 5-minute spots to all candidates, notwithstanding the Commission's directive in the 1978 Report and Order that broadcasters consider "a candidate's desires as to the method of conducting his or her media campaign." 68 F. C. C. 2d, at 1089, n. 14. See App. 44–45, 75–93; n. 2, *supra.* Petitioner CBS responded with its standard offer of separate 5-minute segments, even though the Carter-Mondale Presidential Committee sought 30 minutes of air time to present a comprehensive statement launching President Carter's re-election campaign. Moreover, the Committee's request was made almost two months before the intended date of broadcast, was flexible in that it could be satisfied with any prime time slot during a 4-day period, was accompanied by an offer to pay the normal commercial rate, and was not preceded by other requests from President Carter for access. See App. 27–40; n. 1, *supra.* Although petitioners adverted to the disruption of regular programming and the potential equal time requests from rival candidates in their responses to the Carter-Mondale Presidential Committee's complaint, the Commission rejected these claims as "speculative and unsubstantiated at best." 74 F. C. C. 2d, at 674.

Under these circumstances, we cannot conclude that the Commission abused its discretion in finding that petitioners failed to grant the "reasonable access" required by § 312 (a) (7).[15] See 5 U. S. C. § 706 (2)(A). "[T]he fact that we might not have made the same determination on the same facts does not warrant a substitution of judicial for administrative discretion since Congress has confided the problem to the latter." *FCC* v. *WOKO, Inc.*, 329 U. S. 223, 229 (1946). "[C]ourts should not overrule an administrative decision merely because they disagree with its wisdom." *Radio Corp. of America* v. *United States*, 341 U. S. 412, 420 (1951).

IV

Finally, petitioners assert that § 312 (a)(7) as implemented by the Commission violates the First Amendment rights of broadcasters by unduly circumscribing their editorial discretion. In *Columbia Broadcasting System, Inc.* v. *Democratic National Committee*, 412 U. S., at 117, we stated:

> "Th[e] role of the Government as an 'overseer' and ultimate arbiter and guardian of the public interest and the role of the licensee as a journalistic 'free agent' call for a delicate balancing of competing interests. The maintenance of this balance for more than 40 years has called on both the regulators and the licensees to walk a 'tightrope' to preserve the First Amendment values written

---

[15] As it did here, the Commission, with the approval of broadcasters, engages in case-by-case adjudication of § 312 (a)(7) complaints rather than awaiting license renewal proceedings. See Tr. of Oral Arg. 11–16. Although the penalty provided by § 312 (a)(7) is license revocation, petitioners simply were directed to inform the Commission of how they intended to meet their statutory obligations. See 74 F. C. C. 2d, at 651; 74 F. C. C. 2d, at 676–677. In essence, the Commission entered a declaratory order that petitioners' responses to the Carter-Mondale Presidential Committee constituted a denial of "reasonable access." Such a ruling favors broadcasters by allowing an opportunity for curative action before their conduct is found to be "willful or repeated" and subject to the imposition of sanctions.

into the Radio Act and its successor, the Communications
Act."

Petitioners argue that the Commission's interpretation of
§ 312 (a)(7)'s access requirement disrupts the "delicate bal-
anc[e]" that broadcast regulation must achieve.   We disagree.

A licensed broadcaster is "granted the free and exclusive
use of a limited and valuable part of the public domain;
when he accepts that franchise it is burdened by enforceable
public obligations." *Office of Communication of the United
Church of Christ* v. *FCC*, 123 U. S. App. D. C. 328, 337, 359
F. 2d 994, 1003 (1966).   This Court has noted the limits on
a broadcast license:

> "A license permits broadcasting, but the licensee has no
> constitutional right to be the one who holds the license
> or to monopolize a . . . frequency to the exclusion of
> his fellow citizens.   There is nothing in the First Amend-
> ment which prevents the Government from requiring a
> licensee to share his frequency with others . . . ." *Red
> Lion Broadcasting Co.* v. *FCC*, 395 U. S., at 389.

See also *FCC* v. *National Citizens Comm. for Broadcasting*,
436 U. S. 775, 799–800 (1978).   Although the broadcasting
industry is entitled under the First Amendment to exercise
"the widest journalistic freedom consistent with its public
[duties]," *Columbia Broadcasting System, Inc.* v. *Democratic
National Committee, supra*, at 110, the Court has made clear
that:

> "*It is the right of the viewers and listeners, not the right
> of the broadcasters, which is paramount.* It is the pur-
> pose of the First Amendment to preserve an uninhibited
> marketplace of ideas in which truth will ultimately pre-
> vail, rather than to countenance monopolization of that
> market . . . .   It is the right of the public to receive
> suitable access to social, political, esthetic, moral, and
> other ideas and experiences which is crucial here." *Red*

Lion Broadcasting Co. v. *FCC, supra,* at 390 (citations omitted) (emphasis added).

The First Amendment interests of candidates and voters, as well as broadcasters, are implicated by § 312 (a)(7). We have recognized that "it is of particular importance that candidates have the . . . opportunity to make their views known so that the electorate may intelligently evaluate the candidates' personal qualities and their positions on vital public issues before choosing among them on election day." *Buckley* v. *Valeo,* 424 U. S. 1, 52–53 (1976). Indeed, "speech concerning public affairs is . . . the essence of self-government," *Garrison* v. *Louisiana,* 379 U. S. 64, 74–75 (1964). The First Amendment "has its fullest and most urgent application precisely to the conduct of campaigns for political office." *Monitor Patriot Co.* v. *Roy,* 401 U. S. 265, 272 (1971). Section 312 (a)(7) thus makes a significant contribution to freedom of expression by enhancing the ability of candidates to present, and the public to receive, information necessary for the effective operation of the democratic process.

Petitioners are correct that the Court has never approved a *general* right of access to the media. See, *e. g., FCC* v. *Midwest Video Corp.,* 440 U. S. 689 (1979); *Miami Herald Publishing Co.* v. *Tornillo,* 418 U. S. 241 (1974); *Columbia Broadcasting System, Inc.* v. *Democratic National Committee, supra.* Nor do we do so today. Section 312 (a)(7) creates a *limited* right to "reasonable" access that pertains only to legally qualified federal candidates and may be invoked by them only for the purpose of advancing their candidacies once a campaign has commenced. The Commission has stated that, in enforcing the statute, it will "provide leeway to broadcasters and not merely attempt *de novo* to determine the reasonableness of their judgments . . . ." 74 F. C. C. 2d, at 672. If broadcasters have considered the relevant factors in good faith, the Commission will uphold their decisions. See 202 U. S. App. D. C., at 393, 629 F. 2d, at 25. Further, § 312 (a)(7) does not impair the discretion of broadcasters to present their views on any issue or to carry any particular type of programming.

Section 312 (a)(7) represents an effort by Congress to assure that an important resource—the airwaves—will be used in the public interest. We hold that the statutory right of access, as defined by the Commission and applied in these cases, properly balances the First Amendment rights of federal candidates, the public, and broadcasters.

The judgment of the Court of Appeals is

Affirmed.

PART III

RELIGIOUS FREEDOM

1. WISCONSIN v. YODER et al. (1972).

2. WALZ v. TAX COMMISSION OF THE CITY OF NEW YORK (1970).

3. LEMON et al. v. KURTZMAN, SUPERINTENDENT OF PUBLIC INSTRUCTION OF PENNSYLVANIA, et al. (1971).

4. WOOLEY, CHIEF OF POLICE OF LEBANON, et al. v. MAYNARD et ux. (1977).

5. McDANIEL v. PATY et al. (1978).

6. MARSH, NEBRASKA STATE TREASURER, et al. v. CHAMBERS (1983).

7. LYNCH, MAYOR OF PAWTUCKET, et al. v. DONNELLY et al. (1984).

---oOo--

WISCONSIN v. YODER ET AL.

CERTIORARI TO THE SUPREME COURT OF WISCONSIN

No. 70–110.   Argued December 8, 1971—Decided May 15, 1972

Respondents, members of the Old Order Amish religion and the Conservative Amish Mennonite Church, were convicted of violating Wisconsin's compulsory school-attendance law (which requires a child's school attendance until age 16) by declining to send their children to public or private school after they had graduated from the eighth grade. The evidence showed that the Amish provide continuing informal vocational education to their children designed to prepare them for life in the rural Amish community. The evidence also showed that respondents sincerely believed that high school attendance was contrary to the Amish religion and way of life and that they would endanger their own salvation and that of their children by complying with the law. The State Supreme Court sustained respondents' claim that application of the compulsory school-attendance law to them violated their rights under the Free Exercise Clause of the First Amendment, made applicable to the States by the Fourteenth Amendment. *Held:*

1. The State's interest in universal education is not totally free from a balancing process when it impinges on other fundamental rights, such as those specifically protected by the Free Exercise Clause of the First Amendment and the traditional interest of parents with respect to the religious upbringing of their children. Pp. 213–215.

2. Respondents have amply supported their claim that enforcement of the compulsory formal education requirement after the eighth grade would gravely endanger if not destroy the free exercise of their religious beliefs. Pp. 215–219.

3. Aided by a history of three centuries as an identifiable religious sect and a long history as a successful and self-sufficient segment of American society, the Amish have demonstrated the sincerity of their religious beliefs, the interrelationship of belief with their mode of life, the vital role that belief and daily conduct play in the continuing survival of Old Order Amish communities, and the hazards presented by the State's enforcement of a statute generally valid as to others. Beyond this, they have

391

carried the difficult burden of demonstrating the adequacy of their alternative mode of continuing informal vocational education in terms of the overall interests that the State relies on in support of its program of compulsory high school education. In light of this showing, and weighing the minimal difference between what the State would require and what the Amish already accept, it was incumbent on the State to show with more particularity how its admittedly strong interest in compulsory education would be adversely affected by granting an exemption to the Amish. Pp. 219–229, 234–236.

4. The State's claim that it is empowered, as *parens patriae,* to extend the benefit of secondary education to children regardless of the wishes of their parents cannot be sustained against a free exercise claim of the nature revealed by this record, for the Amish have introduced convincing evidence that accommodating their religious objections by forgoing one or two additional years of compulsory education will not impair the physical or mental health of the child, or result in an inability to be self-supporting or to discharge the duties and responsibilities of citizenship, or in any other way materially detract from the welfare of society. Pp. 229–234.

49 Wis. 2d 430, 182 N. W. 2d 539, affirmed.

BURGER, C. J., delivered the opinion of the Court, in which BRENNAN, STEWART, WHITE, MARSHALL, and BLACKMUN, JJ., joined. STEWART, J., filed a concurring opinion, in which BRENNAN, J., joined, *post,* p. 237. WHITE, J., filed a concurring opinion, in which BRENNAN and STEWART, JJ., joined, *post,* p. 237. DOUGLAS, J., filed an opinion dissenting in part, *post,* p. 241. POWELL and REHNQUIST, JJ., took no part in the consideration or decision of the case.

John W. Calhoun, Assistant Attorney General of Wisconsin, argued the cause for petitioner. With him on the briefs were *Robert W. Warren,* Attorney General, and *William H. Wilker,* Assistant Attorney General.

William B. Ball argued the cause for respondents. With him on the brief was *Joseph G. Skelly.*

Briefs of *amici curiae* urging affirmance were filed by *Donald E. Showalter* for the Mennonite Central Com-

mittee; by *Boardman Noland* and *Lee Boothby* for the
General Conference of Seventh-Day Adventists; by *William S. Ellis* for the National Council of the Churches
of Christ; by *Nathan Lewin* for the National Jewish
Commission on Law and Public Affairs; and by *Leo
Pfeffer* for the Synagogue Council of America et al.

MR. CHIEF JUSTICE BURGER delivered the opinion of
the Court.

On petition of the State of Wisconsin, we granted
the writ of certiorari in this case to review a decision of
the Wisconsin Supreme Court holding that respondents'
convictions of violating the State's compulsory school-
attendance law were invalid under the Free Exercise
Clause of the First Amendment to the United States
Constitution made applicable to the States by the Fourteenth Amendment. For the reasons hereafter stated we
affirm the judgment of the Supreme Court of Wisconsin.

Respondents Jonas Yoder and Wallace Miller are
members of the Old Order Amish religion, and respondent
Adin Yutzy is a member of the Conservative Amish
Mennonite Church. They and their families are residents of Green County, Wisconsin. Wisconsin's compulsory school-attendance law required them to cause
their children to attend public or private school until
reaching age 16 but the respondents declined to send
their children, ages 14 and 15, to public school after they
completed the eighth grade.[1] The children were not enrolled in any private school, or within any recognized
exception to the compulsory-attendance law,[2] and they
are conceded to be subject to the Wisconsin statute.

---

[1] The children, Frieda Yoder, aged 15, Barbara Miller, aged 15,
and Vernon Yutzy, aged 14, were all graduates of the eighth grade
of public school.

[2] Wis. Stat. § 118.15 (1969) provides in pertinent part:

"118.15 *Compulsory school attendance*

"(1)(a) Unless the child has a legal excuse or has graduated from

On complaint of the school district administrator for the public schools, respondents were charged, tried, and convicted of violating the compulsory-attendance law in Green County Court and were fined the sum of $5 each.[3] Respondents defended on the ground that the applica-

high school, any person having under his control a child who is between the ages of 7 and 16 years shall cause such child to attend school regularly during the full period and hours, religious holidays excepted, that the public or private school in which such child should be enrolled is in session until the end of the school term, quarter or semester of the school year in which he becomes 16 years of age.

. . . . . .

"(3) This section does not apply to any child who is not in proper physical or mental condition to attend school, to any child exempted for good cause by the school board of the district in which the child resides or to any child who has completed the full 4-year high school course. The certificate of a reputable physician in general practice shall be sufficient proof that a child is unable to attend school.

"(4) Instruction during the required period elsewhere than at school may be substituted for school attendance. Such instruction must be approved by the state superintendent as substantially equivalent to instruction given to children of like ages in the public or private schools where such children reside.

"(5) Whoever violates this section . . . may be fined not less than $5 nor more than $50 or imprisoned not more than 3 months or both."

Section 118.15 (1)(b) requires attendance to age 18 in a school district containing a "vocational, technical and adult education school," but this section is concededly inapplicable in this case, for there is no such school in the district involved.

[3] Prior to trial, the attorney for respondents wrote the State Superintendent of Public Instruction in an effort to explore the possibilities for a compromise settlement. Among other possibilities, he suggested that perhaps the State Superintendent could administratively determine that the Amish could satisfy the compulsory-attendance law by establishing their own vocational training plan similar to one that has been established in Pennsylvania. Supp. App. 6. Under the Pennsylvania plan, Amish children of high school age are required to attend an Amish vocational school for

tion of the compulsory-attendance law violated their rights under the First and Fourteenth Amendments.[4] The trial testimony showed that respondents believed, in accordance with the tenets of Old Order Amish communities generally, that their children's attendance at high school, public or private, was contrary to the Amish religion and way of life. They believed that by sending their children to high school, they would not only expose themselves to the danger of the censure of the church community, but, as found by the county court, also endanger their own salvation and that of their children. The State stipulated that respondents' religious beliefs were sincere.

In support of their position, respondents presented as expert witnesses scholars on religion and education whose testimony is uncontradicted. They expressed their opinions on the relationship of the Amish belief concerning school attendance to the more general tenets of their religion, and described the impact that compulsory high school attendance could have on the continued survival of Amish communities as they exist in the United States today. The history of the Amish

---

three hours a week, during which time they are taught such subjects as English, mathematics, health, and social studies by an Amish teacher. For the balance of the week, the children perform farm and household duties under parental supervision, and keep a journal of their daily activities. The major portion of the curriculum is home projects in agriculture and homemaking. See generally J. Hostetler & G. Huntington, Children in Amish Society: Socialization and Community Education, c. 5 (1971). A similar program has been instituted in Indiana. *Ibid.* See also Iowa Code § 299.24 (1971); Kan. Stat. Ann. § 72–1111 (Supp. 1971).

The Superintendent rejected this proposal on the ground that it would not afford Amish children "substantially equivalent education" to that offered in the schools of the area. Supp. App. 6.

[4] The First Amendment provides: "Congress shall make no law respecting an establishment of religion, or prohibiting the free exercise thereof . . . ."

sect was given in some detail, beginning with the Swiss
Anabaptists of the 16th century who rejected institutionalized churches and sought to return to the early,
simple, Christian life de-emphasizing material success,
rejecting the competitive spirit, and seeking to insulate
themselves from the modern world. As a result of their
common heritage, Old Order Amish communities today
are characterized by a fundamental belief that salvation
requires life in a church community separate and apart
from the world and worldly influence. This concept of
life aloof from the world and its values is central to
their faith.

A related feature of Old Order Amish communities
is their devotion to a life in harmony with nature
and the soil, as exemplified by the simple life of the
early Christian era that continued in America during much of our early national life. Amish beliefs require members of the community to make their living
by farming or closely related activities. Broadly speaking, the Old Order Amish religion pervades and determines the entire mode of life of its adherents. Their
conduct is regulated in great detail by the *Ordnung,*
or rules, of the church community. Adult baptism,
which occurs in late adolescence, is the time at which
Amish young people voluntarily undertake heavy obligations, not unlike the Bar Mitzvah of the Jews, to
abide by the rules of the church community.[5]

Amish objection to formal education beyond the
eighth grade is firmly grounded in these central religious concepts. They object to the high school, and
higher education generally, because the values they teach

---

[5] See generally J. Hostetler, Amish Society (1968); J. Hostetler
& G. Huntington, Children in Amish Society (1971); Littell, Sec-
tarian Protestantism and the Pursuit of Wisdom: Must Technological
Objectives Prevail?, in Public Controls for Nonpublic Schools 61
(D. Erickson ed. 1969).

are in marked variance with Amish values and the Amish way of life; they view secondary school education as an impermissible exposure of their children to a "worldly" influence in conflict with their beliefs.   The high school tends to emphasize intellectual and scientific accomplishments, self-distinction, competitiveness, worldly success, and social life with other students.   Amish society emphasizes informal learning-through-doing; a life of "goodness," rather than a life of intellect; wisdom, rather than technical knowledge; community welfare, rather than competition; and separation from, rather than integration with, contemporary worldly society.

Formal high school education beyond the eighth grade is contrary to Amish beliefs, not only because it places Amish children in an environment hostile to Amish beliefs with increasing emphasis on competition in class work and sports and with pressure to conform to the styles, manners, and ways of the peer group, but also because it takes them away from their community, physically and emotionally, during the crucial and formative adolescent period of life.   During this period, the children must acquire Amish attitudes favoring manual work and self-reliance and the specific skills needed to perform the adult role of an Amish farmer or housewife.   They must learn to enjoy physical labor.   Once a child has learned basic reading, writing, and elementary mathematics, these traits, skills, and attitudes admittedly fall within the category of those best learned through example and "doing" rather than in a classroom.   And, at this time in life, the Amish child must also grow in his faith and his relationship to the Amish community if he is to be prepared to accept the heavy obligations imposed by adult baptism.   In short, high school attendance with teachers who are not of the Amish faith—and may even be hostile to it—interposes a serious barrier to the integration of the Amish child into

the Amish religious community. Dr. John Hostetler,
one of the experts on Amish society, testified that the
modern high school is not equipped, in curriculum or
social environment, to impart the values promoted by
Amish society.

The Amish do not object to elementary education
through the first eight grades as a general proposition
because they agree that their children must have basic
skills in the "three R's" in order to read the Bible, to
be good farmers and citizens, and to be able to deal with
non-Amish people when necessary in the course of daily
affairs. They view such a basic education as acceptable
because it does not significantly expose their children to
worldly values or interfere with their development in
the Amish community during the crucial adolescent
period. While Amish accept compulsory elementary
education generally, wherever possible they have established their own elementary schools in many respects
like the small local schools of the past. In the Amish
belief higher learning tends to develop values they reject
as influences that alienate man from God.

On the basis of such considerations, Dr. Hostetler testified that compulsory high school attendance could not
only result in great psychological harm to Amish children, because of the conflicts it would produce, but
would also, in his opinion, ultimately result in the destruction of the Old Order Amish church community as
it exists in the United States today. The testimony of
Dr. Donald A. Erickson, an expert witness on education,
also showed that the Amish succeed in preparing their
high school age children to be productive members of the
Amish community. He described their system of learning through doing the skills directly relevant to their
adult roles in the Amish community as "ideal" and perhaps superior to ordinary high school education. The
evidence also showed that the Amish have an excellent

record as law-abiding and generally self-sufficient members of society.

Although the trial court in its careful findings determined that the Wisconsin compulsory school-attendance law "does interfere with the freedom of the Defendants to act in accordance with their sincere religious belief" it also concluded that the requirement of high school attendance until age 16 was a "reasonable and constitutional" exercise of governmental power, and therefore denied the motion to dismiss the charges. The Wisconsin Circuit Court affirmed the convictions. The Wisconsin Supreme Court, however, sustained respondents' claim under the Free Exercise Clause of the First Amendment and reversed the convictions. A majority of the court was of the opinion that the State had failed to make an adequate showing that its interest in "establishing and maintaining an educational system overrides the defendants' right to the free exercise of their religion." 49 Wis. 2d 430, 447, 182 N. W. 2d 539, 547 (1971).

I

There is no doubt as to the power of a State, having a high responsibility for education of its citizens, to impose reasonable regulations for the control and duration of basic education. See, e. g., Pierce v. Society of Sisters, 268 U. S. 510, 534 (1925). Providing public schools ranks at the very apex of the function of a State. Yet even this paramount responsibility was, in Pierce, made to yield to the right of parents to provide an equivalent education in a privately operated system. There the Court held that Oregon's statute compelling attendance in a public school from age eight to age 16 unreasonably interfered with the interest of parents in directing the rearing of their offspring, including their education in church-operated schools. As that case suggests, the values of parental direction of the religious upbringing and education of their children in their early and formative years have a high place in our society. See also *Ginsberg* v. *New York,* 390 U. S. 629, 639 (1968); *Meyer* v. *Nebraska,* 262 U. S. 390 (1923); cf. *Rowan* v. *Post Office Dept.,* 397 U. S. 728 (1970). Thus, a State's interest in universal education, however highly we rank it, is not totally free from a balancing process when it impinges on fundamental rights and interests, such as those specifically protected by the Free Exercise Clause of the First Amendment, and the traditional interest of parents with respect to the religious upbringing of their children so long as they, in the words of *Pierce,* "prepare [them] for additional obligations." 268 U. S., at 535.

It follows that in order for Wisconsin to compel school attendance beyond the eighth grade against a claim that such attendance interferes with the practice of a legitimate religious belief, it must appear either that the State does not deny the free exercise of religious belief by its requirement, or that there is a state interest of sufficient magnitude to override the interest claiming protection under the Free Exercise Clause. Long before there was general acknowledgment of the need for universal formal education, the Religion Clauses had specifically and firmly fixed the right to free exercise of religious beliefs, and buttressing this fundamental right was an equally firm, even if less explicit, prohibition against the establishment of any religion by government. The values underlying these two provisions relating to religion have been zealously protected, sometimes even at the expense of other interests of admittedly high social importance. The invalidation of financial aid to parochial schools by government grants for a salary subsidy for teachers is but one example of the extent to which courts have gone in this regard, notwithstanding that such aid programs were legislatively determined to be in the public interest and the service of sound educational policy by States and by Congress. *Lemon* v.

Kurtzman, 403 U. S. 602 (1971); *Tilton* v. *Richardson,* 403 U. S. 672 (1971). See also *Everson* v. *Board of Education,* 330 U. S. 1, 18 (1947).

The essence of all that has been said and written on the subject is that only those interests of the highest order and those not otherwise served can overbalance legitimate claims to the free exercise of religion. We can accept it as settled, therefore, that, however strong the State's interest in universal compulsory education, it is by no means absolute to the exclusion or subordination of all other interests. *E. g., Sherbert* v. *Verner,* 374 U. S. 398 (1963); *McGowan* v. *Maryland,* 366 U. S. 420, 459 (1961) (separate opinion of Frankfurter, J.); *Prince* v. *Massachusetts,* 321 U. S. 158, 165 (1944).

II

We come then to the quality of the claims of the respondents concerning the alleged encroachment of Wisconsin's compulsory school-attendance statute on their rights and the rights of their children to the free exercise of the religious beliefs they and their forebears have adhered to for almost three centuries. In evaluating those claims we must be careful to determine whether the Amish religious faith and their mode of life are, as they claim, inseparable and interdependent. A way of life, however virtuous and admirable, may not be interposed as a barrier to reasonable state regulation of education if it is based on purely secular considerations; to have the protection of the Religion Clauses, the claims must be rooted in religious belief. Although a determination of what is a "religious" belief or practice entitled to constitutional protection may present a most delicate question,[6] the very concept of ordered liberty precludes

---

[6] See *Welsh* v. *United States,* 398 U. S. 333, 351–361 (1970) (Harlan, J., concurring in result); *United States* v. *Ballard,* 322 U. S. 78 (1944).

allowing every person to make his own standards on matters of conduct in which society as a whole has important interests. Thus, if the Amish asserted their claims because of their subjective evaluation and rejection of the contemporary secular values accepted by the majority, much as Thoreau rejected the social values of his time and isolated himself at Walden Pond, their claims would not rest on a religious basis. Thoreau's choice was philosophical and personal rather than religious, and such belief does not rise to the demands of the Religion Clauses.

Giving no weight to such secular considerations, however, we see that the record in this case abundantly supports the claim that the traditional way of life of the Amish is not merely a matter of personal prefer-. ence, but one of deep religious conviction, shared by an organized group, and intimately related to daily living. That the Old Order Amish daily life and religious practice stem from their faith is shown by the fact that it is in response to their literal interpretation of the Biblical injunction from the Epistle of Paul to the Romans, "be not conformed to this world . . . ." This command is fundamental to the Amish faith. Moreover, for the Old Order Amish, religion is not simply a matter of theocratic belief. As the expert witnesses explained, the Old Order Amish religion pervades and determines virtually their entire way of life, regulating it with the detail of the Talmudic diet through the strictly enforced rules of the church community.

The record shows that the respondents' religious beliefs and attitude toward life, family, and home have remained constant—perhaps some would say static—in a period of unparalleled progress in human knowledge generally and great changes in education.[7] The re-

[7] See generally R. Butts & L. Cremin, A History of Education in American Culture (1953); L. Cremin, The Transformation of the School (1961).

spondents freely concede, and indeed assert as an article of faith, that their religious beliefs and what we would today call "life style" have not altered in fundamentals for centuries. Their way of life in a church-oriented community, separated from the outside world and "worldly" influences, their attachment to nature and the soil, is a way inherently simple and uncomplicated, albeit difficult to preserve against the pressure to conform. Their rejection of telephones, automobiles, radios, and television, their mode of dress, of speech, their habits of manual work do indeed set them apart from much of contemporary society; these customs are both symbolic and practical.

As the society around the Amish has become more populous, urban, industrialized, and complex, particularly in this century, government regulation of human affairs has correspondingly become more detailed and pervasive. The Amish mode of life has thus come into conflict increasingly with requirements of contemporary society exerting a hydraulic insistence on conformity to majoritarian standards. So long as compulsory education laws were confined to eight grades of elementary basic education imparted in a nearby rural schoolhouse, with a large proportion of students of the Amish faith, the Old Order Amish had little basis to fear that school attendance would expose their children to the worldly influence they reject. But modern compulsory secondary education in rural areas is now largely carried on in a consolidated school, often remote from the student's home and alien to his daily home life. As the record so strongly shows, the values and programs of the modern secondary school are in sharp conflict with the fundamental mode of life mandated by the Amish religion; modern laws requiring compulsory secondary education have accordingly engendered great concern and conflict.[8]

---

[8] Hostetler, *supra,* n. 5, c. 9; Hostetler & Huntington, *supra,* n. 5.

The conclusion is inescapable that secondary schooling, by exposing Amish children to worldly influences in terms of attitudes, goals, and values contrary to beliefs, and by substantially interfering with the religious development of the Amish child and his integration into the way of life of the Amish faith community at the crucial adolescent stage of development, contravenes the basic religious tenets and practice of the Amish faith, both as to the parent and the child.

The impact of the compulsory-attendance law on respondents' practice of the Amish religion is not only severe, but inescapable, for the Wisconsin law affirmatively compels them, under threat of criminal sanction, to perform acts undeniably at odds with fundamental tenets of their religious beliefs. See *Braunfeld* v. *Brown*, 366 U. S. 599, 605 (1961). Nor is the impact of the compulsory-attendance law confined to grave interference with important Amish religious tenets from a subjective point of view. It carries with it precisely the kind of objective danger to the free exercise of religion that the First Amendment was designed to prevent. As the record shows, compulsory school attendance to age 16 for Amish children carries with it a very real threat of undermining the Amish community and religious practice as they exist today; they must either abandon belief and be assimilated into society at large, or be forced to migrate to some other and more tolerant region.[9]

---

[9] Some States have developed working arrangements with the Amish regarding high school attendance. See n. 3, *supra*. However, the danger to the continued existence of an ancient religious faith cannot be ignored simply because of the assumption that its adherents will continue to be able, at considerable sacrifice, to relocate in some more tolerant State or country or work out accommodations under threat of criminal prosecution. Forced migration of religious minorities was an evil that lay at the heart of the Religion Clauses. See, *e. g.*, *Everson* v. *Board of Education*, 330 U. S. 1, 9–10 (1947); Madison, Memorial and Remonstrance Against

In sum, the unchallenged testimony of acknowledged experts in education and religious history, almost 300 years of consistent practice, and strong evidence of a sustained faith pervading and regulating respondents' entire mode of life support the claim that enforcement of the State's requirement of compulsory formal education after the eighth grade would gravely endanger if not destroy the free exercise of respondents' religious beliefs.

III

Neither the findings of the trial court nor the Amish claims as to the nature of their faith are challenged in this Court by the State of Wisconsin. Its position is that the State's interest in universal compulsory formal secondary education to age 16 is so great that it is paramount to the undisputed claims of respondents that their mode of preparing their youth for Amish life, after the traditional elementary education, is an essential part of their religious belief and practice. Nor does the State undertake to meet the claim that the Amish mode of life and education is inseparable from and a part of the basic tenets of their religion—indeed, as much a part of their religious belief and practices as baptism, the confessional, or a sabbath may be for others.

Wisconsin concedes that under the Religion Clauses religious beliefs are absolutely free from the State's control, but it argues that "actions," even though religiously grounded, are outside the protection of the First Amendment.[10] But our decisions have rejected the idea that

---

Religious Assessments, 2 Writings of James Madison 183 (G. Hunt ed. 1901).

[10] That has been the apparent ground for decision in several previous state cases rejecting claims for exemption similar to that here. See, *e. g., State* v. *Garber,* 197 Kan. 567, 419 P. 2d 896 (1966), cert. denied, 389 U. S. 51 (1967); *State* v. *Hershberger,* 103 Ohio App. 188, 144 N. E. 2d 693 (1955); *Commonwealth* v. *Beiler,* 168 Pa. Super. 462, 79 A. 2d 134 (1951).

religiously grounded conduct is always outside the protection of the Free Exercise Clause. It is true that
activities of individuals, even when religiously based, are
often subject to regulation by the States in the exercise
of their undoubted power to promote the health, safety,
and general welfare, or the Federal Government in the
exercise of its delegated powers. See, *e. g., Gillette* v.
United States, 401 U. S. 437 (1971); *Braunfeld* v. *Brown,*
366 U. S. 599 (1961); *Prince* v. *Massachusetts,* 321 U. S.
158 (1944); *Reynolds* v. *United States,* 98 U. S. 145
(1879). But to agree that religiously grounded conduct
must often be subject to the broad police power of the
State is not to deny that there are areas of conduct protected by the Free Exercise Clause of the First Amendment and thus beyond the power of the State to control,
even under regulations of general applicability. *E. g.,*
Sherbert v. *Verner,* 374 U. S. 398 (1963); *Murdock* v.
Pennsylvania, 319 U. S. 105 (1943); *Cantwell* v. *Connecticut,* 310 U. S. 296, 303–304 (1940). This case,
therefore, does not become easier because respondents
were convicted for their "actions" in refusing to send
their children to the public high school; in this context
belief and action cannot be neatly confined in logic-tight
compartments. Cf. *Lemon* v. *Kurtzman,* 403 U. S.. at
612.

Nor can this case be disposed of on the grounds that
Wisconsin's requirement for school attendance to age 16
applies uniformly to all citizens of the State and does
not, on its face, discriminate against religions or a particular religion, or that it is motivated by legitimate
secular concerns. A regulation neutral on its face may,
in its application, nonetheless offend the constitutional
requirement for governmental neutrality if it unduly
burdens the free exercise of religion. *Sherbert* v. *Verner,*
supra; cf. *Walz* v. *Tax Commission,* 397 U. S. 664 (1970).
The Court must not ignore the danger that an exception

from a general obligation of citizenship on religious grounds may run afoul of the Establishment Clause, but that danger cannot be allowed to prevent any exception no matter how vital it may be to the protection of values promoted by the right of free exercise. By preserving doctrinal flexibility and recognizing the need for a sensible and realistic application of the Religion Clauses

> "we have been able to chart a course that preserved the autonomy and freedom of religious bodies while avoiding any semblance of established religion. This is a 'tight rope' and one we have successfully traversed." *Walz* v. *Tax Commission, supra,* at 672.

We turn, then, to the State's broader contention that its interest in its system of compulsory education is so compelling that even the established religious practices of the Amish must give way. Where fundamental claims of religious freedom are at stake, however, we cannot accept such a sweeping claim; despite its admitted validity in the generality of cases, we must searchingly examine the interests that the State seeks to promote by its requirement for compulsory education to age 16, and the impediment to those objectives that would flow from recognizing the claimed Amish exemption. See, *e. g., Sherbert* v. *Verner, supra; Martin* v. *City of Struthers,* 319 U. S. 141 (1943); *Schneider* v. *State,* 308 U. S. 147 (1939).

The State advances two primary arguments in support of its system of compulsory education. It notes, as Thomas Jefferson pointed out early in our history, that some degree of education is necessary to prepare citizens to participate effectively and intelligently in our open political system if we are to preserve freedom and independence. Further, education prepares individuals to be self-reliant and self-sufficient participants in society. We accept these propositions.

However, the evidence adduced by the Amish in this case is persuasively to the effect that an additional one or two years of formal high school for Amish children in place of their long-established program of informal vocational education would do little to serve those interests. Respondents' experts testified at trial, without challenge, that the value of all education must be assessed in terms of its capacity to prepare the child for life. It is one thing to say that compulsory education for a year or two beyond the eighth grade may be necessary when its goal is the preparation of the child for life in modern society as the majority live, but it is quite another if the goal of education be viewed as the preparation of the child for life in the separated agrarian community that is the keystone of the Amish faith. See *Meyer* v. *Nebraska,* 262 U. S., at 400.

The State attacks respondents' position as one fostering "ignorance" from which the child must be protected by the State. No one can question the State's duty to protect children from ignorance but this argument does not square with the facts disclosed in the record. Whatever their idiosyncrasies as seen by the majority, this record strongly shows that the Amish community has been a highly successful social unit within our society, even if apart from the conventional "mainstream." Its members are productive and very law-abiding members of society; they reject public welfare in any of its usual modern forms. The Congress itself recognized their self-sufficiency by authorizing exemption of such groups as the Amish from the obligation to pay social security taxes.[11]

[11] Title 26 U. S. C. § 1402 (h) authorizes the Secretary of Health, Education, and Welfare to exempt members of "a recognized religious sect" existing at all times since December 31, 1950, from the obligation to pay social security taxes if they are, by reason of the tenets of their sect, opposed to receipt of such benefits and agree

It is neither fair nor correct to suggest that the Amish are opposed to education beyond the eighth grade level. What this record shows is that they are opposed to conventional formal education of the type provided by a certified high school because it comes at the child's crucial adolescent period of religious development. Dr. Donald Erickson, for example, testified that their system of learning-by-doing was an "ideal system" of education in terms of preparing Amish children for life as adults in the Amish community, and that "I would be inclined to say they do a better job in this than most of the rest of us do." As he put it, "These people aren't purporting to be learned people, and it seems to me the self-sufficiency of the community is the best evidence I can point to—whatever is being done seems to function well." [12]

We must not forget that in the Middle Ages important values of the civilization of the Western World were preserved by members of religious orders who isolated themselves from all worldly influences against great obstacles. There can be no assumption that today's majority is

to waive them, provided the Secretary finds that the sect makes reasonable provision for its dependent members. The history of the exemption shows it was enacted with the situation of the Old Order Amish specifically in view. H. R. Rep. No. 213, 89th Cong., 1st Sess., 101–102 (1965).

The record in this case establishes without contradiction that the Green County Amish had never been known to commit crimes, that none had been known to receive public assistance, and that none were unemployed.

[12] Dr. Erickson had previously written: "Many public educators would be elated if their programs were as successful in preparing students for productive community life as the Amish system seems to be. In fact, while some public schoolmen strive to outlaw the Amish approach, others are being forced to emulate many of its features." Erickson, Showdown at an Amish Schoolhouse: A Description and Analysis of the Iowa Controversy, in Public Controls for Nonpublic Schools 15, 53 (D. Erickson ed. 1969). And see Littell, *supra*, n. 5, at 61.

"right" and the Amish and others like them are "wrong." A way of life that is odd or even erratic but interferes with no rights or interests of others is not to be condemned because it is different.

The State, however, supports its interest in providing an additional one or two years of compulsory high school education to Amish children because of the possibility that some such children will choose to leave the Amish community, and that if this occurs they will be ill-equipped for life. The State argues that if Amish children leave their church they should not be in the position of making their way in the world without the education available in the one or two additional years the State requires. However, on this record, that argument is highly speculative. There is no specific evidence of the loss of Amish adherents by attrition, nor is there any showing that upon leaving the Amish community Amish children, with their practical agricultural training and habits of industry and self-reliance, would become burdens on society because of educational shortcomings. Indeed, this argument of the State appears to rest primarily on the State's mistaken assumption, already noted, that the Amish do not provide any education for their children beyond the eighth grade, but allow them to grow in "ignorance." To the contrary, not only do the Amish accept the necessity for formal schooling through the eighth grade level, but continue to provide what has been characterized by the undisputed testimony of expert educators as an "ideal" vocational education for their children in the adolescent years.

There is nothing in this record to suggest that the Amish qualities of reliability, self-reliance, and dedication to work would fail to find ready markets in today's society. Absent some contrary evidence supporting the

State's position, we are unwilling to assume that persons possessing such valuable vocational skills and habits are doomed to become burdens on society should they determine to leave the Amish faith, nor is there any basis in the record to warrant a finding that an additional one or two years of formal school education beyond the eighth grade would serve to eliminate any such problem that might exist.

Insofar as the State's claim rests on the view that a brief additional period of formal education is imperative to enable the Amish to participate effectively and intelligently in our democratic process, it must fall. The Amish alternative to formal secondary school education has enabled them to function effectively in their day-to-day life under self-imposed limitations on relations with the world, and to survive and prosper in contemporary society as a separate, sharply identifiable and highly self-sufficient community for more than 200 years in this country. In itself this is strong evidence that they are capable of fulfilling the social and political responsibilities of citizenship without compelled attendance beyond the eighth grade at the price of jeopardizing their free exercise of religious belief.[13] When Thomas Jefferson emphasized the need for education as a bulwark of a free people against tyranny, there is nothing to indicate he had in mind compulsory education through any fixed age beyond a basic education. Indeed, the Amish communities singularly parallel and reflect many of the virtues of Jefferson's ideal of the "sturdy yeoman" who would form the basis of what he considered as the

---

[13] All of the children involved in this case are graduates of the eighth grade. In the county court, the defense introduced a study by Dr. Hostetler indicating that Amish children in the eighth grade achieved comparably to non-Amish children in the basic skills. Supp. App. 9–11. See generally Hostetler & Huntington, *supra,* n. 5, at 88–96.

ideal of a democratic society.[14]   Even their idiosyncratic separateness exemplifies the diversity we profess to admire and encourage.

The requirement for compulsory education beyond the eighth grade is a relatively recent development in our history.   Less than 60 years ago, the educational requirements of almost all of the States were satisfied by completion of the elementary grades, at least where the child was regularly and lawfully employed.[15]   The inde-

_____

[14] While Jefferson recognized that education was essential to the welfare and liberty of the people, he was reluctant to directly force instruction of children "in opposition to the will of the parent." Instead he proposed that state citizenship be conditioned on the ability to "read readily in some tongue, native or acquired."   Letter from Thomas Jefferson to Joseph Cabell, Sept. 9, 1817, in 17 Writings of Thomas Jefferson 417, 423–424 (Mem. ed. 1904).   And it is clear that, so far as the mass of the people were concerned, he envisaged that a basic education in the "three R's" would sufficiently meet the interests of the State.   He suggested that after completion of elementary school, "those destined for labor will engage in the business of agriculture, or enter into apprenticeships to such handicraft art as may be their choice."   Letter from Thomas Jefferson to Peter Carr, Sept. 7, 1814, in Thomas Jefferson and Education in a Republic 93–106 (Arrowood ed. 1930).   See also *id.*, at 60–64, 70, 83, 136–137.

[15] See Dept. of Interior, Bureau of Education, Bulletin No. 47, Digest of State Laws Relating to Public Education 527–559 (1916); Joint Hearings on S. 2475 and H. R. 7200 before the Senate Committee on Education and Labor and the House Committee on Labor, 75th Cong., 1st Sess., pt. 2, p. 416.
Even today, an eighth grade education fully satisfies the educational requirements of at least six States.   See Ariz. Rev. Stat. Ann. § 15–321 (B) (4) (1956); Ark. Stat. Ann. § 80–1504 (1947); Iowa Code § 299.2 (1971); S. D. Comp. Laws Ann. § 13–27–1 (1967); Wyo. Stat. Ann. § 21.1–48 (Supp. 1971).   (Mississippi has no compulsory education law.)   A number of other States have flexible provisions permitting children aged 14 or having completed the eighth grade to be excused from school in order to engage in lawful employment.   *E. g.*, Colo. Rev. Stat. Ann. §§ 123–20–5, 80–6–1 to 80–6–12

pendence and successful social functioning of the Amish community for a period approaching almost three centuries and more than 200 years in this country are strong evidence that there is at best a speculative gain, in terms of meeting the duties of citizenship, from an additional one or two years of compulsory formal education. Against this background it would require a more particularized showing from the State on this point to justify the severe interference with religious freedom such additional compulsory attendance would entail.

We should also note that compulsory education and child labor laws find their historical origin in common humanitarian instincts, and that the age limits of both laws have been coordinated to achieve their related objectives.[16] In the context of this case, such considera-

---

(1963); Conn. Gen. Stat. Rev. §§ 10–184, 10–189 (1964); D. C. Code Ann. §§ 31–202, 36–201 to 36–228 (1967); Ind. Ann. Stat. §§ 28–505 to 28–506, 28–519 (1948); Mass. Gen. Laws Ann., c. 76, § 1 (Supp. 1972) and c. 149, § 86 (1971); Mo. Rev. Stat. §§ 167.031, 294.051 (1969); Nev. Rev. Stat. § 392.110 (1968); N. M. Stat. Ann. § 77–10–6 (1968).

An eighth grade education satisfied Wisconsin's formal education requirements until 1933. See Wis. Laws 1927, c. 425, § 97; Laws 1933, c. 143. (Prior to 1933, provision was made for attendance at continuation or vocational schools by working children past the eighth grade, but only if one was maintained by the community in question.) For a general discussion of the early development of Wisconsin's compulsory education and child labor laws, see F. Ensign, Compulsory School Attendance and Child Labor 203–230 (1921).

[16] See, *e. g.,* Joint Hearings, *supra,* n. 15, pt. 1, at 185–187 (statement of Frances Perkins, Secretary of Labor), pt. 2, at 381–387 (statement of Katherine Lenroot, Chief, Children's Bureau, Department of Labor); National Child Labor Committee, 40th Anniversary Report, The Long Road (1944); 1 G. Abbott, The Child and the State 259–269, 566 (Greenwood reprint 1968); L. Cremin, The Transformation of the School, c. 3 (1961); A. Steinhilber & C. Sokolowski, State Law on Compulsory Attendance 3–4 (Dept. of Health, Education, and Welfare 1966).

tions, if anything, support rather than detract from respondents' position. The origins of the requirement for school attendance to age 16, an age falling after the completion of elementary school but before completion of high school, are not entirely clear. But to some extent such laws reflected the movement to prohibit most child labor under age 16 that culminated in the provisions of the Federal Fair Labor Standards Act of 1938.[17] It is true, then, that the 16-year child labor age limit may to some degree derive from a contemporary impression that children should be in school until that age. But at the same time, it cannot be denied that, conversely, the 16-year education limit reflects, in substantial measure, the concern that children under that age not be employed under conditions hazardous to their health, or in work that should be performed by adults.

The requirement of compulsory schooling to age 16 must therefore be viewed as aimed not merely at providing educational opportunities for children, but as an alternative to the equally undesirable consequence of unhealthful child labor displacing adult workers, or, on the other hand, forced idleness.[18] The two kinds of statutes—compulsory school attendance and child labor laws—tend to keep children of certain ages off the labor market and in school; this regimen in turn provides opportunity to prepare for a livelihood of a higher order than that which children could pursue without education and protects their health in adolescence.

In these terms, Wisconsin's interest in compelling the school attendance of Amish children to age 16 emerges as somewhat less substantial than requiring such attend-

---

[17] 52 Stat. 1060, as amended, 29 U. S. C. §§ 201–219.

[18] See materials cited n. 16, *supra;* Casad, Compulsory Education and Individual Rights, in 5 Religion and the Public Order 51, 82 (D. Giannella ed. 1969).

ance for children generally. For, while agricultural employment is not totally outside the legitimate concerns of the child labor laws, employment of children under parental guidance and on the family farm from age 14 to age 16 is an ancient tradition that lies at the periphery of the objectives of such laws.[19] There is no intimation that the Amish employment of their children on family farms is in any way deleterious to their health or that Amish parents exploit children at tender years. Any such inference would be contrary to the record before us. Moreover, employment of Amish children on the family farm does not present the undesirable economic aspects of eliminating jobs that might otherwise be held by adults.

IV

Finally, the State, on authority of *Prince* v. *Massachusetts,* argues that a decision exempting Amish children from the State's requirement fails to recognize the substantive right of the Amish child to a secondary education, and fails to give due regard to the power of the State as *parens patriae* to extend the benefit of secondary education to children regardless of the wishes of their parents. Taken at its broadest sweep, the Court's language in *Prince,* might be read to give support to the State's position. However, the Court was not confronted in *Prince* with a situation comparable to that of the Amish as revealed in this record; this is shown by the

---

[19] See, *e. g.,* Abbott, *supra,* n. 16, at 266. The Federal Fair Labor Standards Act of 1938 excludes from its definition of "[o]ppressive child labor" employment of a child under age 16 by "a parent . . . employing his own child . . . in an occupation other than manufacturing or mining or an occupation found by the Secretary of Labor to be particularly hazardous for the employment of children between the ages of sixteen and eighteen years or detrimental to their health or well-being." 29 U. S. C. § 203 (*l*).

Court's severe characterization of the evils that it thought the legislature could legitimately associate with child labor, even when performed in the company of an adult. 321 U. S., at 169–170. The Court later took great care to confine *Prince* to a narrow scope in *Sherbert* v. *Verner,* when it stated:

> "On the other hand, the Court has rejected challenges under the Free Exercise Clause to governmental regulation of certain overt acts prompted by religious beliefs or principles, for 'even when the action is in accord with one's religious convictions, [it] is not totally free from legislative restrictions.' *Braunfeld* v. *Brown,* 366 U. S. 599, 603. The conduct or actions so regulated have invariably posed some substantial threat to public safety, peace or order. See, *e. g., Reynolds* v. *United States,* 98 U. S. 145; *Jacobson* v. *Massachusetts,* 197 U. S. 11; *Prince* v. *Massachusetts,* 321 U. S. 158 . . . ." 374 U. S., at 402–403.

This case, of course, is not one in which any harm to the physical or mental health of the child or to the public safety, peace, order, or welfare has been demonstrated or may be properly inferred.[20] The record is to the contrary, and any reliance on that theory would find no support in the evidence.

Contrary to the suggestion of the dissenting opinion of MR. JUSTICE DOUGLAS, our holding today in no degree depends on the assertion of the religious interest of the child as contrasted with that of the parents. It is the parents who are subject to prosecution here for failing to cause their children to attend school, and it

---

[20] Cf. *e. g., Jacobson* v. *Massachusetts,* 197 U. S. 11 (1905); *Wright* v. *DeWitt School District,* 238 Ark. 906, 385 S. W. 2d 644 (1965); *Application of President and Directors of Georgetown College, Inc.,* 118 U. S. App. D. C. 80, 87–90, 331 F. 2d 1000, 1007–1010 (in-chambers opinion), cert. denied, 377 U. S. 978 (1964).

is their right of free exercise, not that of their children, that must determine Wisconsin's power to impose criminal penalties on the parent. The dissent argues that a child who expresses a desire to attend public high school in conflict with the wishes of his parents should not be prevented from doing so. There is no reason for the Court to consider that point since it is not an issue in the case. The children are not parties to this litigation. The State has at no point tried this case on the theory that respondents were preventing their children from attending school against their expressed desires, and indeed the record is to the contrary.[21] The State's position from the outset has been that it is empowered to apply its compulsory-attendance law to Amish parents in the same manner as to other parents— that is, without regard to the wishes of the child. That is the claim we reject today.

Our holding in no way determines the proper resolution of possible competing interests of parents, children, and the State in an appropriate state court proceeding in which the power of the State is asserted on the theory that Amish parents are preventing their minor children from attending high school despite their expressed desires to the contrary. Recognition of the claim of the State in such a proceeding would, of course, call into question traditional concepts of parental control over the religious upbringing and education of their minor children recognized in this Court's past decisions. It is clear that such an intrusion by a State into family decisions in the area of religious training would give rise to grave questions of religious freedom comparable to those raised here

---

[21] The only relevant testimony in the record is to the effect that the wishes of the one child who testified corresponded with those of her parents. Testimony of Frieda Yoder, Tr. 92–94, to the effect that her personal religious beliefs guided her decision to discontinue school attendance after the eighth grade. The other children were not called by either side.

and those presented in *Pierce* v. *Society of Sisters*, 268 U. S. 510 (1925). On this record we neither reach nor decide those issues.

The State's argument proceeds without reliance on any actual conflict between the wishes of parents and children. It appears to rest on the potential that exemption of Amish parents from the requirements of the compulsory-education law might allow some parents to act contrary to the best interests of their children by foreclosing their opportunity to make an intelligent choice between the Amish way of life and that of the outside world. The same argument could, of course, be made with respect to all church schools short of college. There is nothing in the record or in the ordinary course of human experience to suggest that non-Amish parents generally consult with children of ages 14–16 if they are placed in a church school of the parents' faith.

Indeed it seems clear that if the State is empowered, as *parens patriae,* to "save" a child from himself or his Amish parents by requiring an additional two years of compulsory formal high school education, the State will in large measure influence, if not determine, the religious future of the child. Even more markedly than in *Prince*, therefore, this case involves the fundamental interest of parents, as contrasted with that of the State, to guide the religious future and education of their children. The history and culture of Western civilization reflect a strong tradition of parental concern for the nurture and upbringing of their children. This primary role of the parents in the upbringing of their children is now established beyond debate as an enduring American tradition. If not the first, perhaps the most significant statements of the Court in this area are found in *Pierce* v. *Society of Sisters,* in which the Court observed:

"Under the doctrine of *Meyer* v. *Nebraska,* 262 U. S. 390, we think it entirely plain that the Act of 1922 unreasonably interferes with the liberty of parents and guardians to direct the upbringing and education of children under their control. As often heretofore pointed out, rights guaranteed by the Constitution may not be abridged by legislation which has no reasonable relation to some purpose within the competency of the State. The fundamental theory of liberty upon which all governments in this Union repose excludes any general power of the State to standardize its children by forcing them to accept instruction from public teachers only. The child is not the mere creature of the State; those who nurture him and direct his destiny have the right, coupled with the high duty, to recognize and prepare him for additional obligations." 268 U. S., at 534–535.

The duty to prepare the child for "additional obligations," referred to by the Court, must be read to include the inculcation of moral standards, religious beliefs, and elements of good citizenship. *Pierce*, of course, recognized that where nothing more than the general interest of the parent in the nurture and education of his children is involved, it is beyond dispute that the State acts "reasonably" and constitutionally in requiring education to age 16 in some public or private school meeting the standards prescribed by the State.

However read, the Court's holding in *Pierce* stands as a charter of the rights of parents to direct the religious upbringing of their children. And, when the interests of parenthood are combined with a free exercise claim of the nature revealed by this record, more than merely a "reasonable relation to some purpose within the competency of the State" is required to sustain the validity of the State's requirement under the First Amendment. To be sure, the power of the parent, even when linked to a free exercise claim, may be subject to limitation under *Prince* if it appears that parental decisions will jeopardize the health or safety of the child, or have a potential for significant social burdens. But in this case, the Amish have introduced persuasive evidence undermining the arguments the State has advanced to support its claims in terms of the welfare of the child and society as a whole. The record strongly indicates that accommodating the religious objections of the Amish by forgoing one, or at most two, additional years of compulsory education will not impair the physical or mental health of the child, or result in an inability to be self-supporting or to discharge the duties and responsibilities of citizenship, or in any other way materially detract from the welfare of society.

In the face of our consistent emphasis on the central values underlying the Religion Clauses in our constitutional scheme of government, we cannot accept a *parens patriae* claim of such all-encompassing scope and with such sweeping potential for broad and unforeseeable application as that urged by the State.

V

For the reasons stated we hold, with the Supreme Court of Wisconsin, that the First and Fourteenth Amendments prevent the State from compelling respondents to cause their children to attend formal high school to age 16.[22] Our disposition of this case, however, in no way

---

[22] What we have said should meet the suggestion that the decision of the Wisconsin Supreme Court recognizing an exemption for the Amish from the State's system of compulsory education constituted an impermissible establishment of religion. In *Walz* v. *Tax Commission,* the Court saw the three main concerns against which the Establishment Clause sought to protect as "sponsorship, financial support, and active involvement of the sovereign in religious activity." 397 U. S. 664, 668 (1970). Accommodating the religious beliefs of the Amish can hardly be characterized as sponsorship or active involvement. The purpose and effect of such an exemption are not

alters our recognition of the obvious fact that courts are not school boards or legislatures, and are ill-equipped to determine the "necessity" of discrete aspects of a State's program of compulsory education. This should suggest that courts must move with great circumspection in performing the sensitive and delicate task of weighing a State's legitimate social concern when faced with religious claims for exemption from generally applicable educational requirements. It cannot be overemphasized that we are not dealing with a way of life and mode of education by a group claiming to have recently discovered some "progressive" or more enlightened process for rearing children for modern life.

Aided by a history of three centuries as an identifiable religious sect and a long history as a successful and self-sufficient segment of American society, the Amish in this case have convincingly demonstrated the sincerity of their religious beliefs, the interrelationship of belief with their mode of life, the vital role that belief and daily conduct play in the continued survival of Old Order Amish communities and their religious organization, and the hazards presented by the State's enforcement of a statute generally valid as to others. Beyond this, they have carried the even more difficult burden of demonstrating the adequacy of their alternative mode of continuing informal vocational education in terms of precisely those overall interests that the State advances in support of its program of compulsory high school education. In light of this con-

_____

to support, favor, advance, or assist the Amish, but to allow their centuries-old religious society, here long before the advent of any compulsory education, to survive free from the heavy impediment compliance with the Wisconsin compulsory-education law would impose. Such an accommodation "reflects nothing more than the governmental obligation of neutrality in the face of religious differences, and does not represent that involvement of religious with secular institutions which it is the object of the Establishment Clause to forestall." *Sherbert* v. *Verner,* 374 U. S. 398, 409 (1963).

vincing showing, one that probably few other religious groups or sects could make, and weighing the minimal difference between what the State would require and what the Amish already accept, it was incumbent on the State to show with more particularity how its admittedly strong interest in compulsory education would be adversely affected by granting an exemption to the Amish. *Sherbert* v. *Verner, supra.*

Nothing we hold is intended to undermine the general applicability of the State's compulsory school-attendance statutes or to limit the power of the State to promulgate reasonable standards that, while not impairing the free exercise of religion, provide for continuing agricultural vocational education under parental and church guidance by the Old Order Amish or others similarly situated. The States have had a long history of amicable and effective relationships with church-sponsored schools, and there is no basis for assuming that, in this related context, reasonable standards cannot be established concerning the content of the continuing vocational education of Amish children under parental guidance, provided always that state regulations are not inconsistent with what we have said in this opinion.[23]

Affirmed.

---

[23] Several States have now adopted plans to accommodate Amish religious beliefs through the establishment of an "Amish vocational school." See n. 3, *supra.* These are not schools in the traditional sense of the word. As previously noted, respondents attempted to reach a compromise with the State of Wisconsin patterned after the Pennsylvania plan, but those efforts were not productive. There is no basis to assume that Wisconsin will be unable to reach a satisfactory accommodation with the Amish in light of what we now hold, so as to serve its interests without impinging on respondents' protected free exercise of their religion.

WALZ v. TAX COMMISSION OF THE CITY OF NEW YORK

APPEAL FROM THE COURT OF APPEALS OF THE STATE OF NEW YORK

No. 135. Argued November 19, 1969—Decided May 4, 1970

Appellant property owner unsuccessfully sought an injunction in the New York courts to prevent the New York City Tax Commission from granting property tax exemptions to religious organizations for properties used solely for religious worship, as authorized by the state constitution and the implementing statute providing for tax exemptions for property used exclusively for religious, educational, or charitable purposes. Appellant contended that the exemptions as applied to religious bodies violated provisions prohibiting establishment of religion under the First and Fourteenth Amendments. *Held:*

1. The First Amendment tolerates neither governmentally established religion nor governmental interference with religion. Pp. 667–672.

2. The legislative purpose of tax exemptions is not aimed at establishing, sponsoring, or supporting religion, and New York's legislation simply spares the exercise of religion from the burden of property taxation levied on private profit institutions. Pp. 672–674.

3. The tax exemption creates only a minimal and remote involvement between church and state, far less than taxation of churches would entail, and it restricts the fiscal relationship between them, thus tending to complement and reinforce the desired separation insulating each from the other. Pp. 674–676.

4. Freedom from taxation for two centuries has not led to an established church or religion and on the contrary has helped to guarantee the free exercise of all forms of religious belief. Pp. 676–680.

24 N. Y. 2d 30, 246 N. E. 2d 517, affirmed.

Edward J. Ennis argued the cause for appellant.

J. Lee Rankin argued the cause for appellee. With him on the brief were *Stanley Buchsbaum* and *Edith I. Spivack.*

Briefs of *amici curiae* urging reversal were filed by *Osmond K. Fraenkel, Marvin M. Karpatkin, Norman Dorsen, Mr. Ennis,* and *Melvin L. Wulf* for the American Civil Liberties Union, and by *Lola Boswell* for Madalyn Murray O'Hair and *James H. Anderson, Jr.,* for the Society of Separationists, Inc.

Briefs of *amici curiae* urging affirmance were filed by *Louis J. Lefkowitz,* Attorney General, *Samuel A. Hirshowitz,* First Assistant Attorney General, and *Julius Greenfield,* Assistant Attorney General, for the State of New York, joined by the Attorneys General for their respective States as follows: *MacDonald Gallion* of Alabama, *Gary K. Nelson* of Arizona, *Joe Purcell* of Arkansas, *Duke W. Dunbar* of Colorado, *Robert K. Killian* of Connecticut, *David P. Buckson* of Delaware, *Earl Faircloth* of Florida, *Bertram T. Kanbara* of Hawaii, *William J. Scott* of Illinois, *Theodore L. Sendak* of Indiana, *Richard C. Turner* of Iowa, *Kent Frizzell* of Kansas, *John B. Breckinridge* of Kentucky, *Jack P. F. Gremillion* of Louisiana, *James S. Erwin* of Maine, *Francis B. Burch* of Maryland, *Frank J. Kelley* of Michigan, *A. F. Summer* of Mississippi, *John C. Danforth* of Missouri, *Robert L. Woodahl* of Montana, *Clarence A. H. Meyer* of Nebraska, *Arthur J. Sills* of New Jersey, *James A. Maloney* of New Mexico, *Robert B. Morgan* of North Carolina, *Helgi Johanneson* of North Dakota, *Paul W. Brown* of Ohio, *William C. Sennett* of Pennsylvania, *Herbert F. De Simone* of Rhode Island, *Gordon Mydland* of South Dakota, *George F. McCanless* of Tennessee, *Crawford C. Martin* of Texas, *James M. Jeffords* of Vermont, *Robert Y. Button* of Virginia, *Slade Gorton* of Washington, *Robert W. War-*

ren of Wisconsin, and *James E. Barrett* of Wyoming, and
by *Santiago C. Soler-Favale*, Attorney General of Puerto
Rico; by *Franklin C. Salisbury* for Protestants and
Other Americans United for Separation of Church and
State; by *Noel Thompson* for the Parish Hall School,
Inc.; by *Charles H. Tuttle* and *Thomas A. Shaw, Jr.*,
for the National Council of the Churches of Christ in
the United States; by *Anthony L. Fletcher, Stephen B.
Clarkson, John Miles Evans, George F. Mackey, William G. Rhines, William Sherman,* and *H. Richard
Schumacher* for the Episcopal Diocese of New York et
al.; by *William R. Consedine, George E. Reed, Alfred L.
Scanlan, Arthur E. Sutherland,* and *Charles M. Whelan*
for the United States Catholic Conference; by *Marvin
Braiterman* for the Synagogue Council of America et al.;
by *Nathan Lewin* and *Julius Berman* for the National
Jewish Commission on Law and Public Affairs; by
Joseph B. Friedman for the Baptist Joint Committee
on Public Affairs; and by *Roy L. Cole* for the Baptist
General Convention of Texas.

Mr. Chief Justice Burger delivered the opinion of
the Court.

Appellant, owner of real estate in Richmond County,
New York, sought an injunction in the New York courts
to prevent the New York City Tax Commission from
granting property tax exemptions to religious organizations for religious properties used solely for religious worship. The exemption from state taxes is authorized by
Art. 16, § 1, of the New York Constitution, which
provides in relevant part:

"Exemptions from taxation may be granted only
by general laws. Exemptions may be altered or
repealed except those exempting real or personal
property used exclusively for religious, educational or

charitable purposes as defined by law and owned by any corporation or association organized or conducted exclusively for one or more of such purposes and not operating for profit." [1]

The essence of appellant's contention was that the New York City Tax Commission's grant of an exemption to church property indirectly requires the appellant to make a contribution to religious bodies and thereby violates provisions prohibiting establishment of religion under the First Amendment which under the Fourteenth Amendment is binding on the States. [2]

Appellee's motion for summary judgment was granted and the Appellate Division of the New York Supreme Court, and the New York Court of Appeals affirmed. We noted probable jurisdiction, 395 U. S. 957 (1969), and affirm.

I

Prior opinions of this Court have discussed the development and historical background of the First Amendment in detail. See *Everson* v. *Board of Education,* 330 U. S. 1 (1947); *Engel* v. *Vitale,* 370 U. S. 421 (1962). It would therefore serve no useful purpose to review in detail the background of the Establishment and Free

_____

[1] Art. 16, § 1, of the New York State Constitution is implemented by § 420, subd. 1, of the New York Real Property Tax Law which states in pertinent part:

"Real property owned by a corporation or association organized exclusively for the moral or mental improvement of men and women, or for religious, bible, tract, charitable, benevolent, missionary, hospital, infirmary, educational, public playground, scientific, literary, bar association, medical society, library, patriotic, historical or cemetery purposes . . . and used exclusively for carrying out thereupon one or more of such purposes . . . shall be exempt from taxation as provided in this section."

[2] The First Amendment to the United States Constitution provides in part that "Congress shall make no law respecting an establishment of religion, or prohibiting the free exercise thereof . . . ."

Exercise Clauses of the First Amendment or to restate what the Court's opinions have reflected over the years.

It is sufficient to note that for the men who wrote the Religion Clauses of the First Amendment the "establishment" of a religion connoted sponsorship, financial support, and active involvement of the sovereign in religious activity.   In England, and in some Colonies at the time of the separation in 1776, the Church of England was sponsored and supported by the Crown as a state, or established, church; in other countries "establishment" meant sponsorship by the sovereign of the Lutheran or Catholic Church.   See *Engel* v. *Vitale*, 370 U. S., at 428 n. 10.   See generally C. Antieau, A. Downey, & E. Roberts, Freedom from Federal Establishment (1964).   The exclusivity of established churches in the 17th and 18th centuries, of course, was often carried to prohibition of other forms of worship.   See *Everson* v. *Board of Education*, 330 U. S., at 9–11; L. Pfeffer, Church, State and Freedom 71 *et seq.* (1967).

The Establishment and Free Exercise Clauses of the First Amendment are not the most precisely drawn portions of the Constitution.   The sweep of the absolute prohibitions in the Religion Clauses may have been calculated; but the purpose was to state an objective, not to write a statute.   In attempting to articulate the scope of the two Religion Clauses, the Court's opinions reflect the limitations inherent in formulating general principles on a case-by-case basis.   The considerable internal inconsistency in the opinions of the Court derives from what, in retrospect, may have been too sweeping utterances on aspects of these clauses that seemed clear in relation to the particular cases but have limited meaning as general principles.

The Court has struggled to find a neutral course between the two Religion Clauses, both of which are cast in absolute terms, and either of which, if expanded to a logical extreme, would tend to clash with the other. For example, in *Zorach* v. *Clauson,* 343 U. S. 306 (1952), Mr. Justice Douglas, writing for the Court, noted:

> "The First Amendment, however, does not say that in every and all respects there shall be a separation of Church and State." *Id.,* at 312.
> "We sponsor an attitude on the part of government that shows no partiality to any one group and that lets each flourish according to the zeal of its adherents and the appeal of its dogma." *Id.,* at 313.

Mr. Justice Harlan expressed something of this in his dissent in *Sherbert* v. *Verner,* 374 U. S. 398 (1963), saying that the constitutional neutrality imposed on us

> "is not so narrow a channel that the slightest deviation from an absolutely straight course leads to condemnation." *Id.,* at 422.

The course of constitutional neutrality in this area cannot be an absolutely straight line; rigidity could well defeat the basic purpose of these provisions, which is to insure that no religion be sponsored or favored, none commanded, and none inhibited. The general principle deducible from the First Amendment and all that has been said by the Court is this: that we will not tolerate either governmentally established religion or governmental interference with religion. Short of those expressly proscribed governmental acts there is room for play in the joints productive of a benevolent neutrality which will permit religious exercise to exist without sponsorship and without interference.

Each value judgment under the Religion Clauses must therefore turn on whether particular acts in question are intended to establish or interfere with religious beliefs and practices or, have the effect of doing so. Adherence to the policy of neutrality that derives from an accommodation of the Establishment and Free Exercise Clauses has prevented the kind of involvement that would tip the balance toward government control of churches or governmental restraint on religious practice.

Adherents of particular faiths and individual churches frequently take strong positions on public issues including, as this case reveals in the several briefs *amici,* vigorous advocacy of legal or constitutional positions. Of course, churches as much as secular bodies and private citizens have that right. No perfect or absolute separation is really possible; the very existence of the Religion Clauses is an involvement of sorts—one that seeks to mark boundaries to avoid excessive entanglement.

The hazards of placing too much weight on a few words or phrases of the Court is abundantly illustrated within the pages of the Court's opinion in *Everson.* MR. JUSTICE BLACK, writing for the Court's majority, said the First Amendment

> "means at least this: Neither a state nor the Federal Government can . . . pass laws which aid one religion, aid all religions, or prefer one religion over another." 330 U. S., at 15.

Yet he had no difficulty in holding that:

> "Measured by these standards, we cannot say that the First Amendment prohibits New Jersey from spending tax-raised funds to pay the bus fares of parochial school pupils as a part of a general program under which it pays the fares of pupils attending public and other schools. *It is undoubtedly true that children are helped to get to church schools. There is even a possibility that some of the children might not be sent to the church schools if the parents were compelled to pay their children's bus fares out of their own pockets . . . ."* *Id.,* at 17. (Emphasis added.)

The Court did not regard such "aid" to schools teaching a particular religious faith as any more a violation of the Establishment Clause than providing "state-paid policemen, detailed to protect children . . . [at the schools] from the very real hazards of traffic . . . ." *Ibid.*

Mr. Justice Jackson, in perplexed dissent in *Everson,* noted that

> "the undertones of the opinion, advocating complete and uncompromising separation . . . seem utterly discordant with its conclusion . . . ." *Id.,* at 19.

Perhaps so. One can sympathize with Mr. Justice Jackson's logical analysis but agree with the Court's eminently sensible and realistic application of the language of the Establishment Clause. In *Everson* the Court declined to construe the Religion Clauses with a literalness that would undermine the ultimate constitutional objective as illuminated by history. Surely, bus transportation and police protection to pupils who receive religious instruction "aid" that particular religion to maintain schools that plainly tend to assure future adherents to a particular faith by having control of their total education at an early age. No religious body that maintains schools would deny this as an affirmative if not dominant policy of church schools. But if as in *Everson* buses can be provided to carry and policemen to protect church school pupils, we fail to see how a broader range of police and fire protection given equally to all churches, along with nonprofit hospitals, art galleries, and libraries receiving the same tax exemption, is different for purposes of the Religion Clauses.

Similarly, making textbooks available to pupils in parochial schools in common with public schools was surely an "aid" to the sponsoring churches because it relieved those churches of an enormous aggregate cost

for those books. Supplying of costly teaching materials
was not seen either as manifesting a legislative purpose
to aid or as having a primary effect of aid contravening
the First Amendment. *Board of Education* v. *Allen,*
392 U. S. 236 (1968).   In so holding the Court was heed-
ing both its own prior decisions and our religious tradition. MR. JUSTICE DOUGLAS, in *Zorach* v. *Clauson, supra,*
after recalling that we "are a religious people whose institutions presuppose a Supreme Being," went on to say:

> "We make room for as wide a variety of beliefs and
> creeds as the spiritual needs of man deem neces-
> sary. . . . *When the state encourages religious
> instruction . . . it follows the best of our traditions.*
> For it then respects the religious nature of our
> people and accommodates the public service to their
> spiritual needs." 343 U. S., at 313–314.   (Emphasis
> added.)

With all the risks inherent in programs that bring
about administrative relationships between public education bodies and church-sponsored schools, we have
been able to chart a course that preserved the autonomy
and freedom of religious bodies while avoiding any sem-
blance of established religion. This is a "tight rope"
and one we have successfully traversed.

II

The legislative purpose of the property tax exemption
is neither the advancement nor the inhibition of religion;
it is neither sponsorship nor hostility. New York, in
common with the other States, has determined that certain entities that exist in a harmonious relationship
to the community at large, and that foster its "moral
or mental improvement," should not be inhibited in
their activities by property taxation or the hazard of
loss of those properties for nonpayment of taxes. It

431

has not singled out one particular church or religious group or even churches as such; rather, it has granted exemption to all houses of religious worship within a broad class of property owned by nonprofit, quasi-public corporations which include hospitals, libraries, playgrounds, scientific, professional, historical, and patriotic groups. The State has an affirmative policy that considers these groups as beneficial and stabilizing influences in community life and finds this classification useful, desirable, and in the public interest. Qualification for tax exemption is not perpetual or immutable; some tax-exempt groups lose that status when their activities take them outside the classification and new entities can come into being and qualify for exemption.

Governments have not always been tolerant of religious activity, and hostility toward religion has taken many shapes and forms—economic, political, and sometimes harshly oppressive. Grants of exemption historically reflect the concern of authors of constitutions and statutes as to the latent dangers inherent in the imposition of property taxes; exemption constitutes a reasonable and balanced attempt to guard against those dangers. The limits of permissible state accommodation to religion are by no means co-extensive with the noninterference mandated by the Free Exercise Clause. To equate the two would be to deny a national heritage with roots in the Revolution itself. See *Sherbert* v. *Verner,* 374 U. S. 398, 423 (1963) (HARLAN, J., dissenting); *Braunfeld* v. *Brown,* 366 U. S. 599, 608 (1961). See generally Kauper, The Constitutionality of Tax Exemptions for Religious Activities in The Wall Between Church and State 95 (D. Oaks ed. 1963). We cannot read New York's statute as attempting to establish religion; it is simply sparing the exercise of religion from the burden of property taxation levied on private profit institutions.

We find it unnecessary to justify the tax exemption on the social welfare services or "good works" that some churches perform for parishioners and others—family counselling, aid to the elderly and the infirm, and to children. Churches vary substantially in the scope of such services; programs expand or contract according to resources and need. As public-sponsored programs enlarge, private aid from the church sector may diminish. The extent of social services may vary, depending on whether the church serves an urban or rural, a rich or poor constituency. To give emphasis to so variable an aspect of the work of religious bodies would introduce an element of governmental evaluation and standards as to the worth of particular social welfare programs, thus producing a kind of continuing day-to-day relationship which the policy of neutrality seeks to minimize. Hence, the use of a social welfare yardstick as a significant element to qualify for tax exemption could conceivably give rise to confrontations that could escalate to constitutional dimensions.

Determining that the legislative purpose of tax exemption is not aimed at establishing, sponsoring, or supporting religion does not end the inquiry, however. We must also be sure that the end result—the effect—is not an excessive government entanglement with religion. The test is inescapably one of degree. Either course, taxation of churches or exemption, occasions some degree of involvement with religion. Elimination of exemption would tend to expand the involvement of government by giving rise to tax valuation of church property, tax liens, tax foreclosures, and the direct confrontations and conflicts that follow in the train of those legal processes.

Granting tax exemptions to churches necessarily operates to afford an indirect economic benefit and also gives rise to some, but yet a lesser, involvement than taxing them. In analyzing either alternative the questions are whether the involvement is excessive, and whether it is a continuing one calling for official and continuing surveillance leading to an impermissible degree of entanglement. Obviously a direct money subsidy would be a relationship pregnant with involvement and, as with most governmental grant programs, could encompass sustained and detailed administrative relationships for enforcement of statutory or administrative standards, but that is not this case. The hazards of churches supporting government are hardly less in their potential than the hazards of government supporting churches;[3] each relationship carries some involvement rather than the desired insulation and separation. We cannot ignore the instances in history when church support of government led to the kind of involvement we seek to avoid.

The grant of a tax exemption is not sponsorship since the government does not transfer part of its revenue to churches but simply abstains from demanding that the church support the state. No one has ever suggested that tax exemption has converted libraries, art galleries, or hospitals into arms of the state or put employees "on the public payroll." There is no genuine nexus between tax exemption and establishment of religion. As Mr. Justice Holmes commented in a related context "a page of

---

[3] The support of religion with direct allocation of public revenue was a common colonial practice. See C. Antieau, A. Downey, & E. Roberts, Freedom from Federal Establishment cc. 1 and 2 (1964). A general assessment proposed in the Virginia Legislature in 1784 prompted the writing of James Madison's Remonstrance. See opinion of MR. JUSTICE DOUGLAS dissenting, post, at 704–706; 716–727. Governmental support of religion is common in many countries. See e. g., R. Murray, A Brief History of the Church of Sweden 75 (1961); G. Codding, The Federal Government of Switzerland 53–54 (1961); M. Scehic, Zbirka Propisa o Doprinosima i Porezima Gradjana 357 (Yugoslavia) (1968).

history is worth a volume of logic." *New York Trust Co.* v. *Eisner,* 256 U. S. 345, 349 (1921). The exemption creates only a minimal and remote involvement between church and state and far less than taxation of churches. It restricts the fiscal relationship between church and state, and tends to complement and reinforce the desired separation insulating each from the other.

Separation in this context cannot mean absence of all contact; the complexities of modern life inevitably produce some contact and the fire and police protection received by houses of religious worship are no more than incidental benefits accorded all persons or institutions within a State's boundaries, along with many other exempt organizations. The appellant has not established even an arguable quantitative correlation between the payment of an ad valorem property tax and the receipt of these municipal benefits.

All of the 50 States provide for tax exemption of places of worship, most of them doing so by constitutional guarantees. For so long as federal income taxes have had any potential impact on churches—over 75 years—religious organizations have been expressly exempt from the tax.[4] Such treatment is an "aid" to churches no more and no less in principle than the real estate tax exemption granted by States. Few concepts are more deeply embedded in the fabric of our national life, beginning with pre-Revolutionary colonial times, than for the government to exercise at the very least this kind of benevolent neutrality toward churches and religious exer-

---

[4] Act of August 27, 1894, § 32, 28 Stat. 556. Following passage of the Sixteenth Amendment, federal income tax acts have consistently exempted corporations and associations, organized and operated exclusively for religious purposes along with eleemosynary groups, from payment of the tax. Act of Oct. 3, 1913, § IIG (a), 38 Stat. 172. See Int. Rev. Code of 1954, § 501 *et seq.,* 26 U. S. C. § 501 *et seq.*

cise generally so long as none was favored over others and none suffered interference.

It is significant that Congress, from its earliest days, has viewed the Religion Clauses of the Constitution as authorizing statutory real estate tax exemption to religious bodies. In 1802 the 7th Congress enacted a taxing statute for the County of Alexandria, adopting the 1800 Virginia statutory pattern which provided tax exemptions for churches. 2 Stat. 194.[5] As early as 1813 the 12th Congress refunded import duties paid by religious societies on the importation of religious articles.[6] During this period the City Council of Washington, D. C., acting under congressional authority, Act of Incorporation, § 7, 2 Stat. 197 (May 3, 1802), enacted a series of real and personal property assessments that uniformly exempted church property.[7] In 1870 the Congress specifically exempted all churches in the District of Colum-

---

[5] In 1798 Congress passed an Act to provide for the valuation of lands and dwelling houses. All existing state exemptions were expressly excluded from the aforesaid valuation and enumeration. Act of July 9, 1798, § 8, 1 Stat. 585. Subsequent levies of direct taxes expressly or impliedly incorporated existing state exemptions. Act of July 14, 1798, § 2, 1 Stat. 598 (express incorporation of state exemption). See Act of Aug. 2, 1813, § 4, 3 Stat. 71; Act of Jan. 9, 1815, § 5, 3 Stat. 166 (express incorporation of state exemptions).

[6] See 6 Stat. 116 (1813), relating to plates for printing Bibles. See also 6 Stat. 346 (1826) relating to church vestments, furniture, and paintings; 6 Stat. 162 (1816), Bible plates; 6 Stat. 600 (1834), and 6 Stat. 675 (1836), church bells.

[7] See, *e. g.,* Acts of the Corporation of the City of Washington, First Council, c. V, approved Oct. 6, 1802, p. 13; Acts of the Corporation of the City of Washington, Second Council, § 1, approved Sept. 12, 1803, p. 13; Acts of the Corporation of the City of Washington, Third Council, § 1, approved Sept. 5, 1804, p. 13. Succeeding Acts of the Corporation impliedly renewed the exemption in subsequent assessments. See, *e. g.,* Acts of the Corporation of the City of Washington, Thirteenth Council, c. 19, § 2, approved July 27, 1815, p. 24.

bia and appurtenant grounds and property "from any
and all taxes or assessments, national, municipal, or
county."   Act of June 17, 1870, 16 Stat. 153.[8]

It is obviously correct that no one acquires a vested
or protected right in violation of the Constitution by long
use, even when that span of time covers our entire
national existence and indeed predates it.   Yet an unbroken practice of according the exemption to churches,
openly and by affirmative state action, not covertly or
by state inaction, is not something to be lightly cast
aside.   Nearly 50 years ago Mr. Justice Holmes stated:

> "If a thing has been practised for two hundred
> years by common consent, it will need a strong case
> for the Fourteenth Amendment to affect it. . . ."
> *Jackman* v. *Rosenbaum Co.*, 260 U. S. 22, 31 (1922).

Nothing in this national attitude toward religious tolerance and two centuries of uninterrupted freedom from
taxation has given the remotest sign of leading to an
established church or religion and on the contrary it has
operated affirmatively to help guarantee the free exercise
of all forms of religious belief.   Thus, it is hardly useful
to suggest that tax exemption is but the "foot in the
door" or the "nose of the camel in the tent" leading to
an established church.   If tax exemption can be seen as
this first step toward "establishment" of religion, as
MR. JUSTICE DOUGLAS fears, the second step has been
long in coming.   Any move that realistically "establishes" a church or tends to do so can be dealt with
"while this Court sits."

Mr. Justice Cardozo commented in The Nature of the
Judicial Process 51 (1921) on the "tendency of a prin-

---

[8] Subsequent Acts of Congress carried over the substance of the
exemption.   Act of July 12, 1876, § 8, 19 Stat. 85; Act of March 3,
1877, § 8, 19 Stat. 399; Act of August 15, 1916, 39 Stat. 514; D. C.
Code Ann. § 47–801a (1967).

ciple to expand itself to the limit of its logic"; such expansion must always be contained by the historical frame of reference of the principle's purpose and there is no lack of vigilance on this score by those who fear religious entanglement in government.

The argument that making "fine distinctions" between what is and what is not absolute under the Constitution is to render us a government of men, not laws, gives too little weight to the fact that it is an essential part of adjudication to draw distinctions, including fine ones, in the process of interpreting the Constitution. We must frequently decide, for example, what are "reasonable" searches and seizures under the Fourth Amendment. Determining what acts of government tend to establish or interfere with religion falls well within what courts have long been called upon to do in sensitive areas.

It is interesting to note that while the precise question we now decide has not been directly before the Court previously, the broad question was discussed by the Court in relation to real estate taxes assessed nearly a century ago on land owned by and adjacent to a church in Washington, D. C.[9] At that time Congress granted real estate tax exemptions to buildings devoted to art, to institutions of public charity, libraries, cemeteries, and "church buildings, and grounds actually occupied by such buildings." In denying tax exemption as to land owned by but not used for the church, but rather to produce income, the Court concluded:

> "In the exercise of this [taxing] power, Congress, like any State legislature unrestricted by constitutional provisions, may at its discretion wholly exempt certain classes of property from taxation, or

---

[9] *Gibbons* v. *District of Columbia,* 116 U. S. 404 (1886). Cf. *Washington Ethical Society* v. *District of Columbia,* 101 U. S. App. D. C. 371, 249 F. 2d 127 (1957)

may tax them at a lower rate than other property."
Gibbons v. *District of Columbia,* 116 U. S. 404, 408
(1886).

It appears that at least up to 1885 this Court, reflecting more than a century of our history and uninterrupted practice, accepted without discussion the proposition that federal or state grants of tax exemption to churches were not a violation of the Religion Clauses of the First Amendment.   As to the New York statute, we now confirm that view.

Affirmed.

LEMON ET AL. *v.* KURTZMAN, SUPERINTENDENT OF PUBLIC INSTRUCTION OF PENN-SYLVANIA, ET AL.

APPEAL FROM THE UNITED STATES DISTRICT COURT FOR THE EASTERN DISTRICT OF PENNSYLVANIA

No. 89.   Argued March 3, 1971—Decided June 28, 1971*

Rhode Island's 1969 Salary Supplement Act provides for a 15% salary supplement to be paid to teachers in nonpublic schools at which the average per-pupil expenditure on secular education is below the average in public schools. Eligible teachers must teach only courses offered in the public schools, using only materials used in the public schools, and must agree not to teach courses in religion. A three-judge court found that about 25% of the State's elementary students attended nonpublic schools, about 95% of whom attended Roman Catholic affiliated schools, and that to date about 250 teachers at Roman Catholic schools are the sole beneficiaries under the Act. The court found that the parochial school system was "an integral part of the religious mission of the Catholic Church," and held that the Act fostered "excessive entanglement" between government and religion, thus violating the Establishment Clause. Pennsylvania's Nonpublic Elementary and Secondary Education Act, passed in 1968, authorizes the state Superintendent of Public Instruction to "purchase" certain "secular educational services" from nonpublic schools, directly reimbursing those schools solely for teachers' salaries, textbooks, and instructional materials. Reimbursement is restricted to courses in specific secular subjects, the textbooks and materials must be approved by the Superintendent, and no payment is to be made for any course containing "any subject matter expressing religious teaching, or the morals or forms of worship of any sect." Contracts were made with schools that have more than 20% of all the students in the State, most of which were affiliated with the Roman Catholic Church. The complaint challenging the constitutionality of

---

*Together with No. 569, *Earley et al.* v. *DiCenso et al.*, and No. 570, *Robinson, Commissioner of Education of Rhode Island, et al.* v. *DiCenso et al.*, on appeal from the United States District Court for the District of Rhode Island.

the Act alleged that the church-affiliated schools are controlled by religious organizations, have the purpose of propagating and promoting a particular religious faith, and conduct their operations to fulfill that purpose. A three-judge court granted the State's motion to dismiss the complaint for failure to state a claim for relief, finding no violation of the Establishment or Free Exercise Clause. *Held:* Both statutes are unconstitutional under the Religion Clauses of the First Amendment, as the cumulative impact of the entire relationship arising under the statutes involves excessive entanglement between government and religion. Pp. 611–625.

(a) The entanglement in the Rhode Island program arises because of the religious activity and purpose of the church-affiliated schools, especially with respect to children of impressionable age in the primary grades, and the dangers that a teacher under religious control and discipline poses to the separation of religious from purely secular aspects of elementary education in such schools. These factors require continuing state surveillance to ensure that the statutory restrictions are obeyed and the First Amendment otherwise respected. Furthermore, under the Act the government must inspect school records to determine what part of the expenditures is attributable to secular education as opposed to religious activity, in the event a nonpublic school's expenditures per pupil exceed the comparable figures for public schools. Pp. 615–620.

(b) The entanglement in the Pennsylvania program also arises from the restrictions and surveillance necessary to ensure that teachers play a strictly nonideological role and the state supervision of nonpublic school accounting procedures required to establish the cost of secular as distinguished from religious education. In addition, the Pennsylvania statute has the further defect of providing continuing financial aid directly to the church-related schools. Historically governmental control and surveillance measures tend to follow cash grant programs, and here the government's post-audit power to inspect the financial records of church-related schools creates an intimate and continuing relationship between church and state. Pp. 620–622.

(c) Political division along religious lines was one of the evils at which the First Amendment aimed, and in these programs, where successive and probably permanent annual appropriations that benefit relatively few religious groups are involved, political fragmentation and divisiveness on religious lines are likely to be intensified. Pp. 622–624.

(d) Unlike the tax exemption for places of religious worship, upheld in *Walz* v. *Tax Commission*, 397 U. S. 664, which was based on a practice of 200 years, these innovative programs have self-perpetuating and self-expanding propensities which provide a warning signal against entanglement between government and religion. Pp. 624–625.

No. 89, 310 F. Supp. 35, reversed and remanded; Nos. 569 and 570, 316 F. Supp. 112, affirmed.

BURGER, C. J., delivered the opinion of the Court, in which BLACK, DOUGLAS, HARLAN, STEWART, MARSHALL (as to Nos. 569 and 570), and BLACKMUN, JJ., joined. DOUGLAS, J., filed a concurring opinion, *post*, p. 625, in which BLACK, J., joined, and in which MARSHALL, J. (as to Nos. 569 and 570), joined, filing a separate statement, *post*, p. 642. BRENNAN, J., filed a concurring opinion, *post*, p. 642. WHITE, J., filed an opinion concurring in the judgment in No. 89 and dissenting in Nos. 569 and 570, *post*, p. 661. MARSHALL, J., took no part in the consideration or decision of No. 89.

Henry W. Sawyer III argued the cause and filed briefs for appellants in No. 89. *Edward Bennett Williams* argued the cause for appellants in No. 569. With him on the brief were *Jeremiah C. Collins* and *Richard P. McMahon. Charles F. Cottam* argued the cause for appellants in No. 570. With him on the brief were *Herbert F. DeSimone*, Attorney General of Rhode Island, and *W. Slater Allen, Jr.*, Assistant Attorney General.

J. Shane Creamer argued the cause for appellees Kurtzman et al. in No. 89. On the brief were *Fred Speaker*, Attorney General of Pennsylvania, *David W. Rutstein*, Deputy Attorney General, and *Edward Friedman. William B. Ball* argued the cause for appellee schools in No. 89. With him on the brief were *Joseph G. Skelly, James E. Gallagher, Jr., C. Clark Hodgson, Jr., Samuel Rappaport, Donald A. Semisch*, and *William D. Valente. Henry T. Reath* filed a brief for appellee Pennsylvania Association of Independent Schools in No. 89. *Leo*

Pfeffer and *Milton Stanzler* argued the cause for appellees in Nos. 569 and 570. With them on the brief were *Harold E. Adams, Jr.,* and *Allan M. Shine.*

Briefs of *amici curiae* urging reversal in No. 89 were filed by *Mr. Pfeffer* for the American Association of School Administrators et al.; by *Henry C. Clausen* for United Americans for Public Schools; by *Samuel Rabinove, Arnold Forster, George Soll, Joseph B. Robison, Paul Hartman,* and *Sol Rabkin* for the American Jewish Committee et al.; by *Franklin C. Salisbury* for Protestants and Other Americans United for Separation of Church and State; by *J. Harold Flannery* for the Center for Law and Education, Harvard University, et al.; and by *Peter L. Costas* and *Paul W. Orth* for the Connecticut State Conference of Branches of the NAACP et al.

Briefs of *amici curiae* urging affirmance in No. 89 were filed by *Acting Solicitor General Friedman, Assistant Attorney General Ruckelshaus, Robert V. Zener,* and *Donald L. Horowitz* for the United States; by *Paul W. Brown,* Attorney General of Ohio, *pro se,* and *Charles S. Lopeman,* First Assistant Attorney General, for the Attorney General of Ohio et al.; by *Levy Anderson* for the City of Philadelphia; by *Robert M. Landis* for the School District of Philadelphia; by the City of Pittsburgh; by *Bruce W. Kauffman, John M. Elliott,* and *Edward F. Mannino* for the City of Erie; by *James A. Kelly* for the School District of the City of Scranton; by *Charles M. Whelan, William R. Consedine, Alfred L. Scanlan, Arthur E. Sutherland,* and *Harmon Burns, Jr.,* for the National Catholic Educational Association et al.; by *Ethan A. Hitchcock* and *I. N. P. Stokes* for the National Association of Independent Schools, Inc.; by *Jerome H. Gerber* for the Pennsylvania State ÁFL–CIO; by *Thomas J. Ford, Edward J. Walsh, Jr.,* and *Theodore D. Hoffmann*

for the Long Island Conference of Religious Elementary
and Secondary School Administrators; by *Nathan Lewin*
for the National Jewish Commission on Law and Public
Affairs; by *Stuart Hubbell* for Citizens for Educational
Freedom; and by *Edward M. Koza, Walter L. Hill, Jr.,
Thomas R. Balaban,* and *William J. Pinkowski* for the
Polish American Congress, Inc., et al.

The National Association of Laymen filed a brief as
amicus curiae in No. 89.

Briefs of *amici curiae* urging reversal in Nos. 569 and
570 were filed by *Acting Solicitor General Friedman, Assistant Attorney General Gray,* and *Messrs. Zener* and
Horowitz for the United States, and by *Jesse H. Choper*
and *Messrs. Consedine, Whelan,* and *Burns* for the National Catholic Educational Association et al.

Briefs of *amici curiae* urging affirmance in Nos. 569
and 570 were filed by *Messrs. Rabinove, Robison, Forster,*
and *Rabkin* for the American Jewish Committee et al.;
by *Mr. Salisbury* for Protestants and Other Americans
United for Separation of Church and State; by *Mr.
Flannery* for the Center for Law and Education, Harvard
University, et al.; and by *Messrs. Costas* and *Orth* for the
Connecticut State Conference of Branches of the NAACP
et al.

MR. CHIEF JUSTICE BURGER delivered the opinion of
the Court.

These two appeals raise questions as to Pennsylvania
and Rhode Island statutes providing state aid to church-
related elementary and secondary schools. Both statutes
are challenged as violative of the Establishment and Free
Exercise Clauses of the First Amendment and the Due
Process Clause of the Fourteenth Amendment.

Pennsylvania has adopted a statutory program that
provides financial support to nonpublic elementary and

secondary schools by way of reimbursement for the cost
of teachers' salaries, textbooks, and instructional materials in specified secular subjects. Rhode Island has
adopted a statute under which the State pays directly to
teachers in nonpublic elementary schools a supplement
of 15% of their annual salary. Under each statute state
aid has been given to church-related educational institutions. We hold that both statutes are unconstitutional.

I

The Rhode Island Statute

The Rhode Island Salary Supplement Act [1] was
enacted in 1969. It rests on the legislative finding that
the quality of education available in nonpublic elementary schools has been jeopardized by the rapidly rising
salaries needed to attract competent and dedicated
teachers. The Act authorizes state officials to supplement the salaries of teachers of secular subjects in nonpublic elementary schools by paying directly to a teacher
an amount not in excess of 15% of his current annual
salary. As supplemented, however, a nonpublic school
teacher's salary cannot exceed the maximum paid to
teachers in the State's public schools, and the recipient
must be certified by the state board of education in
substantially the same manner as public school teachers.

In order to be eligible for the Rhode Island salary
supplement, the recipient must teach in a nonpublic
school at which the average per-pupil expenditure on
secular education is less than the average in the State's
public schools during a specified period. Appellant State
Commissioner of Education also requires eligible schools
to submit financial data. If this information indicates
a per-pupil expenditure in excess of the statutory limita-

---

[1] R. I. Gen. Laws Ann. § 16–51–1 *et seq.* (Supp. 1970).

tion, the records of the school in question must be examined in order to assess how much of the expenditure is attributable to secular education and how much to religious activity.[2]

The Act also requires that teachers eligible for salary supplements must teach only those subjects that are offered in the State's public schools. They must use "only teaching materials which are used in the public schools." Finally, any teacher applying for a salary supplement must first agree in writing "not to teach a course in religion for so long as or during such time as he or she receives any salary supplements" under the Act.

Appellees are citizens and taxpayers of Rhode Island. They brought this suit to have the Rhode Island Salary Supplement Act declared unconstitutional and its operation enjoined on the ground that it violates the Establishment and Free Exercise Clauses of the First Amendment. Appellants are state officials charged with administration of the Act, teachers eligible for salary supplements under the Act, and parents of children in church-related elementary schools whose teachers would receive state salary assistance.

A three-judge federal court was convened pursuant to 28 U. S. C. §§ 2281, 2284. It found that Rhode Island's nonpublic elementary schools accommodated approximately 25% of the State's pupils. About 95% of these pupils attended schools affiliated with the Roman Catholic church. To date some 250 teachers have applied for benefits under the Act. All of them are employed by Roman Catholic schools.

---

[2] The District Court found only one instance in which this breakdown between religious and secular expenses was necessary. The school in question was not affiliated with the Catholic church. The court found it unlikely that such determinations would be necessary with respect to Catholic schools because their heavy reliance on nuns kept their wage costs substantially below those of the public schools.

The court held a hearing at which extensive evidence was introduced concerning the nature of the secular instruction offered in the Roman Catholic schools whose teachers would be eligible for salary assistance under the Act. Although the court found that concern for religious values does not necessarily affect the content of secular subjects, it also found that the parochial school system was "an integral part of the religious mission of the Catholic Church."

The District Court concluded that the Act violated the Establishment Clause, holding that it fostered "excessive entanglement" between government and religion. In addition two judges thought that the Act had the impermissible effect of giving "significant aid to a religious enterprise." 316 F. Supp. 112. We affirm.

The Pennsylvania Statute

Pennsylvania has adopted a program that has some but not all of the features of the Rhode Island program. The Pennsylvania Nonpublic Elementary and Secondary Education Act [3] was passed in 1968 in response to a crisis that the Pennsylvania Legislature found existed in the State's nonpublic schools due to rapidly rising costs. The statute affirmatively reflects the legislative conclusion that the State's educational goals could appropriately be fulfilled by government support of "those purely secular educational objectives achieved through nonpublic education . . . ."

The statute authorizes appellee state Superintendent of Public Instruction to "purchase" specified "secular educational services" from nonpublic schools. Under the "contracts" authorized by the statute, the State directly reimburses nonpublic schools solely for their actual expenditures for teachers' salaries, textbooks, and instructional materials. A school seeking reimbursement must

---

[3] Pa. Stat. Ann., Tit. 24, §§ 5601–5609 (Supp. 1971).

maintain prescribed accounting procedures that identify the "separate" cost of the "secular educational service." These accounts are subject to state audit. The funds for this program were originally derived from a new tax on horse and harness racing, but the Act is now financed by a portion of the state tax on cigarettes.

There are several significant statutory restrictions on state aid. Reimbursement is limited to courses "presented in the curricula of the public schools." It is further limited "solely" to courses in the following "secular" subjects: mathematics, modern foreign languages,[4] physical science, and physical education. Textbooks and instructional materials included in the program must be approved by the state Superintendent of Public Instruction. Finally, the statute prohibits reimbursement for any course that contains "any subject matter expressing religious teaching, or the morals or forms of worship of any sect."

The Act went into effect on July 1, 1968, and the first reimbursement payments to schools were made on September 2, 1969. It appears that some $5 million has been expended annually under the Act. The State has now entered into contracts with some 1,181 nonpublic elementary and secondary schools with a student population of some 535,215 pupils—more than 20% of the total number of students in the State. More than 96% of these pupils attend church-related schools, and most of these schools are affiliated with the Roman Catholic church.

Appellants brought this action in the District Court to challenge the constitutionality of the Pennsylvania statute. The organizational plaintiffs-appellants are associations of persons resident in Pennsylvania declaring

---

[4] Latin, Hebrew, and classical Greek are excluded.

belief in the separation of church and state; individual
plaintiffs-appellants are citizens and taxpayers of Pennsylvania. Appellant Lemon, in addition to being a citizen
and a taxpayer, is a parent of a child attending public
school in Pennsylvania. Lemon also alleges that he
purchased a ticket at a race track and thus had paid
the specific tax that supports the expenditures under
the Act. Appellees are state officials who have the responsibility for administering the Act. In addition seven
church-related schools are defendants-appellees.

A three-judge federal court was convened pursuant to
28 U. S. C. §§ 2281, 2284. The District Court held that
the individual plaintiffs-appellants had standing to challenge the Act, 310 F. Supp. 42. The organizational
plaintiffs-appellants were denied standing under *Flast* v.
Cohen, 392 U. S. 83, 99, 101 (1968).

The court granted appellees' motion to dismiss the
complaint for failure to state a claim for relief.[5] 310
F. Supp. 35. It held that the Act violated neither the
Establishment nor the Free Exercise Clause, Chief Judge
Hastie dissenting. We reverse.

II

In *Everson* v. *Board of Education,* 330 U. S. 1 (1947),
this Court upheld a state statute that reimbursed the
parents of parochial school children for bus transportation

---

[5] Plaintiffs-appellants also claimed that the Act violated the Equal
Protection Clause of the Fourteenth Amendment by providing state
assistance to private institutions that discriminated on racial and
religious grounds in their admissions and hiring policies. The court
unanimously held that no plaintiff had standing to raise this claim
because the complaint did not allege that the child of any plaintiff
had been denied admission to any nonpublic school on racial or
religious grounds. Our decision makes it unnecessary for us to
reach this issue.

expenses. There MR. JUSTICE BLACK, writing for the majority, suggested that the decision carried to "the verge" of forbidden territory under the Religion Clauses. *Id.*, at 16. Candor compels acknowledgment, moreover, that we can only dimly perceive the lines of demarcation in this extraordinarily sensitive area of constitutional law.

The language of the Religion Clauses of the First Amendment is at best opaque, particularly when compared with other portions of the Amendment. Its authors did not simply prohibit the establishment of a state church or a state religion, an area history shows they regarded as very important and fraught with great dangers. Instead they commanded that there should be "no law *respecting* an establishment of religion." A law may be one "respecting" the forbidden objective while falling short of its total realization. A law "respecting" the proscribed result, that is, the establishment of religion, is not always easily identifiable as one violative of the Clause. A given law might not *establish* a state religion but nevertheless be one "respecting" that end in the sense of being a step that could lead to such establishment and hence offend the First Amendment.

In the absence of precisely stated constitutional prohibitions, we must draw lines with reference to the three main-evils against which the Establishment Clause was intended to afford protection: "sponsorship, financial support, and active involvement of the sovereign in religious activity." *Walz* v. *Tax Commission*, 397 U. S. 664, 668 (1970).

Every analysis in this area must begin with consideration of the cumulative criteria developed by the Court over many years. Three such tests may be gleaned from our cases. First, the statute must have a secular legislative purpose; second, its principal or primary effect must be one that neither advances nor inhibits religion, *Board of Education* v. *Allen*, 392 U. S. 236, 243 (1968);

finally, the statute must not foster "an excessive government entanglement with religion." *Walz, supra,* at 674.

Inquiry into the legislative purposes of the Pennsylvania and Rhode Island statutes affords no basis for a conclusion that the legislative intent was to advance religion. On the contrary, the statutes themselves clearly state that they are intended to enhance the quality of the secular education in all schools covered by the compulsory attendance laws. There is no reason to believe the legislatures meant anything else. A State always has a legitimate concern for maintaining minimum standards in all schools it allows to operate. As in *Allen,* we find nothing here that undermines the stated legislative intent; it must therefore be accorded appropriate deference.

In *Allen* the Court acknowledged that secular and religious teachings were not necessarily so intertwined that secular textbooks furnished to students by the State were in fact instrumental in the teaching of religion. 392 U. S., at 248. The legislatures of Rhode Island and Pennsylvania have concluded that secular and religious education are identifiable and separable. In the abstract we have no quarrel with this conclusion.

The two legislatures, however, have also recognized that church-related elementary and secondary schools have a significant religious mission and that a substantial portion of their activities is religiously oriented. They have therefore sought to create statutory restrictions designed to guarantee the separation between secular and religious educational functions and to ensure that State financial aid supports only the former. All these provisions are precautions taken in candid recognition that these programs approached, even if they did not intrude upon, the forbidden areas under the Religion Clauses. We need not decide whether these legislative precautions restrict the principal or primary effect of the programs to the point where they do not offend the Religion

Clauses, for we conclude that the cumulative impact of the entire relationship arising under the statutes in each State involves excessive entanglement between government and religion.

III

In *Walz* v. *Tax Commission, supra,* the Court upheld state tax exemptions for real property owned by religious organizations and used for religious worship. That holding, however, tended to confine rather than enlarge the area of permissible state involvement with religious institutions by calling for close scrutiny of the degree of entanglement involved in the relationship. The objective is to prevent, as far as possible, the intrusion of either into the precincts of the other.

Our prior holdings do not call for total separation between church and state; total separation is not possible in an absolute sense. Some relationship between government and religious organizations is inevitable. *Zorach* v. *Clauson,* 343 U. S. 306, 312 (1952); *Sherbert* v. *Verner,* 374 U. S. 398, 422 (1963) (HARLAN, J., dissenting). Fire inspections, building and zoning regulations, and state requirements under compulsory school-attendance laws are examples of necessary and permissible contacts. Indeed, under the statutory exemption before us in *Walz,* the State had a continuing burden to ascertain that the exempt property was in fact being used for religious worship. Judicial caveats against entanglement must recognize that the line of separation, far from being a "wall," is a blurred, indistinct, and variable barrier depending on all the circumstances of a particular relationship.

This is not to suggest, however, that we are to engage in a legalistic minuet in which precise rules and forms must govern. A true minuet is a matter of pure form and style, the observance of which is itself the substantive end. Here we examine the form of the relationship for the light that it casts on the substance.

In order to determine whether the government entanglement with religion is excessive, we must examine
the character and purposes of the institutions that
are benefited, the nature of the aid that the State provides, and the resulting relationship between the government and the religious authority. MR. JUSTICE HARLAN,
in a separate opinion in *Walz, supra,* echoed the classic
warning as to "programs, whose very nature is apt to
entangle the state in details of administration . . . ."
Id., at 695. Here we find that both statutes foster an
impermissible degree of entanglement.

(a) *Rhode Island program*

The District Court made extensive findings on the
grave potential for excessive entanglement that inheres
in the religious character and purpose of the Roman
Catholic elementary schools of Rhode Island, to date
the sole beneficiaries of the Rhode Island Salary Supplement Act.

The church schools involved in the program are located close to parish churches. This understandably
permits convenient access for religous exercises since instruction in faith and morals is part of the total educational process. The school buildings contain identifying
religious symbols such as crosses on the exterior and
crucifixes, and religious paintings and statues either in the
classrooms or hallways. Although only approximately
30 minutes a day are devoted to direct religious instruction, there are religiously oriented extracurricular activities. Approximately two-thirds of the teachers in these
schools are nuns of various religious orders. Their dedicated efforts provide an atmosphere in which religious instruction and religious vocations are natural and proper
parts of life in such schools. Indeed, as the District
Court found, the role of teaching nuns in enhancing the
religious atmosphere has led the parochial school au-

453

thorities to attempt to maintain a one-to-one ratio between nuns and lay teachers in all schools rather than to permit some to be staffed almost entirely by lay teachers.

On the basis of these findings the District Court concluded that the parochial schools constituted "an integral part of the religious mission of the Catholic Church." The various characteristics of the schools make them "a powerful vehicle for transmitting the Catholic faith to the next generation." This process of inculcating religious doctrine is, of course, enhanced by the impressionable age of the pupils, in primary schools particularly. In short, parochial schools involve substantial religious activity and purpose.[6]

The substantial religious character of these church-related schools gives rise to entangling church-state relationships of the kind the Religion Clauses sought to avoid. Although the District Court found that concern for religious values did not inevitably or necessarily intrude into the content of secular subjects, the considerable religious activities of these schools led the legislature to provide for careful governmental controls and surveillance by state authorities in order to ensure that state aid supports only secular education.

The dangers and corresponding entanglements are enhanced by the particular form of aid that the Rhode Island Act provides. Our decisions from *Everson* to *Allen* have permitted the States to provide church-related schools with secular, neutral, or nonideological services, facilities, or materials. Bus transportation, school lunches, public health services, and secular textbooks supplied in common to all students were not

---

[6] See, *e. g.*, J. Fichter, Parochial School: A Sociological Study 77–108 (1958); Giannella, Religious Liberty, Nonestablishment, and Doctrinal Development, pt. II, The Nonestablishment Principle, 81 Harv. L. Rev. 513, 574 (1968).

thought to offend the Establishment Clause. We note that the dissenters in *Allen* seemed chiefly concerned with the pragmatic difficulties involved in ensuring the truly secular content of the textbooks provided at state expense.

In *Allen* the Court refused to make assumptions, on a meager record, about the religious content of the textbooks that the State would be asked to provide. We cannot, however, refuse here to recognize that teachers have a substantially different ideological character from books. In terms of potential for involving some aspect of faith or morals in secular subjects, a textbook's content is ascertainable, but a teacher's handling of a subject is not. We cannot ignore the danger that a teacher under religious control and discipline poses to the separation of the religious from the purely secular aspects of pre-college education. The conflict of functions inheres in the situation.

In our view the record shows these dangers are present to a substantial degree. The Rhode Island Roman Catholic elementary schools are under the general supervision of the Bishop of Providence and his appointed representative, the Diocesan Superintendent of Schools. In most cases, each individual parish, however, assumes the ultimate financial responsibility for the school, with the parish priest authorizing the allocation of parish funds. With only two exceptions, school principals are nuns appointed either by the Superintendent or the Mother Provincial of the order whose members staff the school. By 1969 lay teachers constituted more than a third of all teachers in the parochial elementary schools, and their number is growing. They are first interviewed by the superintendent's office and then by the school principal. The contracts are signed by the parish priest, and he retains some discretion in negotiating salary levels. Religious authority necessarily pervades the school system.

The schools are governed by the standards set forth in a "Handbook of School Regulations," which has the force of synodal law in the diocese. It emphasizes the role and importance of the teacher in parochial schools: "The prime factor for the success or the failure of the school is the spirit and personality, as well as the professional competency, of the teacher . . . ." The Handbook also states that: "Religious formation is not confined to formal courses; nor is it restricted to a single subject area." Finally, the Handbook advises teachers to stimulate interest in religious vocations and missionary work. Given the mission of the church school, these instructions are consistent and logical.

Several teachers testified, however, that they did not inject religion into their secular classes. And the District Court found that religious values did not necessarily affect the content of the secular instruction. But what has been recounted suggests the potential if not actual hazards of this form of state aid. The teacher is employed by a religious organization, subject to the direction and discipline of religious authorities, and works in a system dedicated to rearing children in a particular faith. These controls are not lessened by the fact that most of the lay teachers are of the Catholic faith. Inevitably some of a teacher's responsibilities hover on the border between secular and religious orientation.

We need not and do not assume that teachers in parochial schools will be guilty of bad faith or any conscious design to evade the limitations imposed by the statute and the First Amendment. We simply recognize that a dedicated religious person, teaching in a school affiliated with his or her faith and operated to inculcate its tenets, will inevitably experience great difficulty in remaining religiously neutral. Doctrines and faith are not inculcated or advanced by neutrals. With the best of intentions such a teacher would find it hard to make a total separation between secular teaching and religious doctrine. What would appear to some to be essential to good citizenship might well for others border on or constitute instruction in religion. Further difficulties are inherent in the combination of religious discipline and the possibility of disagreement between teacher and religious authorities over the meaning of the statutory restrictions.

We do not assume, however, that parochial school teachers will be unsuccessful in their attempts to segregate their religious beliefs from their secular educational responsibilities. But the potential for impermissible fostering of religion is present. The Rhode Island Legislature has not, and could not, provide state aid on the basis of a mere assumption that secular teachers under religious discipline can avoid conflicts. The State must be certain, given the Religion Clauses, that subsidized teachers do not inculcate religion—indeed the State here has undertaken to do so. To ensure that no trespass occurs, the State has therefore carefully conditioned its aid with pervasive restrictions. An eligible recipient must teach only those courses that are offered in the public schools and use only those texts and materials that are found in the public schools. In addition the teacher must not engage in teaching any course in religion.

A comprehensive, discriminating, and continuing state surveillance will inevitably be required to ensure that these restrictions are obeyed and the First Amendment otherwise respected. Unlike a book, a teacher cannot be inspected once so as to determine the extent and intent of his or her personal beliefs and subjective acceptance of the limitations imposed by the First Amendment. These prophylactic contacts will involve excessive and enduring entanglement between state and church.

There is another area of entanglement in the Rhode Island program that gives concern. The statute excludes teachers employed by nonpublic schools whose average per-pupil expenditures on secular education equal or exceed the comparable figures for public schools. In the event that the total expenditures of an otherwise eligible school exceed this norm, the program requires the government to examine the school's records in order to determine how much of the total expenditures is attributable to secular education and how much to religious activity. This kind of state inspection and evaluation of the religious content of a religious organization is fraught with the sort of entanglement that the Constitution forbids. It is a relationship pregnant with dangers of excessive government direction of church schools and hence of churches. The Court noted "the hazards of government supporting churches" in *Walz* v. *Tax Commission, supra,* at 675, and we cannot ignore here the danger that pervasive modern governmental power will ultimately intrude on religion and thus conflict with the Religion Clauses.

(b) *Pennsylvania program*

The Pennsylvania statute also provides state aid to church-related schools for teachers' salaries. The complaint describes an educational system that is very similar to the one existing in Rhode Island. According to the allegations, the church-related elementary and secondary schools are controlled by religious organizations, have the purpose of propagating and promoting a particular religious faith, and conduct their operations to fulfill that purpose. Since this complaint was dismissed for failure to state a claim for relief, we must accept these allegations as true for purposes of our review.

As we noted earlier, the very restrictions and surveillance necessary to ensure that teachers play a strictly nonideological role give rise to entanglements between

church and state. The Pennsylvania statute, like that
of Rhode Island, fosters this kind of relationship. Reimbursement is not only limited to courses offered in
the public schools and materials approved by state officials, but the statute excludes "any subject matter expressing religious teaching, or the morals or forms of
worship of any sect." In addition, schools seeking reimbursement must maintain accounting procedures that
require the State to establish the cost of the secular as
distinguished from the religious instruction.

The Pennsylvania statute, moreover, has the further
defect of providing state financial aid directly to the
church-related school. This factor distinguishes both
Everson and *Allen,* for in both those cases the Court was
careful to point out that state aid was provided to the
student and his parents—not to the church-related school.
Board of Education v. *Allen, supra,* at 243–244; *Everson*
v. *Board of Education, supra,* at 18. In *Walz* v. *Tax
Commission, supra,* at 675, the Court warned of the
dangers of direct payments to religious organizations:

> "Obviously a direct money subsidy would be a rela-
> tionship pregnant with involvement and, as with
> most governmental grant programs, could encompass
> sustained and detailed administrative relationships
> for enforcement of statutory or administrative
> standards . . . ."

The history of government grants of a continuing cash
subsidy indicates that such programs have almost always
been accompanied by varying measures of control and
surveillance. The government cash grants before us now
provide no basis for predicting that comprehensive measures of surveillance and controls will not follow. In
particular the government's post-audit power to inspect
and evaluate a church-related school's financial records
and to determine which expenditures are religious and

which are secular creates an intimate and continuing relationship between church and state.

IV

A broader base of entanglement of yet a different character is presented by the divisive political potential of these state programs. In a community where such a large number of pupils are served by church-related schools, it can be assumed that state assistance will entail considerable political activity. Partisans of parochial schools, understandably concerned with rising costs and sincerely dedicated to both the religious and secular educational missions of their schools, will inevitably champion this cause and promote political action to achieve their goals. Those who oppose state aid, whether for constitutional, religious, or fiscal reasons, will inevitably respond and employ all of the usual political campaign techniques to prevail. Candidates will be forced to declare and voters to choose. It would be unrealistic to ignore the fact that many people confronted with issues of this kind will find their votes aligned with their faith.

Ordinarily political debate and division, however vigorous or even partisan, are normal and healthy manifestations of our democratic system of government, but political division along religious lines was one of the principal evils against which the First Amendment was intended to protect. Freund, Comment, Public Aid to Parochial Schools, 82 Harv. L. Rev. 1680, 1692 (1969). The potential divisiveness of such conflict is a threat to the normal political process. *Walz* v. *Tax Commission, supra,* at 695 (separate opinion of HARLAN, J.). See also *Board of Education* v. *Allen,* 392 U. S., at 249 (HARLAN, J., concurring); *Abington School District* v. *Schempp,* 374 U. S. 203, 307 (1963) (Goldberg, J., concurring). To have States or communities divide on the issues presented by state aid to parochial schools would tend to confuse and obscure other issues of great urgency. We have an expanding array of vexing issues, local and national, domestic and international, to debate and divide on. It conflicts with our whole history and tradition to permit questions of the Religion Clauses to assume such importance in our legislatures and in our elections that they could divert attention from the myriad issues and problems that confront every level of government. The highways of church and state relationships are not likely to be one-way streets, and the Constitution's authors sought to protect religious worship from the pervasive power of government. The history of many countries attests to the hazards of religion's intruding into the political arena or of political power intruding into the legitimate and free exercise of religious belief.

Of course, as the Court noted in *Walz*, "[a]dherents of particular faiths and individual churches frequently take strong positions on public issues." *Walz* v. *Tax Commission, supra,* at 670. We could not expect otherwise, for religious values pervade the fabric of our national life. But in *Walz* we dealt with a status under state tax laws for the benefit of all religious groups. Here we are confronted with successive and very likely permanent annual appropriations that benefit relatively few religious groups. Political fragmentation and divisiveness on religious lines are thus likely to be intensified.

The potential for political divisiveness related to religious belief and practice is aggravated in these two statutory programs by the need for continuing annual appropriations and the likelihood of larger and larger demands as costs and populations grow. The Rhode Island District Court found that the parochial school system's "monumental and deepening financial crisis" would "inescapably" require larger annual appropriations subsidizing greater percentages of the salaries of lay teachers. Although no facts have been developed in this respect in the Pennsylvania case, it appears that such pressures for expanding aid have already required the state legislature to include a portion of the state revenues from cigarette taxes in the program.

V

In *Walz* it was argued that a tax exemption for places of religious worship would prove to be the first step in an inevitable progression leading to the establishment of state churches and state religion. That claim could not stand up against more than 200 years of virtually universal practice imbedded in our colonial experience and continuing into the present.

The progression argument, however, is more persuasive here. We have no long history of state aid to church-related educational institutions comparable to 200 years of tax exemption for churches. Indeed, the state programs before us today represent something of an innovation. We have already noted that modern governmental programs have self-perpetuating and self-expanding propensities. These internal pressures are only enhanced when the schemes involve institutions whose legitimate needs are growing and whose interests have substantial political support. Nor can we fail to see that in constitutional adjudication some steps, which when taken were thought to approach "the verge," have become the platform for yet further steps. A certain momentum develops in constitutional theory and it can be a "downhill thrust" easily set in motion but difficult to retard or stop. Development by momentum is not invariably bad; indeed, it is the way the common law has grown, but it is a force to be recognized and reckoned with. The dangers are increased by the difficulty of perceiving in advance exactly where the "verge" of the precipice lies. As well as constituting an independent evil against which the Religion Clauses were intended to protect, involvement or entanglement between government and religion serves as a warning signal.

Finally, nothing we have said can be construed to disparage the role of church-related elementary and secondary schools in our national life. Their contribution has been and is enormous. Nor do we ignore their economic plight in a period of rising costs and expanding need. Taxpayers generally have been spared vast sums by the maintenance of these educational institutions by religious organizations, largely by the gifts of faithful adherents.

The merit and benefits of these schools, however, are not the issue before us in these cases. The sole question is whether state aid to these schools can be squared with the dictates of the Religion Clauses. Under our system the choice has been made that government is to be entirely excluded from the area of religious instruction and churches excluded from the affairs of government. The Constitution decrees that religion must be a private matter for the individual, the family, and the institutions of private choice, and that while some involvement and entanglement are inevitable, lines must be drawn.

The judgment of the Rhode Island District Court in No. 569 and No. 570 is affirmed. The judgment of the Pennsylvania District Court in No. 89 is reversed, and the case is remanded for further proceedings consistent with this opinion.

WOOLEY, CHIEF OF POLICE OF LEBANON, ET AL. *v.* MAYNARD ET UX.

APPEAL FROM THE UNITED STATES DISTRICT COURT FOR THE DISTRICT OF NEW HAMPSHIRE

No. 75-1453. Argued November 29, 1976—Decided April 20, 1977

New Hampshire statutes require that noncommercial motor vehicles bear license plates embossed with the state motto, "Live Free or Die," and make it a misdemeanor to obscure the motto. Appellees, Maynard and his wife, who are followers of the Jehovah's Witnesses faith, view the motto as repugnant to their moral, religious, and political beliefs, and accordingly they covered up the motto on the license plates of their jointly owned family automobiles. Appellee Maynard was subsequently found guilty in state court of violating the misdemeanor statute on three separate charges and upon refusing to pay the fines imposed was sentenced to, and served, 15 days in jail. Appellees then brought this action in Federal District Court pursuant to 42 U. S. C. § 1983, seeking injunctive and declaratory relief against enforcement of the New Hampshire statutes; a three-judge court enjoined the State from arresting and prosecuting appellees in the future for covering the motto on their license plates. *Held:*

1. The principles of equitable restraint enunciated in *Younger* v. *Harris*, 401 U. S. 37, do not preclude the District Court from exercising jurisdiction. Pp. 709–712.

   (a) When a genuine threat of state prosecutions exists, a litigant is entitled to resort to a federal forum to seek redress for an alleged deprivation of federal rights, and, aside from *Younger* principles, may seek such redress under 42 U. S. C. § 1983. Pp. 709–710.

   (b) When the relief sought is wholly prospective, *i. e.*, to preclude further prosecution under a statute alleged to violate constitutional rights, failure to seek state appellate review of criminal convictions does not bar relief in federal court. *Huffman* v. *Pursue, Ltd.*, 420 U. S. 592, distinguished. Pp. 710–711.

   (c) The threat of repeated prosecutions in the future against both appellees, and the effect of such a continuing threat on their ability to perform the ordinary tasks of daily life that require an automobile, are sufficient to justify injunctive relief, and hence the District Court was not limited to granting declaratory relief. Pp. 711–712.

2. The State may not constitutionally require an individual to par-

ticipate in the dissemination of an ideological message by displaying it on his private property in a manner and for the express purpose that it be observed and read by the public. Pp. 714–717.

(a) New Hampshire's statute, by forcing an individual, as part of his daily life—indeed constantly while his automobile is in public view—to be an instrument for advocating public adherence to an ideological point of view he finds unacceptable, "invades the sphere of intellect and spirit which it is the purpose of the First Amendment . . . to reserve from all official control," *Board of Education* v. *Barnette*, 319 U. S. 624, 642. Pp. 714–715.

(b) The State's claimed interests in requiring display of the state motto on license plates (1) so as to facilitate the identification of passenger vehicles, and (2) so as to promote appreciation of history, individualism, and state pride, are not sufficiently compelling to justify infringement of appellees' First Amendment rights. The purpose of the first interest could be achieved by less drastic means, and the second interest cannot outweigh an individual's First Amendment right to avoid becoming the courier for the State's ideological message. Pp. 715–717.

406 F. Supp. 1381, affirmed.

BURGER, C. J., delivered the opinion of the Court, in which BRENNAN, STEWART, MARSHALL, POWELL, and STEVENS, JJ., joined, and in which WHITE, J., joined, except insofar as it affirms the District Court's issuance of an injunction. WHITE, J., filed an opinion dissenting in part, in which BLACKMUN and REHNQUIST, JJ., joined, *post,* p. 717. REHNQUIST, J., filed a dissenting opinion, in which BLACKMUN, J., joined, *post,* p. 719.

Robert V. Johnson II, Assistant Attorney General of New Hampshire, argued the cause for appellants. With him on the brief was *David H. Souter,* Attorney General.

Richard S. Kohn argued the cause for appellees. With him on the brief were *Jack B. Middleton, R. David DePuy, Melvin L. Wulf,* and *Joel M. Gora.*

MR. CHIEF JUSTICE BURGER delivered the opinion of the Court.

The issue on appeal is whether the State of New Hampshire may constitutionally enforce criminal sanctions against

persons who cover the motto "Live Free or Die" on passenger
vehicle license plates because that motto is repugnant to their
moral and religious beliefs.

(1)

Since 1969 New Hampshire has required that noncommercial vehicles bear license plates embossed with the state motto,
"Live Free or Die." [1] N. H. Rev. Stat. Ann. § 263:1 (Supp.
1975). Another New Hampshire statute makes it a misdemeanor "knowingly [to obscure] . . . the figures or letters
on any number plate." N. H. Rev. Stat. Ann. § 262:27–c
(Supp. 1975). The term "letters" in this section has been interpreted by the State's highest court to include the state
motto. *State* v. *Hoskin,* 112 N. H. 332, 295 A. 2d 454 (1972).

Appellees George Maynard and his wife Maxine are followers of the Jehovah's Witnesses faith. The Maynards consider the New Hampshire State motto to be repugnant to
their moral, religious, and political beliefs,[2] and therefore
assert it objectionable to disseminate this message by displaying it on their automobiles.[3] Pursuant to these beliefs, the

---

[1] License plates are issued without the state motto for trailers, agricultural vehicles, car dealers, antique automobiles, the Governor of New
Hampshire, its Congressional Representatives, its Attorney General, Justices of the State Supreme Court, veterans, chaplains of the state legislature, sheriffs, and others.

[2] Mr. Maynard described his objection to the state motto:

"[B]y religious training and belief, I believe my 'government'—Jehovah's
Kingdom—offers everlasting life. It would be contrary to that belief to
give up my life for the state, even if it meant living in bondage. Although
I obey all laws of the State not in conflict with my conscience, this slogan
is directly at odds with my deeply held religious convictions.

". . . I also disagree with the motto on political grounds. I believe that
life is more precious than freedom." Affidavit of George Maynard, App. 3.

[3] At the time this suit was commenced appellees owned two automobiles,
a Toyota Corolla and a Plymouth station wagon. Both automobiles were
registered in New Hampshire where the Maynards are domiciled.

Maynards began early in 1974 to cover up the motto on their license plates.[4]

On November 27, 1974, Mr. Maynard was issued a citation for violating § 262:27–c. On December 6, 1974, he appeared *pro se* in Lebanon, N. H., District Court to answer the charge. After waiving his right to counsel, he entered a plea of not guilty and proceeded to explain his religious objections to the motto. The state trial judge expressed sympathy for Mr. Maynard's situation, but considered himself bound by the authority of *State* v. *Hoskin, supra,* to hold Maynard guilty. A $25 fine was imposed, but execution was suspended during "good behavior."

On December 28, 1974, Mr. Maynard was again charged with violating § 262:27–c. He appeared in court on January 31, 1975, and again chose to represent himself; he was found guilty, fined $50, and sentenced to six months in the Grafton County House of Corrections. The court suspended this jail sentence but ordered Mr. Maynard to also pay the $25 fine for the first offense. Maynard informed the court that, as a matter of conscience, he refused to pay the two fines. The court thereupon sentenced him to jail for a period of 15 days. He has served the full sentence.

Prior to trial on the second offense Mr. Maynard was charged with yet a third violation of § 262:27–c on January 3, 1975. He appeared on this complaint on the same day as for the second offense, and was, again, found guilty. This conviction was "continued for sentence" so that Maynard received no punishment in addition to the 15 days.

———————

4 In May or June 1974 Mr. Maynard actually snipped the words "or Die" off the license plates, and then covered the resulting hole, as well as the words "Live Free," with tape. This was done, according to Mr. Maynard, because neighborhood children kept removing the tape. The Maynards have since been issued new license plates, and have disavowed any intention of physically mutiliating them.

(2)

On March 4, 1975, appellees brought the present action pursuant to 42 U. S. C. § 1983 in the United States District Court for the District of New Hampshire. They sought injunctive and declaratory relief against enforcement of N. H. Rev. Stat. Ann. §§ 262:27–c, 263:1, insofar as these required displaying the state motto on their vehicle license plates, and made it a criminal offense to obscure the motto.[5] On March 11, 1975, the single District Judge issued a temporary restraining order against further arrests and prosecutions of the Maynards. Because the appellees sought an injunction against a state statute on grounds of its unconstitutionality, a three-judge District Court was convened pursuant to 28 U. S. C. § 2281. Following a hearing on the merits,[6] the District Court entered an order enjoining the State "from arresting and prosecuting [the Maynards] at any time in the future for covering over that portion of their license plates that contains the motto 'Live Free or Die.' "[7]   406 F. Supp. 1381 (1976). We noted probable jurisdiction of the appeal. 426 U. S. 946 (1976).

(3)

Appellants argue that the District Court was precluded from exercising jurisdiction in this case by the principles of

---

[5] Appellees sought (a) injunctions against future criminal prosecutions for violation of the statutes and (b) an injunction requiring that in future years they be issued license plates that do not bear the state motto.

[6] Several months elapsed between the issuance of the temporary restraining order and the hearing on the merits. This delay was occasioned by the request of the State pending consideration of a bill in the New Hampshire Legislature that would have made inclusion of the state motto on passenger vehicle license plates optional with the car owner. The bill failed to gain enactment.

[7] The District Court refused to order the State of New Hampshire to issue the Maynards license plates without the state motto, although it noted that there was evidence on the record that New Hampshire could easily do so. 406 F. Supp., at 1389. See n. 1, supra.

equitable restraint enunciated in *Younger* v. *Harris,* 401 U. S. 37 (1971). In *Younger* the Court recognized that principles of judicial economy, as well as proper state-federal relations, preclude federal courts from exercising equitable jurisdiction to enjoin ongoing state prosecutions. *Id.,* at 43. However, when a genuine threat of prosecution exists, a litigant is entitled to resort to a federal forum to seek redress for an alleged deprivation of federal rights. See *Steffel* v. *Thompson,* 415 U. S. 452 (1974); *Doran* v. *Salem Inn, Inc.,* 422 U. S. 922, 930–931 (1975). *Younger* principles aside, a litigant is entitled to resort to a federal forum in seeking redress under 42 U. S. C. § 1983 for an alleged deprivation of federal rights. *Huffman* v. *Pursue, Ltd.,* 420 U. S. 592, 609–610, n. 21 (1975). Mr. Maynard now finds himself placed "between the Scylla of intentionally flouting state law and the Charybdis of forgoing what he believes to be constitutionally protected activity in order to avoid becoming enmeshed in [another] criminal proceeding." *Steffel* v. *Thompson, supra,* at 462. Mrs. Maynard, as joint owner of the family automobiles, is no less likely than her husband to be subjected to state prosecution. Under these circumstances he cannot be denied consideration of a federal remedy.

Appellants, however, point out that Maynard failed to seek review of his criminal convictions and cite *Huffman* v. *Pursue, Ltd., supra,* for the propositions that "a necessary concomitant of *Younger* is that a party in appellee's posture must exhaust his state appellate remedies before seeking relief in the District Court," 420 U. S., at 608, and that "*Younger* standards must be met to justify federal intervention in a state judicial proceeding as to which a losing litigant has not exhausted his state appellate remedies," *id.,* at 609. *Huffman,* however, is inapposite. There the appellee was seeking to prevent, by means of federal intervention, enforcement of a state-court judgment declaring its theater a nuisance. We held that appellee's failure to exhaust its state appeals barred federal intervention under the principles of *Younger:* "Federal post-trial intervention, in a fashion designed to annul the results of a state trial . . . deprives the States of a function which quite legitimately is left to them, that of overseeing trial court dispositions of constitutional issues which arise in civil litigation over which they have jurisdiction." *Ibid.*

Here, however, the suit is in no way "designed to annul the results of a state trial" since the relief sought is wholly prospective, to preclude further prosecution under a statute alleged to violate appellees' constitutional rights. Maynard has already sustained convictions and has served a sentence of imprisonment for his prior offenses.[8] He does not seek to have his record expunged, or to annul any collateral effects those convictions may have, *e. g.,* upon his driving privileges. The Maynards seek only to be free from prosecutions for future violations of the same statutes. *Younger* does not bar federal jurisdiction.

In their complaint, the Maynards sought both declaratory and injunctive relief against the enforcement of the New Hampshire statutes. We have recognized that although " '[o]rdinarily . . . the practical effect of [injunctive and declaratory] relief will be virtually identical,' " *Doran* v. *Salem Inn, supra,* at 931, quoting *Samuels* v. *Mackell,* 401 U. S. 66, 73 (1971), a "district court can generally protect the interests of a federal plaintiff by entering a declaratory judgment, and therefore the stronger injunctive medicine will be unnecessary." *Doran, supra,* at 931. It is correct that generally a

---

[8] As to the offense which was "continued for sentence," see *supra,* at 708, the District Court found that "[n]o collateral consequences will attach as a result of it unless Mr. Maynard is arrested and prosecuted for the violation of NHRSA 262:27-c at some time in the future." 406 F. Supp., at 1384.

court will not enjoin "the enforcement of a criminal statute even though unconstitutional," *Spielman Motor Co.* v. *Dodge,* 295 U. S. 89, 95 (1935), since "[s]uch a result seriously impairs the State's interest in enforcing its criminal laws, and implicates the concerns for federalism which lie at the heart of *Younger,*" *Doran, supra,* at 931.　But this is not an absolute policy and in some circumstances injunctive relief may be appropriate.　"To justify such interference there must be exceptional circumstances and a clear showing that an injunction is necessary in order to afford adequate protection of constitutional rights." *Spielman Motor Co., supra,* at 95.

We have such a situation here for, as we have noted, three successive prosecutions were undertaken against Mr. Maynard in the span of five weeks.　This is quite different from a claim for federal equitable relief when a prosecution is threatened for the first time.　The threat of repeated prosecutions in the future against both him and his wife, and the effect of such a continuing threat on their ability to perform the ordinary tasks of daily life which require an automobile, is sufficient to justify injunctive relief.　Cf. *Douglas* v. *City of Jeannette,* 319 U. S. 157 (1943).　We are therefore unwilling to say that the District Court was limited to granting declaratory relief.　Having determined that the District Court was not required to stay its hand as to either appellee,[9] we turn to the merits of the Maynards' claim.

---

[9] If the totality of appellants' arguments were accepted, a § 1983 action could never be brought to enjoin state criminal prosecutions.　According to appellants, *Younger* principles bar Mr. Maynard from seeking an injunction because he has already been subjected to prosecution.　As to Mrs. Maynard, they argue, in effect, that the action is premature because no such prosecution has been instituted.　Since the two spouses were similarly situated but for the fact that one has been prosecuted and one has not, we fail to see where appellants' argument would ever leave room for federal intervention under § 1983.

(4)

The District Court held that by covering up the state motto "Live Free or Die" on his automobile license plate, Mr. Maynard was engaging in symbolic speech and that "New Hampshire's interest in the enforcement of its defacement statute is not sufficient to justify the restriction on [appellee's] constitutionally protected expression." 406 F. Supp., at 1389. We find it unnecessary to pass on the "symbolic speech" issue, since we find more appropriate First Amendment grounds to affirm the judgment of the District Court.[10] We turn instead to what in our view is the essence of appellees' objection to the requirement that they display the motto "Live Free or Die" on their automobile license plates. This is succinctly summarized in the statement made by Mr. Maynard in his affidavit filed with the District Court:

> "I refuse to be coerced by the State into advertising a slogan which I find morally, ethically, religiously and politically abhorrent." App. 5.

We are thus faced with the question of whether the State may constitutionally require an individual to participate in the dissemination of an ideological message by displaying it on his private property in a manner and for the express purpose that it be observed and read by the public. We hold that the State may not do so.

---

[10] We note that appellees' claim of symbolic expression is substantially undermined by their prayer in the District Court for issuance of special license plates not bearing the state motto. See n. 5, *supra.* This is hardly consistent with the stated intent to communicate affirmative opposition to the motto. Whether or not we view appellees' present practice of covering the motto with tape as sufficiently communicative to sustain a claim of symbolic expression, display of the "expurgated" plates requested by appellees would surely not satisfy that standard. See n. 1, *supra; Spence* v. *Washington,* 418 U. S. 405, 410–411 (1974), *United States* v. *O'Brien,* 391 U. S. 367, 376 (1968). (MR. JUSTICE BRENNAN does not join in this note.)

A

We begin with the proposition that the right of freedom of thought protected by the First Amendment against state action includes both the right to speak freely and the right to refrain from speaking at all. See *Board of Education* v. *Barnette,* 319 U. S. 624, 633–634 (1943); *id.,* at 645 (Murphy, J., concurring). A system which secures the right to proselytize religious, political, and ideological causes must also guarantee the concomitant right to decline to foster such concepts. The right to speak and the right to refrain from speaking are complementary components of the broader concept of "individual freedom of mind." *Id.,* at 637. This is illustrated by the recent case of *Miami Herald Publishing Co.* v. *Tornillo,* 418 U. S. 241 (1974), where we held unconstitutional a Florida statute placing an affirmative duty upon newspapers to publish the replies of political candidates whom they had criticized. We concluded that such a requirement deprived a newspaper of the fundamental right to decide what to print or omit:

> "Faced with the penalties that would accrue to any newspaper that published news or commentary arguably within the reach of the right-of-access statute, editors might well conclude that the safe course is to avoid controversy. Therefore, under the operation of the Florida statute, political and electoral coverage would be blunted or reduced. Government-enforced right of access inescapably 'dampens the vigor and limits the variety of public debate,' *New York Times Co.* v. *Sullivan,* 376 U. S. [254,] 279 [(1964)]." *Id.,* at 257 (footnote omitted).

The Court in *Barnette, supra,* was faced with a state statute which required public school students to participate in daily public ceremonies by honoring the flag both with words and traditional salute gestures. In overruling its prior decision in *Minersville District* v. *Gobitis,* 310 U. S. 586 (1940), the Court held that "a ceremony so touching matters of opinion and political attitude may [not] be imposed upon the individual by official authority under powers committed to any political organization under our Constitution." 319 U. S., at 636. Compelling the affirmative act of a flag salute involved a more serious infringement upon personal liberties than the passive act of carrying the state motto on a license plate, but the difference is essentially one of degree. Here, as in *Barnette,* we are faced with a state measure which forces an individual, as part of his daily life—indeed constantly while his automobile is in public view—to be an instrument for fostering public adherence to an ideological point of view he finds unacceptable. In doing so, the State "invades the sphere of intellect and spirit which it is the purpose of the First Amendment to our Constitution to reserve from all official control." *Id.,* at 642.

New Hampshire's statute in effect requires that appellees use their private property as a "mobile billboard" for the State's ideological message—or suffer a penalty, as Maynard already has. As a condition to driving an automobile—a virtual necessity for most Americans—the Maynards must display "Live Free or Die" to hundreds of people each day.[11] The fact that most individuals agree with the thrust of New Hampshire's motto is not the test; most Americans also find the flag salute acceptable. The First Amendment protects the right of individuals to hold a point of view different from the majority and to refuse to foster, in the way New Hampshire commands, an idea they find morally objectionable.

B

Identifying the Maynards' interests as implicating First Amendment protections does not end our inquiry however.

---

[11] Some States require that certain documents bear the seal of the State or some other official stamp for purposes of recordation. Such seal might contain, albeit obscurely, a symbol or motto having political or philosophical implications. The purpose of such seal, however, is not to advertise the message it bears but simply to authenticate the document by showing the authority of its origin.

We must also determine whether the State's countervailing interest is sufficiently compelling to justify requiring appellees to display the state motto on their license plates. See, *e. g.,* *United States* v. *O'Brien,* 391 U. S. 367, 376–377 (1968). The two interests advanced by the State are that display of the motto (1) facilitates the identification of passenger vehicles,[12] and (2) promotes appreciation of history, individualism, and state pride.

The State first points out that passenger vehicles, but not commercial, trailer, or other vehicles are required to display the state motto. Thus, the argument proceeds, officers of the law are more easily able to determine whether passenger vehicles are carrying the proper plates. However, the record here reveals that New Hampshire passenger license plates normally consist of a specific configuration of letters and numbers, which makes them readily distinguishable from other types of plates, even without reference to the state motto.[13] Even were we to credit the State's reasons and "even though the governmental purpose be legitimate and substantial, that purpose cannot be pursued by means that broadly stifle fundamental personal liberties when the end can be more narrowly achieved. The breadth of legislative abridgment must be viewed in the light of less drastic means for achieving the

---

[12] The Chief of Police of Lebanon, N. H., testified that "enforcement of the motor vehicle laws is facilitated by the State Motto appearing on non-commercial license plates, the benefits being the ease of distinguishing New Hampshire license plates from those of similar colors of other states and the ease of discovering misuse of license plates, for instance, the use of a 'trailer' license plate on a non-commercial vehicle." Brief for Appellants 20.

[13] New Hampshire passenger vehicle license plates generally consist of two letters followed by four numbers. No other license plate category displays this combination, and no other category bears the state motto. See n. 1, *supra.* However, of the approximately 325,000 passenger plates in New Hampshire, 9,999 do not follow the regular pattern, displaying numbers only, preceded by no letters. App. 50–53.

same basic purpose." *Shelton* v. *Tucker,* 364 U. S. 479, 488 (1960) (footnotes omitted).

The State's second claimed interest is not ideologically neutral. The State is seeking to communicate to others an official view as to proper appreciation of history, state pride, and individualism. Of course, the State may legitimately pursue such interests in any number of ways. However, where the State's interest is to disseminate an ideology, no matter how acceptable to some, such interest cannot outweigh an individual's First Amendment right to avoid becoming the courier for such message.[14]

We conclude that the State of New Hampshire may not require appellees to display the state motto [15] upon their vehicle license plates; and, accordingly, we affirm the judgment of the District Court.

Affirmed.

---

[14] Appellants do not explain why advocacy of these values is enhanced by display on private citizens' cars but not on the cars of officials such as the Governor, Supreme Court Justices, Members of Congress, and sheriffs. See n. 1, *supra.*

[15] It has been suggested that today's holding will be read as sanctioning the obliteration of the national motto, "In God We Trust" from United States coins and currency. That question is not before us today but we note that currency, which is passed from hand to hand, differs in significant respects from an automobile, which is readily associated with its operator. Currency is generally carried in a purse or pocket and need not be displayed to the public. The bearer of currency is thus not required to publicly advertise the national motto.

McDANIEL v. PATY ET AL.

APPEAL FROM THE SUPREME COURT OF TENNESSEE

No. 76–1427.   Argued December 5, 1977—Decided April 19, 1978

Appellee Paty, a candidate for delegate to a Tennessee constitutional convention, sued in the State Chancery Court for a declaratory judgment that appellant, an opponent who was a Baptist minister, was disqualified from serving as delegate by a Tennessee statutory provision establishing the qualifications of constitutional convention delegates to be the same as those for membership in the State House of Representatives, thus invoking a Tennessee constitutional provision barring "[m]inister[s] of the Gospel, or priest[s] of any denomination whatever."   That court held that the statutory provision violated the First and Fourteenth Amendments. The Tennessee Supreme Court reversed, holding that the clergy disqualification imposed no burden on "religious belief" and restricted "religious action . . . [only] in the law making process of government— where religious action is absolutely prohibited by the establishment clause . . . ."   *Held:* The judgment is reversed, and the case is remanded.   Pp. 625–629; 629–642; 642–643; 643–646.

547 S. W. 2d 897, reversed and remanded.

THE CHIEF JUSTICE, joined by MR. JUSTICE POWELL, MR. JUSTICE REHNQUIST, and MR. JUSTICE STEVENS, concluded:

1. The Tennessee disqualification is directed primarily, not at religious belief, but at the status, acts, and conduct of the clergy.   Therefore, the Free Exercise Clause's absolute prohibition against infringements on the "freedom to believe" is inapposite here.   *Torcaso* v. *Watkins*, 367 U. S. 488 (which invalidated a state requirement that an appointee to public office declare his belief in the existence of God), distinguished.   Pp. 626–627.

2. Nevertheless, the challenged provision violates appellant's First Amendment right to the free exercise of his religion made applicable to the States by the Fourteenth Amendment, because it conditions his right to the free exercise of his religion on the surrender of his right to seek office.   *Sherbert* v. *Verner*, 374 U. S. 398, 406.   Though justification is asserted under the Establishment Clause for the statutory restriction on the ground that if elected to public office members of the clergy will necessarily promote the interests of one sect or thwart those of another contrary to the anti-establishment principle of neutrality, Tennessee has failed to demonstrate that its views of the dangers of

clergy participation in the political process have not lost whatever validity they may once have enjoyed. Accordingly, there is no need to inquire whether the State's legislative goal is permissible. Pp. 626; 627–629.

MR. JUSTICE BRENNAN, joined by MR. JUSTICE MARSHALL, concluded:

1. The Free Exercise Clause is violated by the challenged provision. Pp. 630–635.

(a) Freedom of belief protected by that Clause embraces freedom to profess or practice that belief, even including doing so for a livelihood. The Tennessee disqualification establishes as a condition of office the willingness to eschew certain protected religious practices. The provision therefore establishes a religious classification governing eligibility for office that is absolutely prohibited. *Torcaso* v. *Watkins, supra.* Pp. 631–633.

(b) The fact that the law does not directly prohibit religious exercise but merely conditions eligibility for office on its abandonment does not alter the protection afforded by the Free Exercise Clause. "Governmental imposition of such a choice puts the same kind of burden upon the free exercise of religion as would a fine . . . ," *Sherbert* v. *Verner, supra,* at 404, and Tennessee's disqualification provision therefore imposed an unconstitutional penalty on appellant's free exercise. Moreover, "[t]he fact . . . that a person is not compelled to hold public office cannot possibly be an excuse for barring him from office by state-imposed criteria forbidden by the Constitution." *Sherbert* v. *Verner, supra,* at 495–496. Pp. 633–634.

2. The Tennessee disqualification also violates the Establishment Clause. Government generally may not use religion as a basis of classification for the imposition of duties, penalties, privileges, or benefits. Specifically, government may not fence out from political participation, people such as ministers whom it regards as overinvolved in religion. The disqualification provision employed by Tennessee here establishes a religious classification that has the primary effect of inhibiting religion. Pp. 636–642.

MR. JUSTICE STEWART concluded that *Torcaso* v. *Watkins, supra,* controls this case. Except for the fact that Tennessee bases its disqualification, not on a person's statement of belief, but on his decision to pursue a religious vocation as directed by his belief, the situation in *Torcaso* is indistinguishable from the one here. Pp. 642–643.

MR. JUSTICE WHITE concluded that the Tennessee disqualification, while not interfering with appellant's right to exercise his religion as he desires, denies him equal protection. Though that disqualification is based on the State's asserted interest in maintaining the required separation of church and state, it is not reasonably necessary for that objective, which all States except Tennessee have been able to realize without burdening ministers' rights to candidacy. In addition, the statute is both underinclusive and overinclusive. Pp. 643–646.

BURGER, C. J., announced the Court's judgment, and delivered an opinion, in which POWELL, REHNQUIST, and STEVENS, JJ., joined. BRENNAN, J., filed an opinion concurring in the judgment, in which MARSHALL, J., joined, *post*, p. 629. STEWART, J., *post*, p. 642, and WHITE, J., *post*, p. 643, filed opinions concurring in the judgment. BLACKMUN, J., took no part in the consideration or decision of the case.

Frederic S. Le Clercq argued the cause and filed a brief for appellant.

Kenneth R. Herrell, Assistant Attorney General of Tennessee, argued the cause for appellees. With him on the brief for appellees Hassler et al. were *Brooks McLemore,* Attorney General, and *C. Hayes Cooney,* Chief Deputy Attorney General. *Phillip C. Lawrence* filed a brief for appellee Paty.*

MR. CHIEF JUSTICE BURGER announced the judgment of the Court and delivered an opinion in which MR. JUSTICE POWELL, MR. JUSTICE REHNQUIST, and MR. JUSTICE STEVENS joined.

The question presented by this appeal is whether a Tennessee statute barring "Minister[s] of the Gospel, or priest[s] of any denomination whatever" from serving as delegates to the State's limited constitutional convention deprived appellant McDaniel, an ordained minister, of the right to the free exercise of religion guaranteed by the First Amendment and made applicable to the States by the Fourteenth Amendment. The First Amendment forbids all laws "prohibiting the free exercise" of religion.

Leo Pfeffer, Abraham S. Goldstein, Joel Gora, George W. McKeag, John T. Redmond, James W. Respess, and *Thomas A. Shaw* filed a brief for the American Civil Liberties Union et al. as *amici curiae* urging reversal.

I

In its first Constitution, in 1796, Tennessee disqualified ministers from serving as legislators.[1] That disqualifying provision has continued unchanged since its adoption; it is now Art. 9, § 1, of the State Constitution. The state legislature applied this provision to candidates for delegate to the State's 1977 limited constitutional convention when it enacted ch. 848, § 4, of 1976 Tenn. Pub. Acts: "Any citizen of the state who can qualify for membership in the House of Representatives of the General Assembly may become a candidate for delegate to the convention . . . ."

McDaniel, an ordained minister of a Baptist Church in Chattanooga, Tenn., filed as a candidate for delegate to the constitutional convention. An opposing candidate, appellee Selma Cash Paty, sued in the Chancery Court for a declaratory judgment that McDaniel was disqualified from serving as a delegate and for a judgment striking his name from the ballot. Chancellor Franks of the Chancery Court held that § 4 of ch. 848 violated the First and Fourteenth Amendments to the Federal Constitution and declared McDaniel eligible for the office of delegate. Accordingly, McDaniel's name remained on the ballot and in the ensuing election he was elected by a vote almost equal to that of three opposing candidates.

After the election, the Tennessee Supreme Court reversed the Chancery Court, holding that the disqualification of clergy imposed no burden upon "religious belief" and restricted "religious action . . . [only] in the lawmaking process of government—where religious action is absolutely prohibited by the establishment clause . . . ." 547 S. W. 2d 897, 903 (1977).

---

[1] "Whereas Ministers of the Gospel are by their profession, dedicated to God and the care of Souls, and ought not to be diverted from the great duties of their functions; therefore, no Minister of the Gospel, or priest of any denomination whatever, shall be eligible to a seat in either House of the Legislature." Tenn. Const., Art. VIII, § 1 (1796).

The state interests in preventing the establishment of religion and in avoiding the divisiveness and tendency to channel political activity along religious lines, resulting from clergy participation in political affairs, were deemed by that court sufficiently weighty to justify the disqualification, notwithstanding the guarantee of the Free Exercise Clause.

We noted probable jurisdiction.[2] 432 U. S. 905 (1977).

II

A

The disqualification of ministers from legislative office was a practice carried from England by seven of the original States;[3] later six new States similarly excluded clergymen from some political offices. 1 A. Stokes, Church and State in the United States 622 (1950) (hereafter Stokes). In England the practice of excluding clergy from the House of Commons was justified on a variety of grounds: to prevent dual officeholding, that is, membership by a minister in both Parliament and Convocation; to insure that the priest or deacon devoted himself to his "sacred calling" rather than to "such mundane activities as were appropriate to a member of the House of Commons"; and to prevent ministers, who after 1533 were subject to the Crown's powers over the benefices of the clergy, from using membership in Commons to diminish its independence by increasing the influence of the King and the nobility. *In re MacManaway*, [1951] A. C. 161, 164, 170–171.

The purpose of the several States in providing for disqualification was primarily to assure the success of a new political experiment, the separation of church and state. Stokes 622.

---

[2] The judgment of the Tennessee Supreme Court was stayed until final disposition of this appeal. McDaniel is currently serving as a delegate.

[3] Maryland, Virginia, North Carolina, South Carolina, Georgia, New York, and Delaware. L. Pfeffer, Church, State, and Freedom 118 (Rev. ed. 1967). Three of these—New York, Delaware, and South Carolina—barred clergymen from hoiding any political office. *Ibid.*

Prior to 1776, most of the 13 Colonies had some form of an established, or government-sponsored, church. *Id.*, at 364–446. Even after ratification of the First Amendment, which prohibited the Federal Government from following such a course, some States continued pro-establishment provisions. See *id.*, at 408, 418–427, 444. Massachusetts, the last State to accept disestablishment, did so in 1833. *Id.*, at 426–427.

In light of this history and a widespread awareness during that period of undue and often dominant clerical influence in public and political affairs here, in England, and on the Continent, it is not surprising that strong views were held by some that one way to assure disestablishment was to keep clergymen out of public office. Indeed, some of the foremost political philosophers and statesmen of that period held such views regarding the clergy. Earlier, John Locke argued for confining the authority of the English clergy "within the bounds of the church, nor can it in any manner be extended to civil affairs; because the church itself is a thing absolutely separate and distinct from the commonwealth." 5 Works of John Locke 21 (C. Baldwin ed. 1824). Thomas Jefferson initially advocated such a position in his 1783 draft of a constitution for Virginia.[4] James Madison, however, disagreed and vigorously

---

[4] 6 Papers of Thomas Jefferson 297 (J. Boyd ed. 1952). Jefferson later concluded that experience demonstrated there was no need to exclude clergy from elected office. In a letter to Jeremiah Moor in 1800, he stated: "[I]n the same scheme of a constitution [for Virginia which I prepared in 1783, I observe] an abridgment of the right of being elected, which after 17 years more of experience & reflection, I do not approve. It is the incapacitation of a clergyman from being elected. The clergy, by getting themselves established by law, & ingrafted into the machine of government, have been a very formidable engine against the civil and religious rights of man. They are still so in many countries & even in some of these United States. Even in 1783 we doubted the stability of our recent measures for reducing them to the footing of other useful callings. It now appears that our means were effectual. The clergy here seem to have relinquished all pretensions to privilege, and to stand on a footing with

urged the position which in our view accurately reflects the spirit and purpose of the Religion Clauses of the First Amendment. Madison's response to Jefferson's position was:

> "Does not The exclusion of Ministers of the Gospel as such violate a fundamental principle of liberty by punishing a religious profession with the privation of a civil right? does it [not] violate another article of the plan itself which exempts religion from the cognizance of Civil power? does it not violate justice by at once taking away a right and prohibiting a compensation for it? does it not in fine violate impartiality by shutting the door [against] the Ministers of one Religion and leaving it open for those of every other." 5 Writings of James Madison 288 (G. Hunt ed. 1904).

Madison was not the only articulate opponent of clergy disqualification. When proposals were made earlier to prevent clergymen from holding public office, John Witherspoon, a Presbyterian minister, president of Princeton University, and the only clergyman to sign the Declaration of Independence, made a cogent protest and, with tongue in cheek, offered an amendment to a provision much like that challenged here:

> " 'No clergyman, of any denomination, shall be capable of being elected a member of the Senate or House of Representatives, because (here insert the grounds of offensive disqualification, which I have not been able to discover) Provided always, and it is the true intent and meaning of this part of the constitution, that if at any time he shall be completely deprived of the clerical character by those by whom he was invested with it, as by deposition for cursing and swearing, drunkenness or uncleanness, he shall then be fully restored to all the privileges of a free

lawyers, physicians, &c. They ought therefore to possess the same rights." 9 Works of Jefferson 143 (P. Ford ed. 1905).

citizen; his offense [of being a clergyman] shall no more be remembered against him; but he may be chosen either to the Senate or House of Representatives, and shall be treated with all the respect due to his *brethren,* the other members of Assembly.' " Stokes 624–625.

As the value of the disestablishment experiment was perceived, 11 of the 13 States disqualifying the clergy from some types of public office gradually abandoned that limitation. New York, for example, took that step in 1846 after delegates to the State's constitutional convention argued that the exclusion of clergymen from the legislature was an "odious distinction." 2 C. Lincoln, The Constitutional History of New York 111–112 (1906). Only Maryland and Tennessee continued their clergy-disqualification provisions into this century and, in 1974, a District Court held Maryland's provision violative of the First and Fourteenth Amendments' guarantees of the free exercise of religion. *Kirkley* v. *Maryland,* 381 F. Supp. 327. Today Tennessee remains the only State excluding ministers from certain public offices.

The essence of this aspect of our national history is that in all but a few States the selection or rejection of clergymen for public office soon came to be viewed as something safely left to the good sense and desires of the people.

B

This brief review of the history of clergy-disqualification provisions also amply demonstrates, however, that, at least during the early segment of our national life, those provisions enjoyed the support of responsible American statesmen and were accepted as having a rational basis. Against this background we do not lightly invalidate a statute enacted pursuant to a provision of a state constitution which has been sustained by its highest court. The challenged provision came to the Tennessee Supreme Court clothed with the presumption of validity to which that court was bound to give deference.

However, the right to the free exercise of religion unquestionably encompasses the right to preach, proselyte, and perform other similar religious functions, or, in other words, to be a minister of the type McDaniel was found to be. *Murdock* v. *Pennsylvania*, 319 U. S. 105 (1943); *Cantwell* v. *Connecticut*, 310 U. S. 296 (1940). Tennessee also acknowledges the right of its adult citizens generally to seek and hold office as legislators or delegates to the state constitutional convention. Tenn. Const., Art. 2, §§ 9, 25, 26; Tenn. Code Ann. §§ 8–1801, 8–1803 (Supp. 1977). Yet under the clergy-disqualification provision, McDaniel cannot exercise both rights simultaneously because the State has conditioned the exercise of one on the surrender of the other. Or, in James Madison's words, the State is "punishing a religious profession with the privation of a civil right." 5 Writings of James Madison, *supra,* at 288. In so doing, Tennessee has encroached upon McDaniel's right to the free exercise of religion. "[T]o condition the availability of benefits [including access to the ballot] upon this appellant's willingness to violate a cardinal principle of [his] religious faith [by surrendering his religiously impelled ministry] effectively penalizes the free exercise of [his] constitutional liberties." *Sherbert* v. *Verner,* 374 U. S. 398, 406 (1963).

If the Tennessee disqualification provision were viewed as depriving the clergy of a civil right solely because of their religious beliefs, our inquiry would be at an end. The Free Exercise Clause categorically prohibits government from regulating, prohibiting, or rewarding religious beliefs as such. *Id.,* at 402; *Cantwell* v. *Connecticut, supra,* at 304. In *Torcaso* v. *Watkins,* 367 U. S. 488 (1961), the Court reviewed the Maryland constitutional requirement that all holders of "any office of profit or trust in this State" declare their belief in the existence of God. In striking down the Maryland requirement, the Court did not evaluate the interests assertedly justifying it but rather held that it violated freedom of religious belief.

In our view, however, *Torcaso* does not govern. By its

terms, the Tennessee disqualification operates against Mc-
Daniel because of his *status* as a "minister" or "priest." The
meaning of those words is, of course, a question of state law.[5]
And although the question has not been examined extensively
in state-law sources, such authority as is available indicates
that ministerial status is defined in terms of conduct and
activity rather than in terms of belief.[6] Because the Tennessee disqualification is directed primarily at status, acts, and
conduct it is unlike the requirement in *Torcaso,* which focused
on *belief.* Hence, the Free Exercise Clause's absolute prohibition of infringements on the "freedom to believe" is inapposite here.[7]

This does not mean, of course, that the disqualification
escapes judicial scrutiny or that McDaniel's activity does not
enjoy significant First Amendment protection. The Court

---

[5] In this case, the Tennessee Supreme Court concluded that the disqualification of McDaniel did not interfere with his religious *belief.* 547 S. W.
2d 897, 903, 904, 907 (1977). But whether the ministerial status, as defined by state law, implicates the "freedom to act" or the absolute "freedom to believe," *Cantwell* v. *Connecticut,* 310 U. S. 296, 304 (1940), must
be resolved under the Free Exercise Clause. Thus, although we consider
the Tennessee court's resolution of that issue, we are not bound by it.

[6] The Tennessee constitutional provision embodying the disqualification
inferentially defines the ministerial profession in terms of its "duties,"
which include the "care of souls." Tenn. Const., Art. 9, § 1. In this case,
the Tennessee Supreme Court stated that the disqualification reaches those
filling a "leadership role in religion," and those "dedicated to the full time
promotion of the religious objectives of a particular religious sect." 547
S. W. 2d, at 903 (emphasis added). The Tennessee court, in defining
"priest," also referred to the dictionary definition as "one who *performs*
sacrificial, ritualistic, mediatorial, interpretative, or ministerial functions . . . ." *Id.,* at 908 (quoting Webster's Third New International Dictionary 1799–1800 (1971)) (emphasis added).

[7] The absolute protection afforded belief by the First Amendment suggests
that a court should be cautious in expanding the *scope* of that protection
since to do so might leave government powerless to vindicate compelling
state interests.

recently declared in *Wisconsin* v. *Yoder,* 406 U. S. 205, 215 (1972):

> "The essence of all that has been said and written on the subject is that only those interests of the highest order and those not otherwise served can overbalance legitimate claims to the free exercise of religion." [8]

Tennessee asserts that its interest in preventing the establishment of a state religion is consistent with the Establishment Clause and thus of the highest order. The constitutional history of the several States reveals that generally the interest in preventing establishment prompted the adoption of clergy disqualification provisions, see Stokes 622; Tennessee does not appear to be an exception to this pattern. Cf. *post,* at 636 n. 9 (BRENNAN, J., concurring in judgment). There is no occasion to inquire whether promoting such an interest is a permissible legislative goal, however, see *post,* at 636–642, for Tennessee has failed to demonstrate that its views of the dangers of clergy participation in the political process have not lost whatever validity they may once have enjoyed. The essence of the rationale underlying the Tennessee restriction on ministers is that if elected to public office they will necessarily exercise

---

[8] Thus, the courts have sustained government prohibitions on handling venomous snakes or drinking poison, even as part of a religious ceremony, *State ex rel. Swann* v. *Pack,* 527 S. W. 2d 99 (Tenn. 1975), cert. denied, 424 U. S. 954 (1976); *State* v. *Massey,* 229 N. C. 734, 51 S. E. 2d 179, appeal dismissed for want of substantial federal question *sub nom. Bunn* v. *North Carolina,* 336 U. S. 942 (1949), but have precluded the application of criminal sanctions to the religious use of peyote, *People* v. *Woody,* 61 Cal. 2d 716, 394 P. 2d 813 (1964); cf. *Oliver* v. *Udall,* 113 U. S. App. D. C. 212, 306 F. 2d 819 (1962) (not reaching constitutional issue), or the religiously impelled refusal to comply with mandatory education laws past the eighth grade, *Wisconsin* v. *Yoder.*

We need not pass on the conclusions reached in *Pack* and *Woody,* which were not reviewed by this Court. Those cases are illustrative of the general nature of free exercise protections and the delicate balancing required by our decisions in *Sherbert* v. *Verner,* 374 U. S. 398 (1963), and *Wisconsin* v. *Yoder,* when an important state interest is shown.

618

their powers and influence to promote the interests of one sect or thwart the interests of another, thus pitting one against the others, contrary to the anti-establishment principle with its command of neutrality. See *Walz* v. *Tax Comm'n,* 397 U. S. 664 (1970). However widely that view may have been held in the 18th century by many, including enlightened statesmen of that day, the American experience provides no persuasive support for the fear that clergymen in public office will be less careful of anti-establishment interests or less faithful to their oaths of civil office than their unordained counterparts.[9]

We hold that § 4 of ch. 848 violates McDaniel's First Amendment right to the free exercise of his religion made applicable to the States by the Fourteenth Amendment. Accordingly, the judgment of the Tennessee Supreme Court is reversed, and the case is remanded to that court for further proceedings not inconsistent with this opinion.

Reversed and remanded.

---

[9] The struggle for separation of church and state in Virginia, which influenced developments in other States—and in the Federal Government— was waged by others in addition to such secular leaders as Jefferson, Madison, and George Mason; many clergymen vigorously opposed any established church. See Stokes 366–379. This suggests the imprecision of any assumption that, even in the early days of the Republic, most ministers, as legislators, would support measures antithetical to the separation of church and state.

NOTE: Where it is feasible, a syllabus (headnote) will be released, as is being done in connection with this case, at the time the opinion is issued. The syllabus constitutes no part of the opinion of the Court but has been prepared by the Reporter of Decisions for the convenience of the reader. See *United States* v. *Detroit Lumber Co.*, 200 U. S. 321, 337.

SUPREME COURT OF THE UNITED STATES

Syllabus

MARSH, NEBRASKA STATE TREASURER, ET AL. *v.* CHAMBERS

CERTIORARI TO THE UNITED STATES COURT OF APPEALS FOR THE EIGHTH CIRCUIT

No. 82–23. Argued April 20, 1983—Decided July 5, 1983

The Nebraska Legislature begins each of its sessions with a prayer by a chaplain paid by the State with the legislature's approval. Respondent member of the Nebraska Legislature brought an action in Federal District Court, claiming that the legislature's chaplaincy practice violates the Establishment Clause of the First Amendment, and seeking injunctive relief. The District Court held that the Establishment Clause was not breached by the prayer but was violated by paying the chaplain from public funds, and accordingly enjoined the use of such funds to pay the chaplain. The Court of Appeals held that the whole chaplaincy practice violated the Establishment Clause, and accordingly prohibited the State from engaging in any aspect of the practice.

Held: The Nebraska Legislature's chaplaincy practice does not violate the Establishment Clause. Pp. 3–11.

(a) The practice of opening sessions of Congress with prayer has continued without interruption for almost 200 years ever since the First Congress drafted the First Amendment, and a similar practice has been followed for more than a century in Nebraska and many other states. While historical patterns, standing alone, cannot justify contemporary violations of constitutional guarantees, historical evidence in the context of this case sheds light not only on what the drafters of the First Amendment intended the Establishment Clause to mean but also on how they thought that Clause applied to the chaplaincy practice authorized by the First Congress. In applying the First Amendment to the states through the Fourteenth Amendment, it would be incongruous to interpret the Clause as imposing more stringent First Amendment limits on the states than the draftsmen imposed on the Federal Government. In light of the history, there can be no doubt that the practice of opening

I

legislative sessions with prayer has become part of the fabric of our society. To invoke divine guidance on a public body entrusted with making the laws is not, in these circumstances, a violation of the Establishment Clause; it is simply a tolerable acknowledgment of beliefs widely held among the people of this country. Pp. 3–9.

(b) Weighed against the historical background, the facts that a clergyman of only one denomination has been selected by the Nebraska Legislature for 16 years, that the chaplain is paid at public expense, and that the prayers are in the Judeo-Christian tradition do not serve to invalidate Nebraska's practice. Pp. 9–11.

675 F. 2d 228, reversed.

BURGER, C. J., delivered the opinion of the Court, in which WHITE, BLACKMUN, POWELL, REHNQUIST, and O'CONNOR, JJ., joined. BRENNAN, J., filed a dissenting opinion, in which MARSHALL joined. STEVENS, J., filed a dissenting opinion.

SUPREME COURT OF THE UNITED STATES

No. 82–23

FRANK MARSH, STATE TREASURER, ET AL., PETITIONER v. ERNEST CHAMBERS

ON WRIT OF CERTIORARI TO THE UNITED STATES COURT OF APPEALS FOR THE EIGHTH CIRCUIT

[July 5, 1983]

CHIEF JUSTICE BURGER delivered the opinion of the Court.

The question presented is whether the Nebraska Legislature's practice of opening each legislative day with a prayer by a chaplain paid by the State violates the Establishment Clause of the First Amendment.

I

The Nebraska Legislature begins each of its sessions with a prayer offered by a chaplain who is chosen biennially by the Executive Board of the Legislative Council and paid out of public funds.[1] Robert E. Palmer, a Presbyterian minister, has served as chaplain since 1965 at a salary of $319.75 per month for each month the legislature is in session.

Ernest Chambers is a member of the Nebraska Legislature and a taxpayer of Nebraska. Claiming that the Nebraska Legislature's chaplaincy practice violates the Establishment Clause of the First Amendment, he brought this action under 42 U. S. C. § 1983, seeking to enjoin enforcement of the prac-

---

[1] Rules of the Nebraska Unicameral, Rules 1, 2, and 21. These prayers are recorded in the Legislative Journal and, upon the vote of the Legislature, collected from time to time into prayerbooks, which are published at the public expense. In 1975, 200 copies were printed; prayerbooks were also published in 1978 (200 copies), and 1979 (100 copies). In total, publication costs amounted to $458.56.

tice.[2] After denying a motion to dismiss on the ground of
legislative immunity, the District Court held that the Establishment Clause was not breached by the prayers, but was
violated by paying the chaplain from public funds.   It therefore enjoined the Legislature from using public funds to
pay the chaplain; it declined to enjoin the policy of beginning
sessions with prayers.   Cross-appeals were taken.[3]

The Court of Appeals for the Eighth Circuit rejected arguments that the case should be dismissed on Tenth Amendment, legislative immunity, standing or federalism grounds.
On the merits of the chaplaincy issue, the court refused to
treat respondent's challenges as separable issues as the District Court had done.   Instead, the Court of Appeals assessed the practice as a whole because "[p]arsing out [the]
elements" would lead to "an incongruous result."   675 F. 2d
228, 233 (CA8 1982).

Applying the three-part test of *Lemon* v. *Kurtzman,* 403
U. S. 602, 612–613 (1971), as set out in *Committee for Public
Educ. & Religious Liberty* v. *Nyquist,* 413 U. S. 756, 773
(1973), the court held that the chaplaincy practice violated all
three elements of the test: the purpose and primary effect of
selecting the same minister for 16 years and publishing his
prayers was to promote a particular religious expression; use
of state money for compensation and publication led to entanglement.   675 F. 2d, at 234–235.   Accordingly, the Court of
Appeals modified the District Court's injunction and prohibited the State from engaging in any aspect of its established
chaplaincy practice.

---

[2] Respondent named as defendants State Treasurer Frank Marsh,
Chaplain Palmer, and the members of the Executive Board of the Legislative Council in their official capacity.   All appear as petitioners before us.

[3] The District Court also enjoined the State from using public funds to
publish the prayers holding that this practice violated the Establishment
Clause.   Petitioners have represented to us that they did not challenge
this facet of the District Court's decision, Tr. of Oral Arg. 19–20.   Accordingly, no issue as to publishing these prayers is before us.

We granted certiorari limited to the challenge to the practice of opening sessions with prayers by a State-employed clergyman, —— U. S. —— (1982), and we reverse.[4]

II

The opening of sessions of legislative and other deliberative public bodies with prayer is deeply embedded in the history and tradition of this country. From colonial times through the founding of the Republic and ever since, the practice of legislative prayer has coexisted with the principles of disestablishment and religious freedom. In the very courtrooms in which the United States District Judge and later three Circuit Judges heard and decided this case, the proceedings opened with an announcement that concluded, "God save the United States and this Honorable Court." The same invocation occurs at all sessions of this Court.

The tradition in many of the colonies was, of course, linked to an established church,[5] but the Continental Congress, be-

---

[4] Petitioners also sought review of their Tenth Amendment, federalism and immunity claims. They did not, however, challenge the Court of Appeals' decision as to standing and we agree that Chambers, as a member of the Legislature and as a taxpayer whose taxes are used to fund the chaplaincy, has standing to assert this claim.

[5] The practice in colonies with established churches is, of course, not dispositive of the legislative prayer question. The history of Virginia is instructive, however, because that colony took the lead in defining religious rights. In 1776, the Virginia Convention adopted a Declaration of Rights that included, as Article 16, a guarantee of religious liberty that is considered the precursor of both the Free Exercise and Establishment Clauses. 1 B. Schwartz, The Bill of Rights, A Documentary History 231–236 (1971); S. Cobb, The Rise of Religious Liberty in America, 491–492 (1970). Virginia was also among the first to disestablish its church. Both before and after disestablishment, however, Virginia followed the practice of opening legislative sessions with prayer. See *e. g.*, J. of the House of Burgesses 34 (Nov. 20, 1712); Debates in the Convention of the Commonwealth of Va. 470 (June 2, 1788) (ratification convention); J. of the House of Delegates of Va. 3 (June 24, 1788) (state legislature).

Rhode Island's experience mirrored that of Virginia. That colony was

ginning in 1774, adopted the traditional procedure of opening
its sessions with a prayer offered by a paid chaplain.   See
e. g., 1 J. of the Continental Cong. 26 (1774); 2 J. of the Continental Cong. 12 (1775); 5 J. of the Continental Cong. 530
(1776); 6 J. of the Continental Cong. 887 (1776); 27 J. of the
Continental Cong. 683 (1784).   See also 1 A. Stokes, Church
and State in the United States 448–450 (1950).   Although
prayers were not offered during the Constitutional Convention,[6] the First Congress, as one of its early items of business, adopted the policy of selecting a chaplain to open each
session with prayer.   Thus, on April 7, 1789, the Senate appointed a committee "to take under consideration the manner
of electing Chaplains."   J. of the Sen. 10.   On April 9, 1789,
a similar committee was appointed by the House of Representatives.   On April 25, 1789, the Senate elected its first
chaplain, J. of the Sen. 16; the House followed suit on May 1,
1789, J. of the H. R. 26.   A statute providing for the payment of these chaplains was enacted into law on Sept. 22,
1789.[7]   2 Annals of Cong. 2180; 1 Stat. 71.[8]

---

founded by Roger Williams, who was among the first of his era to espouse
the principle of religious freedom.   Cobb, at 426.   As early as 1641, its
Legislature provided for liberty of conscience.   Id., at 430.   Yet the sessions of its ratification convention, like Virginia's, began with prayers,
see W. Staples, Rhode Island in the Continental Congress, 1765–1790 668
(1971) (reprinting May 26, 1790 minutes of the convention).

    [6] History suggests that this may simply have been an oversight.   At
one point, Benjamin Franklin suggested "that henceforth prayers implor-
ing the assistance of Heaven, and its blessings on our deliberations, be held
in this Assembly every morning before we proceed to business."   1 M.
Farrand, Records of the Federal Convention of 1787 452 (1911).   His proposal was rejected not because the Convention was opposed to prayer, but
because it was thought that a mid-stream adoption of the policy would
highlight prior omissions and because "[t]he Convention had no funds."
Ibid.; see also Stokes, at 455–456.

    [7] The statute provided that:

"there shall be allowed to each chaplain of Congress . . . five hundred dollars per annum during the session of Congress."

This salary compares favorably with the congressmen's own salaries of

On Sept. 25, 1789, three days after Congress authorized
the appointment of paid chaplains, final agreement was
reached on the language of the Bill of Rights, J. of the Sen.
88; J. of the H. R. 121.[9] Clearly the men who wrote the
First Amendment Religion Clause did not view paid legislative chaplains and opening prayers as a violation of that
Amendment, for the practice of opening sessions with prayer
has continued without interruption ever since that early session of Congress.[10] It has also been followed consistently in
most of the states,[11] including Nebraska, where the institu-

---

$6.00 for each day of attendance, 1 Stat. 70–71.

[8] It bears note that James Madison, one of the principal advocates of
religious freedom in the colonies and a drafter of the Establishment Clause,
see, e. g., Cobb, supra, at 495–497; Stokes, supra, at 537–552, was one of
those appointed to undertake this task by the House of Representatives,
J. of the H. R. 11–12; Stokes, at 541–549, and voted for the bill authorizing
payment of the chaplains, 1 Annals of Cong. 891.

[9] Interestingly, Sept. 25, 1789 was also the day that the House resolved
to request the President to set aside a Thanksgiving Day to acknowledge
"the many signal favors of Almighty God," J. of the H. R. 123. See also
J. of the Sen. 88.

[10] The chaplaincy was challenged in the 1850's by "sundry petitions pray-
ing Congress to abolish the office of chaplain," S. Rep. No. 376, 32d Cong.,
2d Sess. 1 (1853). After consideration by the Senate Committee on the
Judiciary, the Senate decided that the practice did not violate the Establishment Clause, reasoning that a rule permitting Congress to elect chaplains is not a law establishing a national church and that the chaplaincy was
no different from Sunday Closing Laws, which the Senate thought clearly
constitutional. In addition, the Senate reasoned that since prayer was
said by the very Congress that adopted the Bill of Rights, the Founding
Fathers could not have intended the First Amendment to forbid legislative
prayer or viewed prayer as a step toward an established church. Id., at
2–4. In any event, the 35th Congress abandoned the practice of electing
chaplains in favor of inviting local clergy to officiate, see Cong. Globe, 35th
Cong., 1st Sess. 14, 27–28 (1857). Elected chaplains were reinstituted by
the 36th Congress, Cong. Globe, 36th Cong., 1st Sess. 162 (1859); id., at
1016 (1860).

See Brief of the Nat'l Conference of State Legislatures as Amicus Curiae. Although most state legislatures begin their sessions with prayer,
most do not have a formal rule requiring this procedure. But see, e. g.,

tion of opening legislative sessions with prayer was adopted even before the State attained statehood. Nebraska Journal of the Council at the First Regular Session of the General Assembly 16 (Jan. 22, 1855).

Standing alone, historical patterns cannot justify contemporary violations of constitutional guarantees, but there is far more here than simply historical patterns. In this context, historical evidence sheds light not only on what the draftsmen intended the Establishment Clause to mean, but also on how they thought that Clause applied to the practice authorized by the First Congress—their actions reveal their intent. An act

> "passed by the first Congress assembled under the Constitution, many of whose members had taken part in framing that instrument, . . . is contemporaneous and weighty evidence of its true meaning". *Wisconsin* v. *Pelican Ins. Co.*, 127 U. S. 265, 297 (1888).

Alaska State Leg. Uniform Rule 11 and 17 (1981) (providing for opening invocation); Ark. Rules of Sen 18 (1983); Colo. Legislator's Handbook, House of Rep. Rule 44 (1982); Idaho Rules of the H. R. and Joint Rules 2 and 4 (1982); Ind. H. R. Rule 10 (1983); Kan., Rules of the Sen. 4 (1983); Kan., Rules of the H. R. 103 (1983); Ky. Gen'l Ass. H. Res. 2 (1982); La. Rules of Order, Sen. Rule 10.1 (1983); La. Rules of Order, House Rule 8.1 (1982); Me. Sen. and House Register, Rules of the House 4 (1983); Md., Sen. and House of Delegates Rules 1 (1982 and 1983); Mo., Rules of the Mo. Legislature, Joint Rule 1–1 (1983) N. H. Manual for the Use of the Gen'l Court of N. H., Rules of the House 52 (a) (1981); N. D. Sen. and House Rules 101 and 310 (1983); Ore. Rules of Sen. 4.01 (1983); Ore. Rules of H. R. 4.01 (1983) (opening session only); 104 Pa. Code § 11.11 (1983), 107 Pa. Code § 21.17 (1983); S. D. Official Directory and Rules of the Sen. and H. R. Joint Rules of the Sen. and House 4–1 (1983); Tenn. Permanent Rules of Order of the Sen. 1 and 6 (1981–1982) (provides for admission into Sen. chamber of the "Chaplain of the Day"); Tex. Rules of the H. R. 6 (1983); Utah Rules of the State Sen. and H. R. 4.04 (1983); Va. Manual of the Sen. and House of Delegates, Rules of the Sen. 21(a) (1982) (session opens with "period of devotions"); Wash. Permanent Rules of the H. R. 15 (1983); Wyo. Rules of the Sen. 4–1 (1983); Wyo. Rules of the H. R. 2–1 (1983). See also, Mason's Manual of Legislative Procedure § 586(2) (1979).

In *Walz* v. *Tax Comm'n*, 397 U. S. 664, 678 (1970), we considered the weight to be accorded to history:

> "It is obviously correct that no one acquires a vested or protected right in violation of the Constitution by long use, even when that span of time covers our entire national existence and indeed predates it. Yet an unbroken practice . . . is not something to be lightly cast aside."

No more is Nebraska's practice of over a century, consistent with two centuries of national practice, to be cast aside. It can hardly be thought that in the same week Members of the First Congress voted to appoint and to pay a Chaplain for each House and also voted to approve the draft of the First Amendment for submission to the States, they intended the Establishment Clause of the Amendment to forbid what they had just declared acceptable. In applying the First Amendment to the states through the Fourteenth Amendment, *Cantwell* v. *Connecticut*, 310 U. S. 296 (1940), it would be incongruous to interpret that clause as imposing more stringent First Amendment limits on the States than the draftsmen imposed on the Federal Government.

This unique history leads us to accept the interpretation of the First Amendment draftsmen who saw no real threat to the Establishment Clause arising from a practice of prayer similar to that now challenged. We conclude that legislative prayer presents no more potential for establishment than the provision of school transportation, *Everson* v. *Board of Education*, 330 U. S. 1 (1946), beneficial grants for higher education, *Tilton* v. *Richardson*, 403 U. S. 672 (1971), or tax exemptions for religious organizations, *Walz, supra.*

Respondent cites JUSTICE BRENNAN's concurring opinion in *Abington School Dist.* v. *Schempp*, 374 U. S. 203, 237 (1963), and argues that we should not rely too heavily on "the advice of the Founding Fathers" because the messages of history often tend to be ambiguous and not relevant to a society far more heterogeneous than that of the Framers, *id.*, at 240. Respondent also points out that John Jay and John Rutledge opposed the motion to begin the first session of the Continental Congress with prayer.   Brief for Respondent 60.[12]

We do not agree that evidence of opposition to a measure weakens the force of the historical argument; indeed it infuses it with power by demonstrating that the subject was considered carefully and the action not taken thoughtlessly, by force of long tradition and without regard to the problems posed by a pluralistic society.   Jay and Rutledge specifically grounded their objection on the fact that the delegates to the Congress "were so divided in religious sentiments . . . that [they] could not join in the same act of worship."   Their objection was met by Samuel Adams, who stated that "he was no bigot, and could hear a prayer from a gentleman of piety and virtue, who was at the same time a friend to his country."   C. Adams, Familiar Letters of John Adams and his Wife, Abigail Adams, during the Revolution 37–38, reprinted in Stokes, at 449.

This interchange emphasizes that the delegates did not consider opening prayers as a proselytizing activity or as symbolically placing the government's "official seal of approval on one religious view" cf. 675 F. 2d, at 234.   Rather, the Founding Fathers looked at invocations as "conduct whose . . . effect . . . harmonize[d] with the tenets of some or all religions."   *McGowan* v. *Maryland*, 366 U. S. 420, 442 (1961).   The Establishment Clause does not always bar a state from regulating conduct simply because it "harmonizes with religious canons."   *Id.*, at 462 (Frankfurter, J., concurring).   Here, the individual claiming injury by the practice is

---

[12] It also could be noted that objections to prayer were raised, apparently successfully, in Pennsylvania while ratification of the Constitution was debated, Penn. Herald, Nov. 24, 1787, and that in the 1820s, Madison expressed doubts concerning the chaplaincy practice.   See, L. Pfeffer, Church State and Freedom 248–249 (rev. ed. 1967), quoting E. Fleet, Madison's "Detached Memoranda," III William and Mary Quarterly 558–559 (1946).

an adult, presumably not readily susceptible to "religious in-
doctrination," see *Tilton* 403 U. S., at 686; *Colo* v. *Treasurer
& Receiver Gen'l*, 392 N. E. 2d 1195, 1200 (Mass. 1979), or
peer pressure, *compare, Abington, supra*, 374 U. S., at 290
(BRENNAN, J., concurring).

In light of the unambiguous and unbroken history of more
than 200 years, there can be no doubt that the practice of
opening legislative sessions with prayer has become part of
the fabric of our society.　To invoke Divine guidance on a
public body entrusted with making the laws is not, in these
circumstances, an "establishment" of religion or a step toward establishment; it is simply a tolerable acknowledgment
of beliefs widely held among the people of this country.　As
Justice Douglas observed, "[w]e are a religious people whose
institutions presuppose a Supreme Being." *Zorach* v.
Clauson, 343 U. S. 306, 313 (1952).

III

We turn then to the question of whether any features of
the Nebraska practice violate the Establishment Clause.
Beyond the bare fact that a prayer is offered, three points
have been made: first, that a clergyman of only one denomination—Presbyterian—has been selected for 16 years;[13] second, that the chaplain is paid at public expense; and third,
that the prayers are in the Judeo-Christian tradition.[14]
Weighed against the historical background, these factors do
not serve to invalidate Nebraska's practice.[15]

---

[13] In comparison, the First Congress provided for the appointment of
two chaplains of different denominations who would alternate between the
two chambers on a weekly basis, J. of the Sen. 12; J. of the H. R. 16.

[14] Palmer characterizes his prayers as "nonsectarian," "Judeo Christian,"
and with "elements of the American civil religion."　App. 75 and 87. (Deposition of Robert E. Palmer).　Although some of his earlier prayers were
often explicitly Christian, Palmer removed all references to Christ after a
1980 complaint from a Jewish legislator. *Id.*, at 49.

[15] It is also claimed that Nebraska's practice of collecting the prayers into
books violates the First Amendment.　Because the State did not appeal

The Court of Appeals was concerned that Palmer's long tenure has the effect of giving preference to his religious views. We, no more than Members of the Congresses of this century, can perceive any suggestion that choosing a clergyman of one denomination advances the beliefs of a particular church. To the contrary, the evidence indicates that Palmer was reappointed because his performance and personal qualities were acceptable to the body appointing him.[16] Palmer was not the only clergyman heard by the Legislature; guest chaplains have officiated at the request of various legislators and as substitutes during Palmer's absences. Tr. of Oral Arg. 10. Absent proof that the chaplain's reappointment stemmed from an impermissible motive, we conclude that his long tenure does not in itself conflict with the Establishment Clause.[17]

Nor is the compensation of the chaplain from public funds a reason to invalidate the Nebraska Legislature's chaplaincy; remuneration is grounded in historic practice initiated, as we noted earlier, *ante*, at 4–5, by the same Congress that adopted the Establishment Clause of the First Amendment. The Continental Congress paid its chaplain, see *e. g.*, 6 J. of the Continental Cong. 887 (1776), as did some of the states, see *e. g.*, Debates and other Proceedings of the Convention of Va. 470 (June 26, 1788). Currently, many state legislatures

---

the District Court order enjoining further publications, see n. 3, *supra*, this issue is not before us and we express no opinion on it.

[16] Nebraska's practice is consistent with the manner in which the First Congress viewed its chaplains. Reports contemporaneous with the elections reported only the chaplains' names, and not their religions or church affiliations, see, *e. g.*, II Gazette of the U. S. 18 (April 25, 1789); V Gazette of the U. S. 18 (April 27, 1789) (listing nominees for chaplain of the House); VI Gazette of the U. S. 23 (May 1, 1789). See also S. Rep. 376, *supra*, at 3.

[17] We note that Dr. Edward L. R. Elson served as Chaplain of the Senate of the United States from January 1969 to February 1981, a period of 12 years; Dr. Frederick Brown Harris served from February 1949 to January 1969, a period of 20 years. Senate Library, Chaplains of the Federal Government (rev. 1982).

and the United States Congress provide compensation for
their chaplains, Brief for Nat'l Conference of State Legislatures as *Amicus Curiae* 3; 2 U.S.C. §§ 61d and 84–2; H. R.
Res. 7, 96th Cong., 1st Sess. (1979).[18] Nebraska has paid its
chaplain for well over a century, see 1867 Neb. Laws §§ 2–4
(June 21, 1867), reprinted in, Neb. Gen'l Stat. 459 (1873).
The content of the prayer is not of concern to judges where,
as here, there is no indication that the prayer opportunity has
been exploited to proselytize or advance any one, or to disparage any other, faith or belief.   That being so, it is not for
us to embark on a sensitive evaluation or to parse the content
of a particular prayer.

We do not doubt the sincerity of those, who like respondent, believe that to have prayer in this context risks the beginning of the establishment the Founding Fathers feared.
But this concern is not well founded, for as Justice Goldberg,
aptly observed in his concurring opinion in *Abington*, 374
U. S., at 308:

> "It is of course true that great consequences can grow
> from small beginnings, but the measure of constitutional
> adjudication is the ability and willingness to distinguish
> between real threat and mere shadow."

The unbroken practice for two centuries in the National Con-

---

[18] The states' practices differ widely.   Like Nebraska, several states
choose a chaplain who serves for the entire legislative session.   In other
states, the prayer is offered by a different clergyman each day.   Under
either system, some states pay their chaplains and others do not.   For
states providing for compensation statutorily or by resolution, see, *e. g.*,
Cal. Gov't Code Ann. §§ 9170, 9171, 9320 and Sen. Res. No. 6 (1983); Colo.
House J., 54th Gen. Ass. 17–19 (Jan. 5, 1983); Conn. Gen. Stat. § 2–9
(1982); Geo. H. R. Res. No. 3(1)(e) (1983); Geo. S. Res. No. 3(1)(c)(1983);
Iowa Code § 2.11 (1983); Mo. Rev. Stat. § 21.150 (1969) (West); Nev. Rev.
Stat. § 218.200 (1979); N. J. Stat. Ann. § 52:11–2 (1970) (West); N. M. Stat.
Ann. Const. Art. IV § 9 (1978); Okla. Stat. Tit. 74, §§ 291.12 and 292.1
(West Supp. 1982); Vt. Stat. Ann., Tit. 2, § 19 (1982 Supp.); Wisc. Stat.
§ 13.125 (1982 Supp.).

gress, for more than a century in Nebraska and in many other states, gives abundant assurance that there is no real threat "while this Court sits," *Panhandle Oil Co.* v. *Mississippi ex rel. Knox*, 277 U. S. 218, 223 (1928) (Holmes, J., dissenting).

The judgment of the Court of Appeals is

Reversed.

NOTE: Where it is feasible, a syllabus (headnote) will be released, as is being done in connection with this case, at the time the opinion is issued. The syllabus constitutes no part of the opinion of the Court but has been prepared by the Reporter of Decisions for the convenience of the reader. See *United States* v. *Detroit Lumber Co.*, 200 U. S. 321, 337.

SUPREME COURT OF THE UNITED STATES

Syllabus

LYNCH, MAYOR OF PAWTUCKET, ET AL. *v.* DONNELLY ET AL.

CERTIORARI TO THE UNITED STATES COURT OF APPEALS FOR THE FIRST CIRCUIT

No. 82–1256. Argued October 4, 1983—Decided March 5, 1984

The city of Pawtucket, R. I., annually erects a Christmas display in a park owned by a nonprofit organization and located in the heart of the city's shopping district. The display includes, in addition to such objects as a Santa Claus house, a Christmas tree, and a banner that reads "SEASONS GREETINGS," a crèche or Nativity scene, which has been part of this annual display for 40 years or more. Respondents brought an action in Federal District Court, challenging the inclusion of the crèche in the display on the ground that it violated the Establishment Clause of the First Amendment, as made applicable to the states by the Fourteenth Amendment. The District Court upheld the challenge and permanently enjoined the city from including the crèche in the display. The Court of Appeals affirmed.

Held: Notwithstanding the religious significance of the crèche, Pawtucket has not violated the Establishment Clause. Pp. 3–17.

(a) The concept of a "wall" of separation between church and state is a useful metaphor but is not an accurate description of the practical aspects of the relationship that in fact exists. The Constitution does not require complete separation of church and state; it affirmatively mandates accommodation, not merely tolerance, of all religions, and forbids hostility toward any. Anything less would require the "callous indifference," *Zorach* v. *Clauson*, 343 U. S. 306, 314, that was never intended by the Establishment Clause. Pp. 3–4.

(b) This Court's interpretation of the Establishment Clause comports with the contemporaneous understanding of the Framers' intent. That neither the draftsmen of the Constitution, who were Members of the First Congress, nor the First Congress itself, saw any establishment problem in employing Chaplains to offer daily prayers in the Congress is

503

I

Syllabus

a striking example of the accommodation of religious beliefs intended by the Framers. Pp. 4–5.

(c) Our history is pervaded by official acknowledgment of the role of religion in American life, and equally pervasive is evidence of accommodation of all faiths and all forms of religious expression and hostility toward none. Pp. 5–8.

(d) Rather than taking an absolutist approach in applying the Establishment Clause and mechanically invalidating all governmental conduct or statutes that confer benefits or give special recognition to religion in general or to one faith, this Court has scrutinized challenged conduct or legislation to determine whether, in reality, it establishes a religion or religious faith or tends to do so. In the line-drawing process called for in each case, it has often been found useful to inquire whether the challenged law or conduct has a secular purpose, whether its principal or primary effect is to advance or inhibit religion, and whether it creates an excessive entanglement of government with religion. But this Court has been unwilling to be confined to any single test or criterion in this sensitive area. Pp. 8–9.

(e) Here, the focus of the inquiry must be on the crèche in the context of the Christmas season. Focus exclusively on the religious component of any activity would inevitably lead to its invalidation under the Establishment Clause. Pp. 9–10.

(f) Based on the record in this case, the city has a secular purpose for including the crèche in its Christmas display and has not impermissibly advanced religion or created an excessive entanglement between religion and government. The display is sponsored by the city to celebrate the Holiday recognized by Congress and national tradition and to depict the origins of that Holiday; these are legitimate secular purposes. Whatever benefit to one faith or religion or to all religions inclusion of the crèche in the display effects is indirect, remote, and incidental, and is no more an advancement or endorsement of religion than the congressional and executive recognition of the origins of Christmas, or the exhibition of religious paintings in governmentally supported museums. This Court is unable to discern a greater aid to religion from the inclusion of the crèche than from the substantial benefits previously held not violative of the Establishment Clause. As to administrative entanglement, there is no evidence of contact with church authorities concerning the content or design of the exhibition prior to or since the city's purchase of the crèche. No expenditures for maintenance of the crèche have been necessary, and, since the city owns the crèche, now valued at $200, the tangible material it contributes is de minimis. Political divisiveness alone cannot serve to invalidate otherwise permissible conduct, and, in any event, apart from the instant litigation, there is no evidence of political friction

Syllabus

or divisiveness over the crèche in the 40-year history of the city's Christ-mas celebration. Pp. 10–15.

(g) It would be ironic if the inclusion of the crèche in the display, as part of a celebration of an event acknowledged in the Western World for 20 centuries, and in this country by the people, the Executive Branch, Congress, and the courts for 2 centuries, would so "taint" the exhibition as to render it violative of the Establishment Clause. To forbid the use of this one passive symbol while hymns and carols are sung and played in public places including schools, and while Congress and state legislatures open public sessions with prayers, would be an overreaction contrary to our history and our holdings. Pp. 15–16.

691 F. 2d 1029, reversed.

BURGER, C. J., delivered the opinion of the Court, in which WHITE, POWELL, REHNQUIST, and O'CONNOR, JJ., joined. O'CONNOR, J., filed a concurring opinion. BRENNAN, J., filed a dissenting opinion, in which MARSHALL, BLACKMUN, and STEVENS, JJ., joined. BLACKMUN, J., filed a dissenting opinion, in which STEVENS, J., joined.

SUPREME COURT OF THE UNITED STATES

No. 82–1256

DENNIS LYNCH, ETC., ET AL., PETITIONERS v. DANIEL DONNELLY ET AL.

ON WRIT OF CERTIORARI TO THE UNITED STATES COURT OF APPEALS FOR THE FIRST CIRCUIT

[March 5, 1984]

THE CHIEF JUSTICE delivered the opinion of the Court.

We granted certiorari to decide whether the Establishment Clause of the First Amendment prohibits a municipality from including a crèche, or Nativity scene, in its annual Christmas display.

I

Each year, in cooperation with the downtown retail merchants' association, the City of Pawtucket, Rhode Island, erects a Christmas display as part of its observance of the Christmas holiday season. The display is situated in a park owned by a nonprofit organization and located in the heart of the shopping district. The display is essentially like those to be found in hundreds of towns or cities across the Nation—often on public grounds—during the Christmas season. The Pawtucket display comprises many of the figures and decorations traditionally associated with Christmas, including, among other things, a Santa Claus house, reindeer pulling Santa's sleigh, candy-striped poles, a Christmas tree, carolers, cutout figures representing such characters as a clown, an elephant, and a teddy bear, hundreds of colored lights, a large banner that reads "SEASONS GREETINGS," and the creche at issue here. All components of this display are owned by the City.

The creche, which has been included in the display for 40 or more years, consists of the traditional figures, including the

506

Infant Jesus, Mary and Joseph, angels, shepherds, kings, and animals, all ranging in height from 5″ to 5′. In 1973, when the present crèche was acquired, it cost the City $1365; it now is valued at $200. The erection and dismantling of the crèche costs the City about $20 per year; nominal expenses are incurred in lighting the crèche. No money has been expended on its maintenance for the past 10 years.

Respondents, Pawtucket residents and individual members of the Rhode Island affiliate of the American Civil Liberties Union, and the affiliate itself, brought this action in the United States District Court for Rhode Island, challenging the City's inclusion of the crèche in the annual display. The District Court held that the City's inclusion of the crèche in the display violates the Establishment Clause, *Donnelly* v. *Lynch*, 525 F. Supp. 1150, 1178 (D R. I. 1981), which is binding on the states through the Fourteenth Amendment. The District Court found that, by including the crèche in the Christmas display, the City has "tried to endorse and promulgate religious beliefs," 525 F. Supp., at 1173, and that "erection of the crèche has the real and substantial effect of affiliating the City with the Christian beliefs that the crèche represents." *Id.*, at 1177. This "appearance of official sponsorship," it believed, "confers more than a remote and incidental benefit on Christianity." *Id.*, at 1178. Last, although the court acknowledged the absence of administrative entanglement, it found that excessive entanglement has been fostered as a result of the political divisiveness of including the crèche in the celebration. *Id.*, at 1179–1180. The City was permanently enjoined from including the crèche in the display.

A divided panel of the Court of Appeals for the First Circuit affirmed. *Donnelly* v. *Lynch*, 691 F. 2d 1029 (1982). We granted certiorari, —— U. S. —— (1983), and we reverse.

II

A

This Court has explained that the purpose of the Establishment and Free Exercise Clauses of the First Amendment is

> "to prevent, as far as possible, the intrusion of either [the church or the state] into the precincts of the other." *Lemon* v. *Kurtzman*, 403 U. S. 602, 614 (1971).

At the same time, however, the Court has recognized that

> "total separation is not possible in an absolute sense. Some relationship between government and religious organizations is inevitable." *Ibid.*

In every Establishment Clause case, we must reconcile the inescapable tension between the objective of preventing unnecessary intrusion of either the church or the state upon the other, and the reality that, as the Court has so often noted, total separation of the two is not possible.

The Court has sometimes described the Religion Clauses as erecting a "wall" between church and state, see, *e. g.*, *Everson* v. *Board of Education*, 330 U. S. 1, 18 (1947). The concept of a "wall" of separation is a useful figure of speech probably deriving from views of Thomas Jefferson.[1] The metaphor has served as a reminder that the Establishment Clause forbids an established church or anything approaching it. But the metaphor itself is not a wholly accurate description of the practical aspects of the relationship that in fact exists between church and state.

No significant segment of our society and no institution within it can exist in a vacuum or in total or absolute isolation from all the other parts, much less from government. "It has never been thought either possible or desirable to enforce a regime of total separation. . . ." *Committee for Public*

---

[1] See *Reynolds* v. *United States*, 98 U. S. 145, 164 (1878) (quoting reply from Thomas Jefferson to an address by a committee of the Danbury Baptist Association (January 1, 1802)).

Education & Religious Liberty v. *Nyquist*, 413 U. S. 756, 760 (1973). Nor does the Constitution require complete separation of church and state; it affirmatively mandates accommodation, not merely tolerance, of all religions, and forbids hostility toward any. See, *e. g.*, *Zorach* v. *Clauson*, 343 U. S. 306, 314, 315 (1952); *McCollum* v. *Board of Education*, 333 U. S. 203, 211 (1948). Anything less would require the "callous indifference" we have said was never intended by the Establishment Clause. *Zorach, supra*, at 314. Indeed, we have observed, such hostility would bring us into "war with our national tradition as embodied in the First Amendment's guaranty of the free exercise of religion." *McCollum, supra*, at 211–212.

B

The Court's interpretation of the Establishment Clause has comported with what history reveals was the contemporaneous understanding of its guarantees. A significant example of the contemporaneous understanding of that Clause is found in the events of the first week of the First Session of the First Congress in 1789. In the very week that Congress approved the Establishment Clause as part of the Bill of Rights for submission to the states, it enacted legislation providing for paid chaplains for the House and Senate. In *Marsh* v. *Chambers*, —— U. S. —— (1983), we noted that seventeen Members of that First Congress had been Delegates to the Constitutional Convention where freedom of speech, press and religion and antagonism toward an established church were subjects of frequent discussion. We saw no conflict with the Establishment Clause when Nebraska employed members of the clergy as official Legislative Chaplains to give opening prayers at sessions of the state legislature. *Id.*, at ——.

The interpretation of the Establishment Clause by Congress in 1789 takes on special significance in light of the Court's emphasis that the First Congress "was a Congress whose constitutional decisions have always been regarded, as they should be regarded, as of the greatest weight in the interpretation of that fundamental instument," *Myers* v. *United States*, 272 U. S. 52, 174–175 (1926).

It is clear that neither the seventeen draftsmen of the Constitution who were Members of the First Congress, nor the Congress of 1789, saw any establishment problem in the employment of congressional Chaplains to offer daily prayers in the Congress, a practice that has continued for nearly two centuries. It would be difficult to identify a more striking example of the accommodation of religious belief intended by the Framers.

C

There is an unbroken history of official acknowledgment by all three branches of government of the role of religion in American life from at least 1789. Seldom in our opinions was this more affirmatively expressed than in Justice Douglas' opinion for the Court validating a program allowing release of public school students from classes to attend off-campus religious exercises. Rejecting a claim that the program violated the Establishment Clause, the Court asserted pointedly:

"We are a religious people whose institutions presuppose a Supreme Being." *Zorach* v. *Clauson, supra,* at 313.

See also *Abington School District* v. *Schempp,* 374 U. S. 203, 213 (1963).

Our history is replete with official references to the value and invocation of Divine guidance in deliberations and pronouncements of the Founding Fathers and contemporary leaders. Beginning in the early colonial period long before Independence, a day of Thanksgiving was celebrated as a religious holiday to give thanks for the bounties of Nature as gifts from God. President Washington and his successors proclaimed Thanksgiving, with all its religious overtones, a day of national celebration[2] and Congress made it a National Holiday more than a century ago. Ch. 167, 16 Stat. 168 (1870). That holiday has not lost its theme of expressing thanks for Divine aid[3] any more than has Christmas lost its religious significance.

Executive Orders and other official announcements of Presidents and of the Congress have proclaimed both Christmas and Thanksgiving National Holidays in religious terms. And, by Acts of Congress, it has long been the practice that

---

[2] The day after the First Amendment was proposed, Congress urged President Washington to proclaim "a day of public thanksgiving and prayer, to be observed by acknowledging with grateful hearts, the many and signal favours of Almighty God." See A. Stokes & L. Pfeffer, Church and State in the United States 87 (rev. 1st ed. 1964). President Washington proclaimed November 26, 1789, a day of thanksgiving to "offer[ ] our prayers and supplications to the Great Lord and Ruler of Nations, and beseech Him to pardon our national and other transgressions. . . ." 1 J. Richardson, A Compilation of the Messages and Papers of the Presidents 1789–1897 64 (1899).

Presidents Adams and Madison also issued thanksgiving proclamations, as have almost all our presidents, see 3 A. Stokes, Church and State in the United States 180–193 (1950), through the incumbent, see Proclamation No. 4883, 46 Fed. Reg. 56,153 (1981).

[3] An example is found in President Roosevelt's 1944 Proclamation of Thanksgiving:

"[I]t is fitting that we give thanks with special fervor to our Heavenly Father for the mercies we have received individually and as a nation and for the blessings He has restored, through the victories of our arms and those of our Allies, to His children in other lands.

.   .   .   .   .

To the end that we may bear more earnest witness to our gratitude to Almighty God, I suggest a nationwide reading of the Holy Scriptures during the period from Thanksgiving Day to Christmas." Proclamation No. 2629, 9 Fed. Reg. 13,099 (1944).

President Reagan and his immediate predecessors have issued similar proclamations. See, e. g., Proclamation No. 5098, 48 Fed. Reg. 42,801 (1983); Proclamation No. 4803, 45 Fed. Reg. 75,633 (1980); Proclamation No. 4333, 39 Fed. Reg. 40,003 (1974); Proclamation No. 4093, 36 Fed. Reg. 21,401 (1971); Proclamation No. 3752, 31 Fed. Reg. 13,635 (1966); Proclamation No. 3560, 28 Fed. Reg. 11,871 (1963).

federal employees are released from duties on these National Holidays, while being paid from the same public revenues that provide the compensation of the Chaplains of the Senate and the House and the military services. See J. Res. 5, 23 Stat. 516 (1885). Thus, it is clear that Government has long recognized—indeed it has subsidized—holidays with religious significance.

Other examples of reference to our religious heritage are found in the statutorily prescribed national motto "In God We Trust," 36 U. S. C. § 186, which Congress and the President mandated for our currency, see 31 U. S. C. § 324, and in the language "One nation under God," as part of the Pledge of Allegiance to the American flag. That pledge is recited by thousands of public school children—and adults—every year.

Art galleries supported by public revenues display religious paintings of the 15th and 16th centuries, predominantly inspired by one religious faith. The National Gallery in Washington, maintained with Government support, for example, has long exhibited masterpieces with religious messages, notably the Last Supper, and paintings depicting the Birth of Christ, the Crucifixion, and the Resurrection, among many others with explicit Christian themes and messages.[4] The very chamber in which oral arguments on this case were heard is decorated with a notable and permanent—not seasonal—symbol of religion: Moses with Ten Commandments. Congress has long provided chapels in the Capitol for religious worship and meditation.

There are countless other illustrations of the Government's acknowledgment of our religious heritage and governmental sponsorship of graphic manifestations of that heritage. Congress has directed the President to proclaim a National Day of Prayer each year "on which [day] the people of the United States may turn to God in prayer and meditation at churches, in groups, and as individuals." 36 U. S. C. § 169h. Our

---

[4] The National Gallery regularly exhibits more than 200 similar religious paintings.

Presidents have repeatedly issued such Proclamations.[5]
Presidential Proclamations and messages have also issued to
commemorate Jewish Heritage Week, Proclamation No.
4844, 46 Fed. Reg. 25,077 (1981), and the Jewish High Holy
Days, 17 Weekly Comp. Pres. Doc. 1058 (Sept. 29, 1981).
One cannot look at even this brief resume without finding
that our history is pervaded by expressions of religious beliefs such as are found in Zorach, supra. Equally pervasive
is the evidence of accommodation of all faiths and all forms of
religious expression, and hostility toward none. Through
this accommodation, as Justice Douglas observed, governmental action has "follow[ed] the best of our traditions" and
"respect[ed] the religious nature of our people." Id., at 314.

III

This history may help explain why the Court consistently
has declined to take a rigid, absolutist view of the Establishment Clause. We have refused "to construe the Religion
Clauses with a literalness that would undermine the ultimate
constitutional objective as illuminated by history." Walz v.
Tax Commission, 397 U. S. 664, 671 (1970) (Emphasis
added). In our modern, complex society, whose traditions
and constitutional underpinnings rest on and encourage diversity and pluralism in all areas, an absolutist approach in
applying the Establishment Clause is simplistic and has been
uniformly rejected by the Court.

Rather than mechanically invalidating all governmental
conduct or statutes that confer benefits or give special recognition to religion in general or to one faith—as an absolutist
approach would dictate—the Court has scrutinized challenged legislation or official conduct to determine whether, in
reality, it establishes a religion or religious faith, or tends to

---

[5] See, e. g., Proclamation No. 5017, 48 Fed. Reg. 4261 (1983); Proclamation No. 4795, 45 Fed. Reg. 62,969 (1980); Proclamation No. 4379, 40 Fed.
Reg. 25,429 (1975); Proclamation No. 4087, 36 Fed. Reg. 19,961 (1971);
Proclamation No. 3812, 32 Fed. Reg. 14,015 (1967); Proclamation No. 3501,
27 Fed. Reg. 10,147 (1962).

do so. See *Walz, supra*, at 669. Joseph Story wrote a century and a half ago:

> "The real object of the [First] Amendment was . . . to prevent any national ecclesiastical establishment, which should give to an hierarchy the exclusive patronage of the national government." 3 Story, Commentaries on the Constitution of the United States 728 (1833).

In each case, the inquiry calls for line drawing; no fixed, *per se* rule can be framed. The Establishment Clause like the Due Process Clauses is not a precise, detailed provision in a legal code capable of ready application. The purpose of the Establishment Clause "was to state an objective, not to write a statute." *Walz, supra*, at 668. The line between permissible relationships and those barred by the Clause can no more be straight and unwavering than due process can be defined in a single stroke or phrase or test. The Clause erects a "blurred, indistinct, and variable barrier depending on all the circumstances of a particular relationship." *Lemon, supra*, at 614.

In the line-drawing process we have often found it useful to inquire whether the challenged law or conduct has a secular purpose, whether its principal or primary effect is to advance or inhibit religion, and whether it creates an excessive entanglement of government with religion. *Lemon, supra*. But, we have repeatedly emphasized our unwillingness to be confined to any single test or criterion in this sensitive area. See *e. g. Tilton* v. *Richardson*, 403 U. S. 672, 677–678 (1971); *Nyquist, supra*, 413 U. S., at 773. In two cases, the Court did not even apply the *Lemon* "test." We did not, for example, consider that analysis relevant in *Marsh, supra*. Nor did we find *Lemon* useful in *Larson* v. *Valente*, 456 U. S. 228 (1982), where there was substantial evidence of overt discrimination against a particular church.

In this case, the focus of our inquiry must be on the crèche in the context of the Christmas season. See, *e. g.*, *Stone* v. *Graham*, 449 U. S. 39 (1980) *(per curiam); Abington School*

District v. *Schempp, supra.* In *Stone*, for example, we invalidated a state statute requiring the posting of a copy of the Ten Commandments on public classroom walls. But the Court carefully pointed out that the Commandments were posted purely as a religious admonition, not "integrated into the school curriculum, where the Bible may constitutionally be used in an appropriate study of history, civilization, ethics, comparative religion, or the like." 449 U. S., at 42. Similarly, in *Abington*, although the Court struck down the practices in two States requiring daily Bible readings in public schools, it specifically noted that nothing in the Court's holding was intended to "indicat[e] that such study of the Bible or of religion, when presented objectively as part of a secular program of education, may not be effected consistently with the First Amendment." 374 U. S., at 225. Focus exclusively on the religious component of any activity would inevitably lead to its invalidation under the Establishment Clause.

The Court has invalidated legislation or governmental action on the ground that a secular purpose was lacking, but only when it has concluded there was no question that the statute or activity was motivated wholly by religious considerations. See, *e. g., Stone* v. *Graham, supra,* at 41; *Epperson* v. *Arkansas,* 393 U. S. 97, 107–109 (1968); *Abington School District* v. *Schempp, supra,* at 223–224; *Engel* v. *Vitale,* 370 U. S. 421, 424–425 (1962). Even where the benefits to religion were substantial, as in *Everson, supra; Board of Education* v. *Allen,* 392 U. S. 236 (1968), *Walz, supra,* and *Tilton, supra,* we saw a secular purpose and no conflict with the Establishment Clause. Cf. *Larkin* v. *Grendel's Den,* 459 U. S. 116 (1983).

The District Court inferred from the religious nature of the crèche that the City has no secular purpose for the display. In so doing, it rejected the City's claim that its reasons for including the crèche are essentially the same as its reasons for sponsoring the display as a whole. The District Court

plainly erred by focusing almost exclusively on the crèche.
When viewed in the proper context of the Christmas Holiday
season, it is apparent that, on this record, there is insufficient
evidence to establish that the inclusion of the crèche is a purposeful or surreptitious effort to express some kind of subtle
governmental advocacy of a particular religious message.   In
a pluralistic society a variety of motives and purposes are implicated.   The City, like the Congresses and Presidents,
however, has principally taken note of a significant historical
religious event long celebrated in the Western World.   The
crèche in the display depicts the historical origins of this traditional event long recognized as a National Holiday.   See
Allen v. *Hickel*, 424 F. 2d 944 (CADC 1970); *Citizens Concerned for Separation of Church and State* v. *City and
County of Denver*, 526 F. Supp. 1310 (D Colo. 1981).

The narrow question is whether there is a secular purpose
for Pawtucket's display of the crèche.   The display is sponsored by the City to celebrate the Holiday and to depict the
origins of that Holiday.   These are legitimate secular purposes.[6]   The District Court's inference, drawn from the religious nature of the crèche, that the City has no secular purpose was, on this record, clearly erroneous.[7]

The District Court found that the primary effect of including the crèche is to confer a substantial and impermissible
benefit on religion in general and on the Christian faith in
particular.   Comparisons of the relative benefits to religion
of different forms of governmental support are elusive and

---

[6] The City contends that the purposes of the display are "exclusively
secular."   We hold only that Pawtucket has a secular purpose for its display, which is all that *Lemon* requires.   Were the test that the government must have "exclusively secular" objectives, much of the conduct and
legislation this Court has approved in the past would have been
invalidated.

[7] JUSTICE BRENNAN argues that the City's objectives could have been
achieved without including the crèche in the display, *post*, at 6.   True or
not, that is irrelevant.   The question is whether the display of the crèche
violates the Establishment Clause.

difficult to make. But to conclude that the primary effect of
including the crèche is to advance religion in violation of the
Establishment Clause would require that we view it as more
beneficial to and more an endorsement of religion, for example, than expenditure of large sums of public money for textbooks supplied throughout the country to students attending
church-sponsored schools, *Board of Education* v. *Allen,*
supra;[8] expenditure of public funds for transportation of students to church-sponsored schools, *Everson* v. *Board of Education, supra;*[9] federal grants for college buildings of church-
sponsored institutions of higher education combining secular
and religious education, *Tilton, supra;*[10] noncategorical
grants to church-sponsored colleges and universities, *Roemer*
v. *Board of Public Works,* 426 U. S. 736 (1976); and the tax
exemptions for church properties sanctioned in *Walz, supra.*
It would also require that we view it as more of an endorsement of religion than the Sunday Closing Laws upheld in
McGowan v. *Maryland,* 366 U. S. 420 (1961);[11] the release
time program for religious training in *Zorach, supra;* and the
legislative prayers upheld in *Marsh, supra.*

We are unable to discern a greater aid to religion deriving
from inclusion of the crèche than from these benefits and endorsements previously held not violative of the Establish-

---

[8] The *Allen* Court noted that "[p]erhaps free books make it more likely
that some children choose to attend a sectarian school. . . ."   392 U. S., at
244.

[9] In *Everson,* the Court acknowledged that "[i]t is undoubtedly true that
children are helped to get to church schools," and that "some of the children might not be sent to the church schools if the parents were compelled
to pay their children's bus fares out of their own pockets . . ."   330 U. S.,
at 17.

[10] We recognized in *Tilton* that the construction grants "surely aid[ed]"
the institutions that received them.   403 U. S., at 679.

[11] "In *McGowan* v. *Maryland* . . . Sunday Closing Laws were sustained
even though one of their undeniable effects was to render it somewhat
more likely that citizens would respect religious institutions and even attend religious services."   *Nyquist, supra,* at 776.

ment Clause. What was said about the legislative prayers in *Marsh, supra,* at ——, and implied about the Sunday Closing Laws in *McGowan* is true of the City's inclusion of the crèche: its "reason or effect merely happens to coincide or harmonize with the tenets of some . . . religions." See *McGowan, supra,* at 442.

This case differs significantly from *Larkin* v. *Grendel's Den, supra,* and *McCollum, supra,* where religion was substantially aided. In *Grendel's Den,* important governmental power—a licensing veto authority—had been vested in churches. In *McCollum,* government had made religious instruction available in public school classrooms; the State had not only used the public school buildings for the teaching of religion, it had "afford[ed] sectarian groups an invaluable aid . . . [by] provid[ing] pupils for their religious classes through use of the State's compulsory public school machinery." 333 U. S., at 212. No comparable benefit to religion is discernible here.

The dissent asserts some observers may perceive that the City has aligned itself with the Christian faith by including a Christian symbol in its display and that this serves to advance religion. We can assume, *arguendo,* that the display advances religion in a sense; but our precedents plainly contemplate that on occasion some advancement of religion will result from governmental action. The Court has made it abundantly clear, however, that "not every law that confers an 'indirect,' 'remote,' or 'incidental' benefit upon [religion] is, for that reason alone, constitutionally invalid." *Nyquist, supra,* at 771; see also *Widmar* v. *Vincent,* 454 U. S. 263, 273 (1981). Here, whatever benefit to one faith or religion or to all religions, is indirect, remote and incidental; display of the crèche is no more an advancement or endorsement of religion than the Congressional and Executive recognition of the origins of the Holiday itself as "Christ's Mass," or the exhibition of literally hundreds of religious paintings in governmentally supported museums.

The District Court found that there had been no administrative entanglement between religion and state resulting
from the City's ownership and use of the crèche.   525 F.
Supp., at 1179.   But it went on to hold that some political
divisiveness was engendered by this litigation.   Coupled
with its finding of an impermissible sectarian purpose and effect, this persuaded the court that there was "excessive entanglement."   The Court of Appeals expressly declined to
accept the District Court's finding that inclusion of the creche
has caused political divisiveness along religious lines, and
noted that this Court has never held that political divisiveness alone was sufficient to invalidate government conduct.

Entanglement is a question of kind and degree.   In this
case, however, there is no reason to disturb the District
Court's finding on the absence of administrative entanglement.   There is no evidence of contact with church authorities concerning the content or design of the exhibit prior to or
since Pawtucket's purchase of the crèche.   No expenditures
for maintenance of the crèche have been necessary; and since
the City owns the crèche, now valued at $200, the tangible
material it contributes is *de minimis*.   In many respects the
display requires far less ongoing, day-to-day interaction
between church and state than religious paintings in public
galleries.   There is nothing here, of course, like the "comprehensive, discriminating, and continuing state surveillance" or
the "enduring entanglement" present in *Lemon, supra,* at
619–622.

The Court of Appeals correctly observed that this Court
has not held that political divisiveness alone can serve to invalidate otherwise permissible conduct.   And we decline to
so hold today.   This case does not involve a direct subsidy to
church-sponsored schools or colleges, or other religious institutions, and hence no inquiry into potential political divisiveness is even called for, *Mueller* v. *Allen,* —— U. S. ——, 103
S. Ct. 3062, 3071, n. 11 (1983).   In any event, apart from this
litigation there is no evidence of political friction or divisive-

ness over the crèche in the 40-year history of Pawtucket's Christmas celebration.   The District Court stated that the inclusion of the crèche for the 40 years has been "marked by no apparent dissension" and that the display has had a "calm history."   525 F. Supp., at 1179.   Curiously, it went on to hold that the political divisiveness engendered by this lawsuit was evidence of excessive entanglement.   A litigant cannot, by the very act of commencing a lawsuit, however, create the appearance of divisiveness and then exploit it as evidence of entanglement.

We are satisfied that the City has a secular purpose for including the crèche, that the City has not impermissibly advanced religion, and that including the crèche does not create excessive entanglement between religion and government.

IV

JUSTICE BRENNAN describes the crèche as a "re-creation of an event that lies at the heart of Christian faith," *post*, at 15.   The crèche, like a painting, is passive; admittedly it is a reminder of the origins of Christmas.   Even the traditional, purely secular displays extant at Christmas, with or without a crèche, would inevitably recall the religious nature of the Holiday.   The display engenders a friendly community spirit of good will in keeping with the season.   The crèche may well have special meaning to those whose faith includes the celebration of religious masses, but none who sense the origins of the Christmas celebration would fail to be aware of its religious implications.   That the display brings people into the central city, and serves commercial interests and benefits merchants and their employees, does not, as the dissent points out, determine the character of the display.   That a prayer invoking Divine guidance in Congress is preceded and followed by debate and partisan conflict over taxes, budgets, national defense, and myriad mundane subjects, for example, has never been thought to demean or taint the sacredness of the invocation.[12]

Of course the crèche is identified with one religious faith but no more so than the examples we have set out from prior cases in which we found no conflict with the Establishment Clause. See, *e. g., McGowan, supra; Marsh, supra.* It would be ironic, however, if the inclusion of a single symbol of a particular historic religious event, as part of a celebration acknowledged in the Western World for 20 centuries, and in this country by the people, by the Executive Branch, by the Congress, and the courts for two centuries, would so "taint" the City's exhibit as to render it violative of the Establishment Clause. To forbid the use of this one passive symbol— the crèche—at the very time people are taking note of the season with Christmas hymns and carols in public schools and other public places, and while the Congress and Legislatures open sessions with prayers by paid chaplains would be a stilted over-reaction contrary to our history and to our holdings. If the presence of the crèche in this display violates the Establishment Clause, a host of other forms of taking official note of Christmas, and of our religious heritage, are equally offensive to the Constitution.

The Court has acknowledged that the "fears and political problems" that gave rise to the Religion Clauses in the 18th century are of far less concern today. *Everson, supra,* 330 U. S., at 8. We are unable to perceive the Archbishop of Canterbury, the Vicar of Rome, or other powerful religious leaders behind every public acknowledgment of the religious heritage long officially recognized by the three constitutional branches of government. Any notion that these symbols

---

[12] JUSTICE BRENNAN states that "by focusing on the holiday 'context' in which the crèche appear[s], the Court seeks to "explain away the clear religious import of the crèche," *post,* at 12, and that it has equated the crèche with a Santa's house or a talking wishing well, *post,* at 18. Of course this is not true.

pose a real danger of establishment of a state church is far-fetched indeed.

V

That this Court has been alert to the constitutionally expressed opposition to the establishment of religion is shown in numerous holdings striking down statutes or programs as violative of the Establishment Clause. See, *e. g.*, *McCollum* v. *Board of Education, supra; Epperson* v. *Arkansas, supra; Lemon, supra; Levitt* v. *Committee for Public Education*, 413 U. S. 472 (1973); *Nyquist, supra; Meek* v. *Pittenger*, 421 U. S. 349 (1975); and *Stone* v. *Graham, supra.* The most recent example of this careful scrutiny is found in the case invalidating a municipal ordinance granting to a church a virtual veto power over the licensing of liquor establishments near the church. *Grendel's Den, supra.* Taken together these cases abundantly demonstrate the Court's concern to protect the genuine objectives of the Establishment Clause. It is far too late in the day to impose a crabbed reading of the Clause on the country.

VI

We hold that, notwithstanding the religious significance of the crèche, the City of Pawtucket has not violated the Establishment Clause of the First Amendment.[13] Accordingly, the judgment of the Court of Appeals is reversed.

It is so ordered.

---

[13] The Court of Appeals viewed *Larson* v. *Valente*, 456 U. S. 228 (1982), as commanding a "strict scrutiny" due to the City's ownership of the $200 crèche which it considers as a discrimination between Christian and other religions. It is correct that we require strict scrutiny of a statute or practice patently discriminatory on its face. But we are unable to see this display, or any part of it, as explicitly discriminatory in the sense contemplated in *Larson.*

PART IV

RIGHTS OF THE ACCUSED

1. SOUTH DAKOTA v. OPPERMAN (1976).

2. BIVENS v. SIX UNKNOWN NAMED AGENTS OF FEDE-RAL BUREAU OF NARCOTICS (1971).

3. HARRIS v. NEW YORK (1971).

4. MORRISSEY et al. v. BREWER, WARDEN, et al. (1972).

5. UNITED STATES v. HENRY (1980).

6. LOCKETT v. OHIO (1978).

7. NIX, WARDEN OF THE IOWA STATE PENITENTIARY v. WILLIAMS (1984).

—oOo—

SOUTH DAKOTA *v.* OPPERMAN

CERTIORARI TO THE SUPREME COURT OF SOUTH DAKOTA

No. 75–76.   Argued March 29, 1976—Decided July 6, 1976

After respondent's car had been impounded for multiple parking violations the police, following standard procedures, inventoried the contents of the car. In doing so they discovered marihuana in the glove compartment, for the possession of which respondent was subsequently arrested. His motion to suppress the evidence yielded by the warrantless inventory search was denied, and respondent was thereafter convicted. The State Supreme Court reversed, concluding that the evidence had been obtained in violation of the Fourth Amendment as made applicable to the States by the Fourteenth. *Held:* The police procedures followed in this case did not involve an "unreasonable" search in violation of the Fourth Amendment. The expectation of privacy in one's automobile is significantly less than that relating to one's home or office, *Cardwell* v. *Lewis,* 417 U. S. 583, 590. When vehicles are impounded, police routinely follow caretaking procedures by securing and inventorying the cars' contents. These procedures have been widely sustained as reasonable under the Fourth Amendment. This standard practice was followed here, and there is no suggestion of any investigatory motive on the part of the police. Pp. 367–376.

89 S. D. ——, 228 N. W. 2d 152, reversed and remanded.

BURGER, C. J., delivered the opinion of the Court, in which BLACKMUN, POWELL, REHNQUIST, and STEVENS, JJ., joined. POWELL, J., filed a concurring opinion, *post,* p. 376. WHITE, J., filed a dissenting statement, *post,* p. 396. MARSHALL, J., filed a dissenting opinion, in which BRENNAN and STEWART, JJ., joined, *post,* p. 384.

William J. Janklow, Attorney General of South Dakota, argued the cause for petitioner. With him on the brief was *Earl R. Mettler,* Assistant Attorney General.

Robert C. Ulrich, by appointment of the Court, 423

U. S. 1012, argued the cause for respondent *pro hac vice.*
With him on the brief were *Lee M. McCahren* and
*John F. Hagemann.**

MR. CHIEF JUSTICE BURGER delivered the opinion of
the Court.

We review the judgment of the Supreme Court of
South Dakota, holding that local police violated the
Fourth Amendment to the Federal Constitution, as applicable to the States under the Fourteenth Amendment,
when they conducted a routine inventory search of an
automobile lawfully impounded by police for violations
of municipal parking ordinances.

(1)

Local ordinances prohibit parking in certain areas of
downtown Vermillion, S. D., between the hours of 2 a. m.
and 6 a. m. During the early morning hours of December 10, 1973, a Vermillion police officer observed respondent's unoccupied vehicle illegally parked in the restricted
zone. At approximately 3 a. m., the officer issued an
overtime parking ticket and placed it on the car's wind-
shield. The citation warned:

> "Vehicles in violation of any parking ordinance
> may be towed from the area."

At approximately 10 o'clock on the same morning, an-

---

*Briefs of *amici curiae* urging reversal were filed by *Evelle J.
Younger,* Attorney General, *Jack R. Winkler,* Chief Assistant Attorney General, *S. Clark Moore,* Assistant Attorney General, and
Kent L. Richland and *Robert R. Anderson,* Deputy Attorneys General, for the State of California; by *Theodore L. Sendak,* Attorney
General, and *Donald P. Bogard,* Executive Assistant Attorney General, for the State of Indiana; by *Toney Anaya,* Attorney General,
and *Warren O. F. Harris,* Deputy Attorney General, for the State
of New Mexico; and by *Wayne W. Schmidt* for Americans for Effective Law Enforcement, Inc.

other officer issued a second ticket for an overtime parking violation. These circumstances were routinely reported to police headquarters, and after the vehicle was inspected, the car was towed to the city impound lot.

From outside the car at the impound lot, a police officer observed a watch on the dashboard and other items of personal property located on the back seat and back floorboard. At the officer's direction, the car door was then unlocked and, using a standard inventory form pursuant to standard police procedures, the officer inventoried the contents of the car, including the contents of the glove compartment, which was unlocked. There he found marihuana contained in a plastic bag. All items, including the contraband, were removed to the police department for safekeeping.[1] During the late afternoon of December 10, respondent appeared at the police department to claim his property. The marihuana was retained by police.

Respondent was subsequently arrested on charges of possession of marihuana. His motion to suppress the evidence yielded by the inventory search was denied; he was convicted after a jury trial and sentenced to a fine of $100 and 14 days' incarceration in the county jail. On appeal, the Supreme Court of South Dakota reversed

---

[1] At respondent's trial, the officer who conducted the inventory testified as follows:

"Q. And why did you inventory this car?

"A. Mainly for safekeeping, because we have had a lot of trouble in the past of people getting into the impound lot and breaking into cars and stealing stuff out of them.

"Q. Do you know whether the vehicles that were broken into . . . were locked or unlocked?

"A. Both of them were locked, they would be locked." Record 74.

In describing the impound lot, the officer stated:

"A. It's the old county highway yard. It has a wooden fence partially around part of it, and kind of a dilapidated wire fence, a makeshift fence." *Id.*, at 73.

the conviction. 89 S. D. ——, 228 N. W. 2d 152. The court concluded that the evidence had been obtained in violation of the Fourth Amendment prohibition against unreasonable searches and seizures. We granted certiorari, 423 U. S. 923 (1975), and we reverse.

(2)

This Court has traditionally drawn a distinction between automobiles and homes or offices in relation to the Fourth Amendment. Although automobiles are "effects" and thus within the reach of the Fourth Amendment, *Cady* v. *Dombrowski,* 413 U. S. 433, 439 (1973), warrantless examinations of automobiles have been upheld in circumstances in which a search of a home or office would not. *Cardwell* v. *Lewis,* 417 U. S. 583, 589 (1974); *Cady* v. *Dombrowski, supra,* at 439–440; *Chambers* v. *Maroney,* 399 U. S. 42, 48 (1970).

The reason for this well-settled distinction is twofold. First, the inherent mobility of automobiles creates circumstances of such exigency that, as a practical necessity, rigorous enforcement of the warrant requirement is impossible. *Carroll* v. *United States,* 267 U. S. 132, 153–154 (1925); *Coolidge* v. *New Hampshire,* 403 U. S. 443, 459–460 (1971). But the Court has also upheld warrantless searches where no immediate danger was presented that the car would be removed from the jurisdiction. *Chambers* v. *Maroney, supra,* at 51–52; *Cooper* v. *California,* 386 U. S. 58 (1967). Besides the element of mobility, less rigorous warrant requirements govern because the expectation of privacy with respect to one's automobile is significantly less than that relating to one's home or office.[2] In discharging their varied re-

---

[2] In *Camara* v. *Municipal Court,* 387 U. S. 523 (1967), and *See* v. *City of Seattle,* 387 U. S. 541 (1967), the Court held that a warrant was required to effect an unconsented administrative entry

sponsibilities for ensuring the public safety, law enforcement officials are necessarily brought into frequent contact with automobiles.   Most of this contact is distinctly noncriminal in nature.   *Cady* v. *Dombrowski, supra,* at 442.   Automobiles, unlike homes, are subjected to pervasive and continuing governmental regulation and controls, including periodic inspection and licensing requirements.   As an everyday occurrence, police stop and examine vehicles when license plates or inspection stickers have expired, or if other violations, such as exhaust fumes or excessive noise, are noted, or if headlights or other safety equipment are not in proper working order.

The expectation of privacy as to automobiles is further diminished by the obviously public nature of automobile travel.   Only two Terms ago, the Court noted:

"One has a lesser expectation of privacy in a motor vehicle because its function is transportation and it seldom serves as one's residence or as the repository of personal effects. . . . It travels public thoroughfares where both its occupants and its contents are in plain view." *Cardwell* v. *Lewis, supra,* at 590.

In the interests of public safety and as part of what the Court has called "community caretaking functions," *Cady* v. *Dombrowski, supra,* at 441, automobiles are frequently taken into police custody.   Vehicle accidents present one such occasion.   To permit the uninterrupted flow of traffic and in some circumstances to preserve evidence, disabled or damaged vehicles will often be removed from the highways or streets at the behest of police engaged solely in caretaking and traffic-control activi-

---

into and inspection of private dwellings or commercial premises to ascertain health or safety conditions. In contrast, this procedure has never been held applicable to automobile inspections for safety purposes.

ties. Police will also frequently remove and impound automobiles which violate parking ordinances and which thereby jeopardize both the public safety and the efficient movement of vehicular traffic.[3] The authority of police to seize and remove from the streets vehicles impeding traffic or threatening public safety and convenience is beyond challenge.

When vehicles are impounded, local police departments generally follow a routine practice of securing and inventorying the automobiles' contents. These procedures developed in response to three distinct needs: the protection of the owner's property while it remains in police custody, *United States* v. *Mitchell,* 458 F. 2d 960, 961 (CA9 1972); the protection of the police against claims or disputes over lost or stolen property, *United States* v. *Kelehar,* 470 F. 2d 176, 178 (CA5 1972); and the protection of the police from potential danger, *Cooper* v. *California, supra,* at 61–62. The practice has been viewed as essential to respond to incidents of theft or vandalism. See *Cabbler* v. *Commonwealth,* 212 Va. 520, 522, 184 S. E. 2d 781, 782 (1971), cert. denied, 405 U. S. 1073 (1972); *Warrix* v. *State,* 50 Wis. 2d 368, 376, 184 N. W. 2d 189, 194 (1971). In addition, police frequently attempt to determine whether a vehicle has been stolen and thereafter abandoned.

These caretaking procedures have almost uniformly been upheld by the state courts, which by virtue of the localized nature of traffic regulation have had considerable occasion to deal with the issue.[4] Applying the

---

[3] The New York Court of Appeals has noted that in New York City alone, 108,332 cars were towed away for traffic violations during 1969. *People* v. *Sullivan,* 29 N. Y. 2d 69, 71, 272 N. E. 2d 464, 465 (1971).

[4] In contrast to state officials engaged in everyday caretaking functions:

"The contact with vehicles by federal law enforcement officers

Fourth Amendment standard of "reasonableness," [5] the state courts have overwhelmingly concluded that, even if an inventory is characterized as a "search," [6] the

usually, if not always, involves the detection or investigation of crimes unrelated to the operation of a vehicle." *Cady* v. *Dombrowski*, 413 U. S. 433, 440 (1973).

[5] In analyzing the issue of reasonableness *vel non*, the courts have not sought to determine whether a protective inventory was justified by "probable cause." The standard of probable cause is peculiarly related to criminal investigations, not routine, noncriminal procedures. See generally Note, Warrantless Searches and Seizures of Automobiles, 87 Harv. L. Rev. 835, 850–851 (1974). The probable-cause approach is unhelpful when analysis centers upon the reasonableness of routine administrative caretaking functions, particularly when no claim is made that the protective procedures are a subterfuge for criminal investigations.

In view of the noncriminal context of inventory searches, and the inapplicability in such a setting of the requirement of probable cause, courts have held—and quite correctly—that search warrants are not required, linked as the warrant requirement textually is to the probable-cause concept. We have frequently observed that the warrant requirement assures that legal inferences and conclusions as to probable cause will be drawn by a neutral magistrate unrelated to the criminal investigative-enforcement process. With respect to noninvestigative police inventories of automobiles lawfully within governmental custody, however, the policies underlying the warrant requirement, to which MR. JUSTICE POWELL refers, are inapplicable.

[6] Given the benign noncriminal context of the intrusion, see *Wyman* v. *James*, 400 U. S. 309, 317 (1971), some courts have concluded that an inventory does not constitute a search for Fourth Amendment purposes. See, *e. g., People* v. *Sullivan, supra*, at 77, 272 N. E. 2d, at 469; *People* v. *Willis*, 46 Mich. App. 436, 208 N. W. 2d 204 (1973); *State* v. *Wallen*, 185 Neb. 44, 49–50, 173 N. W. 2d 372, 376, cert. denied, 399 U. S. 912 (1970). Other courts have expressed doubts as to whether the intrusion is classifiable as a search. *State* v. *All*, 17 N. C. App. 284, 286, 193 S. E. 2d 770, 772, cert. denied, 414 U. S. 866 (1973). Petitioner, however, has expressly abandoned the contention that the inventory in this case is exempt from the Fourth Amendment standard of reasonableness. Tr. of Oral Arg. 5.

intrusion is constitutionally permissible. See, *e. g., City of St. Paul* v. *Myles,* 298 Minn. 298, 300–301, 218 N. W. 2d 697, 699 (1974); *State* v. *Tully,* 166 Conn. 126, 136, 348 A. 2d 603, 609 (1974); *People* v. *Trusty,* 183 Colo. 291, 296–297, 516 P. 2d 423, 425–426 (1973); *People* v. *Sullivan,* 29 N. Y. 2d 69, 73, 272 N. E. 2d 464, 466 (1971); *Cabbler* v. *Commonwealth, supra; Warrix* v. *State, supra; State* v. *Wallen,* 185 Neb. 44, 173 N. W. 2d 372, cert. denied, 399 U. S. 912 (1970); *State* v. *Criscola,* 21 Utah 2d 272, 444 P. 2d 517 (1968); *State* v. *Montague,* 73 Wash. 2d 381, 438 P. 2d 571 (1968); *People* v. *Clark,* 32 Ill. App. 3d 898, 336 N. E. 2d 892 (1975); *State* v. *Achter,* 512 S. W. 2d 894 (Mo. Ct. App. 1974); *Bennett* v. *State,* 507 P. 2d 1252 (Okla. Crim. App. 1973); *People* v. *Willis,* 46 Mich. App. 436, 208 N. W. 2d 204 (1973); *State* v. *All,* 17 N. C. App. 284, 193 S. E. 2d 770, cert. denied, 414 U. S. 866 (1973); *Godbee* v. *State,* 224 So. 2d 441 (Fla. Dist. Ct. App. 1969). Even the seminal state decision relied on by the South Dakota Supreme Court in reaching the contrary result, *Mozzetti* v. *Superior Court,* 4 Cal. 3d 699, 484 P. 2d 84 (1971), expressly approved police caretaking activities resulting in the securing of property within the officer's plain view.

The majority of the Federal Courts of Appeals have likewise sustained inventory procedures as reasonable police intrusions. As Judge Wisdom has observed:

> "[W]hen the police take custody of any sort of container [such as] an automobile . . . it is reasonable to search the container to itemize the property to be held by the police. [This reflects] the underlying principle that the fourth amendment proscribes only *unreasonable* searches." *United States* v. *Gravitt,* 484 F. 2d 375, 378 (CA5 1973), cert. denied, 414 U. S. 1135 (1974) (emphasis in original).

See also *Cabbler* v. *Superintendent,* 528 F. 2d 1142 (CA4 1975), cert. pending, No. 75–1463; *Barker* v. *Johnson,* 484 F. 2d 941 (CA6 1973); *United States* v. *Mitchell,* 458 F. 2d 960 (CA9 1972); *United States* v. *Lipscomb,* 435 F. 2d 795 (CA5 1970), cert. denied, 401 U. S. 980 (1971); *United States* v. *Pennington,* 441 F. 2d 249 (CA5), cert. denied, 404 U. S. 854 (1971); *United States* v. *Boyd,* 436 F. 2d 1203 (CA5 1971); *Cotton* v. *United States,* 371 F. 2d 385 (CA9 1967). Accord, *Lowe* v. *Hopper,* 400 F. Supp. 970, 976–977 (SD Ga. 1975); *United States* v. *Spitalieri,* 391 F. Supp. 167, 169–170 (ND Ohio 1975); *United States* v. *Smith,* 340 F. Supp. 1023 (Conn. 1972); *United States* v. *Fuller,* 277 F. Supp. 97 (DC 1967), conviction aff'd, 139 U. S. App. D. C. 375, 433 F. 2d 533 (1970). These cases have recognized that standard inventories often include an examination of the glove compartment, since it is a customary place for documents of ownership and registration, *United States* v. *Pennington, supra,* at 251, as well as a place for the temporary storage of valuables.

(3)

The decisions of this Court point unmistakably to the conclusion reached by both federal and state courts that inventories pursuant to standard police procedures are reasonable. In the first such case, Mr. Justice Black made plain the nature of the inquiry before us:

> "But the question here is not whether the search was *authorized* by state law. The question is rather whether the search was *reasonable* under the Fourth Amendment." *Cooper* v. *California,* 386 U. S., at 61 (emphasis added).

And, in his last writing on the Fourth Amendment, Mr. Justice Black said:

> "[T]he Fourth Amendment does not require that every search be made pursuant to a warrant. It

prohibits only '*unreasonable* searches and seizures.'
The relevant test *is not the reasonableness of the*
opportunity to procure a warrant, but the reasonableness of the seizure under all the circumstances.
The test of reasonableness cannot be fixed by *per se*
rules; each case must be decided on its own facts."
Coolidge v. *New Hampshire,* 403 U. S., at 509–510
(concurring and dissenting) (emphasis added).

In applying the reasonableness standard adopted by
the Framers, this Court has consistently sustained police
intrusions into automobiles impounded or otherwise in
lawful police custody where the process is aimed at securing or protecting the car and its contents. In *Cooper* v.
California, supra, the Court upheld the inventory of a
car impounded under the authority of a state forfeiture
statute. Even though the inventory was conducted in
a distinctly criminal setting [7] and carried out a week
after the car had been impounded, the Court nonetheless found that the car search, including examination of
the glove compartment where contraband was found, was
reasonable under the circumstances. This conclusion
was reached despite the fact that no warrant had issued
and probable cause to search for the contraband in the
vehicle had not been established. The Court said in
language explicitly applicable here:

> "It would be unreasonable to hold that the police,
> having to retain the car in their custody for such
> a length of time, had no right, even for their own
> protection, to search it."   386 U. S., at 61–62.[8]

---

[7] In *Cooper,* the owner had been arrested on narcotics charges,
and the car was taken into custody pursuant to the state forfeiture
statute. The search was conducted several months before the forfeiture proceedings were actually instituted.

[8] There was, of course, no certainty at the time of the search
that forfeiture proceedings would ever be held. Accordingly, there

In the following Term, the Court in *Harris* v. *United States,* 390 U. S. 234 (1968), upheld the introduction of evidence, seized by an officer who, after conducting an inventory search of a car and while taking means to safeguard it, observed a car registration card lying on the metal stripping of the car door.   Rejecting the argument that a warrant was necessary, the Court held that the intrusion was justifiable since it was "taken to protect the car while it was in police custody."   *Id.,* at 236.[9]

Finally, in *Cady* v. *Dombrowski, supra,* the Court upheld a warrantless search of an automobile towed to a private garage even though no probable cause existed to believe that the vehicle contained fruits of a crime.   The sole justification for the warrantless incursion was that it was incident to the caretaking function of the local police to protect the community's safety.   Indeed, the protective search was instituted solely because local police "were under the impression" that the incapacitated driver, a Chicago police officer, was required to carry his service revolver at all times; the police had reasonable grounds to believe a weapon might be in the car, and thus available to vandals.   413 U. S., at 436.   The Court carefully noted that the protective search was

---

was no reason for the police to assume automatically that the automobile would eventually be forfeited to the State.   Indeed, as the California Court of Appeal stated, "[T]he instant record nowhere discloses that forfeiture proceedings were instituted in respect to defendant's car . . . ."   *People* v. *Cooper,* 234 Cal. App. 2d 587, 596, 44 Cal. Rptr. 483, 489 (1965).   No reason would therefore appear to limit *Cooper* to an impoundment pursuant to a forfeiture statute.

[9] The Court expressly noted that the legality of the inventory was not presented, since the evidence was discovered at the point when the officer was taking protective measures to secure the automobile from the elements.   But the Court clearly held that the officer acted properly in opening the car for protective reasons.

carried out in accordance with *standard procedures* in the local police department, *ibid.*, a factor tending to ensure that the intrusion would be limited in scope to the extent necessary to carry out the caretaking function. See *United States* v. *Spitalieri*, 391 F. Supp., at 169. In reaching this result, the Court in *Cady* distinguished *Preston* v. *United States*, 376 U. S. 364 (1964), on the grounds that the holding, invalidating a car search conducted after a vagrancy arrest, "stands only for the proposition that the search challenged there could not be justified as one incident to an arrest." 413 U. S., at 444. *Preston* therefore did not raise the issue of the constitutionality of a protective inventory of a car lawfully within police custody.

The holdings in *Cooper, Harris,* and *Cady* point the way to the correct resolution of this case. None of the three cases, of course, involves the precise situation presented here; but, as in all Fourth Amendment cases, we are obliged to look to all the facts and circumstances of this case in light of the principles set forth in these prior decisions.

> "[W]hether a search and seizure is unreasonable within the meaning of the Fourth Amendment depends upon the facts and circumstances of each case . . . ." *Cooper* v. *California*, 386 U. S., at 59.

The Vermillion police were indisputably engaged in a caretaking search of a lawfully impounded automobile. Cf. *United States* v. *Lawson*, 487 F. 2d 468, 471 (CA8 1973). The inventory was conducted only after the car had been impounded for multiple parking violations. The owner, having left his car illegally parked for an extended period, and thus subject to impoundment, was not present to make other arrangements for the safekeeping of his belongings. The inventory itself was prompted by the presence in plain view of a number of valuables inside the car. As in *Cady,* there is no suggestion whatever that this standard procedure, essentially like that followed throughout the country, was a pretext concealing an investigatory police motive.[10]

On this record we conclude that in following standard police procedures, prevailing throughout the country and approved by the overwhelming majority of courts, the conduct of the police was not "unreasonable" under the Fourth Amendment.

The judgment of the South Dakota Supreme Court is therefore reversed, and the case is remanded for further proceedings not inconsistent with this opinion.

Reversed and remanded.

---

[10]The inventory was not unreasonable in scope. Respondent's motion to suppress in state court challenged the inventory only as to items inside the car not in plain view. But once the policeman was lawfully inside the car to secure the personal property in plain view, it was not unreasonable to open the unlocked glove compartment, to which vandals would have had ready and unobstructed access once inside the car.

The "consent" theory advanced by the dissent rests on the assumption that the inventory is exclusively for the protection of the car owner. It is not. The protection of the municipality and public officers from claims of lost or stolen property and the protection of the public from vandals who might find a firearm, *Cady v. Dombrowski,* or as here, contraband drugs, are also crucial.

BIVENS v. SIX UNKNOWN NAMED AGENTS OF FEDERAL BUREAU OF NARCOTICS

CERTIORARI TO THE UNITED STATES COURT OF APPEALS FOR THE SECOND CIRCUIT

No. 301. Argued January 12, 1971—Decided June 21, 1971

Petitioner's complaint alleged that respondent agents of the Federal Bureau of Narcotics, acting under color of federal authority, made a warrantless entry of his apartment, searched the apartment, and arrested him on narcotics charges. All of the acts were alleged to have been done without probable cause. Petitioner's suit to recover damages from the agents was dismissed by the District Court on the alternative grounds (1) that it failed to state a federal cause of action and (2) that respondents were immune from suit by virtue of their official position. The Court of Appeals affirmed on the first ground alone. *Held:*

1. Petitioner's complaint states a federal cause of action under the Fourth Amendment for which damages are recoverable upon proof of injuries resulting from the federal agents' violation of that Amendment. Pp. 390–397.

2. The Court does not reach the immunity question, which was not passed on by the Court of Appeals. Pp. 397–398.

409 F. 2d 718, reversed and remanded.

BRENNAN, J., delivered the opinion of the Court, in which DOUGLAS, STEWART, WHITE, and MARSHALL, JJ., joined. HARLAN, J., filed an opinion concurring in the judgment, *post,* p. 398. BURGER, C. J., *post,* p. 411, BLACK, J., *post,* p. 427, and BLACKMUN, J., *post,* p. 430, filed dissenting opinions.

Stephen A. Grant argued the cause and filed a brief for petitioner.

Jerome Feit argued the cause for respondents. On the brief were *Solicitor General Griswold, Assistant Attorney General Ruckelshaus,* and *Robert V. Zener.*

Melvin L. Wulf filed a brief for the American Civil Liberties Union as *amicus curiae* urging reversal.

MR. CHIEF JUSTICE BURGER, dissenting.

I dissent from today's holding which judicially creates
a damage remedy not provided for by the Constitution
and not enacted by Congress. We would more surely
preserve the important values of the doctrine of separa-

tion of powers—and perhaps get a better result—by recommending a solution to the Congress as the branch of
government in which the Constitution has vested the
legislative power. Legislation is the business of the
Congress, and it has the facilities and competence for that
task—as we do not. Professor Thayer, speaking of the
limits on judicial power, albeit in another context, had
this to say: [1]

> "And if it be true that the holders of legislative
> power are careless or evil, yet the constitutional duty
> of the court remains untouched; it cannot rightly
> attempt to protect the people, by undertaking a
> function not its own. On the other hand, by adher-
> ing rigidly to its own duty, the court will help, as
> nothing else can, to fix the spot where responsibility
> lies, and to bring down on that precise locality the
> thunderbolt of popular condemnation. . . . For
> that course—the true course of judicial duty al-
> ways—will powerfully help to bring the people
> and their representatives to a sense of their
> own responsibility."

This case has significance far beyond its facts and its
holding. For more than 55 years this Court has enforced a rule under which evidence of undoubted reliability and probative value has been suppressed and
excluded from criminal cases whenever it was obtained
in violation of the Fourth Amendment. *Weeks* v. *United
States,* 232 U. S. 383 (1914); *Boyd* v. *United States,* 116
U. S. 616, 633 (1886) (dictum). This rule was extended
to the States in *Mapp* v. *Ohio,* 367 U. S. 643 (1961).[2]

---

[1] J. Thayer, O. Holmes, & F. Frankfurter, John Marshall 88
(Phoenix ed. 1967).

[2] The Court reached the issue of applying the *Weeks* doctrine
to the States *sua sponte.*

The rule has rested on a theory that suppression of evidence in these circumstances was imperative to deter law enforcement authorities from using improper methods to obtain evidence.

The deterrence theory underlying the suppression doctrine, or exclusionary rule, has a certain appeal in spite of the high price society pays for such a drastic remedy. Notwithstanding its plausibility, many judges and lawyers and some of our most distinguished legal scholars have never quite been able to escape the force of Cardozo's statement of the doctrine's anomalous result:

> "The criminal is to go free because the constable has blundered. . . . A room is searched against the law, and the body of a murdered man is found. . . . The privacy of the home has been infringed, and the murderer goes free." *People* v. *Defore*, 242 N. Y. 13, 21, 23–24, 150 N. E. 585, 587, 588 (1926).[3]

The plurality opinion in *Irvine* v. *California*, 347 U. S. 128, 136 (1954), catalogued the doctrine's defects:

> "Rejection of the evidence does nothing to punish the wrong-doing official, while it may, and likely will, release the wrong-doing defendant. It deprives society of its remedy against one lawbreaker because he has been pursued by another. It protects one against whom incriminating evidence is discovered, but does nothing to protect innocent persons who are the victims of illegal but fruitless searches."

From time to time members of the Court, recognizing the validity of these protests, have articulated varying

---

[3] What Cardozo suggested as an example of the potentially far-reaching consequences of the suppression doctrine was almost realized in *Killough* v. *United States*, 114 U. S. App. D. C. 305, 315 F. 2d 241 (1962).

alternative justifications for the suppression of important evidence in a criminal trial. Under one of these alternative theories the rule's foundation is shifted to the "sporting contest" thesis that the government must "play the game fairly" and cannot be allowed to profit from its own illegal acts. *Olmstead* v. *United States*, 277 U. S. 438, 469, 471 (1928) (dissenting opinions); see *Terry* v. *Ohio*, 392 U. S. 1, 13 (1968). But the exclusionary rule does not ineluctably flow from a desire to ensure that government plays the "game" according to the rules. If an effective alternative remedy is available, concern for official observance of the law does not require adherence to the exclusionary rule. Nor is it easy to understand how a court can be thought to endorse a violation of the Fourth Amendment by allowing illegally seized evidence to be introduced against a defendant if an effective remedy is provided against the government.

The exclusionary rule has also been justified on the theory that the relationship between the Self-Incrimination Clause of the Fifth Amendment and the Fourth Amendment requires the suppression of evidence seized in violation of the latter. *Boyd* v. *United States, supra,* at 633 (dictum); *Wolf* v. *Colorado*, 338 U. S. 25, 47, 48 (1949) (Rutledge, J., dissenting); *Mapp* v. *Ohio, supra,* at 661–666 (Black, J., concurring).

Even ignoring, however, the decisions of this Court that have held that the Fifth Amendment applies only to "testimonial" disclosures, *United States* v. *Wade*, 388 U. S. 218, 221–223 (1967); *Schmerber* v. *California*, 384 U. S. 757, 764 and n. 8 (1966), it seems clear that the Self-Incrimination Clause does not protect a person from the seizure of evidence that is incriminating. It protects a person only from being the conduit by which the police acquire evidence. Mr. Justice Holmes once put it succinctly, "A party is privileged from producing the evidence but not from its production." *Johnson* v. *United States,* 228 U. S. 457, 458 (1913).

It is clear, however, that neither of these theories under-girds the decided cases in this Court. Rather the exclusionary rule has rested on the deterrent rationale—the hope that law enforcement officials would be deterred from unlawful searches and seizures if the illegally seized, albeit trustworthy, evidence was suppressed often enough and the courts persistently enough deprived them of any benefits they might have gained from their illegal conduct.

This evidentiary rule is unique to American jurisprudence. Although the English and Canadian legal systems are highly regarded, neither has adopted our rule. See Martin, The Exclusionary Rule Under Foreign Law—Canada, 52 J. Crim. L. C. & P. S. 271, 272 (1961); Williams, The Exclusionary Rule Under Foreign Law—England, 52 J. Crim. L. C. & P. S. 272 (1961).

I do not question the need for some remedy to give meaning and teeth to the constitutional guarantees against unlawful conduct by government officials. Without some effective sanction, these protections would constitute little more than rhetoric. Beyond doubt the conduct of some officials requires sanctions as cases like *Irvine* indicate. But the hope that this objective could be accomplished by the exclusion of reliable evidence from criminal trials was hardly more than a wistful dream. Although I would hesitate to abandon it until some meaningful substitute is developed, the history of the suppression doctrine demonstrates that it is both conceptually sterile and practically ineffective in accomplishing its stated objective. This is illustrated by the paradox that an unlawful act against a totally innocent person—such as petitioner claims to be—has been left without an effective remedy, and hence the Court finds

it necessary now—55 years later—to construct a remedy
of its own.

Some clear demonstration of the benefits and effectiveness of the exclusionary rule is required to justify it in
view of the high price it extracts from society—the release of countless guilty criminals.   See Allen, Federalism
and the Fourth Amendment: A Requiem for Wolf, 1961
Sup. Ct. Rev. 1, 33 n. 172.   But there is no empirical
evidence to support the claim that the rule actually deters
illegal conduct of law enforcement officials.   Oaks, Studying the Exclusionary Rule in Search and Seizure, 37 U.
Chi. L. Rev. 665, 667 (1970).

There are several reasons for this failure.   The rule
does not apply any direct sanction to the individual official whose illegal conduct results in the exclusion of evidence in a criminal trial.   With rare exceptions law enforcement agencies do not impose direct sanctions on the
individual officer responsible for a particular judicial application of the suppression doctrine.   *Id.*, at 710.
Thus there is virtually nothing done to bring about
a change in his practices.   The immediate sanction trig-
gered by the application of the rule is visited upon the
prosecutor whose case against a criminal is either weak-
ened or destroyed.   The doctrine deprives the police in
no real sense; except that apprehending wrongdoers is
their business, police have no more stake in successful
prosecutions than prosecutors or the public.

The suppression doctrine vaguely assumes that law
enforcement is a monolithic governmental enterprise.
For example, the dissenters in *Wolf* v. *Colorado, supra,*
at 44, argued that:

>"Only by exclusion can we impress upon the zealous
>*prosecutor* that violation of the Constitution will
>do him no good.   And only when that point is driven
>home can the *prosecutor* be expected to emphasize

the importance of observing the constitutional demands in *his instructions to the police.*" (Emphasis added.)

But the prosecutor who loses his case because of police misconduct is not an official in the police department; he can rarely set in motion any corrective action or administrative penalties. Moreover, he does not have control or direction over police procedures or police actions that lead to the exclusion of evidence. It is the rare exception when a prosecutor takes part in arrests, searches, or seizures so that he can guide police action.

Whatever educational effect the rule conceivably might have in theory is greatly diminished in fact by the realities of law enforcement work. Policemen do not have the time, inclination, or training to read and grasp the nuances of the appellate opinions that ultimately define the standards of conduct they are to follow. The issues that these decisions resolve often admit of neither easy nor obvious answers, as sharply divided courts on what is or is not "reasonable" amply demonstrate.[4] Nor can judges, in all candor, forget that opinions sometimes lack helpful clarity.

The presumed educational effect of judicial opinions is also reduced by the long time lapse—often several years—between the original police action and its final judicial evaluation. Given a policeman's pressing responsibilities, it would be surprising if he ever becomes aware of the final result after such a delay. Finally, the exclu-

---

[4] For example, in a case arising under *Mapp, supra,* state judges at every level of the state judiciary may find the police conduct proper. On federal habeas corpus a district judge and a court of appeals might agree. Yet, in these circumstances, this Court, reviewing the case as much as 10 years later, might reverse by a narrow margin. In these circumstances it is difficult to conclude that the policeman has violated some rule that he should have known was a restriction on his authority.

sionary rule's deterrent impact is diluted by the fact
that there are large areas of police activity that do not
result in criminal prosecutions—hence the rule has virtually no applicability and no effect in such situations.
Oaks, *supra*, at 720–724.

Today's holding seeks to fill one of the gaps of the
suppression doctrine—at the price of impinging on the
legislative and policy functions that the Constitution
vests in Congress. Nevertheless, the holding serves the
useful purpose of exposing the fundamental weaknesses
of the suppression doctrine. Suppressing unchallenged
truth has set guilty criminals free but demonstrably has
neither deterred deliberate violations of the Fourth
Amendment nor decreased those errors in judgment that
will inevitably occur given the pressures inherent in police
work having to do with serious crimes.

Although unfortunately ineffective, the exclusionary
rule has increasingly been characterized by a single, monolithic, and drastic judicial response to all official violations of legal norms. Inadvertent errors of judgment
that do not work any grave injustice will inevitably occur
under the pressure of police work. These honest mis-
takes have been treated in the same way as deliberate and
flagrant *Irvine*-type violations of the Fourth Amendment.
For example, in *Miller* v. *United States,* 357 U. S. 301,
309–310 (1958), reliable evidence was suppressed because
of a police officer's failure to say a "few more words" during the arrest and search of a known narcotics peddler.

This Court's decision announced today in *Coolidge* v.
New Hampshire, post, p. 443, dramatically illustrates the
extent to which the doctrine represents a mechanically inflexible response to widely varying degrees of police error
and the resulting high price that society pays. I dissented in *Coolidge* primarily because I do not believe the
Fourth Amendment had been violated. Even on the
Court's contrary premise, however, whatever violation

occurred was surely insufficient in nature and extent to justify the drastic result dictated by the suppression doctrine. A fair trial by jury has resolved doubts as to Coolidge's guilt. But now his conviction on retrial is placed in serious question by the remand for a new trial—years after the crime—in which evidence that the New Hampshire courts found relevant and reliable will be withheld from the jury's consideration. It is hardly surprising that such results are viewed with incomprehension by nonlawyers in this country and lawyers, judges, and legal scholars the world over.

Freeing either a tiger or a mouse in a schoolroom is an illegal act, but no rational person would suggest that these two acts should be punished in the same way. From time to time judges have occasion to pass on regulations governing police procedures. I wonder what would be the judicial response to a police order authorizing "shoot to kill" with respect to every fugitive. It is easy to predict our collective wrath and outrage. We, in common with all rational minds, would say that the police response must relate to the gravity and need; that a "shoot" order might conceivably be tolerable to prevent the escape of a convicted killer but surely not for a car thief, a pickpocket or a shoplifter.

I submit that society has at least as much right to expect rationally graded responses from judges in place of the universal "capital punishment" we inflict on all evidence when police error is shown in its acquisition. See ALI, Model Code of Pre-Arraignment Procedure § SS 8.02 (2), p. 23 (Tent. Draft No. 4, 1971), reprinted in the Appendix to this opinion. Yet for over 55 years, and with increasing scope and intensity as today's *Coolidge* holding shows, our legal system has treated vastly dissimilar cases as if they were the same. Our adherence to the exclusionary rule, our resistance to change, and our refusal even to acknowledge the need for effective enforcement mechanisms bring to mind Holmes' well-known statement:

> "It is revolting to have no better reason for a rule of law than that so it was laid down in the time of Henry IV. It is still more revolting if the grounds upon which it was laid down have vanished long since, and the rule simply persists from blind imitation of the past." Holmes, The Path of the Law, 10 Harv. L. Rev. 457, 469 (1897).

In characterizing the suppression doctrine as an anomalous and ineffective mechanism with which to regulate law enforcement, I intend no reflection on the motivation of those members of this Court who hoped it would be a means of enforcing the Fourth Amendment. Judges cannot be faulted for being offended by arrests, searches, and seizures that violate the Bill of Rights or statutes intended to regulate public officials. But we can and should be faulted for clinging to an unworkable and irrational concept of law. My criticism is that we have taken so long to find better ways to accomplish these desired objectives. And there are better ways.

Instead of continuing to enforce the suppression doctrine inflexibly, rigidly, and mechanically, we should view it as one of the experimental steps in the great tradition of the common law and acknowledge its shortcomings. But in the same spirit we should be prepared to discontinue what the experience of over half a century has shown neither deters errant officers nor affords a remedy to the totally innocent victims of official misconduct.

I do not propose, however, that we abandon the suppression doctrine until some meaningful alternative can be developed. In a sense our legal system has become the captive of its own creation. To overrule *Weeks* and *Mapp,* even assuming the Court was now prepared to

take that step, could raise yet new problems. Obviously
the public interest would be poorly served if law enforcement officials were suddenly to gain the impression, however erroneous, that all constitutional restraints on police
had somehow been removed—that an open season on
"criminals" had been declared. I am concerned lest some
such mistaken impression might be fostered by a flat
overruling of the suppression doctrine cases. For years
we have relied upon it as the exclusive remedy for unlawful official conduct; in a sense we are in a situation akin
to the narcotics addict whose dependence on drugs precludes any drastic or immediate withdrawal of the supposed prop, regardless of how futile its continued use
may be.

Reasonable and effective substitutes can be formulated
if Congress would take the lead, as it did for example in
1946 in the Federal Tort Claims Act. I see no insuper-
able obstacle to the elimination of the suppression doctrine if Congress would provide some meaningful and
effective remedy against unlawful conduct by government
officials.

The problems of both error and deliberate misconduct
by law enforcement officials call for a workable remedy.
Private damage actions against individual police officers
concededly have not adequately met this requirement,
and it would be fallacious to assume today's work of the
Court in creating a remedy will really accomplish its
stated objective. There is some validity to the claims
that juries will not return verdicts against individual
officers except in those unusual cases where the violation
has been flagrant or where the error has been complete,
as in the arrest of the wrong person or the search of the
wrong house. There is surely serious doubt, for example,
that a drug peddler caught packaging his wares will be
able to arouse much sympathy in a jury on the ground
that the police officer did not announce his identity and

purpose fully or because he failed to utter a "few more words." See *Miller* v. *United States, supra.* Jurors may well refuse to penalize a police officer at the behest of a person they believe to be a "criminal" and probably will not punish an officer for honest errors of judgment. In any event an actual recovery depends on finding non-exempt assets of the police officer from which a judgment can be satisfied.

I conclude, therefore, that an entirely different remedy is necessary but it is one that in my view is as much beyond judicial power as the step the Court takes today. Congress should develop an administrative or quasi-judicial remedy against the government itself to afford compensation and restitution for persons whose Fourth Amendment rights have been violated. The venerable doctrine of *respondeat superior* in our tort law provides an entirely appropriate conceptual basis for this remedy. If, for example, a security guard privately employed by a department store commits an assault or other tort on a customer such as an improper search, the victim has a simple and obvious remedy—an action for money damages against the guard's employer, the department store. W. Prosser, The Law of Torts § 68, pp. 470–480 (3d ed. 1964).[5] Such a statutory scheme would have the added advantage of providing some remedy to the completely innocent persons who are sometimes the victims of illegal police conduct—something that the suppression doctrine, of course, can never accomplish.

A simple structure would suffice.[6] For example, Congress could enact a statute along the following lines:

(a) a waiver of sovereign immunity as to the illegal

---

[5] Damage verdicts for such acts are often sufficient in size to provide an effective deterrent and stimulate employers to corrective action.

[6] Electronic eavesdropping presents special problems. See 18 U. S. C. §§ 2510–2520 (1964 ed., Supp. V).

acts of law enforcement officials committed in the performance of assigned duties;

(b) the creation of a cause of action for damages sustained by any person aggrieved by conduct of governmental agents in violation of the Fourth Amendment or statutes regulating official conduct;

(c) the creation of a tribunal, quasi-judicial in nature or perhaps patterned after the United States Court of Claims, to adjudicate all claims under the statute;

(d) a provision that this statutory remedy is in lieu of the exclusion of evidence secured for use in criminal cases in violation of the Fourth Amendment; and

(e) a provision directing that no evidence, otherwise admissible, shall be excluded from any criminal proceeding because of violation of the Fourth Amendment.

I doubt that lawyers serving on such a tribunal would be swayed either by undue sympathy for officers or by the prejudice against "criminals" that has sometimes moved lay jurors to deny claims. In addition to awarding damages, the record of the police conduct that is condemned would undoubtedly become a relevant part of an officer's personnel file so that the need for additional training or disciplinary action could be identified or his future usefulness as a public official evaluated. Finally, appellate judicial review could be made available on much the same basis that it is now provided as to district courts and regulatory agencies. This would leave to the courts the ultimate responsibility for determining and articulating standards.

Once the constitutional validity of such a statute is established,[7] it can reasonably be assumed that the States

---

[7] Any such legislation should emphasize the interdependence between the waiver of sovereign immunity and the elimination of the judicially created exclusionary rule so that if the legislative determination to repudiate the exclusionary rule falls, the entire statutory scheme would fall.

would develop their own remedial systems on the federal model.   Indeed there is nothing to prevent a State from enacting a comparable statutory scheme without waiting for the Congress.   Steps along these lines would move our system toward more responsible law enforcement on the one hand and away from the irrational and drastic results of the suppression doctrine on the other.   Independent of the alternative embraced in this dissenting opinion, I believe the time has come to re-examine the scope of the exclusionary rule and consider at least some narrowing of its thrust so as to eliminate the anomalies it has produced.

In a country that prides itself on innovation, inventive genius, and willingness to experiment, it is a paradox that we should cling for more than a half century to a legal mechanism that was poorly designed and never really worked.   I can only hope now that the Congress will manifest a willingness to view realistically the hard evidence of the half-century history of the suppression doctrine revealing thousands of cases in which the criminal was set free because the constable blundered and virtually no evidence that innocent victims of police error—such as petitioner claims to be—have been afforded meaningful redress.

HARRIS *v.* NEW YORK

CERTIORARI TO THE COURT OF APPEALS OF NEW YORK

No. 206. Argued December 17, 1970—Decided February 24, 1971

Statement inadmissible against a defendant in the prosecution's case
in chief because of lack of the procedural safeguards required by
Miranda v. *Arizona,* 384 U. S. 436, may, if its trustworthiness
satisfies legal standards, be used for impeachment purposes to
attack the credibility of defendant's trial testimony. See *Walder*
v. *United States,* 347 U. S. 62. Pp. 223–226.

25 N. Y. 2d 175, 250 N. E. 2d 349, affirmed.

BURGER, C. J., delivered the opinion of the Court, in which
HARLAN, STEWART, WHITE, and BLACKMUN, JJ., joined. BLACK, J.,
dissented. BRENNAN, J., filed a dissenting opinion, in which DOUG-
LAS and MARSHALL, JJ., joined, *post,* p. 226.

Joel Martin Aurnou argued the cause and filed a brief
for petitioner.

James J. Duggan argued the cause for respondent.
With him on the brief was *Carl A. Vergari.*

Sybil H. Landau argued the cause for the District Attorney of New York County as *amicus curiae* urging
affirmance. With her on the brief were *Frank S. Hogan,
pro se,* and *Michael R. Juviler.*

MR. CHIEF JUSTICE BURGER delivered the opinion of
the Court.

We granted the writ in this case to consider petitioner's
claim that a statement made by him to police under
circumstances rendering it inadmissible to establish the
prosecution's case in chief under *Miranda* v. *Arizona,*
384 U. S. 436 (1966), may not be used to impeach his
credibility.

The State of New York charged petitioner in a two-
count indictment with twice selling heroin to an under-

cover police officer.   At a subsequent jury trial the officer
was the State's chief witness, and he testified as to details
of the two sales.   A second officer verified collateral details of the sales, and a third offered testimony about the
chemical analysis of the heroin.

Petitioner took the stand in his own defense.   He admitted knowing the undercover police officer but denied
a sale on January 4, 1966.   He admitted making a sale
of contents of a glassine bag to the officer on January 6
but claimed it was baking powder and part of a scheme
to defraud the purchaser.

On cross-examination petitioner was asked seriatim
whether he had made specified statements to the police
immediately following his arrest on January 7—statements that partially contradicted petitioner's direct testimony at trial.   In response to the cross-examination,
petitioner testified that he could not remember virtually
any of the questions or answers recited by the prosecutor.   At the request of petitioner's counsel the written
statement from which the prosecutor had read questions
and answers in his impeaching process was placed in the
record for possible use on appeal; the statement was not
shown to the jury.

The trial judge instructed the jury that the statements
attributed to petitioner by the prosecution could be considered only in passing on petitioner's credibility and not
as evidence of guilt.   In closing summations both counsel argued the substance of the impeaching statements.
The jury then found petitioner guilty on the second count
of the indictment.[1]   The New York Court of Appeals
affirmed in a *per curiam* opinion, 25 N. Y. 2d 175, 250
N. E. 2d 349 (1969).

At trial the prosecution made no effort in its case in
chief to use the statements allegedly made by petitioner,

---

[1] No agreement was reached as to the first count.   That count
was later dropped by the State.

conceding that they were inadmissible under *Miranda* v. *Arizona,* 384 U. S. 436 (1966). The transcript of the interrogation used in the impeachment, but not given to the jury, shows that no warning of a right to appointed counsel was given before questions were put to petitioner when he was taken into custody. Petitioner makes no claim that the statements made to the police were coerced or involuntary.

Some comments in the *Miranda* opinion can indeed be read as indicating a bar to use of an uncounseled statement for any purpose, but discussion of that issue was not at all necessary to the Court's holding and cannot be regarded as controlling. *Miranda* barred the prosecution from making its case with statements of an accused made while in custody prior to having or effectively waiving counsel. It does not follow from *Miranda* that evidence inadmissible against an accused in the prosecution's case in chief is barred for all purposes, provided of course that the trustworthiness of the evidence satisfies legal standards.

In *Walder* v. *United States,* 347 U. S. 62 (1954), the Court permitted physical evidence, inadmissible in the case in chief, to be used for impeachment purposes.

> "It is one thing to say that the Government cannot make an affirmative use of evidence unlawfully obtained. It is quite another to say that the defendant can turn the illegal method by which evidence in the Government's possession was obtained to his own advantage, and provide himself with a shield against contradiction of his untruths. Such an extension of the *Weeks* doctrine would be a perversion of the Fourth Amendment.
>
> "[T]here is hardly justification for letting the defendant affirmatively resort to perjurious testimony in reliance on the Government's disability to challenge his credibility." 347 U. S., at 65.

It is true that Walder was impeached as to collateral matters included in his direct examination, whereas petitioner here was impeached as to testimony bearing more directly on the crimes charged. We are not persuaded that there is a difference in principle that warrants a result different from that reached by the Court in *Walder*. Petitioner's testimony in his own behalf concerning the events of January 7 contrasted sharply with what he told the police shortly after his arrest. The impeachment process here undoubtedly provided valuable aid to the jury in assessing petitioner's credibility, and the benefits of this process should not be lost, in our view, because of the speculative possibility that impermissible police conduct will be encouraged thereby. Assuming that the exclusionary rule has a deterrent effect on proscribed police conduct, sufficient deterrence flows when the evidence in question is made unavailable to the prosecution in its case in chief.

Every criminal defendant is privileged to testify in his own defense, or to refuse to do so. But that privilege cannot be construed to include the right to commit perjury. See *United States* v. *Knox,* 396 U. S. 77 (1969); cf. *Dennis* v. *United States,* 384 U. S. 855 (1966). Having voluntarily taken the stand, petitioner was under an obligation to speak truthfully and accurately, and the prosecution here did no more than utilize the traditional truth-testing devices of the adversary process.[2] Had

---

[2] If, for example, an accused confessed fully to a homicide and led the police to the body of the victim under circumstances making his confession inadmissible, the petitioner would have us allow that accused to take the stand and blandly deny every fact disclosed to the police or discovered as a "fruit" of his confession, free from confrontation with his prior statements and acts. The voluntariness of the confession would, on this thesis, be totally irrelevant. We reject such an extravagant extension of the Constitution. Compare *Killough* v. *United States,* 114 U. S. App. D. C. 305, 315 F. 2d 241 (1962).

inconsistent statements been made by the accused to some third person, it could hardly be contended that the conflict could not be laid before the jury by way of cross-examination and impeachment.

The shield provided by *Miranda* cannot be perverted into a license to use perjury by way of a defense, free from the risk of confrontation with prior inconsistent utterances. We hold, therefore, that petitioner's credibility was appropriately impeached by use of his earlier conflicting statements.

Affirmed.

MORRISSEY ET AL. *v.* BREWER, WARDEN, ET AL.

CERTIORARI TO THE UNITED STATES COURT OF APPEALS
FOR THE EIGHTH CIRCUIT

No. 71–5103. Argued April 11, 1972—Decided June 29, 1972

Petitioners in these habeas corpus proceedings claimed that their paroles were revoked without a hearing and that they were thereby deprived of due process. The Court of Appeals, in affirming the District Court's denial of relief, reasoned that under controlling authorities parole is only "a correctional device authorizing service of sentence outside a penitentiary," and concluded that a parolee, who is still "in custody," is not entitled to a full adversary hearing such as would be mandated in a criminal proceeding. *Held:*

1. Though parole revocation does not call for the full panoply of rights due a defendant in a criminal proceeding, a parolee's liberty involves significant values within the protection of the Due Process Clause of the Fourteenth Amendment, and termination of that liberty requires an informal hearing to give assurance that the finding of a parole violation is based on verified facts to support the revocation. Pp. 480–482.

2. Due process requires a reasonably prompt informal inquiry conducted by an impartial hearing officer near the place of the alleged parole violation or arrest to determine if there is reasonable ground to believe that the arrested parolee has violated a parole condition. The parolee should receive prior notice of the inquiry, its purpose, and the alleged violations. The parolee may present relevant information and (absent security considerations) question adverse informants. The hearing officer shall digest the evidence on probable cause and state the reasons for holding the parolee for the parole board's decision. Pp. 484–487.

3. At the revocation hearing, which must be conducted reasonably soon after the parolee's arrest, minimum due process requirements are: (a) written notice of the claimed violations of parole; (b) disclosure to the parolee of evidence against him; (c) opportunity to be heard in person and to present witnesses and documentary evidence; (d) the right to confront and cross-examine adverse witnesses (unless the hearing officer specifically finds good cause for not allowing confrontation); (e) a "neutral and detached" hearing body such as a traditional parole board, members of which need not be judicial officers or lawyers; and (f) a written statement

by the factfinders as to the evidence relied on and reasons for revoking parole. Pp. 487–490.

443 F. 2d 942, reversed and remanded.

BURGER, C. J., delivered the opinion of the Court, in which STEWART, WHITE, BLACKMUN, POWELL, and REHNQUIST, JJ., joined. BRENNAN, J., filed an opinion concurring in the result, in which MARSHALL, J., joined, *post*, p. 490. DOUGLAS, J., filed an opinion dissenting in part, *post*, p. 491.

W. Don Brittin, Jr., by appointment of the Court, 404 U. S. 1036, argued the cause and filed briefs for petitioners.

Lawrence S. Seuferer, Assistant Attorney General of Iowa, argued the cause for respondents. With him on the brief was *Richard C. Turner,* Attorney General.

Briefs of *amici curiae* urging reversal were filed by *William W. Falsgraf* and *Robert J. Kutak* for the American Bar Association; by *Melvin L. Wulf, Herman Schwartz,* and *Robert Plotkin* for the American Civil Liberties Union; and by *Craig Eldon Pinkus* for James H. Russell.

MR. CHIEF JUSTICE BURGER delivered the opinion of the Court.

We granted certiorari in this case to determine whether the Due Process Clause of the Fourteenth Amendment requires that a State afford an individual some opportunity to be heard prior to revoking his parole.

Petitioner Morrissey was convicted of false drawing or uttering of checks in 1967 pursuant to his guilty plea, and was sentenced to not more than seven years' confinement. He was paroled from the Iowa State Penitentiary in June 1968. Seven months later, at the direction of his parole officer, he was arrested in his home town as a parole violator and incarcerated in the county jail. One week later, after review of the parole officer's written report, the Iowa Board of Parole revoked Mor-

rissey's parole, and he was returned to the penitentiary
located about 100 miles from his home. Petitioner asserts he received no hearing prior to revocation of his
parole.

The parole officer's report on which the Board of
Parole acted shows that petitioner's parole was revoked
on the basis of information that he had violated the
conditions of parole by buying a car under an assumed
name and operating it without permission, giving false
statements to police concerning his address and insurance company after a minor accident, obtaining credit
under an assumed name, and failing to report his
place of residence to his parole officer. The report states
that the officer interviewed Morrissey, and that he could
not explain why he did not contact his parole officer
despite his effort to excuse this on the ground that he
had been sick. Further, the report asserts that Morrissey admitted buying the car and obtaining credit
under an assumed name, and also admitted being involved in the accident. The parole officer recommended
that his parole be revoked because of "his continual
violating of his parole rules."

The situation as to petitioner Booher is much the
same. Pursuant to his guilty plea, Booher was convicted of forgery in 1966 and sentenced to a maximum
term of 10 years. He was paroled November 14, 1968.
In August 1969, at his parole officer's direction, he was
arrested in his home town for a violation of his parole
and confined in the county jail several miles away. On
September 13, 1969, on the basis of a written report
by his parole officer, the Iowa Board of Parole revoked
Booher's parole and Booher was recommitted to the
state penitentiary, located about 250 miles from his
home, to complete service of his sentence. Petitioner
asserts he received no hearing prior to revocation of his
parole.

The parole officer's report with respect to Booher recommended that his parole be revoked because he had violated the territorial restrictions of his parole without consent, had obtained a driver's license under an assumed name, operated a motor vehicle without permission, and had violated the employment condition of his parole by failing to keep himself in gainful employment. The report stated that the officer had interviewed Booher and that he had acknowledged to the parole officer that he had left the specified territorial limits and had operated the car and had obtained a license under an assumed name "knowing that it was wrong." The report further noted that Booher had stated that he had not found employment because he could not find work that would pay him what he wanted—he stated he would not work for $2.25 to $2.75 per hour—and that he had left the area to get work in another city.

After exhausting state remedies, both petitioners filed habeas corpus petitions in the United States District Court for the Southern District of Iowa alleging that they had been denied due process because their paroles had been revoked without a hearing. The State responded by arguing that no hearing was required. The District Court held on the basis of controlling authority that the State's failure to accord a hearing prior to parole revocation did not violate due process. On appeal, the two cases were consolidated.

The Court of Appeals, dividing 4 to 3, held that due process does not require a hearing. The majority recognized that the traditional view of parole as a privilege rather than a vested right is no longer dispositive as to whether due process is applicable; however, on a balancing of the competing interests involved, it concluded that no hearing is required. The court reasoned that parole is only "a correctional device authorizing service of sentence outside the penitentiary," 443 F. 2d

942, 947; the parolee is still "in custody." Accordingly,
the Court of Appeals was of the view that prison officials
must have large discretion in making revocation determinations, and that courts should retain their traditional reluctance to interfere with disciplinary matters properly
under the control of state prison authorities. The majority expressed the view that "non-legal, non-adversary considerations" were often the determinative factors in making a parole revocation decision. It expressed concern
that if adversary hearings were required for parole revocation, "with the full panoply of rights accorded in
criminal proceedings," the function of the parole board
as "an administrative body acting in the role of *parens
patriae* would be aborted," *id.,* at 949, and the board would
be more reluctant to grant parole in the first instance—an
apprehension that would not be without some basis if the
choice were between a full-scale adversary proceeding or
no hearing at all. Additionally, the majority reasoned
that the parolee has no statutory right to remain on
parole. Iowa law provides that a parolee may be returned to the institution at any time. Our holding in
Mempa v. *Rhay,* 389 U. S. 128 (1967), was distinguished
on the ground that it involved deferred sentencing upon
probation revocation, and thus involved a stage of the
criminal proceeding, whereas parole revocation was not a
stage in the criminal proceeding. The Court of Appeals'
decision was consistent with many other decisions on
parole revocations.

In their brief in this Court, respondents assert for the first
time that petitioners were in fact granted hearings after
they were returned to the penitentiary. More generally,
respondents say that within two months after the Board
revokes an individual's parole and orders him returned
to the penitentiary, on the basis of the parole officer's
written report it grants the individual a hearing before
the Board. At that time, the Board goes over "each of

the alleged parole violations with the returnee, and he is given an opportunity to orally present his side of the story to the Board." If the returnee denies the report, it is the practice of the Board to conduct a further investigation before making a final determination either affirming the initial revocation, modifying it, or reversing it.[1] Respondents assert that Morrissey, whose parole was revoked on January 31, 1969, was granted a hearing before the Board on February 12, 1969. Booher's parole was revoked on September 13, 1969, and he was granted a hearing on October 14, 1969. At these hearings, respondents tell us—in the briefs—both Morrissey and Booher admitted the violations alleged in the parole violation reports.

Nothing in the record supplied to this Court indicates that respondent claimed, either in the District Court or the Court of Appeals, that petitioners had received hearings promptly after their paroles were revoked, or that in such hearing they admitted the violations; that information comes to us only in the respondents' brief here. Further, even the assertions that respondents make here are not based on any public record but on interviews with two of the members of the parole board. In the interview relied on to show that petitioners admitted their violations, the board member did not assert he could remember that both Morrissey and Booher admitted the parole violations with which they were charged. He stated only that, according to his memory, in the previous several years all but three returnees had admitted commission of the parole infractions al-

---

[1] The hearing required by due process, as defined herein, must be accorded *before* the effective decision. See *Armstrong* v. *Manzo*, 380 U. S. 545 (1965). Petitioners assert here that only one of the 540 revocations ordered most recently by the Iowa Parole Board was reversed after hearing, Petitioners' Reply Brief 7, suggesting that the hearing may not objectively evaluate the revocation decision.

leged and that neither of the petitioners was among the three who denied them.

We must therefore treat this case in the posture and on the record respondents elected to rely on in the District Court and the Court of Appeals. If the facts are otherwise, respondents may make a showing in the District Court that petitioners in fact have admitted the violations charged before a neutral officer.

I

Before reaching the issue of whether due process applies to the parole system, it is important to recall the function of parole in the correctional process.

During the past 60 years, the practice of releasing prisoners on parole before the end of their sentences has become an integral part of the penological system. Note, Parole Revocation in the Federal System, 56 Geo. L. J. 705 (1968). Rather than being an *ad hoc* exercise of clemency, parole is an established variation on imprisonment of convicted criminals. Its purpose is to help individuals reintegrate into society as constructive individuals as soon as they are able, without being confined for the full term of the sentence imposed. It also serves to alleviate the costs to society of keeping an individual in prison.[2] The essence of parole is release from prison, before the completion of sentence, on the condition that the prisoner abide by certain rules during the balance of the sentence. Under some systems, parole is granted automatically after the service of a certain portion of a prison term. Under others, parole is granted by the discretionary action of a board, which evaluates an array of information about a pris-

[2] See Warren, Probation in the Federal System of Criminal Justice, 19 Fed. Prob. 3 (Sept. 1955); Annual Report, Ohio Adult Parole Authority 1964/65, pp. 13–14; Note, Parole: A Critique of Its Legal Foundations and Conditions, 38 N. Y. U. L. Rev. 702, 705–707 (1963).

oner and makes a prediction whether he is ready to
reintegrate into society.

To accomplish the purpose of parole, those who are
allowed to leave prison early are subjected to specified
conditions for the duration of their terms. These conditions restrict their activities substantially beyond the
ordinary restrictions imposed by law on an individual
citizen. Typically, parolees are forbidden to use liquor or
to have associations or correspondence with certain categories of undesirable persons. Typically, also they must
seek permission from their parole officers before engaging
in specified activities, such as changing employment or
living quarters, marrying, acquiring or operating a motor
vehicle, traveling outside the community, and incurring
substantial indebtedness. Additionally, parolees must
regularly report to the parole officer to whom they are
assigned and sometimes they must make periodic written
reports of their activities. Arluke, A Summary of Parole
Rules—Thirteen Years Later, 15 Crime & Delin. 267,
272–273 (1969).

The parole officers are part of the administrative system designed to assist parolees and to offer them guidance. The conditions of parole serve a dual purpose;
they prohibit, either absolutely or conditionally, behavior
that is deemed dangerous to the restoration of the
individual into normal society. And through the requirement of reporting to the parole officer and seeking
guidance and permission before doing many things, the
officer is provided with information about the parolee
and an opportunity to advise him. The combination
puts the parole officer into the position in which he can
try to guide the parolee into constructive development.[3]

The enforcement leverage that supports the parole
conditions derives from the authority to return the pa-

---

[3] Note, Observations on the Administration of Parole, 79 Yale
L. J. 698, 699–700 (1970).

rolee to prison to serve out the balance of his sentence
if he fails to abide by the rules. In practice, not every
violation of parole conditions automatically leads to
revocation. Typically, a parolee will be counseled to
abide by the conditions of parole, and the parole officer ordinarily does not take steps to have parole revoked unless he thinks that the violations are serious
and continuing so as to indicate that the parolee is
not adjusting properly and cannot be counted on to
avoid antisocial activity.[4] The broad discretion accorded
the parole officer is also inherent in some of the quite
vague conditions, such as the typical requirement that
the parolee avoid "undesirable" associations or correspondence. Cf. *Arciniega* v. *Freeman,* 404 U. S. 4
(1971). Yet revocation of parole is not an unusual
phenomenon, affecting only a few parolees. It has been
estimated that 35%–45% of all parolees are subjected
to revocation and return to prison.[5] Sometimes revocation occurs when the parolee is accused of another
crime; it is often preferred to a new prosecution because
of the procedural ease of recommitting the individual on
the basis of a lesser showing by the State.[6]

Implicit in the system's concern with parole violations
is the notion that the parolee is entitled to retain his liberty as long as he substantially abides by the conditions of
his parole. The first step in a revocation decision thus
involves a wholly retrospective factual question: whether
the parolee has in fact acted in violation of one or more
conditions of his parole. Only if it is determined that

---

[4] *Ibid.*

[5] President's Commission on Law Enforcement and Administration of Justice, Task Force Report: Corrections 62 (1967). The
substantial revocation rate indicates that parole administrators often
deliberately err on the side of granting parole in borderline cases.

[6] See *Morrissey* v. *Brewer,* 443 F. 2d 942, at 953–954, n. 5 (CA8
1971) (Lay, J., dissenting); *Rose* v. *Haskins,* 388 F. 2d 91, 104
(CA6 1968) (Celebrezze, J., dissenting).

the parolee did violate the conditions does the second question arise: should the parolee be recommitted to prison or should other steps be taken to protect society and improve chances of rehabilitation? The first step is relatively simple; the second is more complex. The second question involves the application of expertise by the parole authority in making a prediction as to the ability of the individual to live in society without committing antisocial acts. This part of the decision, too, depends on facts, and therefore it is important for the board to know not only that some violation was committed but also to know accurately how many and how serious the violations were. Yet this second step, deciding what to do about the violation once it is identified, is not purely factual but also predictive and discretionary.

If a parolee is returned to prison, he usually receives no credit for the time "served" on parole.[7] Thus, the returnee may face a potential of substantial imprisonment.

II

We begin with the proposition that the revocation of parole is not part of a criminal prosecution and thus the full panoply of rights due a defendant in such a proceeding does not apply to parole revocations. Cf. *Mempa* v. *Rhay,* 389 U. S. 128 (1967). Parole arises after the end of the criminal prosecution, including imposition of sentence. Supervision is not directly by the court but by an administrative agency, which is sometimes an arm of the court and sometimes of the executive. Revocation deprives an individual, not of the absolute liberty to which every citizen is entitled, but only of the conditional liberty properly dependent on observance of special parole restrictions.

---

[7] Arluke, A Summary of Parole Rules—Thirteen Years Later, 15 Crime and Delinquency 267, 271 (1969); Note, Parole Revocation in the Federal System, 56 Geo. L. J. 705, 733 (1968).

We turn, therefore, to the question whether the requirements of due process in general apply to parole revocations. As MR. JUSTICE BLACKMUN has written recently, "this Court now has rejected the concept that constitutional rights turn upon whether a governmental benefit is characterized as a 'right' or as a 'privilege.'" *Graham* v. *Richardson,* 403 U. S. 365, 374 (1971). Whether any procedural protections are due depends on the extent to which an individual will be "condemned to suffer grievous loss." *Joint Anti-Fascist Refugee Committee* v. *McGrath,* 341 U. S. 123, 168 (1951) (Frankfurter, J., concurring), quoted in *Goldberg* v. *Kelly,* 397 U. S. 254, 263 (1970). The question is not merely the "weight" of the individual's interest, but whether the nature of the interest is one within the contemplation of the "liberty or property" language of the Fourteenth Amendment. *Fuentes* v. *Shevin,* 407 U. S. 67 (1972). Once it is determined that due process applies, the question remains what process is due. It has been said so often by this Court and others as not to require citation of authority that due process is flexible and calls for such procedural protections as the particular situation demands. "[C]onsideration of what procedures due process may require under any given set of circumstances must begin with a determination of the precise nature of the government function involved as well as of the private interest that has been affected by governmental action." *Cafeteria & Restaurant Workers Union* v. *McElroy,* 367 U. S. 886, 895 (1961). To say that the concept of due process is flexible does not mean that judges are at large to apply it to any and all relationships. Its flexibility is in its scope once it has been determined that some process is due; it is a recognition that not all situations calling for procedural safeguards call for the same kind of procedure.

We turn to an examination of the nature of the interest

of the parolee in his continued liberty. The liberty of
a parolee enables him to do a wide range of things open
to persons who have never been convicted of any crime.
The parolee has been released from prison based on an
evaluation that he shows reasonable promise of being able
to return to society and function as a responsible, self-
reliant person. Subject to the conditions of his parole,
he can be gainfully employed and is free to be with
family and friends and to form the other enduring at-
tachments of normal life. Though the State properly
subjects him to many restrictions not applicable to other
citizens, his condition is very different from that of confinement in a prison.[8] He may have been on parole for
a number of years and may be living a relatively normal
life at the time he is faced with revocation.[9] The parolee
has relied on at least an implicit promise that parole will
be revoked only if he fails to live up to the parole
conditions. In many cases, the parolee faces lengthy incarceration if his parole is revoked.

We see, therefore, that the liberty of a parolee, although
indeterminate, includes many of the core values of unqualified liberty and its termination inflicts a "grievous
loss" on the parolee and often on others. It is hardly
useful any longer to try to deal with this problem in terms
of whether the parolee's liberty is a "right" or a "privilege." By whatever name, the liberty is valuable and
must be seen as within the protection of the Fourteenth
Amendment. Its termination calls for some orderly
process, however informal.

---

[8] "It is not sophistic to attach greater importance to a person's
justifiable reliance in maintaining his conditional freedom so long as
he abides by the conditions of his release, than to his mere anticipation or hope of freedom." *United States ex rel. Bey* v. *Connecticut
Board of Parole*, 443 F. 2d 1079, 1086 (CA2 1971).

[9] See, *e. g.*, *Murray* v. *Page*, 429 F. 2d 1359 (CA10 1970) (parole
revoked after eight years; 15 years remaining on original term).

Turning to the question what process is due, we find that the State's interests are several. The State has found the parolee guilty of a crime against the people. That finding justifies imposing extensive restrictions on the individual's liberty. Release of the parolee before the end of his prison sentence is made with the recognition that with many prisoners there is a risk that they will not be able to live in society without committing additional antisocial acts. Given the previous conviction and the proper imposition of conditions, the State has an overwhelming interest in being able to return the individual to imprisonment without the burden of a new adversary criminal trial if in fact he has failed to abide by the conditions of his parole.

Yet, the State has no interest in revoking parole without some informal procedural guarantees. Although the parolee is often formally described as being "in custody," the argument cannot even be made here that summary treatment is necessary as it may be with respect to controlling a large group of potentially disruptive prisoners in actual custody. Nor are we persuaded by the argument that revocation is so totally a discretionary matter that some form of hearing would be administratively intolerable. A simple factual hearing will not interfere with the exercise of discretion. Serious studies have suggested that fair treatment on parole revocation will not result in fewer grants of parole.[10]

This discretionary aspect of the revocation decision need not be reached unless there is first an appropriate determination that the individual has in fact breached

[10] Sklar, Law and Practice in Probation and Parole Revocation Hearings, 55 J. Crim. L. C. & P. S. 175, 194 (1964) (no decrease in Michigan, which grants extensive rights); *Rose* v. *Haskins,* 388 F. 2d 91, 102 n. 16 (CA6 1968) (Celebrezze, J., dissenting) (cost of imprisonment so much greater than parole system that procedural requirements will not change economic motivation).

the conditions of parole. The parolee is not the only one who has a stake in his conditional liberty. Society has a stake in whatever may be the chance of restoring him to normal and useful life within the law. Society thus has an interest in not having parole revoked because of erroneous information or because of an erroneous evaluation of the need to revoke parole, given the breach of parole conditions. See *People ex rel. Menechino* v. *Warden,* 27 N. Y. 2d 376, 379, and n. 2, 267 N. E. 2d 238, 239, and n. 2 (1971) (parole board had less than full picture of facts). And society has a further interest in treating the parolee with basic fairness: fair treatment in parole revocations will enhance the chance of rehabilitation by avoiding reactions to arbitrariness.[11]

Given these factors, most States have recognized that there is no interest on the part of the State in revoking parole without any procedural guarantees at all.[12] What is needed is an informal hearing structured to assure that the finding of a parole violation will be based on verified facts and that the exercise of discretion will be informed by an accurate knowledge of the parolee's behavior.

III

We now turn to the nature of the process that is due, bearing in mind that the interest of both State and

---

[11] See President's Commission on Law Enforcement and Administration of Justice, Task Force Report: Corrections 83, 88 (1967).

[12] See n. 15, *infra.* As one state court has written, "Before such a determination or finding can be made it appears that the principles of fundamental justice and fairness would afford the parolee a reasonable opportunity to explain away the accusation of a parole violation. [The parolee] . . . is entitled to a conditional liberty and possessed of a right which can be forfeited only by reason of a breach of the conditions of the grant." *Chase* v. *Page,* 456 P. 2d 590, 594 (Okla. Crim. App. 1969).

parolee will be furthered by an effective but informal
hearing. In analyzing what is due, we see two important
stages in the typical process of parole revocation.

(a) *Arrest of Parolee and Preliminary Hearing.* The
first stage occurs when the parolee is arrested and de-
tained, usually at the direction of his parole officer. The
second occurs when parole is formally revoked. There is
typically a substantial time lag between the arrest and
the eventual determination by the parole board whether
parole should be revoked. Additionally, it may be that
the parolee is arrested at a place distant from the state
institution, to which he may be returned before the final
decision is made concerning revocation. Given these
factors, due process would seem to require that some
minimal inquiry be conducted at or reasonably near the
place of the alleged parole violation or arrest and as
promptly as convenient after arrest while information is
fresh and sources are available. Cf. *Hyser* v. *Reed,* 115
U. S. App. D. C. 254, 318 F. 2d 225 (1963). Such an
inquiry should be seen as in the nature of a "preliminary
hearing" to determine whether there is probable cause
or reasonable ground to believe that the arrested parolee
has committed acts that would constitute a violation of
parole conditions. Cf. *Goldberg* v. *Kelly,* 397 U. S., at
267–271.

In our view, due process requires that after the arrest,
the determination that reasonable ground exists for revocation of parole should be made by someone not directly
involved in the case. It would be unfair to assume that
the supervising parole officer does not conduct an interview with the parolee to confront him with the reasons
for revocation before he recommends an arrest. It would
also be unfair to assume that the parole officer bears
hostility against the parolee that destroys his neutrality; realistically the failure of the parolee is in a sense a

failure for his supervising officer.[13]   However, we need
make no assumptions one way or the other to conclude
that there should be an uninvolved person to make this
preliminary evaluation of the basis for believing the conditions of parole have been violated.   The officer directly
involved in making recommendations cannot always have
complete objectivity in evaluating them.[14]   *Goldberg* v.
Kelly found it unnecessary to impugn the motives of
the caseworker to find a need for an independent
decisionmaker to examine the initial decision.

This independent officer need not be a judicial officer.
The granting and revocation of parole are matters traditionally handled by administrative officers.   In *Goldberg,* the Court pointedly did not require that the hearing
on termination of benefits be conducted by a judicial officer or even before the traditional "neutral and detached"
officer; it required only that the hearing be conducted
by some person *other* than one initially dealing with
the case.   It will be sufficient, therefore, in the parole
revocation context, if an evaluation of whether reasonable cause exists to believe that conditions of parole have
been violated is made by someone such as a parole officer
other than the one who has made the report of parole
violations or has recommended revocation.   A State could
certainly choose some other independent decisionmaker
to perform this preliminary function.

With respect to the preliminary hearing before this
officer, the parolee should be given notice that the hear-

---

[13] Note, Observations on the Administration of Parole, 79 Yale
L. J. 698, 704–706 (1970) (parole officers in Connecticut adopt role
model of social worker rather than an adjunct of police, and exhibit a lack of punitive orientation).

[14] This is not an issue limited to bad motivation. "Parole agents
are human, and it is possible that friction between the agent and
parolee may have influenced the agent's judgment." 4 Attorney
General's Survey on Release Procedures: Parole 246 (1939).

ing will take place and that its purpose is to determine
whether there is probable cause to believe he has committed a parole violation. The notice should state what
parole violations have been alleged. At the hearing
the parolee may appear and speak in his own behalf;
he may bring letters, documents, or individuals who can
give relevant information to the hearing officer. On
request of the parolee, a person who has given adverse
information on which parole revocation is to be based
is to be made available for questioning in his presence.
However, if the hearing officer determines that an informant would be subjected to risk of harm if his identity
were disclosed, he need not be subjected to confrontation
and cross-examination.

The hearing officer shall have the duty of making a
summary, or digest, of what occurs at the hearing
in terms of the responses of the parolee and the substance of the documents or evidence given in support of
parole revocation and of the parolee's position. Based on
the information before him, the officer should determine
whether there is probable cause to hold the parolee for the
final decision of the parole board on revocation. Such a
determination would be sufficient to warrant the parolee's
continued detention and return to the state correctional
institution pending the final decision. As in *Goldberg,*
"the decision maker should state the reasons for his
determination and indicate the evidence he relied on . . ."
but it should be remembered that this is not a final
determination calling for "formal findings of fact and
conclusions of law." 397 U. S., at 271. No interest
would be served by formalism in this process; informality
will not lessen the utility of this inquiry in reducing the
risk of error.

(*b*) *The Revocation Hearing.* There must also be an
opportunity for a hearing, if it is desired by the parolee,
prior to the final decision on revocation by the parole

authority.   This hearing must be the basis for more than
determining probable cause; it must lead to a final
evaluation of any contested relevant facts and consideration of whether the facts as determined warrant revocation.   The parolee must have an opportunity to be
heard and to show, if he can, that he did not violate the
conditions, or, if he did, that circumstances in mitigation
suggest that the violation does not warrant revocation.
The revocation hearing must be tendered within a reasonable time after the parolee is taken into custody.   A
lapse of two months, as respondents suggest occurs in some
cases, would not appear to be unreasonable.

We cannot write a code of procedure; that is the responsibility of each State.   Most States have done so
by legislation, others by judicial decision usually on due
process grounds.[15]   Our task is limited to deciding the

---

[15] Very few States provide no hearing at all in parole revocations.   Thirty States provide in their statutes that a parolee shall
receive some type of hearing.   See Ala. Code, Tit. 42, § 12 (1959);
Alaska Stat. § 33.15.220 (1962); Ariz. Rev. Stat. Ann. § 31–417
(1956); Ark. Stat. Ann. § 43–2810 (Supp. 1971); Del. Code Ann.,
Tit. 11, § 4352 (Supp. 1970); Fla. Stat. Ann. § 947.23 (1) (Supp.
1972); Ga. Code Ann. § 77–519 (Supp. 1971); Haw. Rev. Stat.
§ 353–66 (1968); Idaho Code §§ 20–229, 20–229A (Supp. 1971); Ill.
Ann. Stat., c. 108, §§ 204 (e), 207 (Supp. 1972); Ind. Ann. Stat.
§ 13–1611 (Supp. 1972); Kan. Stat. Ann. § 22–3721 (1971); Ky. Rev.
Stat. Ann. § 439.330 (1)(e) (1962); La. Rev. Stat. Ann. § 15:574.9
(Supp. 1972); Me. Rev. Stat. Ann., Tit. 34, § 1675 (Supp. 1970–
1971); Md. Ann. Code, Art. 41, § 117 (1971); Mich. Comp. Laws
§ 791.240a, Mich. Stat. Ann. § 28.2310 (1) (Supp. 1972); Miss. Code
Ann. § 4004–13 (1956); Mo. Ann. Stat. § 549.265 (Supp. 1971); Mont.
Rev. Codes Ann. §§ 94–9838, 94–9835 (1969); N. H. Rev. Stat. Ann.
§ 607:46 (1955); N. M. Stat. Ann. § 41–17–28 (1972); N. Y. Correc.
Law § 212 subd. 7 (Supp. 1971); N. D. Cent. Code § 12–59–15
(Supp. 1971); Pa. Stat. Ann., Tit. 61, § 331.21a (b) (1964); Tenn.
Code Ann. § 40–3619 (1955); Tex. Code Crim. Proc., Art. 42.12, § 22
(1966); Vt. Stat. Ann., Tit. 28, § 1081 (b) (1970); Wash. Rev.
Code §§ 9.95.120 through 9.95.126 (Supp. 1971); W. Va. Code Ann.
§ 62–12–19 (1966).   Decisions of state and federal courts have re-

minimum requirements of due process. They include
(a) written notice of the claimed violations of parole;
(b) disclosure to the parolee of evidence against him;
(c) opportunity to be heard in person and to present
witnesses and documentary evidence; (d) the right to
confront and cross-examine adverse witnesses (unless the
hearing officer specifically finds good cause for not allowing confrontation); (e) a "neutral and detached" hearing body such as a traditional parole board, members
of which need not be judicial officers or lawyers; and
(f) a written statement by the factfinders as to the
evidence relied on and reasons for revoking parole. We
emphasize there is no thought to equate this second stage
of parole revocation to a criminal prosecution in any
sense. It is a narrow inquiry; the process should be
flexible enough to consider evidence including letters,
affidavits, and other material that would not be admissible in an adversary criminal trial.

We do not reach or decide the question whether the
parolee is entitled to the assistance of retained counsel
or to appointed counsel if he is indigent.[16]

---

quired a number of other States to provide hearings. See *Hutchi-
son* v. *Patterson*, 267 F. Supp. 433 (Colo. 1967) (approving parole
board regulations); *United States ex rel. Bey* v. *Connecticut State
Board of Parole*, 443 F. 2d 1079 (CA2 1971) (requiring counsel to
be appointed for revocation hearings); *State* v. *Holmes*, 109 N. J.
Super. 180, 262 A. 2d 725 (1970); *Chase* v. *Page*, 456 P. 2d 590
(Okla. Crim. App. 1969); *Bearden* v. *South Carolina*, 443 F.
2d 1090 (CA4 1971); *Baine* v. *Beckstead*, 10 Utah 2d 4, 347 P. 2d
554 (1959); *Goolsby* v. *Gagnon*, 322 F. Supp. 460 (ED Wis. 1971).
A number of States are affected by no legal requirement to grant any
kind of hearing.

[16] The Model Penal Code § 305.15 (1) (Proposed Official Draft
1962) provides that "[t]he institutional parole staff shall render
reasonable aid to the parolee in preparation for the hearing and he
shall be permitted to advise with his own legal counsel."

We have no thought to create an inflexible structure for parole revocation procedures. The few basic requirements set out above, which are applicable to future revocations of parole, should not impose a great burden on any State's parole system. Control over the required proceedings by the hearing officers can assure that delaying tactics and other abuses sometimes present in the traditional adversary trial situation do not occur. Obviously a parolee cannot relitigate issues determined against him in other forums, as in the situation presented when the revocation is based on conviction of another crime.

In the peculiar posture of this case, given the absence of an adequate record, we conclude the ends of justice will be best served by remanding the case to the Court of Appeals for its return of the two consolidated cases to the District Court with directions to make findings on the procedures actually followed by the Parole Board in these two revocations. If it is determined that petitioners admitted parole violations to the Parole Board, as respondents contend, and if those violations are found to be reasonable grounds for revoking parole under state standards, that would end the matter. If the procedures followed by the Parole Board are found to meet the standards laid down in this opinion that, too, would dispose of the due process claims for these cases.

We reverse and remand to the Court of Appeals for further proceedings consistent with this opinion.

Reversed and remanded.

UNITED STATES *v.* HENRY

No. 79–121. Argued January 16, 1980—Decided June 16, 1980

After respondent was indicted for armed robbery of a bank, and while
he was in jail pending trial, Government agents contacted an informant
who was then an inmate confined in the same cellblock as respondent.
An agent instructed the informant to be alert to any statements made
by federal prisoners but not to initiate conversations with or question
respondent regarding the charges against him. After the informant had
been released from jail, he reported to the agent that he and respondent
had engaged in conversation and that respondent made incriminating
statements about the robbery. The informant was paid for furnishing
the information. At respondent's trial, which resulted in a conviction,
the informant testified about the incriminating statements that respondent had made to him. Respondent moved to vacate his sentence on the
ground that the introduction of the informant's testimony interfered with
and violated his Sixth Amendment right to the assistance of counsel.
The District Court denied the motion, but the Court of Appeals reversed,
holding that the Government's actions impaired respondent's Sixth
Amendment rights under *Massiah* v. *United States,* 377 U. S. 201.

Held: Respondent's statements to the informant should not have been
admitted at trial. By intentionally creating a situation likely to induce
respondent to make incriminating statements without the assistance of
counsel, the Government violated respondent's Sixth Amendment right
to counsel. Under the facts—particularly the facts that the informant
was acting under instructions as a paid informant for the Government
while ostensibly no more than a fellow inmate, and that respondent was
in custody and under indictment at the time—incriminating statements
were "deliberately elicited" from respondent within the meaning of
Massiah. Since respondent was unaware that the informant was acting
for the Government, he cannot be held to have waived his right to the
assistance of counsel. Pp. 269–275.

590 F. 2d 544, affirmed.

BURGER, C. J., delivered the opinion of the Court, in which BRENNAN,
STEWART, MARSHALL, POWELL, and STEVENS, JJ., joined. POWELL, J.,
filed a concurring opinion, *post,* p. 275. BLACKMUN, J., filed a dissenting

opinion, in which WHITE, J., joined, *post,* p. 277. REHNQUIST, J., filed a dissenting opinion, *post,* p. 289.

Deputy Solicitor General Frey argued the cause for the United States. With him on the brief were *Solicitor General McCree, Assistant Attorney General Heymann,* and *Edwin S. Kneedler.*

Michael E. Geltner argued the cause for respondent. With him on the brief were *Larry J. Ritchie* and *William W. Greenhalgh.*

MR. CHIEF JUSTICE BURGER delivered the opinion of the Court.

We granted certiorari to consider whether respondent's Sixth Amendment right to the assistance of counsel was violated by the admission at trial of incriminating statements made by respondent to his cellmate, an undisclosed Government informant, after indictment and while in custody. 444 U. S. 824 (1979).

I

The Janaf Branch of the United Virginia Bank/Seaboard National in Norfolk, Va., was robbed in August 1972. Witnesses saw two men wearing masks and carrying guns enter the bank while a third man waited in the car. No witnesses were able to identify respondent Henry as one of the participants. About an hour after the robbery, the getaway car was discovered. Inside was found a rent receipt signed by one "Allen R. Norris" and a lease, also signed by Norris, for a house in Norfolk. Two men, who were subsequently convicted of participating in the robbery, were arrested at the rented house. Discovered with them were the proceeds of the robbery and the guns and masks used by the gunmen.

Government agents traced the rent receipt to Henry; on the basis of this information, Henry was arrested in Atlanta, Ga., in November 1972. Two weeks later he was indicted for armed robbery under 18 U. S. C. §§ 2113 (a) and (d). He was held pending trial in the Norfolk city jail. Counsel was appointed on November 27.

On November 21, 1972, shortly after Henry was incarcerated, Government agents working on the Janaf robbery contacted one Nichols, an inmate at the Norfolk city jail, who for some time prior to this meeting had been engaged to provide confidential information to the Federal Bureau of Investigation as a paid informant. Nichols was then serving a sentence on local forgery charges. The record does not disclose whether the agent contacted Nichols specifically to acquire information about Henry or the Janaf robbery.[1]

Nichols informed the agent that he was housed in the same cellblock with several federal prisoners awaiting trial, including Henry. The agent told him to be alert to any statements made by the federal prisoners, but not to initiate any conversation with or question Henry regarding the bank robbery. In early December, after Nichols had been released from jail, the agent again contacted Nichols, who reported that he and Henry had engaged in conversation and that Henry had told him about the robbery of the Janaf bank.[2] Nichols was paid for furnishing the information.

When Henry was tried in March 1973, an agent of the

---

[1] The record does disclose that on November 21, 1972, the same day the agent contacted Nichols, the agent's supervisor interrogated Henry at the jail. After denying participation in the robbery, Henry exercised his right to terminate the interview.

[2] Henry also asked Nichols if he would help him once Nichols was released. Henry requested Nichols to go to Virginia Beach and contact a woman there. He prepared instructions on how to find the woman and wanted Nichols to tell her to visit Henry in the Norfolk jail. He explained that he wanted to ask the woman to carry a message to his partner, who was incarcerated in the Portsmouth city jail. Henry also gave Nichols a telephone number and asked him to contact an individual named "Junior" or "Nail." In addition Henry asked Nichols to provide him with a floor plan of the United States Marshals' office and a handcuff key because Henry intended to attempt an escape.

Federal Bureau of Investigation testified concerning the events surrounding the discovery of the rental slip and the evidence uncovered at the rented house. Other witnesses also connected Henry to the rented house, including the rental agent who positively identified Henry as the "Allen R. Norris" who had rented the house and had taken the rental receipt described earlier. A neighbor testified that prior to the robbery she saw Henry at the rented house with John Luck, one of the two men who had by the time of Henry's trial been convicted for the robbery. In addition, palm prints found on the lease agreement matched those of Henry.

Nichols testified at trial that he had "an opportunity to have some conversations with Mr. Henry while he was in the jail," and that Henry told him that on several occasions he had gone to the Janaf Branch to see which employees opened the vault. Nichols also testified that Henry described to him the details of the robbery and stated that the only evidence connecting him to the robbery was the rental receipt. The jury was not informed that Nichols was a paid Government informant.

On the basis of this testimony,[3] Henry was convicted of bank robbery and sentenced to a term of imprisonment of 25 years. On appeal, he raised no Sixth Amendment claims. His conviction was affirmed, judgt. order reported at 483 F. 2d 1401 (CA4 1973), and his petition to this Court for a writ of certiorari was denied. 421 U. S. 915 (1975).

On August 28, 1975, Henry moved to vacate his sentence pursuant to 28 U. S. C. § 2255.[4] At this stage, he stated that

---

[3] Joseph Sadler, another of Henry's cellmates, also testified at trial. He stated that Henry had told him that Henry had robbed a bank with a man named "Lucky" or "Luck." Sadler testified that on advice of counsel he informed Government agents of the conversation with Henry. Sadler was not a paid informant and had no arrangement to monitor or report on conversations with Henry.

[4] In his § 2255 petition, Henry also alleged that Sadler's testimony was perjurious; that the Government failed to disclose *Brady* material, see

he had just learned that Nichols was a paid Government informant and alleged that he had been intentionally placed in the same cell with Nichols so that Nichols could secure information about the robbery. Thus, Henry contended that the introduction of Nichols' testimony violated his Sixth Amendment right to the assistance of counsel. The District Court denied the motion without a hearing. The Court of Appeals, however, reversed and remanded for an evidentiary inquiry into "whether the witness [Nichols] was acting as a government agent during his interviews with Henry."

On remand, the District Court requested affidavits from the Government agents. An affidavit was submitted describing the agent's relationship with Nichols and relating the following conversation:

> "I recall telling Nichols at this time to be alert to any statements made by these individuals [the federal prisoners] regarding the charges against them. I specifically recall telling Nichols that he was not to question Henry or these individuals about the charges against them, however, if they engaged him in conversation or talked in front of him, he was requested to pay attention to their statements. I recall telling Nichols not to initiate any conversations with Henry regarding the bank robbery charges against Henry, but that if Henry initiated the conversations with Nichols, I requested Nichols to pay attention to the information furnished by Henry."

The agent's affidavit also stated that he never requested anyone affiliated with the Norfolk city jail to place Nichols in the same cell with Henry.

The District Court again denied Henry's § 2255 motion, concluding that Nichols' testimony at trial did not violate Henry's

---

Brady v. *Maryland*, 373 U. S. 83 (1963); that the United States Attorney's argument to the jury was impermissibly prejudicial; and that his trial counsel was incompetent. The District Court rejected each of these grounds, and none of these issues is before this Court.

Sixth Amendment right to counsel. The Court of Appeals reversed and remanded, holding that the actions of the Government impaired the Sixth Amendment rights of the defendant under *Massiah* v. *United States,* 377 U. S. 201 (1964). The court noted that Nichols had engaged in conversation with Henry and concluded that if by association, by general conversation, or both, Nichols had developed a relationship of trust and confidence with Henry such that Henry revealed incriminating information, this constituted interference with the right to the assistance of counsel under the Sixth Amendment.[5]   590 F. 2d 544 (1978).

II

This Court has scrutinized postindictment confrontations between Government agents and the accused to determine whether they are "critical stages" of the prosecution at which the Sixth Amendment right to the assistance of counsel attaches. See, *e. g., United States* v. *Ash,* 413 U. S. 300 (1973); *United States* v. *Wade,* 388 U. S. 218 (1967). The present case involves incriminating statements made by the accused to an undisclosed and undercover Government informant while in custody and after indictment. The Government characterizes Henry's incriminating statements as voluntary and not the result of any affirmative conduct on the part of Government agents to elicit evidence. From this, the Government argues that Henry's rights were not violated, even assuming the Sixth Amendment applies to such surreptitious confrontations; in short, it is contended that the Government has not interfered with Henry's right to counsel.[6]

---

[5] The Court of Appeals acknowledged that the testimony of Sadler, another cellmate of Henry, supported the conviction but was not willing to conclude beyond a reasonable doubt that Nichols' testimony did not influence the jury. *Chapman* v. *California,* 386 U. S. 18, 24 (1967).

[6] Although both the Government, and MR. JUSTICE REHNQUIST in dissent, question the continuing vitality of the *Massiah* branch of the Sixth Amendment, we reject their invitation to reconsider it.

This Court first applied the Sixth Amendment to postindictment communications between the accused and agents of the Government in *Massiah* v. *United States, supra.* There, after the accused had been charged, he made incriminating statements to his codefendant, who was acting as an agent of the Government. In reversing the conviction, the Court held that the accused was denied "the basic protections of [the Sixth Amendment] when there was used against him at his trial evidence of his own incriminating words, which federal agents had deliberately elicted from him." *Id.,* at 206. The *Massiah* holding rests squarely on interference with his right to counsel.

The question here is whether under the facts of this case a Government agent "deliberately elicited" incriminating statements from Henry within the meaning of *Massiah.* Three factors are important. First, Nichols was acting under instructions as a paid informant for the Government; second, Nichols was ostensibly no more than a fellow inmate of Henry; and third, Henry was in custody and under indictment at the time he was engaged in conversation by Nichols.

The Court of Appeals viewed the record as showing that Nichols deliberately used his position to secure incriminating information from Henry when counsel was not present and held that conduct attributable to the Government. Nichols had been a paid Government informant for more than a year; moreover, the FBI agent was aware that Nichols had access to Henry and would be able to engage him in conversations without arousing Henry's suspicion. The arrangement between Nichols and the agent was on a contingent-fee basis; Nichols was to be paid only if he produced useful information.[7]

---

[7] The affidavit of the agent discloses that "Nichols had been paid by the FBI for expenses and services in connection with information he had provided" as an informant for at least a year. The only reasonable inference from this statement is that Nichols was paid when he produced information, not that Nichols was continuously on the payroll of the FBI. Here, the service requested of Nichols was that he obtain incriminating

This combination of circumstances is sufficient to support the Court of Appeals' determination. Even if the agent's statement that he did not intend that Nichols would take affirmative steps to secure incriminating information is accepted, he must have known that such propinquity likely would lead to that result.

The Government argues that the federal agents instructed Nichols not to question Henry about the robbery.[8] Yet according to his own testimony, Nichols was not a passive listener; rather, he had "some conversations with Mr. Henry" while he was in jail and Henry's incriminatory statements were "the product of this conversation." While affirmative interrogation, absent waiver, would certainly satisfy *Massiah,* we are not persuaded, as the Government contends, that *Brewer* v. *Williams,* 430 U. S. 387 (1977), modified *Massiah's* "deliberately elicited" test. See *Rhode Island* v. *Innis,* 446 U. S. 291, 300, n. 4 (1980).[9] In *Massiah,* no inquiry was

---

information from Henry; there is no indication that Nichols would have been paid if he had not performed the requested service.

[8] Two aspects of the agent's affidavit are particularly significant. First, it is clear that the agent in his discussions with Nichols singled out Henry as the inmate in whom the agent had a special interest. Thus, the affidavit relates that "I specifically recall telling Nichols that he was not to question *Henry* or these individuals" and "I recall telling Nichols not to initiate any conversations *with Henry* regarding the bank robbery charges," but to "pay attention to the information furnished *by Henry.*" (Emphasis added.) Second, the agent only instructed Nichols not to question Henry or to initiate conversations regarding the bank robbery charges. Under these instructions, Nichols remained free to discharge his task of eliciting the statements in myriad less direct ways.

[9] The situation where the "listening post" is an inanimate electronic device differs; such a device has no capability of leading the conversation into any particular subject or prompting any particular replies. See, *e. g., United States* v. *Hearst,* 563 F 2d 1331, 1347–1348 (CA9 1977), cert. denied, 435 U. S. 1000 (1978). However, that situation is not presented in this case, and there is no occasion to treat it; nor are we called upon to pass on the situation where an informant is placed in close proximity but makes no effort to stimulate conversations about the crime charged.

made as to whether Massiah or his codefendant first raised the subject of the crime under investigation.[10]

It is quite a different matter when the Government uses undercover agents to obtain incriminating statements from persons not in custody but suspected of criminal activity prior to the time charges are filed. In *Hoffa* v. *United States*, 385 U. S. 293, 302 (1966), for example, this Court held that "no interest legitimately protected by the Fourth Amendment is involved" because "the Fourth Amendment [does not protect] a wrongdoer's misplaced belief that a person to whom he voluntarily confides his wrongdoing will not reveal it." See also *United States* v. *White*, 401 U. S. 745 (1971). Similarly, the Fifth Amendment has been held not to be implicated by the use of undercover Government agents before charges are filed because of the absence of the potential for compulsion. See *Hoffa* v. *United States*, *supra*, at 303–304. But the Fourth and Fifth Amendment claims made in those cases are not relevant to the inquiry under the Sixth Amendment here—whether the Government has interfered with the right to counsel of the accused by "deliberately eliciting" incriminating statements. Our holding today does not modify *White* or *Hoffa*.

It is undisputed that Henry was unaware of Nichols' role as a Government informant. The Government argues that this Court should apply a less rigorous standard under the

---

[10] No doubt the role of the agent at the time of the conversations between Massiah and his codefendant was more active than that of the federal agents here. Yet the additional fact in *Massiah* that the agent was monitoring the conversations is hardly determinative. In both *Massiah* and this case, the informant was charged with the task of obtaining information from an accused. Whether Massiah's codefendant questioned Massiah about the crime or merely engaged in general conversation about it was a matter of no concern to the *Massiah* Court. Moreover, we deem it irrelevant that in *Massiah* the agent had to arrange the meeting between Massiah and his codefendant while here the agents were fortunate enough to have an undercover informant already in close proximity to the accused.

Sixth Amendment where the accused is prompted by an undisclosed undercover informant than where the accused is speaking in the hearing of persons he knows to be Government officers. That line of argument, however, seeks to infuse Fifth Amendment concerns against compelled self-incrimination into the Sixth Amendment protection of the right to the assistance of counsel. An accused speaking to a known Government agent is typically aware that his statements may be used against him. The adversary positions at that stage are well established; the parties are then "arm's-length" adversaries.

When the accused is in the company of a fellow inmate who is acting by prearrangement as a Government agent, the same cannot be said. Conversation stimulated in such circumstances may elicit information that an accused would not intentionally reveal to persons known to be Government agents. Indeed, the *Massiah* Court noted that if the Sixth Amendment "is to have any efficacy it must apply to indirect and surreptitious interrogations as well as those conducted in the jailhouse." The Court pointedly observed that Massiah was more seriously imposed upon because he did not know that his codefendant was a Government agent. 377 U. S., at 206.

Moreover, the concept of a knowing and voluntary waiver of Sixth Amendment rights does not apply in the context of communications with an undisclosed undercover informant acting for the Government. See *Johnson* v. *Zerbst*, 304 U. S. 458 (1938). In that setting, Henry, being unaware that Nichols was a Government agent expressly commissioned to secure evidence, cannot be held to have waived his right to the assistance of counsel.

Finally, Henry's incarceration at the time he was engaged in conversation by Nichols is also a relevant factor.[11] As a ground

---

[11] This is not to read a "custody" requirement, which is a prerequisite to the attachment of *Miranda* rights, into this branch of the Sixth Amend-

for imposing the prophylactic requirements in *Miranda* v. *Arizona*, 384 U. S. 436, 467 (1966), this Court noted the powerful psychological inducements to reach for aid when a person is in confinement. See also *id.*, at 448–454. While the concern in *Miranda* was limited to custodial police interrogation, the mere fact of custody imposes pressures on the accused; confinement may bring into play subtle influences that will make him particularly susceptible to the ploys of undercover Government agents. The Court of Appeals determined that on this record the incriminating conversations between Henry and Nichols were facilitated by Nichols' conduct and apparent status as a person sharing a common plight. That Nichols had managed to gain the confidence of Henry, as the Court of Appeals determined, is confirmed by Henry's request that Nichols assist him in his escape plans when Nichols was released from confinement.[12]

Under the strictures of the Court's holdings on the exclusion of evidence, we conclude that the Court of Appeals did not err in holding that Henry's statements to Nichols should not have been admitted at trial. By intentionally creating a situation likely to induce Henry to make incriminating statements without the assistance of counsel, the Government violated Henry's Sixth Amendment right to counsel.[13] This is

---

ment. Massiah was in no sense in custody at the time of his conversation with his codefendant. Rather, we believe the fact of custody bears on whether the Government "deliberately elicited" the incriminating statements from Henry.

[12] This is admittedly not a case such as *Massiah* where the informant and the accused had a prior longstanding relationship. Nevertheless, there is ample evidence in the record which discloses that Nichols had managed to become more than a casual jailhouse acquaintance. That Henry could be induced to discuss his past crime is hardly surprising in view of the fact that Nichols had so ingratiated himself that Henry actively solicited his aid in executing his next crime—his planned attempt to escape from the jail.

[13] The holding of the Court of Appeals that this was not harmless error is on less firm grounds in view of the strong evidence against Henry, in-

264

not a case where, in Justice Cardozo's words, "the constable . . . blundered," *People* v. *DeFore,* 242 N. Y. 13, 21, 150 N. E. 585, 587 (1926); rather, it is one where the "constable" planned an impermissible interference with the right to the assistance of counsel.[14]

The judgment of the Court of Appeals for the Fourth Circuit is

Affirmed.

---

cluding the testimony of a neutral fellow inmate, Henry's rental of the hideaway house, and his presence there with the other participants in the robbery before the crime. The Government, however, has not argued that the error was harmless, and on balance, we are not inclined to disturb the determination of the Court of Appeals.

[14] Although it does not bear on the constitutional question in this case, we note that Disciplinary Rule 7–104 (A)(1) of the Code of Professional Responsibility provides:

"(A) During the course of his representation of a client a lawyer shall not:

"(1) Communicate or cause another to communicate on the subject of the representation with a party he knows to be represented by a lawyer in that matter unless he has the prior consent of the lawyer representing such other party or is authorized by law to do so."

See also Ethical Consideration 7–18.

LOCKETT *v.* OHIO

CERTIORARI TO THE SUPREME COURT OF OHIO

No. 76–6997.   Argued January 17, 1978—Decided July 3, 1978

The Ohio death penalty statute provides that once a defendant is found
guilty of aggravated murder with at least one of seven specified aggravating circumstances, the death penalty must be imposed unless,
considering "the nature and circumstances of the offense and the history,
character, and condition of the offender," the sentencing judge determines
that at least one of the following circumstances is established by a
preponderance of the evidence: (1) the victim induced or facilitated the
offense; (2) it is unlikely that the offense would have been committed
but for the fact that the offender was under duress, coercion, or strong
provocation; or (3) the offense was primarily the product of the
offender's psychosis or mental deficiency.   Petitioner, whose conviction of
aggravated murder with specifications that it was committed to escape
apprehension for, and while committing or attempting to commit, aggravated robbery, and whose sentence to death were affirmed by the Ohio
Supreme Court, makes various challenges to the validity of her conviction, and attacks the constitutionality of the death penalty statute on
the ground, *inter alia*, that it does not give the sentencing judge a full
opportunity to consider mitigating circumstances in capital cases as
required by the Eighth and Fourteenth Amendments.   *Held:* The judgment is reversed insofar as it upheld the death penalty, and the case
is remanded.   Pp. 594–609; 613–619; 619–621; 624–628.

49 Ohio St. 2d 48, 358 N. E. 2d 1062, reversed in part and remanded.

THE CHIEF JUSTICE delivered the opinion of the Court with respect to
Parts I and II, concluding:

   1. The prosecutor's closing references to the State's evidence as "unrefuted" and "uncontradicted" (no evidence having been introduced to
rebut the prosecutor's case after petitioner decided not to testify) did not
violate the constitutional prohibitions against commenting on an accused's
failure to testify, where petitioner's counsel had already focused the
jury's attention on her silence by promising a defense and telling the jury
that she would testify.   Pp. 594–595.

   2. The exclusion from the venire of four prospective jurors who made
it "unmistakably clear" that, because of their opposition to the death
penalty, they could not be trusted to "abide by existing law" and to

                              589

"follow conscientiously" the trial judge's instructions, *Boulden* v. *Holman,* 394 U. S. 478, 484, did not violate petitioner's Sixth and Fourteenth Amendment rights under the principles of *Witherspoon* v. *Illinois,* 391 U. S. 510, or *Taylor* v. *Louisiana,* 419 U. S. 522. Pp. 595–597.

3. Petitioner's contention that the Ohio Supreme Court's interpretation of the complicity provision of the statute under which she was convicted was so unexpected that it deprived her of fair warning of the crime with which she was charged, is without merit. The court's construction was consistent with both prior Ohio law and the statute's legislative history. P. 597.

THE CHIEF JUSTICE, joined by MR. JUSTICE STEWART, MR. JUSTICE POWELL, and MR. JUSTICE STEVENS, concluded, in Part III, that the limited range of mitigating circumstances that may be considered by the sentencer under the Ohio death penalty statute is incompatible with the Eighth and Fourteenth Amendments. Pp. 597–609.

(a) The Eighth and Fourteenth Amendments require that the sentencer, in all but the rarest kind of capital case, not be precluded from considering *as a mitigating factor,* any aspect of a defendant's character or record and any of the circumstances of the offense that the defendant proffers as a basis for a sentence less than death. Pp. 604–605.

(b) The need for treating each defendant in a capital case with the degree of respect due the uniqueness of the individual is far more important than in noncapital cases, particularly in view of the unavailability with respect to an executed capital sentence of such postconviction mechanisms in noncapital cases as probation, parole, and work furloughs. P. 605.

(c) A statute that prevents the sentencer in capital cases from giving independent mitigating weight to aspects of the defendant's character and record and to the circumstances of the offense proffered in mitigation creates the risk that the death penalty will be imposed in spite of factors that may call for a less severe penalty, and when the choice is between life and death, such risk is unacceptable and incompatible with the commands of the Eighth and Fourteenth Amendments. P. 605.

(d) The Ohio death penalty statute does not permit the type of individualized consideration of mitigating factors required by the Eighth and Fourteenth Amendments. Only the three factors specified in the statute can be considered in mitigation of the defendant's sentence, and once it is determined that none of those factors is present, the statute mandates the death sentence. Pp. 606–608.

MR. JUSTICE WHITE concluded that petitioner's death sentence should be vacated on the ground that the Ohio death penalty statute permits a defendant convicted of aggravated murder with specifications to be sentenced to death, as petitioner was in this case, without a finding that he intended death to result. Pp. 624–628.

MR. JUSTICE MARSHALL, being of the view that the death penalty is, under all circumstances, a cruel and unusual punishment prohibited by the Eighth Amendment, concurred in the judgment insofar as it vacates petitioner's death sentence, and also concurred in the judgment insofar as it affirms her conviction. Pp. 619–621.

MR. JUSTICE BLACKMUN concluded that petitioner's death sentence should be vacated on the grounds that (1) the Ohio death penalty statute is deficient in regard to petitioner, a nontriggerman charged with aiding and abetting a murder, in failing to allow consideration of the extent of petitioner's involvement, or the degree of her *mens rea*, in the commission of the homicide, and (2) the procedure provided by an Ohio Rule of Criminal Procedure giving the sentencing court full discretion to bar the death sentence "in the interests of justice" *if* the defendant pleads guilty or no contest, but no such discretion if the defendant goes to trial, creates an unconstitutional disparity of sentencing alternatives, *United States* v. *Jackson*, 390 U. S. 570. Pp. 613–619.

BURGER, C. J., announced the Court's judgment and delivered an opinion of the Court with respect to Parts I and II, in which STEWART, WHITE, BLACKMUN, POWELL, REHNQUIST, and STEVENS, JJ., joined, and an opinion with respect to Part III, in which STEWART, POWELL, and STEVENS, JJ., joined. BLACKMUN, J., filed an opinion concurring in part and concurring in the judgment, *post*, p. 613. MARSHALL, J., filed an opinion concurring in the judgment, *post*, p. 619. WHITE, J., filed an opinion concurring in part, concurring in the judgment, and dissenting in part, *post*, p. 621. REHNQUIST, J., filed an opinion concurring in part and dissenting in part, *post*, p. 628. BRENNAN, J., took no part in the consideration or decision of the case.

Anthony G. Amsterdam argued the cause for petitioner. With him on the brief were *Max Kravitz, Jack Greenberg, James M. Nabrit III, Joel Berger, David E. Kendall,* and *Peggy C. Davis.*

Carl M. Layman III argued the cause for respondent. With him on the brief were *Stephan M. Gabalac* and *James A. Rudgers.*

MR. CHIEF JUSTICE BURGER delivered the opinion of the
Court with respect to the constitutionality of petitioner's conviction (Parts I and II), together with an opinion (Part III),
in which MR. JUSTICE STEWART, MR. JUSTICE POWELL, and
MR. JUSTICE STEVENS joined, on the constitutionality of the
statute under which petitioner was sentenced to death, and
announced the judgment of the Court.

We granted certiorari in this case to consider, among other
questions, whether Ohio violated the Eighth and Fourteenth
Amendments by sentencing Sandra Lockett to death pursuant
to a statute [1] that narrowly limits the sentencer's discretion
to consider the circumstances of the crime and the record and
character of the offender as mitigating factors.

I

Lockett was charged with aggravated murder with the
aggravating specifications (1) that the murder was "committed
for the purpose of escaping detection, apprehension, trial, or
punishment" for aggravated robbery, and (2) that the murder
was "committed while . . . committing, attempting to commit, or fleeing immediately after committing or attempting to
commit . . . aggravated robbery." That offense was punishable by death in Ohio. See Ohio Rev. Code Ann. §§ 2929.03,
2929.04 (1975). She was also charged with aggravated robbery. The State's case against her depended largely upon the
testimony of a coparticipant, one Al Parker, who gave the
following account of her participation in the robbery and
murder.

Lockett became acquainted with Parker and Nathan Earl
Dew while she and a friend, Joanne Baxter, were in New
Jersey. Parker and Dew then accompanied Lockett, Baxter,
and Lockett's brother back to Akron, Ohio, Lockett's home-

---

[1] The pertinent provisions of the Ohio death penalty statute appear as
an appendix to this opinion.

town.   After they arrived in Akron, Parker and Dew needed
money for the trip back to New Jersey.   Dew suggested that
he pawn his ring.   Lockett overheard his suggestion, but felt
that the ring was too beautiful to pawn, and suggested instead
that they could get some money by robbing a grocery store and
a furniture store in the area.   She warned that the grocery
store's operator was a "big guy" who carried a "45" and that
they would have "to get him real quick."   She also volunteered to get a gun from her father's basement to aid in
carrying out the robberies, but by that time, the two stores
had closed and it was too late to proceed with the plan to rob
them.

Someone, apparently Lockett's brother, suggested a plan for
robbing a pawnshop.   He and Dew would enter the shop and
pretend to pawn a ring.   Next Parker, who had some bullets,
would enter the shop, ask to see a gun, load it, and use it to
rob the shop.   No one planned to kill the pawnshop operator
in the course of the robbery.   Because she knew the owner,
Lockett was not to be among those entering the pawnshop,
though she did guide the others to the shop that night.

The next day Parker, Dew, Lockett, and her brother gath-
ered at Baxter's apartment.   Lockett's brother asked if they
were "still going to do it," and everyone, including Lockett,
agreed to proceed.   The four then drove by the pawnshop
several times and parked the car.   Lockett's brother and Dew
entered the shop.   Parker then left the car and told Lockett
to start it again in two minutes.   The robbery proceeded
according to plan until the pawnbroker grabbed the gun when
Parker announced the "stickup."   The gun went off with
Parker's finger on the trigger, firing a fatal shot into the
pawnbroker.

Parker went back to the car where Lockett waited with the
engine running.   While driving away from the pawnshop,
Parker told Lockett what had happened.   She took the gun
from the pawnshop and put it into her purse.   Lockett and

Parker drove to Lockett's aunt's house and called a taxicab. Shortly thereafter, while riding away in a taxicab, they were stopped by the police, but by this time Lockett had placed the gun under the front seat. Lockett told the police that Parker rented a room from her mother and lived with her family. After verifying this story with Lockett's parents, the police released Lockett and Parker. Lockett hid Dew and Parker in the attic when the police arrived at the Lockett household later that evening.

Parker was subsequently apprehended and charged with aggravated murder with specifications, an offense punishable by death, and aggravated robbery. Prior to trial, he pleaded guilty to the murder charge and agreed to testify against Lockett, her brother, and Dew. In return, the prosecutor dropped the aggravated robbery charge and the specifications to the murder charge, thereby eliminating the possibility that Parker could receive the death penalty.

Lockett's brother and Dew were later convicted of aggravated murder with specifications. Lockett's brother was sentenced to death, but Dew received a lesser penalty because it was determined that his offense was "primarily the product of mental deficiency," one of the three mitigating circumstances specified in the Ohio death penalty statute.

Two weeks before Lockett's separate trial, the prosecutor offered to permit her to plead guilty to voluntary manslaughter and aggravated robbery (offenses which each carried a maximum penalty of 25 years' imprisonment and a maximum fine of $10,000, see Ohio Rev. Code Ann. §§ 2903.03, 2911.01, 2929.11 (1975)) if she would cooperate with the State, but she rejected the offer. Just prior to her trial, the prosecutor offered to permit her to plead guilty to aggravated murder without specifications, an offense carrying a mandatory life penalty, with the understanding that the aggravated robbery charge and an outstanding forgery charge would be dismissed. Again she rejected the offer.

At trial, the opening argument of Lockett's defense counsel summarized what appears to have been Lockett's version of the events leading to the killing. He asserted the evidence would show that, as far as Lockett knew, Dew and her brother had planned to pawn Dew's ring for $100 to obtain money for the trip back to New Jersey. Lockett had not waited in the car while the men went into the pawnshop but had gone to a restaurant for lunch and had joined Parker, thinking the ring had been pawned, after she saw him walking back to the car. Lockett's counsel asserted that the evidence would show further that Parker had placed the gun under the seat in the taxicab and that Lockett had voluntarily gone to the police station when she learned that the police were looking for the pawnbroker's killers.

Parker was the State's first witness. His testimony related his version of the robbery and shooting, and he admitted to a prior criminal record of breaking and entering, larceny, and receiving stolen goods, as well as bond jumping. He also acknowledged that his plea to aggravated murder had eliminated the possibility of the death penalty, and that he had agreed to testify against Lockett, her brother, and Dew as part of his plea agreement with the prosecutor. At the end of the major portion of Parker's testimony, the prosecutor renewed his offer to permit Lockett to plead guilty to aggravated murder without specifications and to drop the other charges against her. For the third time Lockett refused the option of pleading guilty to a lesser offense.

Lockett called Dew and her brother as defense witnesses, but they invoked their Fifth Amendment rights and refused to testify. In the course of the defense presentation, Lockett's counsel informed the court, in the presence of the jury, that he believed Lockett was to be the next witness and requested a short recess. After the recess, Lockett's counsel told the judge that Lockett wished to testify but had decided to accept her mother's advice to remain silent, despite her counsel's warning that, if she followed that advice, she would have no

595

defense except the cross-examination of the State's witnesses. Thus, the defense did not introduce any evidence to rebut the prosecutor's case.

The court instructed the jury that, before it could find Lockett guilty, it had to find that she purposely had killed the pawnbroker while committing or attempting to commit aggravated robbery. The jury was further charged that one who

"purposely aids, helps, associates himself or herself with another for the purpose of committing a crime is regarded as if he or she were the principal offender and is just as guilty as if the person performed every act constituting the offense. . . ."

Regarding the intent requirement, the court instructed:

"A person engaged in a common design with others to rob by force and violence an individual or individuals of their property is presumed to acquiesce in whatever may reasonably be necessary to accomplish the object of their enterprise. . . .

"If the conspired robbery and the manner of its accomplishment would be reasonably likely to produce death, each plotter is equally guilty with the principal offender as an aider and abettor in the homicide . . . . An intent to kill by an aider and abettor may be found to exist beyond a reasonable doubt under such circumstances."

The jury found Lockett guilty as charged.

Once a verdict of aggravated murder with specifications had been returned, the Ohio death penalty statute required the trial judge to impose a death sentence unless, after "considering the nature and circumstances of the offense" and Lockett's "history, character, and condition," he found by a preponderance of the evidence that (1) the victim had induced or facilitated the offense, (2) it was unlikely that Lockett would have committed the offense but for the fact that she "was under duress, coercion, or strong provocation," or (3) the offense was "primarily the product of [Lockett's] psychosis or mental deficiency." Ohio Rev. Code §§ 2929.03–2929.04 (B) (1975).

In accord with the Ohio statute, the trial judge requested a presentence report as well as psychiatric and psychological reports. The reports contained detailed information about Lockett's intelligence, character, and background. The psychiatric and psychological reports described her as a 21-year-old with low-average or average intelligence, and not suffering from a mental deficiency. One of the psychologists reported that "her prognosis for rehabilitation" if returned to society was favorable. The presentence report showed that Lockett had committed no major offenses although she had a record of several minor ones as a juvenile and two minor offenses as an adult. It also showed that she had once used heroin but was receiving treatment at a drug abuse clinic and seemed to be "on the road to success" as far as her drug problem was concerned. It concluded that Lockett suffered no psychosis and was not mentally deficient.[2]

After considering the reports and hearing argument on the penalty issue, the trial judge concluded that the offense had not been primarily the product of psychosis or mental deficiency. Without specifically addressing the other two statutory mitigating factors, the judge said that he had "no alternative, whether [he] like[d] the law or not" but to impose the death penalty. He then sentenced Lockett to death.

II

A

At the outset, we address Lockett's various challenges to the validity of her conviction. Her first contention is that the

---

[2] The presentence report also contained information about the robbery. It indicated that Dew had told the police that he, Parker, and Lockett's brother had planned the holdup. It also indicated that Parker had told the police that Lockett had not followed his order to keep the car running during the robbery and instead had gone to get something to eat.

prosecutor's repeated references in his closing remarks to the State's evidence as "unrefuted" and "uncontradicted" constituted a comment on her failure to testify and violated her Fifth and Fourteenth Amendment rights. See *Griffin* v. *California,* 380 U. S. 609, 615 (1965). We conclude, however, that the prosecutor's closing comments in this case did not violate constitutional prohibitions. Lockett's own counsel had clearly focused the jury's attention on her silence, first, by outlining her contemplated defense in his opening statement and, second, by stating to the court and jury near the close of the case, that Lockett would be the "next witness." When viewed against this background, it seems clear that the prosecutor's closing remarks added nothing to the impression that had already been created by Lockett's refusal to testify after the jury had been promised a defense by her lawyer and told that Lockett would take the stand.

B

Lockett also contends that four prospective jurors were excluded from the venire in violation of her Sixth and Fourteenth Amendment rights under the principles established in *Witherspoon* v. *Illinois,* 391 U. S. 510 (1968), and *Taylor* v. *Louisiana,* 419 U. S. 522, 528 (1975). We do not agree.

On *voir dire,* the prosecutor told the venire that there was a possibility that the death penalty might be imposed, but that the judge would make the final decision as to punishment. He then asked whether any of the prospective jurors were so opposed to capital punishment that "they could not sit, listen to the evidence, listen to the law, [and] make their determination solely upon the evidence and the law without considering the fact that capital punishment" might be imposed. Four of the venire responded affirmatively. The trial judge then addressed the following question to those four veniremen:

> "[D]o you feel that you could take an oath to well and truely [*sic*] try this case . . . and follow the law, or is

your conviction so strong that you cannot take an oath,
knowing that a possibility exists in regard to capital
punishment?"

Each of the four specifically stated twice that he or she would
not "take the oath." They were excused.

In *Witherspoon,* persons generally opposed to capital punishment had been excluded for cause from the jury that convicted
and sentenced the petitioner to death. We did not disturb
the conviction but we held that "a sentence of death cannot
be carried out if the jury that imposed or recommended it was
chosen by excluding veniremen for cause simply because they
voiced general objections to the death penalty or expressed
conscientious or religious scruples against its infliction." 391
U. S., at 522. We specifically noted, however, that nothing in
our opinion prevented the execution of a death sentence when
the veniremen excluded for cause make it "unmistakably
clear . . . that their attitude toward the death penalty would
prevent them from making an impartial decision as to the
defendant's *guilt.*" *Id.,* at 522–523, n. 21.

Each of the excluded veniremen in this case made it "unmistakably clear" that they could not be trusted to "abide by
existing law" and "to follow conscientiously the instructions"
of the trial judge. *Boulden* v. *Holman,* 394 U. S. 478, 484
(1969). They were thus properly excluded under *Witherspoon,*
even assuming, *arguendo,* that *Witherspoon* provides a basis
for attacking the conviction as well as the sentence in a capital
case.

Nor was there any violation of the principles of *Taylor* v.
Louisiana, supra. In *Taylor,* the Court invalidated a jury
selection system that operated to exclude a "grossly disproportionate," 419 U. S., at 525, number of women from jury service
thereby depriving the petitioner of a jury chosen from a "fair
cross-section" of the community, *id.,* at 530. Nothing in
Taylor, however, suggests that the right to a representative
jury includes the right to be tried by jurors who have explicitly

indicated an inability to follow the law and instructions of the trial judge.

C

Lockett's final attack on her conviction, as distinguished from her sentence, merits only brief attention. Specifically she contends that the Ohio Supreme Court's interpretation of the complicity provision of the statute under which she was convicted, Ohio Rev. Code Ann. § 2923.03 (A) (1975), was so unexpected that it deprived her of fair warning of the crime with which she was charged. The opinion of the Ohio Supreme Court belies this claim. It shows clearly that the construction given the statute by the Ohio court was consistent with both prior Ohio law and with the legislative history of the statute.[3] In such circumstances, any claim of inadequate notice under the Due Process Clause of the Fourteenth Amendment must be rejected.

III

Lockett challenges the constitutionality of Ohio's death penalty statute on a number of grounds. We find it necessary to consider only her contention that her death sentence is invalid because the statute under which it was imposed did not permit the sentencing judge to consider, as mitigating factors, her character, prior record, age, lack of specific intent to cause death, and her relatively minor part in the crime. To address her contention from the proper perspective, it is helpful to review the developments in our recent cases where we have applied the Eighth and Fourteenth Amendments to death penalty statutes. We do not write on a "clean slate."

A

Prior to *Furman* v. *Georgia*, 408 U. S. 238 (1972), every State that authorized capital punishment had abandoned

---

[3] See 49 Ohio St. 2d 48, 58–62, 358 N. E. 2d 1062, 1070–1072 (1976); *id.*, at 69–70, 358 N. E. 2d, at 1076 (Stern, J., dissenting).

mandatory death penalties,[4] and instead permitted the jury
unguided and unrestrained discretion regarding the imposition
of the death penalty in a particular capital case.[5] Mandatory
death penalties had proved unsatisfactory, as the plurality
noted in *Woodson* v. *North Carolina,* 428 U. S. 280, 293
(1976), in part because juries, "with some regularity, dis-
regarded their oaths and refused to convict defendants where
a death sentence was the automatic consequence of a guilty
verdict."

This Court had never intimated prior to *Furman* that discretion in sentencing offended the Constitution. See *Pennsylvania ex rel. Sullivan* v. *Ashe,* 302 U. S. 51, 55 (1937);
Williams v. *New York,* 337 U. S. 241, 247 (1949); *Williams* v.
Oklahoma, 358 U. S. 576, 585 (1959). As recently as
McGautha v. *California,* 402 U. S. 183 (1971), the Court had
specifically rejected the contention that discretion in imposing
the death penalty violated the fundamental standards of fairness embodied in Fourteenth Amendment due process, *id.,* at
207–208, and had asserted that States were entitled to assume
that "jurors confronted with the truly awesome responsibility
of decreeing death for a fellow human [would] act with due
regard for the consequences of their decision." *Id.,* at 208.

The constitutional status of discretionary sentencing in
capital cases changed abruptly, however, as a result of the
separate opinions supporting the judgment in *Furman.* The
question in *Furman* was whether "the imposition and carrying
out of the death penalty [in the cases before the Court]
constitute[d] cruel and unusual punishment in violation of the
Eighth and Fourteenth Amendments." 408 U. S., at 239.
Two Justices concluded that the Eighth Amendment prohibited the death penalty altogether and on that ground voted

---

[4] See *Woodson* v. *North Carolina,* 428 U. S. 280, 291–292, and n. 25
(1976) (opinion of STEWART, POWELL, and STEVENS, JJ.).

[5] See *id.,* at 291–292; *McGautha* v. *California,* 402 U. S. 183, 200 n. 11
(1971).

to reverse the judgments sustaining the death penalties. *Id.,*
at 305–306 (Brennan, J., concurring); *id.,* at 370–371
(Marshall, J., concurring). Three Justices were unwilling
to hold the death penalty *per se* unconstitutional under the
Eighth and Fourteenth Amendments, but voted to reverse the
judgments on other grounds. In separate opinions, the three
concluded that discretionary sentencing, unguided by legislatively defined standards, violated the Eighth Amendment
because it was "pregnant with discrimination," *id.,* at 257
(Douglas, J., concurring), because it permitted the death
penalty to be "wantonly" and "freakishly" imposed, *id.,* at 310
(Stewart, J., concurring), and because it imposed the death
penalty with "great infrequency" and afforded "no meaningful
basis for distinguishing the few cases in which it [was]
imposed from the many cases in which it [was] not," *id.,* at
313 (White, J., concurring). Thus, what had been approved
under the Due Process Clause of the Fourteenth Amendment
in *McGautha* became impermissible under the Eighth and
Fourteenth Amendments by virtue of the judgment in *Furman.*
See *Gregg* v. *Georgia,* 428 U. S. 153, 195–196, n. 47 (1976)
(opinion of Stewart, Powell, and Stevens, JJ.).

Predictably,[6] the variety of opinions supporting the judgment in *Furman* engendered confusion as to what was required
in order to impose the death penalty in accord with the Eighth
Amendment.[7] Some States responded to what was thought to

---

[6] See *Furman* v. *Georgia,* 408 U. S. 238, 403 (1972) (Burger, C. J.,
dissenting).

[7] The limits on the consideration of mitigating factors in Ohio's death
penalty statute which Lockett now attacks appear to have been a direct
response to *Furman.* Prior to *Furman,* Ohio had begun to revise its system
of capital sentencing. The Ohio House of Representatives had passed a
bill abandoning the practice of unbridled sentencing discretion and instruct-
ing the sentencer to consider a list of aggravating and mitigating circumstances in determining whether to impose the death penalty. The list of
mitigating circumstances permitted consideration of any circumstance

be the command of *Furman* by adopting mandatory death penalties for a limited category of specific crimes thus eliminating all discretion from the sentencing process in capital cases.[8] Other States attempted to continue the practice of individually assessing the culpability of each individual defendant convicted of a capital offense and, at the same time, to comply with *Furman,* by providing standards to guide the sentencing decision.[9]

Four years after *Furman,* we considered Eighth Amendment

"tending to mitigate the offense, though failing to establish a defense." See Sub. House Bill 511, 109th Ohio General Assembly § 2929.03 (C)(3), passed by the Ohio House on March 22, 1972; Lehman & Norris, Some Legislative History and Comments on Ohio's New Criminal Code, 23 Cleve. St. L. Rev. 8, 10, 16 (1974).

Furman was announced during the Ohio Senate Judiciary Committee's consideration of the Ohio House bill. After *Furman,* the Committee decided to retain the death penalty but to eliminate much of the sentencing discretion permitted by the House bill. As a result, the Ohio Senate developed the current sentencing procedure which requires the imposition of the death penalty if one of seven specific aggravating circumstances and none of three specific mitigating circumstances is found to exist. Confronted with what reasonably would have appeared to be the questionable constitutionality of permitting discretionary weighing of mitigating factors after *Furman,* the sponsors of the Ohio House bill were not in a position to mount a strong opposition to the Senate's amendments, see Lehman & Norris, *supra,* at 18–22, and the statute under which Lockett was sentenced was enacted.

[8] See, *e. g., Woodson, supra,* at 300 (opinion of Stewart, Powell, and Stevens, JJ.); *Rockwell* v. *Superior Court,* 18 Cal. 3d 420, 446–448, 556 P. 2d 1101, 1116–1118 (1976) (Clark, J., concurring) (account of how California and other States enacted unconstitutional mandatory death penalties in response to *Furman*); *State* v. *Spence,* 367 A. 2d 983, 985–986 (Del. 1976) (Delaware Legislature and court interpreted *Furman* as requiring elimination of all sentencing discretion resulting in an unconstitutional statute); Liebman & Shepard, Guiding Capital Sentencing Discretion Beyond the "Boiler Plate": Mental Disorder as a Mitigating Factor, 66 Geo. L. J. 757, 765 n. 43 (1978).

[9] See Note, Discretion and the Constitutionality of the New Death Penalty Statutes, 87 Harv. L. Rev. 1690, 1690–1710 (1974).

issues posed by five of the post-*Furman* death penalty statutes.[10] Four Justices took the position that all five statutes complied with the Constitution; two Justices took the position that none of them complied. Hence, the disposition of each case varied according to the votes of three Justices who delivered a joint opinion in each of the five cases upholding the constitutionality of the statutes of Georgia, Florida, and Texas, and holding those of North Carolina and Louisiana unconstitutional.

The joint opinion reasoned that, to comply with *Furman*, sentencing procedures should not create "a substantial risk that the death penalty [will] be inflicted in an arbitrary and capricious manner." *Gregg* v. *Georgia, supra,* at 188. In the view of the three Justices, however, *Furman* did not require that all sentencing discretion be eliminated, but only that it be "directed and limited," 428 U. S., at 189, so that the death penalty would be imposed in a more consistent and rational manner and so that there would be a "meaningful basis for distinguishing the . . . cases in which it is imposed from . . . the many cases in which it is not." *Id.,* at 188. The plurality concluded, in the course of invalidating North Carolina's mandatory death penalty statute, that the sentencing process must permit consideration of the "character and record of the individual offender and the circumstances of the particular offense as a constitutionally indispensable part of the process of inflicting the penalty of death," *Woodson* v. *North Carolina,* 428 U. S., at 304, in order to ensure the reliability, under Eighth Amendment standards, of the determination that "death is the appropriate punishment in a specific case." *Id.,* at 305; see *Roberts (Harry)* v. *Louisiana,* 431 U. S. 633, 637 (1977); *Jurek* v. *Texas,* 428 U. S. 262, 271–272 (1976).

---

[10] *Gregg* v. *Georgia,* 428 U. S. 153 (1976); *Proffitt* v. *Florida,* 428 U. S. 242 (1976); *Jurek* v. *Texas,* 428 U. S. 262 (1976); *Woodson* v. *North Carolina, supra;* and *Roberts (Stanislaus)* v. *Louisiana,* 428 U. S. 325 (1976).

In the last decade, many of the States have been obliged to
revise their death penalty statutes in response to the various
opinions supporting the judgments in *Furman* and *Gregg* and
its companion cases. The signals from this Court have not,
however, always been easy to decipher. The States now
deserve the clearest guidance that the Court can provide; we
have an obligation to reconcile previously differing views in
order to provide that guidance.

B

With that obligation in mind we turn to Lockett's attack on
the Ohio statute. Essentially she contends that the Eighth
and Fourteenth Amendments require that the sentencer be
given a full opportunity to consider mitigating circumstances
in capital cases and that the Ohio statute does not comply with
that requirement. She relies, in large part, on the plurality
opinions in *Woodson, supra,* at 303–305, and *Roberts (Stanislaus)* v. *Louisiana,* 428 U. S. 325, 333–334 (1976), and the
joint opinion in *Jurek, supra,* at 271–272, but she goes beyond
them.

We begin by recognizing that the concept of individualized
sentencing in criminal cases generally, although not constitutionally required, has long been accepted in this country. See
Williams v. *New York,* 337 U. S., at 247–248; *Pennsylvania ex
rel. Sullivan* v. *Ashe,* 302 U. S., at 55. Consistent with that
concept, sentencing judges traditionally have taken a wide
range of factors into account. That States have authority to
make aiders and abettors equally responsible, as a matter of
law, with principals, or to enact felony-murder statutes is
beyond constitutional challenge. But the definition of crimes
generally has not been thought automatically to dictate what
should be the proper penalty. See *ibid.; Williams* v. *New
York, supra,* at 247–248; *Williams* v. *Oklahoma,* 358 U. S., at
585. And where sentencing discretion is granted, it generally

has been agreed that the sentencing judge's "possession of the fullest information possible concerning the defendant's life and characteristics" is "[h]ighly relevant—*if not essential*—[to the] selection of an appropriate sentence . . . ." *Williams* v. *New York, supra,* at 247 (emphasis added).

The opinions of this Court going back many years in dealing with sentencing in capital cases have noted the strength of the basis for individualized sentencing. For example, Mr. Justice Black, writing for the Court in *Williams* v. *New York, supra,* at 247–248—a capital case—observed that the

> "whole country has traveled far from the period in which the death sentence was an automatic and commonplace result of convictions—even for offenses today deemed trivial."

Ten years later, in *Williams* v. *Oklahoma, supra,* at 585, another capital case, the Court echoed Mr. Justice Black, stating that

> "[i]n discharging his duty of imposing a proper sentence, the sentencing judge is authorized, *if not required,* to consider all of the mitigating and aggravating circumstances involved in the crime." (Emphasis added.)

See also *Furman* v. *Georgia,* 408 U. S., at 245–246 (Douglas, J., concurring); *id.,* at 297–298 (BRENNAN, J., concurring); *id.,* at 339 (MARSHALL, J., concurring); *id.,* at 402–403 (BURGER, C. J., dissenting); *id.,* at 413 (BLACKMUN, J., dissenting); *McGautha* v. *California,* 402 U. S., at 197–203. Most would agree that "the 19th century movement away from mandatory death sentences marked an enlightened introduction of flexibility into the sentencing process." *Furman* v. *Georgia, supra,* at 402 (BURGER, C. J., dissenting).

Although legislatures remain free to decide how much discretion in sentencing should be reposed in the judge or jury in noncapital cases, the plurality opinion in *Woodson,* after reviewing the historical repudiation of mandatory sentencing in capital cases, 428 U. S., at 289–298, concluded that

> "in capital cases the fundamental respect for humanity underlying the Eighth Amendment . . . requires consideration of the character and record of the individual offender and the circumstances of the particular offense as a constitutionally indispensable part of the process of inflicting the penalty of death." *Id.*, at 304.

That declaration rested "on the predicate that the penalty of death is qualitatively different" from any other sentence. *Id.*, at 305. We are satisfied that this qualitative difference between death and other penalties calls for a greater degree of reliability when the death sentence is imposed. The mandatory death penalty statute in *Woodson* was held invalid because it permitted *no* consideration of "relevant facets of the character and record of the individual offender or the circumstances of the particular offense." *Id.*, at 304. The plurality did not attempt to indicate, however, which facets of an offender or his offense it deemed "relevant" in capital sentencing or what degree of consideration of "relevant facets" it would require.

We are now faced with those questions and we conclude that the Eighth and Fourteenth Amendments require that the sentencer, in all but the rarest kind of capital case,[11] not be precluded from considering, *as a mitigating factor,* any aspect of a defendant's character or record and any of the circumstances of the offense that the defendant proffers as a basis for a sentence less than death.[12] We recognize that, in noncapital

---

[11] We express no opinion as to whether the need to deter certain kinds of homicide would justify a mandatory death sentence as, for example, when a prisoner—or escapee—under a life sentence is found guilty of murder. See *Roberts (Harry)* v. *Louisiana,* 431 U. S. 633, 637 n. 5 (1977).

[12] Nothing in this opinion limits the traditional authority of a court to exclude, as irrelevant, evidence not bearing on the defendant's character, prior record, or the circumstances of his offense.

cases, the established practice of individualized sentences rests
not on constitutional commands, but on public policy enacted
into statutes.   The considerations that account for the wide
acceptance of individualization of sentences in noncapital
cases surely cannot be thought less important in capital cases.
Given that the imposition of death by public authority is so
profoundly different from all other penalties, we cannot avoid
the conclusion that an individualized decision is essential in
capital cases.   The need for treating each defendant in a
capital case with that degree of respect due the uniqueness of
the individual is far more important than in noncapital cases.
A variety of flexible techniques—probation, parole, work furloughs, to name a few—and various postconviction remedies
may be available to modify an initial sentence of confinement
in noncapital cases.   The nonavailability of corrective or
modifying mechanisms with respect to an executed capital
sentence underscores the need for individualized consideration
as a constitutional requirement in imposing the death
sentence.[13]

There is no perfect procedure for deciding in which cases
governmental authority should be used to impose death.
But a statute that prevents the sentencer in all capital cases
from giving independent mitigating weight to aspects of the
defendant's character and record and to circumstances of the
offense proffered in mitigation creates the risk that the death
penalty will be imposed in spite of factors which may call for
a less severe penalty.   When the choice is between life and
death, that risk is unacceptable and incompatible with the
commands of the Eighth and Fourteenth Amendments.

---

[13] Sentencing in noncapital cases presents no comparable problems.   We
emphasize that in dealing with standards for imposition of the death
sentence we intimate no view regarding the authority of a State or of the
Congress to fix mandatory, minimum sentences for noncapital crimes.

C

The Ohio death penalty statute does not permit the type of individualized consideration of mitigating factors we now hold to be required by the Eighth and Fourteenth Amendments in capital cases.   Its constitutional infirmities can best be understood by comparing it with the statutes upheld in *Gregg*, *Proffitt*, and *Jurek*.

In upholding the Georgia statute in *Gregg*, Justices Stewart, Powell, and Stevens noted that the statute permitted the jury "to consider any aggravating or mitigating circumstances," see *Gregg*, 428 U. S., at 206, and that the Georgia Supreme Court had approved "open and far-ranging argument" in presentence hearings, *id.*, at 203.[14]   Although the Florida statute approved in *Proffitt* contained a list of mitigating factors, six Members of this Court assumed, in approving the statute, that the range of mitigating factors listed in the statute was not exclusive.[15]   *Jurek* involved a Texas statute which made no explicit reference to mitigating factors.   428 U. S., at 272.   Rather, the jury was required to answer three

---

[14] The statute provided that, in sentencing, the jury should consider "any mitigating circumstances or aggravating circumstances otherwise authorized by law" in addition to 10 specified aggravating circumstances.   See Ga. Code Ann. § 27.2534.1 (b) (Supp. 1975).   Mr. Justice White, who also voted to uphold the statute in an opinion joined by The Chief Justice and Mr. Justice Rehnquist, noted that the Georgia Legislature had decided to permit "the jury to dispense mercy on the basis of factors too intangible to write into a statute."   *Gregg*, 428 U. S., at 222.

[15] The opinion of Justices Stewart, Powell, and Stevens in *Proffitt* noted that the Florida statute "provides that '[a]ggravating circumstances shall be *limited* to . . . [eight specified factors]' " and that there was "no such limiting language introducing the list of statutory mitigating factors." 428 U. S., at 250 n. 8.   Mr. Justice White, joined by The Chief Justice and Mr. Justice Rehnquist, accepted the interpretation of the statute contained in the opinion of Justices Stewart, Powell, and Stevens. See *id.*, at 260.

609

questions in the sentencing process, the second of which was "whether there is a probability that the defendant would commit criminal acts of violence that would constitute a continuing threat to society." Tex. Code Crim. Proc., Art. 37.071 (b) (Supp. 1975–1976); see 428 U. S., at 269. The statute survived the petitioner's Eighth and Fourteenth Amendment attack because three Justices concluded that the Texas Court of Criminal Appeals had broadly interpreted the second question—despite its facial narrowness—so as to permit the sentencer to consider "whatever mitigating circumstances" the defendant might be able to show. *Id.*, at 272–273 (opinion of STEWART, POWELL, and STEVENS, JJ.), citing and quoting, *Jurek* v. *State,* 522 S. W. 2d 934, 939–940 (Tex. Crim. App. 1975). None of the statutes we sustained in *Gregg* and the companion cases clearly operated at that time to prevent the sentencer from considering any aspect of the defendant's character and record or any circumstances of his offense as an independently mitigating factor.

In this regard the statute now before us is significantly different. Once a defendant is found guilty of aggravated murder with at least one of seven specified aggravating circumstances, the death penalty must be imposed unless, considering "the nature and circumstances of the offense and the history, character, and condition of the offender," the sentencing judge determines that at least one of the following mitigating circumstances is established by a preponderance of the evidence:

"(1) The victim of the offense induced or facilitated it.

"(2) It is unlikely that the offense would have been committed, but for the fact that the offender was under duress, coercion, or strong provocation.

"(3) The offense was primarily the product of the offender's psychosis or mental deficiency, though such condition is insufficient to establish the defense of insanity." Ohio Rev. Code Ann. § 2929.04 (B) (1975).

The Ohio Supreme Court has concluded that there is no constitutional distinction between the statute approved in *Proffitt* and Ohio's statute, see *State* v. *Bayless*, 48 Ohio St. 2d 73, 86–87, 357 N. E. 2d 1035, 1045–1046 (1976), because the mitigating circumstances in Ohio's statute are "liberally construed in favor of the accused," *State* v. *Bell*, 48 Ohio St. 2d 270, 281, 358 N. E. 2d 556, 564 (1976) ; see *State* v. *Bayless*, *supra*, at 86, 357 N. E. 2d, at 1046, and because the sentencing judge or judges may consider factors such as the age and criminal record of the defendant in determining whether any of the mitigating circumstances is established, *State* v. *Bell*, *supra*, at 281, 358 N. E. 2d, at 564.   But even under the Ohio court's construction of the statute, only the three factors specified in the statute can be considered in mitigation of the defendant's sentence.   See, 48 Ohio St. 2d, at 281–282, 358 N. E. 2d, at 564–565; *State* v. *Bayless, supra*, at 87 n. 2, 357 N. E. 2d, at 1046 n. 2.   We see, therefore, that once it is determined that the victim did not induce or facilitate the offense, that the defendant did not act under duress or coercion, and that the offense was not primarily the product of the defendant's mental deficiency, the Ohio statute mandates the sentence of death.   The absence of direct proof that the defendant intended to cause the death of the victim is relevant for mitigating purposes only if it is determined that it sheds some light on one of the three statutory mitigating factors.   Similarly, consideration of a defendant's comparatively minor role in the offense, or age, would generally not be permitted, as such, to affect the sentencing decision.

The limited range of mitigating circumstances which may be considered by the sentencer under the Ohio statute is incompatible with the Eighth and Fourteenth Amendments.   To meet constitutional requirements, a death penalty statute must not preclude consideration of relevant mitigating factors.

Accordingly, the judgment under review is reversed to the

586

extent that it sustains the imposition of the death penalty, and the case is remanded for further proceedings.[16]

So ordered.

---

[16] In view of our holding that Lockett was not sentenced in accord with the Eighth Amendment, we need not address her contention that the death penalty is constitutionally disproportionate for one who has not been proved to have taken life, to have attempted to take life, or to have intended to take life, or her contention that the death penalty is disproportionate as applied to her in this case. Nor do we address her contentions that the Constitution requires that the death sentence be imposed by a jury; that the Ohio statutory procedures impermissibly burden the defendant's exercise of his rights to plead not guilty and to be tried by a jury; and that it violates the Constitution to require defendants to bear the risk of nonpersuasion as to the existence of mitigating circumstances in capital cases.

SUPREME COURT OF THE UNITED STATES

Syllabus

NIX, WARDEN OF THE IOWA STATE PENITENTIARY *v.* WILLIAMS

CERTIORARI TO THE UNITED STATES COURT OF APPEALS FOR THE EIGHTH CIRCUIT

No. 82–1651. Argued January 18, 1984—Decided June 11, 1984

Following the disappearance of a 10-year-old girl in Des Moines, Iowa, respondent was arrested and arraigned in Davenport, Iowa. The police informed respondent's counsel that they would drive respondent back to Des Moines without questioning him, but during the trip one of the officers began a conversation with respondent that ultimately resulted in his making incriminating statements and directing the officers to the child's body. A systematic search of the area that was being conducted with the aid of 200 volunteers and that had been initiated before respondent made the incriminating statements was terminated when respondent guided police to the body. Before trial in an Iowa state court for first-degree murder, the court denied respondent's motion to suppress evidence of the body and all related evidence, including the body's condition as shown by an autopsy, respondent having contended that such evidence was the fruit of his illegally obtained statements made during the automobile ride. Respondent was convicted, and the Iowa Supreme Court affirmed, but later federal-court habeas corpus proceedings ultimately resulted in this Court's holding that the police had obtained respondent's incriminating statements through interrogation in violation of his Sixth Amendment right to counsel. *Brewer* v. *Williams*, 430 U. S. 387. However, it was noted that even though the statements could not be admitted at a second trial, evidence of the body's location and condition might be admissible on the theory that the body would have been discovered even if the incriminating statements had not been elicited from respondent. *Id.*, at 407, n. 12. At respondent's second state-court trial, his incriminating statements were not offered in evidence, nor did the prosecution seek to show that respondent had directed the police to the child's body. However, evidence concerning the body's lo-

613   I

cation and condition was admitted, the court having concluded that the
State had proved that if the search had continued the body would have
been discovered within a short time in essentially the same condition as
it was actually found.   Respondent was again convicted of first-degree
murder, and the Iowa Supreme Court affirmed.   In subsequent habeas
corpus proceedings, the Federal District Court, denying relief, also concluded that the body inevitably would have been found.   However, the
Court of Appeals reversed, holding that—even assuming that there is an
inevitable discovery exception to the exclusionary rule—the State had
not met the exception's requirement that it be proved that the police did
not act in bad faith.

Held: The evidence pertaining to the discovery and condition of the victim's body was properly admitted at respondent's second trial on the
ground that it would ultimately or inevitably have been discovered even
if no violation of any constitutional provision had taken place.   Pp. 7–16.

  (a) The core rationale for extending the exclusionary rule to evidence
that is the fruit of unlawful police conduct is that such course is needed to
deter police from violations of constitutional and statutory protections
notwithstanding the high social cost of letting obviously guilty persons
go unpunished.   On this rationale, the prosecution is not to be put in a
better position than it would have been in if no illegality had transpired.
By contrast, the independent source doctrine—allowing admission of evidence that has been discovered by means wholly independent of any constitutional violation—rests on the rationale that society's interest in deterring unlawful police conduct and the public interest in having juries
receive all probative evidence of a crime are properly balanced by
putting the police in the same, not a *worse*, position than they would
have been in if no police error or misconduct had occurred.   Although
the independent source doctrine does not apply here, its rationale is
wholly consistent with and justifies adoption of the ultimate or inevitable
discovery exception to the exclusionary rule.   If the prosecution can establish by a preponderance of the evidence that the information ultimately or inevitably would have been discovered by lawful means—here
the volunteers' search—then the deterrence rationale has so little basis
that the evidence should be received.   Pp. 8–11.

  (b) Under the inevitable discovery exception, the prosecution is not
required to prove the absence of bad faith, since such a requirement
would result in withholding from juries relevant and undoubted truth
that would have been available to police absent any unlawful police activity.   This would put the police in a *worse* position than they would have
been in if no unlawful conduct had transpired, and would fail to take into
account the enormous societal cost of excluding truth in the search for
truth in the administration of justice.   Significant disincentives to ob-

taining evidence illegally—including the possibility of departmental discipline and civil liability—lessen the likelihood that the ultimate or inevitable discovery exception will promote police misconduct.   Pp. 11–12.

(c) There is no merit to respondent's contention that because he did not waive his right to the assistance of counsel, and because the Sixth Amendment exclusionary rule is designed to protect the right to a fair trial, competing values may not be balanced in deciding whether the challenged evidence was properly admitted.   Exclusion of physical evidence that would inevitably have been discovered adds nothing to either the integrity or fairness of a criminal trial.   Nor would suppression ensure fairness on the theory that it tends to safeguard the adversary system of justice.   Pp. 12–15.

(d) The record here supports the finding that the search party ultimately or inevitably would have discovered the victim's body.   The evidence clearly shows that the searchers were approaching the actual location of the body, that the search would have been resumed had respondent not led the police to the body, and that the body inevitably would have been found.   Pp. 15–16.

700 F. 2d 1164, reversed and remanded.

BURGER, C. J., delivered the opinion of the Court, in which WHITE, BLACKMUN, POWELL, REHNQUIST, and O'CONNOR, JJ., joined.   WHITE, J., filed a concurring opinion.   STEVENS, J., filed an opinion concurring in the judgment.   BRENNAN, J., filed a dissenting opinion, in which MARSHALL, J., joined.

SUPREME COURT OF THE UNITED STATES

No. 82–1651

CRISPUS NIX, WARDEN, PETITIONER v. ROBERT ANTHONY WILLIAMS

ON WRIT OF CERTIORARI TO THE UNITED STATES COURT OF APPEALS FOR THE EIGHTH CIRCUIT

[June 11, 1984]

CHIEF JUSTICE BURGER delivered the opinion of the Court.

We granted certiorari to consider whether, at respondent Williams' second murder trial in state court, evidence pertaining to the discovery and condition of the victim's body was properly admitted on the ground that it would ultimately or inevitably have been discovered even if no violation of any constitutional or statutory provision had taken place.

I

A

On December 24, 1968, 10-year-old Pamela Powers disappeared from a YMCA building in Des Moines, Iowa, where she had accompanied her parents to watch an athletic contest. Shortly after she disappeared, Williams was seen leaving the YMCA carrying a large bundle wrapped in a blanket; a 14-year-old boy who had helped Williams open his car door reported that he had seen "two legs in it and they were skinny and white."

Williams' car was found the next day 160 miles east of Des Moines in Davenport, Iowa. Later several items of clothing belonging to the child, some of Williams' clothing, and an army blanket like the one used to wrap the bundle that Williams carried out of the YMCA were found at a rest stop on

616

Interstate 80 near Grinnell, between Des Moines and Davenport.   A warrant was issued for Williams' arrest.

Police surmised that Williams had left Pamela Powers or her body somewhere between Des Moines and the Grinnell rest stop where some of the young girl's clothing had been found.   On December 26, the Iowa Bureau of Criminal Investigation initiated a large-scale search. Two hundred volunteers divided into teams began the search 21 miles east of Grinnell, covering an area several miles to the north and south of Interstate 80.   They moved westward from Poweshiek County, in which Grinnell was located, into Jasper County.   Searchers were instructed to check all roads, abandoned farm buildings, ditches, culverts, and any other place in which the body of a small child could be hidden.

Meanwhile, Williams surrendered to local police in Davenport, where he was promptly arraigned.   Williams contacted a Des Moines attorney who arranged for an attorney in Davenport to meet Williams at the Davenport police station.   Des Moines police informed counsel they would pick Williams up in Davenport and return him to Des Moines without questioning him.   Two Des Moines detectives then drove to Davenport, took Williams into custody, and proceeded to drive him back to Des Moines.

During the return trip, one of the policemen, Detective Leaming, began a conversation with Williams, saying:

> "I want to give you something to think about while we're traveling down the road. . . . They are predicting several inches of snow for tonight, and I feel that you yourself are the only person that knows where this little girl's body is . . . and if you get a snow on top of it you yourself may be unable to find it.   And since we will be going right past the area [where the body is] on the way into Des Moines, I feel that we could stop and locate the body, that the parents of this little girl should be entitled to a Christian burial for the little girl who was snatched away from them on Christmas [E]ve and murdered. . . .

617

[A]fter a snow storm [we may not be] able to find it at all."

Leaming told Williams he knew the body was in the area of Mitchellville—a town they would be passing on the way to Des Moines. He concluded the conversation by saying, "I do not want you to answer me. . . . Just think about it . . . ."

Later, as the police car approached Grinnell, Williams asked Leaming whether the police had found the young girl's shoes. After Leaming replied that he was unsure, Williams directed the police to a point near a service station where he said he had left the shoes; they were not found. As they continued the drive to Des Moines, Williams asked whether the blanket had been found and then directed the officers to a rest area in Grinnell where he said he had disposed of the blanket; they did not find the blanket. At this point Leaming and his party were joined by the officers in charge of the search. As they approached Mitchellville, Williams, without any further conversation, agreed to direct the officers to the child's body.

The officers directing the search had called off the search at 3 p. m., when they left the Grinnell Police Department to join Leaming at the rest area. At that time, one search team near the Jasper County-Polk County line was only two and one-half miles from where Williams soon guided Leaming and his party to the body. The child's body was found next to a culvert in a ditch beside a gravel road in Polk County, about two miles south of Interstate 80, and essentially within the area to be searched.

B

First Trial

In February 1969 Williams was indicted for first-degree murder. Before trial in the Iowa court, his counsel moved to suppress evidence of the body and all related evidence including the condition of the body as shown by the autopsy. The ground for the motion was that such evidence was the "fruit" or product of Williams' statements made during the automo-

bile ride from Davenport to Des Moines and prompted by
Leaming's statements.   The motion to suppress was denied.

The jury found Williams guilty of first-degree murder; the
judgment of conviction was affirmed by the Iowa Supreme
Court.   *State* v. *Williams,* 182 N. W. 2d 396 (1970).   Williams then sought release on habeas corpus in the United
States District Court for the Southern District of Iowa.
That court concluded that the evidence in question had been
wrongly admitted at Williams' trial, *Williams* v. *Brewer,* 375
F. Supp. 170 (1974); a divided panel of the Court of Appeals
for the Eighth Circuit agreed.   509 F. 2d 227 (1974).

We granted certiorari, 432 U. S. 1031 (1975), and a divided
Court affirmed, holding that Detective Leaming had obtained
incriminating statements from Williams by what was viewed
as interrogation in violation of his right to counsel.   *Brewer*
v. *Williams,* 430 U. S. 387 (1977).   This Court's opinion
noted, however, that although Williams' incriminating statements could not be introduced into evidence at a second trial,
evidence of the body's location and condition "might well be
admissible on the theory that the body would have been discovered in any event, even had incriminating statements not
been elicited from Williams."   *Id.,* at 407, n. 12.

C

Second Trial

At Williams' second trial in 1977 in the Iowa court, the
prosecution did not offer Williams' statements into evidence,
nor did it seek to show that Williams had directed the police
to the child's body.   However, evidence of the condition of
her body as it was found, articles and photographs of her
clothing, and the results of post mortem medical and chemical
tests on the body were admitted.   The trial court concluded
that the State had proved by a preponderance of the evidence
that, if the search had not been suspended and Williams had
not led the police to the victim, her body would have been
discovered *"within a short time"* in essentially the same con-

dition as it was actually found. The trial court also ruled that if the police had not located the body, "the search would clearly have been taken up again where it left off, given the extreme circumstances of this case and the body would [have] been found *in short order*." App. 86 (emphasis added).

In finding that the body would have been discovered in essentially the same condition as it was actually found, the court noted that freezing temperatures had prevailed and tissue deterioration would have been suspended. *Id.*, at 87. The challenged evidence was admitted and the jury again found Williams guilty of first-degree murder; he was sentenced to life in prison.

On appeal, the Supreme Court of Iowa again affirmed. 285 N. W. 2d 248 (1979). That court held that there was in fact a "hypothetical independent source" exception to the Exclusionary Rule:

> "After the defendant has shown unlawful conduct on the part of the police, the State has the burden to show by a preponderance of the evidence that (1) the police did not act in bad faith for the purpose of hastening discovery of the evidence in question, and (2) that the evidence in question would have been discovered by lawful means." *Id.*, at 260.

As to the first element, the Iowa Supreme Court, having reviewed the relevant cases, stated:

> "The issue of the propriety of the police conduct in this case, as noted earlier in this opinion, has caused the closest possible division of views in every appellate court which has considered the question. In light of the legitimate disagreement among individuals well versed in the law of criminal procedure who were given the opportunity for calm deliberation, it cannot be said that the actions of the police were taken in bad faith." *Id.*, at 260–261.

The Iowa court then reviewed the evidence *de novo*[1] and concluded that the State had shown by a preponderance of the evidence that, even if Williams had not guided police to the child's body, it would inevitably have been found by lawful activity of the search party before its condition had materially changed.

In 1980 Williams renewed his attack on the state-court conviction by seeking a writ of habeas corpus in the United States District Court for the Southern District of Iowa. The District Court conducted its own independent review of the evidence and concluded, as had the state courts, that the body would inevitably have been found by the searchers in essentially the same condition it was in when Williams led police to its discovery. The District Court denied Williams' petition. 528 F. Supp. 664 (1981).

The Court of Appeals for the Eighth Circuit reversed. 700 F. 2d 1164 (1983); an equally divided court denied rehearing en banc. 700 F. 2d 1175 (1983). That court assumed, without deciding, that there is an inevitable discovery exception to the Exclusionary Rule and that the Iowa Supreme Court correctly stated that exception to require proof that the police did not act in bad faith and that the evidence would have been discovered absent any constitutional violation. In reversing the District Court's denial of habeas relief, the Court of Appeals stated:

> "We hold that the State has not met the first requirement. It is therefore unnecessary to decide whether the state courts' finding that the body would have been discovered anyway is fairly supported by the record. It is also unnecessary to decide whether the State must prove the two elements of the exception by clear and

---

[1] Iowa law provides for *de novo* appellate review of factual as well as legal determinations in cases raising constitutional challenges. See, *e. g.*, *Armento* v. *Baughman*, 290 N. W. 2d 11, 15 (Iowa 1980); *State* v. *Ege*, 274 N. W. 2d 350, 352 (Iowa 1979).

convincing evidence, as defendant argues, or by a preponderance of the evidence, as the state courts held.

"The state trial court, in denying the motion to suppress, made no finding one way or the other on the question of bad faith. Its opinion does not even mention the issue and seems to proceed on the assumption—contrary to the rule of law later laid down by the Supreme Court of Iowa—that the State needed to show only that the body would have been discovered in any event. The Iowa Supreme Court did expressly address the issue . . . and a finding by an appellate court of a state is entitled to the same presumption of correctness that attaches to trial-court findings under 28 U. S. C. § 2254(d). . . . We conclude, however, that the state Supreme Court's finding that the police did not act in bad faith is not entitled to the shield of § 2254(d) . . . ." 700 F. 2d, at 1169–1170 (footnotes omitted).

We granted the State's petition for certiorari, 461 U. S. —— (1983), and we reverse.

II

A

The Iowa Supreme Court correctly stated that the "vast majority" of all courts, both state and federal, recognize an inevitable discovery exception to the Exclusionary Rule.[2]

[2] Every Federal Court of Appeals having jurisdiction over criminal matters, including the Eighth Circuit in a case decided after the instant case, has endorsed the inevitable discovery doctrine. See *Wayne* v. *United States*, 115 U. S. App. D. C. 234, 238, 318 F. 2d 205, 209, cert. denied, 375 U. S. 860 (1963); *United States* v. *Bienvenue*, 632 F. 2d 910, 914 (CA1 1980); *United States* v. *Fisher*, 700 F. 2d 780, 784 (CA2 1983); *Government of Virgin Islands* v. *Gereau*, 502 F. 2d 914, 927–928 (CA3 1974), cert. denied, 420 U. S. 909 (1975); *United States* v. *Seohnlein*, 423 F. 2d 1051, 1053 (CA4), cert. denied, 399 U. S. 913 (1970); *United States* v. *Brookins*, 614 F. 2d 1037, 1042, 1044 (CA5 1980); *Papp* v. *Jago*, 656 F. 2d 221, 222 (CA6 1981); *United States ex rel Owens* v. *Twomey*, 508 F. 2d 858, 865–866 (CA7 1974); *United States* v. *Apker*, 705 F. 2d 293, 306–307 (CA8 1983); *United*

We are now urged to adopt and apply the so-called ultimate or inevitable discovery exception to the Exclusionary Rule.

Williams contends that evidence of the body's location and condition is "fruit of the poisonous tree," *i. e.*, the "fruit" or product of Detective Leaming's plea to help the child's parents give her "a Christian burial," which this Court had already held equated to interrogation. He contends that admitting the challenged evidence violated the Sixth Amendment whether it would have been inevitably discovered or not. Williams also contends that, if the inevitable discovery doctrine is constitutionally permissible, it must include a threshold showing of police good faith.

B

The doctrine requiring courts to suppress evidence as the tainted "fruit" of unlawful governmental conduct had its genesis in *Silverthorne Lumber Co.* v. *United States*, 251 U. S. 385 (1920); there, the Court held that the Exclusionary Rule applies not only to the illegally obtained evidence itself, but also to other incriminating evidence derived from the primary evidence. The holding of *Silverthorne* was carefully limited, however, for the Court emphasized that such information does not automatically become "sacred and inaccessible." *Id.*, at 392.

> "If knowledge of [such facts] is gained from an *independent source*, they may be proved like any others . . . ." *Ibid.* (emphasis added).

Wong Sun v. *United States*, 371 U. S. 471 (1963), extended the Exclusionary Rule to evidence that was the indirect product or "fruit" of unlawful police conduct, but there again the Court emphasized that evidence that has been illegally obtained need not always be suppressed, stating:

States v. *Schmidt*, 573 F. 2d 1057, 1065–1066, n. 9 (CA9), cert. denied, 439 U. S. 881 (1978); *United States* v. *Romero*, 692 F. 2d 699, 704 (CA10 1982); *United States* v. *Roper*, 681 F. 2d 1354, 1358 (CA11 1982).

623

"We need not hold that all evidence is 'fruit of the poisonous tree' simply because it would not have come to light *but for the illegal actions* of the police. Rather, the more apt question in such a case is 'whether, granting establishment of the primary illegality, the evidence to which instant objection is made has been come at by exploitation of that illegality or instead by means sufficiently distinguishable to be purged of the primary taint.' " *Id.*, at 487–488 (emphasis added) (quoting J. Maguire, Evidence of Guilt 221 (1959)).

The Court thus pointedly negated the kind of good-faith requirement advanced by the Court of Appeals in reversing the District Court.

Although *Silverthorne* and *Wong Sun* involved violations of the Fourth Amendment, the "fruit of the poisonous tree" doctrine has not been limited to cases in which there has been a Fourth Amendment violation. The Court has applied the doctrine where the violations were of the Sixth Amendment, see *United States* v. *Wade*, 388 U. S. 218 (1967), as well as of the Fifth Amendment.[3]

The core rationale consistently advanced by this Court for extending the Exclusionary Rule to evidence that is the fruit of unlawful police conduct has been that this admittedly drastic and socially costly course is needed to deter police from

---

[3] In *Murphy* v. *Waterfront Comm'n of New York Harbor*, 378 U. S. 52, 79 (1964), the Court held that "a state witness may not be compelled to give testimony which may be incriminating under federal law unless the compelled testimony and its fruits cannot be used in any manner by federal officials in connection with a criminal prosecution against him." The Court added, however, that "[o]nce a defendant demonstrates that he has testified, under a state grant of immunity, to matters related to the federal prosecution, the federal authorities have the burden of showing that their evidence is not tainted by establishing that they had an independent, legitimate source for the disputed evidence." *Id.*, at 79, n. 18; see *id.*, at 103 (WHITE, J., concurring). Application of the independent source doctrine in the Fifth Amendment context was reaffirmed in *Kastigar* v. *United States*, 406 U. S. 441, 460–461 (1972).

violations of constitutional and statutory protections. This Court has accepted the argument that the way to ensure such protections is to exclude evidence seized as a result of such violations notwithstanding the high social cost of letting persons obviously guilty go unpunished for their crimes. On this rationale, the prosecution is not to be put in a better position than it would have been in if no illegality had transpired.

By contrast, the derivative evidence analysis ensures that the prosecution is not put in a *worse* position simply because of some earlier police error or misconduct. The independent source doctrine allows admission of evidence that has been discovered by means wholly independent of any constitutional violation. That doctrine, although closely related to the inevitable discovery doctrine, does not apply here; Williams' statements to Leaming indeed led police to the child's body, but that is not the whole story. The independent source doctrine teaches us that the interest of society in deterring unlawful police conduct and the public interest in having juries receive all probative evidence of a crime are properly balanced by putting the police in the same, not a *worse*, position than they would have been in if no police error or misconduct had occurred.[4] See *Murphy* v. *Waterfront Comm'n of New York Harbor*, 378 U. S. 52, 79 (1964); *Kastigar* v. *United States*, 406 U. S. 441, 457, 458–459 (1972). When the challenged evidence has an independent source, exclusion of such evidence would put the police in a worse position than they would have been in absent any error or violation. There is a functional similarity between these

---

[4] The ultimate or inevitable discovery exception to the Exclusionary Rule is closely related in purpose to the harmless-error rule of *Chapman* v. *California*, 386 U. S. 18, 22 (1967). The harmless-constitutional-error rule "serve[s] a very useful purpose insofar as [it] block[s] setting aside convictions for small errors or defects that have little, if any, likelihood of having changed the result of the trial." The purpose of the inevitable discovery rule is to block setting aside convictions that would have been obtained without police misconduct.

two doctrines in that exclusion of evidence that would inevitably have been discovered would also put the government in a worse position, because the police would have obtained that evidence if no misconduct had taken place. Thus, while the independent source exception would not justify admission of evidence in this case, its rationale is wholly consistent with and justifies our adoption of the ultimate or inevitable discovery exception to the Exclusionary Rule.

It is clear that the cases implementing the Exclusionary Rule "begin with the premise that the challenged evidence is *in some sense* the product of illegal governmental activity." *United States* v. *Crews*, 445 U. S. 463, 471 (1980) (emphasis added). Of course, this does not end the inquiry. If the prosecution can establish by a preponderance of the evidence that the information ultimately or inevitably would have been discovered by lawful means—here the volunteers' search— then the deterrence rationale has so little basis that the evidence should be received.[5] Anything less would reject logic, experience, and common sense.

---

[5] As to the quantum of proof, we have already established some relevant guidelines. In *United States* v. *Matlock*, 415 U. S. 164, 178, n. 14 (1974) (emphasis added), we stated that "the controlling burden of proof at suppression hearings should impose *no greater burden* than proof by a preponderance of the evidence." In *Lego* v. *Twomey*, 404 U. S. 477, 488 (1972), we observed "from our experience [that] no substantial evidence has accumulated that federal rights have suffered from determining admissibility by a preponderance of the evidence" and held that the prosecution must prove by a preponderance of the evidence that a confession sought to be used at trial was voluntary. We are unwilling to impose added burdens on the already difficult task of proving guilt in criminal cases by enlarging the barrier to placing evidence of unquestioned truth before juries.

Williams argues that the preponderance of the evidence standard used by the Iowa courts is inconsistent with *United States* v. *Wade*, 388 U. S. 218 (1967). In requiring clear and convincing evidence of an independent source for an in-court identification, the Court gave weight to the effect an uncounseled pre-trial identification has in "crystalliz[ing] the witnesses' identification of the defendant for the future reference." *Id.*, at 240. The Court noted as well that possible unfairness at the lineup "may be the sole

The requirement that the prosecution must prove the absence of bad faith, imposed here by the Court of Appeals, would place courts in the position of withholding from juries relevant and undoubted truth that would have been available to police absent any unlawful police activity. Of course, that view would put the police in a *worse* position than they would have been in if no unlawful conduct had transpired. And, of equal importance, it wholly fails to take into account the enormous societal cost of excluding truth in the search for truth in the administration of justice. Nothing in this Court's prior holdings supports any such formalistic, pointless, and punitive approach.

The Court of Appeals concluded, without analysis, that if an absence of bad faith requirement were not imposed, "the temptation to risk deliberate violations of the Sixth Amendment would be too great, and the deterrent effect of the Exclusionary Rule reduced too far." 700 F. 2d, at 1169, n. 5. We reject that view. A police officer who is faced with the opportunity to obtain evidence illegally will rarely, if ever, be in a position to calculate whether the evidence sought would inevitably be discovered. Cf. *United States* v. *Ceccolini,* 435 U. S. 268, 283 (1978):

> "[T]he concept of effective deterrence assumes that the police officer consciously realizes the probable consequences of a presumably impermissible course of conduct." (Opinion concurring in judgment.)

On the other hand, when an officer is aware that the evidence will inevitably be discovered, he will try to avoid engaging in any questionable practice. In that situation, there will be

---

means of attack upon the unequivocal courtroom identification," *ibid.,* and recognized the difficulty of determining whether an in-court identification was based on independent recollection unaided by the lineup identification, *id.,* at 240–241. By contrast, inevitable discovery involves no speculative elements but focuses on demonstrated historical facts capable of ready verification or impeachment and does not require a departure from the usual burden of proof at suppression hearings.

little to gain from taking any dubious "shortcuts" to obtain the evidence. Significant disincentives to obtaining evidence illegally—including the possibility of departmental discipline and civil liability—also lessen the likelihood that the ultimate or inevitable discovery exception will promote police misconduct. See *Bivens* v. *Six Unknown Federal Narcotics Agents*, 403 U. S. 388, 397 (1971). In these circumstances, the societal costs of the Exclusionary Rule far outweigh any possible benefits to deterrence that a good-faith requirement might produce.

Williams contends that because he did not waive his right to the assistance of counsel, the Court may not balance competing values in deciding whether the challenged evidence was properly admitted. He argues that, unlike the Exclusionary Rule in the Fourth Amendment context, the essential purpose of which is to deter police misconduct, the Sixth Amendment Exclusionary Rule is designed to protect the right to a fair trial and the integrity of the factfinding process. Williams contends that, when those interests are at stake, the societal costs of excluding evidence obtained from responses presumed involuntary are irrelevant in determining whether such evidence should be excluded. We disagree.

Exclusion of physical evidence that would inevitably have been discovered adds nothing to either the integrity or fairness of a criminal trial. The Sixth Amendment right to counsel protects against unfairness by preserving the adversary process in which the reliability of proffered evidence may be tested in cross-examination. See *United States* v. *Ash*, 413 U. S. 300, 314 (1973); *Schneckloth* v. *Bustamonte*, 412 U. S. 218, 241 (1973). Here, however, Detective Leaming's conduct did nothing to impugn the reliability of the evidence in question—the body of the child and its condition as it was found, articles of clothing found on the body, and the autopsy. No one would seriously contend that the presence of counsel in the police car when Leaming appealed to Williams' decent human instincts would have had any bearing on the reliability of the body as evidence. Suppression, in these circumstances, would do nothing whatever to promote the integrity of the trial process, but would inflict a wholly unacceptable burden on the administration of criminal justice.

Nor would suppression ensure fairness on the theory that it tends to safeguard the adversary system of justice. To assure the fairness of trial proceedings, this Court has held that assistance of counsel must be available at pretrial confrontations where "the subsequent trial [cannot] cure a[n otherwise] one-sided confrontation between prosecuting authorities and the uncounseled defendant." *United States* v. *Ash, supra,* at 315. Fairness can be assured by placing the State and the accused in the same positions they would have been in had the impermissible conduct not taken place. However, if the government can prove that the evidence would have been obtained inevitably and, therefore, would have been admitted regardless of any overreaching by the police, there is no rational basis to keep that evidence from the jury in order to ensure the fairness of the trial proceedings. In that situation, the State has gained no advantage at trial and the defendant has suffered no prejudice. Indeed, suppression of the evidence would operate to undermine the adversary system by putting the State in a *worse* position than it would have occupied without any police misconduct. Williams' argument that inevitable discovery constitutes impermissible balancing of values is without merit.

More than a half century ago, Judge, later Justice, Cardozo made his seminal observation that under the Exclusionary Rule "[t]he criminal is to go free because the constable has blundered." *People* v. *Defore,* 242 N. Y. 13, 21, 150 N. E. 585, 587 (1926). Prophetically, he went on to consider "how far-reaching in its effect upon society" the Exclusionary Rule would be when "[t]he pettiest peace officer would have it in his power through overzeal or indiscretion to confer immunity upon an offender for crimes the most flagitious." *Id.*, at 23, 150 N. E., at 588.

Some day, Cardozo speculated, some court might press the Exclusionary Rule to the outer limits of its logic—or beyond—and suppress evidence relating to the "body of a murdered" victim because of the means by which it was found. *Id.*, at 23–24, 150 N. E., at 588. Cardozo's prophecy was fulfilled in *Killough* v. *United States*, 114 U. S. App. D. C. 305, 309, 315 F. 2d 241, 245 (1962) (en banc). But when, as here, the evidence in question would inevitably have been discovered without reference to the police error or misconduct, there is no nexus sufficient to provide a taint and the evidence is admissible.

C

The Court of Appeals did not find it necessary to consider whether the record fairly supported the finding that the volunteer search party would ultimately or inevitably have discovered the victim's body. However, three courts independently reviewing the evidence have found that the body of the child inevitably would have been found by the searchers. Williams challenges these findings, asserting that the record contains only the "*post hoc* rationalization" that the search efforts would have proceeded two and one-half miles into Polk County where Williams had led police to the body.

When that challenge was made at the suppression hearing preceeding Williams' second trial, the prosecution offered the testimony of Agent Ruxlow of the Iowa Bureau of Criminal Investigation. Ruxlow had organized and directed some 200 volunteers who were searching for the child's body. Tr. of Hearings on Motion to Suppress in *State* v. *Williams*, No. CR 55805, p. 34 (May 31, 1977). The searchers were instructed "to check all the roads, the ditches, any culverts . . . . If they came upon any abandoned farm buildings, they were instructed to go onto the property and search those abandoned farm buildings or any other places where a small child could be secreted." *Id.*, at 35.   Ruxlow testified that he marked off highway maps of Poweshiek and Jasper Counties in grid fashion, divided the volunteers into teams of four to six persons, and assigned each team to search specific grid areas.   *Id.*, at 34.   Ruxlow also testified that, if the search had not been suspended because of Williams' promised cooperation, it would have continued into Polk County, using the same grid system.   *Id.*, at 36, 39–40.   Although he had previously marked off into grids only the highway maps of Poweshiek and Jasper Counties, Ruxlow had obtained a map of Polk County, which he said he would have marked off in the same manner had it been necessary for the search to continue.   *Id.*, at 39.

The search had commenced at approximately 10 a. m. and moved westward through Poweshiek County into Jasper County.   At approximately 3 p. m., after Williams had volunteered to cooperate with the police, Officer Leaming, who was in the police car with Williams, sent word to Ruxlow and the other Special Agent directing the search to meet him at the Grinnell truck stop and the search was suspended at that time.   *Id.*, at 51–52.   Ruxlow also stated that he was "under the impression that there was a possibility" that Williams would lead them to the child's body at that time.   *Id.*, at 61. The search was not resumed once it was learned that Williams had led the police to the body, *id.*, at 57, which was found two and one-half miles from where the search had stopped in what would have been the easternmost grid to be searched in Polk County, *id.*, at 39.   There was testimony that it would have taken an additional three to five hours to discover the body if the search had continued, *id.*, at 41; the body was found near a culvert, one of the kinds of places the teams had been specifically directed to search.

On this record it is clear that the search parties were approaching the actual location of the body and we are satisfied, along with three courts earlier, that the volunteer search teams would have resumed the search had Williams not earlier led the police to the body and the body inevitably would have been found. The evidence asserted by Williams as newly discovered, *i. e.*, certain photographs of the body and deposition testimony of Agent Ruxlow made in connection with the federal habeas proceeding, does not demonstrate that the material facts were inadequately developed in the suppression hearing in state court or that Williams was denied a full, fair, and adequate opportunity to present all relevant facts at the suppression hearing.[6]

The judgment of the Court of Appeals is reversed, and the case is remanded for further proceedings consistent with this opinion.[7]

It is so ordered.

---

[6] Williams had presented to the District Court newly discovered evidence consisting of "previously overlooked photographs of the body at the site of its discovery and recent deposition testimony of the investigative officer in charge of the search [Ruxlow]." 528 F. Supp., at 671, n. 6. He contends that Ruxlow's testimony was no more than "*post hoc* rationalization" and challenges Ruxlow's credibility. However, the state trial court and federal District Court that heard Ruxlow's testimony credited it. The District Court found that the newly discovered evidence "neither adds much to nor subtracts much from the suppression hearing evidence." *Ibid.*

[7] In view of our holding that the challenged evidence was admissible under the inevitable discovery exception to the Exclusionary Rule, we find it unnecessary to decide whether *Stone* v. *Powell*, 428 U. S. 465 (1976), should be extended to bar federal habeas corpus review of Williams' Sixth Amendment claim and we express no view on that issue.

PART V

EQUAL JUSTICE UNDER LAW:
RACIAL AND NON-RACIAL DISCRIMINATION

--oOo--

REED v. REED, ADMINISTRATOR

APPEAL FROM THE SUPREME COURT OF IDAHO

No. 70–4. Argued October 19, 1971—Decided November 22, 1971

A mandatory provision of the Idaho probate code that gives preference to men over women when persons of the same entitlement class apply for appointment as administrator of a decedent's estate is based solely on a discrimination prohibited by and therefore violative of the Equal Protection Clause of the Fourteenth Amendment.

93 Idaho 511, 465 P. 2d 635, reversed and remanded.

BURGER, C. J., delivered the opinion for a unanimous Court.

Allen R. Derr argued the cause for appellant. With him on the briefs were *Melvin L. Wulf, Ruth Bader Ginsburg, Pauli Murray,* and *Dorothy Kenyon.*

Charles S. Stout argued the cause for appellee. With him on the brief was *Myron E. Anderson.*

Briefs of *amici curiae* urging reversal were filed by *J. Lee Rankin* and *Norman Redlich* for the City of New York; by *Martha W. Griffiths, Phineas Indritz, Leo Kanowitz, Marguerite Rawalt, Sylvia Roberts,* and *Faith Seidenberg* for American Veterans Committee, Inc., et al.; and by *Birch Bayh* for the National Federation of Business and Professional Women's Clubs, Inc.

MR. CHIEF JUSTICE BURGER delivered the opinion of the Court.

Richard Lynn Reed, a minor, died intestate in Ada County, Idaho, on March 29, 1967. His adoptive parents, who had separated sometime prior to his death, are the parties to this appeal. Approximately seven months after Richard's death, his mother, appellant Sally Reed, filed a petition in the Probate Court of Ada County, seeking appointment as administratrix of her son's estate.[1] Prior to the date set for a hearing on the mother's petition, appellee Cecil Reed, the father of the decedent, filed a competing petition seeking to have himself appointed administrator of the son's estate. The probate court held a joint hearing on the two petitions and thereafter ordered that letters of administration be issued to appellee Cecil Reed upon his taking the oath and filing the bond required by law. The court treated §§ 15–312 and 15–314 of the Idaho Code as the controlling statutes and read those sections as compelling a preference for Cecil Reed because he was a male.

Section 15–312[2] designates the persons who are entitled to administer the estate of one who dies intestate. In making these designations, that section lists 11 classes of persons who are so entitled and provides, in substance,

---

[1] In her petition, Sally Reed alleged that her son's estate, consisting of a few items of personal property and a small savings account, had an aggregate value of less than $1,000.

[2] Section 15–312 provides as follows:

"Administration of the estate of a person dying intestate must be granted to some one or more of the persons hereinafter mentioned, and they are respectively entitled thereto in the following order:

"1. The surviving husband or wife or some competent person whom he or she may request to have appointed.

"2. The children.

"3. The father or mother.

"4. The brothers.

"5. The sisters.

"6. The grandchildren.

"7. The next of kin entitled to share in the distribution of the estate.

"8. Any of the kindred.

"9. The public administrator.

"10. The creditors of such person at the time of death.

"11. Any person legally competent.

"If the decedent was a member of a partnership at the time of his decease, the surviving partner must in no case be appointed administrator of his estate."

that the order in which those classes are listed in the section shall be determinative of the relative rights of competing applicants for letters of administration. One of the 11 classes so enumerated is "[t]he father or mother" of the person dying intestate. Under this section, then, appellant and appellee, being members of the same entitlement class, would seem to have been equally entitled to administer their son's estate. Section 15–314 provides, however, that

> "[o]f several persons claiming and equally entitled [under § 15–312] to administer, males must be preferred to females, and relatives of the whole to those of the half blood."

In issuing its order, the probate court implicitly recognized the equality of entitlement of the two applicants under § 15–312 and noted that neither of the applicants was under any legal disability; the court ruled, however, that appellee, being a male, was to be preferred to the female appellant "by reason of Section 15–314 of the Idaho Code." In stating this conclusion, the probate judge gave no indication that he had attempted to determine the relative capabilities of the competing applicants to perform the functions incident to the administration of an estate. It seems clear the probate judge considered himself bound by statute to give preference to the male candidate over the female, each being otherwise "equally entitled."

Sally Reed appealed from the probate court order, and her appeal was treated by the District Court of the Fourth Judicial District of Idaho as a constitutional attack on § 15–314. In dealing with the attack, that court held that the challenged section violated the Equal Protection Clause of the Fourteenth Amendment[3] and was, there-

---

[3] The court also held that the statute violated Art. I, § 1, of the Idaho Constitution.

fore, void; the matter was ordered "returned to the Probate Court for its determination of which of the two parties" was better qualified to administer the estate.

This order was never carried out, however, for Cecil Reed took a further appeal to the Idaho Supreme Court, which reversed the District Court and reinstated the original order naming the father administrator of the estate. In reaching this result, the Idaho Supreme Court first dealt with the governing statutory law and held that under § 15–312 "a father and mother are 'equally entitled' to letters of administration," but the preference given to males by § 15–314 is "mandatory" and leaves no room for the exercise of a probate court's discretion in the appointment of administrators. Having thus definitively and authoritatively interpreted the statutory provisions involved, the Idaho Supreme Court then proceeded to examine, and reject, Sally Reed's contention that § 15–314 violates the Equal Protection Clause by giving a mandatory preference to males over females, without regard to their individual qualifications as potential estate administrators. 93 Idaho 511, 465 P. 2d 635.

Sally Reed thereupon appealed for review by this Court pursuant to 28 U. S. C. § 1257 (2), and we noted probable jurisdiction. 401 U. S. 934. Having examined the record and considered the briefs and oral arguments of the parties, we have concluded that the arbitrary preference established in favor of males by § 15–314 of the Idaho Code cannot stand in the face of the Fourteenth Amendment's command that no State deny the equal protection of the laws to any person within its jurisdiction.[4]

_____

[4] We note that § 15–312, set out in n. 2, *supra*, appears to give a superior entitlement to brothers of an intestate (class 4) than is given to sisters (class 5). The parties now before the Court are not

Idaho does not, of course, deny letters of administration to women altogether. Indeed, under § 15–312, a woman whose spouse dies intestate has a preference over a son, father, brother, or any other male relative of the decedent. Moreover, we can judicially notice that in this country, presumably due to the greater longevity of women, a large proportion of estates, both intestate and under wills of decedents, are administered by surviving widows.

Section 15–314 is restricted in its operation to those situations where competing applications for letters of administration have been filed by both male and female members of the same entitlement class established by § 15–312. In such situations, § 15–314 provides that different treatment be accorded to the applicants on the basis of their sex; it thus establishes a classification subject to scrutiny under the Equal Protection Clause.

In applying that clause, this Court has consistently recognized that the Fourteenth Amendment does not deny to States the power to treat different classes of persons in different ways. *Barbier* v. *Connolly*, 113 U. S. 27 (1885); *Lindsley* v. *Natural Carbonic Gas Co.*, 220 U. S. 61 (1911); *Railway Express Agency* v. *New York*, 336 U. S. 106 (1949); *McDonald* v. *Board of Election Commissioners*, 394 U. S. 802 (1969). The Equal Protection Clause of that amendment does, however, deny to States the power to legislate that different treatment be accorded to persons placed by a statute into

affected by the operation of § 15–312 in this respect, however, and appellant has made no challenge to that section.

We further note that on March 12, 1971, the Idaho Legislature adopted the Uniform Probate Code, effective July 1, 1972. Idaho Laws 1971, c. 111, p. 233. On that date, §§ 15–312 and 15–314 of the present code will, then, be effectively repealed, and there is in the new legislation no mandatory preference for males over females as administrators of estates.

different classes on the basis of criteria wholly unrelated
to the objective of that statute. A classification "must
be reasonable, not arbitrary, and must rest upon some
ground of difference having a fair and substantial relation to the object of the legislation, so that all persons
similarly circumstanced shall be treated alike." *Royster
Guano Co.* v. *Virginia,* 253 U. S. 412, 415 (1920). The
question presented by this case, then, is whether a difference in the sex of competing applicants for letters of
administration bears a rational relationship to a state
objective that is sought to be advanced by the operation
of §§ 15–312 and 15–314.

In upholding the latter section, the Idaho Supreme
Court concluded that its objective was to eliminate one
area of controversy when two or more persons, equally
entitled under § 15–312, seek letters of administration
and thereby present the probate court "with the issue of
which one should be named." The court also concluded
that where such persons are not of the same sex, the elimination of females from consideration "is neither an illogi-
cal nor arbitrary method devised by the legislature to
resolve an issue that would otherwise require a hearing
as to the relative merits . . . of the two or more petitioning relatives . . . ." 93 Idaho, at 514, 465 P. 2d,
at 6̣38.

Clearly the objective of reducing the workload on
probate courts by eliminating one class of contests is not
without some legitimacy. The crucial question, however,
is whether § 15–314 advances that objective in a manner
consistent with the command of the Equal Protection
Clause. We hold that it does not. To give a mandatory
preference to members of either sex over members of the
other, merely to accomplish the elimination of hearings
on the merits, is to make the very kind of arbitrary legislative choice forbidden by the Equal Protection Clause
of the Fourteenth Amendment; and whatever may be

said as to the positive values of avoiding intrafamily controversy, the choice in this context may not lawfully be mandated solely on the basis of sex.

We note finally that if § 15–314 is viewed merely as a modifying appendage to § 15–312 and as aimed at the same objective, its constitutionality is not thereby saved. The objective of § 15–312 clearly is to establish degrees of entitlement of various classes of persons in accordance with their varying degrees and kinds of relationship to the intestate. Regardless of their sex, persons within any one of the enumerated classes of that section are similarly situated with respect to that objective. By providing dissimilar treatment for men and women who are thus similarly situated, the challenged section violates the Equal Protection Clause. *Royster Guano Co.* v. *Virginia, supra.*

The judgment of the Idaho Supreme Court is reversed and the case remanded for further proceedings not inconsistent with this opinion.

Reversed and remanded.

LUBIN v. PANISH, REGISTRAR–RECORDER
OF COUNTY OF LOS ANGELES

CERTIORARI TO THE SUPREME COURT OF CALIFORNIA

No. 71–6852. Argued October 9, 1973—Decided March 26, 1974

Petitioner, an indigent, was denied nomination papers to file as a
candidate for the position of County Supervisor in California
because, although otherwise qualified, he was unable to pay the
filing fee required of all candidates by a California statute. He
brought this class action in California Superior Court for a writ
of mandate against the Secretary of State and the County
Registrar-Recorder, claiming that the statute, by requiring the
filing fee but providing no other way of securing access to the
ballot, deprived him and others similarly situated of the equal
protection guaranteed by the Fourteenth Amendment and rights of
expression and association guaranteed by the First and Fourteenth
Amendments. The Superior Court denied the writ of mandate; the
Court of Appeal and the California Supreme Court also denied
writs. *Held:* Absent reasonable alternative means of ballot access,
a State may not, consistent with constitutional standards, require
from an indigent candidate filing fees that he cannot pay; denying
a person the right to file as a candidate solely because of an inability to pay a fixed fee, without providing any alternative means,
is not reasonably necessary to the accomplishment of the State's
legitimate interest of maintaining the integrity of elections. Pp.
712–719.

Reversed and remanded.

BURGER, C. J., delivered the opinion of the Court, in which DOUG-
LAS, BRENNAN, STEWART, WHITE, MARSHALL, and POWELL, JJ.,
joined. DOUGLAS, J., filed a concurring opinion, *post*, p. 719.
BLACKMUN, J., filed an opinion concurring in part, in which REHN-
QUIST, J., joined, *post*, p. 722.

Marguerite M. Buckley argued the cause for petitioner.
With her on the briefs were *A. L. Wirin* and *Fred Okrand.*

Edward H. Gaylord argued the cause for respondent.
With him on the brief was *John H. Larson.*

MR. CHIEF JUSTICE BURGER delivered the opinion of the Court.

We granted certiorari to consider petitioner's claim that the California statute requiring payment of a filing fee of $701.60 in order to be placed on the ballot in the primary election for nomination to the position of County Supervisor, while providing no alternative means of access to the ballot, deprived him, as an indigent person unable to pay the fee, and others similarly situated, of the equal protection guaranteed by the Fourteenth Amendment and rights of expression and association guaranteed by the First Amendment.

The California Elections Code provides that forms required for nomination and election to congressional, state, and county offices are to be issued to candidates only upon prepayment of a nonrefundable filing fee. Cal. Elections Code § 6551. Generally, the required fees are fixed at a percentage of the salary for the office sought. The fee for candidates for United States Senator, Governor, and other state offices and some county offices, is 2% of the annual salary. Candidates for Representative to Congress, State Senator or Assemblyman, or for judicial office or district attorney, must pay 1%. No filing fee is required of candidates in the presidential primary, or for offices which pay either no fixed salary or not more than $600 annually. §§ 6551, 6552, and 6554.

Under the California statutes in effect at the time this suit was commenced, the required candidate filing fees ranged from $192 for State Assembly, $425 for Congress, $701.60 for Los Angeles County Board of Supervisors, $850 for United States Senator, to $982 for Governor.

The California statute provides for the counting of write-in votes subject to certain conditions. § 18600 *et seq.* (Supp. 1974). Write-in votes are not counted, however, unless the person desiring to be a write-in candidate files a statement to that effect with the Registrar-Recorder at least eight days prior to the election, § 18602, and pays the requisite filing fee, § 18603. The latter section provides that "[n]o name written upon a ballot in any state, county, city, city and county, or district election shall be counted for an office or nomination unless . . . [t]he fee required by Section 6555 is paid when the declaration of write-in candidacy is filed . . . ." Thus, the contested filing fees must be satisfied even under the write-in nomination procedures.

Petitioner commenced this class action on February 17, 1972, by petitioning the Los Angeles Superior Court for a writ of mandate against the Secretary of State and the Los Angeles County Registrar-Recorder. The suit was filed on behalf of petitioner and all those similarly situated persons who were unable to pay the filing fees and who desired to be nominated for public office. In his complaint, petitioner maintained that he was a citizen and a voter and that he had sought nomination as a candidate for membership on the Board of Supervisors of Los Angeles County.[1] Petitioner asserted that on February 15, 1972, he had appeared at the office of James S. Allison, then Registrar-Recorder of the County of Los Angeles, to apply for and secure all necessary nomination papers requisite to his proposed candidacy. Petitioner was denied the requested nomination papers orally and in writing solely because he was unable to pay the $701.60 filing fee required of all would-be candidates for the office of Board of Supervisors.

---

[1] The Board of Supervisors of Los Angeles County is the governing body for Los Angeles County, California. The term is four years, the annual salary $35,080.

The Los Angeles Superior Court denied the requested writ of mandate on March 6, 1972. Petitioner alleged that he was a serious candidate, that he was indigent, and that he was unable to pay the $701.60 filing fee; no evidence was taken during the hearing. The Superior Court found the fees to be "reasonable, as a matter of law." Accordingly, the court made no attempt to determine whether the fees charged were necessary to the State's purpose, or whether the fees, in addition to deterring some frivolous candidates, also prohibited serious but indigent candidates from entering their names on the ballot. The Superior Court also rejected the argument that the State was required by *Bullock* v. *Carter,* 405 U. S. 134 (1972), to provide an alternative means of access to the ballot which did not discriminate on the basis of economic factors.

On March 9, 1972, a second petition for writ of mandate was denied by the Court of Appeal, Second District, and on March 22, 1972, after the deadline for filing nomination papers had passed, the California Supreme Court denied petitioner's third application for a writ of mandate.

Historically, since the Progressive movement of the early 20th century, there has been a steady trend toward limiting the size of the ballot in order to "concentrate the attention of the electorate on the selection of a much smaller number of officials and so afford to the voters the opportunity of exercising more discrimination in their use of the franchise." [2] This desire to limit the size of the ballot has been variously phrased as a desire to minimize voter confusion, *Thomas* v. *Mims,* 317 F. Supp. 179, 181 (SD Ala. 1970), to limit the number of runoff elections, *Spillers* v. *Slaughter,* 325 F. Supp. 550, 553 (MD

---

[2] H. Croly, Progressive Democracy 289 (1914).

Fla. 1971), to curb "ballot flooding," *Jenness* v. *Little,* 306 F. Supp. 925, 927 (ND Ga. 1969), appeal dismissed *sub nom. Matthews* v. *Little,* 397 U. S. 94 (1970), and to prevent the overwhelming of voting machines—the modern counterpart of ballot flooding, *Wetherington* v. *Adams,* 309 F. Supp. 318, 321 (ND Fla. 1970). A majority of States have long required the payment of some form of filing fee,[3] in part to limit the ballot and in part to have candidates pay some of the administrative costs.

In sharp contrast to this fear of an unduly lengthy ballot is an increasing pressure for broader access to the ballot. Thus, while progressive thought in the first half of the century was concerned with restricting the ballot to achieve voting rationality, recent decades brought an enlarged demand for an expansion of political opportunity. The Twenty-fifth Amendment, the Twenty-sixth Amendment, and the Voting Rights Act of 1965, 79 Stat. 437, 42 U. S. C. § 1973 *et seq.,* reflect this shift in emphasis. There has also been a gradual enlargement of the Fourteenth Amendment's equal protection provision in the area of voting rights:

> "It has been established in recent years that the Equal Protection Clause confers the substantive right to participate on an equal basis with other qualified voters whenever the State has adopted an electoral process for determining who will represent any segment of the State's population. See, *e. g., Reynolds* v. *Sims,* 377 U. S. 533; *Kramer* v. *Union School District,* 395 U. S. 621; *Dunn* v. *Blumstein,* 405 U. S. 330, 336." *San Antonio School District* v.

---

[3] See Comment, The Constitutionality of Qualifying Fees for Political Candidates, 120 U. Pa. L. Rev. 109 (1971), for a detailed description of each State's filing-fee requirements.

Rodriguez, 411 U. S. 1, 59 n. 2 (1973) (STEWART, J., concurring).

This principle flows naturally from our recognition that

> "[l]egislators are elected by voters, not farms or cities or economic interests. As long as ours is a representative form of government, and our legislatures are those instruments of government elected directly by and directly representative of the people, the right to elect legislators in a free and unimpaired fashion is a bedrock of our political system." *Reynolds* v. *Sims,* 377 U. S. 533, 562 (1964) (Warren, C. J.).

The present case draws these two means of achieving an effective, representative political system into apparent conflict and presents the question of how to accommodate the desire for increased ballot access with the imperative of protecting the integrity of the electoral system from the recognized dangers of ballots listing so many candidates as to undermine the process of giving expression to the will of the majority. The petitioner stated on oath that he is without assets or income and cannot pay the $701.60 filing fee although he is otherwise legally eligible to be a candidate on the primary ballot. Since his affidavit of indigency states that he has no resources and earned no income whatever in 1972, it would appear that he would make the same claim whether the filing fee had been fixed at $1, $100, or $700. The State accepts this as true but defends the statutory fee as necessary to keep the ballot from being overwhelmed with frivolous or otherwise nonserious candidates, arguing that as to indigents the filing fee is not intended as a test of his pocketbook but the extent of his political support and hence the seriousness of his candidacy.

In *Bullock* v. *Carter*, 405 U. S. 134 (1972),[4] we recognized that the State's interest in keeping its ballots within manageable, understandable limits is of the highest order. *Id.*, at 144–145. The role of the primary election process in California is underscored by its importance as a component of the total electoral process and its special function to assure that fragmentation of voter choice is minimized. That function is served, not frustrated, by a procedure that tends to regulate the filing of frivolous candidates. A procedure inviting or permitting every citizen to present himself to the voters on the ballot without some means of measuring the seriousness of the candidate's desire and motivation would make rational voter choices more difficult because of the size of the ballot and hence would tend to impede the electoral process. That no device can be conjured to eliminate every frivolous candidacy does not undermine the State's effort to eliminate as many such as possible.

That "laundry list" ballots discourage voter participation and confuse and frustrate those who do participate is too obvious to call for extended discussion. The means of testing the seriousness of a given candidacy may be open to debate; the fundamental importance of ballots of reasonable size limited to serious candidates with some prospects of public support is not. Rational results within the framework of our system are not likely

---

[4] *Bullock*, of course, does not completely resolve the present attack upon the California election statutes because it involved filing fees that were so patently exclusionary as to violate traditional equal protection concepts. Cf. *Rosario* v. *Rockefeller*, 410 U. S. 752, 760 (1973); *James* v. *Strange*, 407 U. S. 128 (1972); *Rinaldi* v. *Yeager*, 384 U. S. 305 (1966). Under attack in *Bullock* was a Texas statute that required candidates to pay a flat fee of $50 plus their pro rata share of the costs of the election in order to get on the primary ballot. Tex. Election Code, Art. 13.07a (Supp. 1974). The assessment of costs involved sums as high as $8,900.

to be reached if the ballot for a single office must list a dozen or more aspirants who are relatively unknown or have no prospects of success.

This legitimate state interest, however, must be achieved by a means that does not unfairly or unnecessarily burden either a minority party's or an individual candidate's equally important interest in the continued availability of political opportunity. The interests involved are not merely those of parties or individual candidates; the voters can assert their preferences only through candidates or parties or both and it is this broad interest that must be weighed in the balance. The right of a party or an individual to a place on a ballot is entitled to protection and is intertwined with the rights of voters.

> "[T]he right to vote is heavily burdened if that vote may be cast only for one of two parties at a time when other parties are clamoring for a place on the ballot." *Williams* v. *Rhodes*, 393 U. S. 23, 31 (1968).

This must also mean that the right to vote is "heavily burdened" if that vote may be cast only for one of two candidates in a primary election at a time when other candidates are clamoring for a place on the ballot. It is to be expected that a voter hopes to find on the ballot a candidate who comes near to reflecting his policy preferences on contemporary issues. This does not mean every voter can be assured that a candidate to his liking will be on the ballot, but the process of qualifying candidates for a place on the ballot may not constitutionally be measured solely in dollars.

In *Bullock, supra*, we expressly rejected the validity of filing fees as the sole means of determining a candidate's "seriousness":

> "To say that the filing fee requirement tends to limit

the ballot to the more serious candidates is not enough. There may well be some rational relationship between a candidate's willingness to pay a filing fee and the seriousness with which he takes his candidacy, but the candidates in this case affirmatively alleged that they were *unable*, not simply *unwilling*, to pay the assessed fees, and there was no contrary evidence. It is uncontested that the filing fees exclude legitimate as well as frivolous candidates. . . . If the Texas fee requirement is intended to regulate the ballot by weeding out spurious candidates, it is extraordinarily ill-fitted to that goal; other means to protect those valid interests are available." 405 U. S., at 145–146. (Emphasis in original.) (Footnotes omitted.)

Filing fees, however large, do not, in and of themselves, test the genuineness of a candidacy or the extent of the voter support of an aspirant for public office. A large filing fee may serve the legitimate function of keeping ballots manageable but, standing alone, it is not a certain test of whether the candidacy is serious or spurious. A wealthy candidate with not the remotest chance of election may secure a place on the ballot by writing a check. Merchants and other entrepreneurs have been known to run for public office simply to make their names known to the public. We have also noted that prohibitive filing fees, such as those in *Bullock*, can effectively exclude serious candidates. Conversely, if the filing fee is more moderate, as here, impecunious but serious candidates may be prevented from running. Even in this day of high-budget political campaigns some candidates have demonstrated that direct contact with thousands of voters by "walking tours" is a route to success. Whatever may be the political mood at any given time, our tradition has been one of hospitality toward all candidates without regard to their economic status.

The absence of any alternative means of gaining access to the ballot inevitably renders the California system exclusionary as to some aspirants. As we have noted, the payment of a fee is an absolute, not an alternative, condition, and failure to meet it is a disqualification from running for office. Thus, California has chosen to achieve the important and legitimate interest of maintaining the integrity of elections by means which can operate to exclude some potentially serious candidates from the ballot without providing them with any alternative means of coming before the voters. Selection of candidates solely on the basis of ability to pay a fixed fee without providing any alternative means is not reasonably necessary to the accomplishment of the State's legitimate election interests. Accordingly, we hold that in the absence of reasonable alternative means of ballot access, a State may not, consistent with constitutional standards, require from an indigent candidate filing fees he cannot pay.

In so holding, we note that there are obvious and well-known means of testing the "seriousness" of a candidacy which do not measure the probability of attracting significant voter support solely by the neutral fact of payment of a filing fee. States may, for example, impose on minor political parties the precondition of demonstrating the existence of some reasonable quantum of voter support by requiring such parties to file petitions for a place on the ballot signed by a percentage of those who voted in a prior election. See *American Party of Texas* v. *White, post,* p. 767. Similarly, a candidate who establishes that he cannot pay the filing fee required for a place on the primary ballot may be required to demonstrate the "seriousness" of his candidacy by persuading a substantial number of voters to sign a petition in his behalf.[5] The point, of course, is that ballot access must be genuinely open to all, subject to reasonable requirements. *Jenness* v. *Fortson,* 403 U. S. 431, 439 (1971). California's present system has not met this standard.

Reversed and remanded for further consideration not inconsistent with this opinion.

It is so ordered.

---

[5] It is suggested that a write-in procedure, under § 18600 *et seq.,* without a filing fee would be an adequate alternative to California's present filing-fee requirement. The realities of the electoral process, however, strongly suggest that "access" via write-in votes falls far short of access in terms of having the name of the candidate on the ballot. It would allow an affluent candidate to put his name before the voters on the ballot by paying a filing fee while the indigent, relegated to the write-in provision, would be forced to rest his chances solely upon those voters who would remember his name and take the affirmative step of writing it on the ballot. That disparity would, itself, give rise to constitutional questions and, although we need not decide the issue, the intimation that a write-in provision without the filing fee required by § 18600 *et seq.* would constitute "an acceptable alternative" appears dubious at best.

GRIGGS ET AL. v. DUKE POWER CO.

CERTIORARI TO THE UNITED STATES COURT OF APPEALS FOR THE FOURTH CIRCUIT

No. 124.   Argued December 14, 1970—Decided March 8, 1971

Negro employees at respondent's generating plant brought this action, pursuant to Title VII of the Civil Rights Act of 1964, challenging respondent's requirement of a high school diploma or passing of intelligence tests as a condition of employment in or transfer to jobs at the plant.   These requirements were not directed at or intended to measure ability to learn to perform a particular job or category of jobs.   While § 703 (a) of the Act makes it an unlawful employment practice for an employer to limit, segregate, or classify employees to deprive them of employment opportunities or adversely to affect their status because of race, color, religion, sex, or national origin, § 703 (h) authorizes the use of any professionally developed ability test, provided that it is not designed, intended, or used to discriminate.   The District Court found that respondent's former policy of racial discrimination had ended, and that Title VII, being prospective only, did not reach the prior inequities.   The Court of Appeals reversed in part, rejecting the holding that residual discrimination arising from prior practices was insulated from remedial action, but agreed with the lower court that there was no showing of discriminatory purpose in the adoption of the diploma and test requirements.   It held that, absent such discriminatory purpose, use of the requirements was permitted, and rejected the claim that because a disproportionate number of Negroes was rendered ineligible for promotion, transfer, or employment, the requirements were unlawful unless shown to be job related. *Held:*

1. The Act requires the elimination of artificial, arbitrary, and unnecessary barriers to employment that operate invidiously to discriminate on the basis of race, and, if, as here, an employment practice that operates to exclude Negroes cannot be shown to be related to job performance, it is prohibited, notwithstanding the employer's lack of discriminatory intent.   Pp. 429–433.

2. The Act does not preclude the use of testing or measuring procedures, but it does proscribe giving them controlling force un-

less they are demonstrably a reasonable measure of job performance. Pp. 433–436.

420 F. 2d 1225, reversed in part.

BURGER, C. J., delivered the opinion of the Court, in which all
members joined except BRENNAN, J., who took no part in the consideration or decision of the case.

Jack Greenberg argued the cause for petitioners. With
him on the briefs were *James M. Nabrit III, Norman C.
Amaker, William L. Robinson, Conrad O. Pearson, Julius
LeVonne Chambers,* and *Albert J. Rosenthal.*

George W. Ferguson, Jr., argued the cause for respondent. With him on the brief were *William I. Ward, Jr.,*
and *George M. Thorpe.*

Lawrence M. Cohen argued the cause for the Chamber
of Commerce of the United States as *amicus curiae* urging
affirmance. With him on the brief were *Francis V.
Lowden, Jr., Gerard C. Smetana,* and *Milton A. Smith.*

Briefs of *amici curiae* urging reversal were filed by
*Solicitor General Griswold, Assistant Attorney General
Leonard, Deputy Solicitor General Wallace, David L.
Rose, Stanley Hebert,* and *Russell Specter* for the United
States; by *Louis J. Lefkowitz,* Attorney General, *pro se,
Samuel A. Hirshowitz,* First Assistant Attorney General,
and *George D. Zuckerman* and *Dominick J. Tuminaro,*
Assistant Attorneys General, for the Attorney General
of the State of New York; and by *Bernard Kleiman,
Elliot Bredhoff, Michael H. Gottesman,* and *George H.
Cohen* for the United Steelworkers of America, AFL–CIO.

MR. CHIEF JUSTICE BURGER delivered the opinion of
the Court.

We granted the writ in this case to resolve the question
whether an employer is prohibited by the Civil Rights
Act of 1964, Title VII, from requiring a high school edu-

cation or passing of a standardized general intelligence test as a condition of employment in or transfer to jobs when (a) neither standard is shown to be significantly related to successful job performance, (b) both requirements operate to disqualify Negroes at a substantially higher rate than white applicants, and (c) the jobs in question formerly had been filled only by white employees as part of a longstanding practice of giving preference to whites.[1]

Congress provided, in Title VII of the Civil Rights Act of 1964, for class actions for enforcement of provisions of the Act and this proceeding was brought by a group of incumbent Negro employees against Duke Power Company. All the petitioners are employed at the Company's Dan River Steam Station, a power generating facility located at Draper, North Carolina. At the time this action was instituted, the Company had 95 employees at the Dan River Station, 14 of whom were Negroes; 13 of these are petitioners here.

The District Court found that prior to July 2, 1965, the effective date of the Civil Rights Act of 1964, the

---

[1] The Act provides:

"Sec. 703. (a) It shall be an unlawful employment practice for an employer—

.   .   .   .   .

"(2) to limit, segregate, or classify his employees in any way which would deprive or tend to deprive any individual of employment opportunities or otherwise adversely affect his status as an employee, because of such individual's race, color, religion, sex, or national origin.

.   .   .   .

"(h) Notwithstanding any other provision of this title, it shall not be an unlawful employment practice for an employer . . . to give and to act upon the results of any professionally developed ability test provided that such test, its administration or action upon the results is not designed, intended or used to discriminate because of race, color, religion, sex or national origin. . . ." 78 Stat. 255, 42 U. S. C. § 2000e-2.

Company openly discriminated on the basis of race in
the hiring and assigning of employees at its Dan River
plant. The plant was organized into five operating departments: (1) Labor, (2) Coal Handling, (3) Operations, (4) Maintenance, and (5) Laboratory and Test.
Negroes were employed only in the Labor Department
where the highest paying jobs paid less than the lowest
paying jobs in the other four "operating" departments in
which only whites were employed.[2] Promotions were
normally made within each department on the basis of
job seniority. Transferees into a department usually
began in the lowest position.

In 1955 the Company instituted a policy of requiring
a high school education for initial assignment to any
department except Labor, and for transfer from the Coal
Handling to any "inside" department (Operations, Maintenance, or Laboratory). When the Company abandoned
its policy of restricting Negroes to the Labor Department
in 1965, completion of high school also was made a prerequisite to transfer from Labor to any other department.
From the time the high school requirement was instituted
to the time of trial, however, white employees hired before the time of the high school education requirement
continued to perform satisfactorily and achieve promotions in the "operating" departments. Findings on this
score are not challenged.

The Company added a further requirement for new
employees on July 2, 1965, the date on which Title VII
became effective. To qualify for placement in any but
the Labor Department it became necessary to register
satisfactory scores on two professionally prepared apti-

---

[2] A Negro was first assigned to a job in an operating department
in August 1966, five months after charges had been filed with the
Equal Employment Opportunity Commission. The employee, a high
school graduate who had begun in the Labor Department in 1953,
was promoted to a job in the Coal Handling Department.

tude tests, as well as to have a high school education.
Completion of high school alone continued to render
employees eligible for/transfer to the four desirable departments from which Negroes had been excluded if the
incumbent had been employed prior to the time of the
new requirement. In September 1965 the Company began to permit incumbent employees who lacked a high
school education to qualify for transfer from Labor or
Coal Handling to an "inside" job by passing two tests—
the Wonderlic Personnel Test, which purports to measure
general intelligence, and the Bennett Mechanical Comprehension Test. Neither was directed or intended to
measure the ability to learn to perform a particular job
or category of jobs. The requisite scores used for both
initial hiring and transfer approximated the national
median for high school graduates.[3]

The District Court had found that while the Company
previously followed a policy of overt racial discrimination
in a period prior to the Act, such conduct had ceased.
The District Court also concluded that Title VII was
intended to be prospective only and, consequently, the
impact of prior inequities was beyond the reach of corrective action authorized by the Act.

The Court of Appeals was confronted with a question
of first impression, as are we, concerning the meaning of
Title VII. After careful analysis a majority of that
court concluded that a subjective test of the employer's
intent should govern, particularly in a close case, and
that in this case there was no showing of a discriminatory
purpose in the adoption of the diploma and test requirements. On this basis, the Court of Appeals concluded
there was no violation of the Act.

---

[3] The test standards are thus more stringent than the high school
requirement, since they would screen out approximately half of
all high school graduates.

The Court of Appeals reversed the District Court in part, rejecting the holding that residual discrimination arising from prior employment practices was insulated from remedial action.[4] The Court of Appeals noted, however, that the District Court was correct in its conclusion that there was no showing of a racial purpose or invidious intent in the adoption of the high school diploma requirement or general intelligence test and that these standards had been applied fairly to whites and Negroes alike.   It held that, in the absence of a discriminatory purpose, use of such requirements was permitted by the Act.   In so doing, the Court of Appeals rejected the claim that because these two requirements operated to render ineligible a markedly disproportionate number of Negroes, they were unlawful under Title VII unless shown to be job related.[5]   We granted the writ on these claims.   399 U. S. 926.

The objective of Congress in the enactment of Title VII is plain from the language of the statute.   It was to achieve equality of employment opportunities and re-

---

[4] The Court of Appeals ruled that Negroes employed in the Labor Department at a time when there was no high school or test requirement for entrance into the higher paying departments could not now be made subject to those requirements, since whites hired contemporaneously into those departments were never subject to them. The Court of Appeals also required that the seniority rights of those Negroes be measured on a plantwide, rather than a departmental, basis. However, the Court of Appeals denied relief to the Negro employees without a high school education or its equivalent who were hired into the Labor Department after institution of the educational requirement.

[5] One member of that court disagreed with this aspect of the decision, maintaining, as do the petitioners in this Court, that Title VII prohibits the use of employment criteria that operate in a racially exclusionary fashion and do not measure skills or abilities necessary to performance of the jobs for which those criteria are used.

657

move barriers that have operated in the past to favor
an identifiable group of white employees over other employees. Under the Act, practices, procedures, or tests
neutral on their face, and even neutral in terms of intent,
cannot be maintained if they operate to "freeze" the
status quo of prior discriminatory employment practices.

The Court of Appeals' opinion, and the partial dissent,
agreed that, on the record in the present case, "whites
register far better on the Company's alternative requirements" than Negroes.[6]   420 F. 2d 1225, 1239 n. 6. This
consequence would appear to be directly traceable to
race. Basic intelligence must have the means of articu-
lation to manifest itself fairly in a testing process. Because they are Negroes, petitioners have long received
inferior education in segregated schools and this Court
expressly recognized these differences in *Gaston County
v. United States*, 395 U. S. 285 (1969). There, because
of the inferior education received by Negroes in North
Carolina, this Court barred the institution of a literacy
test for voter registration on the ground that the test
would abridge the right to vote indirectly on account of
race. Congress did not intend by Title VII, however,
to guarantee a job to every person regardless of qualifications. In short, the Act does not command that any

---

[6] In North Carolina, 1960 census statistics show that, while 34%
of white males had completed high school, only 12% of Negro males
had done so. U. S. Bureau of the Census, U. S. Census of Population: 1960, Vol. 1, Characteristics of the Population, pt. 35, Table
47.

Similarly, with respect to standardized tests, the EEOC in one
case found that use of a battery of tests, including the Wonderlic
and Bennett tests used by the Company in the instant case, resulted
in 58% of whites passing the tests, as compared with only 6% of
the blacks. Decision of EEOC, CCH Empl. Prac. Guide, ¶ 17,304.53
(Dec. 2, 1966). See also Decision of EEOC 70–552, CCH Empl.
Prac. Guide, ¶ 6139 (Feb. 19, 1970).

person be hired simply because he was formerly the subject of discrimination, or because he is a member of a minority group. Discriminatory preference for any group, minority or majority, is precisely and only what Congress has proscribed. What is required by Congress is the removal of artificial, arbitrary, and unnecessary barriers to employment when the barriers operate invidiously to discriminate on the basis of racial or other impermissible classification.

Congress has now provided that tests or criteria for employment or promotion may not provide equality of opportunity merely in the sense of the fabled offer of milk to the stork and the fox. On the contrary, Congress has now required that the posture and condition of the job-seeker be taken into account. It has—to resort again to the fable—provided that the vessel in which the milk is proffered be one all seekers can use. The Act proscribes not only overt discrimination but also practices that are fair in form, but discriminatory in operation. The touchstone is business necessity. If an employment practice which operates to exclude Negroes cannot be shown to be related to job performance, the practice is prohibited.

On the record before us, neither the high school completion requirement nor the general intelligence test is shown to bear a demonstrable relationship to successful performance of the jobs for which it was used. Both were adopted, as the Court of Appeals noted, without meaningful study of their relationship to job-performance ability. Rather, a vice president of the Company testified, the requirements were instituted on the Company's judgment that they generally would improve the overall quality of the work force.

The evidence, however, shows that employees who have not completed high school or taken the tests have continued to perform satisfactorily and make progress in departments for which the high school and test criteria are now used.[7] The promotion record of present employees who would not be able to meet the new criteria thus suggests the possibility that the requirements may not be needed even for the limited purpose of preserving the avowed policy of advancement within the Company. In the context of this case, it is unnecessary to reach the question whether testing requirements that take into account capability for the next succeeding position or related future promotion might be utilized upon a showing that such long-range requirements fulfill a genuine business need. In the present case the Company has made no such showing.

The Court of Appeals held that the Company had adopted the diploma and test requirements without any "intention to discriminate against Negro employees." 420 F. 2d, at 1232. We do not suggest that either the District Court or the Court of Appeals erred in examining the employer's intent; but good intent or absence of discriminatory intent does not redeem employment procedures or testing mechanisms that operate as "built-in headwinds" for minority groups and are unrelated to measuring job capability.

The Company's lack of discriminatory intent is suggested by special efforts to help the undereducated employees through Company financing of two-thirds the cost of tuition for high school training. But Congress directed the thrust of the Act to the *consequences* of employment practices, not simply the motivation. More than that, Congress has placed on the employer the burden of showing that any given requirement must have a manifest relationship to the employment in question.

---

[7] For example, between July 2, 1965, and November 14, 1966, the percentage of white employees who were promoted but who were not high school graduates was nearly identical to the percentage of nongraduates in the entire white work force.

The facts of this case demonstrate the inadequacy of broad and general testing devices as well as the infirmity of using diplomas or degrees as fixed measures of capability.   History is filled with examples of men and women who rendered highly effective performance without the conventional badges of accomplishment in terms of certificates, diplomas, or degrees.   Diplomas and tests are useful servants, but Congress has mandated the commonsense proposition that they are not to become masters of reality.

The Company contends that its general intelligence tests are specifically permitted by § 703 (h) of the Act.[8] That section authorizes the use of "any professionally developed ability test" that is not "designed, intended *or used* to discriminate because of race . . . ."   (Emphasis added.)

The Equal Employment Opportunity Commission, having enforcement responsibility, has issued guidelines interpreting § 703 (h) to permit only the use of job-related tests.[9]   The administrative interpretation of the

---

[8] Section 703 (h) applies only to tests. It has no applicability to the high school diploma requirement.

[9] EEOC Guidelines on Employment Testing Procedures, issued August 24, 1966, provide:

"The Commission accordingly interprets 'professionally developed ability test' to mean a test which fairly measures the knowledge or skills required by the particular job or class of jobs which the applicant seeks, or which fairly affords the employer a chance to measure the applicant's ability to perform a particular job or class of jobs. The fact that a test was prepared by an individual or organization claiming expertise in test preparation does not, without more, justify its use within the meaning of Title VII."

The EEOC position has been elaborated in the new Guidelines on Employee Selection Procedures, 29 CFR § 1607, 35 Fed. Reg. 12333 (Aug. 1, 1970). These guidelines demand that employers using tests have available "data demonstrating that the test is predictive of or significantly correlated with important elements of work behavior which comprise or are relevant to the job or jobs for which candidates are being evaluated." *Id.,* at § 1607.4 (c).

Act by the enforcing agency is entitled to great deference. See, *e. g., United States* v. *City of Chicago,* 400 U. S. 8 (1970); *Udall* v. *Tallman,* 380 U. S. 1 (1965); *Power Reactor Co.* v. *Electricians,* 367 U. S. 396 (1961). Since the Act and its legislative history support the Commission's construction, this affords good reason to treat the guidelines as expressing the will of Congress.

Section 703 (h) was not contained in the House version of the Civil Rights Act but was added in the Senate during extended debate. For a period, debate revolved around claims that the bill as proposed would prohibit all testing and force employers to hire unqualified persons simply because they were part of a group formerly subject to job discrimination.[10] Proponents of Title VII sought throughout the debate to assure the critics that the Act would have no effect on job-related tests. Senators Case of New Jersey and Clark of Pennsylvania, comanagers of the bill on the Senate floor, issued a memorandum explaining that the proposed Title VII "expressly protects the employer's right to insist that any prospective applicant, Negro or white, *must meet the applicable job qualifications.* Indeed, the very purpose of title VII is to promote hiring on the basis of job qualifications, rather than on the basis of race or color." 110 Cong. Rec. 7247.[11] (Emphasis added.) Despite

---

[10] The congressional discussion was prompted by the decision of a hearing examiner for the Illinois Fair Employment Commission in *Myart* v. *Motorola Co.* (The decision is reprinted at 110 Cong. Rec. 5662.) That case suggested that standardized tests on which whites performed better than Negroes could never be used. The decision was taken to mean that such tests could never be justified even if the needs of the business required them. A number of Senators feared that Title VII might produce a similar result. See remarks of Senators Ervin, 110 Cong. Rec. 5614–5616; Smathers, *id.,* at 5999–6000; Holland, *id.,* at 7012–7013; Hill, *id.,* at 8447; Tower, *id.,* at 9024; Talmadge, *id.,* at 9025–9026; Fulbright, *id.,* at 9599–9600; and Ellender, *id.,* at 9600.

[11] The Court of Appeals majority, in finding no requirement in Title VII that employment tests be job related, relied in part on a

these assurances, Senator Tower of Texas introduced an amendment authorizing "professionally developed ability tests." Proponents of Title VII opposed the amendment because, as written, it would permit an employer to give any test, "whether it was a good test or not, so long as it was professionally designed. Discrimination could actually exist under the guise of compliance with the statute." 110 Cong. Rec. 13504 (remarks of Sen. Case).

The amendment was defeated and two days later Senator Tower offered a substitute amendment which was adopted verbatim and is now the testing provision of § 703 (h). Speaking for the supporters of Title VII, Senator Humphrey, who had vigorously opposed the first amendment, endorsed the substitute amendment, stating: "Senators on both sides of the aisle who were deeply interested in title VII have examined the text of this

---

quotation from an earlier Clark-Case interpretative memorandum addressed to the question of the constitutionality of Title VII. The Senators said in that memorandum:

"There is no requirement in title VII that employers abandon bona fide qualification tests where, because of differences in background and education, members of some groups are able to perform better on these tests than members of other groups. An employer may set his qualifications as high as he likes, he may test to determine which applicants have these qualifications, and he may hire, assign, and promote on the basis of test performance." 110 Cong. Rec. 7213.

However, nothing there stated conflicts with the later memorandum dealing specifically with the debate over employer testing, 110 Cong. Rec. 7247 (quoted from in the text above), in which Senators Clark and Case explained that tests which measure "applicable job qualifications" are permissible under Title VII. In the earlier memorandum Clark and Case assured the Senate that employers were not to be prohibited from using tests that determine *qualifications.* Certainly a reasonable interpretation of what the Senators meant, in light of the subsequent memorandum directed specifically at employer testing, was that nothing in the Act prevents employers from requiring that applicants be fit for the job.

amendment and have found it to be in accord with the intent and purpose of that title." 110 Cong. Rec. 13724. The amendment was then adopted.[12] From the sum of the legislative history relevant in this case, the conclusion is inescapable that the EEOC's construction of § 703 (h) to require that employment tests be job related comports with congressional intent.

Nothing in the Act precludes the use of testing or measuring procedures; obviously they are useful. What Congress has forbidden is giving these devices and mechanisms controlling force unless they are demonstrably a reasonable measure of job performance. Congress has not commanded that the less qualified be preferred over the better qualified simply because of minority origins. Far from disparaging job qualifications as such, Congress has made such qualifications the controlling factor, so that race, religion, nationality, and sex become irrelevant. What Congress has commanded is that any tests used must measure the person for the job and not the person in the abstract.

The judgment of the Court of Appeals is, as to that portion of the judgment appealed from, reversed.

---

[12] Senator Tower's original amendment provided in part that a test would be permissible "if . . . in the case of any individual who is seeking employment with such employer, such test is designed to determine or predict whether such individual is suitable or trainable with respect to his employment in the particular business or enterprise involved . . . ." 110 Cong. Rec. 13492. This language indicates that Senator Tower's aim was simply to make certain that job-related tests would be permitted. The opposition to the amendment was based on its loose wording which the proponents of Title VII feared would be susceptible of misinterpretation. The final amendment, which was acceptable to all sides, could hardly have required less of a job relation than the first.

CASES ADJUDGED

IN THE

SUPREME COURT OF THE UNITED STATES

AT

OCTOBER TERM, 1970

SWANN ET AL. *v.* CHARLOTTE-MECKLENBURG BOARD OF EDUCATION ET AL.

CERTIORARI TO THE UNITED STATES COURT OF APPEALS FOR THE FOURTH CIRCUIT

No. 281. Argued October 12, 1970—Decided April 20, 1971*

The Charlotte-Mecklenburg school system, which includes the city of Charlotte, North Carolina, had more than 84,000 students in 107 schools in the 1968–1969 school year. Approximately 29% (24,000) of the pupils were Negro, about 14,000 of whom attended 21 schools that were at least 99% Negro. This resulted from a desegregation plan approved by the District Court in 1965, at the commencement of this litigation. In 1968 petitioner Swann moved for further relief based on *Green* v. *County School Board*, 391 U. S. 430, which required school boards to "come forward with a plan that promises realistically to work . . . *now* . . . until it is clear that state-imposed segregation has been completely removed." The District Court ordered the school board in April 1969 to provide a plan for faculty and student desegregation. Finding the board's submission unsatisfactory, the District Court appointed an expert to submit a desegregation plan. In February 1970, the expert and the board presented plans, and the court adopted the board's plan, as modified, for the junior and senior high schools, and the expert's proposed plan for the elementary schools. The Court of Appeals affirmed the District Court's order as to faculty desegregation and the secondary school plans,

---

*Together with No. 349, *Charlotte-Mecklenburg Board of Education et al.* v. *Swann et al.*, also on certiorari to the same court.

1

but vacated the order respecting elementary schools, fearing that the provisions for pairing and grouping of elementary schools would unreasonably burden the pupils and the board. The case was remanded to the District Court for reconsideration and submission of further plans. This Court granted certiorari and directed reinstatement of the District Court's order pending further proceedings in that court. On remand the District Court received two new plans, and ordered the board to adopt a plan, or the expert's plan would remain in effect. After the board "acquiesced" in the expert's plan, the District Court directed that it remain in effect. *Held:*

1. Today's objective is to eliminate from the public schools all vestiges of state-imposed segregation that was held violative of equal protection guarantees by *Brown* v. *Board of Education,* 347 U. S. 483, in 1954. P. 15.

2. In default by the school authorities of their affirmative obligation to proffer acceptable remedies, the district courts have broad power to fashion remedies that will assure unitary school systems. P. 16.

3. Title IV of the Civil Rights Act of 1964 does not restrict or withdraw from the federal courts their historic equitable remedial powers. The proviso in 42 U. S. C. § 2000c–6 was designed simply to foreclose any interpretation of the Act as expanding the existing powers of the federal courts to enforce the Equal Protection Clause. Pp. 16–18.

4. Policy and practice with regard to faculty, staff, transportation, extracurricular activities, and facilities are among the most important indicia of a segregated system, and the first remedial responsibility of school authorities is to eliminate invidious racial distinctions in those respects. Normal administrative practice should then produce schools of like quality, facilities, and staffs. Pp. 18–19.

5. The Constitution does not prohibit district courts from using their equity power to order assignment of teachers to achieve a particular degree of faculty desegregation. *United States* v. *Montgomery County Board of Education,* 395 U. S. 225, was properly followed by the lower courts in this case. Pp. 19–20.

6. In devising remedies to eliminate legally imposed segregation, local authorities and district courts must see to it that future school construction and abandonment are not used and do not serve to perpetuate or re-establish a dual system. Pp. 20–21.

7. Four problem areas exist on the issue of student assignment:

(1) *Racial quotas.* The constitutional command to desegregate schools does not mean that every school in the community must always reflect the racial composition of the system as a whole; here the District Court's very limited use of the racial ratio—not as an inflexible requirement, but as a starting point in shaping a remedy—was within its equitable discretion. Pp. 22–25.

(2) *One-race schools.* While the existence of a small number of one-race, or virtually one-race, schools does not in itself denote a system that still practices segregation by law, the court should scrutinize such schools and require the school authorities to satisfy the court that the racial composition does not result from present or past discriminatory action on their part. Pp. 25–26.

An optional majority-to-minority transfer provision has long been recognized as a useful part of a desegregation plan, and to be effective such arrangement must provide the transferring student free transportation and available space in the school to which he desires to move. Pp. 26–27.

(3) *Attendance zones.* The remedial altering of attendance zones is not, as an interim corrective measure, beyond the remedial powers of a district court. A student assignment plan is not acceptable merely because it appears to be neutral, for such a plan may fail to counteract the continuing effects of past school segregation. The pairing and grouping of noncontiguous zones is a permissible tool; judicial steps going beyond contiguous zones should be examined in light of the objectives to be sought. No rigid rules can be laid down to govern conditions in different localities. Pp. 27–29.

(4) *Transportation.* The District Court's conclusion that assignment of children to the school nearest their home serving their grade would not effectively dismantle the dual school system is supported by the record, and the remedial technique of requiring bus transportation as a tool of school desegregation was within that court's power to provide equitable relief. An objection to transportation of students may have validity when the time or distance of travel is so great as to risk either the health of the children or significantly impinge on the educational process; limits on travel time will vary with many factors, but probably with none more than the age of the students. Pp. 29–31.

8. Neither school authorities nor district courts are constitutionally required to make year-by-year adjustments of the racial composition of student bodies once a unitary system has been achieved. Pp. 31–32.

431 F. 2d 138, affirmed as to those parts in which it affirmed the District Court's judgment. The District Court's order of August 7, 1970, is also affirmed.

BURGER, C. J., delivered the opinion for a unanimous Court.

Julius LeVonne Chambers and *James M. Nabrit III* argued the cause for petitioners in No. 281 and respondents in No. 349. With them on the briefs were *Jack Greenberg, Norman J. Chachkin, C. O. Pearson,* and *Anthony G. Amsterdam.*

William J. Wagonner and *Benjamin S. Horack* argued the cause and filed briefs for respondents in No. 281 and petitioners in No. 349.

Solicitor General Griswold argued the cause for the United States as *amicus curiae* in both cases. With him on the brief was *Assistant Attorney General Leonard.*

Briefs of *amici curiae* in No. 281 were filed by *Earl Faircloth,* Attorney General, *Robert J. Kelly,* Deputy Attorney General, *Ronald W. Sabo,* Assistant Attorney General, and *Rivers Buford* for the State of Florida; by *Andrew P. Miller,* Attorney General, *William G. Broaddus* and *Theodore J. Markow,* Assistant Attorneys General, *Lewis F. Powell, Jr., John W. Riely,* and *Guy K. Tower* for the Commonwealth of Virginia; by *Claude R. Kirk, Jr., pro se,* and *Gerald Mager* for Claude R. Kirk, Jr., Governor of Florida; by *W. F. Womble* for the Winston-Salem/Forsyth County Board of Education; by *Raymond B. Witt, Jr.,* and *Eugene N. Collins* for the Chattanooga Board of Education; by *Kenneth W. Cleary* for the School Board of Manatee County, Florida; by *W. Crosby Few* and *John M. Allison* for the School Board of Hillsborough County, Florida; by *Sam J. Ervin,*

Jr., Charles R. Jonas, and *Ernest F. Hollings* for the
Classroom Teachers Association of the Charlotte-
Mecklenburg School System, Inc.; by *Mark Wells White,
Jr.,* for Mrs. H. W. Cullen et al., members of the Board
of Education of the Houston Independent School Dis-
trict; by *Jack Petree* for the Board of Education of
Memphis City Schools; by *Sherwood W. Wise* for the
Jackson Chamber of Commerce, Inc., et al.; by *Stephen
J. Pollak, Benjamin W. Boley,* and *David Rubin* for the
National Education Association; by *William L. Taylor,
Richard B. Sobol,* and *Joseph L. Rauh, Jr.,* for the United
Negro College Fund, Inc., et al.; by *Owen H. Page* for
Concerned Citizens Association, Inc.; by *Charles S.
Conley, Floyd B. McKissick,* and *Charles S. Scott* for
the Congress of Racial Equality; by the Tennessee Fed-
eration for Constitutional Government et al.; by *William
C. Cramer, pro se,* and *Richard B. Peet,* joined by *Albert
W. Watson* et al., for William C. Cramer; by *Charles E.
Bennett, pro se, James C. Rinaman, Jr.,* and *Yardley D.
Buckman* for Charles E. Bennett; by *Calvin H. Childress*
and *M. T. Bohannon, Jr.,* for David E. Allgood et al.; by
William B. Spong, Jr., and by Newton Collier Estes.

Mr. Chief Justice Burger delivered the opinion of
the Court.

We granted certiorari in this case to review important
issues as to the duties of school authorities and the scope
of powers of federal courts under this Court's mandates
to eliminate racially separate public schools established
and maintained by state action. *Brown* v. *Board of
Education,* 347 U. S. 483 (1954) (*Brown I*).

This case and those argued with it [1] arose in States having a long history of maintaining two sets of schools in a

---

[1] *McDaniel* v. *Barresi,* No. 420, *post,* p. 39; *Davis* v. *Board of
School Commissioners of Mobile County,* No. 436, *post,* p. 33;
Moore v. *Charlotte-Mecklenburg Board of Education,* No. 444, *post,*

single school system deliberately operated to carry out a governmental policy to separate pupils in schools solely on the basis of race. That was what *Brown* v. *Board of Education* was all about. These cases present us with the problem of defining in more precise terms than heretofore the scope of the duty of school authorities and district courts in implementing *Brown I* and the mandate to eliminate dual systems and establish unitary systems at once. Meanwhile district courts and courts of appeals have struggled in hundreds of cases with a multitude and variety of problems under this Court's general directive. Understandably, in an area of evolving remedies, those courts had to improvise and experiment without detailed or specific guidelines. This Court, in *Brown I*, appropriately dealt with the large constitutional principles; other federal courts had to grapple with the flinty, intractable realities of day-to-day implementation of those constitutional commands. Their efforts, of necessity, embraced a process of "trial and error," and our effort to formulate guidelines must take into account their experience.

I

The Charlotte-Mecklenburg school system, the 43d largest in the Nation, encompasses the city of Charlotte and surrounding Mecklenburg County, North Carolina. The area is large—550 square miles—spanning roughly 22 miles east-west and 36 miles north-south. During the 1968–1969 school year the system served more than 84,000 pupils in 107 schools. Approximately 71% of the pupils were found to be white and 29% Negro. As of

p. 47; *North Carolina State Board of Education* v. *Swann*, No. 498, *post*, p. 43. For purposes of this opinion the cross-petitions in Nos. 281 and 349 are treated as a single case and will be referred to as "this case."

June 1969 there were approximately 24,000 Negro students in the system, of whom 21,000 attended schools within the city of Charlotte. Two-thirds of those 21,000—approximately 14,000 Negro students—attended 21 schools which were either totally Negro or more than 99% Negro.

This situation came about under a desegregation plan approved by the District Court at the commencement of the present litigation in 1965, 243 F. Supp. 667 (WDNC), aff'd, 369 F. 2d 29 (CA4 1966), based upon geographic zoning with a free-transfer provision. The present proceedings were initiated in September 1968 by petitioner Swann's motion for further relief based on *Green* v. *County School Board*, 391 U. S. 430 (1968), and its companion cases.[2] All parties now agree that in 1969 the system fell short of achieving the unitary school system that those cases require.

The District Court held numerous hearings and received voluminous evidence. In addition to finding certain actions of the school board to be discriminatory, the court also found that residential patterns in the city and county resulted in part from federal, state, and local government action other than school board decisions. School board action based on these patterns, for example, by locating schools in Negro residential areas and fixing the size of the schools to accommodate the needs of immediate neighborhoods, resulted in segregated education. These findings were subsequently accepted by the Court of Appeals.

In April 1969 the District Court ordered the school board to come forward with a plan for both faculty and student desegregation. Proposed plans were accepted by the court in June and August 1969 on an interim basis

[2] *Raney* v. *Board of Education*, 391 U. S. 443 (1968), and *Monroe* v. *Board of Commissioners*, 391 U. S. 450 (1968).

only, and the board was ordered to file a third plan by
November 1969. In November the board moved for an
extension of time until February 1970, but when that
was denied the board submitted a partially completed
plan. In December 1969 the District Court held that
the board's submission was unacceptable and appointed
an expert in education administration, Dr. John Finger,
to prepare a desegregation plan. Thereafter in February 1970, the District Court was presented with two
alternative pupil assignment plans—the finalized "board
plan" and the "Finger plan."

The Board Plan. As finally submitted, the school
board plan closed seven schools and reassigned their
pupils. It restructured school attendance zones to
achieve greater racial balance but maintained existing
grade structures and rejected techniques such as pairing
and clustering as part of a desegregation effort. The
plan created a single athletic league, eliminated the previously racial basis of the school bus system, provided
racially mixed faculties and administrative staffs, and
modified its free-transfer plan into an optional majority-
to-minority transfer system.

The board plan proposed substantial assignment of
Negroes to nine of the system's 10 high schools, producing 17% to 36% Negro population in each. The projected Negro attendance at the 10th school, Independence,
was 2%. The proposed attendance zones for the high
schools were typically shaped like wedges of a pie, extending outward from the center of the city to the suburban
and rural areas of the county in order to afford residents
of the center city area access to outlying schools.

As for junior high schools, the board plan rezoned the
21 school areas so that in 20 the Negro attendance would
range from 0% to 38%. The other school, located in
the heart of the Negro residential area, was left with an
enrollment of 90% Negro.

The board plan with respect to elementary schools relied entirely upon gerrymandering of geographic zones. More than half of the Negro elementary pupils were left in nine schools that were 86% to 100% Negro; approximately half of the white elementary pupils were assigned to schools 86% to 100% white.

The Finger Plan. The plan submitted by the court-appointed expert, Dr. Finger, adopted the school board zoning plan for senior high schools with one modification: it required that an additional 300 Negro students be transported from the Negro residential area of the city to the nearly all-white Independence High School.

The Finger plan for the junior high schools employed much of the rezoning plan of the board, combined with the creation of nine "satellite" zones.[3] Under the satellite plan, inner-city Negro students were assigned by attendance zones to nine outlying predominately white junior high schools, thereby substantially desegregating every junior high school in the system.

The Finger plan departed from the board plan chiefly in its handling of the system's 76 elementary schools. Rather than relying solely upon geographic zoning, Dr. Finger proposed use of zoning, pairing, and grouping techniques, with the result that student bodies throughout the system would range from 9% to 38% Negro.[4]

The District Court described the plan thus:

"Like the board plan, the Finger plan does as much by rezoning school attendance lines as can reasonably

---

[3] A "satellite zone" is an area which is not contiguous with the main attendance zone surrounding the school.

[4] In its opinion and order of December 1, 1969, later incorporated in the order appointing Dr. Finger as consultant, the District Court stated:

"Fixed ratios of pupils in particular schools will not be set. If the board in one of its three tries had presented a plan for desegregation, the court would have sought ways to approve variabe accomplished. However, unlike the board plan, it does not stop there. It goes further and desegregates all the rest of the elementary schools by the technique of grouping two or three outlying schools with one black inner city school; by transporting black students from grades one through four to the outlying white schools; and by transporting white students from the fifth and sixth grades from the outlying white schools to the inner city black school."

Under the Finger plan, nine inner-city Negro schools were grouped in this manner with 24 suburban white schools.

On February 5, 1970, the District Court adopted the board plan, as modified by Dr. Finger, for the junior and senior high schools. The court rejected the board elementary school plan and adopted the Finger plan as presented. Implementation was partially stayed by the Court of Appeals for the Fourth Circuit on March 5, and this Court declined to disturb the Fourth Circuit's order, 397 U. S. 978 (1970).

On appeal the Court of Appeals affirmed the District Court's order as to faculty desegregation and the secondary school plans, but vacated the order respecting elementary schools. While agreeing that the District Court properly disapproved the board plan concerning these schools, the Court of Appeals feared that the pairing and grouping of elementary schools would place an unreasonable burden on the board and the system's pupils. The case was remanded to the District Court for reconsideration and submission of further plans. 431 F. 2d

---

tions in pupil ratios. In default of any such plan from the school board, the court will start with the thought . . . that efforts should be made to reach a 71–29 ratio in the various schools so that there will be no basis for contending that one school is racially different from the others, but to understand that variations from that norm may be unavoidable." 306 F. Supp. 1299, 1312.

138. This Court granted certiorari, 399 U. S. 926, and directed reinstatement of the District Court's order pending further proceedings in that court.

On remand the District Court received two new plans for the elementary schools: a plan prepared by the United States Department of Health, Education, and Welfare (the HEW plan) based on contiguous grouping and zoning of schools, and a plan prepared by four members of the nine-member school board (the minority plan) achieving substantially the same results as the Finger plan but apparently with slightly less transportation. A majority of the school board declined to amend its proposal. After a lengthy evidentiary hearing the District Court concluded that its own plan (the Finger plan), the minority plan, and an earlier draft of the Finger plan were all reasonable and acceptable. It directed the board to adopt one of the three or in the alternative to come forward with a new, equally effective plan of its own; the court ordered that the Finger plan would remain in effect in the event the school board declined to adopt a new plan. On August 7, the board indicated it would "acquiesce" in the Finger plan, reiterating its view that the plan was unreasonable. The District Court, by order dated August 7, 1970, directed that the Finger plan remain in effect.

II

Nearly 17 years ago this Court held, in explicit terms, that state-imposed segregation by race in public schools denies equal protection of the laws. At no time has the Court deviated in the slightest degree from that holding or its constitutional underpinnings. None of the parties before us challenges the Court's decision of May 17, 1954, that

"in the field of public education the doctrine of 'separate but equal' has no place. Separate educational facilities are inherently unequal. Therefore, we hold that the plaintiffs and others similarly situated . . . are, by reason of the segregation complained of, deprived of the equal protection of the laws guaranteed by the Fourteenth Amendment. . . .

"Because these are class actions, because of the wide applicability of this decision, and because of the great variety of local conditions, the formulation of decrees in these cases presents problems of considerable complexity." *Brown* v. *Board of Education, supra,* at 495.

None of the parties before us questions the Court's 1955 holding in *Brown II,* that

"School authorities have the primary responsibility for elucidating, assessing, and solving these problems; courts will have to consider whether the action of school authorities constitutes good faith implementation of the governing constitutional principles. Because of their proximity to local conditions and the possible need for further hearings, the courts which originally heard these cases can best perform this judicial appraisal. Accordingly, we believe it appropriate to remand the cases to those courts.

"In fashioning and effectuating the decrees, the courts will be guided by equitable principles. Traditionally, equity has been characterized by a practical flexibility in shaping its remedies and by a facility for adjusting and reconciling public and private needs. These cases call for the exercise of these traditional attributes of equity power. At stake is the personal interest of the plaintiffs in admission to public schools as soon as practicable on a nondiscriminatory basis. To effectuate this interest may call for elimination of a variety of obstacles in making the transition to school systems operated in accordance with the constitutional principles set forth in our May 17, 1954, decision. Courts of

equity may properly take into account the public
interest in the elimination of such obstacles in a
systematic and effective manner.   But it should go
without saying that the vitality of these constitutional principles cannot be allowed to yield simply
because of disagreement with them." *Brown* v.
Board of Education, 349 U. S. 294, 299–300 (1955).

Over the 16 years since *Brown II,* many difficulties
were encountered in implementation of the basic constitutional requirement that the State not discriminate
between public school children on the basis of their race.
Nothing in our national experience prior to 1955 prepared
anyone for dealing with changes and adjustments of the
magnitude and complexity encountered since then.   Deliberate resistance of some to the Court's mandates has
impeded the good-faith efforts of others to bring school
systems into compliance.   The detail and nature of these
dilatory tactics have been noted frequently by this Court
and other courts.

By the time the Court considered *Green* v. *County
School Board,* 391 U. S. 430, in 1968, very little progress had been made in many areas where dual school
systems had historically been maintained by operation
of state laws.   In *Green,* the Court was confronted
with a record of a freedom-of-choice program that the
District Court had found to operate in fact to preserve a dual system more than a decade after *Brown II.*
While acknowledging that a freedom-of-choice concept
could be a valid remedial measure in some circumstances,
its failure to be effective in *Green* required that:

"The burden on a school board today is to come forward with a plan that promises realistically to
work . . . *now* . . . until it is clear that state-imposed
segregation has been completely removed." *Green,
supra,* at 439.

677

This was plain language, yet the 1969 Term of Court brought fresh evidence of the dilatory tactics of many school authorities. *Alexander* v. *Holmes County Board of Education,* 396 U. S. 19, restated the basic obligation asserted in *Griffin* v. *School Board,* 377 U. S. 218, 234 (1964), and *Green, supra,* that the remedy must be implemented *forthwith.*

The problems encountered by the district courts and courts of appeals make plain that we should now try to amplify guidelines, however incomplete and imperfect, for the assistance of school authorities and courts.[5] The failure of local authorities to meet their constitutional obligations aggravated the massive problem of converting from the state-enforced discrimination of racially separate school systems. This process has been rendered more difficult by changes since 1954 in the structure and patterns of communities, the growth of student population,[6] movement of families, and other changes, some of which had marked impact on school planning, sometimes neutralizing or negating remedial action before it was fully implemented. Rural areas accustomed for half a century to the consolidated school systems implemented by bus transportation could make adjustments more readily than metropolitan areas with dense and shifting population, numerous schools, congested and complex traffic patterns.

---

[5] The necessity for this is suggested by the situation in the Fifth Circuit where 166 appeals in school desegregation cases were heard between December 2, 1969, and September 24, 1970.

[6] Elementary public school population (grades 1–6) grew from 17,447,000 in 1954 to 23,103,000 in 1969; secondary school population (beyond grade 6) grew from 11,183,000 in 1954 to 20,775,000 in 1969. Digest of Educational Statistics, Table 3, Office of Education Pub. 10024–64; Digest of Educational Statistics, Table 28, Office of Education Pub. 10024–70.

III

The objective today remains to eliminate from the public schools all vestiges of state-imposed segregation. Segregation was the evil struck down by *Brown I* as contrary to the equal protection guarantees of the Constitution. That was the violation sought to be corrected by the remedial measures of *Brown II*. That was the basis for the holding in *Green* that school authorities are "clearly charged with the affirmative duty to take whatever steps might be necessary to convert to a unitary system in which racial discrimination would be eliminated root and branch." 391 U. S., at 437–438.

If school authorities fail in their affirmative obligations under these holdings, judicial authority may be invoked. Once a right and a violation have been shown, the scope of a district court's equitable powers to remedy past wrongs is broad, for breadth and flexibility are inherent in equitable remedies.

> "The essence of equity jurisdiction has been the power of the Chancellor to do equity and to mould each decree to the necessities of the particular case. Flexibility rather than rigidity has distinguished it. The qualities of mercy and practicality have made equity the instrument for nice adjustment and reconciliation between the public interest and private needs as well as between competing private claims." *Hecht Co.* v. *Bowles*, 321 U. S. 321, 329–330 (1944), cited in *Brown II, supra,* at 300.

This allocation of responsibility once made, the Court attempted from time to time to provide some guidelines for the exercise of the district judge's discretion and for the reviewing function of the courts of appeals. However, a school desegregation case does not differ fundamentally from other cases involving the framing of

679

equitable remedies to repair the denial of a constitutional right. The task is to correct, by a balancing of the individual and collective interests, the condition that offends the Constitution.

In seeking to define even in broad and general terms how far this remedial power extends it is important to remember that judicial powers may be exercised only on the basis of a constitutional violation. Remedial judicial authority does not put judges automatically in the shoes of school authorities whose powers are plenary. Judicial authority enters only when local authority defaults.

School authorities are traditionally charged with broad power to formulate and implement educational policy and might well conclude, for example, that in order to prepare students to live in a pluralistic society each school should have a prescribed ratio of Negro to white students reflecting the proportion for the district as a whole. To do this as an educational policy is within the broad discretionary powers of school authorities; absent a finding of a constitutional violation, however, that would not be within the authority of a federal court. As with any equity case, the nature of the violation determines the scope of the remedy. In default by the school authorities of their obligation to proffer acceptable remedies, a district court has broad power to fashion a remedy that will assure a unitary school system.

The school authorities argue that the equity powers of federal district courts have been limited by Title IV of the Civil Rights Act of 1964, 42 U. S. C. § 2000c. The language and the history of Title IV show that it was enacted not to limit but to define the role of the Federal Government in the implementation of the *Brown I* decision. It authorizes the Commissioner of Education to provide technical assistance to local boards in the preparation of desegregation plans, to arrange "training insti-

tutes" for school personnel involved in desegregation
efforts, and to make grants directly to schools to ease the
transition to unitary systems. It also authorizes the
Attorney General, in specified circumstances, to initiate
federal desegregation suits. Section 2000c (b) defines
"desegregation" as it is used in Title IV:

> " 'Desegregation' means the assignment of students
> to public schools and within such schools without
> regard to their race, color, religion, or national origin,
> but 'desegregation' shall not mean the assignment of
> students to public schools in order to overcome racial
> imbalance."

Section 2000c–6, authorizing the Attorney General to institute federal suits, contains the following proviso:

> "nothing herein shall empower any official or court
> of the United States to issue any order seeking to
> achieve a racial balance in any school by requiring
> the transportation of pupils or students from one
> school to another or one school district to another
> in order to achieve such racial balance, or otherwise
> enlarge the existing power of the court to insure
> compliance with constitutional standards."

On their face, the sections quoted purport only to insure that the provisions of Title IV of the Civil Rights
Act of 1964 will not be read as granting new powers. The
proviso in § 2000c–6 is in terms designed to foreclose any
interpretation of the Act as expanding the *existing* powers
of federal courts to enforce the Equal Protection Clause.
There is no suggestion of an intention to restrict those
powers or withdraw from courts their historic equitable
remedial powers. The legislative history of Title IV
indicates that Congress was concerned that the Act
might be read as creating a right of action under the
Fourteenth Amendment in the situation of so-called "de
facto segregation," where racial imbalance exists in the

schools but with no showing that this was brought about
by discriminatory action of state authoritięs. In short,
there is nothing in the Act that provides us material
assistance in answering the question of remedy for state-
imposed segregation in violation of *Brown I.* The basis
of our decision must be the prohibition of the Fourteenth
Amendment that no State shall "deny to any person
within its jurisdiction the equal protection of the laws."

IV

We turn now to the problem of defining with more
particularity the responsibilities of school authorities in
desegregating a state-enforced dual school system in light
of the Equal Protection Clause. Although the several
related cases before us are primarily concerned with problems of student assignment, it may be helpful to begin
with a brief discussion of other aspects of the process.

In *Green,* we pointed out that existing policy and practice with regard to faculty, staff, transportation, extracurricular activities, and facilities were among the most
important indicia of a segregated system. 391 U. S., at
435. Independent of student assignment, where it is
possible to identify a "white school" or a "Negro school"
simply by reference to the racial composition of teachers
and staff, the quality of school buildings and equipment,
or the organization of sports activities, a *prima facie* case
of violation of substantive constitutional rights under
the Equal Protection Clause is shown.

When a system has been dual in these respects, the
first remedial responsibility of school authorities is to
eliminate invidious racial distinctions. With respect to
such matters as transportation, supporting personnel, and
extracurricular activities, no more than this may be necessary. Similar corrective action must be taken with
regard to the maintenance of buildings and the distribution of equipment. In these areas, normal administra-

tive practice should produce schools of like quality, facilities, and staffs. Something more must be said, however, as to faculty assignment and new school construction.

In the companion *Davis* case, *post*, p. 33, the Mobile school board has argued that the Constitution requires that teachers be assigned on a "color blind" basis. It also argues that the Constitution prohibits district courts from using their equity power to order assignment of teachers to achieve a particular degree of faculty desegregation. We reject that contention.

In *United States* v. *Montgomery County Board of Education*, 395 U. S. 225 (1969), the District Court set as a goal a plan of faculty assignment in each school with a ratio of white to Negro faculty members substantially the same throughout the system. This order was predicated on the District Court finding that:

> "The evidence does not reflect any real administrative problems involved in immediately desegregating the substitute teachers, the student teachers, the night school faculties, and in the evolvement of a really legally adequate program for the substantial desegregation of the faculties of all schools in the system commencing with the school year 1968–69." Quoted at 395 U. S., at 232.

The District Court in *Montgomery* then proceeded to set an initial ratio for the whole system of at least two Negro teachers out of each 12 in any given school. The Court of Appeals modified the order by eliminating what it regarded as "fixed mathematical" ratios of faculty and substituted an initial requirement of *"substantially or approximately"* a five-to-one ratio. With respect to the future, the Court of Appeals held that the numerical ratio should be eliminated and that compliance should not be tested solely by the achievement of specified proportions. *Id.*, at 234.

We reversed the Court of Appeals and restored the District Court's order in its entirety, holding that the order of the District Judge

> "was adopted in the spirit of this Court's opinion in *Green* . . . in that his plan 'promises realistically to work, and promises realistically to work *now*.' The modifications ordered by the panel of the Court of Appeals, while of course not intended to do so, would, we think, take from the order some of its capacity to expedite, by means of specific commands, the day when a completely unified, unitary, nondiscriminatory school system becomes a reality instead of a hope. . . . We also believe that under all the circumstances of this case we follow the original plan outlined in *Brown II* . . . by accepting the more specific and expeditious order of [District] Judge Johnson . . . ." 395 U. S., at 235–236 (emphasis in original).

The principles of *Montgomery* have been properly followed by the District Court and the Court of Appeals in this case.

The construction of new schools and the closing of old ones are two of the most important functions of local school authorities and also two of the most complex. They must decide questions of location and capacity in light of population growth, finances, land values, site availability, through an almost endless list of factors to be considered. The result of this will be a decision which, when combined with one technique or another of student assignment, will determine the racial composition of the student body in each school in the system. Over the long run, the consequences of the choices will be far reaching. People gravitate toward school facilities, just as schools are located in response to the needs of people. The location of schools may thus influence the patterns of residential development of a metropolitan area and have important impact on composition of inner-city neighborhoods.

In the past, choices in this respect have been used as a potent weapon for creating or maintaining a state-segregated school system. In addition to the classic pattern of building schools specifically intended for Negro or white students, school authorities have sometimes, since *Brown,* closed schools which appeared likely to become racially mixed through changes in neighborhood residential patterns. This was sometimes accompanied by building new schools in the areas of white suburban expansion farthest from Negro population centers in order to maintain the separation of the races with a minimum departure from the formal principles of "neighborhood zoning." Such a policy does more than simply influence the short-run composition of the student body of a new school. It may well promote segregated residential patterns which, when combined with "neighborhood zoning," further lock the school system into the mold of separation of the races. Upon a proper showing a district court may consider this in fashioning a remedy.

In ascertaining the existence of legally imposed school segregation, the existence of a pattern of school construction and abandonment is thus a factor of great weight. In devising remedies where legally imposed segregation has been established, it is the responsibility of local authorities and district courts to see to it that future school construction and abandonment are not used and do not serve to perpetuate or re-establish the dual system. When necessary, district courts should retain jurisdiction to assure that these responsibilities are carried out. Cf. *United States* v. *Board of Public Instruction,* 395 F. 2d 66 (CA5 1968); *Brewer* v. *School Board,* 397 F. 2d 37 (CA4 1968).

V

The central issue in this case is that of student assignment, and there are essentially four problem areas:

(1) to what extent racial balance or racial quotas may be used as an implement in a remedial order to correct a previously segregated system;

(2) whether every all-Negro and all-white school must be eliminated as an indispensable part of a remedial process of desegregation;

(3) what the limits are, if any, on the rearrangement of school districts and attendance zones, as a remedial measure; and

(4) what the limits are, if any, on the use of transportation facilities to correct state-enforced racial school segregation.

(1) *Racial Balances or Racial Quotas.*

The constant theme and thrust of every holding from *Brown I* to date is that state-enforced separation of races in public schools is discrimination that violates the Equal Protection Clause. The remedy commanded was to dismantle dual school systems.

We are concerned in these cases with the elimination of the discrimination inherent in the dual school systems, not with myriad factors of human existence which can cause discrimination in a multitude of ways on racial, religious, or ethnic grounds. The target of the cases from *Brown I* to the present was the dual school system. The elimination of racial discrimination in public schools is a large task and one that should not be retarded by efforts to achieve broader purposes lying beyond the jurisdiction of school authorities. One vehicle can carry only a limited amount of baggage. It would not serve the important objective of *Brown I* to seek to use school desegregation cases for purposes beyond their scope, although desegregation of schools ultimately will have impact on other forms of discrimination. We do not reach in this case the question whether a showing that school segregation is a consequence of other types of state action, without any discriminatory action by the school authorities, is a constitutional violation requiring remedial action by a school desegregation decree. This case does not present that question and we therefore do not decide it.

Our objective in dealing with the issues presented by these cases is to see that school authorities exclude no pupil of a racial minority from any school, directly or indirectly, on account of race; it does not and cannot embrace all the problems of racial prejudice, even when those problems contribute to disproportionate racial concentrations in some schools.

In this case it is urged that the District Court has imposed a racial balance requirement of 71%–29% on individual schools. The fact that no such objective was actually achieved—and would appear to be impossible—tends to blunt that claim, yet in the opinion and order of the District Court of December 1, 1969, we find that court directing

> "that efforts should be made to reach a 71–29 ratio in the various schools so that there will be no basis for contending that one school is racially different from the others . . . , [t]hat no school [should] be operated with an all-black or predominantly black student body, [and] [t]hat pupils of all grades [should] be assigned in such a way that as nearly as practicable the various schools at various grade levels have about the same proportion of black and white students."

The District Judge went on to acknowledge that variation "from that norm may be unavoidable." This contains intimations that the "norm" is a fixed mathematical

racial balance reflecting the pupil constituency of the
system. If we were to read the holding of the District
Court to require, as a matter of substantive constitutional right, any particular degree of racial balance or
mixing, that approach would be disapproved and we
would be obliged to reverse. The constitutional command to desegregate schools does not mean that every
school in every community must always reflect the racial
composition of the school system as a whole.

As the voluminous record in this case shows,[7] the
predicate for the District Court's use of the 71%–29%
ratio was twofold: first, its express finding, approved by
the Court of Appeals and not challenged here, that a
dual school system had been maintained by the school
authorities at least until 1969; second, its finding, also
approved by the Court of Appeals, that the school board
had totally defaulted in its acknowledged duty to come
forward with an acceptable plan of its own, notwithstanding the patient efforts of the District Judge who, on
at least three occasions, urged the board to submit plans.[8]
As the statement of facts shows, these findings are abun-

---

[7] It must be remembered that the District Court entered nearly
a score of orders and numerous sets of findings, and for the most part
each was accompanied by a memorandum opinion. Considering
the pressure under which the court was obliged to operate we
would not expect that all inconsistencies and apparent inconsistencies
could be avoided. Our review, of course, is on the orders of February 5, 1970, as amended, and August 7, 1970.

[8] The final board plan left 10 schools 86% to 100% Negro and
yet categorically rejected the techniques of pairing and clustering
as part of the desegregation effort. As discussed below, the Charlotte board was under an obligation to exercise every reasonable
effort to remedy the violation, once it was identified, and the
suggested techniques are permissible remedial devices. Additionally,
as noted by the District Court and Court of Appeals, the board plan
did not assign white students to any school unless the student
population of that school was at least 60% white. This was an
arbitrary limitation negating reasonable remedial steps.

dantly supported by the record. It was because of this total failure of the school board that the District Court was obliged to turn to other qualified sources, and Dr. Finger was designated to assist the District Court to do what the board should have done.

We see therefore that the use made of mathematical ratios was no more than a starting point in the process of shaping a remedy, rather than an inflexible requirement. From that starting point the District Court proceeded to frame a decree that was within its discretionary powers, as an equitable remedy for the particular circumstances.[9] As we said in *Green,* a school authority's remedial plan or a district court's remedial decree is to be judged by its effectiveness. Awareness of the racial composition of the whole school system is likely to be a useful starting point in shaping a remedy to correct past constitutional violations. In sum, the very limited use made of mathematical ratios was within the equitable remedial discretion of the District Court.

(2) *One-race Schools.*

The record in this case reveals the familiar phenomenon that in metropolitan areas minority groups are often found concentrated in one part of the city. In some circumstances certain schools may remain all or largely of one race until new schools can be provided or neighborhood patterns change. Schools all or predominately

---

[9] In its August 3, 1970, memorandum holding that the District Court plan was "reasonable" under the standard laid down by the Fourth Circuit on appeal, the District Court explained the approach taken as follows:

"This court has not ruled, and does not rule that 'racial balance' is required under the Constitution; nor that all black schools in all cities are unlawful; nor that all school boards must bus children or violate the Constitution; *nor that the particular order entered in this case would be correct in other circumstances not before this court.*" (Emphasis in original.)

of one race in a district of mixed population will require close scrutiny to determine that school assignments are not part of state-enforced segregation.

In light of the above, it should be clear that the existence of some small number of one-race, or virtually one-race, schools within a district is not in and of itself the mark of a system that still practices segregation by law. The district judge or school authorities should make every effort to achieve the greatest possible degree of actual desegregation and will thus necessarily be concerned with the elimination of one-race schools. No *per se* rule can adequately embrace all the difficulties of reconciling the competing interests involved; but in a system with a history of segregation the need for remedial criteria of sufficient specificity to assure a school authority's compliance with its constitutional duty warrants a presumption against schools that are substantially disproportionate in their racial composition. Where the school authority's proposed plan for conversion from a dual to a unitary system contemplates the continued existence of some schools that are all or predominately of one race, they have the burden of showing that such school assignments are genuinely nondiscriminatory. The court should scrutinize such schools, and the burden upon the school authorities will be to satisfy the court that their racial composition is not the result of present or past discriminatory action on their part.

An optional majority-to-minority transfer provision has long been recognized as a useful part of every desegregation plan. Provision for optional transfer of those in the majority racial group of a particular school to other schools where they will be in the minority is an indispensable remedy for those students willing to transfer to other schools in order to lessen the impact on them of the state-imposed stigma of segregation. In order to be effective, such a transfer arrangement must grant the transferring student free transportation and space must be made available in the school to which he desires to move. Cf. *Ellis* v. *Board of Public Instruction*, 423 F. 2d 203, 206 (CA5 1970). The court orders in this and the companion *Davis* case now provide such an option.

(3) *Remedial Altering of Attendance Zones.*

The maps submitted in these cases graphically demonstrate that one of the principal tools employed by school planners and by courts to break up the dual school system has been a frank—and sometimes drastic—gerrymandering of school districts and attendance zones. An additional step was pairing, "clustering," or "grouping" of schools with attendance assignments made deliberately to accomplish the transfer of Negro students out of formerly segregated Negro schools and transfer of white students to formerly all-Negro schools. More often than not, these zones are neither compact [10] nor contiguous; indeed they may be on opposite ends of the city. As an interim corrective measure, this cannot be said to be beyond the broad remedial powers of a court.

---

[10] The reliance of school authorities on the reference to the "revision of . . . attendance areas into *compact* units," *Brown II*, at 300 (emphasis supplied), is misplaced. The enumeration in that opinion of considerations to be taken into account by district courts was patently intended to be suggestive rather than exhaustive. The decision in *Brown II* to remand the cases decided in *Brown I* to local courts for the framing of specific decrees was premised on a recognition that this Court could not at that time foresee the particular means which would be required to implement the constitutional principles announced. We said in *Green, supra,* at 439:

"The obligation of the district courts, as it always has been, is to assess the effectiveness of a proposed plan in achieving desegregation. There is no universal answer to complex problems of desegregation; there is obviously no one plan that will do the job in every case. The matter must be assessed in light of the circumstances present and the options available in each instance."

419-882 O - 72 - 7

Absent a constitutional violation there would be no basis for judicially ordering assignment of students on a racial basis. All things being equal, with no history of discrimination, it might well be desirable to assign pupils to schools nearest their homes. But all things are not equal in a system that has been deliberately constructed and maintained to enforce racial segregation. The remedy for such segregation may be administratively awkward, inconvenient, and even bizarre in some situations and may impose burdens on some; but all awkwardness and inconvenience cannot be avoided in the interim period when remedial adjustments are being made to eliminate the dual school systems.

No fixed or even substantially fixed guidelines can be established as to how far a court can go, but it must be recognized that there are limits. The objective is to dismantle the dual school system. "Racially neutral" assignment plans proposed by school authorities to a district court may be inadequate; such plans may fail to counteract the continuing effects of past school segregation resulting from discriminatory location of school sites or distortion of school size in order to achieve or maintain an artificial racial separation. When school authorities present a district court with a "loaded game board," affirmative action in the form of remedial altering of attendance zones is proper to achieve truly nondiscriminatory assignments. In short, an assignment plan is not acceptable simply because it appears to be neutral.

In this area, we must of necessity rely to a large extent, as this Court has for more than 16 years, on the informed judgment of the district courts in the first instance and on courts of appeals.

We hold that the pairing and grouping of noncontiguous school zones is a permissible tool and such action is to be considered in light of the objectives sought. Ju-

dicial steps in shaping such zones going beyond combinations of contiguous areas should be examined in light
of what is said in subdivisions (1), (2), and (3) of this
opinion concerning the objectives to be sought. Maps
do not tell the whole story since noncontiguous school
zones may be more accessible to each other in terms
of the critical travel time, because of traffic patterns and
good highways, than schools geographically closer together. Conditions in different localities will vary so
widely that no rigid rules can be laid down to govern
all situations.

(4) *Transportation of Students.*

The scope of permissible transportation of students as
an implement of a remedial decree has never been defined
by this Court and by the very nature of the problem it
cannot be defined with precision. No rigid guidelines as
to student transportation can be given for application to
the infinite variety of problems presented in thousands
of situations. Bus transportation has been an integral
part of the public education system for years, and was
perhaps the single most important factor in the transition from the one-room schoolhouse to the consolidated
school. Eighteen million of the Nation's public school
children, approximately 39%, were transported to their
schools by bus in 1969–1970 in all parts of the country.

The importance of bus transportation as a normal and
accepted tool of educational policy is readily discernible
in this and the companion case, *Davis, supra.*[11] The

---

[11] During 1967–1968, for example, the Mobile board used 207
buses to transport 22,094 students daily for an average round trip
of 31 miles. During 1966–1967, 7,116 students in the metropolitan
area were bused daily. In Charlotte-Mecklenburg, the system as
a whole, without regard to desegregation plans, planned to bus
approximately 23,000 students this year, for an average daily round
trip of 15 miles. More elementary school children than high school
children were to be bused, and four- and five-year-olds travel the
longest routes in the system.

Charlotte school authorities did not purport to assign
students on the basis of geographically drawn zones until
1965 and then they allowed almost unlimited transfer
privileges. The District Court's conclusion that assignment of children to the school nearest their home serving
their grade would not produce an effective dismantling
of the dual system is supported by the record.

Thus the remedial techniques used in the District
Court's order were within that court's power to provide
equitable relief; implementation of the decree is well
within the capacity of the school authority.

The decree provided that the buses used to implement
the plan would operate on direct routes. Students would
be picked up at schools near their homes and transported
to the schools they were to attend. The trips for elementary school pupils average about seven miles and
the District Court found that they would take "not over
35 minutes at the most." [12] This system compares favorably with the transportation plan previously operated
in Charlotte under which each day 23,600 students on all
grade levels were transported an average of 15 miles one
way for an average trip requiring over an hour. In these
circumstances, we find no basis for holding that the local
school authorities may not be required to employ bus
transportation as one tool of school desegregation. Desegregation plans cannot be limited to the walk-in school.

An objection to transportation of students may have
validity when the time or distance of travel is so great
as to either risk the health of the children or significantly

---

[12] The District Court found that the school system would have
to employ 138 more buses than it had previously operated. But
105 of those buses were already available and the others could
easily be obtained. Additionally, it should be noted that North
Carolina requires provision of transportation for all students who
are assigned to schools more than one and one-half miles from their
homes. N. C. Gen. Stat. § 115–186 (b) (1966).

impinge on the educational process. District courts must
weigh the soundness of any transportation plan in light
of what is said in subdivisions (1), (2), and (3) above.
It hardly needs stating that the limits on time of travel
will vary with many factors, but probably with none
more than the age of the students. The reconciliation of
competing values in a desegregation case is, of course, a
difficult task with many sensitive facets but fundamentally no more so than remedial measures courts of equity
have traditionally employed.

VI

The Court of Appeals, searching for a term to define
the equitable remedial power of the district courts, used
the term "reasonableness." In *Green, supra,* this Court
used the term "feasible" and by implication, "workable,"
"effective," and "realistic" in the mandate to develop "a
plan that promises realistically to work, and . . . to work
now." On the facts of this case, we are unable to conclude that the order of the District Court is not reasonable, feasible and workable. However, in seeking to
define the scope of remedial power or the limits on
remedial power of courts in an area as sensitive as we
deal with here, words are poor instruments to convey the
sense of basic fairness inherent in equity. Substance,
not semantics, must govern, and we have sought to
suggest the nature of limitations without frustrating the
appropriate scope of equity.

At some point, these school authorities and others like
them should have achieved full compliance with this
Court's decision in *Brown I.* The systems would then be
"unitary" in the sense required by our decisions in *Green*
and *Alexander.*

It does not follow that the communities served by
such systems will remain demographically stable, for
in a growing, mobile society, few will do so. Neither

school authorities nor district courts are constitutionally required to make year-by-year adjustments of the racial composition of student bodies once the affirmative duty to desegregate has been accomplished and racial discrimination through official action is eliminated from the system. This does not mean that federal courts are without power to deal with future problems; but in the absence of a showing that either the school authorities or some other agency of the State has deliberately attempted to fix or alter demographic patterns to affect the racial composition of the schools, further intervention by a district court should not be necessary.

For the reasons herein set forth, the judgment of the Court of Appeals is affirmed as to those parts in which it affirmed the judgment of the District Court. The order of the District Court, dated August 7, 1970, is also affirmed.

It is so ordered.

MILLIKEN, GOVERNOR OF MICHIGAN, ET AL. v.
BRADLEY ET AL.

CERTIORARI TO THE UNITED STATES COURT OF APPEALS FOR
THE SIXTH CIRCUIT

No. 73–434. Argued February 27, 1974—Decided July 25, 1974*

Respondents brought this class action, alleging that the Detroit
public school system is racially segregated as a result of the official
policies and actions of petitioner state and city officials, and seeking implementation of a plan to eliminate the segregation and
establish a unitary nonracial school system. The District Court,
after concluding that various acts by the petitioner Detroit Board
of Education had created and perpetuated school segregation in
Detroit, and that the acts of the Board, as a subordinate entity
of the State, were attributable to the State, ordered the Board
to submit Detroit-only desegregation plans. The court also
ordered the state officials to submit desegregation plans encompassing the three-county metropolitan area, despite the fact that
the 85 outlying school districts in these three counties were not parties to the action and there was no claim that they had committed
constitutional violations. Subsequently, outlying school districts were allowed to intervene, but were not permitted to assert
any claim or defense on issues previously adjudicated or to reopen
any issue previously decided, but were allowed merely to advise
the court as to the propriety of a metropolitan plan and to submit
any objections, modifications, or alternatives to any such plan.
Thereafter, the District Court ruled that it was proper to consider
metropolitan plans, that Detroit-only plans submitted by the
Board and respondents were inadequate to accomplish desegregation, and that therefore it would seek a solution beyond the limits of
the Detroit School District, and concluded that "[s]chool district
lines are simply matters of political convenience and may not be
used to deny constitutional rights." Without having evidence
that the suburban school districts had committed acts of *de jure*
segregation, the court appointed a panel to submit a plan for the

---

*Together with No. 73–435, *Allen Park Public Schools et al.* v.
Bradley et al., and No. 73–436, *Grosse Pointe Public School System*
v. *Bradley et al.*, also on certiorari to the same court.

Detroit schools that would encompass an entire designated deseg-regation area consisting of 53 of the 85 suburban school districts plus Detroit, and ordered the Detroit Board to acquire at least 295 school buses to provide transportation under an interim plan to be developed for the 1972–1973 school year. The Court of Appeals, affirming in part, held that the record supported the District Court's finding as to the constitutional violations com-mitted by the Detroit Board and the state officials; that therefore the District Court was authorized and required to take effective measures to desegregate the Detroit school system; and that a metropolitan area plan embracing the 53 outlying districts was the only feasible solution and was within the District Court's equity powers. But the court remanded so that all suburban school districts that might be affected by a metropolitan remedy could be made parties and have an opportunity to be heard as to the scope and implementation of such a remedy, and vacated the order as to the bus acquisitions, subject to its reimposition at an appropriate time. *Held:* The relief ordered by the District Court and affirmed by the Court of Appeals was based upon erroneous standards and was unsupported by record evidence that acts of the outlying districts had any impact on the discrimination found to exist in the Detroit schools. A federal court may not impose a multidistrict, areawide remedy for single-district *de jure* school segregation violations where there is no finding that the other included school districts have failed to operate unitary school systems or have committed acts that effected segregation within the other districts, there is no claim or finding that the school district boundary lines were established with the purpose of foster-ing racial segregation, and there is no meaningful opportunity for the included neighboring school districts to present evidence or be heard on the propriety of a multidistrict remedy or on the question of constitutional violations by those districts. Pp. 737–753.

(a) The District Court erred in using as a standard the declared objective of development of a metropolitan area plan which, upon implementation, would leave "no school, grade or classroom . . . substantially disproportionate to the overall pupil racial composi-tion" of the metropolitan area as a whole. The clear import of *Swann* v. *Board of Education,* 402 U. S. 1, is that desegregation, in the sense of dismantling a dual school system, does not require any particular racial balance. Pp. 739–741.

(b) While boundary lines may be bridged in circumstances where there has been a constitutional violation calling for inter-district relief, school district lines may not be casually ignored or treated as a mere administrative convenience; substantial local control of public education in this country is a deeply rooted tradition. Pp. 741–742.

(c) The interdistrict remedy could extensively disrupt and alter the structure of public education in Michigan, since that remedy would require, in effect, consolidation of 54 independent school districts historically administered as separate governmental units into a vast new super school district, and, since—entirely apart from the logistical problems attending large-scale transportation of students—the consolidation would generate other problems in the administration, financing, and operation of this new school system. Pp. 742–743.

(d) From the scope of the interdistrict plan itself, absent a complete restructuring of the Michigan school district laws, the District Court would become, first, a *de facto* "legislative author-ity" to resolve the complex operational problems involved and thereafter a "school superintendent" for the entire area, a task which few, if any, judges are qualified to perform and one which would deprive the people of local control of schools through elected school boards. Pp. 743–744.

(e) Before the boundaries of separate and autonomous school districts may be set aside by consolidating the separate units for remedial purposes or by imposing a cross-district remedy, it must be first shown that there has been a constitutional violation within one district that produces a significant segregative effect in another district; *i. e.,* specifically, it must be shown that racially discrimi-natory acts of the state or local school districts, or of a single school district have been a substantial cause of interdistrict segre-gation. Pp. 744–745.

(f) With no showing of significant violation by the 53 outlying school districts and no evidence of any interdistrict violation or effect, the District Court transcended the original theory of the case as framed by the pleadings, and mandated a metropolitan area remedy, the approval of which would impose on the outlying districts, not shown to have committed any constitutional viola-tion, a standard not previously hinted at in any holding of this Court. P. 745.

(g) Assuming, *arguendo,* that the State was derivatively respon-sible for Detroit's segregated school conditions, it does not follow that an interdistrict remedy is constitutionally justified or required, since there has been virtually no showing that either the State or any of the 85 outlying districts engaged in any activity that had a cross-district effect. Pp. 748–749.

(h) An isolated instance of a possible segregative effect as between two of the school districts involved would not justify the broad metropolitanwide remedy contemplated, particularly since that remedy embraced 52 districts having no responsibility for the arrangement and potentially involved 503,000 pupils in addition to Detroit's 276,000 pupils. Pp. 749–750.

484 F. 2d 215, reversed and remanded.

BURGER, C. J., delivered the opinion of the Court, in which STEWART, BLACKMUN, POWELL, and REHNQUIST, JJ., joined. STEWART, J., filed a concurring opinion, post, p. 753. DOUGLAS, J., filed a dissenting opinion, post, p. 757. WHITE, J., filed a dissenting opinion, in which DOUGLAS, BRENNAN, and MARSHALL, JJ., joined, post, p. 762. MARSHALL, J., filed a dissenting opinion, in which DOUGLAS, BRENNAN, and WHITE, JJ., joined, post, p. 781.

Frank J. Kelley, Attorney General of Michigan, argued the cause for petitioners in No. 73–434. With him on the brief were *Robert A. Derengoski,* Solicitor General, and *Eugene Krasicky, Gerald F. Young, George L. McCargar,* and *Thomas F. Schimpf,* Assistant Attorneys General. *William M. Saxton* argued the cause for petitioners in Nos. 73–435 and 73–436. With him on the brief in No. 73–435 were *John B. Weaver, Robert M. Vercruysse,* and *Xhafer Orhan. Douglas H. West* filed a brief for petitioner in No. 73–436.

J. Harold Flannery and *Nathaniel R. Jones* argued the cause for respondents in all cases. With them on the brief for respondents Bradley et al. were *Jack Greenberg, Norman Chachkin,* and *Louis R. Lucas. George T. Roumell, Jr.,* and *C. Nicholas Revelos* filed a brief for respondents Board of Education for the School District of the city of Detroit et al. *John Bruff* and *William Ross* filed a brief for respondent Professional Personnel of Van

Dyke.   *Robert J. Lord* filed a brief for respondents Green et al.

Solicitor General Bork argued the cause for the United States as *amicus curiae* urging reversal. With him on the brief was *Assistant Attorney General Pottinger.*†

Mr. Chief Justice Burger delivered the opinion of the Court.

We granted certiorari in these consolidated cases to determine whether a federal court may impose a multi-district, areawide remedy to a single-district *de jure* segregation problem absent any finding that the other included school districts have failed to operate unitary school systems within their districts, absent any claim or finding that the boundary lines of any affected school district were established with the purpose of fostering racial segregation in public schools, absent any finding that the included districts committed acts which effected segregation within the other districts, and absent a

_____

†Briefs of *amici curiae* urging reversal were filed by *Theodore L. Sendak,* Attorney General, *Donald P. Bogard,* Deputy Attorney General, and *William F. Harvey* for the State of Indiana; by *Lewis C. Bose* and *William M. Evans* for the Metropolitan School District of Lawrence Township, Indiana, et al.; by *Richard D. Wagner* and *Richard L. Brown* for the town of Speedway, Indiana, et al.; and by *Harold H. Fuhrman* for the National Suburban League, Ltd.

Briefs of *amici curiae* urging affirmance were filed by *Leonard P. Strickman* for the city of Boston, Massachusetts; by *Alexander A. Goldfarb* for the city of Hartford, Connecticut; by *Sanford Jay Rosen* for the Mexican American Legal Defense and Educational Fund; and by Inter-Faith Centers for Racial Justice, Inc.

Briefs of *amici curiae* were filed by *Charles F. Clippert, Charles E. Keller, Thomas H. Schwarze, John F. Shantz, Raymond McPeters, Walter J. Guth, Jr., Raymond G. Glime, Tony Ferris,* and *Perry Christy* for Bloomfield Hills School District et al.; by *Stephen J. Pollak, Richard M. Sharp,* and *David Rubin* for the National Education Assn.; and by *David I. Caplan* for the Jewish Rights Council.

meaningful opportunity for the included neighboring
school districts to present evidence or be heard on the
propriety of a multidistrict remedy or on the question
of constitutional violations by those neighboring districts.[1]

I

The action was commenced in August 1970 by the
respondents, the Detroit Branch of the National Association for the Advancement of Colored People [2] and individual parents and students, on behalf of a class later
defined by order of the United States District Court for
the Eastern District of Michigan, dated February 16,
1971, to include "all school children in the City of Detroit,
Michigan, and all Detroit resident parents who have
children of school age." The named defendants in the
District Court included the Governor of Michigan, the
Attorney General, the State Board of Education, the
State Superintendent of Public Instruction, the Board of
Education of the city of Detroit, its members, and the
city's former superintendent of schools. The State of
Michigan as such is not a party to this litigation and
references to the State must be read as references to
the public officials, state and local, through whom
the State is alleged to have acted. In their complaint respondents attacked the constitutionality of a
statute of the State of Michigan known as Act 48
of the 1970 Legislature on the ground that it put the
State of Michigan in the position of unconstitutionally
interfering with the execution and operation of a voluntary plan of partial high school desegregation, known as
the April 7, 1970, Plan, which had been adopted by the
Detroit Board of Education to be effective beginning

---

[1] 484 F. 2d 215 (CA6), cert. granted, 414 U. S. 1038 (1973).

[2] The standing of the NAACP as a proper party plaintiff was not
contested in the trial court and is not an issue in this case.

with the fall 1970 semester. The complaint also alleged
that the Detroit Public School System was and is segregated on the basis of race as a result of the official policies
and actions of the defendants and their predecessors in
office, and called for the implementation of a plan that
would eliminate "the racial identity of every school in
the [Detroit] system and . . . maintain now and hereafter a unitary, nonracial school system."

Initially the matter was tried on respondents' motion
for a preliminary injunction to restrain the enforcement
of Act 48 so as to permit the April 7 Plan to be implemented. On that issue, the District Court ruled that
respondents were not entitled to a preliminary injunction since at that stage there was no proof that Detroit
had a dual segregated school system. On appeal, the
Court of Appeals found that the "implementation of the
April 7 plan was [unconstitutionally] thwarted by State
action in the form of the Act of the Legislature of
Michigan," 433 F. 2d 897, 902 (CA6 1970), and that such
action could not be interposed to delay, obstruct, or
nullify steps lawfully taken for the purpose of protecting
rights guaranteed by the Fourteenth Amendment. The
case was remanded to the District Court for an expedited
trial on the merits.

On remand, the respondents moved for immediate
implementation of the April 7 Plan in order to remedy
the deprivation of the claimed constitutional rights. In
response, the School Board suggested two other plans,
along with the April 7 Plan, and urged that top priority
be assigned to the so-called "Magnet Plan" which was
"designed to attract children to a school because of its
superior curriculum." The District Court approved the
Board's Magnet Plan, and respondents again appealed to
the Court of Appeals, moving for summary reversal.
The Court of Appeals refused to pass on the merits of
the Magnet Plan and ruled that the District Court had

not abused its discretion in refusing to adopt the April 7
Plan without an evidentiary hearing. The case was again
remanded with instructions to proceed immediately to a
trial on the merits of respondents' substantive allegations
concerning the Detroit school system. 438 F. 2d 945
(CA6 1971).

The trial of the issue of segregation in the Detroit
school system began on April 6, 1971, and continued
through July 22, 1971, consuming some 41 trial days.
On September 27, 1971, the District Court issued its findings and conclusions on the issue of segregation, finding
that "Governmental actions and inaction at all levels,
federal, state and local, have combined, with those of
private organizations, such as loaning institutions and
real estate associations and brokerage firms, to establish
and to maintain the pattern of residential segregation
throughout the Detroit metropolitan area." 338 F. Supp.
582, 587 (ED Mich. 1971). While still addressing a
Detroit-only violation, the District Court reasoned:

> "While it would be unfair to charge the present de-
> fendants with what other governmental officers or
> agencies have done, it can be said that the actions or
> the failure to act by the responsible school authori-
> ties, both city and state, were linked to that of these
> other governmental units. When we speak of gov-
> ernmental action we should not view the different
> agencies as a collection of unrelated units. Perhaps
> the most that can be said is that all of them, includ-
> ing the school authorities, are, in part, responsible
> for the segregated condition which exists. And we
> note that just as there is an interaction between
> residential patterns and the racial composition of
> the schools, so there is a corresponding effect on the
> residential pattern by the racial composition of the
> schools." *Ibid.*

The District Court found that the Detroit Board of Education created and maintained optional attendance zones [3] within Detroit neighborhoods undergoing racial transition and between high school attendance areas of opposite predominant racial compositions. These zones, the court found, had the "natural, probable, foreseeable and actual effect" of allowing white pupils to escape identifiably Negro schools. *Ibid.* Similarly, the District Court found that Detroit school attendance zones had been drawn along north-south boundary lines despite the Detroit Board's awareness that drawing boundary lines in an east-west direction would result in significantly greater desegregation. Again, the District Court concluded, the natural and actual effect of these acts was the creation and perpetuation of school segregation within Detroit.

The District Court found that in the operation of its school transportation program, which was designed to relieve overcrowding, the Detroit Board had admittedly bused Negro Detroit pupils to predominantly Negro schools which were beyond or away from closer white schools with available space. [4] This practice was found to have continued in recent years despite the Detroit Board's avowed policy, adopted in 1967, of utilizing transportation to increase desegregation:

"With one exception (necessitated by the burning of a white school), defendant Board has never bused

---

[3] Optional zones, sometimes referred to as dual zones or dual overlapping zones, provide pupils living within certain areas a choice of attendance at one of two high schools.

[4] The Court of Appeals found record evidence that in at least one instance during the period 1957–1958, Detroit served a suburban school district by contracting with it to educate its Negro high school students by transporting them away from nearby suburban white high schools, and past Detroit high schools which were predominantly white, to all-Negro or predominantly Negro Detroit schools. 484 F. 2d, at 231.

white children to predominantly black schools. The
Board has not bused white pupils to black schools
despite the enormous amount of space available in
inner-city schools. There were 22,961 vacant seats
in schools 90% or more black." *Id.*, at 588.

With respect to the Detroit Board of Education's practices in school construction, the District Court found that
Detroit school construction generally tended to have a segregative effect with the great majority of schools being
built in either overwhelmingly all-Negro or all-white
neighborhoods so that the new schools opened as predominantly one-race schools. Thus, of the 14 schools
which opened for use in 1970–1971, 11 opened over 90%
Negro and one opened less than 10% Negro.

The District Court also found that the State of Michigan had committed several constitutional violations with
respect to the exercise of its general responsibility for, and
supervision of, public education.[5] The State, for example, was found to have failed, until the 1971 Session of
the Michigan Legislature, to provide authorization or

---

[5] School districts in the State of Michigan are instrumentalities of
the State and subordinate to its State Board of Education and legislature. The Constitution of the State of Michigan, Art. 8, § 2,
provides in relevant part:

"The legislature shall maintain and support a system of free public
elementary and secondary schools as defined by law."

Similarly, the Michigan Supreme Court has stated: "The school
district is a State agency. Moreover, it is of legislative creation. . . ." *Attorney General ex rel. Kies* v. *Lowrey,* 131 Mich. 639,
644, 92 N. W. 289, 290 (1902); " 'Education in Michigan belongs to
the State. It is no part of the local self-government inherent in the
township or municipality, except so far as the legislature may choose
to make it such. The Constitution has turned the whole subject over
to the legislature. . . .'" *Attorney General ex rel. Zacharias* v. *Detroit Board of Education,* 154 Mich. 584, 590, 118 N. W. 606, 609
(1908).

funds for the transportation of pupils within Detroit regardless of their poverty or distance from the school to which they were assigned; during this same period the State provided many neighboring, mostly white, suburban districts the full range of state-supported transportation.

The District Court found that the State, through Act 48, acted to "impede, delay and minimize racial integration in Detroit schools." The first sentence of § 12 of Act 48 was designed to delay the April 7, 1970, desegregation plan originally adopted by the Detroit Board. The remainder of § 12 sought to prescribe for each school in the eight districts criteria of "free choice" and "neighborhood schools," which, the District Court found, "had as their purpose and effect the maintenance of segregation." 338 F. Supp., at 589.[6]

The District Court also held that the acts of the Detroit Board of Education, as a subordinate entity of the State, were attributable to the State of Michigan, thus creating a vicarious liability on the part of the State. Under Michigan law, Mich. Comp. Laws § 388.851 (1970), for example, school building construction plans had to be approved by the State Board of Education, and, prior to 1962, the State Board had specific statutory authority to supervise schoolsite selection. The proofs concerning the effect of Detroit's school construction program were,

---

[6] "Sec. 12. The implementation of any attendance provisions for the 1970–71 school year determined by any first class school district board *shall be delayed* pending the date of commencement of functions by the first class school district boards established under the provisions of this amendatory act but such provision shall not impair the right of any such board to determine and implement prior to such date such changes in attendance provisions as are mandated by practical necessity. . . ." Act No. 48, § 12, Mich. Pub. Acts of 1970; Mich. Comp. Laws § 388.182 (1970) (emphasis added).

therefore, found to be largely applicable to show state responsibility for the segregative results.[7]

Turning to the question of an appropriate remedy for these several constitutional violations, the District Court deferred a pending motion [8] by intervening parent de-

---

[7] The District Court briefly alluded to the possibility that the State, along with private persons, had caused, in part, the housing patterns of the Detroit metropolitan area which, in turn, produced the predominantly white and predominantly Negro neighborhoods that characterize Detroit:

"It is no answer to say that restricted practices grew gradually (as the black population in the area increased between 1920 and 1970), or that since 1948 racial restrictions on the ownership of real property have been removed. The policies pursued by both government and private persons and agencies have a continuing and present effect upon the complexion of the community—as we know, the choice of a residence is a relatively infrequent affair. For many years FHA and VA openly advised and advocated the maintenance of 'harmonious' neighborhoods, i. e., racially and economically harmonious. The conditions created continue." 338 F. Supp. 582, 587 (ED Mich. 1971).

Thus, the District Court concluded:

"The affirmative obligation of the defendant Board has been and is to adopt and implement pupil assignment practices and policies that compensate for and avoid incorporation into the school system the effects of residential racial segregation." Id., at 593.

The Court of Appeals, however, expressly noted that:

"In affirming the District Judge's findings of constitutional violations by the Detroit Board of Education and by the State defendants resulting in segregated schools in Detroit, we have not relied at all upon testimony pertaining to segregated housing except as school construction programs helped cause or maintain such segregation." 484 F. 2d, at 242.

Accordingly, in its present posture, the case does not present any question concerning possible state housing violations.

[8] On March 22, 1971, a group of Detroit residents, who were parents of children enrolled in the Detroit public schools, were permitted to intervene as parties defendant. On June 24, 1971, the District Judge alluded to the "possibility" of a metropolitan school system stating: "[A]s I have said to several witnesses in this case:

fendants to join as additional parties defendant the 85 outlying school districts in the three-county Detroit metropolitan area on the ground that effective relief could not be achieved without their presence.[9] The District Court concluded that this motion to join was "premature," since it "has to do with relief" and no reasonably specific desegregation plan was before the court. 338 F. Supp., at 595. Accordingly, the District Court proceeded to order the Detroit Board of Education to submit desegregation plans limited to the segregation problems found to be existing within the city of Detroit. At the same time, however, the state defendants were directed to submit desegregation plans encompassing the three-county metropolitan area [10] despite the fact that the 85 outlying school

---

'How do you desegregate a black city, or a black school system.' " Petitioners' Appendix 243a (hereinafter Pet. App.). Subsequently, on July 16, 1971, various parents filed a motion to require joinder of all of the 85 outlying independent school districts within the tri-county area.

[9] The respondents, as plaintiffs below, opposed the motion to join the additional school districts, arguing that the presence of the state defendants was sufficient and all that was required, even if, in shaping a remedy, the affairs of these other districts was to be affected. 338 F. Supp., at 595.

[10] At the time of the 1970 census, the population of Michigan was 8,875,083, almost half of which, 4,199,931, resided in the tri-county area of Wayne, Oakland, and Macomb. Oakland and Macomb Counties abut Wayne County to the north, and Oakland County abuts Macomb County to the west. These counties cover 1,952 square miles, Michigan Statistical Abstract (9th ed. 1972), and the area is approximately the size of the State of Delaware (2,057 square miles), more than half again the size of the State of Rhode Island (1,214 square miles) and almost 30 times the size of the District of Columbia (67 square miles). Statistical Abstract of the United States (93d ed. 1972). The populations of Wayne, Oakland, and Macomb Counties were 2,666,751; 907,871; and 625,309, respectively, in 1970. Detroit, the State's largest city, is located in Wayne County.

In the 1970–1971 school year, there were 2,157,449 children enrolled in school districts in Michigan. There are 86 independent, districts of these three counties were not parties to the action and despite the fact that there had been no claim that these outlying districts had committed constitutional violations.[11]   An effort to appeal these orders to the Court of Appeals was dismissed on the ground that the orders were not appealable.   468 F. 2d 902 (CA6), cert. denied, 409 U. S. 844 (1972).   The sequence of the ensuing actions and orders of the District Court are significant factors and will therefore be catalogued in some detail.

Following the District Court's abrupt announcement that it planned to consider the implementation of a multidistrict, metropolitan area remedy to the segregation problems identified within the city of Detroit, the District Court was again requested to grant the outlying school districts intervention as of right on the ground that the District Court's new request for multidistrict plans "may, as a practical matter, impair or impede [the intervenors'] ability to protect" the welfare of their students.   The District Court took the motions to intervene under advisement pending submission of the requested desegregation plans by Detroit and the state officials. On March 7, 1972, the District Court notified all parties and the petitioner school districts seeking intervention, that March 14, 1972, was the deadline for submission of recommendations for conditions of intervention and the

legally distinct school districts within the tri-county area, having a total enrollment of approximately 1,000,000 children.   In 1970, the Detroit Board of Education operated 319 schools with approximately 276,000 students.

[11] In its formal opinion, subsequently announced, the District Court candidly recognized:

"It should be noted that the court has taken no proofs with respect to the establishment of the boundaries of the 86 public school districts in the counties of Wayne, Oakland and Macomb, nor on the issue of whether, with the exclusion of the city of Detroit school district, such school districts have committed acts of de jure segregation."   345 F. Supp. 914, 920 (ED Mich. 1972).

date of the commencement of hearings on Detroit-only desegregation plans. On the second day of the scheduled hearings, March 15, 1972, the District Court granted the motions of the intervenor school districts [12] subject, *inter alia*, to the following conditions:

"1. No intervenor will be permitted to assert any claim or defense previously adjudicated by the court.

"2. No intervenor shall reopen any question or issue which has previously been decided by the court.

.   .   .   .   .

"7. New intervenors are granted intervention for two principal purposes: (a) To advise the court, by brief, of the legal propriety or impropriety of considering a metropolitan plan; (b) To review any plan or plans for the desegregation of the so-called larger Detroit Metropolitan area, and submitting objections, modifications or alternatives to it or them, and in accordance with the requirements of the United States Constitution and the prior orders of this court." 1 Joint Appendix 206 (hereinafter App.).

Upon granting the motion to intervene, on March 15, 1972, the District Court advised the petitioning intervenors that the court had previously set March 22, 1972, as the date for the filing of briefs on the legal propriety of a "metropolitan" plan of desegregation and, accordingly, that the intervening school districts would have one week to muster their legal arguments on the issue.[13]

----

[12] According to the District Court, intervention was permitted under Fed. Rule Civ. Proc. 24 (a), "Intervention of Right," and also under Rule 24(b), "Permissive Intervention."

[13] This rather abbreviated briefing schedule was maintained despite the fact that the District Court had deferred consideration of a motion made eight months earlier, to bring the suburban districts into the case. See text accompanying n. 8, *supra*.

Thereafter, and following the completion of hearings on the Detroit-only desegregation plans, the District Court issued the four rulings that were the principal issues in the Court of Appeals.

(a) On March 24, 1972, two days after the intervenors' briefs were due, the District Court issued its ruling on the question of whether it could "consider relief in the form of a metropolitan plan, encompassing not only the City of Detroit, but the larger Detroit metropolitan area." It rejected the state defendants' arguments that no state action caused the segregation of the Detroit schools, and the intervening suburban districts' contention that interdistrict relief was inappropriate unless the suburban districts themselves had committed violations. The court concluded:

> "[I]t is proper for the court to consider metropolitan plans directed toward the desegregation of the Detroit public schools as an alternative to the present intra-city desegregation plans before it and, in the event that the court finds such intra-city plans inadequate to desegregate such schools, the court is of the opinion that it is required to consider a metropolitan remedy for desegregation." Pet. App. 51a.

(b) On March 28, 1972, the District Court issued its findings and conclusions on the three Detroit-only plans submitted by the city Board and the respondents. It found that the best of the three plans "would make the Detroit school system more identifiably Black . . . thereby increasing the flight of Whites from the city and the system." *Id.*, at 55a. From this the court concluded that the plan "would not accomplish desegregation . . . within the corporate geographical limits of the city." *Id.*, at 56a. Accordingly, the District Court held that it "must look beyond the limits of the Detroit school district for a solution to the problem," and that "[s]chool district lines are simply matters of political convenience and may not be used to deny constitutional rights." *Id.,* at 57a.

(c) During the period from March 28 to April 14, 1972, the District Court conducted hearings on a metropolitan plan. Counsel for the petitioning intervenors was allowed to participate in these hearings, but he was ordered to confine his argument to "the size and expanse of the metropolitan plan" without addressing the intervenors' opposition to such a remedy or the claim that a finding of a constitutional violation by the intervenor districts was an essential predicate to any remedy involving them. Thereafter, on June 14, 1972, the District Court issued its ruling on the "desegregation area" and related findings and conclusions. The court acknowledged at the outset that it had "taken no proofs with respect to the establishment of the boundaries of the 86 public school districts in the counties [in the Detroit area], nor on the issue of whether, with the exclusion of the city of Detroit school district, such school districts have committed acts of de jure segregation." Nevertheless, the court designated 53 of the 85 suburban school districts plus Detroit as the "desegregation area" and appointed a panel to prepare and submit "an effective desegregation plan" for the Detroit schools that would encompass the entire desegregation area.[14] The plan was to be based on 15 clusters, each containing part of the Detroit system and two or more suburban districts,

---

[14] As of 1970, the 53 school districts outside the city of Detroit that were included in the court's "desegregation area" had a combined student population of approximately 503,000 students compared to Detroit's approximately 276,000 students. Nevertheless, the District Court directed that the intervening districts should be represented by only one member on the desegregation panel while the Detroit Board of Education was granted three panel members. 345 F. Supp., at 917.

and was to "achieve the greatest degree of actual desegregation to the end that, upon implementation, no school,
grade or classroom [would be] substantially disproportionate to the overall pupil racial composition." 345 F.
Supp. 914, 918 (ED Mich. 1972).

(d) On July 11, 1972, and in accordance with a recommendation by the court-appointed desegregation panel,
the District Court ordered the Detroit Board of Education to purchase or lease "at least" 295 school buses for
the purpose of providing transportation under an interim
plan to be developed for the 1972–1973 school year. The
costs of this acquisition were to be borne by the state
defendants. Pet. App. 106a–107a.

On June 12, 1973, a divided Court of Appeals, sitting
en banc, affirmed in part, vacated in part, and remanded
for further proceedings. 484 F. 2d 215 (CA6).[15]
The Court of Appeals held, first, that the record supported the District Court's findings and conclusions on
the constitutional violations committed by the Detroit
Board, id., at 221–238, and by the state defendants, id.,
at 239–241.[16] It stated that the acts of racial discrimina-

---

[15] The District Court had certified most of the foregoing rulings for
interlocutory review pursuant to 28 U. S. C. § 1292 (b) (1 App. 265–
266) and the case was initially decided on the merits by a panel of
three judges. However, the panel's opinion and judgment were
vacated when it was determined to rehear the case en banc, 484 F. 2d,
at 218.

[16] With respect to the State's violations, the Court of Appeals
held: (1) that, since the city Board is an instrumentality of the
State and subordinate to the State Board, the segregative actions of
the Detroit Board "are the actions of an agency of the State,"
id., at 238; (2) that the state legislation rescinding Detroit's
voluntary desegregation plan contributed to increasing segregation
in the Detroit schools, ibid.; (3) that under state law prior to 1962
the State Board had authority over school construction plans and
therefore had to be held responsible "for the segregative results,"

tion shown in the record are "causally related to the substantial amount of segregation found in the Detroit school system," *id.*, at 241, and that "the District Court was therefore authorized and required to take effective measures to desegregate the Detroit Public School System." *Id.*, at 242.

The Court of Appeals also agreed with the District Court that "any less comprehensive a solution than a metropolitan area plan would result in an all black school system immediately surrounded by practically all white suburban school systems, with an overwhelmingly white majority population in the total metropolitan area." *Id.*, at 245. The court went on to state that it could "not see how such segregation can be any less harmful to the minority students than if the same result were accomplished within one school district." *Ibid.*

Accordingly, the Court of Appeals concluded that "the only feasible desegregation plan involves the crossing of the boundary lines between the Detroit School District and adjacent or nearby school districts for the limited purpose of providing an effective desegregation plan." *Id.*, at 249. It reasoned that such a plan would be appropriate because of the State's violations, and could be implemented because of the State's authority to control local school districts. Without further elaboration, and without any discussion of the claims that no constitutional violation by the outlying districts had been

---

ibid.; (4) that the "State statutory scheme of support of transportation for school children directly discriminated against Detroit," *id.*, at 240, by not providing transportation funds to Detroit on the same basis as funds were provided to suburban districts, *id.*, at 238; and (5) that the transportation of Negro students from one suburban district to a Negro school in Detroit must have had the "approval, tacit or express, of the State Board of Education," *ibid.*

shown and that no evidence on that point had been allowed, the Court of Appeals held:

> "[T]he State has committed de jure acts of segregation and . . . the State controls the instrumentalities whose action is necessary to remedy the harmful effects of the State acts." *Ibid.*

An interdistrict remedy was thus held to be "within the equity powers of the District Court." *Id.*, at 250.[17]

The Court of Appeals expressed no views on the propriety of the District Court's composition of the metropolitan "desegregation area." It held that all suburban school districts that might be affected by any metropolitanwide remedy should, under Fed. Rule Civ. Proc. 19, be made parties to the case on remand and be given an opportunity to be heard with respect to the scope and implementation of such a remedy. 484 F. 2d, at 251–252. Under the terms of the remand, however, the District Court was not "required" to receive further evidence on the issue of segregation in the Detroit schools or on the propriety of a Detroit-only remedy, or on the question of whether the affected districts had committed any violation of the constitutional rights of Detroit pupils or others. *Id.*, at 252. Finally, the Court of Appeals vacated the District Court's order directing the acquisition of school buses, subject to the right of the District Court to consider reimposing the order "at the appropriate time." *Ibid.*

---

[17] The court sought to distinguish *Bradley* v. *School Board of the City of Richmond*, 462 F. 2d 1058 (CA4 1972), aff'd by an equally divided Court, 412 U. S. 92 (1973), on the grounds that the District Court in that case had ordered an actual consolidation of three school districts and that Virginia's Constitution and statutes, unlike Michigan's, gave the local boards exclusive power to operate the public schools. 484 F. 2d, at 251.

II

Ever since *Brown* v. *Board of Education,* 347 U. S.
483 (1954), judicial consideration of school desegregation
cases has begun with the standard:

> "[I]n the field of public education the doctrine of
> 'separate but equal' has no place. Separate educa-
> tional facilities are inherently unequal." *Id.,* at 495.

This has been reaffirmed time and again as the meaning
of the Constitution and the controlling rule of law.

The target of the *Brown* holding was clear and forth-
right: the elimination of state-mandated or deliberately
maintained dual school systems with certain schools for
Negro pupils and others for white pupils. This duality
and racial segregation were held to violate the Constitution in the cases subsequent to 1954, including particularly *Green* v. *County School Board of New Kent County,*
391 U. S. 430 (1968); *Raney* v. *Board of Education,* 391
U. S. 443 (1968); *Monroe* v. *Board of Comm'rs,* 391
U. S. 450 (1968); *Swann* v. *Charlotte-Mecklenburg Board
of Education,* 402 U. S. 1 (1971); *Wright* v. *Council of
the City of Emporia,* 407 U. S. 451 (1972); *United
States* v. *Scotland Neck Board of Education,* 407 U. S.
484 (1972).

The *Swann* case, of course, dealt

> "with the problem of defining in more precise terms
> than heretofore the scope of the duty of school au-
> thorities and district courts in implementing *Brown I*
> and the mandate to eliminate dual systems and
> establish unitary systems at once." 402 U. S., at 6.

In *Brown* v. *Board of Education,* 349 U. S. 294 (1955)
(*Brown II*), the Court's first encounter with the problem
of remedies in school desegregation cases, the Court noted:

> "In fashioning and effectuating the decrees, the
> courts will be guided by equitable principles. Tra-

ditionally, equity has been characterized by a practical flexibility in shaping its remedies and by a facility for adjusting and reconciling public and private needs." *Id.*, at 300 (footnotes omitted).

In further refining the remedial process, *Swann* held, the task is to correct, by a balancing of the individual and collective interests, "the condition that offends the Constitution." A federal remedial power may be exercised "only on the basis of a constitutional violation" and, "[a]s with any equity case, the nature of the violation determines the scope of the remedy." 402 U. S., at 16.

Proceeding from these basic principles, we first note that in the District Court the complainants sought a remedy aimed at the *condition* alleged to offend the Constitution—the segregation within the Detroit City School District.[18] The court acted on this theory of the case and in its initial ruling on the "Desegregation Area" stated:

> "The task before this court, therefore, is now, and . . . has always been, how to desegregate the Detroit public schools." 345 F. Supp., at 921.

Thereafter, however, the District Court abruptly rejected the proposed Detroit-only plans on the ground that "while [they] would provide a racial mix more in keeping with the Black-White proportions of the student population [they] would accentuate the racial identifiability of the

---

[18] Although the list of issues presented for review in petitioners' briefs and petitions for writs of certiorari do not include arguments on the findings of segregative violations on the part of the Detroit defendants, two of the petitioners argue in brief that these findings constitute error. This Court's Rules 23 (1)(c) and 40 (1)(d)(2), at a minimum, limit our review of the Detroit violation findings to "plain error," and, under our decision last Term in *Keyes* v. *School District No. 1, Denver, Colorado*, 413 U. S. 189 (1973), the findings appear to be correct.

[Detroit] district as a Black school system, and would not accomplish desegregation." Pet. App. 56a. "[T]he racial composition of the student body is such," said the court, "that the plan's implementation would clearly make the entire Detroit public school system racially identifiable" (*id.*, at 54a), "leav[ing] many of its schools 75 to 90 per cent Black." *Id.*, at 55a. Consequently, the court reasoned, it was imperative to "look beyond the limits of the Detroit school district for a solution to the problem of segregation in the Detroit public schools . . ." since "[s]chool district lines are simply matters of political convenience and may not be used to deny constitutional rights." *Id.*, at 57a. Accordingly, the District Court proceeded to redefine the relevant area to include areas of predominantly white pupil population in order to ensure that "upon implementation, no school, grade or classroom [would be] substantially disproportionate to the overall pupil racial composition" of the entire metropolitan area.

While specifically acknowledging that the District Court's findings of a condition of segregation were limited to Detroit, the Court of Appeals approved the use of a metropolitan remedy largely on the grounds that it is

> "impossible to declare 'clearly erroneous' the District Judge's conclusion that any Detroit only segregation plan will lead directly to a single segregated Detroit school district overwhelmingly black in all of its schools, surrounded by a ring of suburbs and suburban school districts overwhelmingly white in composition in a State in which the racial composition is 87 per cent white and 13 per cent black." 484 F. 2d, at 249.

Viewing the record as a whole, it seems clear that the District Court and the Court of Appeals shifted the pri-

mary focus from a Detroit remedy to the metropolitan
area only because of their conclusion that total desegregation of Detroit would not produce the racial balance
which they perceived as desirable. Both courts proceeded on an assumption that the Detroit schools could
not be truly desegregated—in their view of what constituted desegregation—unless the racial composition of
the student body of each school substantially reflected
the racial composition of the population of the metropolitan area as a whole. The metropolitan area was
then defined as Detroit plus 53 of the outlying school
districts. That this was the approach the District Court
expressly and frankly employed is shown by the order
which expressed the court's view of the constitutional
standard:

> "Within the limitations of reasonable travel time
> and distance factors, pupil reassignments shall be
> effected within the clusters described in Exhibit
> P. M. 12 so as to achieve the greatest degree of actual
> desegregation to the end that, upon implementation,
> *no school, grade or classroom* [will be] substantially
> disproportionate to the overall pupil racial composi-
> tion." 345 F. Supp., at 918 (emphasis added).

In *Swann*, which arose in the context of a single independent school district, the Court held:

> "If we were to read the holding of the District Court
> to require, as a matter of substantive constitutional
> right, any particular degree of racial balance or
> mixing, that approach would be disapproved and we
> would be obliged to reverse." 402 U. S., at 24.

The clear import of this language from *Swann* is that
desegregation, in the sense of dismantling a dual school
system, does not require any particular racial balance in

each "school, grade or classroom." [19] See *Spencer* v. *Kugler,* 404 U. S. 1027 (1972).

Here the District Court's approach to what constituted "actual desegregation" raises the fundamental question, not presented in *Swann,* as to the circumstances in which a federal court may order desegregation relief that embraces more than a single school district. The court's analytical starting point was its conclusion that school district lines are no more than arbitrary lines on a map drawn "for political convenience." Boundary lines may be bridged where there has been a constitutional violation calling for interdistrict relief, but the notion that school district lines may be casually ignored or treated as a mere administrative convenience is contrary to the history of public education in our country. No single tradition in public education is more deeply rooted than local control over the operation of schools; local autonomy has long been thought essential both to the maintenance of community concern and support for public schools and to

---

[19] Disparity in the racial composition of pupils within a single district may well constitute a "signal" to a district court at the outset, leading to inquiry into the causes accounting for a pronounced racial identifiability of schools within one school system. In *Swann,* for example, we were dealing with a large but single independent school system, and a unanimous Court noted: "Where the ... proposed plan for conversion from a dual to a unitary system contemplates the continued existence of some schools that are all or predominantly of one race [the school authority has] the burden of showing that such school assignments are genuinely nondiscriminatory." 402 U. S., at 26. See also *Keyes, supra,* at 208. However, the use of significant racial imbalance in schools within an autonomous school district as a signal which operates simply to shift the burden of proof, is a very different matter from equating racial imbalance with a constitutional violation calling for a remedy. *Keyes, supra,* also involved a remedial order within a single autonomous school district.

quality of the educational process.   See *Wright* v. *Council of the City of Emporia*, 407 U. S., at 469.   Thus, in *San Antonio School District* v. *Rodriguez*, 411 U. S. 1, 50 (1973), we observed that local control over the educational process affords citizens an opportunity to participate in decisionmaking, permits the structuring of school programs to fit local needs, and encourages "experimentation, innovation, and a healthy competition for educational excellence."

The Michigan educational structure involved in this case, in common with most States, provides for a large measure of local control,[20] and a review of the scope and character of these local powers indicates the extent to which the interdistrict remedy approved by the two courts could disrupt and alter the structure of public edu-

---

[20] Under the Michigan School Code of 1955, the local school district is an autonomous political body corporate, operating through a Board of Education popularly elected.   Mich. Comp. Laws §§ 340.27, 340.55, 340.107, 340.148, 340.149, 340.188.   As such, the day-to-day affairs of the school district are determined at the local level in accordance with the plenary power to acquire real and personal property, §§ 340.26, 340.77, 340.113, 340.165, 340.192, 340.352; to hire and contract with personnel, §§ 340.569, 340.574; to levy taxes for operations, § 340.563; to borrow against receipts, § 340.567; to determine the length of school terms, § 340.575; to control the admission of nonresident students, § 340.582; to determine courses of study, § 340.583; to provide a kindergarten program, § 340.584; to establish and operate vocational schools, § 340.585; to offer adult education programs, § 340.586; to establish attendance areas, § 340.-589; to arrange for transportation of nonresident students, § 340.-591; to acquire transportation equipment, § 340.594; to receive gifts and bequests for educational purposes, § 340.605; to employ an attorney, § 340.609; to suspend or expel students, § 340.613; to make rules and regulations for the operation of schools, § 340.614; to cause to be levied authorized millage, § 340.643a; to acquire property by eminent domain, § 340.711 *et seq.;* and to approve and select textbooks, § 340.882.

cation in Michigan. The metropolitan remedy would require, in effect, consolidation of 54 independent school districts historically administered as separate units into a vast new super school district. See n. 10, *supra.* Entirely apart from the logistical and other serious problems attending large-scale transportation of students, the consolidation would give rise to an array of other problems in financing and operating this new school system. Some of the more obvious questions would be: What would be the status and authority of the present popularly elected school boards? Would the children of Detroit be within the jurisdiction and operating control of a school board elected by the parents and residents of other districts? What board or boards would levy taxes for school operations in these 54 districts constituting the consolidated metropolitan area? What provisions could be made for assuring substantial equality in tax levies among the 54 districts, if this were deemed requisite? What provisions would be made for financing? Would the validity of long-term bonds be jeopardized unless approved by all of the component districts as well as the State? What body would determine that portion of the curricula now left to the discretion of local school boards? Who would establish attendance zones, purchase school equipment, locate and construct new schools, and indeed attend to all the myriad day-to-day decisions that are necessary to school operations affecting potentially more than three-quarters of a million pupils? See n. 10, *supra.*

It may be suggested that all of these vital operational problems are yet to be resolved by the District Court, and that this is the purpose of the Court of Appeals' proposed remand. But it is obvious from the scope of the interdistrict remedy itself that absent a complete restructuring of the laws of Michigan relating to school districts the District Court will become first, a *de facto* "legislative authority" to resolve these complex questions, and then the "school superintendent" for the entire area.   This is a task which few, if any, judges are qualified to perform and one which would deprive the people of control of schools through their elected representatives.

Of course, no state law is above the Constitution. School district lines and the present laws with respect to local control, are not sacrosanct and if they conflict with the Fourteenth Amendment federal courts have a duty to prescribe appropriate remedies.   See, *e. g., Wright* v. *Council of the City of Emporia,* 407 U. S. 451 (1972); *United States* v. *Scotland Neck Board of Education,* 407 U. S. 484 (1972) (state or local officials prevented from carving out a new school district from an existing district that was in process of dismantling a dual school system); cf. *Haney* v. *County Board of Education of Sevier County,* 429 F. 2d 364 (CA8 1970) (State contributed to separation of races by drawing of school district lines); *United States* v. *Texas,* 321 F. Supp. 1043 (ED Tex. 1970), aff'd, 447 F. 2d 441 (CA5 1971), cert. denied *sub nom. Edgar* v. *United States,* 404 U. S. 1016 (1972) (one or more school districts created and maintained for one race).   But our prior holdings have been confined to violations and remedies within a single school district.   We therefore turn to address, for the first time, the validity of a remedy mandating cross-district or interdistrict consolidation to remedy a condition of segregation found to exist in only one district.

The controlling principle consistently expounded in our holdings is that the scope of the remedy is determined by the nature and extent of the constitutional violation. *Swann,* 402 U. S., at 16.   Before the boundaries of separate and autonomous school districts may be set aside by consolidating the separate units for remedial purposes or by imposing a cross-district remedy, it must

first be shown that there has been a constitutional violation within one district that produces a significant segregative effect in another district. Specifically, it must be
shown that racially discriminatory acts of the state or
local school districts, or of a single school district have
been a substantial cause of interdistrict segregation.
Thus an interdistrict remedy might be in order where
the racially discriminatory acts of one or more school districts caused racial segregation in an adjacent district, or
where district lines have been deliberately drawn on the
basis of race. In such circumstances an interdistrict
remedy would be appropriate to eliminate the interdistrict segregation directly caused by the constitutional violation. Conversely, without an interdistrict violation
and interdistrict effect, there is no constitutional wrong
calling for an interdistrict remedy.

The record before us, voluminous as it is, contains
evidence of *de jure* segregated conditions only in the Detroit schools; indeed, that was the theory on which the
litigation was initially based and on which the District
Court took evidence. See *supra*, at 725–726. With no
showing of significant violation by the 53 outlying school
districts and no evidence of any interdistrict violation or
effect, the court went beyond the original theory of the
case as framed by the pleadings and mandated a metropolitan area remedy. To approve the remedy ordered by
the court would impose on the outlying districts, not
shown to have committed any constitutional violation, a
wholly impermissible remedy based on a standard not
hinted at in *Brown I* and *II* or any holding of this Court.

In dissent, MR. JUSTICE WHITE and MR. JUSTICE MAR-
SHALL undertake to demonstrate that agencies having
statewide authority participated in maintaining the dual
school system found to exist in Detroit. They are apparently of the view that once such participation is

shown, the District Court should have a relatively free hand to reconstruct school districts outside of Detroit in fashioning relief. Our assumption, *arguendo,* see *infra,* at 748, that state agencies did participate in the maintenance of the Detroit system, should make it clear that it is not on this point that we part company.[21] The difference between us arises instead from established doctrine laid down by our cases. *Brown, supra; Green, supra; Swann, supra; Scotland Neck, supra;* and *Emporia, supra,* each addressed the issue of constitutional wrong in terms of an established geographic and administrative school system populated by both Negro and white children. In such a context, terms such as "unitary" and "dual" systems, and "racially identifiable schools," have meaning, and the necessary federal authority to remedy the constitutional wrong is firmly established. But the remedy is necessarily designed, as all remedies are, to restore the victims of discriminatory conduct to the position they would have occupied in the absence of such conduct. Disparate treatment of white and Negro students occurred within the Detroit school system, and not elsewhere, and on this record the remedy must be limited to that system. *Swann, supra,* at 16.

The constitutional right of the Negro respondents residing in Detroit is to attend a unitary school system in that district. Unless petitioners drew the district lines in a discriminatory fashion, or arranged for white stu-

---

[21] Since the Court has held that a resident of a school district has a fundamental right protected by the Federal Constitution to vote in a district election, it would seem incongruous to disparage the importance of the school district in a different context. *Kramer v. Union Free School District No. 15,* 395 U. S. 621, 626 (1969). While the district there involved was located in New York, none of the facts in our possession suggest that the relation of school districts to the State is significantly different in New York from that in Michigan.

dents residing in the Detroit District to attend schools in Oakland and Macomb Counties, they were under no constitutional duty to make provisions for Negro students to do so. The view of the dissenters, that the existence of a dual system in *Detroit* can be made the basis for a decree requiring cross-district transportation of pupils, cannot be supported on the grounds that it represents merely the devising of a suitably flexible remedy for the violation of rights already established by our prior decisions. It can be supported only by drastic expansion of the constitutional right itself, an expansion without any support in either constitutional principle or precedent.[22]

---

[22] The suggestion in the dissent of MR. JUSTICE MARSHALL that schools which have a majority of Negro students are not "desegregated," whatever the racial makeup of the school district's population and however neutrally the district lines have been drawn and administered, finds no support in our prior cases. In *Green* v. *County School Board of New Kent County*, 391 U. S. 430 (1968), for example, this Court approved a desegregation plan which would have resulted in each of the schools within the district having a racial composition of 57% Negro and 43% white. In *Wright* v. *Council of the City of Emporia*, 407 U. S. 451 (1972), the optimal desegregation plan would have resulted in the schools' being 66% Negro and 34% white, substantially the same percentages as could be obtained under one of the plans involved in this case. And in *United States* v. *Scotland Neck Board of Education*, 407 U. S. 484, 491 n. 5 (1972), a desegregation plan was implicitly approved for a school district which had a racial composition of 77% Negro and 22% white. In none of these cases was it even intimated that "actual desegregation" could not be accomplished as long as the number of Negro students was greater than the number of white students.

The dissents also seem to attach importance to the metropolitan character of Detroit and neighboring school districts. But the constitutional principles applicable in school desegregation cases cannot vary in accordance with the size or population dispersal of the particular city, county, or school district as compared with neighboring areas.

III

We recognize that the six-volume record presently under consideration contains language and some specific incidental findings thought by the District Court to afford a basis for interdistrict relief. However, these comparatively isolated findings and brief comments concern only one possible interdistrict violation and are found in the context of a proceeding that, as the District Court conceded, included no proof of segregation practiced by any of the 85 suburban school districts surrounding Detroit. The Court of Appeals, for example, relied on five factors which, it held, amounted to unconstitutional state action with respect to the violations found in the Detroit system:

(1) It held the State derivatively responsible for the Detroit Board's violations on the theory that actions of Detroit as a political subdivision of the State were attributable to the State. Accepting, *arguendo,* the correctness of this finding of state responsibility for the segregated conditions within the city of Detroit, it does not follow that an interdistrict remedy is constitutionally justified or required. With a single exception, discussed later, there has been no showing that either the State or any of the 85 outlying districts engaged in activity that had a cross-district effect. The boundaries of the Detroit School District, which are coterminous with the boundaries of the city of Detroit, were established over a century ago by neutral legislation when the city was incorporated; there is no evidence in the record, nor is there any suggestion by the respondents, that either the original boundaries of the Detroit School District, or any other school district in Michigan, were established for the purpose of creating, maintaining, or perpetuating segregation of races. There is no claim and there is no evidence hinting that petitioner outlying school districts and their

predecessors, or the 30-odd other school districts in the tricounty area—but outside the District Court's "desegregation area"—have ever maintained or operated anything but unitary school systems. Unitary school systems have been required for more than a century by the Michigan Constitution as implemented by state law.[23] Where the schools of only one district have been affected, there is no constitutional power in the courts to decree relief balancing the racial composition of that district's schools with those of the surrounding districts.

(2) There was evidence introduced at trial that, during the late 1950's, Carver School District, a predominantly Negro suburban district, contracted to have Negro high school students sent to a predominantly Negro school in Detroit. At the time, Carver was an independent school district that had no high school because, according to the trial evidence, "Carver District . . . did not have a place for adequate high school facilities." 484 F. 2d, at 231. Accordingly, arrangements were made with Northern High School in the abutting Detroit School District so that the Carver high school students could obtain a secondary school education. In 1960 the Oak Park School District, a predominantly white suburban district, annexed the predominantly Negro Carver School District, through the initiative of local officials.

---

[23] *People ex rel. Workman* v. *Board of Education of Detroit,* 18 Mich. 400 (1869); Act 34, § 28, Mich. Pub. Acts of 1867. The Michigan Constitution and laws provide that "[e]very school district shall provide for the education of its pupils without discrimination as to religion, creed, race, color or national origin," Mich. Const. 1963, Art. 8, § 2; that "[n]o separate school or department shall be kept for any person or persons on account of race or color," Mich. Comp. Laws § 340.355; and that "[a]ll persons, residents of a school district . . . shall have an equal right to attend school therein," *id.,* § 340.356. See also Act 319, Part II, c. 2, § 9, Mich. Pub. Acts of 1927.

Ibid. There is, of course, no claim that the 1960 annexation had a segregative purpose or result or that Oak Park now maintains a dual system.

According to the Court of Appeals, the arrangement during the late 1950's which allowed Carver students to be educated within the Detroit District was dependent upon the "tacit or express" approval of the State Board of Education and was the result of the refusal of the white suburban districts to accept the Carver students. Although there is nothing in the record supporting the Court of Appeals' supposition that suburban white schools refused to accept the Carver students, it appears that this situation, whether with or without the State's consent, may have had a segregative effect on the school populations of the two districts involved. However, since "the nature of the violation determines the scope of the remedy," *Swann,* 402 U. S., at 16, this isolated instance affecting two of the school districts would not justify the broad metropolitanwide remedy contemplated by the District Court and approved by the Court of Appeals, particularly since it embraced potentially 52 districts having no responsibility for the arrangement and involved 503,000 pupils in addition to Detroit's 276,000 students.

(3) The Court of Appeals cited the enactment of state legislation (Act 48) which had the effect of rescinding Detroit's voluntary desegregation plan (the April 7 Plan). That plan, however, affected only 12 of 21 Detroit high schools and had no causal connection with the distribution of pupils by race between Detroit and the other school districts within the tri-county area.

(4) The court relied on the State's authority to supervise schoolsite selection and to approve building construction as a basis for holding the State responsible for the segregative results of the school construction program in Detroit. Specifically, the Court of Appeals asserted

that during the period between 1949 and 1962 the State Board of Education exercised general authority as overseer of site acquisitions by local boards for new school construction, and suggested that this state-approved school construction "fostered segregation throughout the Detroit Metropolitan area." 484 F. 2d, at 241. This brief comment, however, is not supported by the evidence taken at trial since that evidence was specifically limited to proof that schoolsite acquisition and school construction within the city of Detroit produced *de jure* segregation *within* the city itself. *Id.*, at 235–238. Thus, there was no evidence suggesting that the State's activities with respect to either school construction or site acquisition within Detroit affected the racial composition of the school population outside Detroit or, conversely, that the State's school construction and site acquisition activities within the outlying districts affected the racial composition of the schools within Detroit.

(5) The Court of Appeals also relied upon the District Court's finding:

> "This and other financial limitations, such as those on bonding and the working of the state aid formula whereby suburban districts were able to make far larger per pupil expenditures despite less tax effort, have created and perpetuated systematic educational inequalities." *Id.*, at 239.

However, neither the Court of Appeals nor the District Court offered any indication in the record or in their opinions as to how, if at all, the availability of state-financed aid for some Michigan students outside Detroit, but not for those within Detroit, might have affected the racial character of any of the State's school districts. Furthermore, as the respondents recognize, the application of our recent ruling in *San Antonio School District* v. *Rodriguez*, 411 U. S. 1 (1973), to this state education financing system is questionable, and this issue was not addressed by either the Court of Appeals or the District Court. This, again, underscores the crucial fact that the theory upon which the case proceeded related solely to the establishment of Detroit city violations as a basis for desegregating Detroit schools and that, at the time of trial, neither the parties nor the trial judge was concerned with a foundation for interdistrict relief.[24]

IV

Petitioners have urged that they were denied due process by the manner in which the District Court limited their participation after intervention was allowed, thus precluding adequate opportunity to present evidence that they had committed no acts having a segregative effect in Detroit. In light of our holding that, absent an interdistrict violation, there is no basis for an interdistrict remedy, we need not reach these claims. It is clear, however, that the District Court, with the approval of the Court of Appeals, has provided an interdistrict remedy in the face of a record which shows no constitutional violations that would call for equitable relief except within the city of Detroit. In these circumstances there was no occasion for the parties to address, or for the District Court to consider whether there were racially discriminatory acts for which any of the 53 outlying districts were responsible and which had direct and significant segregative effect on schools of more than one district.

We conclude that the relief ordered by the District Court and affirmed by the Court of Appeals was based upon an erroneous standard and was unsupported by record evidence that acts of the outlying districts effected the discrimination found to exist in the schools of De-

---

[24] Apparently, when the District Court, *sua sponte*, abruptly altered the theory of the case to include the possibility of multidistrict relief, neither the plaintiffs nor the trial judge considered amending the complaint to embrace the new theory.

troit. Accordingly, the judgment of the Court of Appeals is reversed and the case is remanded for further proceedings consistent with this opinion leading to prompt formulation of a decree directed to eliminating the segregation found to exist in Detroit city schools, a remedy which has been delayed since 1970.

Reversed and remanded.

NORWOOD ET AL. *v.* HARRISON ET AL.

APPEAL FROM THE UNITED STATES DISTRICT COURT FOR THE NORTHERN DISTRICT OF MISSISSIPPI

No. 72–77. Argued February 20–21, 1973—Decided June 25, 1973

A three-judge District Court sustained the validity of a Mississippi statutory program, begun in 1940, under which textbooks are purchased by the State and lent to students in both public and private schools, without reference to whether any participating private school has racially discriminatory policies. The number of private secular schools in Mississippi, with a virtually all-white student population, has greatly increased in recent years. *Held:*

1. Private schools have the right to exist and to operate, *Pierce* v. *Society of Sisters,* 268 U. S. 510, but the State is not required by the Equal Protection Clause to provide assistance to private schools equivalent to that it provides to public schools without regard to whether the private schools discriminate on racial grounds. Pp. 461–463.

2. Free textbooks, like tuition grants directed to students in private schools, are a form of tangible financial assistance benefiting the schools themselves, and the State's constitutional obligation requires it to avoid not only operating the old dual system of racially segregated schools but also providing tangible aid to schools that practice racial or other invidious discrimination. Pp. 463–468.

3. Assistance carefully limited so as to avoid the prohibitions of the "effect" and "entanglement" tests may be confined to the secular functions of sectarian schools and does not substantially promote the religious mission of those schools in violation of the Establishment Clause. In this case, however, the legitimate educational function of private discriminatory schools cannot be isolated from their alleged discriminatory practices; discriminatory treatment exerts a pervasive influence on the entire educational process. *Brown* v. *Board of Education,* 347 U. S. 483. The Establishment Clause permits a greater degree of state assistance to sectarian schools than may be given to private schools which engage in discriminatory practices. *Everson* v. *Board of Education,* 330 U. S. 1, and *Board of Education* v. *Allen,* 392 U. S. 236, distinguished. Pp. 468–470.

4. Proper injunctive relief can be granted without implying that all the private schools alleged to be receiving textbook aid have restrictive admission policies. The District Court can direct appellees to submit for approval a certification procedure whereby schools may apply for textbooks on behalf of pupils, affirmatively declaring admission policies and practices, and stating the number of their racially and religiously identifiable minority students, and other relevant data. Certification of eligibility will be subject to judicial review. Pp. 470–471.

340 F. Supp. 1003, vacated and remanded.

BURGER, C. J., delivered the opinion of the Court, in which STEWART, WHITE, MARSHALL, BLACKMUN, POWELL, and REHNQUIST, JJ., joined. DOUGLAS and BRENNAN, JJ., concurred in the result.

Melvyn R. Leventhal argued the cause for appellants. With him on the briefs were *Jack Greenberg, James M. Nabrit III, Charles Stephen Ralston, Norman J. Chachkin,* and *Anthony G. Amsterdam.*

William A. Allain, First Assistant Attorney General of Mississippi, argued the cause for appellees. With him on the brief were *A. F. Summer,* Attorney General, and *Heber Ladner, Jr.,* Special Assistant Attorney General.*

MR. CHIEF JUSTICE BURGER delivered the opinion of the Court.

A three-judge District Court sustained the validity of a Mississippi statutory program under which textbooks are purchased by the State and lent to students in both public and private schools, without reference to whether any participating private school has racially discriminatory policies. 340 F. Supp. 1003 (ND Miss. 1972). We noted probable jurisdiction, 409 U. S. 839.

Solicitor General Griswold, Assistant Attorney General Pottinger, Deputy Solicitor General Wallace, Harriet S. Shapiro, Brian K. Landsberg, and *Thomas M. Keeling* filed a memorandum for the United States as *amicus curiae* urging reversal.

I

Appellants, who are parents of four schoolchildren in Tunica County, Mississippi, filed a class action on behalf of students throughout Mississippi to enjoin in part the enforcement of the Mississippi textbook lending program. The complaint alleged that certain of the private schools excluded students on the basis of race and that, by supplying textbooks to students attending such private schools, appellees, acting for the State, have provided direct state aid to racially segregated education. It was also alleged that the textbook aid program thereby impeded the process of fully desegregating public schools, in violation of appellants' constitutional rights.

Private schools in Mississippi have experienced a marked growth in recent years. As recently as the 1963–1964 school year, there were only 17 private schools other than Catholic schools; the total enrollment was 2,362 students. In these nonpublic schools 916 students were Negro, and 192 of these were enrolled in special schools for retarded, orphaned, or abandoned children.[1] By September 1970, the number of private non-Catholic schools had increased to 155 with a student population estimated at 42,000, virtually all white. Appellees do not challenge the statement, which is fully documented in appellants' brief, that "the creation and enlargement of these [private] academies occurred simultaneously with major events in the desegregation of public schools . . . ."[2]

This case does not raise any question as to the right of citizens to maintain private schools with admission limited to students of particular national origins, race, or religion or of the authority of a State to allow such

_____
[1] App. 40–41.
[2] Brief for Appellants 8–9.

736

schools. See *Pierce* v. *Society of Sisters*, 268 U. S. 510
(1925). The narrow issue before us, rather, is a particular form of tangible assistance the State provides to
students in private schools in common with all other students by lending textbooks under the State's 33-year-
old program for providing free textbooks to all the
children of the State. The program dates back to a 1940
appeal for improved educational facilities by the Governor of Mississippi to the state legislature. The legislature then established a state textbook purchasing board
and authorized it to select, purchase, and distribute
free textbooks for all schoolchildren through the first
eight grades.[3] In 1942, the program was extended to
cover all high school students, and, as codified, the statutory authorization remains substantially unchanged.
Miss. Code Ann. § 6634 *et seq.* (1942).

Administration of the textbook program is vested in
the Mississippi Textbook Purchasing Board, whose members include the Governor, the State Superintendent of
Education, and three experienced educators appointed by
the Governor for four-year terms. *Id.*, §§ 6634, 6641.
The Board employs a full-time administrator as its Executive Secretary. Textbooks may be purchased only "for
use in those courses set up in the state course of study
adopted by the State Board of Education, or courses
established by special acts of the Legislature." *Id.*, § 6646.
For each course of study, there is a "rating committee"
composed of appointed members, *id.*, § 6641 (1)(d), and
only those books approved by the relevant rating committee may be purchased from publishers at a price which
cannot "be higher than the lowest prices at which the
same books are being sold anywhere in the United States."
Id., § 6646 (1).

___

[3] See *Norwood* v. *Harrison,* 340 F. Supp. 1003, 1007 (ND Miss.
1972).

The books are kept at a central book repository in Jackson. *Id.,* § 6641 (1)(f). Appellees send to each school district, and, in recent years, to each private school⁴ requisition forms listing approved textbooks available from the State for free distribution to students. The local school district or the private school sends a requisition form to the Purchasing Board for approval by the Executive Secretary, who in turn forwards the approved form to the Jackson book repository where the order is routinely filled and the requested books shipped directly to the school district or the private school.

The District Court found that "34,000 students are presently receiving state-owned textbooks while attending 107 all-white, nonsectarian private schools which have been formed throughout the state since the incep-

---

⁴ The regulation for distribution of state-owned textbooks from 1940 through 1970 provided as follows:

"For the distribution of free textbooks the local control will be placed in the hands of the County Superintendent of Education. All requisitions for books shall be made through him and all shipments of books shall be invoiced through him. At his discretion he may set up certain regulations governing the distribution of books within the county, such regulations not to conflict with the regulations adopted by the State Textbook Board or provisions of the Free Textbook Act."

This regulation was revised on October 14, 1970, to read as follows:

"*Public Schools.* The administration of the textbook program in the public schools shall be the responsibility of the administrative heads of the county units, consolidated districts, and municipal separate districts set up by the Legislature. All textbook transactions between the public schools and the State shall be carried on through them. It shall be the duty of these local custodians to render all reports required by the State; to place orders for textbooks for the pupils in their schools . . . .

"*Private Schools.* Private and parochial school programs shall be the responsibility of the State Textbook Board. All textbook transactions will be carried out between the Board and the administrative heads of these schools. Their duties shall be the same as outlined above for public schools."

tion of public school desegregation." 340 F. Supp., at
1011.[5]. During the 1970–1971 school year, these schools
held 173,424 books, for which Mississippi paid $490,239.
The annual expenditure for replacements or new texts
is approximately $6 per pupil, or a total of approximately
$207,000 for the students enrolled in the participating
private segregated academies, exclusive of mailing costs
which are borne by the State as well.

In dismissing the complaint the District Court stressed,
first, that the statutory scheme was not motivated by a
desire to further racial segregation in the public schools,
having been enacted first in 1940, long before this Court's
decision in *Brown* v. *Board of Education*, 347 U. S. 483
(1954), and consequently, long before there was any
occasion to have a policy or reason to foster the development of racially segregated private academies. Second, the District Court took note that providing textbooks to private *sectarian* schools had been approved by
this Court in *Board of Education* v. *Allen*, 392 U. S. 236
(1968), and that "[t]he essential inquiry, therefore, is
whether we should apply a more stringent standard for
determining what constitutes state aid to a school in the
context of the Fourteenth Amendment's ban against denial of the equal protection of the law than the Supreme
Court has applied in First Amendment cases." 340 F.
Supp., at 1011. The District Court held no more stringent standard should apply on the facts of this case, since,
as in *Allen*, the books were provided to the students and
not to the schools. Finally, the District Court concluded
that the textbook loans did not interfere with or impede
the State's acknowledged duty to establish a unitary

---

[5] The variation in the figures as to schools and students is accounted for by the District Court's omission of particular kinds of
schools in making the findings. The earlier and higher figures are
found in the briefs and are not disputed.

school system under this Court's holding in *Green* v.
County School Board, 391 U. S. 430, 437 (1968), since

> "[d]epriving any segment of school children of
> state-owned textbooks at this point in time is not
> necessary for the establishment or maintenance of
> state-wide unitary schools.   Indeed, the public
> schools which plaintiffs acknowledge were fully es-
> tablished as unitary schools throughout the state no
> later than 1970–71, continue to attract 90% of the
> state's educable children.   There is no showing that
> any child enrolled in private school, if deprived of
> free textbooks, would withdraw from private school
> and subsequently enroll in the public schools."   340
> F. Supp., at 1013.

II

In *Pierce* v. *Society of Sisters,* 268 U. S. 510 (1925), the
Court held that a State's role in the education of its
citizens must yield to the right of parents to provide an
equivalent education for their children in a privately
operated school of the parents' choice.   In the 1971 Term
we reaffirmed the vitality of *Pierce,* in *Wisconsin* v. *Yoder,*
406 U. S. 205, 213 (1972), and there has been no suggestion in the present case that we alter our view of *Pierce.*
Yet the Court's holding in *Pierce* is not without limits.
As MR. JUSTICE WHITE observed in his concurring opinion
in *Yoder, Pierce* "held simply that while a State may posit
[educational] standards, it may not pre-empt the educational process by requiring children to attend public
schools."   *Id.,* at 239.

Appellees fail to recognize the limited scope of *Pierce*
when they urge that the right of parents to send their
children to private schools under that holding is at stake
in this case.   The suggestion is made that the rights of
parents under *Pierce* would be undermined were the lending of free textbooks denied to those who attend private

schools—in other words, that schoolchildren who attend
private schools might be deprived of the equal protection of the laws were they invidiously classified under
the state textbook loan program simply because their
parents had exercised the constitutionally protected
choice to send the children to private schools.

We do not see the issue in appellees' terms.　In *Pierce,*
the Court affirmed the right of private schools to exist
and to operate; it said nothing of any supposed right of
private or parochial schools to share with public schools
in state largesse, on an equal basis or otherwise.　It has
never been held that if private schools are not given
some share of public funds allocated for education that
such schools are isolated into a classification violative of
the Equal Protection Clause.　It is one thing to say that
a State may not prohibit the maintenance of private
schools and quite another to say that such schools must,
as a matter of equal protection, receive state aid.

The appellees intimate that the State *must* provide
assistance to private schools equivalent to that which it
provides to public schools without regard to whether the
private schools discriminate on racial grounds.　Clearly,
the State need not.　Even as to church-sponsored schools
whose policies are nondiscriminatory, any absolute right
to equal aid was negated, at least by implication, in
Lemon v. *Kurtzman,* 403 U. S. 602 (1971).　The Religion
Clauses of the First Amendment strictly confine state aid
to sectarian education.　Even assuming, therefore, that
the Equal Protection Clause might require state aid to be
granted to private nonsectarian schools in some circumstances—health care or textbooks, for example—a State
could rationally conclude as a matter of legislative policy
that constitutional neutrality as to sectarian schools
might best be achieved by withholding all state assistance.　See *San Antonio Independent School District* v.
Rodriguez, 411 U. S. 1 (1973).　In the same way, a

State's special interest in elevating the quality of education in both public and private schools does not mean that the State must grant aid to private schools without regard to constitutionally mandated standards forbidding state-supported discrimination. That the Constitution may compel toleration of private discrimination in some circumstances does not mean that it requires state support for such discrimination.

III

The District Court's holding therefore raises the question whether and on what terms a State may—as a matter of legislative policy—provide tangible assistance to students attending private schools. Appellants assert, not only that the private schools are in fact racially discriminatory, but also that aid to them in any form is in derogation of the State's obligation not to support discrimination in education.

This Court has consistently affirmed decisions enjoining state tuition grants to students attending racially discriminatory private schools.[6] A textbook lending program is not legally distinguishable from the forms of state assistance foreclosed by the prior cases. Free textbooks, like tuition grants directed to private school

---

[6] *Brown* v. *South Carolina Board of Education,* 296 F. Supp. 199 (SC), aff'd *per curiam,* 393 U. S. 222 (1968); *Poindexter* v. *Louisiana Financial Assistance Comm'n,* 275 F. Supp. 833 (ED La. 1967), aff'd *per curiam,* 389 U. S. 571 (1968). See *Wallace* v. *United States,* 389 U. S. 215 (1967), aff'g *Lee* v. *Macon County Board of Education,* 267 F. Supp. 458, 475 (MD Ala.). Mississippi's tuition grant programs were invalidated in *Coffey* v. *State Educational Finance Comm'n,* 296 F. Supp. 1389 (SD Miss. 1969); *Coffey* v. *State Educational Finance Comm'n,* SD Miss., CA No. 2906, decided Sept. 2, 1970 (unreported). The latter case involved a statute which provided for tuition loans rather than tuition grants. See *Green* v. *Connally,* 330 F. Supp. 1150 (DC), aff'd *sub nom. Coit* v. *Green,* 404 U. S. 997 (1971).

students, are a form of financial assistance inuring to the benefit of the private schools themselves.[7] An inescapable educational cost for students in both public and private schools is the expense of providing all necessary learning materials. When, as here, that necessary expense is borne by the State, the economic consequence is to give aid to the enterprise; if the school engages in discriminatory practices the State by tangible aid in the

---

[7] Appellees misperceive the "child benefit" theory of our cases decided under the Religion Clauses of the First Amendment. See, e. g., *Cochran* v. *Louisiana Board of Education,* 281 U. S. 370 (1930), and *Board of Education* v. *Allen,* 392 U. S. 236 (1968). In those cases the Court observed that the direct financial benefit of textbook loans to students is "to parents and children, not to schools," *id.,* at 244, in the sense that parents and children—not schools— would in most instances be required to procure their textbooks if the State did not. But the Court has never denied that "free books make it more likely that some children choose to attend a sectarian school," *ibid.,* just as in other cases involving aid to sectarian schools we have acknowledged that the various forms of state assistance "surely aid these [religious] institutions . . . in the sense that religious bodies would otherwise have been forced to find other sources from which to finance these services." *Tilton* v. *Richardson,* 403 U. S. 672, 679 (1971). Plainly, religion benefits indirectly from governmental aid to parents and children; nevertheless, "[t]hat religion may indirectly benefit from governmental aid . . . does not convert that aid into an impermissible establishment of religion." *Lemon* v. *Kurtzman,* 403 U. S. 602, 664 (1971) (opinion of WHITE, J.).

The leeway for indirect aid to sectarian schools has no place in defining the permissible scope of state aid to private racially discriminatory schools. "State support of segregated schools through any arrangement, management, funds, or property cannot be squared with the [Fourteenth] Amendment's command that no State shall deny to any person within its jurisdiction the equal protection of the laws." *Cooper* v. *Aaron,* 358 U. S. 1, 19 (1958). Thus MR. JUSTICE WHITE, the author of the Court's opinion in *Allen, supra,* and a dissenter in *Lemon* v. *Kurtzman, supra,* noted there that in his view, legislation providing assistance to any sectarian school which restricted entry on racial or religious grounds would, to that extent, be unconstitutional. *Lemon, supra,* at 671 n. 2. See Part IV, *infra.*

form of textbooks thereby gives support to such discrimination. Racial discrimination in state-operated schools is barred by the Constitution and "[i]t is also axiomatic that a state may not induce, encourage or promote private persons to accomplish what it is constitutionally forbidden to accomplish." *Lee* v. *Macon County Board of Education,* 267 F. Supp. 458, 475–476 (MD Ala. 1967).

We do not suggest that a State violates its constitutional duty merely because it has provided *any* form of state service that benefits private schools said to be racially discriminatory. Textbooks are a basic educational tool and, like tuition grants, they are provided only in connection with schools; they are to be distinguished from generalized services government might provide to schools in common with others. Moreover, the textbooks provided to private school students by the State in this case are a form of assistance readily available from sources entirely independent of the State— unlike, for example, "such necessities of life as electricity, water, and police and fire protection." *Moose Lodge No. 107* v. *Irvis,* 407 U. S. 163, 173 (1972). The State has neither an absolute nor operating monopoly on the procurement of school textbooks; anyone can purchase them on the open market.

The District Court laid great stress on the absence of a showing by appellants that "any child enrolled in private school, if deprived of free textbooks, would withdraw from private school and subsequently enroll in the public schools." 340 F. Supp., at 1013. We can accept this factual assertion; we cannot and do not know, on this record at least, whether state textbook assistance is the determinative factor in the enrollment of any students in any of the private schools in Mississippi. We do not agree with the District Court in its analysis of the legal consequences of this uncertainty, for the Constitution does not permit the State to aid discrimination even when there is no precise causal relationship between state financial aid to a private school and the continued well-being of that school. A State may not grant the type of tangible financial aid here involved if that aid has a significant tendency to facilitate, reinforce, and support private discrimination. "[D]ecisions on the constitutionality of state involvement in private discrimination do not turn on whether the state aid adds up to 51 percent or adds up to only 49 per cent of the support of the segregated institution." *Poindexter* v. *Louisiana Financial Assistance Comm'n*, 275 F. Supp. 833, 854 (ED La. 1967).[8]

The recurring theme of appellees' argument is a sympathetic one—that the State's textbook loan program is extended to students who attend racially segregated private schools only because the State sincerely wishes to foster quality education for all Mississippi children, and, to that end, has taken steps to insure that no sub-group of schoolchildren will be deprived of an important educational tool merely because their parents have chosen to enroll them in segregated private schools. We need not assume that the State's textbook aid to private schools has been motivated by other than a sincere interest in the educational welfare of all Mississippi children. But good intentions as to one valid objective do not serve to negate the State's involvement in violation of a constitutional duty. "The existence of a permissible purpose cannot sustain an action that has an impermissible effect." *Wright* v. *Council of City of Emporia*, 407 U. S. 451, 462 (1972). The Equal Protection Clause would

---

[8] Accord, *Griffin* v. *State Board of Education*, 296 F. Supp. 1178, 1181 (ED Va. 1969), superseding *Griffin* v. *State Board of Education*, 239 F. Supp. 560 (ED Va. 1965); *Brown* v. *South Carolina Board of Education, supra.*

be a sterile promise if state involvement in possible private activity could be shielded altogether from constitutional scrutiny simply because its ultimate end was not discrimination but some higher goal.

The District Court offered as further support for its holding the finding that Mississippi's public schools "were fully established as unitary schools throughout the state no later than 1970–71 [and] continue to attract 90% of the state's educable children." 340 F. Supp., at 1013. We note, however, that overall statewide attendance figures do not fully and accurately reflect the impact of private schools in particular school districts.[9] In any event, the constitutional infirmity of the Mississippi textbook program is that it significantly aids the organization and continuation of a separate system of private schools which, under the District Court holding, may discriminate if they so desire. A State's constitutional obligation requires it to steer clear, not only of operating the old dual system of racially segregated schools, but also of giving significant aid to institutions that practice racial or other invidious discrimination.

---

[9] In Tunica County, for example, where appellants reside, in response to *Green* v. *Connally, supra,* and *Alexander* v. *Holmes County Board of Education,* 396 U. S. 19 (1969), all white children were withdrawn from public schools and placed in a private academy housed in local church facilities and staffed by the principal and 17 high school teachers of the county system, who resigned in mid-year to accept jobs at the new academy. See *United States* v. *Tunica County School District,* 323 F. Supp. 1019 (ND Miss. 1970), aff'd, 440 F. 2d 377 (CA5 1971). As of the time of the filing of this lawsuit, the successor Tunica Institute of Learning enrolled 495 students, all white, and would not attest to an open enrollment policy. Similar histories of Holmes County, Canton Municipal Separate School District, Jackson Municipal Separate School District, Amite County, Indianola Municipal Separate School District, and Grenada Municipal Separate School District are recited, without challenge by appellees, in Brief for Appellants 14–19.

That the State's public schools are now fully unitary, as the District Court found, is irrelevant.

IV

Appellees and the District Court also placed great reliance on our decisions in *Everson* v. *Board of Education*, 330 U. S. 1 (1947), and *Board of Education* v. *Allen*, 392 U. S. 236 (1968). In *Everson*, we held that the Establishment Clause of the First Amendment did not prohibit New Jersey from "spending tax-raised funds to pay the bus fares of parochial school pupils as a part of a general program under which it pays the fares of pupils attending public and other schools." 330 U. S., at 17. *Allen*, following *Everson*, sustained a New York law requiring school textbooks to be lent free of charge to all students, including those in attendance at parochial schools, in specified grades.

Neither *Allen* nor *Everson* is dispositive of the issue before us in this case. Religious schools "pursue two goals, religious instruction and secular education." *Board of Education* v. *Allen, supra*, at 245. And, where carefully limited so as to avoid the prohibitions of the "effect" and "entanglement" tests, States may assist church-related schools in performing their secular functions, *Committee for Public Education* v. *Nyquist, post*, at 774, 775; *Levitt* v. *Committee for Public Education, post*, at 481, not only because the States have a substantial interest in the quality of education being provided by private schools, see *Cochran* v. *Louisiana Board of Education*, 281 U. S. 370, 375 (1930), but more importantly because assistance properly confined to the secular functions of sectarian schools does not substantially promote the readily identifiable religious mission of those schools and it does not interfere with the free exercise rights of others.

Like a sectarian school, a private school—even one

that discriminates—fulfills an important educational function; however, the difference is that in the context of this case the legitimate educational function cannot be isolated from discriminatory practices—if such in fact exist. Under *Brown* v. *Board of Education,* 347 U. S. 483 (1954), discriminatory treatment exerts a pervasive influence on the entire educational process. The private school that closes its doors to defined groups of students on the basis of constitutionally suspect criteria manifests, by its own actions, that its educational processes are based on private belief that segregation is desirable in education. There is no reason to discriminate against students for reasons wholly unrelated to individual merit unless the artificial barriers are considered an essential part of the educational message to be communicated to the students who are admitted. Such private bias is not barred by the Constitution, nor does it invoke any sanction of laws, but neither can it call on the Constitution for material aid from the State.

Our decisions under the Establishment Clause reflect the "internal tension in the First Amendment between the Establishment Clause and the Free Exercise Clause," *Tilton* v. *Richardson,* 403 U. S. 672, 677 (1971). This does not mean, as we have already suggested, that a State is constitutionally obligated to provide even "neutral" services to sectarian schools. But the transcendent value of free religious exercise in our constitutional scheme leaves room for "play in the joints" to the extent of cautiously delineated secular governmental assistance to religious schools, despite the fact that such assistance touches on the conflicting values of the Establishment Clause by indirectly benefiting the religious schools and their sponsors.

In contrast, although the Constitution does not proscribe private bias, it places no value on discrimination as

it does on the values inherent in the Free Exercise Clause.
Invidious private discrimination may be characterized as
a form of exercising freedom of association protected by
the First Amendment, but it has never been accorded
affirmative constitutional protections. And even some
private discrimination is subject to special remedial legislation in certain circumstances under § 2 of the Thirteenth Amendment; Congress has made such discrimination unlawful in other significant contexts.[10] However
narrow may be the channel of permissible state aid to
sectarian schools, *Nyquist, supra; Levitt, supra,* it permits a greater degree of state assistance than may be
given to private schools which engage in discriminatory
practices that would be unlawful in a public school
system.

                              V

At oral argument, appellees expressed concern over the
process of determining the scope of relief to be granted
should appellants prevail on the merits. That aspect
of the case presents problems but the procedural details
need not be fully resolved here. The District Court's
assumption that textbook loans were permissible, even
to racially discriminating private schools, obviated any
necessity for that court to determine whether some of
the private schools could properly be classified as "racially discriminatory" and how that determination might
best be made. We construe the complaint as contemplating an individual determination as to each private
school in Mississippi whose students now receive text-

---

[10] See, *e. g., Griffin* v. *Breckenridge,* 403 U. S. 88 (1971); *Jones* v.
Alfred H. Mayer Co., 392 U. S. 409 (1968); 42 U. S. C. § 2000a *et seq.*
(barring discrimination in public accommodations); 42 U. S. C.
§ 2000e *et seq.* (barring discrimination in private employment); 42
U. S. C. § 3601 *et seq.* (barring discrimination in private housing
transactions).

books under the State's textbook loan program; relief on an assumption that all private schools were discriminating, thus foreclosing individualized consideration, would not be appropriate.

The proper injunctive relief can be granted without implying a finding that all the private schools alleged to be receiving textbook aid are in fact practicing restrictive admission policies. Private schools are not fungible and the fact that some or even most may practice discrimination does not warrant blanket condemnation. The District Court can appropriately direct the appellees to submit for approval a certification procedure under which any school seeking textbooks for its pupils may apply for participation on behalf of pupils. The certification by the school to the Mississippi Textbook Purchasing Board should, among other factors, affirmatively declare its admission policies and practices, state the number of its racially and religiously identifiable minority students and such other relevant data as is consistent with this opinion. The State's certification of eligibility would, of course, be subject to judicial review.

This school-by-school determination may be cumbersome but no more so than the State's process of ascertaining compliance with educational standards. No presumptions flow from mere allegations; no one can be required, consistent with due process, to prove the absence of violation of law.

The judgment of the District Court is vacated and the case is remanded for further proceedings consistent with this opinion.

So ordered.

(Slip Opinion)

SUPREME COURT OF THE UNITED STATES

Syllabus

BOB JONES UNIVERSITY *v.*
UNITED STATES

CERTIORARI TO THE UNITED STATES COURT OF APPEALS FOR
THE FOURTH CIRCUIT

No. 81–3.   Argued October 12, 1982—Decided May 24, 1983*

Section 501(c)(3) of the Internal Revenue Code of 1954 (IRC) provides that "[c]orporations . . . organized and operated exclusively for religious, charitable . . . or educational purposes" are entitled to tax exemption. Until 1970, the Internal Revenue Service (IRS) granted tax-exempt status under § 501(c)(3) to private schools, independent of racial admissions policies, and granted charitable deductions for contributions to such schools under § 170 of the IRC.   But in 1970, the IRS concluded that it could no longer justify allowing tax-exempt status under § 501(c)(3) to private schools that practiced racial discrimination, and in 1971 issued Revenue Ruling 71–447 providing that a private school not having a racially nondiscriminatory policy as to students is not "charitable" within the common-law concepts reflected in §§ 170 and 50l(c)(3).   In No. 81–3, petitioner Bob Jones University, while permitting unmarried Negroes to enroll as students, denies admission to applicants engaged in an interracial marriage or known to advocate interracial marriage or dating.   Because of this admissions policy, the IRS revoked the University's tax-exempt status.   After paying a portion of the federal unemployment taxes for a certain taxable year, the University filed a refund action in Federal District Court, and the Government counterclaimed for unpaid taxes for that and other taxable years.   Holding that the IRS exceeded its powers in revoking the University's tax-exempt status and violated the University's rights under the Religion Clauses of the First Amendment, the District Court ordered the IRS to refund the taxes paid and rejected the counterclaim.   The Court of Appeals reversed.   In No.

*Together with No. 81–1, *Goldsboro Christian Schools, Inc.* v. *United States*, also on certiorari to the same court.

81–1, petitioner Goldsboro Christian Schools maintains a racially discriminatory admissions policy based upon its interpretation of the Bible, accepting for the most part only Caucasian students. The IRS determined that Goldsboro was not an organization described in § 501(c)(3) and hence was required to pay federal social security and unemployment taxes. After paying a portion of such taxes for certain years, Goldsboro filed a refund suit in Federal District Court, and the IRS counterclaimed for unpaid taxes. The District Court entered summary judgment for the Government, rejecting Goldsboro's claim to tax-exempt status under § 501(c)(3) and also its claim that the denial of such status violated the Religion Clauses of the First Amendment. The Court of Appeals affirmed.

Held: Neither petitioner qualifies as a tax-exempt organization under § 501(c)(3). Pp. 9–29.

(a) An examination of the IRC's framework and the background of congressional purposes reveals unmistakable evidence that underlying all relevant parts of the IRC is the intent that entitlement to tax exemption depends on meeting certain common-law standards of charity— namely, that an institution seeking tax-exempt status must serve a public purpose and not be contrary to established public policy. Thus, to warrant exemption under § 501(c)(3), an institution must fall within a category specified in that section and must demonstrably serve and be in harmony with the public interest, and the institution's purpose must not be so at odds with the common community conscience as to undermine any public benefit that might otherwise be conferred. Pp. 9–16.

(b) The IRS's 1970 interpretation of § 501(c)(3) was correct. It would be wholly incompatible with the concepts underlying tax exemption to grant tax-exempt status to racially discriminatory private educational entities. Whatever may be the rationale for such private schools' policies, racial discrimination in education is contrary to public policy. Racially discriminatory educational institutions cannot be viewed as conferring a public benefit within the above "charitable" concept or within the congressional intent underlying § 501(c)(3). Pp. 16–19.

(c) The IRS did not exceed its authority when it announced its interpretation of § 501(c)(3) in 1970 and 1971. Such interpretation is wholly consistent with what Congress, the Executive, and the courts had previously declared. And the actions of Congress since 1970 leave no doubt that the IRS reached the correct conclusion in exercising its authority. Pp. 20–25.

(d) The Government's fundamental, overriding interest in eradicating racial discrimination in education substantially outweighs whatever burden denial of tax benefits places on petitioners' exercise of their religious beliefs. Petitioners' asserted interests cannot be accommodated with that compelling governmental interest, and no less restrictive means are available to achieve the govermental interest. Pp. 26–27.

(e) The IRS properly applied its policy to both petitioners. Goldsboro admits that it maintains racially discriminatory policies, and, contrary to Bob Jones University's contention that it is not racially discriminatory, discrimination on the basis of racial affiliation and association is a form of racial discrimination. Pp. 28–29.

No. 81–1, 644 F. 2d 870, and No. 81–3, 639 F. 2d 147, affirmed.

BURGER, C. J., delivered the opinion of the Court, in which BRENNAN, WHITE, MARSHALL, BLACKMUN, STEVENS, and O'CONNOR, JJ., joined, and in Part III of which POWELL, J., joined. POWELL, J., filed an opinion concurring in part and concurring in the judgment. REHNQUIST, J., filed a dissenting opinion.

SUPREME COURT OF THE UNITED STATES

Nos. 81–3 AND 81–1

81–3

BOB JONES UNIVERSITY, PETITIONER
v.
UNITED STATES

81–1

GOLDSBORO CHRISTIAN SCHOOLS, INC., PETITIONER
v.
UNITED STATES

ON WRITS OF CERTIORARI TO THE UNITED STATES COURT OF APPEALS FOR THE FOURTH CIRCUIT

[May 24, 1983]

CHIEF JUSTICE BURGER delivered the opinion of the Court.

We granted certiorari to decide whether petitioners, non-profit private schools that prescribe and enforce racially discriminatory admissions standards on the basis of religious doctrine, qualify as tax-exempt organizations under §501(c)(3) of the Internal Revenue Code of 1954.

I

A

Until 1970, the Internal Revenue Service granted tax-exempt status to private schools, without regard to their racial admissions policies, under §501(c)(3) of the Internal Revenue Code, 26 U. S. C. §501(c)(3),[1] and granted chari-

---

[1] Section 501(c)(3) lists the following organizations, which, pursuant to

table deductions for contributions to such schools under § 170 of the Code, 26 U. S. C. § 170.[2]

On January 12, 1970, a three-judge District Court for the District of Columbia issued a preliminary injunction prohibiting the IRS from according tax-exempt status to private schools in Mississippi that discriminated as to admissions on the basis of race. *Green* v. *Kennedy,* 309 F. Supp. 1127 (D. D. C.), *app. dismissed sub nom. Cannon* v. *Green,* 398 U. S. 956 (1970). Thereafter, in July 1970, the IRS concluded that it could "no longer legally justify allowing tax-exempt status [under § 501(c)(3)] to private schools which practice racial discrimination." IRS News Release (7/10/70), reprinted in App. in No. 81–3, p. A235. At the same time, the IRS announced that it could not "treat gifts to such schools as charitable deductions for income tax purposes [under § 170]." *Ibid.* By letter dated November 30, 1970, the IRS formally notified private schools, including those involved in this case, of this change in policy, "applicable to all private schools in the United States at all levels of education." See *id.,* at A232.

_____

§ 501(a), are exempt from taxation unless denied tax exemptions under other specified sections of the Code:

"Corporations, and any community chest, fund, or foundation, *organized and operated exclusively for religious, charitable,* scientific, testing for public safety, literary, *or educational purposes,* or to foster national or international amateur sports competition (but only if no part of its activities involve the provision of athletic facilities or equipment), or for the prevention of cruelty to children or animals, no part of the net earnings of which inures to the benefit of any private shareholder or individual, no substantial part of the activities of which is carrying on propaganda, or otherwise attempting, to influence legislation . . . , and which does not participate in, or intervene in (including the publishing or distributing of statements), any political campaign on behalf of any candidate for public office." (Emphasis added).

[2] Section 170(a) allows deductions for certain "charitable contributions." Section 170(c)(2)(B) includes within the definition of "charitable contribution" a contribution or gift to or for the use of a corporation "organized and

On June 30, 1971, the three-judge District Court issued its opinion on the merits of the Mississippi challenge. *Green* v. *Connally*, 330 F. Supp. 1150 (D. D. C.), *aff'd sub nom. Coit* v. *Green*, 404 U. S. 997 (1971) *(per curiam)*. That court approved the IRS' amended construction of the Tax Code. The court also held that racially discriminatory private schools were not entitled to exemption under § 501(c)(3) and that donors were not entitled to deductions for contributions to such schools under § 170. The court permanently enjoined the Commissioner of Internal Revenue from approving tax-exempt status for any school in Mississippi that did not publicly maintain a policy of nondiscrimination.

The revised policy on discrimination was formalized in Revenue Ruling 71–447, 1971–2 Cum. Bull. 230:

> "Both the courts and the Internal Revenue Service have long recognized that the statutory requirement of being 'organized and operated exclusively for religious, charitable, . . . or educational purposes' was intended to express the basic common law concept [of 'charity']. . . . All charitable trusts, educational or otherwise, are subject to the requirement that the purpose of the trust may not be illegal or contrary to public policy." *Id.*, at 230.

Based on the "national policy to discourage racial discrimination in education," the IRS ruled that "a private school not having a racially nondiscriminatory policy as to students is not 'charitable' within the common law concepts reflected in sections 170 and 501(c)(3) of the Code." *Id.*, at 231.[3]

---

operated exclusively for religious, charitable, scientific, literary, or educational purposes. . . ."

[3] Revenue Ruling 71–447, 1971–2 Cum. Bull. 230, defined "racially nondiscriminatory policy as to students" as meaning that:
"[T]he school admits the students of any race to all the rights, privileges, programs, and activities generally accorded or made available to students at that school and that the school does not discriminate on the basis of race in administration of its educational policies, admissions policies, scholarship

The application of the IRS construction of these provisions to petitioners, two private schools with racially discriminatory admissions policies, is now before us.

B

No. 81-3, Bob Jones University v. *United States*

Bob Jones University is a nonprofit corporation located in Greenville, South Carolina.[4]   Its purpose is "to conduct an institution of learning . . . , giving special emphasis to the Christian religion and the ethics revealed in the Holy Scriptures."   Certificate of Incorporation, Bob Jones University, Inc., of Greenville, S. C., *reprinted in* App. in No. 81-3, pp. A118-A119.   The corporation operates a school with an enrollment of approximately 5,000 students, from kindergarten through college and graduate school.   Bob Jones University is not affiliated with any religious denomination, but is dedicated to the teaching and propagation of its fundamentalist Christian religious beliefs.   It is both a religious and educational institution.   Its teachers are required to be devout Christians, and all courses at the University are taught according to the Bible.   Entering students are screened as to their religious beliefs, and their public and private conduct is strictly regulated by standards promulgated by University authorities.

The sponsors of the University genuinely believe that the Bible forbids interracial dating and marriage.   To effectuate these views, Negroes were completely excluded until 1971. From 1971 to May 1975, the University accepted no applications from unmarried Negroes,[5] but did accept applications from Negroes married within their race.

---

and loan programs, and athletic and other school-administered programs."

[4] Bob Jones University was founded in Florida in 1927.   It moved to Greenville, South Carolina, in 1940, and has been incorporated as an eleemosynary institution in South Carolina since 1952.

[5] Beginning in 1973, Bob Jones University instituted an exception to

Following the decision of the United States Court of Appeals for the Fourth Circuit in *McCrary* v. *Runyon,* 515 F. 2d 1082 (CA4 1975), *aff'd* 427 U. S. 160 (1976), prohibiting racial exclusion from private schools, the University revised its policy. Since May 29, 1975, the University has permitted unmarried Negroes to enroll; but a disciplinary rule prohibits interracial dating and marriage. That rule reads:

There is to be no interracial dating

1. Students who are partners in an interracial marriage will be expelled.

2. Students who are members of or affiliated with any group or organization which holds as one of its goals or advocates interracial marriage will be expelled.

3. Students who date outside their own race will be expelled.

4. Students who espouse, promote, or encourage others to violate the University's dating rules and regulations will be expelled. App. in No. 81–3, p. A197.

The University continues to deny admission to applicants engaged in an interracial marriage or known to advocate interracial marriage or dating. *Id.,* at A277.

Until 1970, the IRS extended tax-exempt status to Bob Jones University under § 501(c)(3). By the letter of November 30, 1970, that followed the injunction issued in *Green* v. *Kennedy, supra,* the IRS formally notified the University of the change in IRS policy, and announced its intention to challenge the tax-exempt status of private schools practicing racial discrimination in their admissions policies.

After failing to obtain an assurance of tax exemption through administrative means, the University instituted an action in 1971 seeking to enjoin the IRS from revoking the school's tax-exempt status. That suit culminated in *Bob*

---

this rule, allowing applications from unmarried Negroes who had been members of the University staff for four years or more.

Jones University v. *Simon*, 416 U. S. 725 (1974), in which this Court held that the Anti-Injunction Act of the Internal Revenue Code, 26 U. S. C. § 7421(a), prohibited the University from obtaining judicial review by way of injunctive action before the assessment or collection of any tax. |

Thereafter, on April 16, 1975, the IRS notified the University of the proposed revocation of its tax-exempt status. On January 19, 1976, the IRS officially revoked the University's tax-exempt status, effective as of December 1, 1970, the day after the University was formally notified of the change in IRS policy. The University subsequently filed returns under the Federal Unemployment Tax Act for the period from December 1, 1970, to December 31, 1975, and paid a tax totalling $21.00 on one employee for the calendar year of 1975. After its request for a refund was denied, the University instituted the present action, seeking to recover the $21.00 it had paid to the IRS. The Government counterclaimed for unpaid federal unemployment taxes for the taxable years 1971 through 1975, in the amount of $489,675.59, plus interest.

The United States District Court for the District of South Carolina held that revocation of the University's tax-exempt status exceeded the delegated powers of the IRS, was improper under the IRS rulings and procedures, and violated the University's rights under the Religion Clauses of the First Amendment. 468 F. Supp. 890, 907 (D. S. C. 1978). The court accordingly ordered the IRS to pay the University the $21.00 refund it claimed and rejected the IRS counterclaim.

The Court of Appeals for the Fourth Circuit, in a divided opinion, reversed. 639 F. 2d 147 (CA4 1980). Citing *Green* v. *Connally, supra,* with approval, the Court of Appeals concluded that § 501(c)(3) must be read against the background of charitable trust law. To be eligible for an exemption under that section, an institution must be "charitable" in the common law sense, and therefore must not be contrary to public policy. In the court's view, Bob Jones University did not meet this requirement, since its "racial policies violated the clearly defined public policy, rooted in our Constitution, condemning racial discrimination and, more specifically, the government policy against subsidizing racial discrimination in education, public or private." *Id.*, at 151. The court held that the IRS acted within its statutory authority in revoking the University's tax-exempt status. Finally, the Court of Appeals rejected petitioner's arguments that the revocation of the tax exemption violated the Free Exercise and Establishment Clauses of the First Amendment. The case was remanded to the District Court with instructions to dismiss the University's claim for a refund and to reinstate the Government's counterclaim.

C

No. 81–1, Goldsboro Christian Schools, Inc. v. *United States*

Goldsboro Christian Schools is a nonprofit corporation located in Goldsboro, North Carolina. Like Bob Jones University, it was established "to conduct an institution of learning . . . , giving special emphasis to the Christian religion and the ethics revealed in the Holy scriptures." Articles of Incorporation, ¶ 3(a); see Complaint, ¶ 6, reprinted in App. in No. 81–1, pp. 5–6. The school offers classes from kindergarten through high school, and since at least 1969 has satisfied the State of North Carolina's requirements for secular education in private schools. The school requires its high school students to take Bible-related courses, and begins each class with prayer.

Since its incorporation in 1963, Goldsboro Christian Schools has maintained a racially discriminatory admissions policy based upon its interpretation of the Bible.[6] Golds-

---

[6] According to the interpretation espoused by Goldsboro, race is determined by descendance from one of Noah's three sons—Ham, Shem and Japheth. Based on this interpretation, Orientals and Negroes are Hamitic, Hebrews are Shemitic, and Caucasians are Japhethitic. Cultural

boro has for the most part accepted only Caucasians.   On occasion, however, the school has accepted children from racially mixed marriages in which one of the parents is Caucasian.

Goldsboro never received a determination by the IRS that it was an organization entitled to tax exemption under § 501(c)(3).   Upon audit of Goldsboro's records for the years 1969 through 1972, the IRS determined that Goldsboro was not an organization described in § 501(c)(3), and therefore was required to pay taxes under the Federal Insurance Contribution Act and the Federal Unemployment Tax Act.

Goldsboro paid the IRS $3,459.93 in withholding, social security, and unemployment taxes with respect to one employee for the years 1969 through 1972.   Thereafter, Goldsboro filed a suit seeking refund of that payment, claiming that the school had been improperly denied § 501(c)(3) exempt status.[7]   The IRS counterclaimed for $160,073.96 in unpaid social security and unemployment taxes for the years 1969 through 1972, including interest and penalties.[8]

The District Court for the Eastern District of North Carolina decided the action on cross-motions for summary judgment.   436 F. Supp. 1314 (E. D. N. C. 1977).   In addressing the motions for summary judgment, the court assumed that Goldsboro's racially discriminatory admissions policy was based upon a sincerely held religious belief.   The court

---

or biological mixing of the races is regarded as a violation of God's command.   App. in No. 81–1, pp. 40–41.

[7] Goldsboro also asserted that it was not obliged to pay taxes on lodging furnished to its teachers.   Petitioner does not ask this Court to review the rejection of that claim.

[8] By stipulation, the IRS agreed to abate its assessment for 1969 and most of 1970 to reflect the fact that the IRS did not begin enforcing its policy of denying tax-exempt status to racially discriminatory private schools until November 30, 1970.   As a result, the amount of the counterclaim was reduced to $116,190.99.   App. in No. 81–1, pp. 104, 110.

nevertheless rejected Goldsboro's claim to tax-exempt status under § 501(c)(3), finding that "private schools maintaining racially discriminatory admissions policies violate clearly declared federal policy and, therefore, must be denied the federal tax benefits flowing from qualification under Section 501(c)(3)." *Id.*, at 1318.   The court also rejected Goldsboro's arguments that denial of tax-exempt status violated the Free Exercise and Establishment Clauses of the First Amendment.   Accordingly, the court entered summary judgment for the Government on its counterclaim.

The Court of Appeals for the Fourth Circuit affirmed, No. 80–1473 (CA4 Feb. 24, 1981) *(per curiam).*   That court found an "identity for present purposes" between the *Goldsboro* case and the *Bob Jones University* case, which had been decided shortly before by another panel of that court, and affirmed for the reasons set forth in *Bob Jones University.*

We granted certiorari in both cases, 454 U. S. 892 (1981),[9] and we affirm in each.

II

A

In Revenue Ruling 71–447, the IRS formalized the policy

---

[9] After the Court granted certiorari, the Government filed a motion to dismiss, informing the Court that the Department of Treasury intended to revoke Revenue Ruling 71–447 and other pertinent rulings and to recognize § 501(c)(3) exemptions for petitioners.   The Government suggested that these actions were therefore moot.   Before this Court ruled on that motion, however, the United States Court of Appeals for the District of Columbia Circuit enjoined the Government from granting § 501(c)(3) tax-exempt status to any school that discriminates on the basis of race. *Wright* v. *Regan*, No. 80–1124 (CADC Feb. 18, 1982) *(per curiam* order). Thereafter, the Government informed the Court that it would not revoke the revenue rulings and withdrew its request that the actions be dismissed as moot.   The Government continues to assert that the IRS lacked authority to promulgate Revenue Ruling 71–447, and does not defend that aspect of the rulings below.

first announced in 1970, that § 170 and § 501(c)(3) embrace the common law "charity" concept.   Under that view, to qualify for a tax exemption pursuant to § 501(c)(3), an institution must show, first, that it falls within one of the eight categories expressly set forth in that section, and second, that its activity is not contrary to settled public policy.

Section 501(c)(3) provides that "[c]orporations . . . organized and operated exclusively for religious, charitable . . . or educational purposes" are entitled to tax exemption.   Petitioners argue that the plain language of the statute guarantees them tax-exempt status.   They emphasize the absence of any language in the statute expressly requiring all exempt organizations to be "charitable" in the common law sense, and they contend that the disjunctive "or" separating the categories in § 501(c)(3) precludes such a reading.   Instead, they argue that if an institution falls within one or more of the specified categories it is automatically entitled to exemption, without regard to whether it also qualifies as "charitable."   The Court of Appeals rejected that contention and concluded that petitioners' interpretation of the statute "tears section 501(c)(3) from its roots."   *United States* v. *Bob Jones University, supra*, 639 F. 2d, at 151.

It is a well-established canon of statutory construction that a court should go beyond the literal language of a statute if reliance on that language would defeat the plain purpose of the statute:

> "The general words used in the clause . . . , taken by themselves, and literally construed, without regard to the object in view, would seem to sanction the claim of the plaintiff.   But this mode of expounding a statute has never been adopted by any enlightened tribunal—because it is evident that in many cases it would defeat the object which the Legislature intended to accomplish. And it is well settled that, in interpreting a statute, the court will not look merely to a particular clause in which

general words may be used, *but will take in connection with it the whole statute . . . and the objects and policy of the law. . . ."* Brown v. Duchesne, 19 How. 183, 194 (1857) (emphasis added).

Section 501(c)(3) therefore must be analyzed and construed within the framework of the Internal Revenue Code and against the background of the Congressional purposes. Such an examination reveals unmistakable evidence that, underlying all relevant parts of the Code, is the intent that entitlement to tax exemption depends on meeting certain common law standards of charity—namely, that an institution seeking tax-exempt status must serve a public purpose and not be contrary to established public policy.

This "charitable" concept appears explicitly in § 170 of the Code. That section contains a list of organizations virtually identical to that contained in § 501(c)(3). It is apparent that Congress intended that list to have the same meaning in both sections.[10] In § 170, Congress used the list of organizations in defining the term "charitable contributions." On its face,

---

[10] The predecessor of § 170 originally was enacted in 1917, as part of the War Revenue Act of 1917, ch. 63, § 1201(2), 40 Stat. 300, 330 (1917), whereas the predecessor of § 501(c)(3) dates back to the income tax law of 1894, Act of August 27, 1894, ch. 349, 28 Stat. 509, see n. 14, *infra.* There are minor differences between the lists of organizations in the two sections, see generally Liles & Blum, Development of the Federal Tax Treatment of Charities, 39 L. & Contemp. Prob. 6, 24–25 (No. 4, 1975) (hereinafter Liles & Blum). Nevertheless, the two sections are closely related; both seek to achieve the same basic goal of encouraging the development of certain organizations through the grant of tax benefits. The language of the two sections is in most respects identical, and the Commissioner and the courts consistently have applied many of the same standards in interpreting those sections. See 5 J. Mertens, The Law of Federal Income Taxation § 31.12 (1980); 6 *id.* §§ 34.01–34.13 (1975); B. Bittker & L. Stone, Federal Income Taxation 220–222 (5th ed. 1980). To the extent that § 170 "aids in ascertaining the meaning" of § 501(c)(3), therefore, it is "entitled to great weight," *United States* v. *Stewart,* 311 U. S. 60, 64–65 (1940). See *Harris* v. *Commissioner,* 340 U. S. 106, 107 (1950).

therefore, § 170 reveals that Congress' intention was to provide tax benefits to organizations serving charitable purposes.[11]   The form of § 170 simply makes plain what common sense and history tell us: in enacting both § 170 and § 501(c)(3), Congress sought to provide tax benefits to charitable organizations, to encourage the development of private institutions that serve a useful public purpose or supplement or take the place of public institutions of the same kind.

Tax exemptions for certain institutions thought beneficial to the social order of the country as a whole, or to a particular community, are deeply rooted in our history, as in that of England.   The origins of such exemptions lie in the special privileges that have long been extended to charitable trusts.[12]

More than a century ago, this Court announced the caveat

---

[11] The dissent suggests that the Court "quite adeptly avoids the statute it is construing," *post*, at 1, and "seeks refuge . . . by turning to § 170," *post*, at 2.   This assertion dissolves when one sees that § 501(c)(3) and § 170 are construed together, as they must be.   The dissent acknowledges that the two sections are "mirror" provisions; surely there can be no doubt that the Court properly looks to § 170 to determine the meaning of § 501(c)(3).   It is also suggested that § 170 is "at best of little usefulness in finding the meaning of § 501(c)(3)," since "§ 170(c) simply tracks the requirements set forth in § 501(c)(3)," *post*, at 3.   That reading loses sight of the fact that § 170(c) defines the term "charitable contribution."   The plain language of § 170 reveals that Congress' objective was to employ tax exemptions and deductions to promote certain *charitable* purposes.   While the eight categories of institutions specified in the statute are indeed presumptively charitable in nature, the IRS properly considered principles of charitable trust law in determining whether the institutions in question may truly be considered "charitable," for purposes of entitlement to the tax benefits conferred by § 170 and § 501(c)(3).

[12] The form and history of the charitable exemption and deduction sections of the various income tax acts reveal that Congress was guided by the common law of charitable trusts.   See Simon, The Tax-Exempt Status of Racially Discriminatory Religious Schools, 36 Tax L. Rev. 477, 485–489 (1981) (hereinafter Simon).   Congress acknowledged as much in 1969. The House Report on the Tax Reform Act of 1969, Pub. L. 91–172, 83 Stat. 487, stated that the § 501(c)(3) exemption was available only to institutions that served "the specified charitable purposes," H. R. Rep. No. 413 (Part

that is critical in this case:

> "[I]t has now become an established principle of American law, that courts of chancery will sustain and protect ... a gift ... to public charitable uses, *provided the same is consistent with local laws and public policy.* ..." *Perin* v. *Carey*, 24 How. 465, 501 (1861) (emphasis added).

Soon after that, in 1878, the Court commented:

> "A charitable use, *where neither law nor public policy forbids*, may be applied to almost any thing *that tends to promote the well-doing and well-being of social man.*" *Ould* v. *Washington Hospital for Foundlings*, 95 U. S. 303, 311 (1878) (emphasis added). See also, *e. g., Jackson* v. *Phillips*, 96 Mass. 539, 556 (1867).

In 1891, in a restatement of the English law of charity [13] which has long been recognized as a leading authority in this country, Lord MacNaghten stated:

> "'Charity' in its legal sense comprises four principal divisions: trusts for the relief of poverty; *trusts for the advancement of education*; trusts for the advancement of religion; and trusts for other purposes beneficial to the community, not falling under any of the preceding heads." *Commissioners* v. *Pemsel*, [1891] A. C. 531, 583 (emphasis added). See, *e. g.*, 4 A. Scott, The Law

---

1), 91st Cong., 1st Sess. 35 (1969), and described "charitable" as "a term that has been used in the law of trusts for hundreds of years." *Id.*, at 43. We need not consider whether Congress intended to incorporate into the Internal Revenue Code any aspects of charitable trust law other than the requirements of public benefit and a valid public purpose.

[13] The draftsmen of the 1894 income tax law, which included the first charitable exemption provision, relied heavily on English concepts of taxation; and the list of exempt organizations appears to have been patterned upon English income tax statutes. See 26 Cong. Rec. 584–588, 6612–6615 (1894).

of Trusts § 368, at 2853–2854 (3d ed. 1967) (hereinafter
Scott).

These statements clearly reveal the legal background against
which Congress enacted the first charitable exemption statute in 1894:[14] charities were to be given preferential treatment because they provide a benefit to society.

What little floor debate occurred on the charitable exemption provision of the 1894 Act and similar sections of later
statutes leaves no doubt that Congress deemed the specified
organizations entitled to tax benefits because they served desirable public purposes.   See, *e. g.*, 26 Cong. Rec. 585–586
(1894); *id.*, at 1727.   In floor debate on a similar provision in
1917, for example, Senator Hollis articulated the rationale:

> "For every dollar that a man contributes to these public
> charities, educational, scientific, or otherwise, the public
> gets 100 percent." 55 *id.*, at 6728 (1917).   See also,
> *e. g.*, 44 *id.*, at 4150 (1909); 50 *id.*, at 1305–1306 (1913).

In 1924, this Court restated the common understanding of
the charitable exemption provision:

> "Evidently the exemption is made in recognition of the
> benefit which the public derives from corporate activities
> of the class named, and is intended to aid them when
> not conducted for private gain." *Trinidad* v. *Sagrada
> Orden*, 263 U. S. 578, 581 (1924).[15]

---

[14] Act of August 27, 1894, ch. 349, § 32, 28 Stat. 509, 556–557 (1894).
The income tax system contained in the 1894 Act was declared unconstitutional, *Pollock* v. *Farmers' Loan and Trust Co.*, 158 U. S. 601 (1895), for
reasons unrelated to the charitable exemption provision.   The terms of
that exemption were in substance included in the corporate income tax contained in the Payne Aldrich Tariff Act of 1909, ch. 6, § 38, 36 Stat. 11, 112
(1909).   A similar exemption has been included in every income tax act
since the adoption of the Sixteenth Amendment, beginning with the Revenue Act of 1913, ch. 16, § II(G), 38 Stat. 114, 172 (1913).   See generally
Reiling, Federal Taxation: What Is a Charitable Organization?, 44 ABA J.
525 (1958); Liles & Blum.

[15] That same year, the Bureau of Internal Revenue expressed a similar

In enacting the Revenue Act of 1938, ch. 289, 52 Stat. 447 (1938), Congress expressly reconfirmed this view with respect to the charitable deduction provision:

"The exemption from taxation of money and property devoted to charitable and other purposes is based on the theory that the Government is compensated for the loss of revenue by its relief from financial burdens which would otherwise have to be met by appropriations from other public funds, and by the benefits resulting from the promotion of the general welfare." H. R. Rep. No. 1860, 75th Cong., 3d Sess. 19 (1938).[16]

A corollary to the public benefit principle is the requirement, long recognized in the law of trusts, that the purpose of a charitable trust may not be illegal or violate established public policy. In 1861, this Court stated that a public charitable use must be "consistent with local laws and public policy," *Perin* v. *Carey, supra,* 24 How., at 501. Modern commentators and courts have echoed that view. See, *e. g.,* Restatement (Second) of Trusts, § 377, comment c (1959); 4 Scott § 377, and cases cited therein; Bogert § 378, at

---

view of the charitable deduction section of the estate tax contained in the Revenue Act of 1918, ch. 18, § 403(a)(3), 40 Stat. 1057, 1098 (1919). The Solicitor of Internal Revenue looked to the common law of charitable trusts in construing that provision, and noted that "generally bequests for the benefit and advantage of the general public are valid as charities." Sol. Op. 159, III-1 C. B. 480 (1924).

[16] The common law requirement of public benefit is universally recognized by commentators on the law of trusts. For example, Bogert states: "In return for the favorable treatment accorded charitable gifts which imply some disadvantage to the community, the courts must find in the trust which is to be deemed 'charitable' some real advantages to the public which more than offset the disadvantages arising out of special privileges accorded charitable trusts." G. Bogert & G. Bogert, The Law of Trusts and Trustees § 361, at 3 (rev. 2d ed. 1977) (hereinafter Bogert).

For other statements of this principle, see, *e. g.,* 4 Scott § 348, at 2770; Restatement (Second) of Trusts § 368, comment b (1959); E. Fisch, D. Freed & E. Schachter, Charities and Charitable Foundations § 256 (1974).

191–192.[17]

When the Government grants exemptions or allows deductions all taxpayers are affected; the very fact of the exemption or deduction for the donor means that other taxpayers can be said to be indirect and vicarious "donors." Charitable exemptions are justified on the basis that the exempt entity confers a public benefit—a benefit which the society or the community may not itself choose or be able to provide, or which supplements and advances the work of public institutions already supported by tax revenues.[18] History buttresses logic to make clear that, to warrant exemption under

---

[17] Cf. *Tank Truck Rentals, Inc.* v. *Commissioner*, 356 U. S. 30, 35 (1958), in which this Court referred to "the presumption against congressional intent to encourage violation of declared public policy" in upholding the Commissioner's disallowance of deductions claimed by a trucking company for fines it paid for violations of state maximum weight laws.

[18] The dissent acknowledges that "Congress intended . . . to offer a tax benefit to organizations . . . providing a public benefit," *post*, at 3, but suggests that Congress itself fully defined what organizations provide a public benefit, through the list of eight categories of exempt organizations contained in § 170 and § 501(c)(3). Under that view, any nonprofit organization that falls within one of the specified categories is automatically entitled to the tax benefits, provided it does not engage in expressly prohibited lobbying or political activities. *Post*, at 6. The dissent thus would have us conclude, for example, that any nonprofit organization that does not engage in prohibited lobbying activities is entitled to tax exemption as an "educational" institution if it is organized for the "instruction or training of the individual for the purpose of improving or developing his capabilities," 26 CFR § 1.501(c)(3)–1(d)(3). See *post*, at 12. As Judge Leventhal noted in *Green* v. *Connally*, 330 F. Supp. 1150, 1160 (D. D. C.), *aff'd sub nom. Coit* v. *Green*, 404 U. S. 997 (1971) (*per curiam*), Fagin's school for educating English boys in the art of picking pockets would be an "educational" institution under that definition. Similarly, a band of former military personnel might well set up a school for intensive training of subversives for guerrilla warfare and terrorism in other countries; in the abstract, that "school" would qualify as an "educational" institution. Surely Congress had no thought of affording such an unthinking, wooden meaning to § 170 and § 501(c)(3) as to provide tax benefits to "educational" organizations that do not serve a public, charitable purpose.

§ 501(c)(3), an institution must fall within a category specified in that section and must demonstrably serve and be in harmony with the public interest.[19]   The institution's purpose must not be so at odds with the common community conscience as to undermine any public benefit that might otherwise be conferred.

B

We are bound to approach these questions with full awareness that determinations of public benefit and public policy are sensitive matters with serious implications for the institutions affected; a declaration that a given institution is not "charitable" should be made only where there can be no doubt that the activity involved is contrary to a fundamental public policy.   But there can no longer be any doubt that racial discrimination in education violates deeply and widely accepted views of elementary justice.   Prior to 1954, public education in many places still was conducted under the pall of *Plessy* v. *Ferguson*, 163 U. S. 537 (1896); racial segregation in primary and secondary education prevailed in many parts of the country.   See, *e. g.*, Segregation and the Fourteenth Amendment in the States (B. Reams & P. Wilson, eds. 1975).[20]   This Court's decision in *Brown* v. *Board of Educa-*

---

[19] The Court's reading of § 501(c)(3) does not render meaningless Congress' action in specifying the eight categories of presumptively exempt organizations, as petitioners suggest.   See Brief of Petitioner Goldsboro Christian Schools 18–24.   To be entitled to tax-exempt status under § 501(c)(3), an organization must first fall within one of the categories specified by Congress, and in addition must serve a valid charitable purpose.

[20] In 1894, when the first charitable exemption provision was enacted, racially segregated educational institutions would not have been regarded as against public policy.   Yet contemporary standards must be considered in determining whether given activities provide a public benefit and are entitled to the charitable tax exemption.   In *Walz* v. *Tax Comm'n*, 397 U. S. 664, 672–673 (1970), we observed:

"Qualification for tax exemption is not perpetual or immutable; some tax-exempt groups lose that status when their activities take them outside the

tion, 347 U. S. 483 (1954), signalled an end to that era. Over
the past quarter of a century, every pronouncement of this
Court and myriad Acts of Congress and Executive Orders attest a firm national policy to prohibit racial segregation and
discrimination in public education.

An unbroken line of cases following *Brown* v. *Board of
Education* establishes beyond doubt this Court's view that
racial discrimination in education violates a most fundamental
national public policy, as well as rights of individuals.

> "The right of a student not to be segregated on racial
> grounds in schools . . . is indeed so fundamental and per-
> vasive that it is embraced in the concept of due process
> of law." *Cooper* v. *Aaron,* 358 U. S. 1, 19 (1958).

In *Norwood* v. *Harrison,* 413 U. S. 455, 468–469 (1973), we
dealt with a non-public institution:

> "[A] private school—even one that discriminates—fulfills
> an important educational function; *however,* . . . *[that]
> legitimate educational function cannot be isolated from
> discriminatory practices* . . . *[D]iscriminatory treat-
> ment exerts a pervasive influence on the entire educa-
> tional process."* (Emphasis added). See also *Runyon*
> v. *McCrary,* 427 U. S. 160 (1976); *Griffin* v. *County
> School Board,* 377 U. S. 218 (1964).

Congress, in Titles IV and VI of the Civil Rights Act of
1964, Pub. L. 88–352, 78 Stat. 241, 42 U. S. C. §§ 2000c,
2000c–6, 2000–d, clearly expressed its agreement that racial
discrimination in education violates a fundamental public policy. Other sections of that Act, and numerous enactments
since then, testify to the public policy against racial dis-

---

classification and new entities can come into being and qualify for the
exemption."

Charitable trust law also makes clear that the definition of "charity" depends upon contemporary standards. See, *e. g.,* Restatement (Second) of
Trusts, § 374, comment a (1959); Bogert § 369, at 65–67; 4 Scott § 368, at
2855–2856.

crimination.   See, *e. g.*, the Voting Rights Act of 1965, Pub.
L. 89–110, 79 Stat. 437, 42 U. S. C. §§ 1971 *et seq.*; Title VIII
of the Civil Rights Act of 1968, Pub. L. 90–284, 82 Stat. 81,
42 U. S. C. §§ 3601 *et seq.*; the Emergency School Aid Act of
1972, Pub. L. 92–318, 86 Stat. 354 (repealed effective Sept.
30, 1979; replaced by similar provisions in the Emergency
School Aid Act of 1978, Pub. L. 95–561, 92 Stat. 2252, 20
U. S. C. §§ 3191–3207 (1980 Supp.)).

The Executive Branch has consistently placed its support
behind eradication of racial discrimination.   Several years
before this Court's decision in *Brown* v. *Board of Education*,
supra, President Truman issued Executive Orders prohibiting racial discrimination in federal employment decisions,
Exec. Order No. 9980, 3 CFR 720 (1943–1948 Comp.), and in
classifications for the Selective Service, Exec. Order No.
9988, *id.* 726, 729.   In 1957, President Eisenhower employed
military forces to ensure compliance with federal standards in
school desegregation programs.   Exec. Order No. 10730, 3
CFR 389 (1954–1958 Comp.).   And in 1962, President Kennedy announced:

> "[T]he granting of federal assistance for . . . housing and
> related facilities from which Americans are excluded be-
> cause of their race, color, creed, or national origin is
> unfair, unjust, and inconsistent with the public policy of
> the United States as manifested in its Constitution and
> laws."   Exec. Order No. 11063, 3 CFR 652 (1959–1963
> Comp.).

These are but a few of numerous Executive Orders over the
past three decades demonstrating the commitment of the Executive Branch to the fundamental policy of eliminating racial
discrimination.   See, *e. g.*, Exec. Order No. 11197, 3 CFR
278 (1964–1965 Comp.); Exec. Order No. 11478, 3 CFR 803
(1966–1970 Comp.); Exec. Order No. 11764, 3 CFR 849
(1971–1975 Comp.); Exec. Order No. 12250, 3 CFR 298
(1981).

Few social or political issues in our history have been more vigorously debated and more extensively ventilated than the issue of racial discrimination, particularly in education. Given the stress and anguish of the history of efforts to escape from the shackles of the "separate but equal" doctrine of *Plessy* v. *Ferguson, supra,* it cannot be said that educational institutions that, for whatever reasons, practice racial discrimination, are institutions exercising "beneficial and stabilizing influences in community life," *Walz* v. *Tax Comm'n,* 397 U. S. 664, 673 (1970), or should be encouraged by having all taxpayers share in their support by way of special tax status.

There can thus be no question that the interpretation of § 170 and § 501(c)(3) announced by the IRS in 1970 was correct. That it may be seen as belated does not undermine its soundness. It would be wholly incompatible with the concepts underlying tax exemption to grant the benefit of tax-exempt status to racially discriminatory educational entities, which "exer[t] a pervasive influence on the entire educational process." *Norwood* v. *Harrison, supra,* 413 U. S., at 469. Whatever may be the rationale for such private schools' policies, and however sincere the rationale may be, racial discrimination in education is contrary to public policy. Racially discriminatory educational institutions cannot be viewed as conferring a public benefit within the "charitable" concept discussed earlier, or within the Congressional intent underlying § 170 and § 501(c)(3).[21]

C

Petitioners contend that, regardless of whether the IRS

---

[21] In view of our conclusion that racially discriminatory private schools violate fundamental public policy and cannot be deemed to confer a benefit on the public, we need not decide whether an organization providing a public benefit and otherwise meeting the requirements of § 501(c)(3) could nevertheless be denied tax-exempt status if certain of its activities violated a law or public policy.

properly concluded that racially discriminatory private schools violate public policy, only Congress can alter the scope of § 170 and § 501(c)(3). Petitioners accordingly argue that the IRS overstepped its lawful bounds in issuing its 1970 and 1971 rulings.

Yet ever since the inception of the tax code, Congress has seen fit to vest in those administering the tax laws very broad authority to interpret those laws. In an area as complex as the tax system, the agency Congress vests with administrative responsibility must be able to exercise its authority to meet changing conditions and new problems. Indeed as early as 1918, Congress expressly authorized the Commissioner "to make all needful rules and regulations for the enforcement" of the tax laws. Revenue Act of 1918, ch. 18, § 1309, 40 Stat. 1057, 1143 (1919). The same provision, so essential to efficient and fair administration of the tax laws, has appeared in tax codes ever since, see 26 U. S. C. § 7805(a) (1976); and this Court has long recognized the primary authority of the IRS and its predecessors in construing the Internal Revenue Code, see, *e. g.*, *Commissioner* v. *Portland Cement Co.*, 450 U. S. 156, 169 (1981); *United States* v. *Correll*, 389 U. S. 299, 306–307 (1967); *Boske* v. *Comingore*, 177 U. S. 459, 469–470 (1900).

Congress, the source of IRS authority, can modify IRS rulings it considers improper; and courts exercise review over IRS actions. In the first instance, however, the responsibility for construing the Code falls to the IRS. Since Congress cannot be expected to anticipate every conceivable problem that can arise or to carry out day-to-day oversight, it relies on the administrators and on the courts to implement the legislative will. Administrators, like judges, are under oath to do so.

In § 170 and § 501(c)(3), Congress has identified categories of traditionally exempt institutions and has specified certain additional requirements for tax exemption. Yet the need for continuing interpretation of those statutes is unavoidable.

For more than 60 years, the IRS and its predecessors have constantly been called upon to interpret these and comparable provisions, and in doing so have referred consistently to principles of charitable trust law. In Treas. Reg. 45, art. 517(1) (1921), for example, the IRS denied charitable exemptions on the basis of proscribed political activity before the Congress itself added such conduct as a disqualifying element. In other instances, the IRS has denied charitable exemptions to otherwise qualified entities because they served too limited a class of people and thus did not provide a truly "public" benefit under the common law test. See, *e. g.*, *Crellin* v. *Commissioner*, 46 B. T. A. 1152, 1155–1156 (1942); *James Sprunt Benevolent Trust* v. *Commissioner*, 20 B. T. A. 19, 24–25 (1930). See also Treas. Reg. § 1.501(c)(3)–1(d)(1)(ii) (1959). Some years before the issuance of the rulings challenged in these cases, the IRS also ruled that contributions to community recreational facilities would not be deductible and that the facilities themselves would not be entitled to tax-exempt status, unless those facilities were open to all on a racially nondiscriminatory basis. See Rev. Rul. 67–325, 1967–2 Cum. Bull. 113. These rulings reflect the Commissioner's continuing duty to interpret and apply the Internal Revenue Code. See also *Textile Mills Securities Corp.* v. *Commissioner*, 314 U. S. 326, 337–338 (1941).

Guided, of course, by the Code, the IRS has the responsibility, in the first instance, to determine whether a particular entity is "charitable" for purposes of § 170 and § 501(c)(3).[22] This in turn may necessitate later determinations of whether given activities so violate public policy that the entities involved cannot be deemed to provide a public benefit worthy of "charitable" status. We emphasize, however, that these sensitive determinations should be made only where there is

---

[22] In the present case, the IRS issued its rulings denying exemptions to racially discriminatory schools only after a three-judge District Court had issued a preliminary injunction. See *supra*, at 2–3.

no doubt that the organization's activities violate fundamental public policy.

On the record before us, there can be no doubt as to the national policy. In 1970, when the IRS first issued the ruling challenged here, the position of all three branches of the Federal Government was unmistakably clear. The correctness of the Commissioner's conclusion that a racially discriminatory private school "is not 'charitable' within the common law concepts reflected in . . . the Code," Rev. Rul. 71–447, 1972–2 Cum. Bull., at 231, is wholly consistent with what Congress, the Executive and the courts had repeatedly declared before 1970. Indeed, it would be anomalous for the Executive, Legislative and Judicial Branches to reach conclusions that add up to a firm public policy on racial discrimination, and at the same time have the IRS blissfully ignore what all three branches of the Federal Government had declared.[23] Clearly an educational institution engaging in practices affirmatively at odds with this declared position of the whole government cannot be seen as exercising a "beneficial and stabilizing influenc[e] in community life," *Walz* v. *Tax Comm'n, supra*, 397 U. S., at 673, and is not "charitable," within the meaning of § 170 and § 501(c)(3). We therefore hold that the IRS did not exceed its authority when it announced its interpretation of § 170 and § 501(c)(3) in 1970 and 1971.[24]

---

[23] JUSTICE POWELL misreads the Court's opinion when he suggests that the Court implies that "the Internal Revenue Service is invested with authority to decide which public policies are sufficiently 'fundamental' to require denial of tax exemptions," *post*, at 6. The Court's opinion does not warrant that interpretation. JUSTICE POWELL concedes that "if any national policy is sufficiently fundamental to constitute such an overriding limitation on the availability of tax-exempt status under § 501(c)(3), it is the policy against racial discrimination in education." *Post*, at 2. Since that policy is sufficiently clear to warrant JUSTICE POWELL's concession and for him to support our finding of longstanding Congressional acquiescence, it should be apparent that his concerns about the Court's opinion are unfounded.

[24] Many of the *amici curiae*, including Amicus William T. Coleman, Jr.

D

The actions of Congress since 1970 leave no doubt that the IRS reached the correct conclusion in exercising its authority. It is, of course, not unknown for independent agencies or the Executive Branch to misconstrue the intent of a statute; Congress can and often does correct such misconceptions, if the courts have not done so. Yet for a dozen years Congress has been made aware—acutely aware—of the IRS rulings of 1970 and 1971. As we noted earlier, few issues have been the subject of more vigorous and widespread debate and discussion in and out of Congress than those related to racial segregation in education. Sincere adherents advocating contrary views have ventilated the subject for well over three decades. Failure of Congress to modify the IRS rulings of 1970 and 1971, of which Congress was, by its own studies and by public discourse, constantly reminded; and Congress' awareness of the denial of tax-exempt status for racially discriminatory schools when enacting other and related legislation make out an unusually strong case of legislative acquiescence in and ratification by implication of the 1970 and 1971 rulings.

Ordinarily, and quite appropriately, courts are slow to attribute significance to the failure of Congress to act on particular legislation. See, *e. g., Aaron* v. *SEC*, 446 U. S. 680, 694 n. 11 (1980). We have observed that "unsuccessful attempts at legislation are not the best of guides to legislative intent," *Red Lion Broadcasting Co.* v. *FCC*, 395 U. S. 367, 381–382 n. 11 (1969). Here, however, we do not have an ordinary claim of legislative acquiescence. Only one month

---

(appointed by the Court), argue that denial of tax-exempt status to racially discriminatory schools is independently required by the equal protection component of the Fifth Amendment. In light of our resolution of this case, we do not reach that issue. See, *e. g., United States* v. *Clark*, 445 U. S. 23, 27 (1980); *NLRB* v. *Catholic Bishop of Chicago*, 440 U. S. 490, 504 (1979).

after the IRS announced its position in 1970, Congress held its first hearings on this precise issue. *Equal Educational Opportunity: Hearings Before the Senate Select Comm. on Equal Educational Opportunity*, 91st Cong., 2d Sess. 1991 (1970). Exhaustive hearings have been held on the issue at various times since then. These include hearings in February 1982, after we granted review in this case. *Administration's Change in Federal Policy Regarding the Tax Status of Racially Discriminatory Private Schools: Hearing Before the House Comm. on Ways and Means*, 97th Cong., 2d Sess. (1982).

Non-action by Congress is not often a useful guide, but the non-action here is significant. During the past 12 years there have been no fewer than 13 bills introduced to overturn the IRS interpretation of § 501(c)(3).[25] Not one of these bills has emerged from any committee, although Congress has enacted numerous other amendments to § 501 during this same period, including an amendment to § 501(c)(3) itself. Tax Reform Act of 1976, Pub. L. 94–455, § 1313(a), 90 Stat. 1520, 1730 (1976). It is hardly conceivable that Congress—and in this setting, any Member of Congress—was not abundantly aware of what was going on. In view of its prolonged and acute awareness of so important an issue, Congress' failure to act on the bills proposed on this subject provides added support for concluding that Congress acquiesced in the IRS rulings of 1970 and 1971. See, *e. g.*, *Merrill, Lynch, Pierce, Fenner & Smith, Inc.* v. *Curran*, 456 U. S. 353, 379–382 (1982); *Haig* v. *Agee*, 453 U. S. 280, 300–301 (1981); *Herman*

---

[25] H. R. 1096, 97th Cong., 1st Sess. (1981); H. R. 802, 97th Cong., 1st Sess. (1981); H. R. 498, 97th Cong., 1st Sess. (1981); H. R. 332, 97th Cong., 1st Sess. (1981); H. R. 95, 97th Cong., 1st Sess. (1981); S. 995, 96th Cong., 1st Sess. (1979); H. R. 1905, 96th Cong., 1st Sess. (1979); H. R. 96, 96th Cong., 1st Sess. (1979); H. R. 3225, 94th Cong., 1st Sess. (1975); H. R. 1394, 93d Cong., 1st Sess. (1973); H. R. 5350, 92d Cong., 1st Sess. (1971); H. R. 2352, 92d Cong., 1st Sess. (1971); H. R. 68, 92d Cong., 1st Sess. (1971).

& *MacLean* v. *Huddleston,* —— U. S. ——, —— (1983); *United States* v. *Rutherford,* 442 U. S. 544, 554 n. 10 (1979).

The evidence of Congressional approval of the policy embodied in Revenue Ruling 71–447 goes well beyond the failure of Congress to act on legislative proposals. Congress affirmatively manifested its acquiescence in the IRS policy when it enacted the present § 501(i) of the Code, Act of October 20, 1976, Pub. L. 94–568, 90 Stat. 2697 (1976). That provision denies tax-exempt status to social clubs whose charters or policy statements provide for "discrimination against any person on the basis of race, color, or religion."[26] Both the House and Senate committee reports on that bill articulated the national policy against granting tax exemptions to racially discriminatory private clubs. S. Rep. No. 1318, 94th Cong., 2d Sess., 8 (1976); H. R. Rep. No. 1353, 94th Cong., 2d Sess., 8 (1976).

Even more significant is the fact that both reports focus on this Court's affirmance of *Green* v. *Connally, supra,* as having established that "discrimination on account of race is inconsistent with an *educational institution's* tax exempt status." S. Rep. No. 1318, *supra,* at 7–8 and n. 5; H. R. Rep. No. 1353, *supra,* at 8 and n. 5 (emphasis added). These references in Congressional committee reports on an enactment denying tax exemptions to racially discriminatory private social clubs cannot be read other than as indicating approval of the standards applied to racially discriminatory private schools by the IRS subsequent to 1970, and specifically of Revenue Ruling 71–447.[27]

---

[26] Prior to the introduction of this legislation, a three-judge district court had held that segregated social clubs were entitled to tax exemptions. *McGlotten* v. *Connally,* 338 F. Supp. 448 (D. D. C. 1972). Section 501(i) was enacted primarily in response to that decision. See S. Rep. No. 1318, 94th Cong., 2d Sess., 7–8 (1976); H. R. Rep. No. 1353, 94th Cong., 2d Sess., 8 (1976).

[27] Reliance is placed on scattered statements in floor debate by Con-

III

Petitioners contend that, even if the Commissioner's policy is valid as to nonreligious private schools, that policy cannot constitutionally be applied to schools that engage in racial discrimination on the basis of sincerely held religious beliefs.[28]

---

gressmen critical of the IRS' adoption of Revenue Ruling 71–447. See, *e. g.*, Brief of Petitioner Goldsboro Christian Schools 27–28. Those views did not prevail. That several Congressmen, expressing their individual views, argued that the IRS had no authority to take the action in question, is hardly a balance for the overwhelming evidence of Congressional awareness of and acquiescence in the IRS rulings of 1970 and 1971. Petitioners also argue that the Ashbrook and Dornan Amendments to the Treasury, Postal Service, and General Government Appropriations Act of 1980; Pub. L. 96–74; §§ 103, 614, 615; 93 Stat. 559, 562, 576–577 (1979), reflect Congressional opposition to the IRS policy formalized in Revenue Ruling 71–447. Those amendments, however, are directly concerned only with limiting more aggressive enforcement procedures proposed by the IRS in 1978 and 1979 and preventing the adoption of more stringent substantive standards. The Ashbrook Amendment, § 103 of the Act, applies only to procedures, guidelines or measures adopted after August 22, 1978, and thus in no way affects the status of Revenue Ruling 71–447. In fact, both Congressman Dornan and Congressman Ashbrook explicitly stated that their amendments would have no effect on prior IRS policy, including Revenue Ruling 71–447, see 125 Cong. Rec. H5982 (daily ed. July 16, 1979) (Cong. Dornan: "[M]y amendment will not affect existing IRS rules which IRS has used to revoke tax exemptions of white segregated academies under Revenue Ruling 71–447. . . ."); 125 Cong. Rec. H5882 (daily ed. July 13, 1979) (Cong. Ashbrook: "My amendment very clearly indicates on its face that all the regulations in existence as of August 22, 1978, would not be touched."). These amendments therefore do not indicate Congressional rejection of Revenue Ruling 71–447 and the standards contained therein.

[28] The District Court found, on the basis of a full evidentiary record, that the challenged practices of petitioner Bob Jones University were based on a genuine belief that the Bible forbids interracial dating and marriage. 468 F. Supp., at 894. We assume, as did the District Court, that the same is true with respect to petitioner Goldsboro Christian Schools. See 436 F. Supp., at 1317.

As to such schools, it is argued that the IRS construction of §170 and §501(c)(3) violates their free exercise rights under the Religion Clauses of the First Amendment. This contention presents claims not heretofore considered by this Court in precisely this context.

This Court has long held the Free Exercise Clause of the First Amendment an absolute prohibition against governmental regulation of religious beliefs, *Wisconsin* v. *Yoder*, 406 U. S. 205, 219 (1972); *Sherbert* v. *Verner*, 374 U. S. 398, 402 (1963); *Cantwell* v. *Connecticut*, 310 U. S. 296, 303 (1940). As interpreted by this Court, moreover, the Free Exercise Clause provides substantial protection for lawful conduct grounded in religious belief, see *Wisconsin* v. *Yoder*, *supra*, 406 U. S., at 220; *Thomas* v. *Review Board of the Indiana Emp. Security Div.*, 450 U. S. 707 (1981); *Sherbert* v. *Verner*, *supra*, 374 U. S., at 402–403. However, "[n]ot all burdens on religion are unconstitutional. . . . The state may justify a limitation on religious liberty by showing that it is essential to accomplish an overriding governmental interest." *United States* v. *Lee*, 455 U. S. 252, 257–258 (1982) (citations omitted). See, *e. g.*, *McDaniel* v. *Paty*, 435 U. S. 618, 628 and n. 8 (1978); *Wisconsin* v. *Yoder*, *supra*, 406 U. S., at 215; *Gillette* v. *United States*, 401 U. S. 437 (1971).

On occasion this Court has found certain governmental interests so compelling as to allow even regulations prohibiting religiously based conduct. In *Prince* v. *Massachusetts*, 321 U. S. 158 (1944), for example, the Court held that neutrally cast child labor laws prohibiting sale of printed materials on public streets could be applied to prohibit children from dispensing religious literature. The Court found no constitutional infirmity in "excluding [Jehovah's Witness children] from doing there what no other children may do." *Id.*, at 170. See also *Reynolds* v. *United States*, 98 U. S. 145 (1878); *United States* v. *Lee, supra*; *Gillette* v. *United States, supra.* Denial of tax benefits will inevitably have a substantial impact on the operation of private religious schools, but will not prevent those schools from observing their religious tenets.

The governmental interest at stake here is compelling. As discussed in Part II(B), *supra*, the Government has a fundamental, overriding interest in eradicating racial discrimination in education[29]—discrimination that prevailed, with official approval, for the first 165 years of this Nation's history. That governmental interest substantially outweighs whatever burden denial of tax benefits places on petitioners' exercise of their religious beliefs. The interests asserted by petitioners cannot be accommodated with that compelling governmental interest, see *United States* v. *Lee, supra*, 455 U. S., at 259–260; and no "less restrictive means," see *Thomas* v. *Review Board, supra*, 450 U. S., at 718, are available to achieve the governmental interest.[30]

---

[29] We deal here only with religious *schools*—not with churches or other purely religious institutions; here, the governmental interest is in denying public support to racial discrimination in education. As noted earlier, racially discriminatory schools "exer[t] a pervasive influence on the entire educational process," outweighing any public benefit that they might otherwise provide, *Norwood* v. *Harrison*, 413 U. S. 455, 469 (1973). See generally Simon 495–496.

[30] Bob Jones University also contends that denial of tax exemption violates the Establishment Clause by preferring religions whose tenets do not require racial discrimination over those which believe racial intermixing is forbidden. It is well settled that neither a State nor the Federal Government may pass laws which "prefer one religion over another," *Everson* v. *Board of Education*, 330 U. S. 1, 15 (1947), but "[i]t is equally true" that a regulation does not violate the Establishment Clause merely because it "happens to coincide or harmonize with the tenets of some or all religions." *McGowan* v. *Maryland*, 366 U. S. 420, 442 (1961). See *Harris* v. *McRae*, 448 U. S. 297, 319–320 (1980). The IRS policy at issue here is founded on a "neutral, secular basis," *Gillette* v. *United States*, 401 U. S. 437, 452 (1971), and does not violate the Establishment Clause. See generally U. S. Comm'n on Civil Rights, Discriminatory Religious Schools and Tax Exempt Status 10–17 (1982). In addition, as the Court of Appeals noted, "the uniform application of the rule to all religiously operated schools *avoids* the necessity for a potentially entangling inquiry into whether a racially restrictive practice is the result of sincere religious belief." *United States* v. *Bob Jones Univ.*, 639 F. 2d 147, 155 (CA4 1980) (emphasis in orig-

IV

The remaining issue is whether the IRS properly applied its policy to these petitioners. Petitioner Goldsboro Christian Schools admits that it "maintain[s] racially discriminatory policies," Brief of Petitioner, Goldsboro Christian Schools, No. 81–1, at 10, but seeks to justify those policies on grounds we have fully discussed. The IRS properly denied tax-exempt status to Goldsboro Christian Schools.

Petitioner Bob Jones University, however, contends that it is not racially discriminatory. It emphasizes that it now allows all races to enroll, subject only to its restrictions on the conduct of all students, including its prohibitions of association between men and women of different races, and of interracial marriage.[31] Although a ban on intermarriage or interracial dating applies to all races, decisions of this Court firmly establish that discrimination on the basis of racial affiliation and association is a form of racial discrimination, see, *e. g.*, *Loving* v. *Virginia*, 388 U. S. 1 (1967); *McLaughlin* v. *Florida*, 379 U. S. 184 (1964); *Tillman* v. *Wheaton-Haven Recreation Ass'n*, 410 U. S. 431 (1973). We therefore find that the IRS properly applied Revenue Ruling 71–447 to Bob Jones University.[32]

The judgments of the Court of Appeals are, accordingly,

Affirmed.

---

inal). Cf. *NLRB* v. *Catholic Bishop of Chicago*, 440 U. S. 490 (1979). But see generally Note, 90 Yale L. J. 350 (1980).

[31] This argument would in any event apply only to the final eight months of the five tax years at issue in this case. Prior to May 1975, Bob Jones University's admissions policy was racially discriminatory on its face, since the University excluded unmarried Negro students while admitting unmarried Caucasians.

[32] Bob Jones University also argues that the IRS policy should not apply to it because it is entitled to exemption under § 501(c)(3) as a "religious" organization, rather than as an "educational" institution. The record in this case leaves no doubt, however, that Bob Jones University is both an educational institution and a religious institution. As discussed previously, the IRS policy properly extends to all private schools, including religious schools. See n. 29, *supra*. The IRS policy thus was properly applied to Bob Jones University.

FULLILOVE ET AL. *v.* KLUTZNICK, SECRETARY OF COMMERCE, ET AL.

CERTIORARI TO THE UNITED STATES COURT OF APPEALS FOR THE SECOND CIRCUIT

No. 78–1007. Argued November 27, 1979—Decided July 2, 1980

The "minority business enterprise" (MBE) provision of the Public Works Employment Act of 1977 (1977 Act) requires that, absent an administrative waiver, at least 10% of federal funds granted for local public works projects must be used by the state or local grantee to procure services or supplies from businesses owned by minority group members, defined as United States citizens "who are Negroes, Spanish-speaking, Orientals, Indians, Eskimos, and Aleuts." Under implementing regulations and guidelines, grantees and their private prime contractors are required, to the extent feasible, in fulfilling the 10% MBE requirement, to seek out all available, qualified, bona fide MBE's, to provide technical assistance as needed, to lower or waive bonding requirements where feasible, to solicit the aid of the Office of Minority Business Enterprise, the Small Business Administration, or other sources for assisting MBE's in obtaining required working capital, and to give guidance through the intricacies of the bidding process. The administrative program, which recognizes that contracts will be awarded to bona fide MBE's even though they are not the lowest bidders if their bids reflect merely attempts to cover costs inflated by the present effects of prior disadvantage and discrimination, provides for handling grantee applications for administrative waiver of the 10% MBE requirement on a case-by-case basis if infeasibility is demonstrated by a showing that, despite affirmative efforts, such level of participation cannot be achieved without departing from the program's objectives. The program also provides an administrative mechanism to ensure that only bona fide MBE's are encompassed by the program, and to prevent unjust participation by minority firms whose access to public contracting opportunities is not impaired by the effects of prior discrimination.

Petitioners, several associations of construction contractors and subcontractors and a firm engaged in heating, ventilation, and air conditioning work, filed suit for declaratory and injunctive relief in Federal District Court, alleging that they had sustained economic injury due to enforcement of the MBE requirement and that the MBE provision on its face violated, *inter alia*, the Equal Protection Clause of the Fourteenth Amendment and the equal protection component of the Due Process Clause of the Fifth Amendment. The District Court upheld the validity of the MBE program, and the Court of Appeals affirmed.

Held: The judgment is affirmed. Pp. 456–492; 517–522.

584 F. 2d 600, affirmed.

MR. CHIEF JUSTICE BURGER, joined by MR. JUSTICE WHITE and MR. JUSTICE POWELL, concluded that the MBE provision of the 1977 Act, on its face, does not violate the Constitution. Pp. 456–492.

(a) Viewed against the legislative and administrative background of the 1977 Act, the legislative objectives of the MBE provision and of the administrative program thereunder were to ensure—without mandating the allocation of federal funds according to inflexible percentages solely based on race or ethnicity—that, to the extent federal funds were granted under the 1977 Act, grantees who elected to participate would not employ procurement practices that Congress had decided might result in perpetuation of the effects of prior discrimination which had impaired or foreclosed access by minority businesses to public contracting opportunities. Pp. 456–472.

(b) In considering the constitutionality of the MBE provision, it first must be determined whether the *objectives* of the legislation are within Congress' power. Pp. 472–480.

(i) The 1977 Act, as primarily an exercise of Congress' Spending Power under Art. I, § 8, cl. 1, "to provide for the . . . general Welfare," conditions receipt of federal moneys upon the receipt's compliance with federal statutory and administrative directives. Since the reach of the Spending Power is at least as broad as Congress' regulatory powers, if Congress, pursuant to its regulatory powers, could have achieved the objectives of the MBE program, then it may do so under the Spending Power. Pp. 473–475.

(ii) Insofar as the MBE program pertains to the actions of private prime contractors, including those not responsible for any violation of antidiscrimination laws, Congress could have achieved its objectives under the Commerce Clause. The legislative history shows that there was a rational basis for Congress to conclude that the subcontracting practices of prime contractors could perpetuate the prevailing impaired access by minority businesses to public contracting opportunities, and that this inequity has an effect on interstate commerce. Pp. 475–476.

(iii) Insofar as the MBE program pertains to the actions of state and local grantees, Congress could have achieved its objectives by use of its power under § 5 of the Fourteenth Amendment "to enforce, by appropriate legislation" the equal protection guarantee of that Amendment. Congress had abundant historical basis from which it could conclude that traditional procurement practices, when applied to minority businesses, could perpetuate the effects of prior discrimination, and that the prospective elimination of such barriers to minority-firm access to public contracting opportunities was appropriate to ensure that those businesses were not denied equal opportunity to participate in federal grants to state and local governments, which is one aspect of the equal protection of the laws. Cf., *e. g., Katzenbach* v. *Morgan,* 384 U. S. 641; *Oregon* v. *Mitchell,* 400 U. S. 112. Pp. 476–478.

(iv) Thus, the *objectives* of the MBE provision are within the scope of Congress' Spending Power. Cf. *Lau* v. *Nichols,* 414 U. S. 563. Pp. 479–480.

(c) Congress' use here of racial and ethnic criteria as a condition attached to a federal grant is a valid *means* to accomplish its constitutional objectives, and the MBE provision on its face does not violate the equal protection component of the Due Process Clause of the Fifth Amendment. Pp. 480–492.

(i) In the MBE program's remedial context, there is no requirement that Congress act in a wholly "color-blind" fashion. Cf., *e. g., Swann* v. *Charlotte-Mecklenberg Board of Education,* 402 U. S. 1; *McDaniel* v. *Barresi,* 402 U. S. 39; *North Carolina Board of Education* v. *Swann,* 402 U. S. 43. Pp. 482–484.

(ii) The MBE program is not constitutionally defective because it may disappoint the expectations of access to a portion of government contracting opportunities of nonminority firms who may themselves be innocent of any prior discriminatory actions. When effectuating a limited and properly tailored remedy to cure the effects of prior discrimination, such "a sharing of the burden" by innocent parties is not impermissible. *Franks* v. *Bowman Transportation Co.,* 424 U. S. 747, 777. Pp. 484–485.

(iii) Nor is the MBE program invalid as being underinclusive in that it limits its benefit to specified minority groups rather than extending its remedial objectives to all businesses whose access to government contracting is impaired by the effects of disadvantage or discrimination. Congress has not sought to give select minority groups a preferred standing in the construction industry, but has embarked on a remedial program to place them on a more equitable footing with respect to public contracting opportunities, and there has been no showing that Congress inadvertently effected an invidious discrimination by excluding from coverage an identifiable minority group that has been the victim of a degree of disadvantage and discrimination equal to or greater than that suffered by the groups encompassed by the MBE program. Pp. 485–486.

(iv) The contention that the MBE program, on its face, is overinclusive in that it bestows a benefit on businesses identified by racial or ethnic criteria which cannot be justified on the basis of competitive criteria or as a remedy for the present effects of identified prior discrimination, is also without merit. The MBE provision, with due account for its administrative program, provides a reasonable assurance that application of racial or ethnic criteria will be narrowly limited to accomplishing Congress' remedial objectives and that misapplications of the program will be promptly and adequately remedied administratively. In particular, the administrative program provides waiver and exemption procedures to identify and eliminate from participation MBE's who are not "bona fide," or who attempt to exploit the remedial aspects of the program by charging an unreasonable price not attributable to the present effects of past discrimination. Moreover, grantees may obtain a waiver if they demonstrate that their best efforts will not achieve or have not achieved the 10% target for minority firm participation within the limitations of the program's remedial objectives. The MBE provision may be viewed as a pilot project, appropriately limited in extent and duration and subject to reassessment and re-evaluation by the Congress prior to any extension or re-enactment. Pp. 486–489.

(d) In the continuing effort to achieve the goal of equality of economic opportunity, Congress has latitude to try new techniques such as the limited use of racial and ethnic criteria to accomplish remedial objectives, especially in programs where voluntary cooperation is induced by placing conditions on federal expenditures. When a program narrowly tailored by Congress to achieve its objectives comes under judicial review, it should be upheld if the courts are satisfied that the legislative objectives and projected administration of the program give reasonable assurance that the program will function within constitutional limitations. Pp. 490–492.

Mr. Justice Marshall, joined by Mr. Justice Brennan and Mr. Justice Blackmun, concurring in the judgment, concluded that the proper inquiry for determining the constitutionality of racial classifications that provide benefits to minorities for the purpose of remedying the present effects of past racial discrimination is whether the classifications serve important governmental objectives and are substantially related to achievement of those objectives, *University of California Regents* v. *Bakke,* 438 U. S. 265, 359 (opinion of Brennan, White, Marshall, and Blackmun, JJ., concurring in judgment in part and dissenting in part), and that, judged under this standard, the 10% minority set-aside provision of the 1977 Act is plainly constitutional, the racial classifications being substantially related to the achievement of the important and congressionally articulated goal of remedying the present effects of past racial discrimination. Pp. 517–521.

BURGER, C. J., announced the judgment of the Court and delivered an opinion, in which WHITE and POWELL, JJ., joined. POWELL, J., filed a concurring opinion, *post*, p. 495. MARSHALL, J., filed an opinion concurring in the judgment, in which BRENNAN and BLACKMUN, JJ., joined, *post*, p. 517. STEWART, J., filed a dissenting opinion, in which REHNQUIST, J., joined, *post*, p. 522. STEVENS, J., filed a dissenting opinion, *post*, p. 532.

Robert G. Benisch argued the cause for petitioners Fullilove et al. With him on the briefs was *Robert J. Fink. Robert J. Hickey* argued the cause for petitioner General Building Contractors of New York State, Inc., the New York State Building Chapter, Associated General Contractors of America, Inc. With him on the briefs was *Peter G. Kilgore.*

Assistant Attorney General Days argued the cause for respondents. With him on the brief for respondent Secretary of Commerce were *Solicitor General McCree, Deputy Solicitor General Wallace, Brian K. Landsberg, Jessica Dunsay Silver,* and *Vincent F. O'Rourke, Jr. Robert Abrams,* Attorney General of New York, *Shirley Adelson Siegel,* Solicitor General, and *Arnold D. Fleischer* and *Barbara E. Levy,* Assistant Attorneys General, filed a brief for respondent State of New York. *Allen G. Schwartz, James G. Greilsheimer, L. Kevin Sheridan,* and *Frances M. Morris* filed a brief for respondents City of New York et al.*

---

*Briefs of *amici curiae* urging reversal were filed by *Kenneth C. McGuiness, Douglas S. McDowell,* and *Daniel R. Levinson* for the Equal Employment Advisory Council; and by *Ronald A. Zumbrun* and *John H. Findley* for the Pacific Legal Foundation.

Briefs of *amici curiae* urging affirmance were filed by *Julian B. Wilkins* and *Jewel S. Lafontant* for Alpha Kappa Alpha Sorority, Inc.; by *E. Richard Larson, Burt Neuborne, Frank Askin,* and *Robert Sedler* for the American Civil Liberties Union et al.; by *Ronald J. Greene* for the American Savings & Loan League, Inc., et al.; by *Bill Lann Lee* for the Asian American Legal Defense and Education Fund, Inc.; by *John B. Jones, Jr., Norman Redlich, William L. Robinson, Richard T. Seymour, Norman J. Chachkin, Laurence S. Fordham, Henry P. Monaghan,* and

MR. CHIEF JUSTICE BURGER announced the judgment of the Court and delivered an opinion, in which MR. JUSTICE WHITE and MR. JUSTICE POWELL joined.

We granted certiorari to consider a facial constitutional challenge to a requirement in a congressional spending program that, absent an administrative waiver, 10% of the federal funds granted for local public works projects must be used by the state or local grantee to procure services or supplies from businesses owned and controlled by members of statutorily identified minority groups. 441 U. S. 960 (1979).

I

In May 1977, Congress enacted the Public Works Employment Act of 1977, Pub. L. 95–28, 91 Stat. 116, which amended the Local Public Works Capital Development and Investment Act of 1976, Pub. L. 94–369, 90 Stat. 999, 42 U. S. C. § 6701 *et seq.* The 1977 amendments authorized an additional $4 billion appropriation for federal grants to be made by the Secretary of Commerce, acting through the Economic Development Administration (EDA), to state and local governmental entities for use in local public works projects. Among the changes made was the addition of the provision that has

---

Robert D. Goldstein for the Lawyers' Committee for Civil Rights Under Law; by *Vilma S. Martinez, Morris J. Baller,* and *Joel G. Contreras* for the Mexican American/Hispanic Contractors and Truckers Association, Inc., et al.; by *Daniel T. Ingram, Jr.,* for the Minority Contractors Assistance Project, Inc.; by *Nathaniel R. Jones, J. Francis Pohlhaus,* and *John A. Fillion* for the National Association for the Advancement of Colored People et al.; by *Jack Greenberg, James M. Nabrit III, Eric Schnapper, Vernon E. Jordan, Jr.,* and *Robert L. Harris* for the NAACP Legal Defense and Educational Fund, Inc., et al.; and by *Robert T. Pickett* for the National Bar Association, Inc., et al.

Briefs of *amici curiae* were filed by *Arthur Kinoy* for the Affirmative Action Coordinating Center et al.; by *Robert A. Helman, Justin J. Finger, Jeffrey P. Sinensky,* and *Richard A. Weisz* for the Anti-Defamation League of B'nai B'rith; by *Walter R. Echo-Hawk* and *Robert S. Pelcyger* for the Minority Contractors Association, Inc.; and by *Bernard Parks* and *Lenwood A. Jackson* for the National Conference of Black Mayors, Inc.

become the focus of this litigation. Section 103 (f)(2) of the 1977 Act, referred to as the "minority business enterprise" or "MBE" provision, requires that: [1]

> "Except to the extent that the Secretary determines otherwise, no grant shall be made under this Act for any local public works project unless the applicant gives satisfactory assurance to the Secretary that at least 10 per centum of the amount of each grant shall be expended for minority business enterprises. For purposes of this paragraph, the term 'minority business enterprise' means a business at least 50 per centum of which is owned by minority group members or, in case of a publicly owned business, at least 51 per centum of the stock of which is owned by minority group members. For the purposes of the preceding sentence, minority group members are citizens of the United States who are Negroes, Spanish-speaking, Orientals, Indians, Eskimos, and Aleuts."

In late May 1977, the Secretary promulgated regulations governing administration of the grant program which were amended two months later.[2] In August 1977, the EDA issued guidelines supplementing the statute and regulations with respect to minority business participation in local public works grants,[3] and in October 1977, the EDA issued a technical bulletin promulgating detailed instructions and information to assist grantees and their contractors in meeting the 10% MBE requirement.[4]

---

[1] 91 Stat. 116, 42 U. S. C. § 6705 (f)(2) (1976 ed., Supp. II).

[2] 42 Fed. Reg. 27432 (1977), as amended by 42 Fed. Reg. 35822 (1977); 13 CFR Part 317 (1978).

[3] U. S. Dept. of Commerce, Economic Development Administration, Local Public Works Program, Round II, Guidelines For 10% Minority Business Participation In LPW Grants (1977) (hereinafter Guidelines); App. 156a–167a.

[4] U. S. Dept. of Commerce, Economic Development Administration, EDA Minority Business Enterprise (MBE) Technical Bulletin (Additional

On November 30, 1977, petitioners filed a complaint in the United States District Court for the Southern District of New York seeking declaratory and injunctive relief to enjoin enforcement of the MBE provision. Named as defendants were the Secretary of Commerce, as the program administrator, and the State and City of New York, as actual and potential project grantees. Petitioners are several associations of construction contractors and subcontractors, and a firm engaged in heating, ventilation, and air conditioning work. Their complaint alleged that they had sustained economic injury due to enforcement of the 10% MBE requirement and that the MBE provision on its face violated the Equal Protection Clause of the Fourteenth Amendment, the equal protection component of the Due Process Clause of the Fifth Amendment, and various statutory antidiscrimination provisions.[5]

After a hearing held the day the complaint was filed, the District Court denied a requested temporary restraining order and scheduled the matter for an expedited hearing on the merits. On December 19, 1977, the District Court issued a memorandum opinion upholding the validity of the MBE program and denying the injunctive relief sought. *Fullilove* v. *Kreps,* 443 F. Supp. 253 (1977).

The United States Court of Appeals for the Second Circuit affirmed, 584 F. 2d 600 (1978), holding that "even under the most exacting standard of review the MBE provision passes constitutional muster." *Id.,* at 603. Considered in the context of many years of governmental efforts to remedy past racial and ethnic discrimination, the court found it

---

Assistance and Information Available to Grantees and Their Contractors In Meeting The 10% MBE Requirement) (1977) (hereinafter Technical Bulletin); App. 129a–155a.

[5] 42 U. S. C. §§ 1981, 1983, 1985; Title VI, § 601 of the Civil Rights Act of 1964, 78 Stat. 252, 42 U. S. C. § 2000d; Title VII, § 701 *et seq.* of the Civil Rights Act of 1964, 78 Stat. 253, as amended, 42 U. S. C. § 2000e *et seq.*

"difficult to imagine" any purpose for the program other than to remedy such discrimination. *Id.*, at 605. In its view, a number of factors contributed to the legitimacy of the MBE provision, most significant of which was the narrowed focus and limited extent of the statutory and administrative program, in size, impact, and duration, *id.*, at 607–608; the court looked also to the holdings of other Courts of Appeals and District Courts that the MBE program was constitutional, *id.*, at 608–609.[6] It expressly rejected petitioners' contention that the 10% MBE requirement violated the equal protection guarantees of the Constitution.[7] *Id.*, at 609.

II

A

The MBE provision was enacted as part of the Public Works Employment Act of 1977, which made various amendments to Title I of the Local Public Works Capital Development and Investment Act of 1976. The 1976 Act was in-

---

[6] *Ohio Contractors Assn.* v. *Economic Development Administration,* 580 F. 2d 213 (CA6 1978); *Constructors Assn.* v. *Kreps,* 573 F. 2d 811 (CA3 1978); *Rhode Island Chapter, Associated General Contractors* v. *Kreps,* 450 F. Supp. 338 (RI 1978); *Associated General Contractors* v. *Secretary of Commerce,* No. 77–4218 (Kan. Feb. 9, 1978); *Carolinas Branch, Associated General Contractors* v. *Kreps,* 442 F. Supp. 392 (SC 1977); *Ohio Contractors Assn.* v. *Economic Development Administration,* 452 F. Supp. 1013 (SD Ohio 1977); *Montana Contractors' Assn.* v. *Secretary of Commerce,* 439 F. Supp. 1331 (Mont. 1977); *Florida East Coast Chapter* v. *Secretary of Commerce,* No. 77–8351 (SD Fla. Nov. 3, 1977); but see *Associated General Contractors* v. *Secretary of Commerce,* 441 F. Supp. 955 (CD Cal. 1977), vacated and remanded for consideration of mootness, 438 U. S. 909 (1978), on remand, 459 F. Supp. 766 (CD Cal.), vacated and remanded *sub nom. Armistead* v. *Associated General Contractors of California, post,* p. 908.

[7] Both the Court of Appeals and the District Court rejected petitioners' various statutory arguments without extended discussion. 584 F. 2d, at 608, n. 15; 443 F. Supp., at 262.

tended as a short-term measure to alleviate the problem of national unemployment and to stimulate the national economy by assisting state and local governments to build needed public facilities.[8] To accomplish these objectives, the Congress authorized the Secretary of Commerce, acting through the EDA, to make grants to state and local governments for construction, renovation, repair, or other improvement of local public works projects.[9] The 1976 Act placed a number of restrictions on project eligibility designed to assure that federal moneys were targeted to accomplish the legislative purposes.[10] It established criteria to determine grant priorities and to apportion federal funds among political jurisdictions.[11] Those criteria directed grant funds toward areas of high unemployment.[12] The statute authorized the appropriation of up to $2 billion for a period ending in September 1977; [13] this appropriation was soon consumed by grants made under the program.

Early in 1977, Congress began consideration of expanded appropriations and amendments to the grant program. Under administration of the 1976 appropriation, referred to as "Round I" of the local public works program, applicants seeking some $25 billion in grants had competed for the $2 billion in available funds; of nearly 25,000 applications, only some 2,000 were granted.[14] The results provoked widespread

---

[8] H. R. Rep. No. 94–1077, p. 2 (1976). The bill discussed in this Report was accepted by the Conference Committee in preference to the Senate version. S. Conf. Rep. No. 94–939, p. 1 (1976); H. R. Conf. Rep. No. 94–1260, p. 1 (1976).

[9] 90 Stat. 999, 42 U. S. C. § 6702.

[10] 90 Stat. 1000, 42 U. S. C. § 6705.

[11] 90 Stat. 1000, 42 U. S. C. § 6707.

[12] 90 Stat. 1001, 42 U. S. C. § 6707 (c).

[13] 90 Stat. 1002, 42 U. S. C. § 6710. The actual appropriation of the full amount authorized was made several weeks later. Pub. L. 94–447, 90 Stat. 1497.

[14] 123 Cong. Rec. 2136 (1977) (remarks of Sen. Randolph).

concern for the fairness of the allocation process.[15] Because
the 1977 Act would authorize the appropriation of an additional $4 billion to fund "Round II" of the grant program,[16]
the congressional hearings and debates concerning the amendments focused primarily on the politically sensitive problems
of priority and geographic distribution of grants under the
supplemental appropriation.[17] The result of this attention
was inclusion in the 1977 Act of provisions revising the allocation criteria of the 1976 legislation. Those provisions, however, retained the underlying objective to direct funds into
areas of high unemployment.[18] The 1977 Act also added new
restrictions on applicants seeking to qualify for federal
grants; [19] among these was the MBE provision.

The origin of the provision was an amendment to the House
version of the 1977 Act, H. R. 11, offered on the floor of the
House on February 23, 1977, by Representative Mitchell of
Maryland.[20] As offered, the amendment provided: [21]

> "Notwithstanding any other provision of law, no grant
> shall be made under this Act for any local public works
> project unless at least 10 per centum of the articles,
> materials, and supplies which will be used in such project
> are procured from minority business enterprises. For
> purposes of this paragraph, the term 'minority business

---

[15] See, e. g., Hearings on H. R. 11 and Related Bills before the Subcom-
mittee on Economic Development of the House Committee on Public
Works and Transportation, 95th Cong., 1st Sess. (1977); H. R. Rep.
No. 95–20 (1977); S. Rep. No. 95–38 (1977).

[16] 91 Stat. 119, 42 U. S. C. § 6710 (1976 ed., Supp. II). The actual
appropriation of the full authorized amount was made the same day.
Pub. L. 95–29, 91 Stat. 123.

[17] E. g., Hearings, supra n. 15; 123 Cong. Rec. 5290–5353 (1977); id.,
at 7097–7176.

[18] 91 Stat. 117, 42 U. S. C. § 6707 (1976 ed., Supp. II).

[19] 91 Stat. 116, 42 U. S. C. § 6705 (1976 ed., Supp. II).

[20] 123 Cong. Rec. 5097 (1977) (remarks of Rep. Mitchell).

[21] Id., at 5098.

enterprise' means a business at least 50 percent of which is owned by minority group members or, in case of publicly owned businesses, at least 51 percent of the stock of which is owned by minority group members. For the purposes of the preceding sentence, minority group members are citizens of the United States who are Negroes, Spanish-speaking, Orientals, Indians, Eskimos, and Aleuts."

The sponsor stated that the objective of the amendment was to direct funds into the minority business community, a sector of the economy sorely in need of economic stimulus but which, on the basis of past experience with Government procurement programs, could not be expected to benefit significantly from the public works program as then formulated.[22] He cited the marked statistical disparity that in fiscal year 1976 less than 1% of all federal procurement was concluded with minority business enterprises, although minorities comprised 15–18% of the population.[23] When the amendment was put forward during debate on H. R. 11,[24] Representative Mitchell reiterated the need to ensure that minority firms would obtain a fair opportunity to share in the benefits of this Government program.[25]

The amendment was put forward not as a new concept, but rather one building upon prior administrative practice.

---

[22] *Id.*, at 5097–5098.

[23] *Id.*, at 5098.

[24] *Id.*, at 5327. As reintroduced, the first sentence of the amendment was modified to provide:

"Notwithstanding any other provision of law, no grant shall be made under this Act for any local public works project unless at least 10 per centum of the dollar volume of each contract shall be set aside for minority business enterprise and, or, unless at least 10 per centum of the articles, materials, and supplies which will be used in such project are procured from minority business enterprises."

[25] *Id.*, at 5327–5328.

In his introductory remarks, the sponsor rested his proposal squarely on the ongoing program under § 8 (a) of the Small Business Act, Pub. L. 85–536, § 2, 72 Stat. 389, which, as will become evident, served as a model for the administrative program developed to enforce the MBE provision: [26]

> "The first point in opposition will be that you cannot have a set-aside. Well, Madam Chairman, we have been doing this for the last 10 years in Government. The 8–A set-aside under SBA has been tested in the courts more than 30 times and has been found to be legitimate and bona fide. We are doing it in this bill."

Although the proposed MBE provision on its face appeared mandatory, requiring compliance with the 10% minority participation requirement "[n]otwithstanding any other provision of law," its sponsor gave assurances that existing administrative practice would ensure flexibility in administration if, with respect to a particular project, compliance with the 10% requirement proved infeasible.[27] Representative Roe of New Jersey then suggested a change of language expressing the twin intentions (1) that the federal administrator would have discretion to waive the 10% requirement where its application was not feasible, and (2) that the grantee would be mandated to achieve at least 10% participation by minority businesses unless infeasibility was demonstrated.[28] He proposed as a substitute for the first sentence of the amendment the language that eventually was enacted: [29]

> "Except to the extent that the Secretary determines otherwise, no grant shall be made under this Act for any local public works project unless the applicant gives satisfactory assurance to the Secretary that at least 10 per-

---

[26] *Id.*, at 5327.
[27] *Id.*, at 5327–5328.
[28] *Id.*, at 5328 (remarks of Rep. Roe).
[29] *Ibid.*

cent of the amount of each grant shall be expended for minority business enterprises."

The sponsor fully accepted the suggested clarification because it retained the directive that the initial burden of compliance would fall on the grantee. That allocation of burden was necessary because, as he put it, "every agency of the Government has tried to figure out a way to avoid doing this very thing. Believe me, these bureaucracies can come up with 10,000 ways to avoid doing it." [30]

Other supporters of the MBE amendment echoed the sponsor's concern that a number of factors, difficult to isolate or quantify, seemed to impair access by minority businesses to public contracting opportunities. Representative Conyers of Michigan spoke of the frustration of the existing situation, in which, due to the intricacies of the bidding process and through no fault of their own, minority contractors and businessmen were unable to gain access to government contracting opportunities. [31]

Representative Biaggi of New York then spoke to the need for the amendment to "promote a sense of economic equality in this Nation." He expressed the view that without the amendment, "this legislation may be potentially inequitable to minority businesses and workers" in that it would perpetuate the historic practices that have precluded minority businesses from effective participation in public contracting opportunities. [32] The amendment was accepted by the House. [33]

Two weeks later, the Senate considered S. 427, its package of amendments to the Local Public Works Capital Development and Investment Act of 1976. At that time Senator Brooke of Massachusetts introduced an MBE amendment,

---

[30] *Id.,* at 5329 (remarks of Rep. Mitchell).
[31] *Id.,* at 5330 (remarks of Rep. Conyers).
[32] *Id.,* at 5331 (remarks of Rep. Biaggi).
[33] *Id.,* at 5332.

worded somewhat differently than the House version, but aimed at achieving the same objectives.[34] His statement in support of the 10% requirement reiterated and summarized the various expressions on the House side that the amendment was necessary to ensure that minority businesses were not deprived of access to the government contracting opportunities generated by the public works program.[35]

The Senate adopted the amendment without debate.[36] The Conference Committee, called to resolve differences between the House and Senate versions of the Public Works Employment Act of 1977, adopted the language approved by the House for the MBE provision.[37] The Conference Reports added only the comment: "This provision shall be dependent on the availability of minority business enterprises located in the project area." [38]

The device of a 10% MBE participation requirement, subject to administrative waiver, was thought to be required to assure minority business participation; otherwise it was thought that repetition of the prior experience could be ex-

---

[34] *Id.*, at 7155–7156 (remarks of Sen. Brooke). The first paragraph of Senator Brooke's formulation was identical to the version originally offered by Representative Mitchell, quoted in the text, *supra*, at 458–459. A second paragraph of Senator Brooke's amendment provided:

"This section shall not be interpreted to defund projects with less than 10 percent minority participation in areas with minority population of less than 5 percent. In that event, the correct level of minority participation will be predetermined by the Secretary in consultation with EDA and based upon its lists of qualified minority contractors and its solicitation of competitive bids from all minority firms on those lists." 123 Cong. Rec. 7156 (1977).

[35] *Ibid.*

[36] *Ibid.*

[37] S. Conf. Rep. No. 95–110, p. 11 (1977); H. R. Conf. Rep. No. 95–230, p. 11 (1977).

[38] *Ibid.* The Conference Committee bill was agreed to by the Senate, 123 Cong. Rec. 12941–12942 (1977), and by the House, *id.*, at 13242–13257, and was signed into law on May 13, 1977.

pected, with participation by minority business accounting for an inordinately small percentage of government contracting. The causes of this disparity were perceived as involving the longstanding existence and maintenance of barriers impairing access by minority enterprises to public contracting opportunities, or sometimes as involving more direct discrimination, but not as relating to lack—as Senator Brooke put it—"of capable and qualified minority enterprises who are ready and willing to work." [39] In the words of its sponsor, the MBE provision was "designed to begin to redress this grievance that has been extant for so long." [40]

B

The legislative objectives of the MBE provision must be considered against the background of ongoing efforts directed toward deliverance of the century-old promise of equality of economic opportunity. The sponsors of the MBE provision in the House and the Senate expressly linked the provision to the existing administrative programs promoting minority opportunity in government procurement, particularly those related to § 8 (a) of the Small Business Act of 1953.[41] Section 8 (a) delegates to the Small Business Administration (SBA) an authority and an obligation "whenever it determines such action is necessary" to enter into contracts with any procurement agency of the Federal Government to furnish required goods or services, and, in turn, to enter into subcontracts with small businesses for the performance of such contracts. This authority lay dormant for a decade. Commencing in 1968, however, the SBA was directed by the President [42] to develop a program pursuant to its § 8 (a) authority to assist small

---

[39] *Id.,* at 7156 (remarks of Sen. Brooke).

[40] *Id.,* at 5330 (remarks of Rep. Mitchell).

[41] *Id.,* at 5327; *id.,* at 7156 (remarks of Sen. Brooke).

[42] Exec. Order No. 11375, 3 CFR 684 (1966–1970 Comp.); Exec. Order No. 11518, 3 CFR 907 (1966–1970 Comp.).

business concerns owned and controlled by "socially or economically disadvantaged" persons to achieve a competitive
position in the economy.

At the time the MBE provision was enacted, the regulations governing the § 8 (a) program defined "social or economic disadvantage" as follows: [43]

> "An applicant concern must be owned and controlled
> by one or more persons who have been deprived of the
> opportunity to develop and maintain a competitive posi-
> tion in the economy because of social or economic disad-
> vantage. Such disadvantage may arise from cultural,
> social, chronic economic circumstances or background, or
> other similar cause. Such persons include, but are not
> limited to, black Americans, American Indians, Spanish-
> Americans, oriental Americans, Eskimos, and Aleuts. . . ."

The guidelines accompanying these regulations provided that
a minority business could not be maintained in the program,
even when owned and controlled by members of the identified
minority groups, if it appeared that the business had not been
deprived of the opportunity to develop and maintain a competitive position in the economy because of social or economic
disadvantage.[44]

---

[43] 13 CFR § 124.8–1 (c)(1) (1977).

[44] U. S. Small Business Administration, Office of Business Development,
Section 8 (a) Program, Standard Operating Procedure 15–16 (1976); see
H. R. Rep. No. 94–468, p. 30 (1975) ("[T]he relevant rules and regulations require such applicant to identify with the disadvantages of his or
her racial group generally, and that such disadvantages must have personally affected the applicant's ability to enter into the mainstream of the
business system"); U. S. Small Business Administration, Office of Minority
Small Business and Capital Ownership Development, MSB & COD Programs, Standard Operating Procedure 20 (1979) ("The social disadvantage
of individuals, including those within the above-named [racial and ethnic]
groups, shall be determined by SBA on a case-by-case basis. Membership alone in any group is not conclusive that an individual is socially
disadvantaged").

As the Congress began consideration of the Public Works Employment Act of 1977, the House Committee on Small Business issued a lengthy Report summarizing its activities, including its evaluation of the ongoing § 8 (a) program.[45] One chapter of the Report, entitled "Minority Enterprises and Allied Problems of Small Business," summarized a 1975 Committee Report of the same title dealing with this subject matter.[46] The original Report, prepared by the House Subcommittee on SBA Oversight and Minority Enterprise, observed: [47]

> "The subcommittee is acutely aware that the economic policies of this Nation must function within and be guided by our constitutional system which guarantees 'equal protection of the laws.' *The effects of past inequities stemming from racial prejudice have not remained in the past. The Congress has recognized the reality that past discriminatory practices have, to some degree, adversely affected our present economic system.*

> "While minority persons comprise about 16 percent of the Nation's population, of the 13 million businesses in the United States, only 382,000, or approximately 3.0 percent, are owned by minority individuals. The most recent data from the Department of Commerce also indicates that the gross receipts of all businesses in this country totals about $2,540.8 billion, and of this amount only $16.6 billion, or about 0.65 percent was realized by minority business concerns.

> "These statistics are not the result of random chance. The presumption must be made that past discriminatory systems have resulted in present economic inequities. In order to right this situation, the Congress has formulated certain remedial programs designed to uplift those socially

---

[45] H. R. Rep. No. 94–1791 (1977).
[46] *Id.,* at 124–149.
[47] H. R. Rep. No. 94–468, pp. 1–2 (1975) (emphasis added).

or economically disadvantaged persons to a level where they may effectively participate in the business mainstream of our economy.*

"*For the purposes of this report the term 'minority' shall include only such minority individuals as are considered to be economically or socially disadvantaged." [48]

The 1975 Report gave particular attention to the § 8 (a) program, expressing disappointment with its limited effectiveness.[49] With specific reference to Government construction contracting, the Report concluded, "there are substantial § 8 (a) opportunities in the area of Federal construction, but . . . the practices of some agencies preclude the realization of this potential." [50] The Subcommittee took "full notice . . . as evidence for its consideration" of reports submitted to the Congress by the General Accounting Office and by the U. S. Commission on Civil Rights, which reflected a similar dissatisfaction with the effectiveness of the § 8 (a) program.[51] The

---

[48] Another chapter of the 1977 Report of the House Committee on Small Business summarized a review of the SBA's Security Bond Guarantee Program, making specific reference to minority business participation in the construction industry:

"The very basic problem disclosed by the testimony is that, over the years, there has developed a business system which has traditionally excluded measurable minority participation. In the past more than the present, this system of conducting business transactions overtly precluded minority input. Currently, we more often encounter a business system which is racially neutral on its face, but because of past overt social and economic discrimination is presently operating, in effect, to perpetuate these past inequities. Minorities, until recently, have not participated to any measurable extent, in our total business system generally, or in the construction industry, in particular." H. R. Rep. No. 94–1791, p. 182 (1977), summarizing H. R. Rep. No. 94–840, p. 17 (1976).

[49] H. R. Rep. No. 94–468, pp. 28–30 (1975).

[50] Id., at 29.

[51] Id., at 11; U. S. General Accounting Office, Questionable Effectiveness of the § 8 (a) Procurement Program, GGD–75–57 (1975); U. S. Comm'n on Civil Rights, Minorities and Women as Government Contractors (May 1975).

Civil Rights Commission report discussed at some length the barriers encountered by minority businesses in gaining access to government contracting opportunities at the federal, state, and local levels. [52] Among the major difficulties confronting minority businesses were deficiencies in working capital, inability to meet bonding requirements, disabilities caused by an inadequate "track record," lack of awareness of bidding opportunities, unfamiliarity with bidding procedures, preselection before the formal advertising process, and the exercise of discretion by government procurement officers to disfavor minority businesses.[53]

The Subcommittee Report also gave consideration to the operations of the Office of Minority Business Enterprise, an agency of the Department of Commerce organized pursuant to Executive Orders [54] to formulate and coordinate federal efforts to assist the development of minority businesses. The Report concluded that OMBE efforts were "totally inadequate" to achieve its policy of increasing opportunities for subcontracting by minority businesses on public contracts. OMBE efforts were hampered by a "glaring lack of specific objectives which each prime contractor should be required to achieve," by a "lack of enforcement provisions," and by a "lack of any meaningful monitoring system." [55]

Against this backdrop of legislative and administrative programs, it is inconceivable that Members of both Houses were not fully aware of the objectives of the MBE provision and of the reasons prompting its enactment.

---

[52] Id., at 16–28, 86–88.

[53] Ibid.

[54] Exec. Order No. 11458, 3 CFR 779 (1966–1970 Comp.); Exec. Order No. 11625, 3 CFR 616 (1971–1975 Comp.).

[55] H. R. Rep. No. 94–468, p. 32 (1975). For other congressional observations with respect to the effect of past discrimination on current business opportunities for minorities, see, e. g., H. R. Rep. No. 92–1615, p. 3 (1972); H. R. Rep. No. 95–949, p. 8 (1978); S. Rep. No. 95–1070, pp. 14–15 (1978); S. Rep. No. 96–31, pp. 107, 123–124 (1979); see also, e. g., H. R. Doc. No. 92–169, p. 4 (1971); H. R. Doc. No. 92–194, p. 1 (1972).

C

Although the statutory MBE provision itself outlines only the bare bones of the federal program, it makes a number of critical determinations: the decision to initiate a limited racial and ethnic preference; the specification of a minimum level for minority business participation; the identification of the minority groups that are to be encompassed by the program; and the provision for an administrative waiver where application of the program is not feasible. Congress relied on the administrative agency to flesh out this skeleton, pursuant to delegated rulemaking authority, and to develop an administrative operation consistent with legislative intentions and objectives.

As required by the Public Works Employment Act of 1977, the Secretary of Commerce promulgated regulations to set into motion "Round II" of the federal grant program.[56] The regulations require that construction projects funded under the legislation must be performed under contracts awarded by competitive bidding, unless the federal administrator has made a determination that in the circumstances relating to a particular project some other method is in the public interest. Where competitive bidding is employed, the regulations echo the statute's requirement that contracts are to be awarded on the basis of the "lowest responsive bid submitted by a bidder meeting established criteria of responsibility," and they also restate the MBE requirement.[57]

EDA also has published guidelines devoted entirely to the administration of the MBE provision. The guidelines outline the obligations of the grantee to seek out all available, qualified, bona fide MBE's, to provide technical assistance as needed, to lower or waive bonding requirements where

---

[56] 91 Stat. 117, 42 U. S. C. § 6706 (1976 ed., Supp. II); 13 CFR Part 317 (1978).

[57] 91 Stat. 116, 42 U. S. C. § 6705 (e) (1) (1976 ed., Supp. II); 13 CFR § 317.19 (1978).

feasible, to solicit the aid of the Office of Minority Business Enterprise, the SBA, or other sources for assisting MBE's in obtaining required working capital, and to give guidance through the intricacies of the bidding process.[58]

EDA regulations contemplate that, as anticipated by Congress, most local public works projects will entail the award of a predominant prime contract, with the prime contractor assuming the above grantee obligations for fulfilling the 10% MBE requirement.[59] The EDA guidelines specify that when prime contractors are selected through competitive bidding, bids for the prime contract "shall be considered by the Grantee to be responsive only if at least 10 percent of the contract funds are to be expended for MBE's."[60] The administrative program envisions that competitive incentive will motivate aspirant prime contractors to perform their obligations under the MBE provision so as to qualify as "responsive" bidders. And, since the contract is to be awarded to the lowest responsive bidder, the same incentive is expected to motivate prime contractors to seek out the most competitive of the available, qualified, bona fide minority firms. This too is consistent with the legislative intention.[61]

The EDA guidelines also outline the projected administration of applications for waiver of the 10% MBE requirement, which may be sought by the grantee either before or during the bidding process.[62] The Technical Bulletin issued by EDA discusses in greater detail the processing of waiver requests, clarifying certain issues left open by the guidelines. It specifies that waivers may be total or partial, depending on

---

[58] Guidelines 2–7; App. 157a–160a. The relevant portions of the Guidelines are set out in the Appendix to this opinion, ¶ 1.

[59] Guidelines 2; App. 157a; see 123 Cong. Rec. 5327–5328 (1977) (remarks of Rep. Mitchell and Rep. Roe).

[60] Guidelines 8; App. 161a.

[61] See 123 Cong. Rec. 5327–5328 (1977) (remarks of Rep. Mitchell and Rep. Roe).

[62] Guidelines 13–16; App. 165a–167a. The relevant portions of the Guidelines are set out in the Appendix to this opinion, ¶ 2.

the circumstances,[63] and it illustrates the projected operation of the waiver procedure by posing hypothetical questions with projected administrative responses. One such hypothetical is of particular interest, for it indicates the limitations on the scope of the racial or ethnic preference contemplated by the federal program when a grantee or its prime contractor is confronted with an available, qualified, bona fide minority business enterprise who is not the lowest competitive bidder. The hypothetical provides: [64]

> "*Question:* Should a request for waiver of the 10% requirement based on an unreasonable price asked by an MBE ever be granted?
>
> "*Answer:* It is possible to imagine situations where an MBE might ask a price for its product or services that is unreasonable and where, therefore, a waiver is justified. However, before a waiver request will be honored, the following determinations will be made:
>
> "a) The MBE's quote is unreasonably priced. This determination should be based on the nature of the product or service of the subcontractor, the geographic location of the site and of the subcontractor, prices of similar products or services in the relevant market area, and general business conditions in the market area. Furthermore, a subcontractor's price should not be considered unreasonable if he is merely trying to cover his costs because the price results from disadvantage which affects the MBE's cost of doing business or results from discrimination.
>
> "b) The contractor has contacted other MBEs and has no meaningful choice but to accept an unreasonably high price."

This announced policy makes clear the administrative understanding that a waiver or partial waiver is justified (and will

[63] Technical Bulletin 5; App. 136a.
[64] Technical Bulletin 9–10; App. 143a.

be granted) to avoid subcontracting with a minority business enterprise at an "unreasonable" price, *i. e.*, a price above competitive levels which cannot be attributed to the minority firm's attempt to cover costs inflated by the present effects of disadvantage or discrimination.

This administrative approach is consistent with the legislative intention. It will be recalled that in the Report of the House Subcommittee on SBA Oversight and Minority Enterprise the Subcommittee took special care to note that when using the term "minority" it intended to include "only such minority individuals as are considered to be economically or socially disadvantaged." [65] The Subcommittee also was cognizant of existing administrative regulations designed to ensure that firms maintained on the lists of bona fide minority business enterprises be those whose competitive position is impaired by the effects of disadvantage and discrimination. In its Report, the Subcommittee expressed its intention that these criteria continue to govern administration of the SBA's § 8 (a) program.[66] The sponsors of the MBE provision, in their reliance on prior administrative practice, intended that the term "minority business enterprise" would be given that same limited application; this even found expression in the legislative debates, where Representative Roe made the point: [67]

> "[W]hen we are talking about companies held by minority groups . . . [c]ertainly people of a variety of backgrounds are included in that. That is not really a measurement. They are talking about people in the minority and deprived."

The EDA Technical Bulletin provides other elaboration of the MBE provision. It clarifies the definition of "minority

---

[65] Text accompanying n. 48, *supra*.
[66] H. R. Rep. No. 94–468, p. 30 (1975).
[67] 123 Cong. Rec. 5330 (1977) (remarks of Rep. Roe).

group members." [68]   It also indicates EDA's intention "to
allow credit for utilization of MBEs only for those contracts
in which involvement constitutes a basis for strengthening
the long-term and continuing participation of the MBE in the
construction and related industries." [69]   Finally, the Bulletin
outlines a procedure for the processing of complaints of
"unjust participation by an enterprise or individuals in the
MBE program," or of improper administration of the MBE
requirement.[70]

III

When we are required to pass on the constitutionality
of an Act of Congress, we assume "the gravest and most
delicate duty that this Court is called on to perform."
Blodgett v. *Holden,* 275 U. S. 142, 148 (1927) (opinion of
Holmes, J.).   A program that employs racial or ethnic criteria, even in a remedial context, calls for close examination;
yet we are bound to approach our task with appropriate
deference to the Congress, a co-equal branch charged by
the Constitution with the power to "provide for the . . .
general Welfare of the United States" and "to enforce, by
appropriate legislation," the equal protection guarantees of
the Fourteenth Amendment.   Art. I, § 8, cl. 1; Amdt. 14,
§ 5.   In *Columbia Broadcasting System, Inc.* v. *Democratic
National Committee,* 412 U. S. 94, 102 (1973), we accorded
"great weight to the decisions of Congress" even though
the legislation implicated fundamental constitutional rights
guaranteed by the First Amendment.   The rule is not different when a congressional program raises equal protection
concerns.   See, *e. g., Cleland* v. *National College of Business,*
435 U. S. 213 (1978); *Mathews* v. *De Castro,* 429 U. S. 181
(1976).

---

[68] Technical Bulletin 1; App. 131a–132a.   These definitions are set out
in the Appendix to this opinion, ¶ 3.

[69] Technical Bulletin 3; App. 135a.

[70] Technical Bulletin 19; App. 155a.   The relevant portions of the Technical Bulletin are set out in the Appendix to this opinion, ¶ 4.

Here we pass, not on a choice made by a single judge or a school board, but on a considered decision of the Congress and the President. However, in no sense does that render it immune from judicial scrutiny, and it "is not to say we 'defer' to the judgment of the Congress . . . on a constitutional question," or that we would hesitate to invoke the Constitution should we determine that Congress has overstepped the bounds of its constitutional power. *Columbia Broadcasting, supra,* at 103.

The clear objective of the MBE provision is disclosed by our necessarily extended review of its legislative and administrative background. The program was designed to ensure that, to the extent federal funds were granted under the Public Works Employment Act of 1977, grantees who elect to participate would not employ procurement practices that Congress had decided might result in perpetuation of the effects of prior discrimination which had impaired or foreclosed access by minority businesses to public contracting opportunities. The MBE program does not mandate the allocation of federal funds according to inflexible percentages solely based on race or ethnicity.

Our analysis proceeds in two steps. At the outset, we must inquire whether the *objectives* of this legislation are within the power of Congress. If so, we must go on to decide whether the limited use of racial and ethnic criteria, in the context presented, is a constitutionally permissible *means* for achieving the congressional objectives and does not violate the equal protection component of the Due Process Clause of the Fifth Amendment.

A

(1)

In enacting the MBE provision, it is clear that Congress employed an amalgam of its specifically delegated powers. The Public Works Employment Act of 1977, by its very nature, is primarily an exercise of the Spending Power. U. S.

Const., Art. I, § 8, cl. 1. This Court has recognized that the power to "provide for the . . . general Welfare" is an independent grant of legislative authority, distinct from other broad congressional powers. *Buckley* v. *Valeo,* 424 U. S. 1, 90–91 (1976); *United States* v. *Butler,* 297 U. S. 1, 65–66 (1936). Congress has frequently employed the Spending Power to further broad policy objectives by conditioning receipt of federal moneys upon compliance by the recipient with federal statutory and administrative directives. This Court has repeatedly upheld against constitutional challenge the use of this technique to induce governments and private parties to cooperate voluntarily with federal policy. *E. g., California Bankers Assn.* v. *Shultz,* 416 U. S. 21 (1974); *Lau* v. *Nichols,* 414 U. S. 563 (1974); *Oklahoma* v. *CSC,* 330 U. S. 127 (1947); *Helvering* v. *Davis,* 301 U. S. 619 (1937); *Steward Machine Co.* v. *Davis,* 301 U. S. 548 (1937).

The MBE program is structured within this familiar legislative pattern. The program conditions receipt of public works grants upon agreement by the state or local governmental grantee that at least 10% of the federal funds will be devoted to contracts with minority businesses, to the extent this can be accomplished by overcoming barriers to access and by awarding contracts to bona fide MBE's. It is further conditioned to require that MBE bids on these contracts are competitively priced, or might have been competitively priced but for the present effects of prior discrimination. Admittedly, the problems of administering this program with respect to these conditions may be formidable. Although the primary responsibility for ensuring minority participation falls upon the grantee, when the procurement practices of the grantee involve the award of a prime contract to a general or prime contractor, the obligations to assure minority participation devolve upon the private contracting party; this is a contractual condition of eligibility for award of the prime contract.

Here we need not explore the outermost limitations on the objectives attainable through such an application of the Spending Power. The reach of the Spending Power, within its sphere, is at least as broad as the regulatory powers of Congress. If, pursuant to its regulatory powers, Congress could have achieved the objectives of the MBE program, then it may do so under the Spending Power. And we have no difficulty perceiving a basis for accomplishing the objectives of the MBE program through the Commerce Power insofar as the program objectives pertain to the action of private contracting parties, and through the power to enforce the equal protection guarantees of the Fourteenth Amendment insofar as the program objectives pertain to the action of state and local grantees.

(2)

We turn first to the Commerce Power. U. S. Const., Art. I, § 8, cl. 3. Had Congress chosen to do so, it could have drawn on the Commerce Clause to regulate the practices of prime contractors on federally funded public works projects. *Katzenbach* v. *McClung,* 379 U. S. 294 (1964); *Heart of Atlanta Motel, Inc.* v. *United States,* 379 U. S. 241 (1964). The legislative history of the MBE provision shows that there was a rational basis for Congress to conclude that the subcontracting practices of prime contractors could perpetuate the prevailing impaired access by minority businesses to public contracting opportunities, and that this inequity has an effect on interstate commerce. Thus Congress could take necessary and proper action to remedy the situation. *Ibid.*

It is not necessary that these prime contractors be shown responsible for any violation of antidiscrimination laws. Our cases dealing with application of Title VII of the Civil Rights Act of 1964, 78 Stat. 253, as amended, express no doubt of the congressional authority to prohibit practices "challenged as perpetuating the effects of [not unlawful] discrimination occurring prior to the effective date of the Act." *Franks* v.

Bowman Transportation Co., 424 U. S. 747, 761 (1976); see
California Brewers Assn. v. *Bryant*, 444 U. S. 598 (1980);
Teamsters v. *United States*, 431 U. S. 324 (1977); *Albemarle
Paper Co.* v. *Moody*, 422 U. S. 405 (1975); *Griggs* v. *Duke
Power Co.*, 401 U. S. 424 (1971). Insofar as the MBE pro-
gram pertains to the actions of private prime contractors, the
Congress could have achieved its objectives under the Com-
merce Clause. We conclude that in this respect the objec-
tives of the MBE provision are within the scope of the
Spending Power.

(3)

In certain contexts, there are limitations on the reach of
the Commerce Power to regulate the actions of state and
local governments. *National League of Cities* v. *Usery*, 426
U. S. 833 (1976). To avoid such complications, we look to
§ 5 of the Fourteenth Amendment for the power to regulate
the procurement practices of state and local grantees of federal funds. *Fitzpatrick* v. *Bitzer*, 427 U. S. 445 (1976). A
review of our cases persuades us that the objectives of the
MBE program are within the power of Congress under § 5
"to enforce, by appropriate legislation," the equal protection
guarantees of the Fourteenth Amendment.

In *Katzenbach* v. *Morgan*, 384 U. S. 641 (1966), we equated
the scope of this authority with the broad powers expressed
in the Necessary and Proper Clause, U. S. Const., Art. I, § 8,
cl. 18. "Correctly viewed, § 5 is a positive grant of legislative
power authorizing Congress to exercise its discretion in determining whether and what legislation is needed to secure
the guarantees of the Fourteenth Amendment." 384 U. S.,
at 651. In *Katzenbach*, the Court upheld § 4 (e) of the Voting Rights Act of 1965, 79 Stat. 439, 42 U. S. C. § 1973b (e),
which prohibited application of state English-language literacy requirements to otherwise qualified voters who had completed the sixth grade in an accredited American school in

which a language other than English was the predominant medium of instruction. To uphold this exercise of congressional authority, the Court found no prerequisite that application of a literacy requirement violate the Equal Protection Clause. 384 U. S., at 648–649. It was enough that the Court could perceive a basis upon which Congress could reasonably predicate a judgment that application of literacy qualifications within the compass of § 4 (e) would discriminate in terms of access to the ballot and consequently in terms of access to the provision or administration of governmental programs. *Id.*, at 652–653.

Four years later, in *Oregon* v. *Mitchell*, 400 U. S. 112 (1970), we upheld § 201 of the Voting Rights Act Amendments of 1970, 84 Stat. 315, which imposed a 5-year nationwide prohibition on the use of various · voter-qualification tests and devices in federal, state, and local elections. The Court was unanimous, albeit in separate opinions, in concluding that Congress was within its authority to prohibit the use of such voter qualifications; Congress could reasonably determine that its legislation was an appropriate method of attacking the perpetuation of prior purposeful discrimination, even though the use of these tests or devices might have discriminatory effects only. See *City of Rome* v. *United States*, 446 U. S. 156, 176–177 (1980). Our cases reviewing the parallel power of Congress to enforce the provisions of the Fifteenth Amendment, U. S. Const., Amdt. 15, § 2, confirm that congressional authority extends beyond the prohibition of purposeful discrimination to encompass state action that has discriminatory impact perpetuating the effects of past discrimination. *South Carolina* v. *Katzenbach*, 383 U. S. 301 (1966); cf. *City of Rome, supra.*

With respect to the MBE provision, Congress had abundant evidence from which it could conclude that minority businesses have been denied effective participation in public contracting opportunities by procurement practices that perpetuated the effects of prior discrimination. Congress, of course, may legislate without compiling the kind of "record" appropriate with respect to judicial or administrative proceedings. Congress had before it, among other data, evidence of a long history of marked disparity in the percentage of public contracts awarded to minority business enterprises. This disparity was considered to result not from any lack of capable and qualified minority businesses, but from the existence and maintenance of barriers to competitive access which had their roots in racial and ethnic discrimination, and which continue today, even absent any intentional discrimination or other unlawful conduct. Although much of this history related to the experience of minority businesses in the area of federal procurement, there was direct evidence before the Congress that this pattern of disadvantage and discrimination existed with respect to state and local construction contracting as well. In relation to the MBE provision, Congress acted within its competence to determine that the problem was national in scope.

Although the Act recites no preambulary "findings" on the subject, we are satisfied that Congress had abundant historical basis from which it could conclude that traditional procurement practices, when applied to minority businesses, could perpetuate the effects of prior discrimination. Accordingly, Congress reasonably determined that the prospective elimination of these barriers to minority firm access to public contracting opportunities generated by the 1977 Act was appropriate to ensure that those businesses were not denied equal opportunity to participate in federal grants to state and local governments, which is one aspect of the equal protection of the laws. Insofar as the MBE program pertains to the actions of state and local grantees, Congress could have achieved its objectives by use of its power under § 5 of the Fourteenth Amendment. We conclude that in this respect the objectives of the MBE provision are within the scope of the Spending Power.

(4)

There are relevant similarities between the MBE program and the federal spending program reviewed in *Lau* v. *Nichols*, 414 U. S. 563 (1974). In *Lau*, a language barrier "effectively foreclosed" non-English-speaking Chinese pupils from access to the educational opportunities offered by the San Francisco public school system. *Id.*, at 564–566. It had not been shown that this had resulted from any discrimination, purposeful or otherwise, or from other unlawful acts. Nevertheless, we upheld the constitutionality of a federal regulation applicable to public school systems receiving federal funds that prohibited the utilization of "criteria or methods of administration *which have the effect* . . . of defeating or substantially impairing accomplishment of the objectives of the [educational] program as respect individuals of a particular race, color, or national origin." *Id.*, at 568 (emphasis added). Moreover, we upheld application to the San Francisco school system, as a recipient of federal funds, of a requirement that "[w]here inability to speak and understand the English language excludes national origin-minority group children from effective participation in the educational program offered by a school district, the district must take affirmative steps to rectify the language deficiency in order to open its instructional program to these students." *Ibid.*

It is true that the MBE provision differs from the program approved in *Lau* in that the MBE program directly employs racial and ethnic criteria as a means to accomplish congressional objectives; however, these objectives are essentially the same as those approved in *Lau*. Our holding in *Lau* is instructive on the exercise of congressional authority by way of the MBE provision. The MBE program, like the federal regulations reviewed in *Lau*, primarily regulates state action in the use of federal funds voluntarily sought and accepted by the grantees subject to statutory and administrative conditions. The MBE participation requirement is directed at the utilization of criteria, methods, or practices thought by Congress to have the effect of defeating, or substantially impairing, access by the minority business community to public funds made available by congressional appropriations.

B

We now turn to the question whether, as a *means* to accomplish these plainly constitutional objectives, Congress may use racial and ethnic criteria, in this limited way, as a condition attached to a federal grant. We are mindful that "[i]n no matter should we pay more deference to the opinion of Congress than in its choice of instrumentalities to perform a function that is within its power," *National Mutual Insurance Co.* v. *Tidewater Transfer Co.*, 337 U. S. 582, 603 (1949) (opinion of Jackson, J.). However, Congress may employ racial or ethnic classifications in exercising its Spending or other legislative powers only if those classifications do not violate the equal protection component of the Due Process Clause of the Fifth Amendment. We recognize the need for careful judicial evaluation to assure that any congressional program that employs racial or ethnic criteria to accomplish the objective of remedying the present effects of past discrimination is narrowly tailored to the achievement of that goal.

Again, we stress the limited scope of our inquiry. Here we are not dealing with a remedial decree of a court but with the legislative authority of Congress. Furthermore, petitioners have challenged the constitutionality of the MBE provision on its face; they have not sought damages or other specific relief for injury allegedly flowing from specific applications of the program; nor have they attempted to show that as applied in identified situations the MBE provision violated the constitutional or statutory rights of any party to this case.[71] In

---

[71] In their complaint, in order to establish standing to challenge the validity of the program, petitioners alleged as "[s]pecific examples" of economic injury three instances where one of their number assertedly

these circumstances, given a reasonable construction and in light of its projected administration, if we find the MBE program on its face to be free of constitutional defects, it must be upheld as within congressional power. *Parker* v. *Levy*, 417 U. S. 733, 760 (1974); *Fortson* v. *Dorsey*, 379 U. S. 433, 438–439 (1965); *Aptheker* v. *Secretary of State*, 378 U. S. 500, 515 (1964); see *United States* v. *Raines*, 362 U. S. 17, 20–24 (1960).

Our review of the regulations and guidelines governing administration of the MBE provision reveals that Congress enacted the program as a strictly remedial measure; moreover, it is a remedy that functions prospectively, in the manner of an injunctive decree. Pursuant to the administrative program, grantees and their prime contractors are required to seek out all available, qualified, bona fide MBE's; they are required to provide technical assistance as needed, to lower or waive bonding requirements where feasible, to solicit the aid of the Office of Minority Business Enterprise, the SBA, or other sources for assisting MBE's to obtain required working capital, and to give guidance through the intricacies of the bidding process. *Supra*, at 468–469. The program assumes that grantees who undertake these efforts in good faith will obtain at least 10% participation by minority business enterprises. It is recognized that, to achieve this target, contracts will be awarded to available, qualified, bona fide MBE's even though they are not the lowest competitive bidders, so long as their higher bids, when challenged, are found to reflect merely attempts to cover costs inflated by the present effects of prior disadvantage and discrimination. *Supra*, at 470–471. There is available to the grantee a provision authorized by Congress for administrative waiver on

would have been awarded a public works contract but for enforcement of the MBE provision. Petitioners requested only declaratory and injunctive relief against continued enforcement of the MBE provision; they did not seek any remedy for these specific instances of assertedly unlawful discrimination. App. 12a–13a, 17a–19a.

a case-by-case basis should there be a demonstration that,
despite affirmative efforts, this level of participation cannot
be achieved without departing from the objectives of the
program. *Supra,* at 469–470. There is also an administrative
mechanism, including a complaint procedure, to ensure that
only bona fide MBE's are encompassed by the remedial program, and to prevent unjust participation in the program by
those minority firms whose access to public contracting opportunities is not impaired by the effects of prior discrimination. *Supra,* at 471–472.

(1)

As a threshold matter, we reject the contention that in
the remedial context the Congress must act in a wholly
"color-blind" fashion. In *Swann* v. *Charlotte-Mecklenburg
Board of Education,* 402 U. S. 1, 18–21 (1971), we rejected
this argument in considering a court-formulated school desegregation remedy on the basis that examination of the racial
composition of student bodies was an unavoidable starting
point and that racially based attendance assignments were
permissible so long as no absolute racial balance of each
school was required. In *McDaniel* v. *Barresi,* 402 U. S. 39,
41 (1971), citing *Swann,* we observed: "In this remedial
process, steps will almost invariably require that students
be assigned 'differently because of their race.' Any other
approach would freeze the status quo that is the very target
of all desegregation processes." (Citations omitted.) And
in *North Carolina Board of Education* v. *Swann,* 402 U. S. 43
(1971), we invalidated a state law that absolutely forbade
assignment of any student on account of race because it foreclosed implementation of desegregation plans that were designed to remedy constitutional violations. We held that
"[j]ust as the race of students must be considered in determining whether a constitutional violation has occurred, so also
must race be considered in formulating a remedy." *Id.,* at
46.

In these school desegregation cases we dealt with the authority of a federal court to formulate a remedy for unconstitutional racial discrimination. However, the authority of a court to incorporate racial criteria into a remedial decree also extends to statutory violations. Where federal antidiscrimination laws have been violated, an equitable remedy may in the appropriate case include a racial or ethnic factor. *Franks* v. *Bowman Transportation Co.,* 424 U. S. 747 (1976); see *Teamsters* v. *United States,* 431 U. S. 324 (1977); *Albemarle Paper Co.* v. *Moody,* 422 U. S. 405 (1975). In another setting, we have held that a state may employ racial criteria that are reasonably necessary to assure compliance with federal voting rights legislation, even though the state action does not entail the remedy of a constitutional violation. *United Jewish Organizations of Williamsburgh, Inc.* v. *Carey,* 430 U. S. 144, 147–165 (1977) (opinion of WHITE, J., joined by BRENNAN, BLACKMUN, and STEVENS, JJ.); *id.,* at 180–187 (BURGER, C. J., dissenting on other grounds).

When we have discussed the remedial powers of a federal court, we have been alert to the limitation that "[t]he power of the federal courts to restructure the operation of local and state governmental entities 'is not plenary. . . .' [A] federal court is required to tailor 'the scope of the remedy' to fit the nature and extent of the . . . violation." *Dayton Board of Education* v. *Brinkman,* 433 U. S. 406, 419–420 (1977) (quoting *Milliken* v. *Bradley,* 418 U. S. 717, 738 (1974), and *Swann* v. *Charlotte-Mecklenburg Board of Education, supra,* at 16).

Here we deal, as we noted earlier, not with the limited remedial powers of a federal court, for example, but with the broad remedial powers of Congress. It is fundamental that in no organ of government, state or federal, does there repose a more comprehensive remedial power than in the Congress, expressly charged by the Constitution with competence and authority to enforce equal protection guarantees. Congress not only may induce voluntary action to assure compliance

with existing federal statutory or constitutional antidiscrimination provisions, but also, where Congress has authority to
declare certain conduct unlawful, it may, as here, authorize
and induce state action to avoid such conduct.   *Supra*, at
473–480.

(2)

A more specific challenge to the MBE program is the
charge that it impermissibly deprives nonminority businesses
of access to at least some portion of the government contracting opportunities generated by the Act.   It must be conceded that by its objective of remedying the historical impairment of access, the MBE provision can have the effect of
awarding some contracts to MBE's which otherwise might be
awarded to other businesses, who may themselves be innocent
of any prior discriminatory actions.   Failure of nonminority
firms to receive certain contracts is, of course, an incidental
consequence of the program, not part of its objective; similarly, past impairment of minority-firm access to public contracting opportunities may have been an incidental consequence of "business as usual" by public contracting agencies
and among prime contractors.

It is not a constitutional defect in this program that
it may disappoint the expectations of nonminority firms.
When effectuating a limited and properly tailored remedy
to cure the effects of prior discrimination, such "a sharing
of the burden" by innocent parties is not impermissible.
Franks, supra, at 777; see *Albemarle Paper Co., supra; United
Jewish Organizations, supra.*   The actual "burden" shouldered
by nonminority firms is relatively light in this connection
when we consider the scope of this public works program as
compared with overall construction contracting opportunities.[72]   Moreover, although we may assume that the com-

---

[72] The Court of Appeals relied upon Department of Commerce statistics to calculate that the $4.2 billion in federal grants conditioned upon
compliance with the MBE provision amounted to about 2.5% of the total

plaining parties are innocent of any discriminatory conduct, it was within congressional power to act on the assumption that in the past some nonminority businesses may have reaped competitive benefit over the years from the virtual exclusion of minority firms from these contracting opportunities.

(3)

Another challenge to the validity of the MBE program is the assertion that it is underinclusive—that it limits its benefit to specified minority groups rather than extending its remedial objectives to all businesses whose access to government contracting is impaired by the effects of disadvantage or discrimination. Such an extension would, of course, be appropriate for Congress to provide; it is not a function for the courts.

Even in this context, the well-established concept that a legislature may take one step at a time to remedy only part of a broader problem is not without relevance. See *Dandridge* v. *Williams,* 397 U. S. 471 (1970); *Williamson* v. *Lee Optical Co.,* 348 U. S. 483 (1955). We are not reviewing a federal program that seeks to confer a preferred status upon a nondisadvantaged minority or to give special assistance to only one of several groups established to be similarly disadvantaged minorities. Even in such a setting, the Congress is not without a certain authority. See, *e. g., Personnel Administrator of Massachusetts* v. *Feeney,* 442 U. S. 256 (1979); *Califano* v. *Webster,* 430 U. S. 313 (1977); *Morton* v. *Mancari,* 417 U. S. 535 (1974).

The Congress has not sought to give select minority groups a preferred standing in the construction industry, but has

---

of nearly $170 billion spent on construction in the United States during 1977. Thus, the 10% minimum minority business participation contemplated by this program would account for only 0.25% of the annual expenditure for construction work in the United States. *Fullilove* v. *Kreps,* 584 F. 2d, at 607.

embarked on a remedial program to place them on a more
equitable footing with respect to public contracting opportunities. There has been no showing in this case that Congress has
inadvertently effected an invidious discrimination by excluding from coverage an identifiable minority group that
has been the victim of a degree of disadvantage and discrimination equal to or greater than that suffered by the groups
encompassed by the MBE program. It is not inconceivable
that on very special facts a case might be made to challenge
the congressional decision to limit MBE eligibility to the
particular minority groups identified in the Act. See *Vance*
v. *Bradley,* 440 U. S. 93, 109–112 (1979); *Oregon* v. *Mitchell,*
400 U. S., at 240 (opinion of Brennan, White, and Marshall, JJ.). But on this record we find no basis to hold
that Congress is without authority to undertake the kind of
limited remedial effort represented by the MBE program.
Congress, not the courts, has the heavy burden of dealing with
a host of intractable economic and social problems.

(4)

It is also contended that the MBE program is overinclusive—that it bestows a benefit on businesses identified by
racial or ethnic criteria which cannot be justified on the basis
of competitive criteria or as a remedy for the present effects of
identified prior discrimination. It is conceivable that a particular application of the program may have this effect; however, the peculiarities of specific applications are not before
us in this case. We are not presented here with a challenge
involving a specific award of a construction contract or the
denial of a waiver request; such questions of specific application must await future cases.

This does not mean that the claim of overinclusiveness
is entitled to no consideration in the present case. The
history of governmental tolerance of practices using racial or
ethnic criteria for the purpose or with the effect of imposing
an invidious discrimination must alert us to the deleterious

effects of even benign racial or ethnic classifications when they stray from narrow remedial justifications. Even in the context of a facial challenge such as is presented in this case, the MBE provision cannot pass muster unless, with due account for its administrative program, it provides a reasonable assurance that application of racial or ethnic criteria will be limited to accomplishing the remedial objectives of Congress and that misapplications of· the program will be promptly and adequately remedied administratively.

It is significant that the administrative scheme provides for waiver and exemption. Two fundamental congressional assumptions underlie the MBE program: (1) that the present effects of past discrimination have impaired the competitive position of businesses owned and controlled by members of minority groups; and (2) that affirmative efforts to eliminate barriers to minority-firm access, and to evaluate bids with adjustment for the present effects of past discrimination, would assure that at least 10% of the federal funds granted under the Public Works Employment Act of 1977 would be accounted for by contracts with available, qualified, bona fide minority business enterprises. Each of these assumptions may be rebutted in the administrative process.

The administrative program contains measures to effectuate the congressional objective of assuring legitimate participation by disadvantaged MBE's. Administrative definition has tightened some less definite aspects of the statutory identification of the minority groups encompassed by the program.[73] There is administrative scrutiny to identify and

---

[73] The MBE provision, 42 U. S. C. § 6705 (f) (2) (1976 ed., Supp. II), classifies as a minority business enterprise any "business at least 50 per centum of which is owned by minority group members or, in the case of a publicly owned business, at least 51 per centum of the stock of which is owned by minority group members." Minority group members are defined as "citizens of the United States who are Negroes, Spanish-speaking, Orientals, Indians, Eskimos and Aleuts." The administrative definitions are set

eliminate from participation in the program MBE's who are not "bona fide" within the regulations and guidelines; for example, spurious minority-front entities can be exposed. A significant aspect of this surveillance is the complaint procedure available for reporting "unjust participation by an enterprise or individuals in the MBE program." *Supra*, at 472. And even as to specific contract awards, waiver is available to avoid dealing with an MBE who is attempting to exploit the remedial aspects of the program by charging an unreasonable price, *i. e.*, a price not attributable to the present effects of past discrimination. *Supra*, at 469–471. We must assume that Congress intended close scrutiny of false claims and prompt action on them.

Grantees are given the opportunity to demonstrate that their best efforts will not succeed or have not succeeded in achieving the statutory 10% target for minority firm participation within the limitations of the program's remedial objectives. In these circumstances a waiver or partial waiver is available once compliance has been demonstrated. A waiver may be sought and granted at any time during the contracting process, or even prior to letting contracts if the facts warrant.

---

out in the Appendix to this opinion, ¶ 3. These categories also are classified as minorities in the regulations implementing the nondiscrimination requirements of the Railroad Revitalization and Regulatory Reform Act of 1976, 45 U. S. C. § 803, see 49 CFR § 265.5 (i) (1978), on which Congress relied as precedent for the MBE provision. See 123 Cong. Rec. 7156 (1977) (remarks of Sen. Brooke). The House Subcommittee on SBA Oversight and Minority Enterprise, whose activities played a significant part in the legislative history of the MBE provision, also recognized that these categories were included within the Federal Government's definition of "minority business enterprise." H. R. Rep. No. 94–468, pp. 20–21 (1975). The specific inclusion of these groups in the MBE provision demonstrates that Congress concluded they were victims of discrimination. Petitioners did not press any challenge to Congress' classification categories in the Court of Appeals; there is no reason for this Court to pass upon the issue at this time.

Nor is the program defective because a waiver may be sought only by the grantee and not by prime contractors who may experience difficulty in fulfilling contract obligations to assure minority participation. It may be administratively cumbersome, but the wisdom of concentrating responsibility at the grantee level is not for us to evaluate; the purpose is to allow the EDA to maintain close supervision of the operation of the MBE provision. The administrative complaint mechanism allows for grievances of prime contractors who assert that a grantee has failed to seek a waiver in an appropriate case. Finally, we note that where private parties, as opposed to governmental entities, transgress the limitations inherent in the MBE program, the possibility of constitutional violation is more removed. See *Steelworkers* v. *Weber,* 443 U. S. 193, 200 (1979).

That the use of racial and ethnic criteria is premised on assumptions rebuttable in the administrative process gives reasonable assurance that application of the MBE program will be limited to accomplishing the remedial objectives contemplated by Congress and that misapplications of the racial and ethnic criteria can be remedied. In dealing with this facial challenge to the statute, doubts must be resolved in support of the congressional judgment that this limited program is a necessary step to effectuate the constitutional mandate for equality of economic opportunity. The MBE provision may be viewed as a pilot project, appropriately limited in extent and duration, and subject to reassessment and reevaluation by the Congress prior to any extension or re-enactment.[74] Miscarriages of administration could have only a transitory economic impact on businesses not encompassed by the program, and would not be irremediable.

---

[74] Cf. GAO, Report to the Congress, Minority Firms on Local Public Works Projects—Mixed Results, CED–79–9 (Jan. 16, 1979); U. S. Dept. of Commerce, Economic Development Administration, Local Public Works Program Interim Report on 10 Percent Minority Business Enterprise Requirement (Sept. 1978).

IV

Congress, after due consideration, perceived a pressing need to move forward with new approaches in the continuing effort to achieve the goal of equality of economic opportunity. In this effort, Congress has necessary latitude to try new techniques such as the limited use of racial and ethnic criteria to accomplish remedial objectives; this is especially so in programs where voluntary cooperation with remedial measures is induced by placing conditions on federal expenditures. That the program may press the outer limits of congressional authority affords no basis for striking it down.

Petitioners have mounted a facial challenge to a program developed by the politically responsive branches of Government. For its part, the Congress must proceed only with programs narrowly tailored to achieve its objectives, subject to continuing evaluation and reassessment; administration of the programs must be vigilant and flexible; and, when such a program comes under judicial review, courts must be satisfied that the legislative objectives and projected administration give reasonable assurance that the program will function within constitutional limitations. But as Mr. Justice Jackson admonished in a different context in 1941: [75]

"The Supreme Court can maintain itself and succeed in its tasks only if the counsels of self-restraint urged most earnestly by members of the Court itself are humbly and faithfully heeded. After the forces of conservatism and liberalism, of radicalism and reaction, of emotion and of self-interest are all caught up in the legislative process and averaged and come to rest in some compromise measure such as the Missouri Compromise, the N. R. A., the A. A. A., a minimum-wage law, or some other legislative policy, a decision striking it down closes an area of compromise in which conflicts have actually, if only

---

[75] R. Jackson, The Struggle for Judicial Supremacy 321 (1941).

temporarily, been composed. Each such decision takes away from our democratic federalism another of its defenses against domestic disorder and violence. The vice of judicial supremacy, as exerted for ninety years in the field of policy, has been its progressive closing of the avenues to peaceful and democratic conciliation of our social and economic conflicts."

Mr. Justice Jackson reiterated these thoughts shortly before his death in what was to be the last of his Godkin Lectures: [76]

> "I have said that in these matters the Court must respect the limitations on its own powers because judicial usurpation is to me no more justifiable and no more promising of permanent good to the country than any other kind. So I presuppose a Court that will not depart from the judicial process, will not go beyond resolving cases and controversies brought to it in conventional form, and will not consciously encroach upon the functions of its coordinate branches."

In a different context to be sure, that is, in discussing the latitude which should be allowed to states in trying to meet social and economic problems, Mr. Justice Brandeis had this to say:

> "To stay experimentation in things social and economic is a grave responsibility. Denial of the right to experiment may be fraught with serious consequences to the Nation." *New State Ice Co.* v. *Liebmann,* 285 U. S. 262, 311 (1932) (dissenting opinion).

Any preference based on racial or ethnic criteria must necessarily receive a most searching examination to make sure that it does not conflict with constitutional guarantees. This case is one which requires, and which has received, that kind

---

[76] R. Jackson, The Supreme Court in the American System of Government 61–62 (1955).

448 U. S.

of examination.   This opinion does not adopt, either expressly
or implicitly, the formulas of analysis articulated in such cases
as *University of California Regents* v. *Bakke,* 438 U. S. 265
(1978).   However, our analysis demonstrates that the MBE
provision would survive judicial review under either "test"
articulated in the several *Bakke* opinions.   The MBE provision of the Public Works Employment Act of 1977 does not
violate the Constitution.[77]

Affirmed.

---

[77] Although the complaint alleged that the MBE program violated several federal statutes, n. 5, *supra,* the only statutory argument urged upon
us is that the MBE provision is inconsistent with Title VI of the Civil
Rights Act of 1964.   We perceive no inconsistency between the requirements of Title VI and those of the MBE provision.   To the extent any
statutory inconsistencies might be asserted, the MBE provision—the later,
more specific enactment—must be deemed to control. See, *e. g., Morton*
v. *Mancari,* 417 U. S. 535, 550–551 (1974); *Preiser* v. *Rodriguez,* 411
U. S. 475, 489–490 (1973); *Bulova Watch Co.* v. *United States,* 365 U. S.
753, 758 (1961); *United States* v. *Borden Co.,* 308 U. S. 188, 198–202
(1939).

H. L. *v.* MATHESON, GOVERNOR OF UTAH, ET AL.

APPEAL FROM THE SUPREME COURT OF UTAH

No. 79–5903. Argued October 6, 1980—Decided March 23, 1981

A Utah statute requires a physician to "[n]otify, if possible," the parents or guardian of a minor upon whom an abortion is to be performed. Appellant, while an unmarried minor living with and dependent on her parents, became pregnant. A physician advised her that an abortion would be in her best medical interest but, because of the statute, refused to perform the abortion without first notifying her parents. Believing that she should proceed with the abortion without notifying her parents, appellant instituted a suit in state court seeking a declaration that the statute is unconstitutional and an injunction against its enforcement. She sought to represent a class consisting of unmarried minors "who are suffering unwanted pregnancies and desire to terminate the pregnancies but may not do so" because of their physicians' insistence on complying with the statute. The trial court upheld the statute as not unconstitutionally restricting a minor's right of privacy to obtain an abortion or to enter into a doctor-patient relationship. The Utah Supreme Court affirmed.

Held:

1. Since appellant did not allege or offer evidence that either she or any member of her class is mature or emancipated, she lacks standing to challenge the Utah statute as being unconstitutional on its face on the ground of overbreadth in that it could be construed to apply to all unmarried minor girls, including those who are mature and emancipated. *Harris* v. *McRae*, 448 U. S. 297. Moreover, the State is bound by a ruling in another case that the statute does not apply to emancipated minors, and the Utah Supreme Court has had no occasion to consider the statute's application to mature minors. Pp. 405–407.

2. As applied to an unemancipated minor girl living with and dependent upon her parents, and making no claim or showing as to maturity or as to her relations with her parents, the Utah statute serves important state interests, is narrowly drawn to protect only those interests, and does not violate any guarantees of the Constitution. Pp. 407–413.

(a) Although a state may not constitutionally legislate a blanket, unreviewable power of parents to veto their daughter's abortion, *Bellotti* v. *Baird*, 443 U. S. 622; *Planned Parenthood of Central Mo.* v. *Danforth*, 428 U. S. 52, a statute setting out a mere requirement of parental notice when possible does not violate the constitutional rights of an immature, dependent minor. Pp. 407–410.

(b) The Utah statute does not give parents a veto power over the minor's abortion decision. As applied to immature and dependent minors, the statute serves important considerations of family integrity and protecting adolescents as well as providing an opportunity for parents to supply essential medical and other information to the physician. The statute is not unconstitutional for failing to specify what information parents may furnish to physicians, or to provide for a mandatory period of delay after the physician notifies the parents; or because the State allows a pregnant minor to consent to other medical procedures without formal notice to her parents if she carries the child to term; or because the notice requirement may inhibit some minors from seeking abortions. Pp. 411–413.

604 P. 2d 907, affirmed.

BURGER, C. J., delivered the opinion of the Court, in which STEWART, WHITE, POWELL, and REHNQUIST, JJ., joined. POWELL, J., filed a concurring opinion, in which STEWART, J., joined, *post*, p. 413. STEVENS, J., filed an opinion concurring in the judgment, *post*, p. 420. MARSHALL, J., filed a dissenting opinion, in which BRENNAN and BLACKMUN, JJ., joined, *post*, p. 425.

David S. Dolowitz argued the cause and filed a brief for appellant.

Paul M. Tinker, Assistant Attorney General of Utah, argued the cause for appellees. With him on the brief was *Robert B. Hansen*, Attorney General.*

CHIEF JUSTICE BURGER delivered the opinion of the Court.

The question presented in this case is whether a state statute which requires a physician to "[n]otify, if possible,"

---

*Briefs of *amici curiae* urging reversal were filed by *Abigail English* and *Pauline H. Tesler* for the Coalition for the Medical Rights of Women et al.; and by *Eve W. Paul* and *Harriet F. Pilpel* for the Planned Parenthood Federation of America, Inc., et al.

Dennis J. Horan, Victor G. Rosenblum, John D. Gorby, Patrick A. Trueman, and *Dolores V. Horan* filed a brief for Americans United for Life as *amicus curiae* urging affirmance.

Lynn D. Wardle and *Robert W. Barker* filed a brief for the Utah Association of Women et al. as *amici curiae*.

the parents of a dependent, unmarried minor girl prior to performing an abortion on the girl violates federal constitutional guarantees.

I

In the spring of 1978, appellant was an unmarried 15-year-old girl living with her parents in Utah and dependent on them for her support. She discovered she was pregnant. She consulted with a social worker and a physician. The physician advised appellant that an abortion would be in her best medical interest. However, because of Utah Code Ann. § 76–7–304 (1978), he refused to perform the abortion without first notifying appellant's parents.

Section 76–7–304, enacted in 1974, provides:

"To enable the physician to exercise his best medical judgment [in considering a possible abortion], he shall:

"(1) Consider all factors relevant to the well-being of the woman upon whom the abortion is to be performed including, but not limited to,

"(a) Her physical, emotional and psychological health and safety,

"(b) Her age,

"(c) Her familial situation.

"(2) *Notify, if possible, the parents or guardian of the woman upon whom the abortion is to be performed, if she is a minor* or the husband of the woman, if she is married." (Emphasis supplied.) [1]

---

[1] Whether parents of a minor are liable under Utah law for the expense of an abortion and related aftercare is not disclosed by the record.

Utah also provides by statute that no abortion may be performed unless a "voluntary and informed written consent" is first obtained by the attending physician from the patient. In order for such a consent to be "voluntary and informed," the patient must be advised at a minimum about available adoption services, about fetal development, and about foreseeable complications and risks of an abortion. See Utah Code Ann. § 76–7–305 (1978). In *Planned Parenthood of Central Mo.* v. *Danforth,*

Violation of this section is a misdemeanor punishable by imprisonment for not more than one year or a fine of not more than $1,000.[2]

Appellant believed "for [her] own reasons" that she should proceed with the abortion without notifying her parents. According to appellant, the social worker concurred in this decision.[3] While still in the first trimester of her pregnancy, appellant instituted this action in the Third Judicial District Court of Utah.[4] She sought a declaration that § 76–7–304 (2) is unconstitutional and an injunction prohibiting appellees, the Governor and the Attorney General of Utah, from enforcing the statute. Appellant sought to represent a class consisting of unmarried "minor women who are suffering unwanted pregnancies and desire to terminate the pregnancies but may not do so" because of their physicians' insistence on complying with § 76–7–304 (2). The trial judge declined to grant a temporary restraining order or a preliminary injunction.[5]

The trial judge held a hearing at which appellant was the only witness. Appellant affirmed the allegations of the complaint by giving monosyllabic answers to her attorney's

---

428 U. S. 52, 65–67 (1976), we rejected a constitutional attack on written consent provisions.

[2] Utah Code Ann. §§ 76–7–314 (3), 76–3–204 (1), 76–3–301 (3) (1978).

[3] Appellant's counsel stated in his jurisdictional statement and again in his brief that the physician concluded not only that an abortion would be in appellant's best interests, but also that parental notification would not be in appellant's best interests. However, at oral argument, counsel corrected this statement and conceded that there is no evidence to support this assertion. Tr. of Oral Arg. 8, 17.

[4] The record does not reveal whether appellant proceeded with the abortion.

[5] The trial judge allowed appellant to proceed without appointment of a guardian *ad litem.* He noted that a guardian would be required to notify the parents.

leading questions.[6]   However, when the State attempted to
cross-examine appellant about her reasons for not wishing
to notify her parents, appellant's counsel vigorously ob-

_____

[6] The testimony was as follows:

"BY MR. DOLOWITZ [appellant's counsel]:

"Q At the time that the Complaint in this matter was signed, you were
pregnant?

"A Yes.

"Q You had consulted with a counselor about that pregnancy?

"A Yeah.

"Q You had determined after talking to the counselor that you felt
you should get an abortion?

"A Yes.

"Q You felt that you did not want to notify your parents—

"A Right.

"Q —of that decision? You did not feel for your own reasons that
you could discuss it with them?

"A Right.

"Q After discussing the matter with a counselor, you still believed that
you should not discuss it with your parents?

"A Right.

"Q And they shouldn't be notified?

"A Right.

"Q After talking the matter over with a counselor, the counselor concurred in your decision that your parents should not be notified?

"A Right.

"Q You were advised that an abortion couldn't be performed without
notifying them?

"A Yes.

"Q You then came to me to see about filing a suit?

"A Right.

"Q You and I discussed it as to whether or not you had a right to do
what you wanted to do?

"A Yes.

"Q You decided that, after our discussion, you should still proceed with
the action to try to obtain an abortion without notifying your parents?

"A Right.

"Q Now, at the time that you signed the Complaint and spoke with
the counselor and spoke with me, you were in the first trimester of pregnancy, within your first twelve weeks of pregnancy?

jected,[7] insisting that "the specifics of the reasons are really irrelevant to the Constitutional issue."[8] The only constitutionally permissible prerequisites for performance of an abortion, he insisted, were the desire of the girl and the medi-

---

"A Yes.

"Q You feel that, from talking to the counselor and thinking the situation over and discussing it with me, that you could make the decision on your own that you wished to abort the pregnancy?

"A Yes.

"Q You are living at home?

"A Yes.

"Q You still felt, even though you were living at home with your parents, that you couldn't discuss the matter with them?

"A Right."

Tr. 5–7.

[7] "BY MR. McCARTHY [counsel for the State]:

"Q . . . Are you still living at home?

"A Yes.

"Q Are you dependent on your parents?

"A Yes.

"Q All your money comes from them?

"A Yes.

"Q How old are you now?

"A Fifteen.

"Q Aside from the issue of abortion, do you have any reason to feel that you can't talk to your parents about other problems?

"A Yes.

"Q What are those reasons?

"MR. DOLOWITZ: Now you are moving into the problem area that I indicated. . . ."

Id., at 8.

[8] *Id.*, at 10. Appellant repeatedly pressed this point despite the trial court's statements that it could "conceive of a situation where a child probably wouldn't have to tell the parents" and that the statute "might be [u]nconstitutional as it relates to a particular fact situation but [c]onstitutional as it relates to another fact situation." *Id.*, at 10, 17. There is no evidence to support the "surmise" in the dissent, *post*, at 438, n. 24, that "appellant expects family conflict over the abortion decision."

cal approval of a physician.[9] The trial judge sustained the
objection, tentatively construing the statute to require appellant's physician to notify her parents "if he is able to
physically contact them."

Thereafter, the trial judge entered findings of fact and
conclusions of law. He concluded that appellant "is an appropriate representative to represent the class she purports
to represent."[10] He construed the statute to require notice
to appellant's parents "if it is physically possible." He concluded that § 76–7–304 (2) "do[es] not unconstitutionally restrict the right of privacy of a minor to obtain an abortion
or to enter into a doctor-patient relationship."[11] Accordingly, he dismissed the complaint.

On appeal, the Supreme Court of Utah unanimously upheld
the statute. 604 P. 2d 907 (1979). Relying on our decisions in *Planned Parenthood of Central Mo.* v. *Danforth,* 428
U. S. 52 (1976), *Carey* v. *Population Services International,*
431 U. S. 678 (1977), and *Bellotti* v. *Baird,* 443 U. S. 622
(1979) (*Bellotti II*), the court concluded that the statute
serves "significant state interest[s]" that are present with
respect to minors but absent in the case of adult women.

The court looked first to subsection (1) of § 76–7–304.
This provision, the court observed, expressly incorporates the
factors we identified in *Doe* v. *Bolton,* 410 U. S. 179 (1973),
as pertinent to exercise of a physician's best medical judgment
in making an abortion decision. In *Doe,* we stated:

> "We agree with the District Court . . . that the medi-
> cal judgment may be exercised in the light of *all factors—
> physical, emotional, psychological, familial, and the wom-*

---

[9] Tr. 18.

[10] The trial judge adopted, verbatim, findings of fact and conclusions
of law prepared by appellant. The findings, the conclusions, and the
opinion of the State Supreme Court make no mention whatsoever of the
precise limits of the class.

[11] The trial judge also ruled that the statute does not violate 42 U. S. C.
§ 1983.

an's age—relevant to the well-being of the patient. All
these factors may relate to health. This allows the attending physician the room he needs to make his best
medical judgment." *Id.,* at 192 (emphasis supplied).

Section 76–7–304 (1) of the Utah statute suggests that the
legislature sought to reflect the language of *Doe.*

The Utah Supreme Court held that notifying the parents
of a minor seeking an abortion is "substantially and logically
related" to the *Doe* factors set out in § 76–7–304 (1) because
parents ordinarily possess information essential to a physician's exercise of his best medical judgment concerning the
child. 604 P. 2d, at 909–910. The court also concluded that
encouraging an unmarried pregnant minor to seek the advice
of her parents in making the decision of whether to carry her
child to term promotes a significant state interest in supporting the important role of parents in child-rearing. *Id.,* at
912. The court reasoned that since the statute allows no
veto power over the minor's decision, it does not unduly
intrude upon a minor's rights.

The Utah Supreme Court also rejected appellant's argument that the phrase "if possible" in § 76–7–304 (2) should be
construed to give the physician discretion whether to notify
appellant's parents. The court concluded that the physician
is required to notify parents "if under the circumstances, in
the exercise of reasonable diligence, he can ascertain their
identity and location and it is feasible or practicable to give
them notification." The court added, however, that "the time
element is an important factor, for there must be sufficient
expedition to provide an effective opportunity for an abortion." 604 P. 2d, at 913.

II

Appellant challenges the statute as unconstitutional on its
face. She contends it is overbroad in that it can be construed
to apply to all unmarried minor girls, including those who are
mature and emancipated. We need not reach that question

since she did not allege or proffer any evidence that either
she or any member of her class is mature or emancipated.[12]
The trial court found that appellant "is unmarried, fifteen
years of age, resides at home and is a dependent of her parents." That affords an insufficient basis for a finding that
she is either mature or emancipated. Under *Harris* v.
McRae, 448 U. S. 297, 320 (1980), she therefore lacks "the
personal stake in the controversy needed to confer standing"
to advance the overbreadth argument.

There are particularly strong reasons for applying established rules of standing in this case. The United States District Court for Utah has held that § 76-7-304 (2) does not
apply to emancipated minors and that, if so applied, it would
be unconstitutional. *L. R.* v. *Hansen*, Civil No. C-80-0078J
(Feb. 8, 1980). Since there was no appeal from that ruling, it is controlling on the State. We cannot assume that
the statute, when challenged in a proper case, will not be construed also to exempt demonstrably mature minors.[13] See
Bellotti v. *Baird*, 428 U. S. 132, 146-148 (1976) (*Bellotti I*).
Nor is there any reason to assume that a minor in need of
emergency treatment will be treated in any way different from

---

[12] In *Bellotti II*, by contrast, the principal class consisted of "unmarried
[pregnant] minors in Massachusetts *who have adequate capacity to give
a valid and informed consent* [to abortion], and who do not wish to involve
their parents." 443 U. S., at 626 (emphasis supplied). The courts considered the rights of "all pregnant minors who might be affected" by the
statute. *Id.*, at 627, n. 5.

[13] The record shows that the State unsuccessfully argued in the trial
court that it should be permitted to inquire into appellant's degree of
maturity. Tr. 11.

JUSTICE STEVENS and the dissent argue that the Utah Supreme Court
held that the statute may validly be applied to all members of the class
described in the complaint. *Post*, at 421, 430, 431, 432-433. However, as
we have shown, neither of the state courts mentioned the scope or limits of
the class. See n. 10, *supra*. Moreover, appellant's counsel prepared the
findings and conclusions. In addition to considerations of standing, we
construe the ambiguity against appellant.

a similarly situated adult.[14] The Utah Supreme Court has
had no occasion to consider the application of the statute
to such situations. In *Bellotti I, supra,* we unanimously
declined to pass on constitutional challenges to an abortion
regulation statute because the statute was "susceptible of a
construction by the state judiciary 'which might avoid in
whole or in part the necessity for federal constitutional adjudication, or at least materially change the nature of the problem.'" *Id.,* at 147, quoting *Harrison* v. *NAACP,* 360 U. S.
167, 177 (1959). See *Kleppe* v. *New Mexico,* 426 U. S. 529,
546–547 (1976); *Ashwander* v. *TVA,* 297 U. S. 288, 346–347
(1936) (concurring opinion). We reaffirm that approach
and find it controlling here insofar as appellant challenges a
purported statutory exclusion of mature and emancipated
minors.

The only issue before us, then, is the facial constitutionality
of a statute requiring a physician to give notice to parents,
"if possible," prior to performing an abortion on their minor
daughter, (a) when the girl is living with and dependent upon
her parents, (b) when she is not emancipated by marriage or
otherwise, and (c) when she has made no claim or showing
as to her maturity or as to her relations with her parents.

III

A

Appellant contends the statute violates the right to privacy
recognized in our prior cases with respect to abortions. She

---

[14] There is no authority for the view expressed in the dissent that the
statute would apply to "minors with emergency health care needs." *Post,*
at 450–451. Appellant does not so contend, and the Utah Supreme Court
in this case took pains to say that time is of the essence in an abortion
decision. 604 P. 2d 907, 913 (1979). When the specific question was
properly posed in *Bellotti II,* the Massachusetts statute was construed by
the state court not to apply in such cases. 443 U. S., at 630.

The same is true for minors with hostile home situations, a class referred to by appellant's *amici curiae* and by the dissent, *post,* at 437–441.

places primary reliance on *Bellotti II,* 443 U. S., at 642, 655. In *Danforth,* we struck down state statutes that imposed a requirement of prior written *consent* of the patient's spouse and of a minor patient's parents as a prerequisite for an abortion. We held that a state

> "does not have the constitutional authority to give a third party an absolute, and possibly arbitrary, veto over the decision of the physician and his patient to terminate the patient's pregnancy, regardless of the reason for withholding the consent." 428 U. S., at 74.

We emphasized, however, "that our holding . . . does not suggest that every minor, regardless of age or maturity, may give effective consent for termination of her pregnancy." *Id.,* at 75, citing *Bellotti I, supra.* There is no logical relationship between the capacity to become pregnant and the capacity for mature judgment concerning the wisdom of an abortion.

In *Bellotti II,* dealing with a class of concededly mature pregnant minors, we struck down a Massachusetts statute requiring parental or judicial consent before an abortion could be performed on any unmarried minor. There the State's highest court had construed the statute to allow a court to overrule the minor's decision even if the court found that the minor was capable of making, and in fact had made, an informed and reasonable decision to have an abortion. We held, among other things, that the statute was unconstitutional for failure to allow mature minors to decide to undergo abortions without parental consent. Four Justices concluded that the flaws in the statute were that, as construed by the state court, (a) it permitted overruling of a mature minor's decision to abort her pregnancy; and (b) "it requires parental consultation or notification in every instance, without affording the pregnant minor an opportunity to receive an independent judicial determination that she is mature enough to

consent or that an abortion would be in her best interests."
443 U. S., at 651. Four other Justices concluded that the defect was in making the abortion decision of a minor subject
to veto by a third party, whether parent or judge, "no matter
how mature and capable of informed decisionmaking" the
minor might be. *Id.*, at 653–656.

Although we have held that a state may not constitutionally legislate a blanket, unreviewable power of parents to veto
their daughter's abortion,[15] a statute setting out a "mere requirement of parental notice" does not violate the constitutional rights of an immature, dependent minor.[16] Four Justices in *Bellotti II* joined in stating:

"[Plaintiffs] suggest . . . that the mere requirement of
parental notice [unduly burdens the right to seek an
abortion]. As stated in Part II above, however, parental
notice and consent are qualifications that typically may
be imposed by the State on a minor's right to make important decisions. As immature minors often lack the
ability to make fully informed choices that take account
of both immediate and long-range consequences, a State
reasonably may determine that parental consultation
often is desirable and in the best interest of the minor.
It may further determine, as a general proposition, that
such consultation is particularly desirable with respect to
the abortion decision—one that for some people raises
profound moral and religious concerns. . . .

" 'There can be little doubt that the State furthers a
constitutionally permissible end by encouraging an unmarried pregnant minor to seek the help and advice of

---

[15] *Bellotti II*, 443 U. S., at 642–643, 653–656; *Danforth*, 428 U. S., at 74.
[16] *Bellotti II*, *supra*, at 640, 649; *id.*, at 657 (dissenting opinion);
Danforth, *supra*, at 90–91 (concurring opinion); see *Bellotti* v. *Baird*, 428
U. S. 132, 145, 147 (1976) (*Bellotti I*); cf. *Carey* v. *Population Services
International*, 431 U. S. 678, 709–710 (1977).

her parents in making the very important decision
whether or not to bear a child.   That is a grave decision,
and a girl of tender years, under emotional stress, may be
ill-equipped to make it without mature advice and emotional support.   It seems unlikely that she will obtain
adequate counsel and support from the attending physician at an abortion clinic, where abortions for pregnant
minors frequently take place.' "   *Id.*, at 640–641 (footnotes omitted), quoting *Danforth*, 428 U. S., at 91 (concurring opinion).

Accord, 443 U. S., at 657 (dissenting opinion).

In addition, "constitutional interpretation has consistently
recognized that the parents' claim to authority in their own
household to direct the rearing of their children is basic in
the structure of our society."   *Ginsberg* v. *New York*, 390
U. S. 629, 639 (1968).   In *Quilloin* v. *Walcott*, 434 U. S. 246
(1978), the Court expanded on this theme:

"We have recognized on numerous occasions that the
relationship between parent and child is constitutionally
protected.   See, *e. g.*, *Wisconsin* v. *Yoder*, 406 U. S.
205, 231–233 (1972); *Stanley* v. *Illinois*, [405 U. S. 645
(1972)]; *Meyer* v. *Nebraska*, 262 U. S. 390, 399–401
(1923).   'It is cardinal with us that the custody, care
and nurture of the child reside first in the parents, whose
primary function and freedom include preparation for
obligations the state can neither supply nor hinder.' "
Id., at 255, quoting *Prince* v. *Massachusetts*, 321 U. S.
158, 166 (1944).

See also *Parham* v. *J. R.*, 442 U. S. 584, 602 (1979); *Pierce* v.
Society of Sisters, 268 U. S. 510, 535 (1925).   We have recognized that parents have an important "guiding role" to play
in the upbringing of their children, *Bellotti II*, *supra*, at
633–639, which presumptively includes counseling them on
important decisions.

B

The Utah statute gives neither parents nor judges a veto power over the minor's abortion decision.[17] As in *Bellotti I*, "we are concerned with a statute directed toward minors, as to whom there are unquestionably greater risks of inability to give an informed consent." 428 U. S., at 147. As applied to immature and dependent minors, the statute plainly serves the important considerations of family integrity [18] and protecting adolescents [19] which we identified in *Bellotti II*. In addition, as applied to that class, the statute serves a significant state interest by providing an opportunity for parents to supply essential medical and other information to a physician. The medical, emotional, and psychological consequences of an abortion are serious and can be lasting; this is particularly so when the patient is immature.[20] An adequate medical and psychological case history is important to the physician. Parents can provide medical and psychological data, refer the physician to other sources of medical history, such as family physicians, and authorize family physicians to give relevant data.

---

[17] The main premise of the dissent seems to be that a requirement of notice to the parents is the functional equivalent of a requirement of parental consent. See *post*, at 437–441. In *Bellotti II*, however, we expressly declined to equate notice requirements with consent requirements. 443 U. S., at 640, 657.

[18] *Bellotti II, supra,* at 637–639. The short shrift given by the dissent to "parental authority and family integrity," *post*, at 447, runs contrary to a long line of constitutional cases in this Court. See cases cited *supra*, at 410.

[19] *Bellotti II, supra,* at 634–637.

[20] Abortion is associated with an increased risk of complication in subsequent pregnancies. Maine, Does Abortion Affect Later Pregnancies?, 11 Family Planning Perspectives 98 (1979). The emotional and psychological effects of the pregnancy and abortion experience are markedly more severe in girls under 18 than in adults. Wallerstein, Kurtz, & Bar-Din, Psychosocial Sequelae of Therapeutic Abortion in Young Unmarried Women, 27 Arch. Gen. Psychiatry 828 (1972); see also Babikian & Goldman, A Study in Teen-Age Pregnancy, 128 Am. J. Psychiatry 755 (1971).

Appellant intimates that the statute's failure to declare, in terms, a detailed description of what information parents may provide to physicians, or to provide for a mandatory period of delay after the physician notifies the parents,[21] renders the statute unconstitutional. The notion that the statute must itemize information to be supplied by parents finds no support in logic, experience, or our decisions. And as the Utah Supreme Court recognized, 604 P. 2d, at 913, time is likely to be of the essence in an abortion decision. The Utah statute is reasonably calculated to protect minors in appellant's class by enhancing the potential for parental consultation concerning a decision that has potentially traumatic and permanent consequences.[22]

Appellant also contends that the constitutionality of the statute is undermined because Utah allows a pregnant minor to consent to other medical procedures without formal notice to her parents if she carries the child to term.[23] But a state's interests in full-term pregnancies are sufficiently different to justify the line drawn by the statutes. Cf. *Maher* v. *Roe*, 432 U. S. 464, 473–474 (1977). If the pregnant girl elects to carry her child to term, the *medical* decisions to be made entail few—perhaps none—of the potentially grave

---

[21] At least five States have enacted parental notification statutes containing brief mandatory waiting periods. See La. Rev. Stat. Ann. § 40:-1299.35.5 (West Supp. 1981) (24 hours' actual notice or 72 hours' constructive notice except for court-authorized abortions); Mass. Gen. Laws Ann., ch. 112, § 12S (West Supp. 1981) (24 hours); Me. Rev. Stat. Ann., Tit. 22, § 1597 (1980) (24 hours); N. D. Cent. Code § 14–02.1–03 (Supp. 1979) (24 hours); Tenn. Code Ann. § 39–302 (Supp. 1979) (two days).

[22] Members of the particular class now before us in this case have no constitutional right to notify a court in lieu of notifying their parents. See *Bellotti II*, *supra*, at 647. This case does not require us to decide in what circumstances a state must provide alternatives to parental notification.

[23] See Utah Code Ann. § 78–14–5 (4)(f) (1977) (permitting any female to give informed consent "to any health care not prohibited by law . . . in connection with her pregnancy or childbirth").

398

emotional and psychological consequences of the decision to abort.

That the requirement of notice to parents may inhibit some minors from seeking abortions is not a valid basis to void the statute as applied to appellant and the class properly before us. The Constitution does not compel a state to fine-tune its statutes so as to encourage or facilitate abortions. To the contrary, state action "encouraging childbirth except in the most urgent circumstances" is "rationally related to the legitimate governmental objective of protecting potential life." *Harris* v. *McRae,* 448 U. S., at 325. Accord, *Maher* v. *Roe, supra,* at 473–474.[24]

As applied to the class properly before us, the statute plainly serves important state interests, is narrowly drawn to protect only those interests, and does not violate any guarantees of the Constitution.[25] The judgment of the Supreme Court of Utah is

Affirmed.

---

[24] See also *Bellotti II,* 443 U. S., at 643–644; *Bellotti I,* 428 U. S., at 148–149; *Danforth,* 428 U. S., at 65–67, 79–81; *Connecticut* v. *Menillo,* 423 U. S. 9, 11 (1975); *West Side Women's Services, Inc.* v. *City of Cleveland,* 450 F. Supp. 796, 798 (ND Ohio), affirmance order, 582 F. 2d 1281 (CA6), cert. denied, 439 U. S. 983 (1978).

[25] Appellant argues that the statute violates her right to secure necessary treatment from a physician who, in the exercise of his best medical judgment, does not believe the parents should be notified. Since there is no evidence that the physician had such an opinion, we decline to reach this question. See *supra,* at 401, n. 3, and 405–407.

CASES ADJUDGED

IN THE

SUPREME COURT OF THE UNITED STATES

AT

OCTOBER TERM, 1971

THE BREMEN ET AL. v. ZAPATA OFF-SHORE CO.

CERTIORARI TO THE UNITED STATES COURT OF APPEALS FOR THE FIFTH CIRCUIT

No. 71-322. Argued March 21, 1972—Decided June 12, 1972

Petitioner Unterweser made an agreement to tow respondent's drilling rig from Louisiana to Italy. The contract contained a forum-selection clause providing for the litigation of any dispute in the High Court of Justice in London. When the rig under tow was damaged in a storm, respondent instructed Unterweser to tow the rig to Tampa, the nearest port of refuge. There, respondent brought suit in admiralty against petitioners. Unterweser invoked the forum clause in moving for dismissal for want of jurisdiction and brought suit in the English court, which ruled that it had jurisdiction under the contractual forum provision. The District Court, relying on *Carbon Black Export, Inc.* v. *The Monrosa*, 254 F. 2d 297, held the forum-selection clause unenforceable, and refused to decline jurisdiction on the basis of *forum non conveniens*. The Court of Appeals affirmed. *Held:* The forum-selection clause, which was a vital part of the towing contract, is binding on the parties unless respondent can meet the heavy burden of showing that its enforcement would be unreasonable, unfair, or unjust. Pp. 8–20.

428 F. 2d 888 and 446 F. 2d 907, vacated and remanded.

BURGER, C. J., delivered the opinion of the Court, in which BRENNAN, STEWART, WHITE, MARSHALL, BLACKMUN, POWELL, and REHNQUIST, JJ., joined. WHITE, J., filed a concurring statement, *post*, p. 20. DOUGLAS, J., filed a dissenting opinion, *post*, p. 20.

David C. G. Kerr argued the cause for petitioners. With him on the briefs was *Jack C. Rinard.*

James K. Nance argued the cause for respondent. With him on the brief was *Dewey R. Villareal, Jr.*

MR. CHIEF JUSTICE BURGER delivered the opinion of the Court.

We granted certiorari to review a judgment of the United States Court of Appeals for the Fifth Circuit declining to enforce a forum-selection clause governing disputes arising under an international towage contract between petitioners and respondent. The circuits have differed in their approach to such clauses.[1] For the reasons stated hereafter, we vacate the judgment of the Court of Appeals.

In November 1967, respondent Zapata, a Houston-based American corporation, contracted with petitioner Unterweser, a German corporation, to tow Zapata's ocean-going, self-elevating drilling rig *Chaparral* from Louisiana to a point off Ravenna, Italy, in the Adriatic Sea, where Zapata had agreed to drill certain wells.

Zapata had solicited bids for the towage, and several companies including Unterweser had responded. Unterweser was the low bidder and Zapata requested it to submit a contract, which it did. The contract submitted by Unterweser contained the following provision, which is at issue in this case:

> "Any dispute arising must be treated before the London Court of Justice."

---

[1] Compare, *e. g., Central Contracting Co.* v. *Maryland Casualty Co.*, 367 F. 2d 341 (CA3 1966), and *Wm. H. Muller & Co.* v. *Swedish American Line Ltd.*, 224 F. 2d 806 (CA2), cert. denied, 350 U. S. 903 (1955), with *Carbon Black Export, Inc.* v. *The Monrosa*, 254 F. 2d 297 (CA5 1958), cert. dismissed, 359 U. S. 180 (1959).

In addition the contract contained two clauses purporting to exculpate Unterweser from liability for damages to the towed barge.[2]

After reviewing the contract and making several changes, but without any alteration in the forum-selection or exculpatory clauses, a Zapata vice president executed the contract and forwarded it to Unterweser in Germany, where Unterweser accepted the changes, and the contract became effective.

On January 5, 1968, Unterweser's deep sea tug *Bremen* departed Venice, Louisiana, with the *Chaparral* in tow bound for Italy. On January 9, while the flotilla was in international waters in the middle of the Gulf of Mexico, a severe storm arose. The sharp roll of the *Chaparral* in Gulf waters caused its elevator legs, which had been raised for the voyage, to break off and fall into the sea, seriously damaging the *Chaparral*. In this emergency situation Zapata instructed the *Bremen* to tow its damaged rig to Tampa, Florida, the nearest port of refuge.

On January 12, Zapata, ignoring its contract promise to litigate "any dispute arising" in the English courts, commenced a suit in admiralty in the United States

[2] The General Towage Conditions of the contract included the following:

"1. . . . [Unterweser and its] masters and crews are not responsible for defaults and/or errors in the navigation of the tow.

"2. . . .

"b) Damages suffered by the towed object are in any case for account of its Owners."

In addition, the contract provided that any insurance of the *Chaparral* was to be "for account of" Zapata. Unterweser's initial telegraphic bid had also offered to "arrange insurance covering towage risk for rig if desired." As Zapata had chosen to be self-insured on all its rigs, the loss in this case was not compensated by insurance.

District Court at Tampa, seeking $3,500,000 damages
against Unterweser *in personam* and the *Bremen in rem,*
alleging negligent towage and breach of contract.[3] Unterweser responded by invoking the forum clause of the
towage contract, and moved to dismiss for lack of jurisdiction or on *forum non conveniens* grounds, or in the
alternative to stay the action pending submission of the
dispute to the "London Court of Justice." Shortly thereafter, in February, before the District Court had ruled
on its motion to stay or dismiss the United States
action, Unterweser commenced an action against Zapata
seeking damages for breach of the towage contract in
the High Court of Justice in London, as the contract
provided. Zapata appeared in that court to contest
jurisdiction, but its challenge was rejected, the English
courts holding that the contractual forum provision
conferred jurisdiction.[4]

---

[3] The *Bremen* was arrested by a United States marshal acting
pursuant to Zapata's complaint immediately upon her arrival in
Tampa. The tug was subsequently released when Unterweser furnished security in the amount of $3,500,000.

[4] Zapata appeared specially and moved to set aside service of
process outside the country. Justice Karminski of the High Court
of Justice denied the motion on the ground the contractual choice-
of-forum provision conferred jurisdiction and would be enforced,
absent a factual showing it would not be "fair and right" to do
so. He did not believe Zapata had made such a showing, and held
that it should be required to "stick to [its] bargain." App. 206, 211,
213. The Court of Appeal dismissed an appeal on the ground that
Justice Karminski had properly applied the English rule. Lord
Justice Willmer stated that rule as follows:

"The law on the subject, I think, is not open to doubt . . . . It is
always open to parties to stipulate . . . that a particular Court
shall have jurisdiction over any dispute arising out of their contract. Here the parties chose to stipulate that disputes were to
be referred to the 'London Court,' which I take as meaning the
High Court in this country. *Prima facie* it is the policy of the
Court to hold parties to the bargain into which they have en-

In the meantime, Unterweser was faced with a dilemma in the pending action in the United States court at Tampa. The six-month period for filing action to limit its liability to Zapata and other potential claimants was about to expire,[5] but the United States District Court in Tampa had not yet ruled on Unterweser's motion to dismiss or stay Zapata's action. On July 2, 1968, confronted with difficult alternatives, Unterweser filed an action to limit its liability in the District Court in Tampa. That court entered the customary injunction against proceedings outside the limitation court, and Zapata refiled its initial claim in the limitation action.[6]

---

tered. . . . But that is not an inflexible rule, as was shown, for instance, by the case of *The Fehmarn,* [1957] 1 Lloyd's Rep. 511; (C. A.) [1957] 2 Lloyd's Rep. 551 . . . .

"I approach the matter, therefore, in this way, that the Court has a discretion, but it is a discretion which, in the ordinary way and in the absence of strong reason to the contrary, will be exercised in favour of holding parties to their bargain. The question is whether sufficient circumstances have been shown to exist in this case to make it desirable, on the grounds of balance of convenience, that proceedings should not take place in this country . . . ." [1968] 2 Lloyd's Rep. 158, 162–163.

[5] 46 U. S. C. §§ 183, 185. See generally G. Gilmore & C. Black, Admiralty § 10–15 (1957).

[6] In its limitation complaint, Unterweser stated it "reserve[d] all rights" under its previous motion to dismiss or stay Zapata's action, and reasserted that the High Court of Justice was the proper forum for determining the entire controversy, including its own right to limited liability, in accord with the contractual forum clause. Unterweser later counterclaimed, setting forth the same contractual cause of action as in its English action and a further cause of action for salvage arising out of the *Bremen's* services following the casualty. In its counterclaim, Unterweser again asserted that the High Court of Justice in London was the proper forum for determining all aspects of the controversy, including its counterclaim.

It was only at this juncture, on July 29, after the six-month period for filing the limitation action had run, that the District Court denied Unterweser's January motion to dismiss or stay Zapata's initial action. In denying the motion, that court relied on the prior decision of the Court of Appeals in *Carbon Black Export, Inc.* v. *The Monrosa,* 254 F. 2d 297 (CA5 1958), cert. dismissed, 359 U. S. 180 (1959). In that case the Court of Appeals had held a forum-selection clause unenforceable, reiterating the traditional view of many American courts that "agreements in advance of controversy whose object is to oust the jurisdiction of the courts are contrary to public policy and will not be enforced." 254 F. 2d, at 300–301.[7] Apparently concluding that it was bound by the *Carbon Black* case, the District Court gave the forum-selection clause little, if any, weight. Instead, the court treated the motion to dismiss under normal *forum non conveniens* doctrine applicable in the absence of such a clause, citing *Gulf Oil Corp.* v. *Gilbert,* 330 U. S. 501 (1947). Under that doctrine "unless the balance is strongly in favor of the defendant, the plaintiff's choice of forum should rarely be disturbed." *Id.,* at 508. The District Court concluded: "The balance of conveniences here is not strongly in favor of [Unterweser] and [Zapata's] choice of forum should not be disturbed."

Thereafter, on January 21, 1969, the District Court denied another motion by Unterweser to stay the limitation action pending determination of the controversy in the High Court of Justice in London and granted Zapata's motion to restrain Unterweser from litigating

---

[7] The *Carbon Black* court went on to say that it was, in any event, unnecessary for it to reject the more liberal position taken in *Wm. H. Muller & Co.* v. *Swedish American Line Ltd.,* 224 F. 2d 806 (CA2), cert. denied, 350 U. S. 903 (1955), because the case before it had a greater nexus with the United States than that in *Muller.*

further in the London court. The District Judge ruled
that, having taken jurisdiction in the limitation proceeding, he had jurisdiction to determine all matters relating
to the controversy. He ruled that Unterweser should
be required to "do equity" by refraining from also litigating the controversy in the London court, not only
for the reasons he had previously stated for denying
Unterweser's first motion to stay Zapata's action, but
also because Unterweser had invoked the United States
court's jurisdiction to obtain the benefit of the Limitation Act.

On appeal, a divided panel of the Court of Appeals
affirmed, and on rehearing *en banc* the panel opinion
was adopted, with six of the 14 *en banc* judges dissenting. As had the District Court, the majority
rested on the *Carbon Black* decision, concluding that
" 'at the very least' " that case stood for the proposition
that a forum-selection clause " 'will not be enforced unless the selected state would provide a more convenient
forum than the state in which suit is brought.' " From
that premise the Court of Appeals proceeded to conclude that, apart from the forum-selection clause, the
District Court did not abuse its discretion in refusing
to decline jurisdiction on the basis of *forum non conveniens*. It noted that (1) the flotilla never "escaped
the Fifth Circuit's mare nostrum, and the casualty occurred in close proximity to the district court"; (2) a
considerable number of potential witnesses, including
Zapata crewmen, resided in the Gulf Coast area; (3) preparation for the voyage and inspection and repair work
had been performed in the Gulf area; (4) the testimony of the *Bremen* crew was available by way of
deposition; (5) England had no interest in or contact
with the controversy other than the forum-selection
clause. The Court of Appeals majority further noted
that Zapata was a United States citizen and "[t]he dis-

cretion of the district court to remand the case to a
foreign forum was consequently limited"—especially
since it appeared likely that the English courts would
enforce the exculpatory clauses.[8] In the Court of Appeals' view, enforcement of such clauses would be contrary to public policy in American courts under *Bisso* v.
Inland Waterways Corp., 349 U. S. 85 (1955), and *Dixilyn
Drilling Corp.* v. *Crescent Towing & Salvage Co.*, 372
U. S. 697 (1963). Therefore, "[t]he district court was
entitled to consider that remanding Zapata to a foreign forum, with no practical contact with the controversy, could raise a bar to recovery by a United States
citizen which its own convenient courts would not
countenance." [9]

We hold, with the six dissenting members of the Court
of Appeals, that far too little weight and effect were given
to the forum clause in resolving this controversy. For
at least two decades we have witnessed an expansion of
overseas commercial activities by business enterprises
based in the United States. The barrier of distance that
once tended to confine a business concern to a modest
territory no longer does so. Here we see an American

---

[8] The record contains an undisputed affidavit of a British solicitor
stating an opinion that the exculpatory clauses of the contract would
be held "prima facie valid and enforceable" against Zapata in any
action maintained in England in which Zapata alleged that defaults
or errors in Unterweser's tow caused the casualty and damage to
the *Chaparral*.

In addition, it is not disputed that while the limitation fund
in the District Court in Tampa amounts to $1,390,000, the limita-
tion fund in England would be only slightly in excess of $80,000
under English law.

[9] The Court of Appeals also indicated in passing that even if it
took the view that choice-of-forum clauses were enforceable unless
"unreasonable" it was "doubtful" that enforcement would be proper
here because the exculpatory clauses would deny Zapata relief to
which it was "entitled" and because England was "seriously inconvenient" for trial of the action.

company with special expertise contracting with a foreign company to tow a complex machine thousands of miles across seas and oceans. The expansion of American business and industry will hardly be encouraged if, notwithstanding solemn contracts, we insist on a parochial concept that all disputes must be resolved under our laws and in our courts. Absent a contract forum, the considerations relied on by the Court of Appeals would be persuasive reasons for holding an American forum convenient in the traditional sense, but in an era of expanding world trade and commerce, the absolute aspects of the doctrine of the *Carbon Black* case have little place and would be a heavy hand indeed on the future development of international commercial dealings by Americans. We cannot have trade and commerce in world markets and international waters exclusively on our terms, governed by our laws, and resolved in our courts.

Forum-selection clauses have historically not been favored by American courts. Many courts, federal and state, have declined to enforce such clauses on the ground that they were "contrary to public policy," or that their effect was to "oust the jurisdiction" of the court.[10] Al-

---

[10] Many decisions reflecting this view are collected in Annot., 56 A. L. R. 2d 300, 306–320 (1957), and Later Case Service (1967).

For leading early cases, see, *e. g., Nute* v. *Hamilton Mutual Ins. Co.,* 72 Mass. (6 Gray) 174 (1856); *Nashua River Paper Co.* v. *Hammermill Paper Co.,* 223 Mass. 8, 111 N. E. 678 (1916); *Benson* v. *Eastern Bldg. & Loan Assn.,* 174 N. Y. 83, 66 N. E. 627 (1903). The early admiralty cases were in accord. See, *e. g., Wood & Selick, Inc.* v. *Compagnie Generale Transatlantique,* 43 F. 2d 941 (CA2 1930); *The Ciano,* 58 F. Supp. 65 (ED Pa. 1944); *Kuhnhold* v. *Compagnie Generale Transatlantique,* 251 F. 387 (SDNY 1918); *Prince Steam-Shipping Co.* v. *Lehman,* 39 F. 704 (SDNY 1889).

In *Insurance Co.* v. *Morse,* 20 Wall. 445 (1874), this Court broadly stated that "agreements in advance to oust the courts of the jurisdiction conferred by law are illegal and void." *Id.,* at 451. But the holding of that case was only that the State of Wisconsin could not by statute force a foreign corporation to "agree" to surrender its federal though this view apparently still has considerable acceptance, other courts are tending to adopt a more hospitable attitude toward forum-selection clauses. This view, advanced in the well-reasoned dissenting opinion in the instant case, is that such clauses are prima facie valid and should be enforced unless enforcement is shown by the resisting party to be "unreasonable" under the circumstances.[11] We believe this is the correct doctrine to be followed by federal district courts sitting in admiralty. It is merely the other side of the proposition recognized by this Court in *National Equipment Rental, Ltd.* v. *Szukhent,* 375 U. S. 311 (1964), holding that in federal courts a party may validly consent to be sued in a juris-

---

statutory right to remove a state court action to the federal courts as a condition of doing business in Wisconsin. Thus, the case is properly understood as one in which a state statutory requirement was viewed as imposing an unconstitutional condition on the exercise of the federal right of removal. See, *e. g., Wisconsin* v. *Philadelphia & Reading Coal Co.,* 241 U. S. 329 (1916).

As Judge Hand noted in *Krenger* v. *Pennsylvania R. Co.,* 174 F. 2d 556 (CA2 1949), even at that date there was in fact no "absolute taboo" against such clauses. See, *e. g., Mittenthal* v. *Mascagni,* 183 Mass. 19, 66 N. E. 425 (1903); *Daley* v. *People's Bldg., Loan & Sav. Assn.,* 178 Mass. 13, 59 N. E. 452 (1901) (Holmes, J.). See also *Cerro de Pasco Copper Corp.* v. *Knut Knutsen, O. A. S.,* 187 F. 2d 990 (CA2 1951).

[11] *E. g., Central Contracting Co.* v. *Maryland Casualty Co.,* 367 F. 2d 341 (CA3 1966); *Anastasiadis* v. *S. S. Little John,* 346 F. 2d 281 (CA5 1965) (by implication); *Wm. H. Muller & Co.* v. *Swedish American Line Ltd.,* 224 F. 2d 806 (CA2), cert. denied, 350 U. S. 903 (1955); *Cerro de Pasco Copper Corp.* v. *Knut Knutsen, O. A. S.,* 187 F. 2d 990 (CA2 1951); *Central Contracting Co.* v. *C. E. Youngdahl & Co.,* 418 Pa. 122, 209 A. 2d 810 (1965).

The *Muller* case was overruled in *Indussa Corp.* v. *S. S. Ranborg,* 377 F. 2d 200 (CA2 1967), insofar as it held that the forum clause was not inconsistent with the "lessening of liability" provision of the Carriage of Goods by Sea Act, 46 U. S. C. § 1303 (8), which was applicable to the transactions in *Muller, Indussa,* and *Carbon Black.* That Act is not applicable in this case.

diction where he cannot be found for service of process through contractual designation of an "agent" for receipt of process in that jurisdiction.   In so holding, the Court stated:

> "[I]t is settled . . . that parties to a contract may agree in advance to submit to the jurisdiction of a given court, to permit notice to be served by the opposing party, or even to waive notice altogether."
> *Id.*, at 315–316.

This approach is substantially that followed in other common-law countries including England.[12] It is the view advanced by noted scholars and that adopted by the Restatement of the Conflict of Laws.[13] It accords with ancient concepts of freedom of contract and reflects an appreciation of the expanding horizons of American contractors who seek business in all parts of the world. Not surprisingly, foreign businessmen prefer, as do we, to

---

[12] In addition to the decision of the Court of Appeal in the instant case, *Unterweser Reederei G. m. b. H.* v. *Zapata Off-Shore Co.* [*The Chaparral*], [1968] 2 Lloyd's Rep. 158 (C. A.), see *e. g., Mackender* v. *Feldia A. G.,* [1967] 2 Q. B. 590 (C. A.); *The Fehmarn,* [1958] 1 W. L. R. 159 (C. A.); *Law* v. *Garrett,* [1878] 8 Ch. D. 26 (C. A.); *The Eleftheria,* [1970] P. 94. As indicated by the clear statements in *The Eleftheria* and of Lord Justice Willmer in this case, *supra,* n. 4, the decision of the trial court calls for an exercise of discretion. See generally A. Dicey & J. Morris, The Conflict of Laws 979–980, 1087–1088 (8th ed. 1967); Cowen & Mendes da Costa, The Contractual Forum: Situation in England and the British Commonwealth, 13 Am. J. Comp. Law 179 (1964); Reese, The Contractual Forum: Situation in the United States, *id.,* at 187, 190 n. 13; Graupner, Contractual Stipulations Conferring Exclusive Jurisdiction Upon Foreign Courts in the Law of England and Scotland, 59 L. Q. Rev. 227 (1943).

[13] Restatement (Second) of the Conflict of Laws § 80 (1971); Reese, The Contractual Forum: Situation in the United States, 13 Am. J. Comp. Law 187 (1964); A. Ehrenzweig, Conflict of Laws § 41 (1962). See also Model Choice of Forum Act (National Conference of Commissioners on Uniform State Laws 1968).

have disputes resolved in their own courts, but if that choice is not available, then in a neutral forum with expertise in the subject matter. Plainly, the courts of England meet the standards of neutrality and long experience in admiralty litigation. The choice of that forum was made in an arm's-length negotiation by experienced and sophisticated businessmen, and absent some compelling and countervailing reason it should be honored by the parties and enforced by the courts.

The argument that such clauses are improper because they tend to "oust" a court of jurisdiction is hardly more than a vestigial legal fiction. It appears to rest at core on historical judicial resistance to any attempt to reduce the power and business of a particular court and has little place in an era when all courts are overloaded and when businesses once essentially local now operate in world markets. It reflects something of a provincial attitude regarding the fairness of other tribunals. No one seriously contends in this case that the forum-selection clause "ousted" the District Court of jurisdiction over Zapata's action. The threshold question is whether that court should have exercised its jurisdiction to do more than give effect to the legitimate expectations of the parties, manifested in their freely negotiated agreement, by specifically enforcing the forum clause.

There are compelling reasons why a freely negotiated private international agreement, unaffected by fraud, undue influence, or overweening bargaining power,[14] such

---

[14] The record here refutes any notion of overweening bargaining power. Judge Wisdom, dissenting, in the Court of Appeals noted:

"Zapata has neither presented evidence of nor alleged fraud or undue bargaining power in the agreement. Unterweser was only one of several companies bidding on the project. No evidence contradicts its Managing Director's affidavit that it specified English courts 'in an effort to meet Zapata Off-Shore Company half way.' Zapata's Vice President has declared by affidavit that no specific negotiations concerning the forum clause took place. But this was not simply a form contract with boilerplate language that Zapata as that involved here, should be given full effect. In this case, for example, we are concerned with a far from routine transaction between companies of two different nations contemplating the tow of an extremely costly piece of equipment from Louisiana across the Gulf of Mexico and the Atlantic Ocean, through the Mediterranean Sea to its final destination in the Adriatic Sea. In the course of its voyage, it was to traverse the waters of many jurisdictions. The *Chaparral* could have been damaged at any point along the route, and there were countless possible ports of refuge. That the accident occurred in the Gulf of Mexico and the barge was towed to Tampa in an emergency were mere fortuities. It cannot be doubted for a moment that the parties sought to provide for a neutral forum for the resolution of any disputes arising during the tow. Manifestly much uncertainty and possibly great inconvenience to both parties could arise if a suit could be maintained in any jurisdiction in which an accident might occur or if jurisdiction were left to any place where the *Bremen* or Unterweser might happen to be found.[15] The elimination of all such uncertainties by agreeing in advance on a forum acceptable to both parties is an indispensable element in international trade,

had no power to alter. The towing of an oil rig across the Atlantic was a new business. Zapata did make alterations to the contract submitted by Unterweser. The forum clause could hardly be ignored. It is the final sentence of the agreement, immediately preceding the date and the parties' signatures. . . ." 428 F. 2d 888, 907.

[15] At the very least, the clause was an effort to eliminate all uncertainty as to the nature, location, and outlook of the forum in which these companies of differing nationalities might find themselves. Moreover, while the contract here did not specifically provide that the substantive law of England should be applied, it is the general rule in English courts that the parties are assumed, absent contrary indication, to have designated the forum with the view that it should apply its own law. See, *e. g., Tzortzis* v. *Monark Line A/B,* [1968] 1 W. L. R. 406 (C. A.); see generally 1 T. Carver, Carriage by Sea 496–497 (12th ed. 1971); G. Cheshire, Private International Law 193 (7th ed. 1965); A. Dicey & J. Morris, The Conflict

commerce, and contracting. There is strong evidence
that the forum clause was a vital part of the agreement,[16]
and it would be unrealistic to think that the parties did
not conduct their negotiations, including fixing the mone-
tary terms, with the consequences of the forum clause
figuring prominently in their calculations. Under these
circumstances, as Justice Karminski reasoned in sustaining jurisdiction over Zapata in the High Court of
Justice, "[t]he force of an agreement for litigation in this
country, freely entered into between two competent parties, seems to me to be very powerful."

---

of Laws 705, 1046 (8th ed. 1967); Collins, Arbitration Clauses and
Forum Selecting Clauses in the Conflict of Laws: Some Recent Developments in England, 2 J. Mar. L. & Comm. 363, 365–370 and
n. 7 (1971). It is therefore reasonable to conclude that the forum
clause was also an effort to obtain certainty as to the applicable
substantive law.

The record contains an affidavit of a Managing Director of
Unterweser stating that Unterweser considered the choice-of-forum
provision to be of "overriding importance" to the transaction. He
stated that Unterweser towage contracts ordinarily provide for
exclusive German jurisdiction and application of German law, but
that "[i]n this instance, in an effort to meet [Zapata] half way,
[Unterweser] proposed the London Court of Justice. Had this
provision not been accepted by [Zapata], [Unterweser] would not
have entered into the towage contract . . . ." He also stated that
the parties intended, by designating the London forum, that English
law would be applied. A responsive affidavit by Hoyt Taylor, a
vice president of Zapata, denied that there were any discussions
between Zapata and Unterweser concerning the forum clause or the'
question of the applicable law.

[16] See nn. 14–15, *supra*. Zapata has denied specifically discussing
the forum clause with Unterweser, but, as Judge Wisdom pointed
out, Zapata made numerous changes in the contract without altering the forum clause, which could hardly have escaped its attention. Zapata is clearly not unsophisticated in such matters. The
contract of its wholly owned subsidiary with an Italian corporation covering the contemplated drilling operations in the Adriatic
Sea provided that all disputes were to be settled by arbitration in
London under English law, and contained broad exculpatory clauses.
App. 306–311.

Thus, in the light of present-day commercial realities and expanding international trade we conclude that the forum clause should control absent a strong showing that it should be set aside. Although their opinions are not altogether explicit, it seems reasonably clear that the District Court and the Court of Appeals placed the burden on Unterweser to show that London would be a more convenient forum than Tampa, although the contract expressly resolved that issue. The correct approach would have been to enforce the forum clause specifically unless Zapata could clearly show that enforcement would be unreasonable and unjust, or that the clause was invalid for such reasons as fraud or overreaching. Accordingly, the case must be remanded for reconsideration.

We note, however, that there is nothing in the record presently before us that would support a refusal to enforce the forum clause. The Court of Appeals suggested that enforcement would be contrary to the public policy of the forum under *Bisso* v. *Inland Waterways Corp.*, 349 U. S. 85 (1955), because of the prospect that the English courts would enforce the clauses of the towage contract purporting to exculpate Unterweser from liability for damages to the *Chaparral*. A contractual choice-of-forum clause should be held unenforceable if enforcement would contravene a strong public policy of the forum in which suit is brought, whether declared by statute or by judicial decision. See, *e. g.*, *Boyd* v. *Grand Trunk W. R. Co.*, 338 U. S. 263 (1949). It is clear, however, that whatever the proper scope of the policy expressed in *Bisso*,[17] it does not reach this case. *Bisso* rested on considerations with respect to the towage business strictly in

---

[17] *Dixilyn Drilling Corp.* v. *Crescent Towing & Salvage Co.*, 372 U. S. 697 (1963) (*per curiam*), merely followed *Bisso* and declined to subject its rule governing towage contracts in American waters to "indeterminate exceptions" based on delicate analysis of the facts of each case. See 372 U. S., at 698 (Harlan, J., concurring).

American waters, and those considerations are not controlling in an international commercial agreement. Speaking for the dissenting judges in the Court of Appeals, Judge Wisdom pointed out:

"[W]e should be careful not to over-emphasize the strength of the [*Bisso*] policy. . . . [T]wo concerns underlie the rejection of exculpatory agreements: that they may be produced by overweening bargaining power; and that they do not sufficiently discourage negligence. . . . Here the conduct in question is that of a foreign party occurring in international waters outside our jurisdiction. The evidence disputes any notion of overreaching in the contractual agreement. And for all we know, the uncertainties and dangers in the new field of transoceanic towage of oil rigs were so great that the tower was unwilling to take financial responsibility for the risks, and the parties thus allocated responsibility for the voyage to the tow. It is equally possible that the contract price took this factor into account. I conclude that we should not invalidate the forum selection clause here unless we are firmly convinced that we would thereby significantly encourage negligent conduct within the boundaries of the United States." 428 F. 2d, at 907–908. (Footnotes omitted.)

Courts have also suggested that a forum clause, even though it is freely bargained for and contravenes no important public policy of the forum, may nevertheless be "unreasonable" and unenforceable if the chosen forum is *seriously* inconvenient for the trial of the action. Of course, where it can be said with reasonable assurance that at the time they entered the contract, the parties to a freely negotiated private international commercial agreement contemplated the claimed inconvenience, it is difficult to see why any such claim of inconvenience should be heard to render the forum clause unenforceable.

We are not here dealing with an agreement between two Americans to resolve their essentially local disputes in a remote alien forum. In such a case, the serious inconvenience of the contractual forum to one or both of the parties might carry greater weight in determining the reasonableness of the forum clause. The remoteness of the forum might suggest that the agreement was an adhesive one, or that the parties did not have the particular controversy in mind when they made their agreement; yet even there the party claiming should bear a heavy burden of proof.[18] Similarly, selection of a remote forum to apply differing foreign law to an essentially American controversy might contravene an important public policy of the forum. For example, so long as *Bisso* governs American courts with respect to the towage business in American waters, it would quite arguably be improper to permit an American tower to avoid that policy by providing a foreign forum for resolution of his disputes with an American towee.

This case, however, involves a freely negotiated international commercial transaction between a German and an American corporation for towage of a vessel from the Gulf of Mexico to the Adriatic Sea. As noted, selection of a London forum was clearly a reasonable effort to bring vital certainty to this international transaction and to provide a neutral forum experienced and capable in the resolution of admiralty litigation. Whatever "inconvenience" Zapata would suffer by being forced to litigate in the contractual forum as it agreed to do was clearly

------

[18] See, *e. g.*, Model Choice of Forum Act § 3 (3), *supra*, n. 13, comment: "On rare occasions, the state of the forum may be a substantially more convenient place for the trial of a particular controversy than the chosen state. If so, the present clause would permit the action to proceed. This result will presumably be in accord with the desires of the parties. It can be assumed that they did not have the particular controversy in mind when they made the choice-of-forum agreement since they would not consciously have agreed to have the action brought in an inconvenient place."

foreseeable at the time of contracting. In such circumstances it should be incumbent on the party seeking to escape his contract to show that trial in the contractual forum will be so gravely difficult and inconvenient that he will for all practical purposes be deprived of his day in court. Absent that, there is no basis for concluding that it would be unfair, unjust, or unreasonable to hold that party to his bargain.

In the course of its ruling on Unterweser's second motion to stay the proceedings in Tampa, the District Court did make a conclusory finding that the balance of convenience was "strongly" in favor of litigation in Tampa. However, as previously noted, in making that finding the court erroneously placed the burden of proof on Unterweser to show that the balance of convenience was strongly in its favor.[19] Moreover, the finding falls far short of a conclusion that Zapata would be effectively deprived of its day in court should it be

---

[19] Applying the proper burden of proof, Justice Karminski in the High Court of Justice at London made the following findings, which appear to have substantial support in the record:

"[Zapata] pointed out that in this case the balance of convenience so far as witnesses were concerned pointed in the direction of having the case heard and tried in the United States District Court at Tampa in Florida because the probability is that most, but not necessarily all, of the witnesses will be American. The answer, as it seems to me, is that a substantial minority at least of witnesses are likely to be German. The tug was a German vessel and was, as far as I know, manned by a German crew . . . . Where they all are now or are likely to be when this matter is litigated I do not know, because the experience of the Admiralty Court here strongly points out that maritime witnesses in the course of their duties move about freely. The homes of the German crew presumably are in Germany. There is probably a balance of numbers in favour of the Americans, but not, as I am inclined to think, a very heavy balance." App. 212.

It should also be noted that if the exculpatory clause is enforced in the English courts, many of Zapata's witnesses on the questions of negligence and damage may be completely unnecessary.

forced to litigate in London. Indeed, it cannot even be assumed that it would be placed to the expense of transporting its witnesses to London. It is not unusual for important issues in international admiralty cases to be dealt with by deposition. Both the District Court and the Court of Appeals majority appeared satisfied that Unterweser could receive a fair hearing in Tampa by using deposition testimony of its witnesses from distant places, and there is no reason to conclude that Zapata could not use deposition testimony to equal advantage if forced to litigate in London as it bound itself to do. Nevertheless, to allow Zapata opportunity to carry its heavy burden of showing not only that the balance of convenience is strongly in favor of trial in Tampa (that is, that it will be far more inconvenient for Zapata to litigate in London than it will be for Unterweser to litigate in Tampa), but also that a London trial will be so manifestly and gravely inconvenient to Zapata that it will be effectively deprived of a meaningful day in court, we remand for further proceedings.

Zapata's remaining contentions do not require extended treatment. It is clear that Unterweser's action in filing its limitation complaint in the District Court in Tampa was, so far as Zapata was concerned, solely a defensive measure made necessary as a response to Zapata's breach of the forum clause of the contract. When the six-month statutory period for filing an action to limit its liability had almost run without the District Court's having ruled on Unterweser's initial motion to dismiss or stay Zapata's action pursuant to the forum clause, Unterweser had no other prudent alternative but to protect itself by filing for limitation of its liability.[20] Its action in so doing was a direct consequence

---

[20] Zapata has suggested that Unterweser was not in any way required to file its "affirmative" limitation complaint because it

of Zapata's failure to abide by the forum clause of the towage contract. There is no basis on which to conclude that this purely necessary defensive action by Unterweser should preclude it from relying on the forum clause it bargained for.

For the first time in this litigation, Zapata has suggested to this Court that the forum clause should not be construed to provide for an exclusive forum or to include *in rem* actions. However, the language of the clause is clearly mandatory and all-encompassing; the language of the clause in the *Carbon Black* case was far different.[21]

The judgment of the Court of Appeals is vacated and the case is remanded for further proceedings consistent with this opinion.

Vacated and remanded.

---

could just as easily have pleaded limitation of liability by way of defense in Zapata's initial action, either before or after the six-month period. That course of action was not without risk, however, that Unterweser's attempt to limit its liability by answer would be held invalid. See G. Gilmore & C. Black, Admiralty § 10–15 (1957). We do not believe this hazardous option in any way deprived Unterweser's limitation complaint of its essentially defensive character so far as Zapata was concerned.

[21] See 359 U. S., at 182.

NOTE: Where it is feasible, a syllabus (headnote) will be released, as is being done in connection with this case, at the time the opinion is issued. The syllabus constitutes no part of the opinion of the Court but has been prepared by the Reporter of Decisions for the convenience of the reader. See *United States* v. *Detroit Lumber Co.*, 200 U. S. 321, 337.

SUPREME COURT OF THE UNITED STATES

Syllabus

HISHON *v.* KING & SPALDING

CERTIORARI TO THE UNITED STATES COURT OF APPEALS FOR THE ELEVENTH CIRCUIT

No. 82–940.   Argued October 31, 1983—Decided May 22, 1984

Petitioner, a woman lawyer, was employed in 1972 as an associate with respondent law firm, a general partnership, but her employment was terminated in 1979 after respondent decided not to invite her to become a partner.   Petitioner filed a charge with the Equal Employment Opportunity Commission, claiming that respondent had discriminated against her on the basis of her sex in violation of Title VII of the Civil Rights Act of 1964.   After the Commission issued a notice of right to sue, petitioner brought this action in Federal District Court under Title VII.   Her complaint included allegations that respondent used the possibility of ultimate partnership as a recruiting device to induce her and other young lawyers to become associates at the firm; that respondent represented that advancement to partnership after five or six years was "a matter of course" for associates who received satisfactory evaluations and that associates would be considered for partnership "on a fair and equal basis"; that she relied on these representations when she accepted employment with respondent; that respondent's promise to consider her on a "fair and equal basis" created a binding employment contract; and that respondent discriminated against her on the basis of her sex when it failed to invite her to become a partner.   The District Court dismissed the complaint on the ground that Title VII was inapplicable to the selection of partners by a partnership, and the Court of Appeals affirmed.

Held: Petitioner's complaint states a claim cognizable under Title VII, and she therefore is entitled to her day in court to prove her allegations. Pp. 3–9.

(a) Once a contractual employment relationship is established, the provisions of Title VII attach, forbidding unlawful discrimination as to the "terms, conditions, or privileges of employment," which clearly include benefits that are part of the employment contract.   If the evidence at trial establishes petitioner's allegation that the parties contracted to have her considered for partnership, that promise clearly was a term, condition, or privilege of her employment.   Independent of the alleged contract, Title VII would then bind respondent to consider petitioner for partnership as the statute provides, *i.e.*, without regard to her sex. Moreover, an employer may provide its employees with benefits that it is under no obligation to furnish by any express or implied contract. Such a benefit, though not a contractual *right* of employment, may qualify as a "privilege" of employment under Title VII that may not be granted or withheld in a discriminatory fashion.   Pp. 3–6.

(b) Even if respondent is correct in its assertion that a partnership invitation is not itself an offer of employment, Title VII would nonetheless apply.   The benefit a plaintiff is denied need not *be* employment to fall within Title VII's protection; it need only be a term, condition, or privilege *of* employment.   It is also of no consequence that employment as an associate necessarily ends upon elevation to partnership; a benefit need not accrue before a person's employment is completed to be a term, condition, or privilege of that employment relationship.   Nor does the statute or its legislative history support a *per se* exemption of partnership decisions from scrutiny.   And respondent has not shown how application of Title VII in this case would infringe its constitutional rights of expression or association.   Moreover, "[i]nvidious private discrimination may be characterized as a form of exercising freedom of association protected by the First Amendment, but it has never been accorded affirmative constitutional protections."   *Norwood* v. *Harrison,* 413 U. S. 455, 470.   Pp. 6–8.

678 F. 2d 1022, reversed and remanded.

BURGER, C. J., delivered the opinion for a unanimous Court.   POWELL, J., filed a concurring opinion.

SUPREME COURT OF THE UNITED STATES

No. 82–940

ELIZABETH ANDERSON HISHON, PETITIONER
v. KING & SPALDING

ON WRIT OF CERTIORARI TO THE UNITED STATES COURT OF APPEALS FOR THE ELEVENTH CIRCUIT

[May 22, 1984]

CHIEF JUSTICE BURGER delivered the opinion of the Court.

We granted certiorari to determine whether the District Court properly dismissed a Title VII complaint alleging that a law partnership discriminated against petitioner, a woman lawyer employed as an associate, when it failed to invite her to become a partner.

I

A

In 1972 petitioner Elizabeth Anderson Hishon accepted a position as an associate with respondent, a large Atlanta law firm established as a general partnership. When this suit was filed in 1980, the firm had more than 50 partners and employed approximately 50 attorneys as associates. Up to that time, no woman had ever served as a partner at the firm.

Petitioner alleges that the prospect of partnership was an important factor in her initial decision to accept employment with respondent. She alleges that respondent used the possibility of ultimate partnership as a recruiting device to induce petitioner and other young lawyers to become associates at the firm. According to the complaint, respondent represented that advancement to partnership after five or six years was "a matter of course" for associates "who receive[d] satisfactory evaluations" and that associates were promoted

867

to partnership "on a fair and equal basis."   Petitioner alleges that she relied on these representations when she accepted employment with respondent.   The complaint further alleges that respondent's promise to consider her on a "fair and equal basis" created a binding employment contract.

In May 1978 the partnership considered and rejected Hishon for admission to the partnership; one year later, the partners again declined to invite her to become a partner.[1] Once an associate is passed over for partnership at respondent's firm, the associate is notified to begin seeking employment elsewhere.   Petitioner's employment as an associate terminated on December 31, 1979.

B

Hishon filed a charge with the Equal Employment Opportunity Commission on November 19, 1979, claiming that respondent had discriminated against her on the basis of her sex in violation of Title VII of the Civil Rights Act of 1964, 78 Stat. 241, as amended, 42 U. S. C. §§ 2000e *et seq.* (1976 ed. and Supp. V).   Ten days later the Commission issued a notice of right to sue, and on February 27, 1980, Hishon brought this action in the United States District Court for the Northern District of Georgia.   She sought declaratory and injunctive relief, back pay, and compensatory damages "in lieu of reinstatement and promotion to partnership." This, of course, negates any claim for specific performance of the contract alleged.

The District Court dismissed the complaint on the ground that Title VII was inapplicable to the selection of partners by

---

[1] The parties dispute whether the partnership actually reconsidered the 1978 decision at the 1979 meeting.   Respondent claims it voted not to reconsider the question and that Hishon therefore was required to file her claim with the Equal Employment Opportunity Commission within 180 days of the May 1978 meeting, not the meeting one year later, see 42 U. S. C. § 2000e–5(e).   The District Court's disposition of the case made it unnecessary to decide that question, and we do not reach it.

a partnership.[2]   24 Fair Empl. Prac. Cas. (BNA) 1303 (ND
Ga. 1980).   A divided panel of the United States Court of
Appeals for the Eleventh Circuit affirmed.   678 F. 2d 1022
(1982).   We granted certiorari, ――― U. S. ――― (1983), and
we reverse.

II

At this stage of the litigation, we must accept petitioner's
allegations as true.   A court may dismiss a complaint only if
it is clear that no relief could be granted under any set of
facts that could be proved consistent with the allegations.
Conley v. *Gibson*, 355 U. S. 41, 45–46 (1957).   The issue before us is whether petitioner's allegations state a claim under
Title VII, the relevant portion of which provides as follows:

> "(a) *It shall be an unlawful employment practice for
> an employer—*
> (1) to fail or refuse to hire or to discharge any individ-
> ual, or otherwise *to discriminate against any individual
> with respect to his* compensation, *terms, conditions, or
> privileges of employment, because of such individual's*
> race, color, religion, *sex*, or national origin."   42
> U. S. C. § 2000e–2(a) (emphasis added).

A

Petitioner alleges that respondent is an "employer" to
whom Title VII is addressed.[3]   She then asserts that consid-

---

[2] The District Court dismissed under Fed. Rule Civ. Proc. 12(b)(1) on
the ground that it lacked subject-matter jurisdiction over petitioner's
claim.   Although limited discovery previously had taken place concerning
the manner in which respondent was organized, the court did not find any
"jurisdictional facts" in dispute.   See *Thomson* v. *Gaskill*, 315 U. S. 442,
446 (1942).   Its reasoning makes clear that it dismissed petitioner's complaint on the ground that her allegations did not state a claim cognizable
under Title VII.   Our disposition makes it unnecessary to consider the
wisdom of the District Court's invocation of Rule 12(b)(1), as opposed to
Rule 12(b)(6).

[3] The statute defines an "employer" as a "person engaged in an industry
affecting commerce who has fifteen or more employees for each working

eration for partnership was one of the "terms, conditions, or privileges of employment" as an associate with respondent.[4] See § 2000e–2(a)(1). If this is correct, respondent could not base an adverse partnership decision on "race, color, religion, sex, or national origin."

Once a contractual relationship of employment is established, the provisions of Title VII attach and govern certain aspects of that relationship.[5] In the context of Title VII, the contract of employment may be written or oral, formal or informal; an informal contract of employment may arise by the simple act of handing a job applicant a shovel and providing a workplace. The contractual relationship of employment triggers the provision of Title VII governing "terms, conditions, or privileges of employment." Title VII in turn forbids discrimination on the basis of "race, color, religion, sex, or national origin."

Because the underlying employment relationship is contractual, it follows that the "terms, conditions, or privileges of employment" clearly include benefits that are part of an employment contract. Here, petitioner in essence alleges that respondent made a contract to consider her for partnership.[6] Indeed, this promise was allegedly a key contractual

---

day in each of twenty or more calendar weeks in the current or preceding calendar year," § 2000e(b), and a "person" is explicitly defined to include "partnerships," § 2000e(a) (1976 ed., Supp. V). The complaint alleges that respondent's partnership satisfies these requirements. Joint Appendix (J. A.) 6.

[4] Petitioner has raised other theories of Title VII liability which, in light of our disposition, need not be addressed.

[5] Title VII also may be relevant in the absence of an existing employment relationship, as when an employer *refuses* to hire someone. See § 2000e–2(a)(1). However, discrimination in that circumstance does not concern the "terms, conditions, or privileges of employment," which is the focus of the present case.

[6] Petitioner not only alleges that respondent promised to consider her for partnership, but also that it promised to consider her on a "fair and equal basis." This latter promise is not necessary to petitioner's Title VII claim. Even if the employment contract did not afford a basis for an implied condi-

provision which induced her to accept employment.   If the evidence at trial establishes that the parties contracted to have petitioner considered for partnership, that promise clearly was a term, condition, or privilege of her employ-ment.   Title VII would then bind respondents to consider petitioner for partnership as the statute provides, i. e., with-out regard to petitioner's sex.   The contract she alleges would lead to the same result.

Petitioner's claim that a contract was made, however, is not the only allegation that would qualify respondent's con-sideration of petitioner for partnership as a term, condition, or privilege of employment.   An employer may provide its employees with many benefits that it is under no obligation to furnish by any express or implied contract.   Such a benefit, though not a contractual *right* of employment, may qualify as a "privileg[e]" of employment under Title VII.   A benefit that is part and parcel of the employment relationship may not be doled out in a discriminatory fashion, even if the em-ployer would be free under the employment contract simply not to provide the benefit at all.   Those benefits that com-prise the "incidents of employment," S. Rep. No. 867, 88th Cong., 2d Sess. 11 (1964),[7] or that form "an aspect of the relationship between the employer and employees," *Allied Chemical & Alkali Workers* v. *Pittsburgh Plate Glass Co.,*

---

tion that the ultimate decision would be fairly made on the merits, Title VII itself would impose such a requirement.   If the promised consider-ation for partnership is a term, condition, or privilege of employment, then the partnership decision must be without regard to "race, color, religion, sex, or national origin."

[7] Senate Report 867 concerned S. 1937, which the Senate postponed in-definitely after it amended a House version of what ultimately became the Civil Rights Act of 1964.   See 110 Cong. Rec. 14,602 (1964).   The report is relevant here because S. 1937 contained language similar to that ultimately found in the Civil Rights Act. It guaranteed "equal employment opportu-nity," which was defined to "include all the compensation, terms, condi-tions, and privileges of employment."   S. Rep. No. 867, 88th Cong., 2d Sess. 24 (1964).

404 U. S. 157, 178 (1971),[8] may not be afforded in a manner contrary to Title VII.

Several allegations in petitioner's complaint would support the conclusion that the opportunity to become a partner was part and parcel of an associate's status as an employee at respondent's firm, independent of any allegation that such an opportunity was included in associates' employment contracts. Petitioner alleges that respondent's associates could regularly expect to be considered for partnership at the end of their "apprenticeships," and it appears that lawyers outside the firm were not routinely so considered.[9] Thus, the benefit of partnership consideration was allegedly linked directly with an associate's status as an employee, and this linkage was far more than coincidental: petitioner alleges that respondent explicitly used the prospect of ultimate partnership to induce young lawyers to join the firm. Indeed, the importance of the partnership decision to a lawyer's status as an associate is underscored by the allegation that associates' employment is terminated if they are not elected to become partners. These allegations, if proved at trial, would suffice to show that partnership consideration was a term, condition, or privilege of an associate's employment at respondent's

---

[8] *Allied Chemical* pertains to Section 8(d) of the National Labor Relations Act (NLRA), which describes the obligation of employers and unions to meet and confer regarding "wages, hours, and other terms and conditions of employment." 49 Stat. 452, as added, 29 U. S. C. § 158(d). The meaning of this analogous language sheds light on the Title VII provision at issue here. We have drawn analogies to the NLRA in other Title VII contexts, see *Franks* v. *Bowman Transportation Co.*, 424 U. S. 747, 768–770 (1976), and have noted that certain sections of Title VII were expressly patterned after the NLRA, see *Albemarle Paper Co.* v. *Moody*, 422 U. S. 405, 419 (1975).

[9] Respondent's own submissions indicate that most of respondent's partners in fact were selected from the ranks of associates who had spent their entire prepartnership legal careers (excluding judicial clerkships) with the firm. See J. A. 45.

firm, and accordingly that partnership consideration must be without regard to sex.

B

Respondent contends that advancement to partnership may never qualify as a term, condition, or privilege of employment for purposes of Title VII. First, respondent asserts that elevation to partnership entails a change in status from an "employee" to an "employer." However, even if respondent is correct that a partnership invitation is not itself an offer of employment, Title VII would nonetheless apply and preclude discrimination on the basis of sex. The benefit a plaintiff is denied need not *be* employment to fall within Title VII's protection; it need only be a term, condition, or privilege *of* employment. It is also of no consequence that employment as an associate necessarily ends when an associate becomes a partner. A benefit need not accrue before a person's employment is completed to be a term, condition, or privilege of that employment relationship. Pension benefits, for example, qualify as terms, conditions, or privileges of employment even though they are received only after employment terminates. *Arizona Governing Committee for Tax Deferred Annuity & Deferred Compensation Plans* v. *Norris,* —— U. S. ——, —— (1983). Accordingly, nothing in the change in status that advancement to partnership might entail means that partnership consideration falls outside the terms of the statute. See *Lucido* v. *Cravath, Swaine & Moore,* 425 F. Supp. 123, 128–129 (SDNY 1977).

Second, respondent argues that Title VII categorically exempts partnership decisions from scrutiny. However, respondent points to nothing in the statute or the legislative history that would support such a *per se* exemption.[10] When

---

[10] The only legislative history respondent offers to support its position is Senator Cotton's defense of an unsuccessful amendment to limit Title VII to businesses with 100 or more employees. In this connection the Senator stated:

Congress wanted to grant an employer complete immunity, it expressly did so.[11]

Third, respondent argues that application of Title VII in this case would infringe constitutional rights of expression or association. Although we have recognized that the activities of lawyers may make a "distinctive contribution . . . to the ideas and beliefs of our society," *NAACP* v. *Button*, 371 U. S. 415, 431 (1963), respondent has not shown how its ability to fulfill such a function would be inhibited by a requirement that it consider petitioner for partnership on her merits. Moreover, as we have held in another context, "[i]nvidious private discrimination may be characterized as a form of exercising freedom of association protected by the First Amendment, but it has never been accorded affirmative constitutional protections." *Norwood* v. *Harrison*, 413 U. S. 455, 470 (1973). There is no constitutional right, for example, to discriminate in the selection of who may attend a private school or join a labor union. *Runyon* v. *McCrary*, 427 U. S. 160 (1976); *Railway Mail Association* v. *Corsi*, 326 U. S. 88, 93–94 (1945).

"[W]hen a small businessman who employs 30 or 25 or 26 persons selects an employee, he comes very close to selecting a partner; and when a businessman selects a partner, he comes dangerously close to the situation he faces when he selects a wife."   110 Cong. Rec. 13,085 (1964); accord 118 Cong. Rec. 1524, 2391 (1972).

Because Senator Cotton's amendment failed, it is unclear to what extent Congress shared his concerns about selecting partners.   In any event, his views hardly conflict with our narrow holding today: that in appropriate circumstances partnership consideration may qualify as a term, condition, or privilege of a person's employment with an employer large enough to be covered by Title VII.

[11] For example, Congress expressly exempted Indian tribes and certain agencies of the District of Columbia, 42 U. S. C. § 2000e(b)(1), small businesses and bona fide private membership clubs, § 2000e(b)(2), and certain employees of religious organizations, § 2000e–1.   Congress initially exempted certain employees of educational institutions, § 702, 78 Stat. 255 (1964), but later revoked that exemption, Equal Employment Opportunity Act of 1972, § 3, 86 Stat. 103.

III

We conclude that petitioner's complaint states a claim cognizable under Title VII.   Petitioner therefore is entitled to her day in court to prove her allegations.   The judgment of the Court of Appeals is reversed, and the case is remanded for further proceedings consistent with this opinion.

It is so ordered.